The Roman Gladius and the Ancient Fighting Techniques

Sit romana potens Italia virtute propago.
(Let the Roman offspring be powerful by Italic valor)

Virgil, *Aeneid*, XII, 827

The Roman Gladius and the Ancient Fighting Techniques

Volume 1: Monarchy and Consular Age

Fabrizio Casprini & Marco Saliola

FRONTLINE BOOKS

First published in Great Britain in 2022 by
Frontline Books
An imprint of
Pen & Sword Books Ltd
Yorkshire – Philadelphia

Copyright © Fabrizio Casprini & Marco Saliola 2022

ISBN 978 1 52677 833 8

The right of Fabrizio Casprini & Marco Saliola to be identified as Authors of this work has been asserted by them in accordance with the Copyright, Designs and Patents Act 1988.

A CIP catalogue record for this book is
available from the British Library.

All rights reserved. No part of this book may be reproduced or transmitted in any form or by any means, electronic or mechanical including photocopying, recording or by any information storage and retrieval system, without permission from the Publisher in writing.

Typeset by Mac Style
Printed in the UK by CPI Group (UK) Ltd, Croydon, CR0 4YY.

Pen & Sword Books Limited incorporates the imprints of Atlas, Archaeology, Aviation, Discovery, Family History, Fiction, History, Maritime, Military, Military Classics, Politics, Select, Transport, True Crime, Air World, Frontline Publishing, Leo Cooper, Remember When, Seaforth Publishing, The Praetorian Press, Wharncliffe Local History, Wharncliffe Transport, Wharncliffe True Crime and White Owl.

For a complete list of Pen & Sword titles please contact

PEN & SWORD BOOKS LIMITED
47 Church Street, Barnsley, South Yorkshire, S70 2AS, England
E-mail: enquiries@pen-and-sword.co.uk
Website: www.pen-and-sword.co.uk

Or

PEN AND SWORD BOOKS
1950 Lawrence Rd, Havertown, PA 19083, USA
E-mail: Uspen-and-sword@casematepublishers.com
Website: www.penandswordbooks.com

Contents

List of Colour Plates   vii
Acknowledgments   viii
Preface   x
Introduction and Etymology   xii

Chapter I: The Archaic Period   1
I.1 Historical Framework – *De Origine Gentium*   1
I.2 Archaic Fighting Techniques   12
I.3 Bronze Swords in the Italic Territory   24
I.4 The Archaic Period: Conclusions   36

Chapter II: The Monarchical Period (753–509 BC)   39
II.1 Historical Framework   39
II.2 Fighting in the Monarchical Period   52
II.3 The Monarchical *Gladius* or Sword with Cross Hilt   83
II.4 The Monarchical Period: Conclusions   112

Chapter III: The Consular Age   114
III (A) The High and Middle Consular Age (End Sixth–Early First Century BC)   114
   III (A).1 Historical Framework   114
   III (A).2 The Fighting in the Early–Middle Consular Age   129
   III (A).3 The *Gladius* of the Early and Middle Consular Age   168
III (B) The Late Consular Age (First Century BC)   189
   III (B).1 Historical Framework   189
   III (B).2 The Fighting in the First Century BC   200
   III (B).3 The Late Consular *Gladius*   219
III (C) The Consular Age: Conclusions   265

Chapter IV: 'De Falsis Originibus': On the Erroneous Derivation of the *Gladius* from Non-Italic People   267
IV.1 About the Hellenic Origins – The Sword with Cross Hilt in Hellenic Lands   267
IV.2 About the Hispanic Origins – The Correct Interpretation of '*Gladius Hispaniensis*'   296
IV.3 Conclusions   311

Chapter V: The Symbolic Value of the *Gladius*   314
V.1 The *Bellum Sacrum* and the Symbolism of the Sword in the Pre-Roman Age   314
V.2 Roman Pragmatism: *Bellum Iustum* and the *Gladius*   317
V.3 The Sword, from Weapon to Political Propaganda   318
V.4 The *Gladius*, a Democratic Sword   324
V.5 The Symbology of the *Gladius* for the Romans   326
V.6 The Symbolism of the Sword after the Fall of the Roman Empire   332

Conclusion   334

Notes   339
Bibliography   379

List of Colour Plates

Plate 1: The Romulean *legio*. (*Author's drawing*)
Plate 2: The *Legio Serviana*. (*Author's drawing*)
Plate 3: The Livian *legio*. (*Author's drawing*)
Plate 4: The Polybian *legio*. (*Author's drawing*)
Plate 5: The battle array of the manipular legion in '*quincunx*'.
Plate 6: A cohortal legion of the first century BC.
Plate 7: Mars and Venus, fresco from the homonymous House of Pompeii, VII, 9, 47 (*National Archaeological Museum of Naples*)
Plate 8: Various swords present in Central Italic territory from the Bronze Age to the late Consular one.

Acknowledgments

As always in any book, the acknowledgments page is the one where you involuntarily risk doing something wrong, forgetting someone deserving. This book was written and published thanks to over five years of research work and study with the support of many friends and the talented suggestions of experts in the field.

First of all, we would like to thank Alessandro Fo, who, by distracting him from the lofty poetics of Catullus and the wonderful songs of Virgil, we have involved in advice and translations of classical texts on military matters, which for all their tragedy, are part of human history. Filomena Giannotti, a disciple and delightful collaborator of Fo, also helped us with our request and who learned from her teacher not only cultural skills but also being generous with her time. We would also like to point out that we assume all responsibility for any errors or inaccuracies that may be found in some Latin phrases or quotations, since these passages were not analysed by them.

We extend heartfelt thanks to our dear friend and companion on our cultural travels Tommaso Tanzilli, who like us, is a lover of Roman culture and has carried out the precious work of 'beta reader', thus giving us valuable suggestions and stimuli on the continuation and improvement of this work.

Important help came from Raffaele D'Amato, who, with his usual great availability and competence, drafted the presentation of this book and provided significant suggestions, improving the English edition and translation together with Mrs Tanja Hammond, to whom therefore our gratitude goes.

Special thanks go to Maria Ruggeri Giove, archaeologist and profound connoisseur of the Picenian people, who has devoted much of her life to the discovery and study of numerous tombs, bringing to light many cross-hilted swords. With her generosity and profound knowledge she opened the doors of the wonderful Museum of Chieti and its storage, allowing us a direct understanding of the famous Monarchical *gladius*, of the Stami dagger with its loom scabbard and of the Apennine culture.

In the context of understanding the archaeological finds, the availability of the various directors of museums was fundamental, to whom we are grateful; and we would also like to extend our heartfelt gratitude to their staff and to the scholars who followed us in our research. Because of their patience and willingness, we were allowed to examine many objects to understand them and to photograph them, making it possible for us to shed light on many shadows of our Italic history.

In alphabetical order by location, but not by importance, heartfelt thanks go to:

Museo Villa Ferrajoli (Albano);
Museo archeologico Statale of Ascoli Piceno;
Museo archeologico of Bologna;
Museo archeologico Nazionale of Cagliari;
Museo archeologico Nazionale of Campli;
Museo archeologico Nazionale of Cassino;
MAC Museo Archeologico of Chianciano (Siena);
Museo archeologico Nazionale D'Abruzzo – Villa Frigerj (Chieti);
Museo MAEC of Cortona;
Museo archeologico Nazionale of Firenze;
Museo archeologico of Lavinium;
Museo archeologico Nazionale of Melfi Massimo Pallottino;
Museo archeologico etnologico of Modena;
Museo archeologico Nazionale of Napoli;
Museo archeologico Nazionale of Orvieto;
Museo archeologico Nazionale dell'Umbria (Perugia);
Museo archeologico Nazionale of Sassari G. A. Sanna;
Museo archeologico Nazionale of Siena;
Museo Civico archeologico Villanoviano (Rimini);
Museo Medaniene of Riofreddo;
Museo archeologico nazionale delle Terme di Diocleziano (Roma);
Museo archeologico Verrucchio (Rimini).

Our high regard goes to a group of authors, who more than others, have left a mark on our book. The works of Marco Bettalli, Armando Cherici, Maurizio Martinelli, Vincenzo D'Ercole and Gianluca Tagliamonte have significantly contributed to shedding light on the historical and military dynamics of the people who lived on the Italic soil in this historical period, and thanks to their rigour, deep analysis and cultural clarity, they have allowed us to complete our work.

Our personal thanks also go to Francesco Caratelli because, as for the birth of our previous book, *Pugio, gladius brevis est*, he did his utmost in IT research by patiently sacrificing his free time, and above all for his invaluable information.

Let us not forget Giorgio Koutifaris, who, for the love of culture and his homeland, put the utmost effort into researching the traces of the cross-hilted sword in the Hellenic territory, meeting specialists in the sector and scouring museums and sites to collect as much data, texts and documents relating to it as possible.

Equally valuable is the contribution of Vincenzo Lemmo who, with his vast experience as an archaeologist, helped us to correctly interpret some important steles.

Finally, we wish with our affectionate love, to apologise to our wives and families who have long endured our preoccupation. We cannot deny how the dedication to our research has often taken us physically and mentally far away, evading us from our family duties and all for the great joy that came from facing this long and fascinating journey.

Marco Saliola
Fabrizio Casprini

Preface

The study of Roman fighting techniques and weapons dates back to the Romans themselves. Already from ancient times the need was felt not only to glorify the power and majesty of Rome, or the historical facts that led a small city of shepherds to extend their rule from the borders of Britain to the deserts of Mesopotamia, but also to understand how this could technically happen. Thus historians such as Polybius, Caesar and Plutarch and military tacticians such as Frontinus, Vegetius and many others unfortunately anonymous, by analysing Roman military structures, organisation and techniques also described in a meticulous and wide-ranging manner the weapons that had given the children of the Capitoline Wolf victory over military structures considered invincible in the ancient world, such as the Macedonian phalanx. Today this study has not been lost, but it has been taken up critically since the nineteenth century, also with the help of archaeology and with the right critical view of the literary and artistic sources handed down from antiquity. A study that requires patience, sacrifice, passion: the work that Marco Saliola and Fabrizio Casprini are offering to us. A thorough, detailed and precise work, which speaks of the most famous weapon of classical antiquity, the *gladius*, the lethal sword of the Roman legionary.

Studying the *gladius* does not only mean analysing archaeological finds in their historical context, in order to research their evolution: it means first of all to understand how the society from which such a weapon arose was structured, and what were the social, economic and political bases and the technological capacities that, intertwined over the centuries, led to its forging and its supremacy for four centuries in the Mediterranean world.

The authors investigate the origins of the sword and definitely row against the current. A brave novelty, which tries to make people understand how this weapon was not merely adopted from an external technology but derived, in its most famous and known form, from the contribution of various cultural influences present in the Italic Peninsula. Celts, Greeks, Etruscans, Samnites: all peoples that the Romans fought and defeated for the supremacy of the Mediterranean, but from whom they were able to draw the necessary cues to forge their civilisation and their material culture, including – and above all – the military. This is why, reading this book, you will discover that *gladius hispaniensis* is not *gladius hispanicus*.

To achieve their purpose the authors analysed historical sources that are often unpublished or misinterpreted, or deliberately ignored; they looked at countless finds, and have written not only a book about the *gladius* and its origins, but a real treatise about all the various forms of cutting weapons that, since the late Bronze Age, transformed the sword into the main weapon, next to the spear, of the Italic warrior and later of the Roman legionary. They revisited the technology of the ancient world, and its etymology, often quickly passed over in the study of ancient weapons. Not content with just this, they have also addressed the vast theme of the system of production and construction of these weapons, answering many of the questions often asked by fans of this topic: how a Roman sword was constructed, as it appeared in different eras, how precise was the Greek and Roman terminology which designated it, and how very often the concept of relegating certain definitions to purely literary and poetic aspects is completely wrong. The Romans, and this is one of the messages that comes from this book, were extremely practical, and every definition, every technical evolution, every modification, was a response to practical and contingent needs that had to be faced and overcome. War was not a game, but a preponderant part of life and was tackled with the same pragmatism with which an aqueduct or an *insula* was built. This does not mean that a weapon – whatever it was – did not have also religious, mystical or symbolic aspects, especially in a civilisation born out from the rural and superstitious environments of the *Latium Vetus*. This aspect is not overlooked by Casprini and Saliola, who indeed show how symbolism and religion were one of the psychological factors spurring the creation of such an effective and ferocious weapon of war.

This is why the authors do not neglect another of the most important arguments that a modern scholar of Roman military antiquities cannot overlook: fighting techniques, the use of the sword, and the tactical ability of the Romans to adapt these to the different circumstances met time after time in their thousand-year military history.

The book has chronological limits, from an era prior to the origins of Rome until the end of the Consular Age. However, if the *gladius* then underwent further evolutions in its form in the Imperial Age, the basic principles and modes of its use remained unchanged, until the diversity of the fighting techniques and the ever-increasing presence of Celtic auxiliaries and Germans brought the *spatha* to the fore, marking its supremacy on the late-ancient battlefield. For this reason the authors are already working on a second volume, which, in addition to analysis of the subsequent evolutionary stages of the *gladius*, will explain its transition and transformation in the imperial, late-ancient and early Middle Ages.

The *gladius*, ultimately, did not cease to exist, while its name, until the late Middle Ages, remained to indicate in the barbarised West Latin any type of sword, so great had been its importance and fame in the ancient world. The work you are about to read is the prized fruit of a spasmodic search, at times even fanatical, of all that the *gladius* was, of what it represented for the civilisation that forged it, of the military values that it transmitted which were part of the greatest eclectic culture of the ancient world, the only one that was able, and not for a short time, to bring the peoples of three continents under one rule.

Dr Raffaele D'Amato
Comitato Scientifico del Laboratorio Antiche Province Danubiane
Università di Ferrara

Introduction and Etymology

An in-depth treatise on an ancient weapon such as the Roman *gladius* could prove to be a purely academic study, of interest only to specialists in the field. So what is the reason that lead us to write a treatise like this and why should it be read? We must first understand that an ancient weapon often shows only a very small part of itself, because modern people are used to looking at it as if it was a contemporary object and therefore can only perceive its technical-functional aspect, at most with some historical context. In reality, the *gladius* is a significant medium that can allow us to grasp the mentality of the people who created it. Through its study, we will be able to understand in depth not only the weapon itself but also the Capitoline *gens* in more detail – its history, its social and military characteristics, the fighting techniques of the army and consequently the different enemies faced at various times by the social composition, the economic level and, ultimately, by the traditions to which the Romans were linked. If properly understood, this weapon will be both the purpose and the means of this book and will provide us with a complete overview of the society of those centuries.

From this observation, another question arises: how should this study be carried out to achieve this correct and complete point of view? In this case it is necessary to make a preliminary reflection; when a weapon becomes the protagonist of a specific culture, like in the present case, it also becomes a typifying element. But as the society changes and its needs are transformed, the weapon itself changes and evolves, thus generating an inextricable and reciprocal relationship between these two subjects. To understand the *gladius* we will have to study its technical characteristics, its history and evolution, but also the military situations of the centuries in which it was used and the general characteristics of the army, which were, especially in antiquity, a direct expression of the society they came from. The right path of study could thus in some way be defined as 'circular', composed of three subjects that are closely related and of equal importance to each other, *gladius* – army – society. To fully comprehend the first, the study of the others is necessary.

The greatest difficulties arise when an artefact is the result of a mixture of influences between several contiguous facies, where we are faced with a cultural tangle of which it is sometimes no longer possible to understand the origin. Probably some changes are the result of a transformation no longer attributable to a single culture and the attempt to frame it in favour of the dominant one would risk giving rise to a historical error. This is exactly the case of the Italic territory where, since the second millennium BC, there was an almost inextricable jumble of different peoples, who often coexisted peacefully but just as often clashed in bloody and interminable wars, still reciprocally profoundly influencing each other, with one culture merging with the other. We will see how our weapon and the Roman army itself emerge slowly from this mixture of cultures.

The work we are proposing here is an attempt to evidence everything the Roman sword was, not only in its technology, morphology and history, but also in what it represented then and now. We will certainly talk about battles, wars, armies and ways of fighting but also – and perhaps above all – about an exceptional society, of millenary migrations, of people arriving from remote places, of religion and superstition.

From this point of view, we have tried to present and study new information and also new points of view, but treating them critically and looking for documented proof for each statement. By adopting this method of study we have shown that many 'certainties' are questionable or even completely wrong, based on archaeological and documented information. One of the major efforts of this work has been to disprove some erroneous clichés, generated by the regrettable and frequent phenomenon of uncritically reporting previous false statements, which has the effect of making the 'quoted' statement more true by consolidating the error. Over the years the *vox populi* with so many uncritical mentions, is thus transformed into *vox Dei*, and as such accepted by all even if it is unsupported by any scientific proof.

Given the scale and complexity of the subject, in this first volume we will focus on the most archaic centuries, an extremely stimulating theme for the scholar, although not easy to look at considering the great distance in time. The period analysed is from the first millennium BC to the period preceding the birth of Rome and to the end of the Consular Age – the Early Empire. The *gladius* will be studied in its technological and constructional aspects, its evolution and use, but also in close correlation with the birth of the Italic peoples and their characteristics, the symbolic and mystical aspect that they attributed to this weapon, as well as the evolution of Roman combat over time and consequently the army's approach to this sword.

To begin our journey, we require a preliminary presentation of our weapon, which can certainly begin with the etymology of its name. '*Gladius*' is the only meaning in the Latin context to define an infantry sword. This statement is based on the fact that the terms *ensis* and *mucro*[1] are essentially poetic forms, while *ferrum* is generally used to indicate any metal weapon, such as the spear, dagger, sword or axe, while the word *spatha* relates to the longer cavalry sword. This is in contrast with the Greeks, in whose language there are various words to define the 'sword', since there were many types, such as single or double-edged blade, curved or straight, short or long, etc.[2]

The different way of expressing the name of the same weapon in two different cultures derives from the fact that for the Romans there was always a single type of sword, resulting in the fact that the authors never felt the need to have it distinguished with different terms. Of course, the *gladius* evolved over time, so much so that we modern people find ourselves in the need to classify them according to their various characteristics. This was a need that never existed in antiquity, most likely because the individual variants of the *gladius* were not relevant to the purposes of its definition.

When analysing the etymology of the word *gladius*, we note that it has a very ancient origin. According to Corrsen,[3] the term is linked to the root word *krad* (*klad*) which means 'shake', 'vibrate', from which derives the Italian words '*cardine*' (hinge) and '*cuore*' (heart), whilst most scholars prefer to connect it to a European root word *kal*, *kla*, which means 'to beat', 'to break', 'to destroy'. The action that this word implies is that of the 'percussion', typical of the staff's stroke, as we can deduce from the Latin word '*càl-a*' which means 'piece of wood', from which came the term *clàva*, meaning 'club'. From the same European lineage derives the Greek word *klào*, from which the noun *clà-des* comes, meaning 'slaughtering' and the Irish word (deduced from the Celtic) *cla-ibed*, meaning 'sword'.[4]

Already in Roman times, the real etymological meaning of the word *gladius* had been lost, so much so that we are witnesses of ancient interpretations or logical connections with elements that in nature had a similar form or function, in sometimes bizarre attempts to give an explanation to the matter. Varro (Rieti, 116 BC – Rome, 27 BC) believed that *gladius* came from the aforementioned *clades* with the change of the consonant 'c' to 'g', because the sword was made to slaughter enemies.[5]

Much more imaginative was the etymological description of Isidore, Bishop of Seville, from the end of the sixth–early seventh century AD, who said (*Etymologies*, XVIII, VI) that 'Properly it is called *gladius* because "*gulamdividit*", for '"it divides the throat", that is, cuts the neck. It was made for this purpose first, for other limbs are more efficiently cut by battle-axes, but the neck only by the *gladius*.'[6]

Pliny Secundus, known as the Elder (23–79 AD), in his *Naturalis Historia* (XXI, 68)[7] states more convincingly to us that 'Gladiolus simile nomini' for 'the gladiolus one (the leaf) that its name suggests', while the Greeks assert that they called it '*Xifio*'. The association between the leaves of this plant and the Roman dagger was assumed both by Dioscorides, a Greek physician and botanist who practiced in Rome during the reign of Nero (*De materia medica*), as well as by Isidore of Seville. Pier Andrea Mattioli (Siena 12 March 1501 – Trento, 1578) translated the work of Dioscorides into Italian, describing that *'Xiphio chiamanoi Latini Gladiolo, è cosìstataquestapiantachiamatadalla forma di spadachehanno le sue frondi. Sarebbestata simile all'iride se le frondinon fosseropiùbrevi e piùstretteappuntate a modo di coltello* (Xiphio

Drawing of the Gladiolus plant (extract from '*I discorsi di Pietro Andrea Mattioli*' ('The speeches of Andrea Mattioli'), p. 467.

call the Latins the Gladiolus, so it was this plant called by the sword shape that its fronds have. It would have been similar to the iris if the branches were not shorter and narrower pinned like a knife)'.

The term *gladius* not only had counterparts in botany, but also in the animal kingdom, since Pliny (IX, 54) affirms that *gladius* is a genus of fish 'the fish called *gladius*',[8] referring to the swordfish[9] and to the inner shell of many cephalopods of the superorder Decapodiformes (in particular of the squid) which is called *gladius*, in analogy to their shape.

The brief etymological discussion that we have reported requires an important reflection. The word *gladius* has an ancient origin, prior to the Roman era, probably used to define the sword in a general sense, but in the Latin context, it will indicate the weapon par excellence, the protagonist of this study. However, deriving its meaning from the word 'beat, break, break', we can deduce an action opposite to that typical of *gladius*, that is, to thrust with the point. We can thus hypothesise that this term entered the Latin vocabulary in very remote times and it was used to define the ancestral weapons that preceded the *gladius* itself. The word remaining unchanged in the many centuries of Roman history, even if the action that it implied had changed in the meantime.

We can now begin our study, in the hope that it may contribute to the knowledge of Rome and of the Italic people, perhaps only modestly but, as a Latin proverb says, '*De minimisgranis fit magnusacervus*', 'From the smallest grains comes a big heap'.

Chapter I

The Archaic Period

I.1 HISTORICAL FRAMEWORK – *DE ORIGINE GENTIUM*

The study of the origins of an object, of its modifications and improvements over time, cannot be separated from the study of the history of the people who used it and with whom it came into contact, since an object is the fruit of the needs of its creators. It also expresses certain characteristics of the typical form and aesthetics of the traditions and material culture of the people.

The *gladius* had an influential role in the development of Roman culture, so much so that it is possible to define the relationship as reciprocal: it adapted to the socio-political needs of the culture, which varied over time, and at the same time it became the most typical element of their identity (the fighting style of the Roman soldier was based on the use of the *gladius* and it was the characteristic weapon of the Roman soldier). To understand this concept better, it is necessary to reflect on the fact that 'man has a double relationship, concrete and transposed, functional and metaphorical, from the beginning with things; a dense network of connivance, complicity and exchanges runs between men and things, and turns them into values and signs'.[1]

For this reason, it is impossible to start the discussion of the *gladius* without the inclusion of the Centro-Italic people, for whom the need for the development and use of this weapon were different from those of the people who inhabited the north and south of the Italian peninsula.

I.1,1 Birth of the Italic people

The Indo-European migration and the formation of the early Centro-Italic people
The variegated population of ancient Italy was gradually delineated due to two millennia of influence and migration of populations, originating from the steppes of southern Russia (Marija Gimbutas defined them as proto-Indo-Europeans or the Kurgan, from the name of the Russian region from which they originated),[2] which enabled the Indo-Europeanisation of Europe from the fifth millennium BC. This process should be considered as an almost uninterrupted infiltration that favoured 'an inextricable tangle of movements of populations … whose result was that of an intense hybridisation and mixture of races, languages and cultures'.[3]

These people had already mastered the technology of bronze, which gave them supremacy over the farmers of ancient Europe – the peaceful, sedentary population based on a 'matriarchate' dedicated to the cult of the Mother Goddess, defined by the later Latin people as *Magna Mater*.

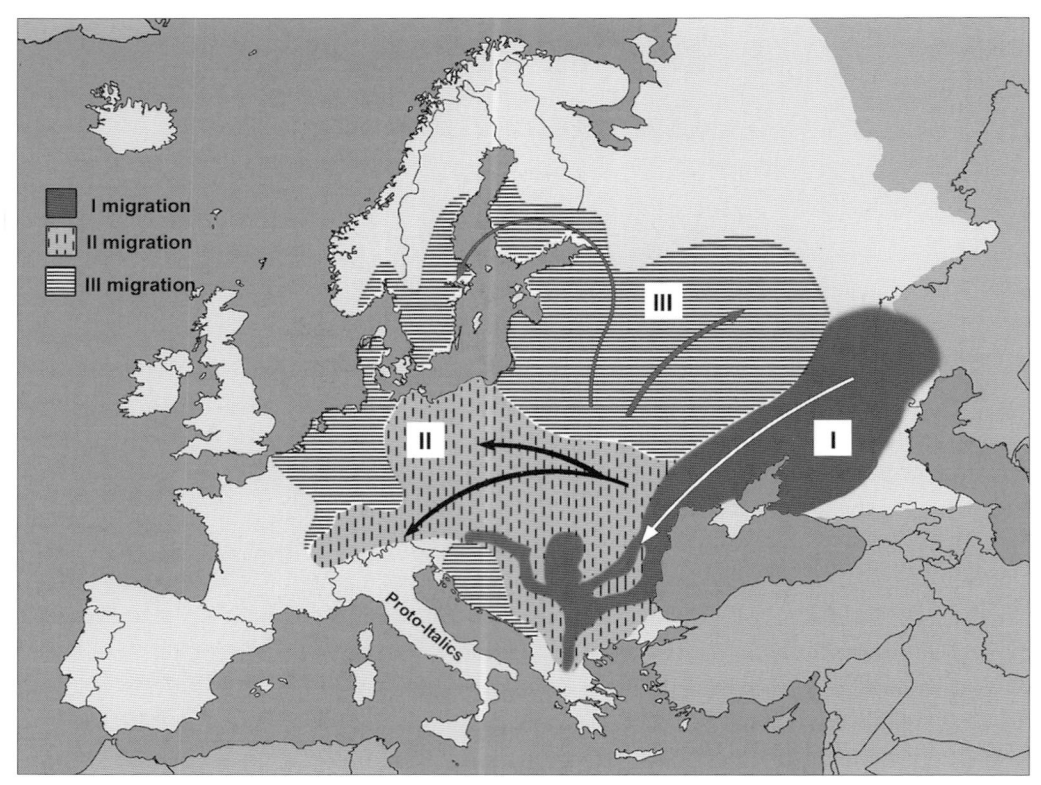

2　The Roman Gladius and the Ancient Fighting Techniques

Fig 1: Kurgan migration patterns. The first wave (I) (between 4300–3500 BC) started from the steppes of the lower course of the Volga, spreading across the Danubian plain and influencing the territories of present-day Bulgaria, Macedonia and up to the Hungarian prairies.

The second wave (II) (between 3500–3000 BC) originated in the Don and Volga basin, and spread throughout Central Europe, giving rise to new cultural groups.

Finally, the third wave (III) (between 3000–2900 BC), with its infiltration in Central and Eastern Europe, had migratory effects that involved the Adriatic coast of the Balkans and the Peloponnese. From these migrations the embryo was created from which derived the various 'people' that populated Europe. (*Author's drawing*)

The clash between the two cultures was disruptive, in some cases resulting in cohabitation, but more frequently in a defeat and a resulting migration of the farming people towards the adjacent territories. Metaphorically this can be described as a billiard stroke, where the Kurgan were the cue ball and the farmers of ancient Europe the coloured balls which at the moment of impact scatter away.[4] According to this theory, the Kurgan established themselves as the elite of ancient Europe, which favoured the spread of their Indo-European language.

Archaeologically it is possible to demonstrate three successive phases of migration, although it is difficult to establish who the derived Indo-European people were,[5] as in the Italian territory there were no clear contours. In fact, in the course of two millennia,[6] at different times and in different ways, there were fractions of numerous lineages, understood as small movements of people, with infiltrations into sparsely-populated areas, which gave rise to settlements of heterogeneous but coexisting populations.[7]

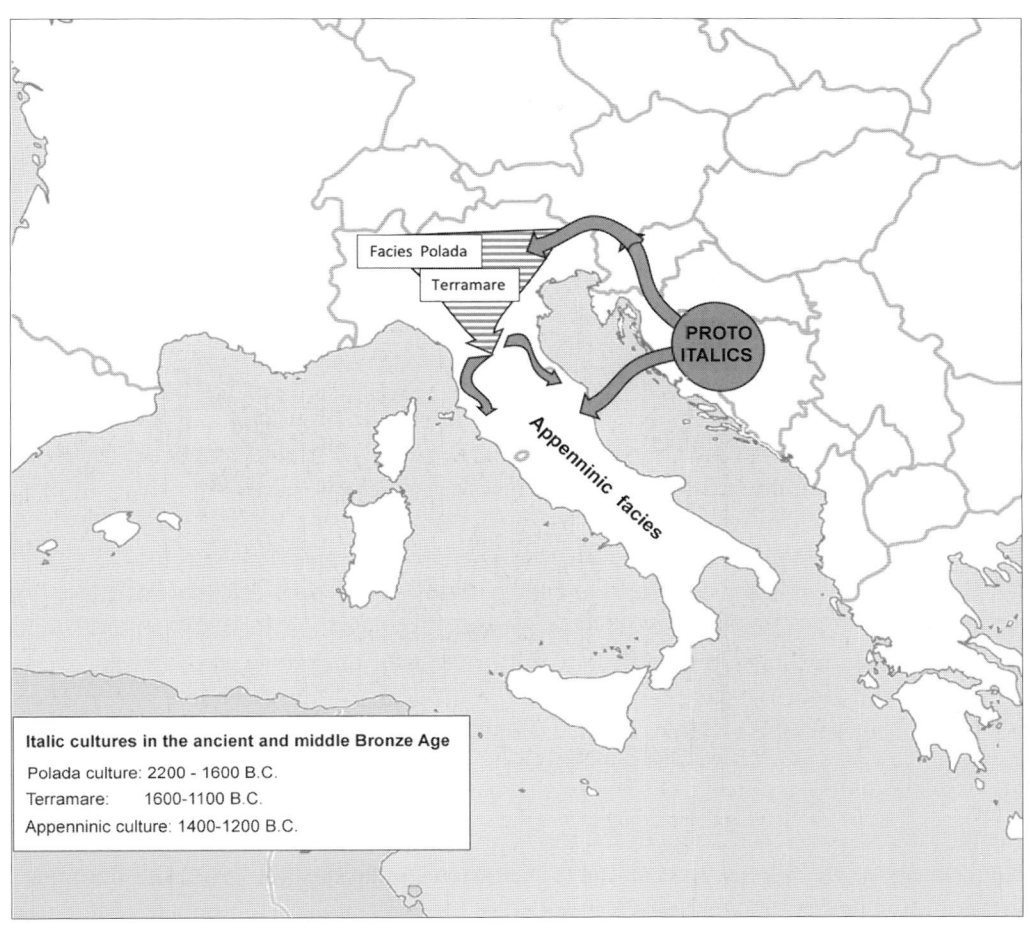

Fig. 2: In the diagram the main migratory movements of the proto-Italic people are shown (indicated by the arrows), influenced by the pressure of the steppe peoples who lived east of the Danube. Some populations entered Italian territory through the Julian Alps, while others crossed the Adriatic Sea to reach the coast of Abruzzo. This movement caused the formation of numerous archaeological areas that spread mainly from north to south and from east to west. (*Author's drawing*)

The most important migration period is, however, the third wave which developed after 3000 BC and induced displacements of populations that later colonised Italian soil and who were for this reason, defined as the 'proto-Italic people'. These multitudes reached Italian territory by two routes: the first, in the north, by the easy passes of the Julian Alps (going up the Adriatic coast or further inland along the Sava river), thus allowing their arrival in the Po Valley and the second, crossing the Adriatic Sea and arriving on the coast of Abruzzo.

The Indo-European origin of the weapons: 'year zero'
If proto-Indo-European migrations can be considered as 'year zero' from the ethnic point of view, the same consideration can also be applied to weapons. The weapons of Kurgan

society[8] are represented by daggers with copper and bronze hilts and triangular blades (the shape deriving from the previous knives made of flint), socketed halberds and axes.

The latter two were the most important weapons and during the Etruscan and Roman period, once all military connotations were mainly (but not completely) lost, they became a symbol of power in the context of the *Fasces Lictorii*, who were appointed to carry out the death penalty.

The Bronze Age weapons developed from the aforementioned maintained a certain homogeneity in their characteristics; both because they were temporally close to the aforementioned 'year zero', and because of the technological limits of materials and construction methods.

The concept of considering all Indo-European weapons being similar in having a unique cultural origin is very important, as it allows us to understand how, in their development amongst people, they can present common or similar characteristics with those manufactured by people from other territories, even if geographically distant.

I.1,2 The Italic People during the Bronze Age

During the Bronze Age we witness the formation of numerous cultures on Italic soil, whose progressive temporal, as well as geographical, change in a north–south and east–west direction, witnesses the slow but implacable migratory wave lasting over a thousand years. During this period, the Indo-European migratory people were carriers of the Hallstatt culture and influenced and interacted with the pre-existing indigenous cultures, creating the base for the development of the central Italic civilisations of the Iron Age. This dissertation becomes indispensable in understanding the mosaic of people and the respective facies of the Italian peninsula, and above all in understanding the concept of the objects that characterised them, including the *gladius*. These facts are not attributable to a single factor, but were the fruit of an evolutionary syncretism to which many cultures contributed.

The Italic territory is distinguished by its fertility and abundance of raw materials. It has favoured the prosperity of the inhabiting people, and at the same time due to its geographical characteristics, it has allowed the development of numerous archaeological facies, well defined in antiquity and existing today in the form of dialects, cultures and traditions. It appears to have been divided into various zones, each characterised by its own identity[9] and a conflict with neighbouring areas, where the factors that allowed communication and the forming of relationships were mainly constituted by transhumance (a semi-nomadic form of pastoralism with a seasonal nature),[10] through markets, from religious pilgrimages to temples to obtain blessings, from raids and finally from mercenary activity,[11] a very important Italic (but not Roman) reality.

The ethnogenesis of the Italic people
Ancient (2300–1600 BC) and Middle (1700–1350 BC) Bronze Age
In northern Italy, north of river Po, during the Bronze Age the Polada culture was formed, a pile-dwelling population with characteristic archaeological facies, followed by the Terramare (1600–1200 BC), who gradually colonised the Po Valley, south of the

Fig. 3:
1) Weapons from the royal tomb of Mala Gruda (Montenegro) showing a golden dagger with a triangular blade fitted with holes for the fitting of an organic handle secured by a system of rivets, and a socketed silver axe.
2) Weapons belonging to the Yamna culture (Pontic-Caspian steppes): bronze dagger with a triangular tanged blade and two flint daggers with triangular blades to which a wooden handle was secured (5000 BC).
3) Stele of Kernosovka, Ukraine (late 4000–mid 3000 BC) depicting two carved halberds and a double-edged axe.
4) Stele of Kurgan of Bagnolo, Valcamonica, Italy (3000 BC), with a crude anthropomorphic appearance in which are depicted solar symbols (the head?), an upturned breastplate, two halberds with handles and two daggers, a ploughing scene with two yoked oxen and seven animals.
(*Author's drawings after* The Civilisation of the Goddess, the World of Ancient Europe *by Marija Gimbutas*)

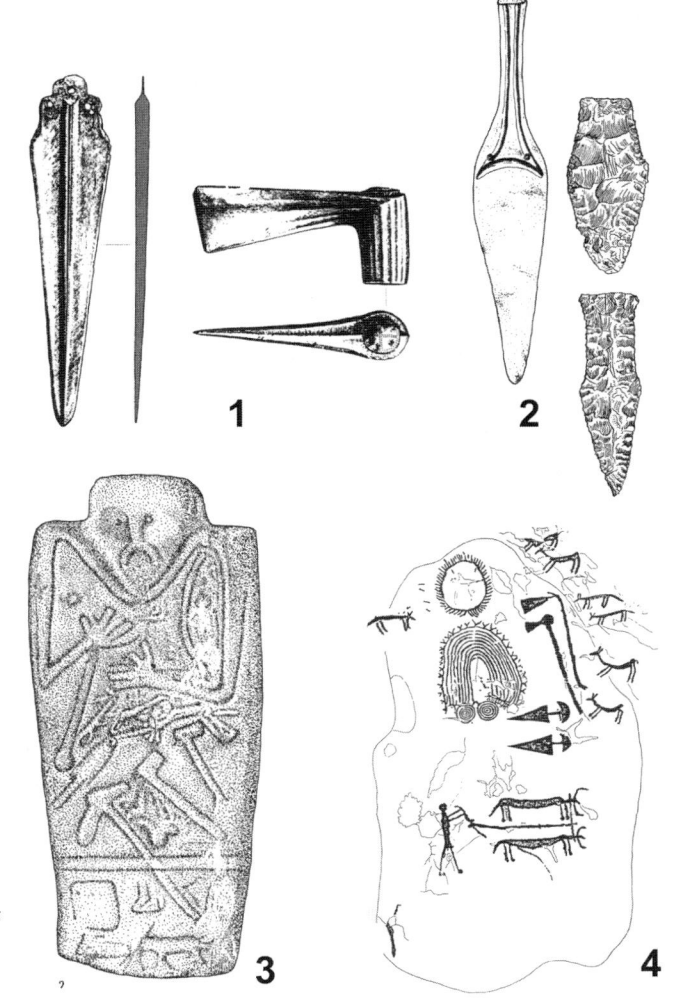

river, which had remained scarcely inhabited until then. The characteristic of the latter culture was the construction of a settlement delimited by a moat and an embankment, often preceded by a palisade, created, as Pigorini stated, 'for contingencies linked to the lake nature of the places, from a high yield agricultural production, possible thanks to the control of the water network and the realisation of massive deforestation works'. According to the Italian paleoethnologist Dr Pigomi we can find the origin of ancient Rome in the people of the Terramare, since their settlements present the fundamental characteristics of a *castrum* (square villages with *cardo*, *decumanus* and *insulae*).[12] Many scholars today dispute this suggestive hypothesis, but it is undeniable that their influence spread in a decisive way up to the Apennines and along the Adriatic coast, eventually disappearing probably due to various factors such as the slight deterioration of climatic conditions, general political instability in Europe, and a probable inability to manage the resulting crisis.[13]

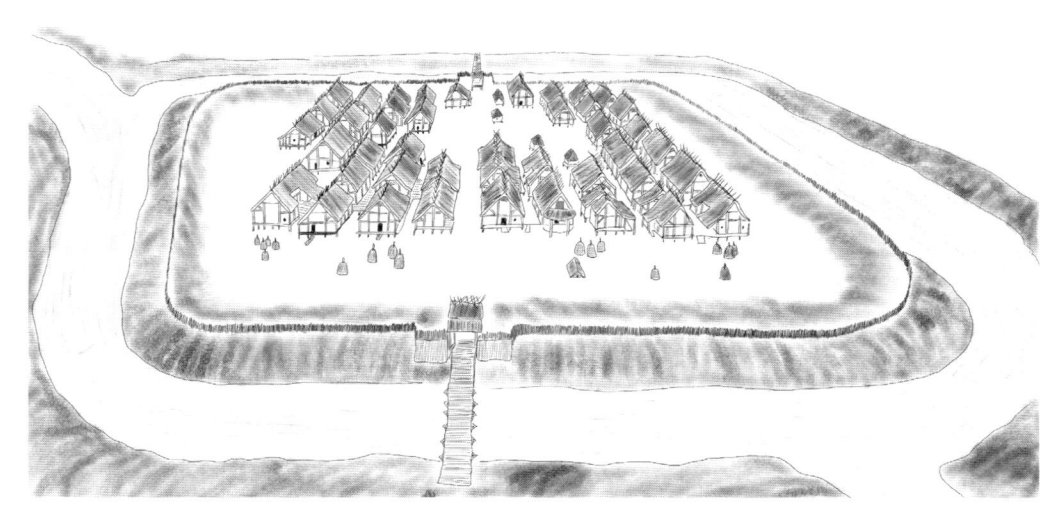

Fig. 4: Terramare village showing the principles that dictated the characteristics of the *Castra Romana*: the *vallum*, the *cardo* and the *decumanus*, the precise arrangement of the stilts in *insulae*. Not all scholars accept the cultural connection between Terramare and Rome, but the hypothesis is very suggestive. (*Drawing by the author, made on the basis of the reconstruction made by the Parco archeologico e Museoall'aperto della Terramare di Montale*)

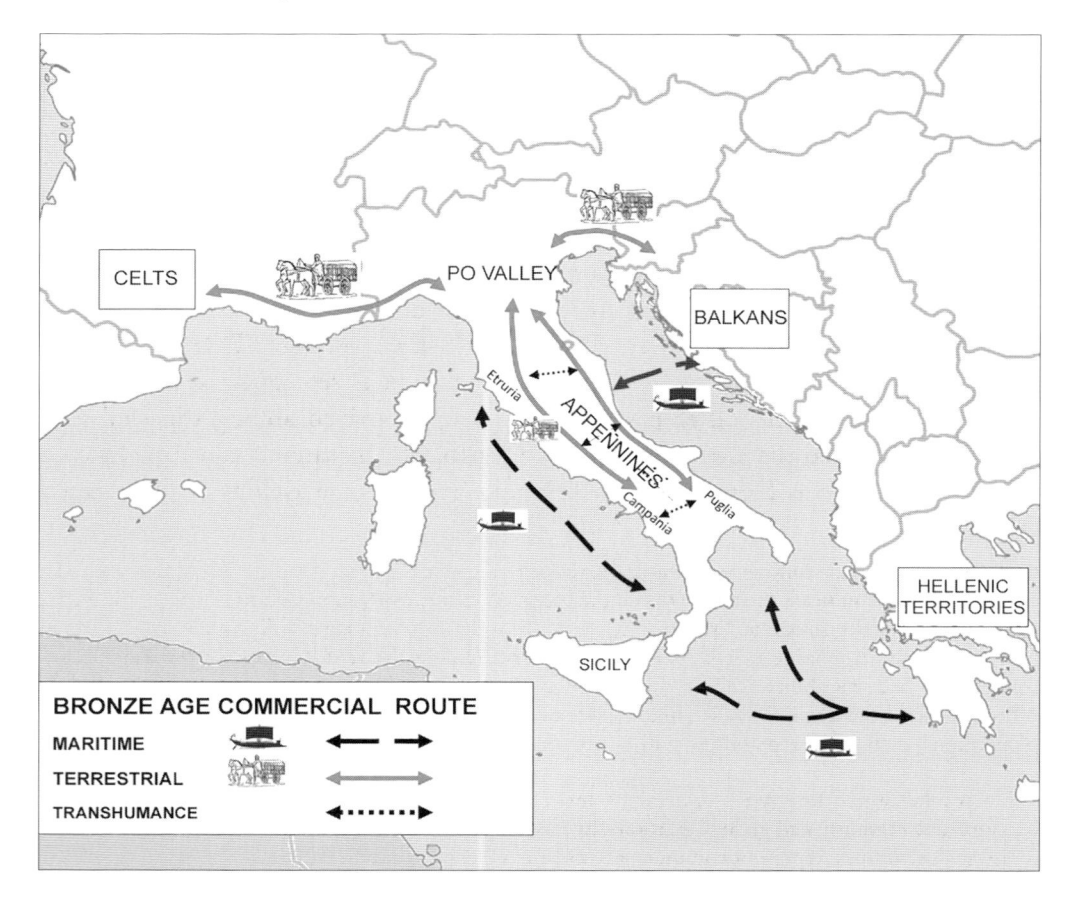

While the Terramare culture spread throughout the territory of northern Italy, the Apennine facies[14] flourished in the central-southern area from the eighteenth to the twelfth century BC, defining its spread along the homonymous mountain chain. Although presenting a homogeneous political-territorial entity, it consisted of individual communities with limited territorial influence, but having an important role in controlling communication routes.[15] The economy of these populations was mainly pastoral, its communities practising seasonal semi-nomadism and burying their dead.

We would like to draw the reader's attention to the group of Apennine *gentes*, as they are the result of a long process of development, born in northern Italy within the Polada culture, then migrated further south and evolved in the Terremare, developed in central Italy, in the mountainous territory of the Apennines, to the homologous culture. From this territory and from these *gentes*, the need for combat techniques based on the sword, and the birth of the *gladius*, arose.

Late Middle (1350–1200 BC) and Late (1200–1000 BC) Bronze Age
According to ancient historians, at the time of the Trojan War, Italy was inhabited by the Umbrians (Oμβρικοι)[16] who the Romans called Aborigines, to indicate that they had existed since the 'origins'. Pliny confirms them to be the oldest Italic lineage, very old *gens antiquissima Italiae*.[17]

The Paleoumbri[18] (based on the common archaic language spoken to distinguish them from the Iron Age Umbrians) were *gentes* of Indo-European origin, despite their language having unusual characteristics. The supremacy of these Apennine populations was challenged in the tenth century BC by the Anatolian people, called Tirreni according to the name of the son of the king who led them, arriving on the west coast (a phenomenon linked to the movements of the so-called 'Sea Peoples' since the twelfth century BC), and reaching the coasts and the territory of Tuscany. These foreign people, with a tradition of cremating their dead, imposed themselves on the Aborigines, giving rise to the Etruscan people in the Iron Age. This hypothesis is affirmed by Pliny the Elder, who writes that the Lydians set sail in search of a land and means to live, until after passing many people, arrived among the Umbrians, where they founded the cities that they still inhabit.[19] The same is confirmed also by other authors such as Herodotus,[20] and Pseudo-Scymnus[21] as well as by Dionysius of

Opposite: Fig. 5: Trade routes in the Italian peninsula.
Continuous lines: indicate the terrestrial communication routes, both extra-peninsular, with the Balkan populations and the southern French coast, and intra-peninsular along the Tyrrhenian and Adriatic coast, along the Apennine ridge. As early as the Bronze Age the first Mycenaean settlements were formed and had the ability to prevail over the local culture in Sicily and the Aeolian Islands. This colonisation took place on the coast, but failed to penetrate inland due to the resistance by the aboriginal populations, such as the Apennines, with whom they did not integrate.

- Horizontal dotted line (trans-Apennine): represents the communications related to transhumance, which until recently had great importance in cultural and commercial diffusion;
- Large dotted lines: represent communications by sea.

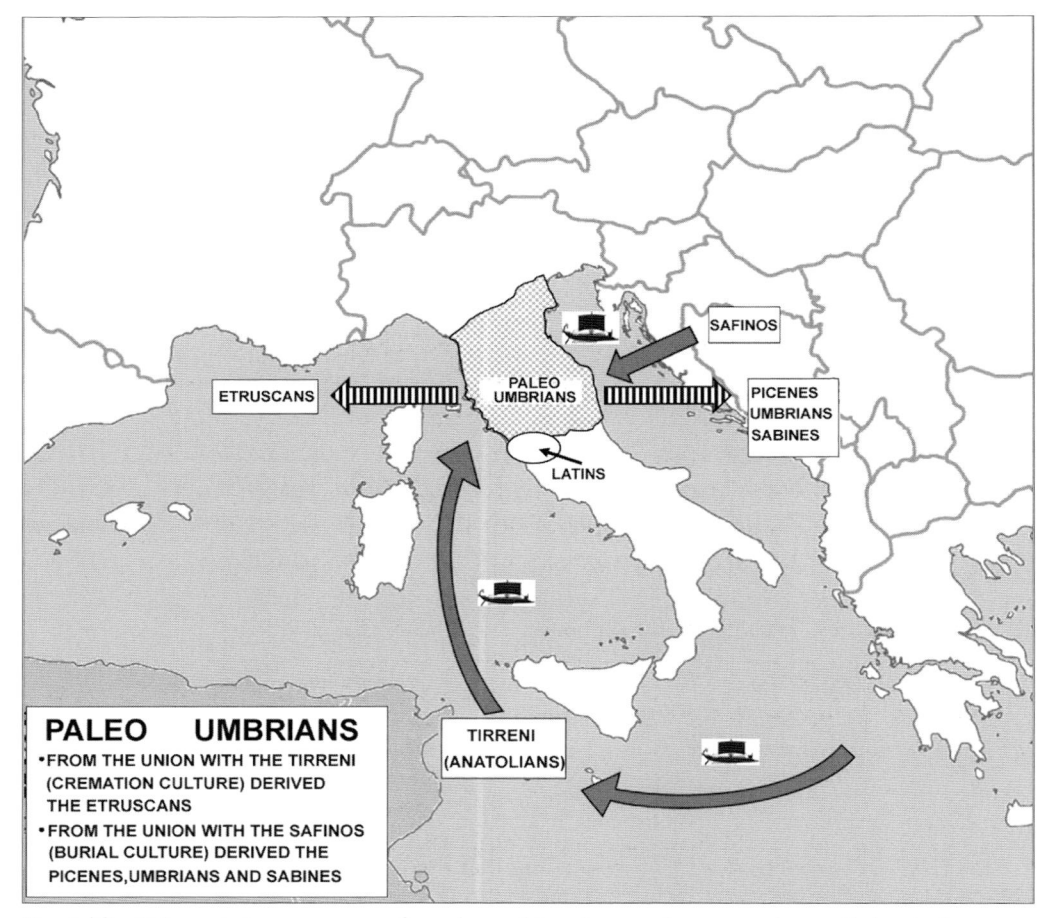

8   The Roman Gladius and the Ancient Fighting Techniques

Fig. 6: The Paleoumbri were a group of people speaking the same language who, until the ninth century BC, dominated the central northern part of the Italic peninsula. Defined by Pliny as 'the most ancient population of Italy' (*gens antiquissima Italiae*) they were Indo-Europeans with distinctive characteristics and very different from the Latin people. Migrations of foreign people, confronting the Paleoumbri people, gave rise to new archaeological facies: the Etruscans developed from the encounter with *gentes* of Anatolian origin, whilst the Picenes, the Umbrians and the Sabines were born from the encounter with the Safine population.

Halicarnassus.[22] In the ninth century BC the domain of the Paleoumbri was also on the east coast, when the Safinos, an Indo-European people of Balkan origin with a tradition of burying their dead, arrived on the Marche and northern Abruzzi coasts, giving rise to various populations such as the Picenes, the Umbrians and the Sabines. Unlike the Safinos, the Osci people developed from the merger of the Safini with the Opici, a proto-Latin people who lived in pre-Roman Campania.

Focusing our attention on the Latium region, which was inhabited by the Latins, reputedly an Indo-European population pre-existing the Paleoumbri, whilst the oldest human settlements on the top of the Capitolium Hill date back to the seventeenth and sixteenth centuries BC.[23]

The Latium area, having no metal deposits like in Etruria, was poorer and consequently less important than the Villanova-Etruscan area. Metal objects were purchased from travelling blacksmiths, who sold their wares and produced some on commission, essentially mainly prestigious goods and weapons, generally axes with raised edges, and bronze 'simple base' daggers with fused handles.

Only during the late Bronze Age will we see an important increase in materials in the inhabited areas, confirming the presence of craftsmen within the community,[24] as found on the Palatine Hill. A gradual process of social differentiation within the population, forming a new elite class, is evident from the presence of monumental tumulus tombs, with the appearance of collective burials and with the presence of weapons in male outfits. This suggests that during this period there was a tendency towards the formation of kinship groups, differentiated from the rest of the community, and the presence of a high level of conflict between the individual family groups. In every necropolis only one armed figure was present and because of this, in a context where it was prohibited to bury weapons with the ashes of the deceased, it has been interpreted by scholars that each group had a single political leader.

I.1,3 The *Latium Vetus* in the Late Bronze Age and Early Iron Age

Period	Age	Main Event	Grave Characteristics
I LATIAL PERIOD	Late Bronze Age tenth century BC	Alban Period	I Cremation Graves near the villages (Capitoline and Palatine Hills) Miniature weapons
II LATIAL PERIOD	Early Iron Age, first period 900–775 BC IIa 900–830 BC IIb 830–770 BC	Villanovian period	IIa Cremation Graves near the villages (Capitoline and Palatine Hills) Miniature and actual weapons ――――――――――――――――― IIb Burials Graves along the road axis (Esquiline) Interdiction of all weapons
III LATIAL PERIOD	Early Iron Age 770–720 BC IIIa 770–750 BC IIIb 750–720 BC	Romulean Age Foundation of Rome Increase of population Foundation of Pithekoussai Pre-colonial Greek contacts	III Burial (Cremation of high-level people) Actual weapons Luxury grave goods
IV LATIAL PERIOD	Iron Age – second period 720–580 BC	Orientalising Period (Eastern–Greek influxes) Servius Tullius	IV Burial (Cremation of high-level people) Actual weapons Modest funerary goods

Table 1: The four periods in which the *Latium Vetus* is historically distinguished, highlighting the main events that characterised each period and the type of burial.

The Latin people lived in the territory between the Tiber to the north (bordering Etruria), the river Garigliano to the south (the border with Campania), the Apennine mountains to the east and finally the Tyrrhenian sea to the west.[25] This ancient territory, called the *Latium Vetus*,[26] was the cradle of the Roman people, distinguished archaeologically in four historical phases ranging from the Late Bronze Age (first phase, about tenth century BC), to the second Iron Age (last phase, 720–580 BC, corresponding to the Roman Monarchical Period). In the most archaic phase of the history of Latium (I Latial Period) the marshy territory was poor, depending on Proto-Villanovan Etruria and its mineral resources to the extent that the two archaeological facies can be superimposed. This analogy is found both in the burial rituals and in the type of cremation, for which use of the urn is typical, and in the limited presence of weapons within the burials, unique to eminent persons who had centralised control over the rest of the population.[27]

During this period the Latial region had only secondary importance, representing the only road link between Etruria and the south, to the extent that the first phase of development took place along the coastal plain only. This decentralisation of roads was also favoured by the fact that at the time, the most important city was Cerveteri (called Caisra by the Etruscans and Caere by the Romans). It favoured the ford of the Tiber

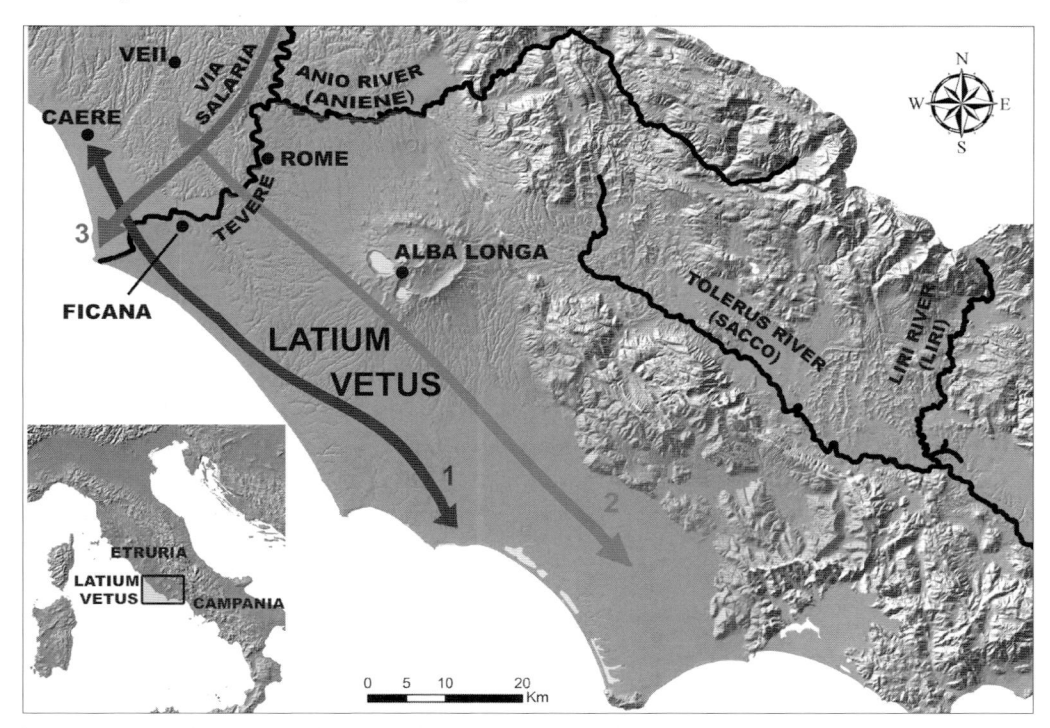

Fig. 7: Line 1 indicates the oldest route between Etruria and southern Italy, through the *Latium Vetus*, passing through the ford near Ficana on the Tevere; line 2 highlights the path that became prominent in the ninth–tenth century BC, through the ford of the Tiber Island on the Tiber, passing through the Alban Hills. Line 3 indicates the 'horizontal' route essentially linked to transhumance and the salt trade, which follows the future *Via Salaria*. (*Salaria road*)

river, barriers and natural limes between Etruria and the *Latium Vetus*, in its vicinity, in Ficana,[28] a town near Acilia, located towards the Latial coast.

Subsequently, the combination of the two factors, first being the Etruscan city of Veii becoming increasingly important at the expense of Cerveteri, and the second being that the Alban Hills (located in the central part of the region) rose to be an important religious and political centre (with the sanctuary of *Iuppiter Latiaris*[29] and the creation of a federation, that of the '*populi albenses*'), resulted in a new, more internal, road layout being created.

It is during this historical period, with the growing importance of the Latial region, that Rome was probably born, a group of 'frontier' villages controlling the ford on the River Tiber,[30] on this new route of communication that led from southern Etruria in the south of Italy through the Alban Hills. The ford of the Tiber at the height of the Tiber Island and the area of the *Forum Olitorium* favoured human aggregation and the appearance of settlements on the Capitoline Hill, where the cult of Saturn arose, worshipping the god who had taught the cultivation of fields and the first laws.

With the passage to the II Latial Period, the archaeological facies became the Villanovian one, with funerary rituals based on cremation, with specific connotations able to highlight their individuality: while in Etruria it was prohibited to put weapons with the remains to be cremated, in Latium many of the male burials appear to contain ritualistically-deposited miniature objects (including weapons), suggesting that 'the holders of miniature objects were possessors of a social role and a rank, distinguishing them from the other members of the society'.[31]

At this time, before the foundation of Rome, the population was made up of rough individuals, dedicated to an agro-pastoral life reflecting the description by Varro who, although in a different context, describes them as men 'of a sturdy sort, swift, nimble, with supple limbs; men who can not only follow the herd but can also protect it from beasts and robbers, who can lift loads to the backs of pack animals, who can dash out, and who can hurl the javelin'.[32]

We must understand that the sword did not yet exist as a typically Roman weapon and way of fighting, and that it was essentially seen only as an object with certain symbolic and rank characteristics. This sword was not an object of everyday use, since it was not useful in the context of maintaining an agro-pastoral life, unlike axes, slings, bows, spears and daggers. Only a leading figure in the society, belonging to the warrior elite, would have had the time and the resources to learn hand-to-hand combat skills.[33]

I.2 ARCHAIC FIGHTING TECHNIQUES

From the Late Bronze Age (fourteenth–thirteenth century BC) to the early Iron Age (tenth–eighth century BC)

The fighting techniques of these archaic *gentes* is a difficult topic to analyse as the information regarding how the weapons were used has been lost. However, some incontrovertible archaeological and iconographic evidence remains, which should be subject to interpretation. Unfortunately, the ancient literature is frequently incomplete,[34] a problem with no easy solution that has led many modern studies to develop various, sometimes contradictory, theories.

First of all, we must be aware that in ancient times the evolution of weapons and the progress of combat techniques was a very slow process compared to what we have witnessed in modern times, so much so that, to use the words of Jon E. Lendon, 'A soldier who went to sleep in his war gear in the fifth century BC would have been able to fight at no disadvantage in that equipment if he awoke in the fourth century AD, eight hundred years later'.[35] This was more evident during ancient times, in which the basic nature of the weapons allowed only simple attack and defence moves compared to those of later ages.

The relative similarity of the weapons leading up to the Late Bronze Age (1350–1200 BC), was the result of limited metal alloys and production techniques, which in turn allowed only rather limited variety in their employment. This contributed to the conventional definition of 'year zero', a period in which the weapons and the fighting techniques used were fairly homogeneous across the European continent.

The concept of tradition – linking every population to certain habits and customs – has its importance in explaining this slow technological progress. The transmission has always assumed the idea of 'delivery' (Cicero), 'teaching' (Quintilian) and 'narration' (Tacitus), and this concept of passing something from hand to hand, meant that over time a certain degree of uniformity was preserved.[36] This moral phenomenon, almost contractual, determined the identity and certain features in the use of weapons, and maintained a degree of invariability within individual peoples.

The concept of universality between different peoples, distant not only geographically but also temporally, can also be explained by human nature which, in its most instinctive forms, tends to manifest the same behaviours, thus explaining many common factors among the events narrated in the ancient Homeric world with some facts from the biblical period and certain attitudes of the present-day indigenous people of New Guinea. We can therefore say that, except for some differences related to the various cultural facies, archaic combat was based on standardised weapons and anthropologically superimposable rituals.

Based on these considerations, we will try to describe how central-Italic archaic combat developed, and even if we are often forced to speculate, our speculations will always be supported by historical and anthropological contexts that will make them very probable.

I.2,1 The *pater familias* and his armed community.
During this archaic era, before the birth of Rome (I – II Latial Period), the inability to produce a surplus of food prohibited the maintenance of a permanent army. This type of economy forced the communities to be defensive of their livelihoods and assets instead of being offensive. The people lived in '*familiae*' and the housing units had in their immediate vicinity a '*castrum*', an area of enclosed land, the word deriving from the Osco '*kastru*', meaning 'estate'.[37] Various '*familiae*' who lived within a territory, defined as '*acnu*' in Osco-Umbrian (from which it seems that the Latin agrarian unit '*acnua*' was derived), possessed a sacred common place, subjected to divine protection, which as a place of worship, also had a defensive and a market function during certain religious holidays.[38] As we can see, the Latin terminologies used to define domestic life, some of which also entered the military world, derive from Osco-Umbrian, thus demonstrating the mixture of the Apennine populations with those who inhabited the *Latium Vetus*. This notion is fundamental in understanding the influence of the central-Italic populations on the Romans, explaining how the diffusion of goods and culture in the following Monarchical Period also favoured the diffusion of the use of the archetypal Roman sword, the *gladius*.

PATER FAMILIAS
(HUT URN)

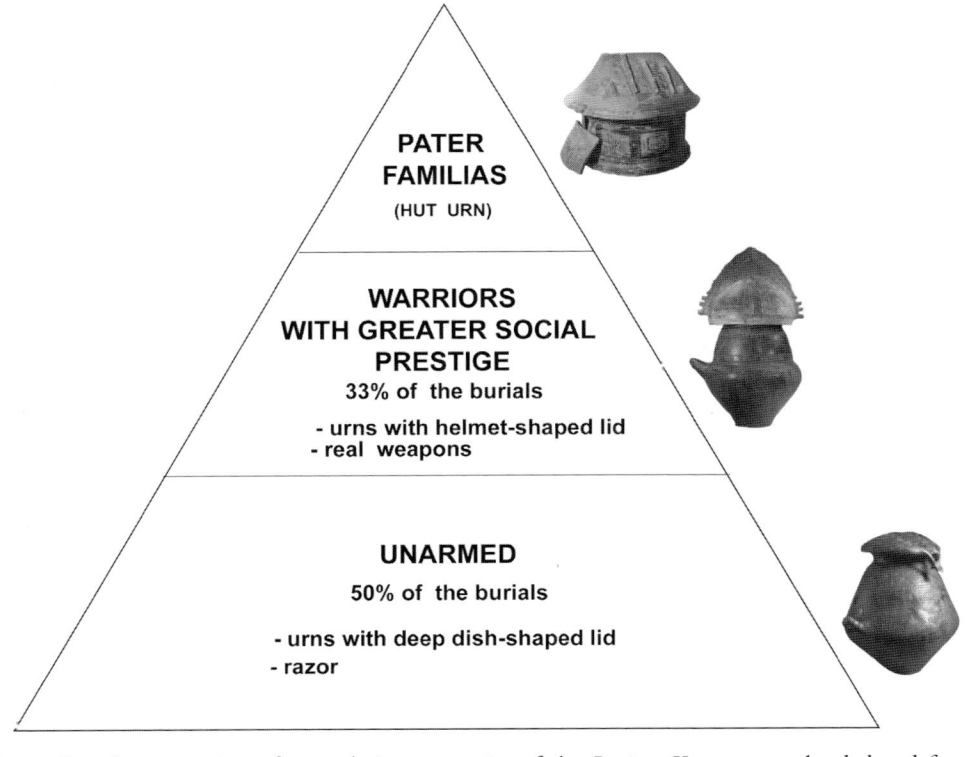

WARRIORS WITH GREATER SOCIAL PRESTIGE
33% of the burials
- urns with helmet-shaped lid
- real weapons

UNARMED
50% of the burials
- urns with deep dish-shaped lid
- razor

Fig. 1: Social organisation of an archaic community of the *Latium Vetus*, as can be deduced from a Tarquinian necropolis of the ninth century BC. At the top of the hierarchy is the *pater familias*, recognisable from the tombs with the hut urn; beneath it are the warriors of greater social prestige (33 per cent of the burials), buried with urns covered by a helmet-shaped lid and miniature or real weapons; at the base of the community are the unarmed (50 per cent of the total), probably identified as young people, possibly only armed with wooden *hastae*, of which no trace remains.

The social organisation can be inferred from burials, which mirrored the military hierarchy,[39] showing that during this time, there was no military organisation distinguishable from the social structure. In fact, the life of every citizen was marked by activities such as work, family, social participation, hunting and war. But to be recognised as an integral part of the community, the individual had to take part in its protection. This aspect can be extracted from the study of the Tarquinian necropolis of the ninth century BC, which we treat as a theoretical reference point. Male burials were differentiated according to the degree of kinship and the age of individuals; the head of the community being recognised as the top of the hierarchy.

The burials of the *pater familias* are recognisable from the gabled urn (typical of Latium and southern Etruria) which symbolises the high status of the person. Their rarity is contrasted by the large number of other members, including those of the warriors of greatest social prestige, which comprise 33 per cent of the overall number. The burials of the warrior caste are identifiable by cinerary urns with a helmet-shaped lid (in clay or bronze) and weapons, among which swords are rare, whether combined with a spear or not; pottery items are usually absent. Finally, at the base of the social hierarchy are the burials of the unarmed, with bowl-lidded urns, occasionally accompanied by a simple set of vessels, comprising approximately 50 per cent of the total number.

The *pater familias* was the head of a group of people consisting of his wife, natural and adopted children, with their wives and their children, as well as slaves.[40] He was the living progenitor of a kinship rank system, the *familia*; the *gens* consisted of several *familiae*, and was linked together by a kinship bond to a mythical and imaginary progenitor. The *pater familias* was not only the administrator of civil life, but also the commander during military operations and assumed the duties of a priest as well. With these prerogatives, in the context of a war (a sacral event), he became the link, the '*pontifex*', between the human and the divine reality. His function was to obtain and preserve divine favour, by taking care of the acts and behaviour of individuals and the community because 'men and gods are debtors and creditors the ones of the others', so to justify the expression '*do ut des*'.[41]

If we analyse some passages of the *Iliad*,[42] not only can we better understand this concept, but we can try to identify ourselves with this ancient mentality where divine actions influenced the fate of ordinary mortals on a daily basis, continually at the mercy of capricious fate. For example, when an arrow was shot, it was believed to be guided by a god, such as the one described by Hector:

> … for verily mine eyes have seen how Zeus hath brought to naught the shafts of a man that is a chieftain. Full easy to discern is the aid Zeus giveth to men, both to whom so he vouch safe the glory of victory, and whom so again he minisheth, and hath no mind to aid … [43]

Indeed, during a battle the leader always needed divine help, as Apollo says: 'Nay, warrior, come, pray thou also to the gods that are forever.'[44]

The authority of the *pater* was fuelled by the fact that during the Late Bronze Age, only a few could afford weapons training. Consequently, tactics were elementary and the wars had to be short, as most of the soldiers had a life characterised by agricultural activity. Maintaining a permanent army required too much manpower – men were needed in the fields and at home – nor was it possible to produce enough resources to maintain such an army in in the field.[45] From this context arises the big difference between the hero and the common soldier, the one who had the wealth to allow him military training and a panoply, and the one who had to work hard for survival and could only arm himself with a spear. In the eyes of these simple peasants, the warriors seemed superhuman to them. They were experienced and equipped with shiny and expensive weapons, lead and protected their family, and fought with a skill that seemed 'divine' to them. That the *pater familias*, the Homeric hero, was from a time when only a few skilled warriors existed can be understood from the fact that during this period, the outcome of a battle was frequently decided by a duel. The clash between individual heroes, so frequently described in the *Iliad*, was not only a poetic refinement, but also a means that allowed the just and noble achievement of victory, the hero essentially representing the *familia* and being the essence of the army.

The *pater familias*, or the hero who represented him, was the leader of the army, and Homer, when speaking about Hector, calls him 'shepherd of the host',[46] an individual who is superior in strength and ability compared to other men, guiding them to the fight in a way that the poet compares to a swollen river '… cometh down upon a plain, … driven on by the rain of Zeus, and many a dry oak and many a pine it beareth in its course, and much drift it casteth into the sea; even so glorious Aias charged tumultuously over the plain on that day, slaying horses and men'.[47]

We believe that Homeric duels were also fought in pre-Roman central Italy, as the tradition of duels still persisted in the following Monarchical Period, and the institution of the '*spoliae*' existed,[48] an honour given in homage to the soldier who killed an enemy general in single combat.[49] These archaic reminiscences of Roman history explain the value of individual combat during ancient times and how it was historically part of their way of fighting.

I.2,2 Offensive weapons: spear, sword and axe

In the *Iliad*, the fighting is mainly conducted 'with spear and sword and great stones',[50] while the employment of the bow is ascribed to 'one that is a weakling and a man of naught'.[51] Compared to a blow of a spear, the sword was less fatal (though more so than an arrow or a stone). From the analysis by BottoMicca,[52] who compared the deadly wounds in Homeric fighting, the following can be concluded:

	Spear	Sword	Arrow	Stone
Head	28	17	5	4
Chest	27		4	
Abdomen	25	4	1	
Upper limbs	9	2		
Lower limbs	2			
Total	91	23	10	4

Table 1: Location of fatal injuries, according to the different weapons, from the analysis of Homeric clashes by Augusto BottoMicca.

16   The Roman Gladius and the Ancient Fighting Techniques

Of 128 fatal blows, 91 of these (71 per cent) were caused by spears and only 23 (17.9 per cent) by the sword, showing how at the end of the Bronze Age, combat based on the sword was secondary, or more correctly an accessory, to the spear as will be shown later.

The archaeological finds confirm the prevalence of the spear as a widespread weapon among the tombs of the warriors. According to the description of the Homeric poem, the spears were around 180–220cm in length with a bronze laurel leaf-shaped point and a butt spike called '*sauroter*'.

We can deduce that the spear was the main weapon in the pre-Roman period from ancient Roman traditions where it continued to have a role in both military and civil life.[53] Adam and Rouveret have outlined in their studies how the spear signified a citizen authorised to manage weapons[54] and traditionally the name of the Roman people derived from this weapon, as can be seen in *Carmen Saliare*,[55] in which they are called '*pilum noepoploe*',[56] identifying them with the use of this weapon, while according to Plutarch, the spear possessed the name *quiris*, a word of Sabine origin, from which the appellative *quirites* would have derived.[57]

Many military events are traditionally connected to the *hasta*, an attribute of the god Mars, called *Hasta Martia*, an esteemed award during war for the most valiant soldiers,[58] so much so that it was defined by Festus as '*hasta summa armorum et imperii est*',[59] i.e. the highest expression of weapons and command. In addition, the *hasta pura*, a spear without a metal head, was the weapon with which the youngest warriors of the archaic age armed themselves with, the same with which the Fetiales priests entered enemy territory to declare war ('*hasta ferrata aut sanguine apraesta*' bloody and burnt on top).

The warrior deities, the Greek Ares and Athena, the Roman Mars and Minerva, are all depicted armed with a spear but not with a sword; this continued also in the following ages, when the sword had become the main weapon, since the cult tradition prevailed over the evolution of fighting techniques.

Fig. 2:
A) Etruscan votive bronze statuette representing 'Attacking Mars', from Umbria, of stylized form (sixth–fourth century BC), now in the Museum of Villa Giulia – Rome.
B) Etruscan bronze statue of 'Attacking Minerva', produced by the workshops of northern Etruria, former collection of the Dukes of Este, exhibited in the Galleria Estense in Modena. Fifth century BC.

   In all of the bronze statuettes depicting the two divinities, the right arm is raised in the act of brandishing the (lost) spear, while the left is leaning forward to hold the shield, present only in some specimens. (*Photos and drawing by the author*)

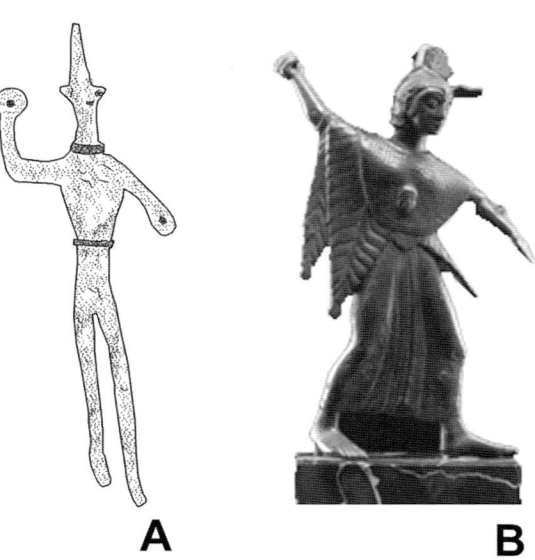

A   **B**

The importance of the spear also pervaded many aspects of the civil world, such as the saying *'recare Hastam rectam'* with the meaning of 'enjoy the civil rights'.[60] Mythologically speaking, the sacred cornel wood, revered at the *Scalae Caci*, originated from the javelin thrown by Romulus;[61] the *Hasta caelibaris* was used during weddings to ritually comb the hair of the *nubentes*,[62] while in public sales of slaves or confiscated property, the auctioneer placed one on the ground before starting an auction (*vendere, venire su hasta*), perhaps to show that this sale took place under the aegis of the state, a term still used today.[63] Finally, we can see how the spear has continuously armed warriors from Neolithic times up to the twentieth century, when it was in the hands of squadrons of mounted lancers. The popularity of this weapon is linked to its high effectiveness and ease of use, not requiring a lot of training.

When analysing the use of the sword in the text of the *Iliad*, we can see that it has many names (ξίφος,[64] ξιφίδιον,[65] φάσγγανον,[66] μάχαιρα, Ἄορ) according to typology and use (thrusting or cutting weapon), and we find it as part of hand-to-hand combat, especially in duels or as a means of breaking the shaft of a spear or arrow needing to be extracted from a body, or finally as a weapon to deliver the *coup de grâce* to a wounded enemy.

If we try to understand what the real sword fighting described in the *Iliad* was like, and if it was based on the thrust or cutting blow, we could probably deduce that both coexisted, but that slashing blows predominated. The duel between Hector and Achilles shows that the fight was not based on fencing techniques but essentially on the '*furor*' and physical prowess of the combatants. The Greek hero was inspired by a god, transforming the fight between the two armies into a trial by combat, in which the gods indicate the side they recognise as the right one.[67] Hector is likened to an eagle when in combat: 'he drew his sharp sword that hung beside his flank, a great sword and a mighty, and gathering himself together swooped like an eagle of lofty flight that darteth to the plain through the dark clouds to seize a tender lamb or a cowering hare.'[68]

In this same duel, the blows of the sword appear to be thrusting ones (Hector shakes the weapon suggesting slashing blows) in the context of a fight with different weapons, where Achilles responds to the attack with the *hasta* (which he doesn't throw and lose unlike his rival), and with which he pierces the throat of the Trojan after violently striking his helmet:

> even so Hector swooped, brandishing his sharp sword. And Achilles rushed upon him, his heart full of savage wrath, and before his breast he made a covering of his shield, fair and richly-dight, and tossed his bright four-horned helm; and fair about it waved the plumes wrought of gold, that Hephaestus had set thick about the crest. As a star goeth forth amid stars in the darkness of night, the star of evening, that is set in heaven as the fairest of all; even so went forth a gleam from the keen spear that Achilles poised in his right hand, as he devised evil for goodly Hector, looking the while upon his fair flesh to find where it was most open to

a blow. Now all the rest of his flesh was covered by the armour of bronze, the goodly armour that he had stripped from mighty Patroclus when he slew him; but there was an opening where the collar bones part the neck and shoulders, even the gullet, where destruction of life cometh most speedily; even there, as he rushed upon him, goodly Achilles let drive with his spear; and clean out through the tender neck went the point.[69]

According to the Homeric descriptions, fighting with the spear and throwing it at the opponent preceded fighting with the sword, the *extrema ratio* based on hand-to-hand combat.[70] The preferred target was the head, sometimes protected by a helmet, which was usually attacked with thrusts rather than cuts.

If the spear and the sword were the most important offensive weapons of the central Italic warriors, the axe was progressively abandoned from archaic times onwards since it involved cutting and piercing blows which were not suited to the type of combat being fought. But this phenomenon was not common amongst other people,[71] where its use lasted longer, as suggested by the Ode of Horace[72] for example, referring to its military employment by the central Alpine population of the fourth to first centuries BC.

I.2,3 The fighting

The *casus belli* that triggered a battle could have been a cattle raid (like the one by Caco against the oxen of Geryon in the possession of Hercules[73]) or a failure to respect territorial boundaries, as the sacral divisions of the land were defined by the Book of Vegoia.[74] We are still far from the epic battles of Republican Rome, since the ideology of the individual *familiae* was that of survival, where the weapons were owned and used according to the requirements of age and economic capacity – it was as important to be able to afford a sword as it was to have the time to train with it, making it impossible for the majority of the people to have. In fact, as Hobbs argues, war meant diverting physical resources to a fight with a minimum supply of weapons, and without proper equipment or adequate technical preparation, but only for short periods at a time as maintaining both crops and flocks would not allow the men to be away for long.[75] The manpower that was required for agricultural work was high and no adequate surplus was produced to maintain a deployment-ready army, resulting in the clashes being more of an extended skirmish, lasting from minutes to a period of a few hours,[76] supported by an army of individuals belonging to a family group, gathered when a particular need or emergency rose.

The descriptions of fighting given by Homer in the *Iliad* are poetically very beautiful but above all, appear realistic despite the fact that the events recalled date back to the thirteenth/twelfth century BC[77] and the poem is believed to have been written in the eighth century BC. Although various academic controversies still exist about these dates, the work remains an inexhaustible source of information, albeit to be taken with due caution.[78]

The close analogy that emerges between the Homeric fights described and those of the indigenous people of Papua New Guinea is very interesting, so much so that

Hans van Wees affirms that the behavioural mechanism follows 'mainly the same schema'. The study of these will therefore allow us to have a clear idea of the ancient ones. The London author says that before the clash, the warriors gathered around their leaders, ran towards the battlefield after a harangue, dispersed and slowed down as they approach the enemy, until they got within range of the opposing lines. At this point the warriors are in loose order and continuously moving, not only from side to side to avoid being an easy target, but also forward and backward: the men come forward, stay for a while to fight, then retire to rest. They fight with bows or spears, depending on their personal preference. The spears, as in Homer, are both thrusting and throwing weapons. At any time, only about a third of each army takes an active part in the battle, while two-thirds remain standing or sitting behind and observe the progress of the action. During this disorderly skirmish, the front line continues to fluctuate, moving forward and backward depending on whether one of the hosts organises a charge. As the afternoon approaches, the rhythm of the fight develops into a series of relatively short fights and breaks between them. On average, a day of battle consists of ten or twenty fights between the opposing ranks, lasting 10 to 15 minutes each. As the action unfolds, the forces expand into a 'scattered formation', closing up again if the situation requires it.[79]

In the light of these studies, we can reconstruct the actions in battle of the various *patres familiarum*, each followed by their own *familiae*. Each group fought in a swarm on the battlefield, assembling and breaking up, forming groups or maniples, concentrating on the throwing of javelins, scattering to avoid being hit by the opponents' javelins, making *impetus* on the enemy and dispersing in individual duels on the field.[80] The *Iliad* describes a type of combat that is metaphorically represented as a swarm of bees;[81] it was an instinctive, unorganised way of fighting, where the soldiers were not well aware of the progress of the battle, as happens to Hector:

> Nor did Hector as yet know aught thereof, for he was fighting on the left of all the battle by the banks of the river Scamander, where chiefly [500] the heads of warriors were falling, and a cry unquenchable arose, round about great Nestor and warlike Idomeneus.[82]

However, there are also some passages in the *Iliad* describing combat 'consisting of a group of warriors united with each other', such as those found in Books XIII (vv 126–135) and XVI (vv 211–217), fighting in tight formations, armed with longer spears and large shields, even being exalted in the Homeric work as superior to single combat with small shields, which made it more agile and suitable for less talented warriors.[83] This narrative does not contradict what has been said so far, as such a compact deployment was not normal in archaic battles. The description of infantrymen who fought in this way must not make one to believe that hoplite deployment was already in use, as was typical of the subsequent period, from the seventh to the middle of the fourth century BC. Bettalli explains how the citizen of hoplite rank, endowed with the resources capable of providing him of the necessary surplus to purchase the panoply, coincides with an 'Aristotelian middle class', a factor of democratisation in comparison to the wars between the heroes of the Homeric age and also a valid bulwark against the ever-present danger of the *Demos*, owners of almost nothing.[84]

But even if we exclude hoplitism, we cannot deny the existence of primordial compact formations, as described by Hans van Wees during the clashes between Papua New Guineans, and which can be seen on the Banner of Ur and on the frescoes of Santorini. During certain times, for example when it was necessary to penetrate an enemy camp, it is evident that more organised fighting techniques were required. Spearmen equipped with shields, who usually formed one-tenth of an army, advanced in tight formation, holding on to each other to protect themselves from the flanks. The archer shot arrows over their heads, or from the flanks.[85] Such formations recall the organisation of the Greek and Roman armies, sowing the seed that Greece was the birthplace of hoplitism and Rome to maniples of soldiers.

The contrast between an instinctive fight based on the *furor* and the one based on organised ranks is present in the archaic period, so much so that it induced the ancients to venerate two distinct warrior deities, each of them representing a special aspect of war. For the Greeks, Ares represented fighting and bloodlust, the fury that led to the massacre in battle, but was also the god who suffered a defeat by Athena, the goddess who was born armed from the head of Zeus. In fact, Athena, called *Promachos*, 'the one who leads the armies into battle', represents mind over instinct, symbolising organised

Fig. 3: The Capitoline triad, Jupiter–Juno–Minerva, sculptural work of the second century BC from Guidonia, Rome. (*Author's photo, courtesy of the 'Rodolfo Lanciani' Archaeological Civic Museum of Montecelio*)

combat. In the Roman world, on the other hand, the *furor*'s divinity was Mars, who was part of the first Capitoline triad, together with Jupiter and Quirinus, and who was later replaced by Minerva who, together with Jupiter and Juno, formed the triad of the new major divinities.

The replacement of Mars with Minerva, the goddess of war, strategy, wisdom and intelligence, underlined the change in the way of fighting, which evolved in favour of organised methods like the one we will see as the main one in Monarchical Rome.

We can deduce that the battles were fought between two opposing sides, each composed of many small groups of warriors, and in each group we can see a glimpse of the archaic form of the future Roman maniple. The warriors forming the armed group were united by family bonds and were led by a hero, the *pater familias* or, if he was too old himself, the warrior who represented him (a sort of centurion *in nuce*). The battles were essentially based on physical strength and the main difference between a recruit and a veteran was that the former, the youngest, only engaged in long-range fighting, unlike the older ones (skilled and brave) who also sought physical contact with the enemy. The spear, which even in the *Iliad* is the most lethal and commonly-used weapon, was thrown by the younger ones while swarming from the rear towards the front of the fight, and used for thrusts over- or under-hand by the veterans in direct combat with the enemy. In the second phase of the clash, the older warriors threw their spears at their opponent, before moving onto hand-to-hand combat, in which the sword became the decisive element. As described by Maurizio Martinelli, only with time did the 'choral' organisation of the armed men (a fight led by Athena/Minerva) prevailed over the uncertainty of the clashes, linked both to fear and instinct even as the *furor* of the individual warriors (represented by Ares/Mars) became less and less decisive for the outcome of the battle.

I.2,4 From spear to sword through the duel with the buckler ('*brocchiero*')

In the Greek world the monomachies were clashes essentially based on the employment of the *hasta* between two contenders, the heroes, whilst the sword was the weapon relegated to the melee, when the distance between the duellists was too close, making the spear useless. Thanks to the *Iliad*, we have a clear idea of the development of an archaic Greek duel, but on the contrary, we have no testimony attesting how it could have taken place in the Italian peninsula. However, relative to eighth-century BC archaeological evidence, the existence of fights exclusively based on the sword and a small shield in the territory of northern and central Italy appears, which in some cases had very particular features reminiscent of the fighting with the medieval buckler ('*brocchiero*'). According to the Renaissance treatise of Maestro Francesco di Sandro Altoni,[86] the diameter of the shield had to be equal 'to the distance of the shoulder joints, that is, equal to the person's chest'. This small shield, which the treatise describes as 'having a very ancient origin', was made of steel or, as probably in the archaic period in question, wood or leather, and often equipped with one or more bosses on the surface, the so-called '*brocco*', useful for blocking an enemy's sword.

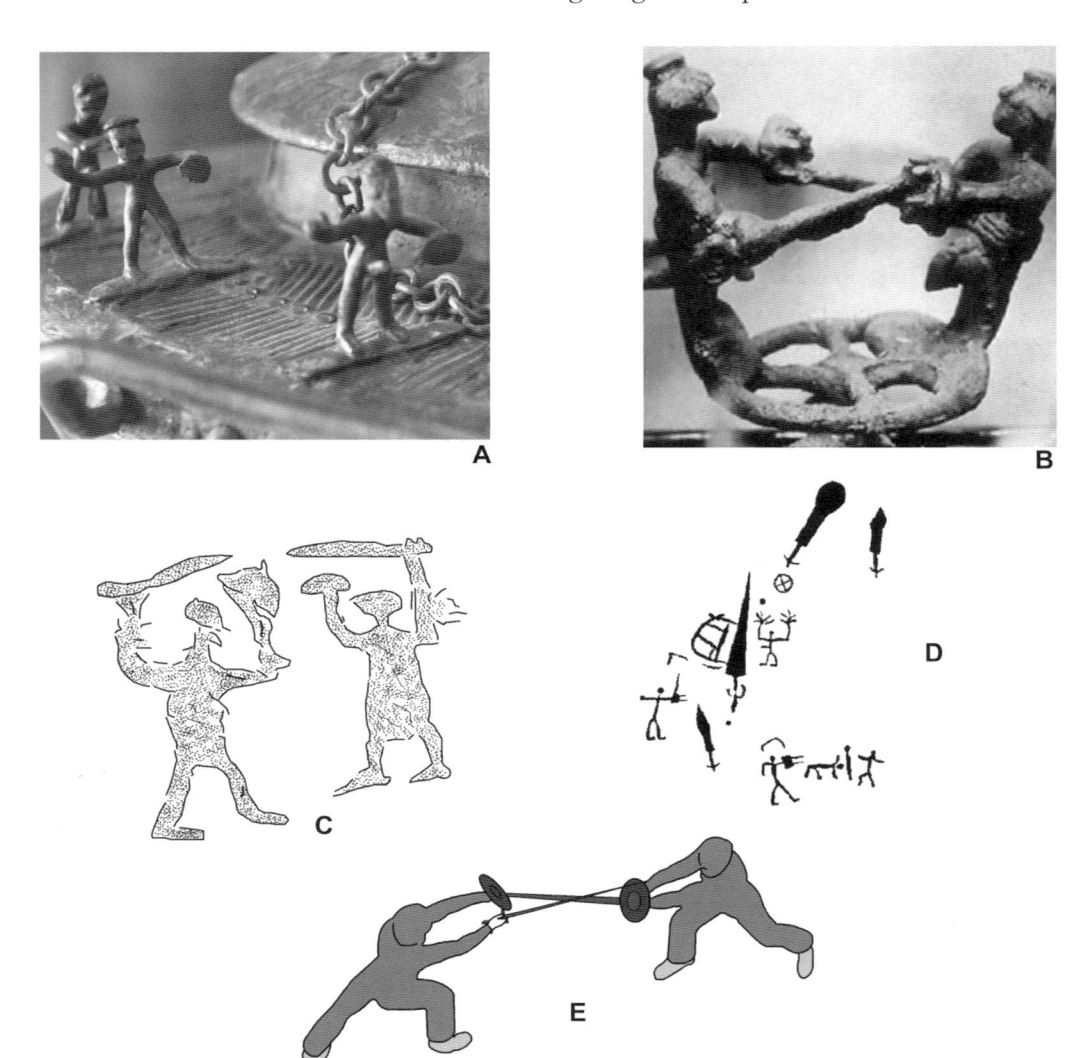

22 The Roman Gladius and the Ancient Fighting Techniques

Fig. 4:
A) Detail of the Bisenzio vessel (from Lake Bolsena – VT) now in the Museum of Villa Giulia (Rome), eighth century BC.
B) Detail of the bronze incense cart from the Olmo Bello necropolis, Bisenzio (Viterbo), in the Museum of Villa Giulia (Rome). On both, we see figures of warriors performing ritual dances. Note the extremely small size of the shields, used to protect against strikes in the context of ritual duels with the sword.
C) Valcamonica rock carvings representing duels with sword and small round shield (*brocchiero*). The armed men are represented dressed while undertaking a high guard position.
D) Rock carvings in Torri del Benaco on Lake Garda with two armed with bucklers. The shield is represented with the '*brocco*', bosses employed to block the opponent's sword during the duel. Rock engravings of Valcamonica representing duels with sword and small round shield (buckler). The armed men are represented dressed while assuming a high guard position.
E) The guard position defined as 'straight line with straight line' taken from Antonio Manciolino's fencing manual. The prints are taken from the Achille Marozzo Manual.

Archaeological evidence attesting to this type of combat can be found on the rock carvings of Valcamonica[87] and Torri del Benaco on Lake Garda[88] (both sites located in the central Alpine valleys of Northern Italy and dating back to the eighth–seventh century BC), in addition to two bronze finds from the Olmo Bello Necropolis,[89] in southern Etruria, on the border with Lazio[90] (Fig. 4).

From these findings we can deduce that during the eighth century BC, the combat with the *brocchiero* was practiced both in a religious and purely ritual way, and also in war, even if limited to the armed 'heroes', confirmed by the archaeological finds that testify its use, even if without the '*brocchi*'. The fighting style is suggested by the Olmo Bello Necropolis censer, where the duellists are cast bronze figures on a rotating wheel, showing how the fencers fought in a circular pattern during a duel. We can guess, as well, that buckler (the small shield with or without '*brocchi*') and *kardiophylax* (a bronze plate the same size as the buckler, used as a warrior's chest protection, were the main elements of a dynamic combat, performed with small and light armour aiding the fencer's agility. The protagonist of this duel was the sword, with its striking blows (warded off by the breastplate and intercepted by the buckler), but not the spear or other hand weapons. In these areas, the duel would therefore appear to differ from that described in the *Iliad*, in which we know that the sword took the main role only after the spear became useless.

I.3 BRONZE SWORDS IN THE ITALIC TERRITORY

This ancestral jumble of people and cultures in the Italian peninsula, with its equally numerous ways of understanding an armed conflict, generated a multitude of weapons, and as Hanson states, 'Tactics more often create, rather than merely respond to, weaponry'.[91]

Towards the Middle Bronze Age (fourteenth–thirteenth century BC) a characteristic development of swords began, that would slowly but surely lead to the appearance of the *gladius* as understood today. The importance of what happened in these distant centuries is considerably greater than what is normally considered, so much so that we can say with a certain confidence that all the main characteristics of the *gladius*, and of the Roman military organisation in its complexities, were already present and distinct at the time that Rome was founded.

We can say that the *gladius* was by no means a sudden invention nor the adoption of a weapon of another people, but the result of a cultural, social and military development that lasted centuries, taking place in a progressive and unconscious way, like continuous warfare. An in-depth study of Bronze Age Italic swords and of their complementary defensive equipment will confirm this fundamental proclamation.

I.3,1 Classification

The first organised conflicts probably began in Mesopotamia between 2300 and 1550 BC,[92] when bronze was available in sufficient quantities to be supplied to the troops; but in Europe, the first significant appearances of bronze swords are recorded slightly later, towards the sixteenth–fifteenth century BC.

Their classification is not simple: a first attempt was made by Luigi Campi[93] followed by the studies of Undset[94] and Naue at the end of the nineteenth century.[95] Only a few years later they attained a certain maturity with Colini[96] and most importantly with a second work by Naue,[97] which was considered the best for a long time. Finally, in much more recent times, we have the complex and well-articulated classification of V.B. Peroni, which, although limited to the swords of continental Italy, is exhaustive.[98]

For the purposes of a summary, which is well suited to the needs of our study, it is possible to divide the bronze swords into the following main groups:

- 'Simple base' swords: often characterised by a triangular blade with rounded or trapezoidal shoulders, fixed to the handle in a simple way with two or more bronze rivets (Fig. 1-A; 2-A). They are the most archaic, essentially the first to appear on the European scene, in the Middle Bronze Age.[99]
- Swords with herringbone tang: characterised by blades of often variable shape and type but always equipped with a simple solid barrel-shaped tang (Fig. 1-B; 2-B) which was inserted inside the handle. Also very archaic, they appear almost simultaneously with those with a simple base.
- Naue swords: having blades made in a single piece with a tang, the latter having a flat shape with raised edges. They appear after the first two types, around 1200 BC.

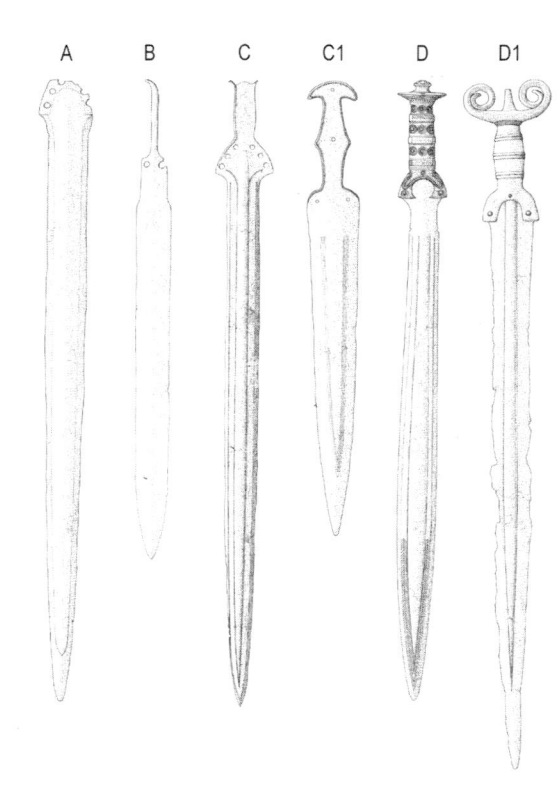

Fig. 1: Main types of bronze swords:

A) 'Simple base' sword, from Biganello (Mantua), length 61cm, Pigorini museum, Rome (MBA, early LBAII).
B) 'Plug tang sword', length 46.5cm, ex F. Marganoni collection (LBAII).
C) 'Grip tongue' sword, Treviso, length 61.5cm, Treviso Civic Museum (MBA–LBA IIB).
C1) 'Grip tongue' sword of Etruscan type, Latina (Rome), length 44cm. Tomb XVI of Satricum (end of LBAIIb–IA1).
D) 'Full handle' sword, Bernate (Como), length 60cm. Civic Museum of Como (from EBF to IA1);
D1) Sword 'with full handle, subtype' with antennae, Rome, length 68.5cm. Esquiline necropolis (from the end of LBA IIB to IA1).

Drawings from Peroni, *Die Schwerter in Italien*.

For simplicity we also include the daggers commonly found in Etruscan territory in this group (Fig. 1-C, C1).
- Full handle swords: having a solid bronze handle, usually heavily decorated, in use from the Late Bronze Age to the early Iron Age. The so-called 'antennae' swords are also included in this group (Fig.1-D, D1).

I.3,2 The influence of bronze sword technology on fighting techniques

One of the main characteristics of bronze swords is the lesser strength of the material, due to which blades longer than 50–55cm would be easily damaged. In the most archaic period, when the 'simple base' types were still widespread, this problem was accentuated by the poor system for fixing the handle to the blade (Fig. 2-A) using only simple rivets, which would easily break.[100] The shortness of the weapon forced it to be used practically only as a stabbing weapon.

Things began to change around 1200 BC, with the arrival of a sword with innovative technology, the so-called 'grip tongue'.[101] The big innovation was not in the metallurgical characteristics of the material used, which for a long time was always bronze, but in the system of how the blade and handle were united. The blade extended into the handle forming a sort of a metal tongue (Fig. 1-C; 2-C; 3) as wide as the handle and with slightly raised edges, which considerably increased its strength and rigidity. The grip, made of organic material, was then fixed to it with rivets (Fig. 2-C). This solution

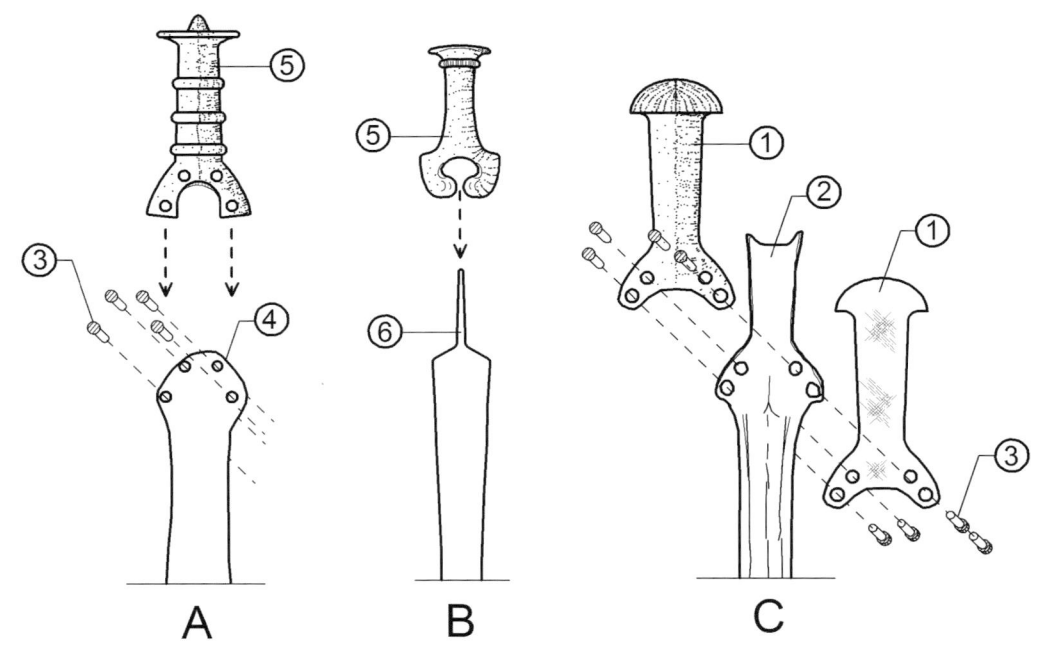

Fig. 2: Simplified diagram of the assembly of the hilts of the different bronze sword types:
'Simple base' sword.
'Thorn tang' sword.
'Grip tongue' sword.

Key:
1) Grip of organic material.
2) Metal tongue.
3) Bronze rivets.
4) Portion of the blade that slipped into the hilt.
5) Bronze hilt cast as a single piece.
6) Tang.

made the sword extremely solid, averting the lethal danger that, following a heavy impact, the hilt would separate from the blade.

This innovation generated an important change in the way of fighting. Since making a longer blade was now possible, the weapon could also be used for slashing blows (meaning both the cutting action and the impact, fracturing action) and no longer just for thrusting with the point.[102] European fighters, especially in Central Europe but also in the Aegean-Anatolian area, took advantage of this development; this is unsurprising since, as we know, a man's instinct is to hit his enemy with a sabre, following the instinctive rotational movement of the arm from the shoulder.[103] This way of striking was well suited to warriors of sufficiently robust build and of good height such as those of Halstattian stock, since the sword, although technically simple and instinctive, required a fair amount of muscular power to be lethal and effective. On the other hand, the people of central Italy had less physical stature which made them less suited to this. In this regard, we recall the words of Julius Caesar in *De Bello*

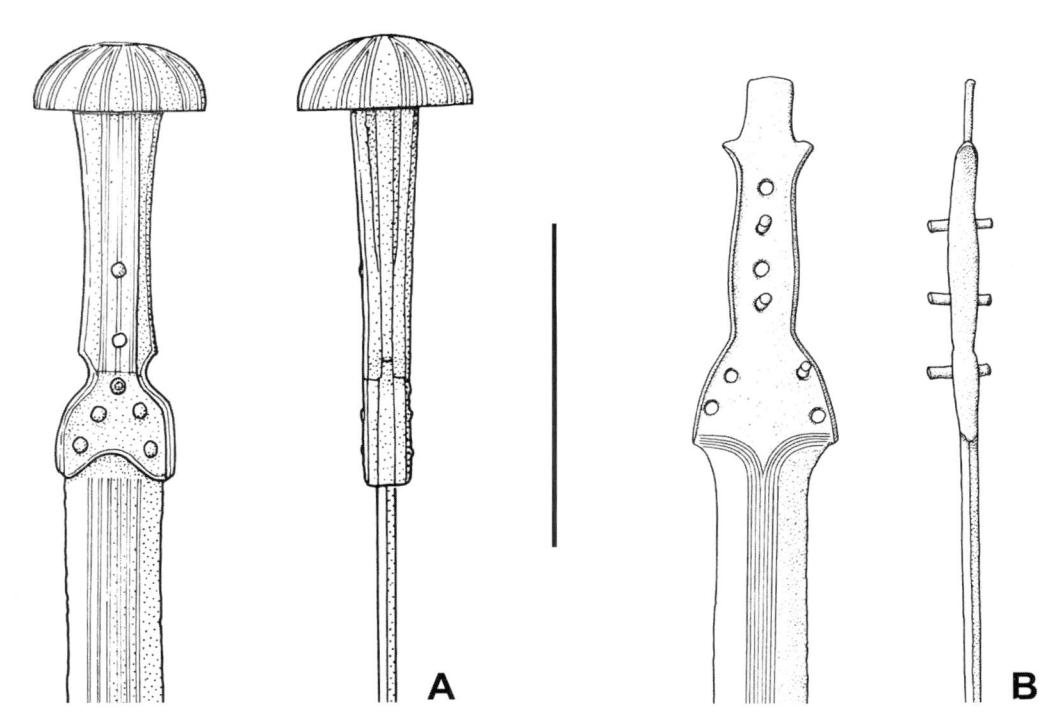

Fig. 3: A) A rare example of a grip tongue sword hilt with an ivory handle (length 442mm, British Museum, PRB 11-10-1). B) Analogous example, which only retains the rivets used to fix the grips (length 400mm, British Museum, PRB WG1143). Drawings from *Prehistoric Metal Artefacts from Italy in the British Museum*, by Anna Maria Bietti Sestieri and Ellen Macnamara.

Gallico, even though they refer to much more recent times: 'men, especially of so puny a stature (for, as a rule, our stature, short by comparison with their own huge physique, is despised of the Gauls)'[104] and 'The Suebi are by far the largest and the most warlike nation among the Germans ... the regular exercise ... nurses their strength and makes men of immense bodily stature'.[105]

Consequently, a fundamental difference began to emerge, which conditioned the way sword fighting developed. The Central Italic people did not tend towards the slashing blow like rest of the Europe, but continued to remain faithful to pointed weapons, which could be equally lethal, if not even more so, without the need for great physical power.[106] In the words of V. D'Ercole,

> around the year 1000 BC, in the transition phase between the Bronze Age and the Iron Age, the length of bronze swords undergoes a drastic decrease in central Italy, passing from 65 to 40cm [almost all of the grip tongue type] ... Not only have the dimensions of the sword changed but it is above all its shape and profile that makes us understand how its use in combat has profoundly changed, from preferably edged weapons to exclusively pointed weapons. This fundamental change in war tactics becomes even more evident with the early Iron Age, in which only short swords, so-called Italic, are attested.[107]

However, the fact that the Italians did not stray far from thrusting combat meant that the tongue sword, no matter how effective, never completely replaced the first two models in central Italy[108] (the simple and pin tang), which still remained compatible with this type of fighting, even if they were less reliable. In the archaeological panorama of these areas there are numerous finds, especially of the simple-based type, coeval with those of the grip tongue type, all being rather short and without any type of bronze hardening,[109] which in the rest of Europe we see disappearing.

I.3,3 The types of swords in the Italic territory and their distribution

Therefore, we have identified that how around 1200 BC, a certain differentiation began between the use of swords in Italy, which remains thrusting with the point, and that of the rest of Europe, which begins to veer towards slashing. It is now interesting to investigate in detail the spread and distribution of swords in Italy.

As a starting point, we want to begin with a series of data in the two maps in Fig. 4 and 5 and in Table 2. In the first (Fig. 4) we report the location of 245 specimens for which the place of discovery and the period is certain. Although not complete, the data that we have is still sufficient to provide us with significant information: first of all the distribution of the finds corresponds to the migratory path of the Indo-European people as discussed above and as shown on the map by the overlapping of sword finds with arrows indicating these paths.

The second map (Fig. 5), on the other hand, is a detailed version of the first, in which we can see a differentiated geographical distribution of the various sword types with chronological periods. Finally, Table 2 presents the numerical evidence. From this data we immediately notice some interesting facts:

- the distribution of swords is by no means ubiquitous throughout the peninsula, but concentrated in certain areas of the north, north-east and centre. In the southern part, as well as in that area roughly coinciding with the Villanovan-Etruscan territory, their presence is minimal;
- considering the various types of weapons distributed in these latter territories, southern and Etruscan, we realise that here the swords, in addition to being scarce, are almost exclusively Etruscan-type grip-tongue daggers (Fig. 1 – C1), with any other type being absent. The only significant exception is a fair amount of specimens with grip tongues (Fig. 1 – C), now held in a storage room in Peschici (Gargano – Puglia)
- On the contrary, the Etruscan-type grip tongue specimens are completely absent in the north of the peninsula.

The Archaic Period

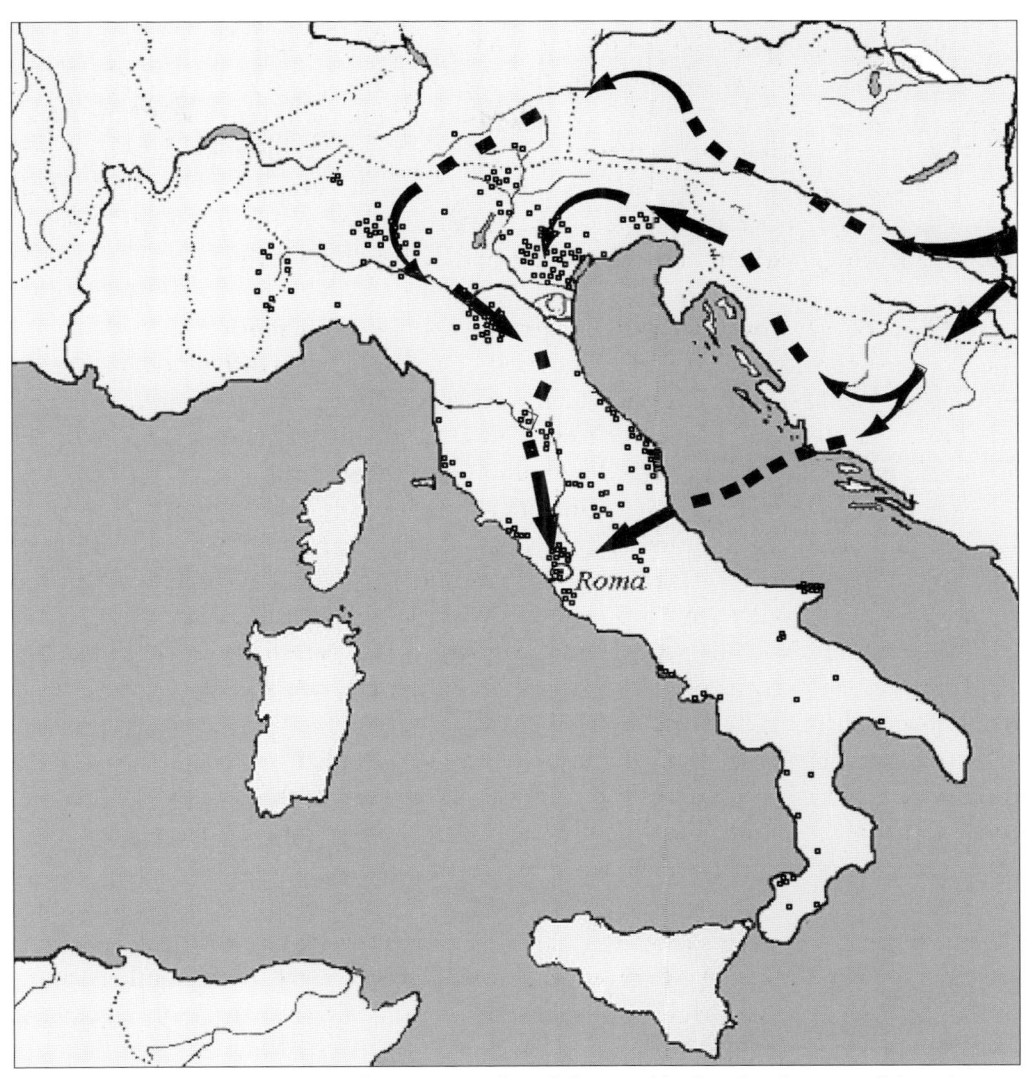

Fig. 4: Overall view of the finds of bronze swords and daggers (dots) and indication of the migratory flows of Indo-European people on Italian territory (arrows).

Type	North	Centre	South
Plug tang sword	26	6	0
Simple base	37	6	2
Grip tongue	32	25	13
Etruscan grip tongue	0	41	7
Antennae sword	15	11	2
Full handle sword	22	0	0
TOTAL	132	89	24

Table 2: Numerical subdivision by type of sword and location. For a better understanding, read this in relation to the detailed maps (Fig. 5)

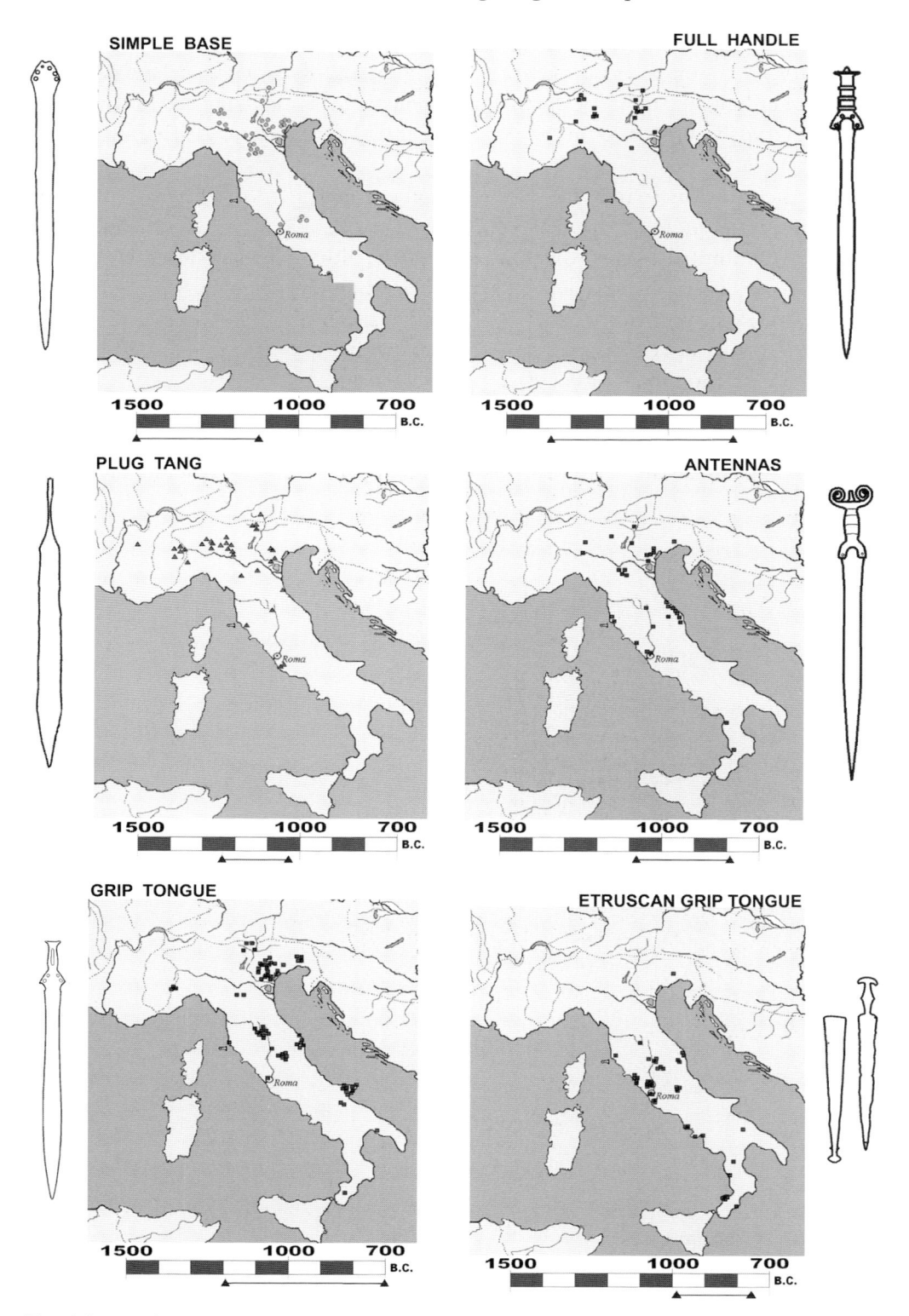

Fig. 5: Detailed view of the distribution of the various types of bronze swords on Italian territory, with indications of the chronological period of diffusion.

The analysis of blade lengths also provides important information. The data of all the specimens examined are summarised in Fig. 6, and show us how there is a clear prevalence of long blades in the north, a preference for the medium ones in the centre and finally for the short ones in the south and in Etruria, better classified as daggers rather than real swords.

Conclusions and more important information can be made from a further study. A particular subtype of 'simple base' swords, called 'Pertosa' (Fig. 7, fourteenth-thirteenth century BC) is limited to the Apennine and partly, although very modestly, Sicilian territories. This is very limited as all the other contemporary 'simple base' subtypes are concentrated exclusively in the north of the Italian peninsula, with this one exception. We note that only the latter is a short and pointed weapon, and the remaining northern ones are, on the contrary, used for slashing.[110]

The subsequent evolution of the grip tongue specimens is similar. During the first period of their existence they were of substantial length and were used as slashing weapons, widespread in the north-east of the peninsula (the 'Allerona' subtype,

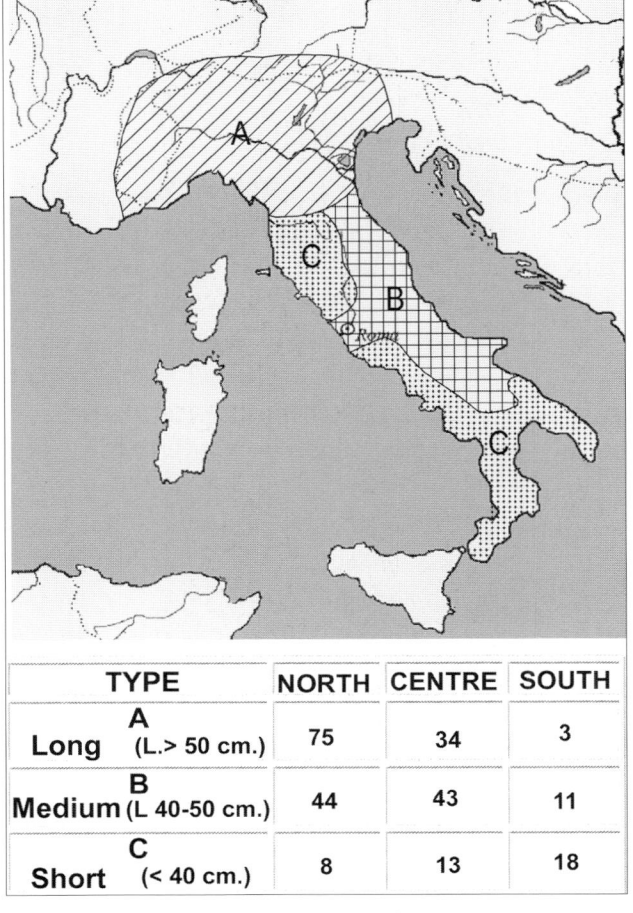

TYPE	NORTH	CENTRE	SOUTH
A Long (L.> 50 cm.)	75	34	3
B Medium (L 40-50 cm.)	44	43	11
C Short (< 40 cm.)	8	13	18

Fig. 6: Locations of swords on Italian soil based on the average length of the blade.

A) Long swords (blade >50cm).
B) Medium swords (blade 40cm–50cm).
C) Short swords (with blade <40cm).

Fig. 7: Various types of bronze swords from Italy (from Peroni, *Die Schwerter in Italien*):
Pertosa type: specimen from Manacora, length 42cm.
Terontola type: specimen from the Montono River, length 44.5cm.
Frassineto type: Treviso, length 45.3cm.
Allerona type: location unknown, length 64.3cm.
Contigliano type: provenance unknown, length 414mm.
Castellace type: from Castellace, length 44.8cm.

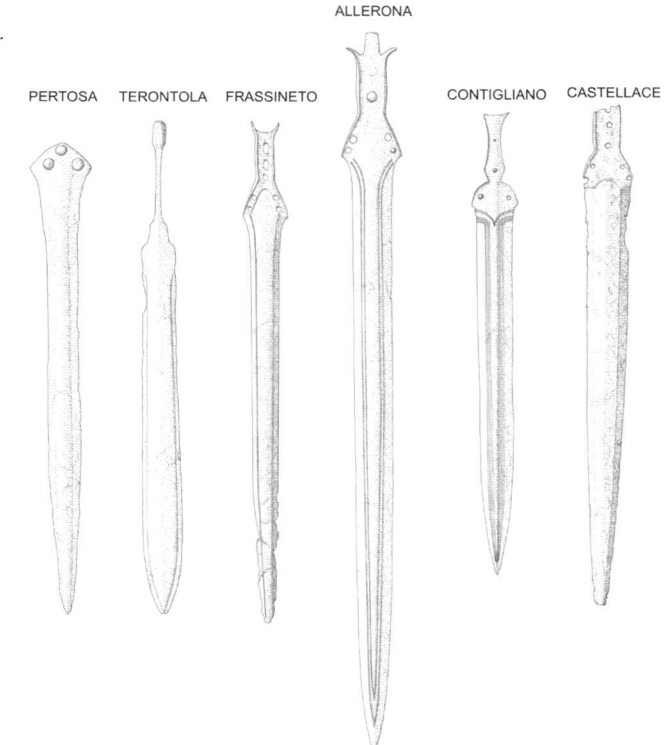

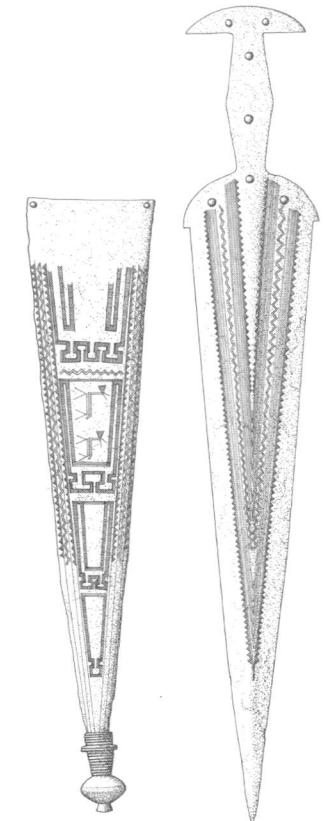

Fig. 7), and at the end of their evolution they were shorter and more pointed (the 'Frassineto' subtype, Fig. 7), no longer only found in their territories of origin but present in central Italy, in the Apennines. A very similar situation also occurs with the 'Castellace' and 'Contigliano' subtypes (Fig. 7), the presence of which is limited to the central areas of the peninsula and marginally in the southern ones. They are a prelude to the Italic iron sword and are once again short and undoubtedly for thrusting use. Therefore, it is confirmed that 'already during the last stages of the final Bronze Age, the use of short swords is generalised in central-southern Italy, while in northern Italy the spread of long slashing swords continues: an important cultural differentiation that will continue in the early Iron Age'.[111]

It is therefore evident that since about the tenth–ninth century BC swords were not distributed at random in

Fig. 8: Dagger with scabbard from Tarquinia, Monterozzi, tomb excavated on 23 March 1883. Length of the dagger 42.5cm, the scabbard 31.5cm. Note the refinement of the decorations (drawing from Peroni, *Die Schwerter in Italien*).

Italian territory: on the contrary, a clear distinction was already consolidated in the various territories, probably linked to the different methods of combat of the numerous populations and cultures.

The geometry of the 'spear' or 'lanceolate' blades deserves a mention. In the initial phase of their appearance, we find them mainly in the territories of the Po Valley, but they were progressively abandoned in favour of subsequent and decisive diffusion with the Apennine culture, especially with a subtype of the 'plug tang' called 'Terontola' (Fig. 7). This data, apparently of little significance, assumes instead that if we consider all the other subtypes of the 'thorn tang', similar but lacking the lanceolate form, remaining confined to their territories of origin, without any penetration into the Apennine one, it confirms that the lanceolate blades were much appreciated by the people of central Italy. We will later see how this is of fundamental importance, an unusual trait that will remain with the *gladius* for centuries.

Our study continues with the Etruscan-type grip tongue daggers, which include various subtypes, all very similar to each other. They are characterised by their modest length (almost always less than 40cm) and by the refinement of the decoration of both the blades and especially of the scabbards. We have little data on the hilts, only rare fragments in ivory and bone, which show similar refinements. We have mentioned that these weapons are almost exclusively found in the territory of Etruscan influence, in which practically all of the finds are attested, while on the other hand they are completely unknown in the north of the peninsula, where long slashing swords persist in the same period.

Numerous clues lead us to believe with reasonable certainty that they were not only used as battle weapons but also signified the status of their owner.[112] Often, as for example in tombs number 34, 36, 147, 149, 194, 197 and 199 of the necropolis of Torre Galli, we find them buried on the left side of the deceased, i.e. on the secondary side, while on the right side, considered as the main one, we find spears and javelins. Equally often they are accompanied by a rich funeral outfit, with spears, greaves, bracelets, helmets and other elements typical of high-ranking Villanovan warriors. Unusually, they were also recorded inside children's or women's tombs (tomb number 313 Torre Galli, tomb number 89, Caracupa), all this confirming that, unlike the swords of the rest of the peninsula, they had mainly a representative function.

The evolutionary process of the swords and of the related fighting techniques, which took place until the end of the Bronze Age, shows us how the Italic territory was divided into three distinct parts (Fig. 6): the north, where the influence of the Halstattian culture was more marked and showing a clear prevalence of long blades, a distinct indication of a tendency to slash and the related fighting style; the centre (with the exception of the Villanovan–Etruscan areas), subjected more to the migration of the Safini people across the Adriatic and where the blades indicate a clear preference for the medium-length weapon and the pointed type, therefore to a more technical and close-combat style; finally, Etruria and the south, which were most influenced by the Greeks and where the swords appear short, as symbols, not having a particular tactical function which was mainly entrusted to the spear instead.

I.3,4 The suspension of the scabbards and the carrying of the weapon in archaic Italy

In the study of swords, particularly important aspects are the scabbards and their various methods of suspension, used for the easy and safe transport of the weapon hanging from the soldier's body. As a general rule, they vary greatly due to various factors, such as the intended use of the weapon itself, tactical needs and the ways of fighting, all obviously related to the historical period. The information useful for our study relating to such an archaic period is, as expected, very scarce. The classical literature does not assist us, never referring to such remote ages; the main source of information is iconographic representations and rare finds of scabbards. In general, it is conceivable that all suspension systems were still quite simple, without any sophisticated technological devices. The main types can be summarised into two groups.

Belt suspensions

Perhaps the most archaic type for which very little information remains, but which can be seen on the steles of Lunigiana,[113] datable to the first half of the second millennium BC. Although the weapon is not a sword but a dagger or a knife, it still provides valuable information as this type of suspension was still in use in Roman culture many centuries later, as depicted in the *stele* of the centurion Minucius Lorarius (*Legio III Martia*, 43 BC). These protohistoric works clearly show the weapon carried against the upper body in a horizontal position, probably tied to a simple belt (Fig. 10-1). However, the steles are not very detailed, preventing any further investigation.

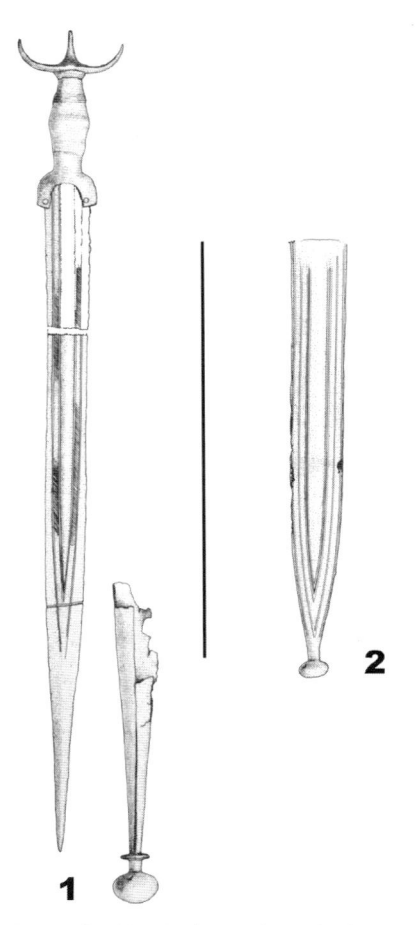

Fig. 9: Scabbards dating from the late Bronze Age – early Iron Age.
1) Sword with antennae with fragment of scabbard, ex Castellani collection.
2) Bronze scabbard, probably from Campania.
Drawings by Sestieri and Macnamara, *Prehistoric Metal Artefacts from Italy*.

The archaeological finds also seem to lead us towards this type of simple suspension. The sheaths are mostly for Etruscan-type daggers, which typically never present any type of metal element for the connection to the belt (or baldric), and the surfaces are always completely smooth. This suggests that simple straps of leather or fabric were used, tightly tied around the scabbard itself.[114]

Suspension with the balteus

One of the first evidence of the existence of this type of suspension can be seen in the numerous Sardinian bronzes depicting tribal chiefs/priests, mostly dating back

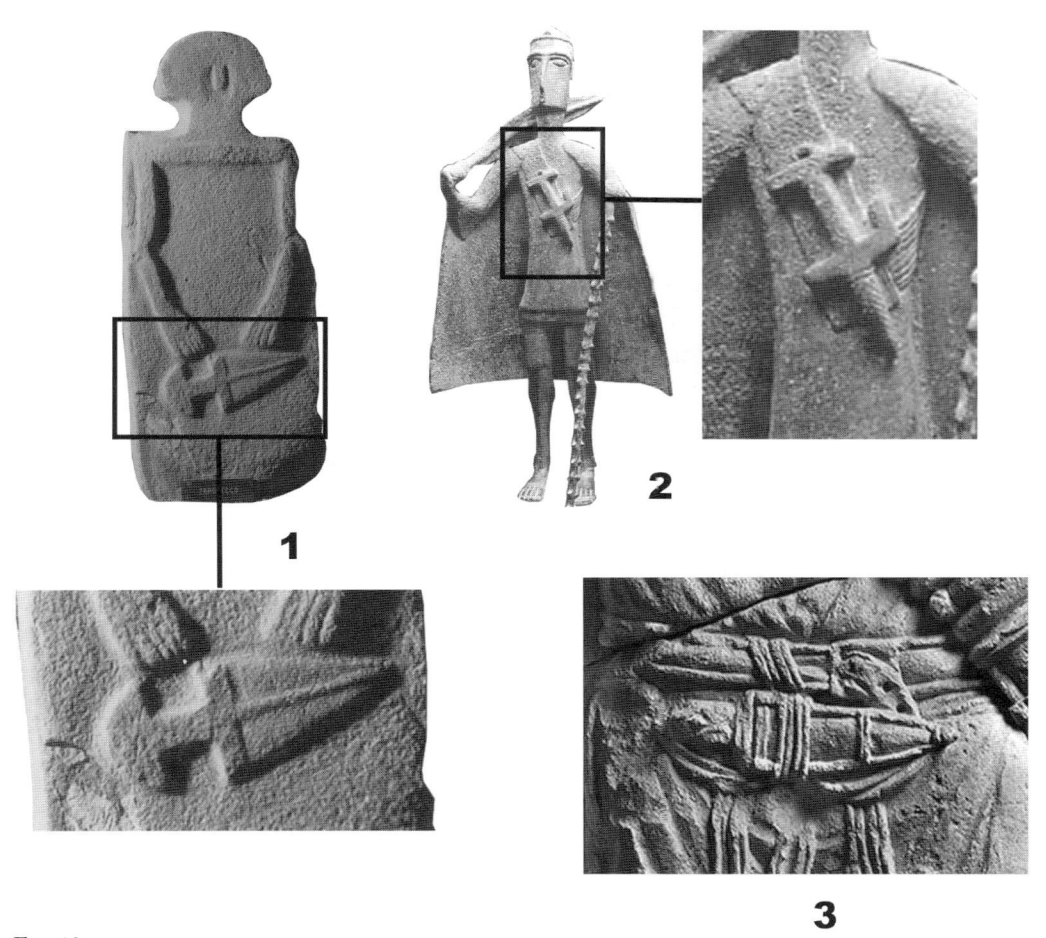

Fig. 10:
1) Lunigiana *stele*– mid-second millennium BC.
2) Nuragic bronze statue representing a tribal chief – ninth seventh century BC.
3) Detail of the *stele* of the Centurion Minucius Lorarius, 43 BC. Note how the *pugio* is worn in a very similar way to the dagger on the Lunigiana *stele*.

to a period shortly after the Lunigiana steles (about ninth–seventh century BC). They frequently show a dagger carried on the chest, tilted towards the shoulder, supported by a generously-sized baldric, a system whose value is demonstrated by the fact that we will see it take root in the culture of the peninsula in the following centuries.

However, both in the Sardinian population of the Nuragic period and in that of Lunigiana, these weapons represented the individual's social status which could be either political (tribal chief) or religious (priest), or very often both (Fig. 10-2).[115] Therefore, it is possible that this suspension system did not have a significant practical military function, which is perfectly compatible with the previously discussed figure of the *pater familias* and all of his social and martial characteristics.

Although these two suspension systems were still primitive, all those that will develop in the following centuries will only be refinements of them, therefore we can consider them to be the forerunners of all the others.

I.4 THE ARCHAIC PERIOD: CONCLUSIONS

The Roman people were just one of the many Italic *gentes* which developed over the course of a slow, but imposing, migratory wave of European populations. During the proto-historic period, numerous new people established themselves on Italian soil, fuelled by the migrations that arrived in the north through the passes of the Julian Alps and in the centre through crossing the Adriatic. The study of the Apennine populations of central Italy, the Paleoumbri, from which the main protagonists of the Iron Age will descend, is fundamental for understanding the origins of the *gladius*. The Latin people, inhabitants of the *Latium Vetus*, were the result of further archaic migrations, which scholars estimate preceded those of the Paleoumbri. These people was characterised by a rich ethnic polycentrism, defined by different dialectal varieties linked to the difference in place (diatopic variation). This was documented by Pliny the Elder when he spoke of fifty-three populations of ancient Latium disappearing without a trace.[116]

In this historical period, the sword was a symbol of power in the hands of the *pater familias* or his closest family members, because of its intrinsic value and the hours dedicate to learning its use, taken from agro-pastoral activities (a critical issue, given that such production was in direct relation to survival). These factors effectively prevented its spread among the wider community. During the Bronze Age the cornerstone of society was the *familia*, in which the civilian, who lived on agricultural and pastoral resources, coincided with the military man, who defended the society from the attacks of neighbouring populations. Those defending the livestock and food reserves of the *familia* comprised 'non-professional' fighters normally dedicated to agro-pastoral activities, who followed the 'Lords', i.e. the *pater familias* and the adult males closest to him.

In general, it is possible say that the armies of Indo-European origin fought mainly in open 'swarm-like' formations, based on an instinctive approach, but also occasionally used closer formations protected by united shields, anticipating the hoplites of ancient Greece. In this context, the spear was the main weapon, which distinguished the warrior from his initiation into civil society, which was used both for throwing and for thrusting during hand-to-hand combat. However, in northern and central Italy this combat style was integrated with another, which over time became increasingly widespread and predominant. Archaeological elements dating back to the eighth century BC testify the remarkable presence of monomachies – duels between heroes, like those sung of by Homer, resolving larger conflicts, in which the main weapon was not the spear but the pointed sword, which essentially decided the final outcome. These duels present many analogies with Renaissance duels based on the sword and buckler, probably sometimes carried out almost as a ritual, revealing the development of a particular type of combat, typical to the warriors of these areas.

From the archaeological studies of Bronze Age swords and their related defensive equipment, it is evident that the Italic territory was divided into three main areas, the north, the centre (limited to the Middle Adriatic, Apennine and Middle Tyrrhenian areas, with the exclusion of the areas of Etruscan culture), and finally the south, each with different characteristics. They clearly tell us that the medium-length sword for thrusting combat was typical only to the populations that lived in the central areas. The type of sword and the consequent way of using it was always tied into the history of the culture and never an import, as E. Oakeshott said, stating that it was an exclusive evolution of central Italy.[117] While the rest of the Europe and Italy abandoned the medium-length sword and concentrated on longer types or other weapons as soon as metallurgical knowledge permitted it, central Italy never did so. On the contrary, it highlighted its status as a weapon of privilege, almost entirely ignoring the longer-bladed weapons. The lanceolate-shaped blade deserves a specific mention as, although only visible in a limited way, it was greatly employed in Europe and especially in central Italy, and was not abandoned for centuries.

All this gives us an innate, remote and almost primordial predisposition of the central Italic people of the middle Adriatic, Apennine and Latium areas, having agile and dynamic, very technical and sophisticated sword-fighting techniques. It is useful to make some reflections on how unusual and almost unique this was in the ancient world.

The infantryman who relied on the rapier sword was not common during the Bronze Age and among the armies of the East, Middle East, Egypt and so on, where the battlefield was first dominated by archers and then by javelinmen, both on foot or mounted in chariots.[118] However, it should be remembered that in the Aegean world, the numerous findings of rapier swords in Crete and on the Greek continent demonstrate that the first Greeks used both military techniques, as is evident from the multiple seals representing scenes of sword duelling. We can find many references in the *Iliad*, where, alongside the duels of the heroes (a Greek tradition uninterrupted since the sixteenth century BC) numerous characters are described as archers (Paris, Odysseus, Teukros, Pandaros and Helenos). Some infantry troops are described being armed with missile weapons too,[119] like those from Locri, made up almost exclusively of archers and slingers[120] or like the Argives, mentioned as 'fighters with arrows'.[121] Robert Drews argues that throughout the Bronze Age, infantrymen were so poorly disciplined and trained that they could have had no ability to manoeuvre effectively on the battlefield, even though his claims obviously clash with the near-perfect Egyptian military organisation. Certainly for many people such as the Hittites, the Mitanni and the Assyrians of the early period, the main function of infantry was only to form a secure line behind which the charioteers could withdraw if necessary, while the main role was reserved for the archers.[122]

Hence, with the exception of the Aegean world, there was predominantly a clear preference for ranged combat, without favouring close combat and the sophisticated melee techniques required by a sword capable of thrusting (which instead is clearly visible in Greek seals since the sixteenth century BC). In the entire ancient world, sword fighting was not adopted at first, not even when, towards the end of the Bronze Age, the archers were replaced by javelinmen, probably due to the improvement of armour, now impenetrable to arrows but not to the more powerful javelin.[123] Neither did it happened with the adoption of archers on horseback by the Assyrians, nor finally with the transition in Greece towards the hoplite phalanx.

It is also worth remembering the comparison with the orientalising part of the Mediterranean, where since the archaic age fighting techniques were aimed towards much heavier and more static combat. The armour of Dendra, from the fifteenth century BC, is an excellent evidence of the need to protect the warrior from both missiles and swords aimed at the throat (as is evident by the high collar), as are the bronze corselets of the Achaeans, described in the *Iliad*, where the heroes fight both in chariots and on foot in single duels. The subsequent bronze corselets and the large hoplite shields, as mentioned above, are the antithesis of the agile combat carried out by the swordsman, and aimed to protect ranks of armed men as a whole rather than the single warrior.

From these factors we can clearly identify the starting point of an evolution that, without too many changes, will lead to the typical Roman way of fighting and to the *gladius* itself, which therefore ultimately has deep roots in the military and social culture of Central Italy. In the next chapters we will see that their entire history and evolution will never depart from these fundamental principles, already established during the Bronze Age. In conclusion we can say that the prodromes of the *gladius* have existed since the end of the Bronze Age.

Chapter II

The Monarchical Period (753–509 BC)

II.1 HISTORICAL FRAMEWORK

Period	Age	Main Event	Grave Characteristics
I LATIAL PERIOD	Late Bronze Age tenth century BC	Alban Period	Cremation Burials near the villages (Capitoline and Palatine Hill) Miniature weapons
II LATIAL PERIOD	Early Iron Age 900–775 BC IIa 900–830 BC IIb 830–770 BC	Villanovan period	IIa Cremation Burials near the villages (Capitoline and Palatine Hill) Miniature and real weapons IIb Burials Burial along roads (Esquiline) No weapons
III LATIAL PERIOD	Early Iron Age 770–720 BC IIIa 770–750 BC IIIb 750–720 BC	Romulean Age Foundation of Rome Population increasing Foundation of Pithekoussai Pre-colonial Greek contacts	IIIa Burial (cremation) Real weapons IIIb Cremation Real weapons Increase of luxury goods in the graves
IV LATIAL PERIOD	Middle Iron Age 720–580 BC	Orientalising period (Eastern Greek contacts) - Servius Tullius	

Table 1: The division of the *Latium Vetus* into four periods, highlighting the main events that characterised the individual periods and the type of burial (traditional chronology Colonna 1976, acts 1980, modified by the AA). The III and IV Latial Periods are highlighted as the two ages are covered in this chapter.

The Late Bronze Age and the early Iron Age were a period of sensational events, which made the *Latium Vetus* region the optimal *pabulum* for the origin and development of Rome as a commercial, political and religious centre.

In the eighth century BC (III Latial Period in the chronology of the *Latium Vetus*), Rome became the centre of power in Latium, replacing the Alban Hills, with the consequence that economic relations with Etruria became the most important, while those with the southern communities became secondary.

Rome, therefore, evolved from a frontier village to a primary centre for its rich and powerful Etruscan neighbours, due to the easy ford of Tiber Island. Indeed, the rich and powerful Villanovan facies (which later evolved into the Etruscan one) in their trade with the rich southern territories of the peninsula (which would become *Etruria Campana* and the future *Magna Graecia*), had to pass through Rome, making the people, or rather the leading noble families who controlled central-south communications, richer and more powerful.

In addition to the north-south trade, a fundamental factor in the development of Rome was the east-west movement linked to transhumance, identified by the 'via

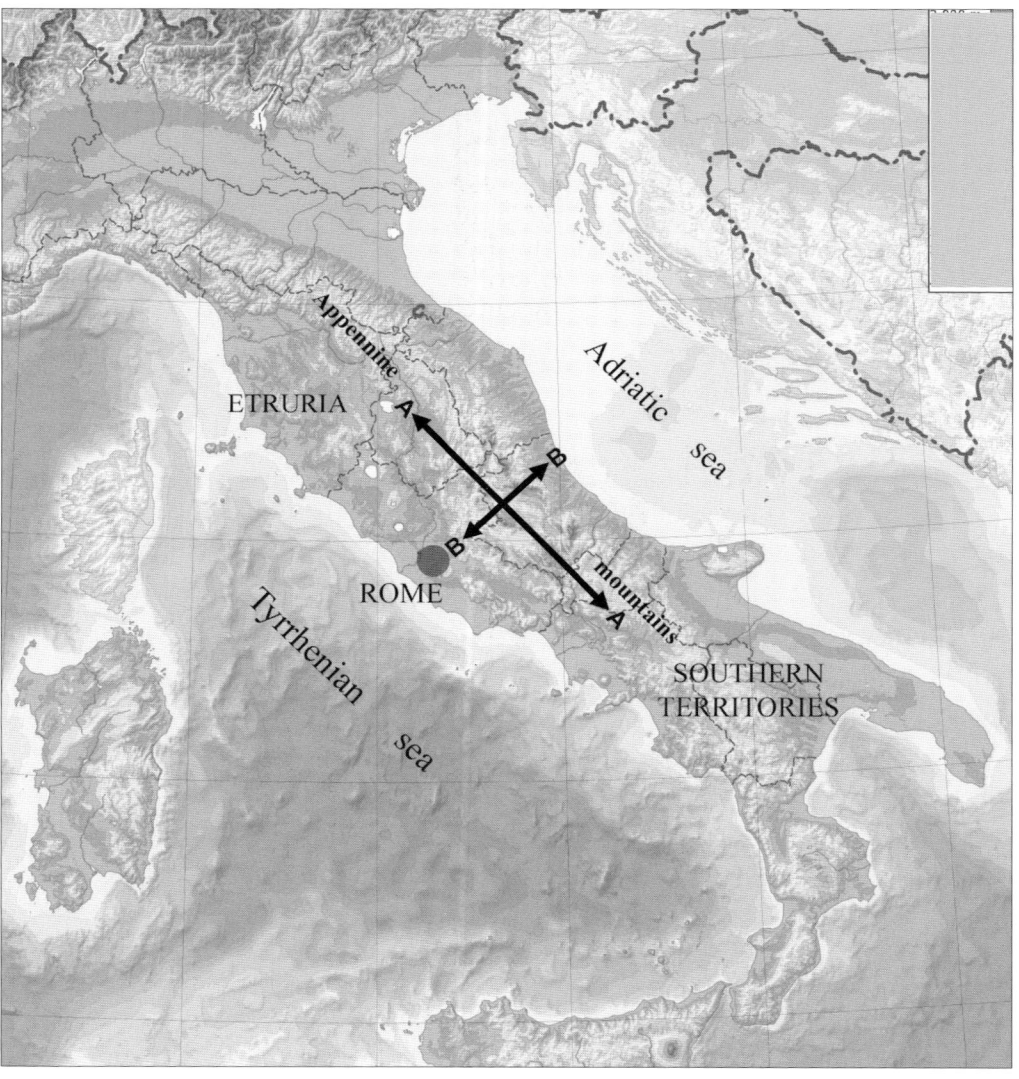

Fig. 1: The two main commercial and cultural routes of Rome: A-A = vertical component, representing the trade of Etruria with the rich southern regions; B-B = horizontal component, representing transhumance, which favoured contacts with Sabine populations. (*Author's drawing*)

The Monarchical Period (753–509 BC)   41

Salaria'. This communication route, which connected the Tyrrhenian and Adriatic coasts of the central Italic area, allowed the transport of salt from Rome to Sabina and at the same time the salt marshes located along the Tiber river[1] were the destination of the herds of the Apennine shepherds, who in the autumn came to graze in a milder climate.

This commercial route was important for the sharing of facies between the Roman and Sabine people, witnessing the frictions and ties between these two *gentes*[2] since the birth of Rome, the numerous wars against the Sabine people and their influence on the formation of the Roman community was equally decisive. The impact they had can be deduced from the fact that the first kings of Rome were of Sabine origin (Titus Tatius, Numa Pompilius and Ancus Marcius), while only the last monarchs

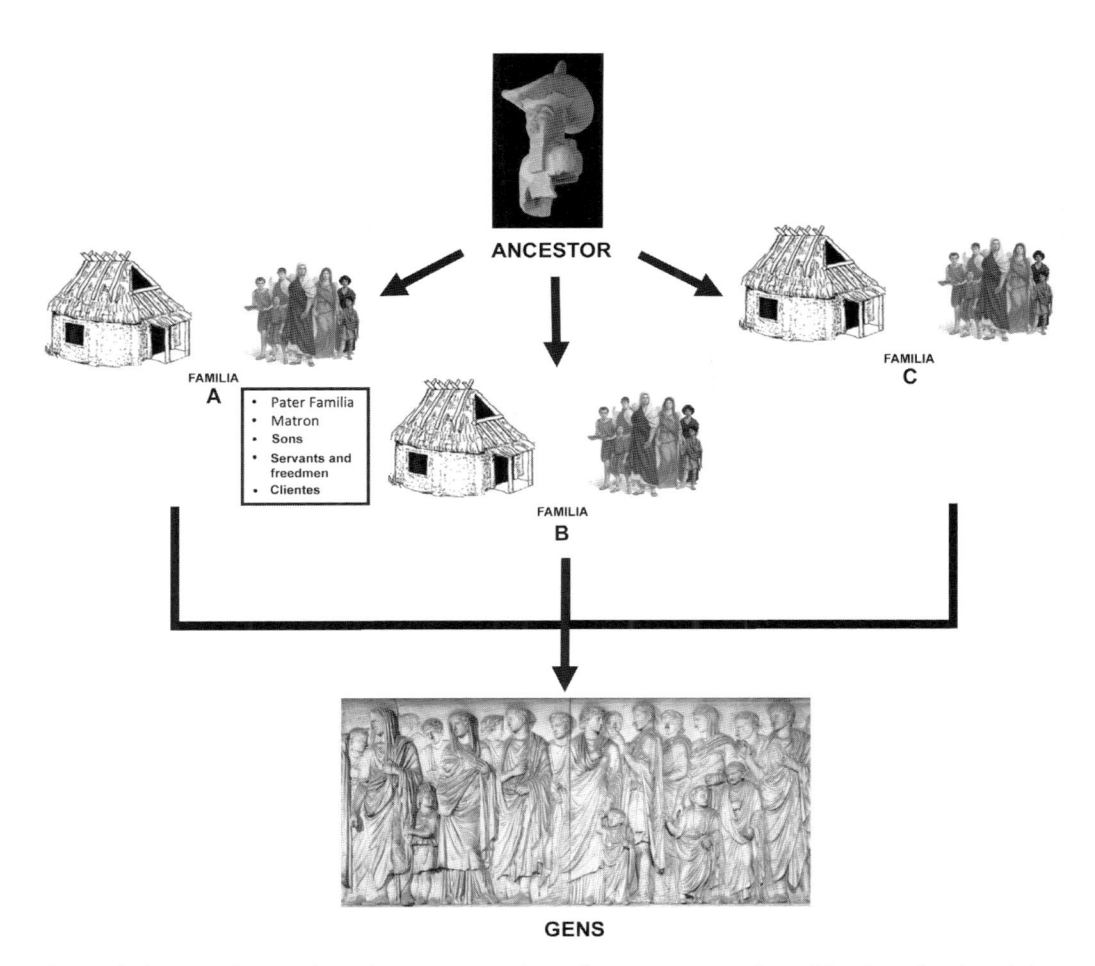

Fig. 2: A diagram showing how the *gens* was made up from varying number of *familiae* who shared the same *nomen*, but a different *cognomen*. All recognised themselves as having a common ancestor and practised common cults. A group of *gens* constituted a *curia* (in this illustration, the *Ara Pacis* frieze representing the *Gens Iulia*, with Agrippa, Gaius Caesar, Julia, Tiberius, Antonia, Germanicus and Drusus). (*Author's drawing*)

(Tarquinius Priscus, Servius Tullius and Tarquinius Superbus) were of Etruscan origin. This suggests that the Apennine influence, followed by the Etruscan one, had been prevalent in the early stages of the history of Rome.

Beyond that, these 'political' forces had had to have been present as distinct entities from the beginning, since the new Roman people were divided by Romulus into three tribes, in which the *Tities* were composed of the Osco-Umbrian people and the *Luceres* were the people of Etruscan origin, to distinguish them from the *Ramnes* who were the Latins, the indigenous people.[3]

The Romulean division of citizenship into three tribes represented the ideal solution for aggregating people of different ethnic origins, even if the cornerstone of the new order was always the '*familia*'. Each tribe was in turn divided into ten *curiae*, and each of them was made up of a variable number of *gentes*, referring to a very specific territory, as reported by various ancient authors (e.g. Dionysius of Halicarnassus,[4] Varro[5] and Livy[6]). Each *gens* was made up of a group of *familiae* who recognised themselves having a common ancestor and whose members were linked by mutual protection and organised in a religious sense.

II.1,1 The immigration phenomenon in the *Latium Vetus*

Between the end of the eighth and sixth centuries BC (IV Latial Period), commercial exchanges with Greek merchants increased. The mining products of Etruria and creation of new marketplaces brought about the spread of the influence of Greek culture to such an extent that scholars define this period as 'Orientalising'.

This intense commercial phenomenon changed the balance of power, favouring the enrichment of the *familiae* more closely linked to metallurgical activity, but also generated the need to defend the communities from the impact of foreign migration, whose presence changed the future fortunes of many Italic people. In fact, the phenomenon of colonisation, meaning the loss of indigenous identity in favour of the culturally-influential foreigners, manifested itself above all in the south of Italy, where it led to the birth of *Magna Graecia*. On the contrary, in central Italy, eastern migration was limited to major influence/interpenetration, which was more important in Etruria with the formation of the Etruscan people than in Latium, where Rome was born.

The contact between indigenous and foreign peoples is described by the ancient authors as a military confrontation, since inevitably the arrival of these refugees to the Lazio coast jeopardised both the possession of goods and the identity of the people. We know from Dionysius of Halicarnassus that these Greek migrations were not planned, but often the result of an emergency, such as the outbreak of a popular uprising. As Livy points out, it was not an entirely peaceful invasion, since 'the Trojans disembarked, and as their almost infinite wanderings had left them nothing but their arms and their ships, they began to plunder the neighbourhood. The Aborigines, who occupied the country, with their king Latinus at their head came hastily together from the city and the country districts to repel the inroads of the strangers by force of arms.'[7]

These 'Trojans' (Anatolian populations heavily influenced by the Aegean people) and Greek groups such as the Arcadians, who arrived on the coast of Latium, had a devastating impact on the local population. This wasn't necessarily because of the type of weapons or because of their numerical superiority, but above all because of their way of fighting in close formation, a successful tactic against the scattered 'swarm' formation of the natives.

This innovative form of battle array, which Greeks would evolve into the classical hoplite formation described by Tirteus in the seventh century BC, would profoundly change the way of fighting in the *Latium Vetus*, even if it would never be assimilated entirely but only reworked. Greek military superiority led the Latins to avoid confrontation and to prefer to receive 'the Arcadians, who were but few in number with great friendship and gave them as much of his own land as they desired ... on a hill, not far from the Tiber, which is now near the middle of the city of Rome ... The Arcadians named the town Pallantium after their mother-city in Arcadia; now, however, the Romans call it Palatium.'[8] However, one should bear in mind that the aboriginals, although fighting in a primitive way, did so effectively so as to counter and prevent the colonisation of the territory by foreigners, Greeks and Phoenicians in the first instance.[9]

The ancient authors agree that the Trojans were bearers of civilisation, as can be deduced from Dionysius, who narrates that 'a certain divinity of the place appeared to Latinus in his sleep and bade him receive the Greeks into his land to dwell with his own subjects, adding that their coming was a great advantage to him'.[10] Ultimately, the historical reality is that in central Italy there was an integration between migrants and aboriginal peoples, and not a prevalence of the former over the latter.

II.1,2 The foundation of Rome: the transition from monomachy to organised combat
The foundation of Rome took place in a climate of great socio-economic instability. The people of the *Latium Vetus* were engaged in continuous conflict, so much so that the Latin derivation of the verb *populare* vindicating the action of looting (devastation, booty) and the related noun *populous* (people) will define this armed community from the beginning.[11] The precarious way the archaic communities lived can be concluded from historical sources, which talk about the worst elements of individual cities,[12] how gangs of brigands[13] or armies were inclined 'to robbing and plundering each other ...' and 'killed or took prisoner',[14] or 'plunder the fields'[15] and attacked the husbandmen,[16] capturing 'no small number of oxen, beasts of burden, and other cattle ... [destroying] the corn that was found there, the iron tools and the other implements with which the land is tilled ... [setting] fire to the country-houses, so that it would be a long time before those who had lost them could restore them'.[17] Usually the effects of such incursions were limited and 'no great disaster occurred nor any wholesale slaughter, and none of their cities went through the experience of being razed or enslaved or suffer any other irreparable calamity as the result of being captured in war; but making incursions into one another's country when the corn was ripe, they foraged it, and then returning home with their armies, exchanged prisoners'.[18] The aim of these clashes was not so much territorial expansion (the defeated people, in fact, retained full authority and autonomy over the remaining territory) but loot, which always was a modest target.

To these continuous battles between the *gentes* living on the borders, was also added the pressure of migrants, thus creating the need for the association of individual *familiae*. It was only by the formation of cities that communities developed that were able to cope with various military situations. If the aborigines of the Latial region wanted to survive, they had to develop a greater awareness of community and aim towards their aggregation/fusion. Dionysius says that 'By these institutions Romulus sufficiently regulated and suitably disposed the city both for peace and for war: and he made it large and populous by the following means'.[19] In fact, the association of several *gentes* would have strengthened their ability to fight, but this could only happen within a disciplined and organised military structure, as the Greek author specifies in the following statements: 'in foreign wars, strength in arms, which is acquired by courage and exercise … those who practise warlike exercises and at the same time are masters of their passions are the greatest ornaments to their country, and these are the men who provide both the commonwealth with impregnable walls and themselves in their private lives with safe refuges';[20] on the other hand, the lack of planning risked causing the whole institution to implode: '… besides, anarchy, in all probability, and sedition, growing out of anarchy, will seize them and soon confound and bring to naught their counsels.[21]

The moment that a society determines the passage from a tribal structure to a town, it follows in its development a logic that is common to all civilisations and it should be noted that it is from that moment that we witness a true characterisation of each people and the acquisition of a specific military and combat organisation. The interesting concept is that Rome was born by the action of the *gladius*. Diodorus Siculus tells that Celer, one of the labourers of the '*sulcus primigenius*', while pushing back Remus, who against the orders of Romulus jumped over the ditch, 'raised his sword, and striking Remus on the head, slew him'.[22] In this case we highlight how a man who apparently did not belong to the nobility is in possession of a blade (therefore we are witnessing a diffusion of its possession) and how it was used instinctively, with a slashing blow and not a thrust, an indication of a lack of specific training.

II.1,3 The transition from the *pater familias* to the *princeps gentis*
The economic enrichment of the *Latium Vetus*, its increase in population and the intensification of military pressure by neighbouring and foreign people led to important social and political changes. William Vernon Harris[23] wrote that that the birth of Rome was connected to military activity, and the figure of the *pater familias*, no longer sufficient to maintain control and command of the group, was gradually replaced by that of the *princeps gentis*. In fact, because of economic prosperity, the *familia* was growing, expanding to include external members defined as *clients*, who came of their own will or as freed slaves (*liberti*), making up the *gens* as a whole. The development of these forms of aggregation was soon insufficient to counter the danger of the neighbouring people attacking and colonising, who were becoming more and more numerous and better armed. Consequently, the individual *patres familiae* found themselves obliged to interact with other family entities (other *gentes*) that made up the *curia* (understood as

a village community, the *pagus*), leading them to the political aggregation of several *gentes* to avoid succumbing. This situation favoured the establishment of the *princeps* and consequently the birth of Rome, a fact that was transformed into a myth but as such, even the Imperial historians themselves question its mythological narrative and dating.[24] We personally believe that in historical reality, Rome should be considered not only as the creation of a congregation of villages, but essentially as the birth of a political-administrative organisation, aimed at ensuring 'under the colour of religion, to protect those who fled to it from suffering any harm at the hands of their enemies'.[25]

The transformation from *multitude* (multitude) to *populus* (people) led to a change in social practices that were governed by discipline, defined by 'law' in civil society and 'by the axe and the fascii' in the military, as explained by Theodor Mommsen. Livy also remembers that

> As nothing could unite them [the *populus*] into one political body but the observance of common laws and customs, he [Romulus] gave them a body of laws, which he thought would only be respected by a rude and uncivilised race of men if he inspired them with awe by assuming the outward symbols of power. He surrounded himself with greater state, and in particular he called into his service twelve lictors ...[26]

The creation of the monarchy became necessary, and this political phenomenon was the consequence of a natural requirement, which followed universal rules, so much so that in Hobbs' words we find the causes that led to the formation of the Roman monarchy well explained, even if used to describe the evolution of the Jewish state. According to Hobbs, the innovation of monarchy was firstly to respond to a military threat, and secondly the deliberate militarisation. On the other hand, the style of war evolved from a strategy of defence of an individual's territory and of themselves to an offensive strategy, in which the surrounding nations were subjected and new symbols were developed, and loyalty was expected to the new rulership.[27]

Religion was probably the means of unification of this multitude of people, although from different backgrounds and of various origins, allowing their coexistence and permeating the definition of their identity.[28] Precisely for this reason, the survival of Rome became essential to contrast the religious power of Alba Longa, city of the *Latium Vetus* where the *Feriae Latinae* took place. It was a religious ceremony that brought together all the confederate Latin people, located in the temple of *Iuppiter Latiaris* on the *Mons Albanus* (nowadays called Monte Cavo). Being a religious centre meant it was the true economic engine of the region, relegating the Capitoline city to a secondary position. It was only in the first half of the seventh century BC that the Romans, under their king Tullius Ostilius, established the political, economic and religious primacy of Rome over the Latin people by destroying the city of Ascanius and Numitor.[29]

Therefore, political power was intertwined with religious power and the leading figures who represented them stood out from rest because they wore, as Livy mentioned

Fig. 3: Representations of monarchs with large wide-brimmed hats: A) Detail from the *Situla della Certosa*, sixth century BC (Venetian culture–Po Valley Etruria); B) Capestrano warrior, sixth century BC (Picenian culture); C) Fictile decoration of the roof of the palace of Murlo (SI), sixth century BC (Etruscan culture). (*Author's photo*)

(I, 8, 1–4), insignia and objects that symbolically enhanced their role. The monarch was most likely identified by a large wide-brimmed hat with pointed *apex*, as worn by the chief shepherds belonging to various cultures of this era,[30] while we can deduce the other garments from the figure of the *Salii*,[31] because, according to Torelli,[32] it is possible to recognise the archaic features of the ancient warrior leaders[33] of the eighth century BC in them. The sacred insignia included:

- The *tunica picta* (the direct forerunner of the triumphal *toga picta*).
- *Aeneum pectori tegumen* (a bronze plate upon the breast).
- *Trabea* held with *latus clavus* (an embroidered purple tunic, fastened by a fibula).
- *Apex* on the head.[34]
- *Gladius* at the belt.
- Spear or staff, called by Plutarch *encheiridion*, in the right hand for striking the shield (forerunner of the triumphator's *sceptrum*).
- The *ancile*[35] shield in the left hand.
- The axe.[36]

We can note that the *gladius* was one of the elements designated for the religious symbolic figure of the *Salii* priests, linked to a military divinity, but also a symbol of power of the archaic figure of the warrior of the eighth century BC.[37]

The need to build a stronger military force, in face of the new requirements of war, implied the establishment of a larger army than what the individual *familiae* were able to field, allowing the birth of the *Legio Romulea* with the king at the head of the army.

II.1,4 The Umbrian–Sabine–Picenian influence

The immigration of the Balkan populations of the *Safine Gentes* on the eastern coasts of the peninsula was the main factor of the evolution of the Paleoumbri in Umbri. These maintained dominion over the Adriatic coast and the Apennine belt for as long as the Sabines, a very ancient and indigenous people,[38] although according to Dionysius 'they just came into the country which they now inhabit, and changing their name with their place of habitation, from Umbrians were called Sabines'.[39] From these communities several other populations were formed through the ritual of the *Ver Sacrum* (sacred spring), a type of sacral migration which Strabo described to us.[40] This ancient ritual was practised by the Umbrian-Sabine populations in emergency situations, such as famine, epidemic, war, excessive population growth, etc., situations in which man was unable to prevail against natural or generally adverse forces, which therefore put socio-economic and demographic stability in crisis. During the rite, the ones born in the following spring were consecrated to a divinity, usually Mars; but while the animals were sacrificed, the male children, as soon as they became adults, were forced to leave the community to found a colony, usually led by an animal that took on a totemic meaning.

As we can see from the map (Fig. 4), the *Ver Sacrum* favoured the colonisation of central Italy, which on the Adriatic side gave rise to the Piceni,[41] Vestini, Peligni, Marrucini and Frentani; from the direction of the Tyrrhenian Sea to the Sabini Tiberini;[42] while migrating towards the south, these populations were the origin of the Equi, Marsi, Carricini, Pentri, Irpini[43] and Caudini. From the latter, four Italic groups originated from the central-southern part of the Italian peninsula, the Samnite population,[44] whose history would intertwine and clash with the Roman one until the third century BC, when they were finally completely subdued.

The geographical environment has always had a great influence on the people who inhabit the land, but in the case of the Apennine people this was particularly so, and heavily influenced their social development, practices and customs. The Apennine chain is composed of rugged mountains covered with forests, often impenetrable, with deep valleys alternating with highlands, relegating the fertile plains to a limited area of the coast: in short it was a very hard place to live,[45] and these difficulties forged these people into a very militarily-strong group over the centuries.[46] Pliny the Elder describes them as '*gentes fortissimae Italiae*',[47] while Livy accuses the Volsci of having a natural inclination for war,[48] the Samnites to be '*durati usu armorum*',[49] emphasising how their belligerence is similar to the nature of their land,[50] while the inhabitants of ancient Bruttium appear as ανδρικωτατα, 'real men', to Strabo,[51] and finally Dionysius of Halicarnassus, describing the lifestyle of the Sabines, describes them as φιλοπόλεμοι, 'fighters' or 'war lovers'.[52]

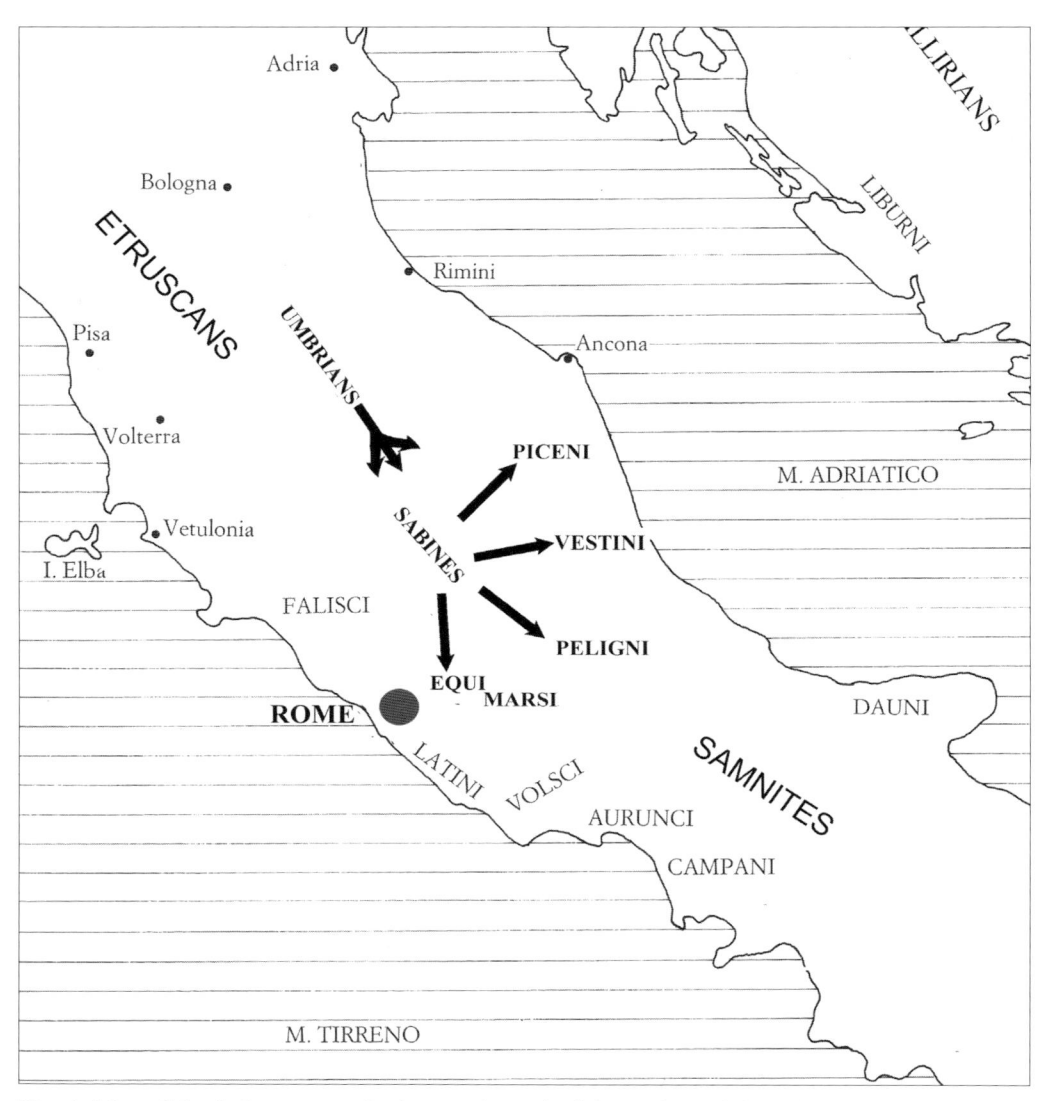

Fig. 4: Map of the Italian peninsula showing how the Sabines derived from the Umbrians and from them, through the *Ver Sacrum*, all the other peoples of the Apennine belt, including the Samnites. The Etruscan people developed within the territory of the Villanovan facies. The Latin people found themselves in close contact with both the Etruscans and Sabines, two groups who greatly influenced the development of the Roman people. (*Author's drawing*)

The most archaic weapons from the burials of the Umbrian people appear similar to those of Villanovan Etruria from Bologna and Verrucchio (Villanovan-type helmet or pointed cap, a breastplate, sword and spear), while in the Orientalising period the affinity tends progressively move towards the Picenian facies, adopting the use of iron rather earlier compared to Etruria. Extremely important are the finds of four combinations of weapons in male burials, testimony of how the outfit expressed the social level of the deceased, which in descending order of social/warrior importance, are:

1. Sword and spear.
2. Sword alone.
3. Spear alone.
4. No weapons.

Later, in the seventh and sixth centuries BC, the male Picenian graves show a continuation of the predominant role of weapons, that testifies to the social rank and military prestige of the deceased. In this regard, it is important to underline the presence of an almost constant archaeological documentation of weapons, in the sense that the burials that lack them are very rare.[53]

It is very indicative is that within these populations, the sword assumes a completely different meaning compared to the other *gentes*. Indeed, among the people of the Polada facies, Terramare and the Villanovans, swords are rarely found, relegated to the burial of the *pater familias*, with more symbolic than military attributes. In these Apennine populations, 'the wide spread of the sword, also visible in the child graves, shows how its meaning has now changed: no longer a symbol of the role of an individual but of an entire social class, which we could therefore define as aristocratic'.[54] This concept is the keystone of the cultural and social revolution present within the Apennine people and which, spreading later in the *Latium Vetus*, will create the basis for a new way of conceiving combat in Rome.

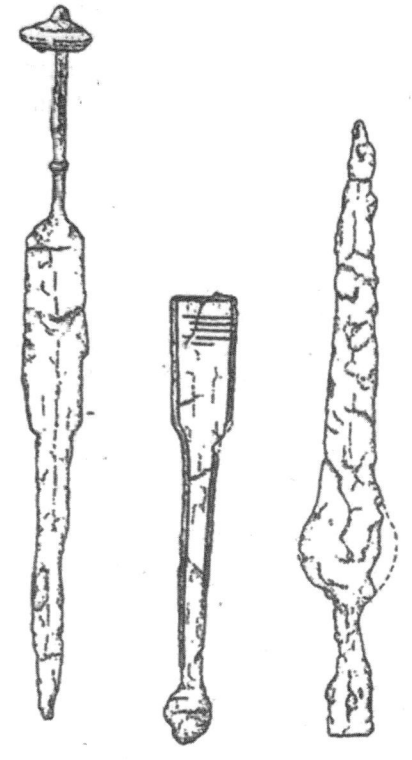

Fig. 5: The finds from the Early Iron Age male graves from the necropolis of Fossa (L'Aquila) usually include a combination of iron objects made up of the short sword (or dagger), with its sheath and elements for suspension, a spear or javelin head and a knife. (*Author's drawing from Sestieri,* L'Italia nell'età del bronzo e del ferro)

II.1,5 The Etruscan people and relations with Rome

The Rasenna (this is the name used by the Etruscans for themselves) distinguished themselves from other Italic populations by greater technological development as well as economic and military power. They were able to exploit the abundant mineral resources present in their territory and their ability in metalworking to obtain profitable contacts and mercantile power with neighbouring territories (primarily the Latin people) and with the economic powers of the time, namely the Greeks and the Carthaginians. At the same time, the Hellenes were as much in need of the Etruscans' metals as they themselves were willing to follow their example. In fact, the Rasenna presented a certain analogy with Levantine politics, based on a monarchical regime with a well-centralised economy, as well as the aesthetic taste of loving Greek luxury products.

The display of wealth and luxury constituted an instrument of aristocratic identification which, associated with the assertion of the divine origin of one's own lineage typical of many ancient civilisations legitimising aristocratic power, automatically excluded the members of the lower class and the small merchants and craftsmen, considered as little more than slaves by the political powerful.

The major difference that emerges between Etruscan and Roman societies is that the former was 'closed', with a clear distinction between nobles and people, who were almost enslaved. The latter instead developed into a 'fluid' society, where the plebeians, although disadvantaged compared to the patricians, enjoyed freedom and political rights allowing them to advance and establish themselves in the Roman society. This different setting of aristocratic domination in the two societies, Etruscan and Roman, had profound influences both on the structure of their armies and on policies of territorial control.

The Etruscan army mirrored its extremely hierarchical society, made up of a small elite, armed with a complete panoply and with the ability to employ the sword, and a vast mass of almost enslaved infantrymen, protected by limited armour and with limited fighting ability. An army like this, considering the important Greek influences to which the Etruscans were very sensitive to, was most likely based on a fighting style similar to the hoplitic one, consisting of infantrymen with very little experience in combat commanded by an aristocratic elite. This hypothesis is confirmed by Dionysius who affirms how the Etruscan soldiers fought 'in the same step, with order and discipline, under the aegis of Ομόνοια [deified personification of concord and especially of political concord]', characteristics that typically distinguish an army of hoplites, made up of companions, friends and affiliates.

On the contrary, the more open-minded Roman monarchy led to a greater spread of the sword among the fighters, to the point that all the *principes* of the *Legio Romulea* and the majority of the infantrymen of the Servian one were armed with it, even

Fig. 6: From the second half of the seventh century BC some elements of the Etruscan panoply were connected with those of Greek hoplites: Corinthian helmets, two-handled shields, greaves, short sword and at least three spears. Often the burials contain associated local and Greek weapons: the *stele* of Aule Feluske from Vetulonia (Bambagini necropolis) is an example, where the warrior, with his head covered by a Corinthian helmet, holds a shield of the hoplite type, but at the same time a typically Etruscan double axe, certainly not suitable for fighting in hoplitic formation. The princely tombs of Etruria are typically characterised by the insignia of power of the aristocratic elite such as chariots, horses, skewers, wings and weapons, as well as ivory furnishings and bronze vases, especially of Levantine origin. (*Author's drawing*)

those that were not part of an aristocratic entourage, provided that they belonged to a class allowing an adequate armament. The ending of Etruscan power by the Romans coincided with various events, beginning with the fall of Veii in 396 BC, continuing with the Battle of Sentinum in 295 BC, and then ending definitively in 90 BC in the context of the Social War, when the Tyrrhenians lost their autonomy, becoming Roman citizens under the *Lex Julia*.

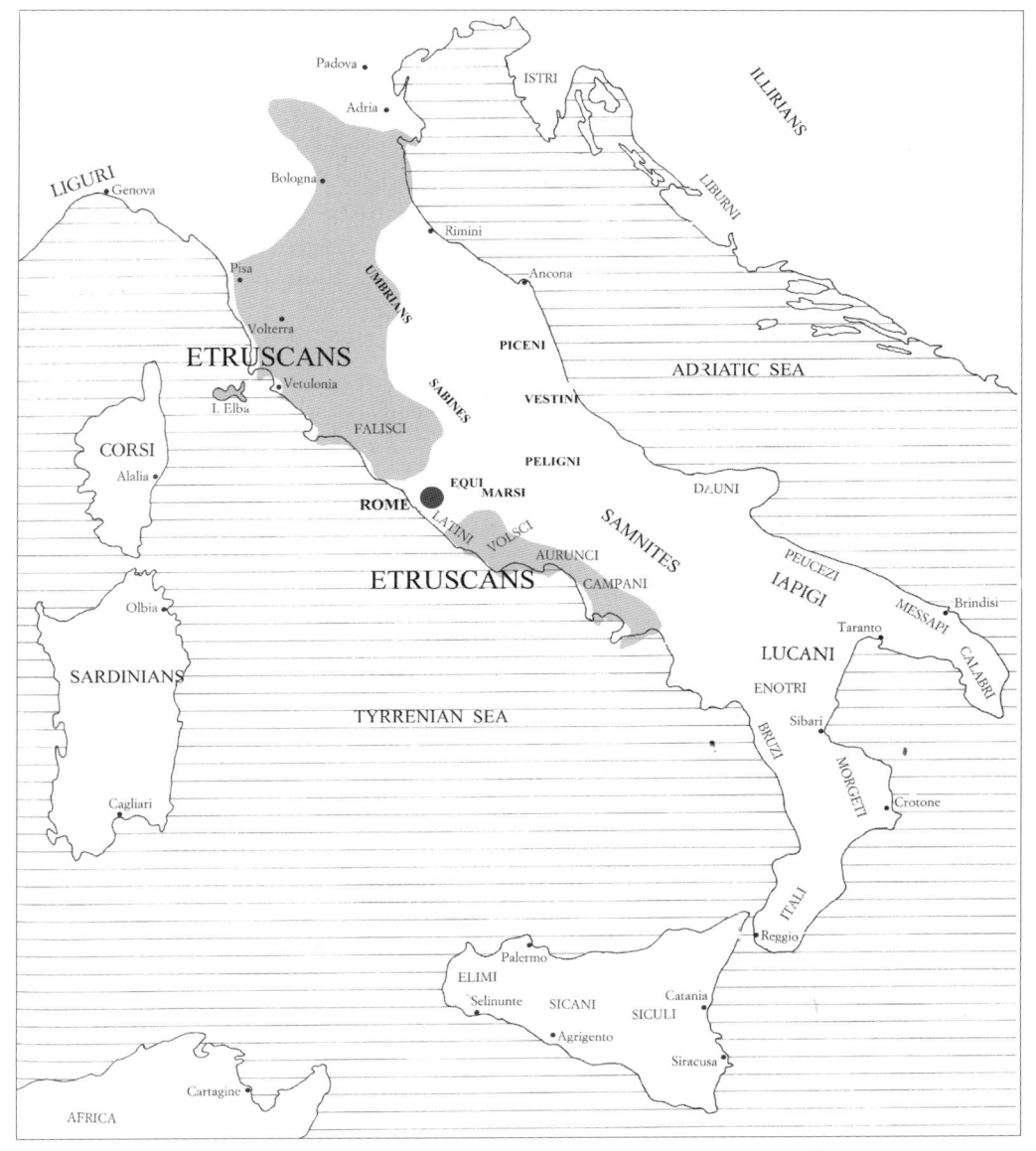

Fig. 7: Map of Italy showing the maximum expansion of the Etruscan domain. The *Latium Vetus* was the crossroads in the relations between Etruria and its colonies in Campania, and Rome's control of the Tiber ford made the Capitoline city strategically very important, so as to attract commercial interests and political control, as well as military, by the Etruscans, until the increase in conflict after the expulsion of King Tarquinius Superbus. (*Author's drawing*)

II.2 FIGHTING IN THE MONARCHICAL PERIOD

II.2,1 The *Legio Romulea* (eighth century BC)

The birth of a new civil and military institution
One of the most impressive things about the Romans was their capability for organisation, present in all aspects of their society since the beginning of their history. Because of this, over time the Romans developed a special way of fighting which enabled their armies to become stronger. As reported by ancient authors, a fight based essentially on impetus and improvisation is much less effective than one well set up and coordinated. Indeed, reporting the story of the attack by the people of Cenina, a city of the *Latium Vetus*, as a reaction for the abduction of the Sabine women, Livy explains how the Romans routed them since fury (*ira*) is worth nothing if strength (*vis*[55]), understood as 'control, ability to command events', is absent. The Latin author confirms this belief by showing the superiority of an ordered battle array over a looser disposition, describing how the Romans 'surprised' the Antemnates[56] 'as they were scattered[57] over the fields. At the very first battle-shout … the enemy were routed and their city captured', more precisely 'not finding the enemy on their soil … prepared and determined to fight a decisive battle'.[58]

The conflicts sustained by single *familiae*, sometimes united in temporary alliances as already described, were no longer militarily competitive, so it became 'naturally' necessary to move to a progressive ordering of the single groups to form a large army. As described by Hobbs for the people of Israel, when the army of ancient Israel passed into the Monarchical Period,[59] the troops were arranged 'uniformly', using similar weapons, and organised in ranks for the advance (cf. 1 Samuel 17). Individual action was regulated by the needs of the group, and relied on the stability of one's companions in the line, which gave an additional sense of security, but increased the level of insecurity and potential panic when the ranks broke. The order of the state was now reflected in the order on the field, and centralisation of the state was reflected in the centralised command, for a certain period being the king and later the general. Thus, control became important and at the same time the need for obedience on the battlefield. Individual initiative now became dangerous as it disturbed the line, and a single warrior would easily become lost.[60]

The combat evolved from a duel to a collective fight and what is described by Hobbs for the army of Israel can be found in the army of Rome, with the unusual fact that the monomachy of the *patres familiarum*, based on the sword, will be regulated, perfected and standardised to the point of becoming the basis of combat no longer limited to some soldiers but extended to the entire army. As we will see, this evolution will last for the entire Monarchical Period and the first part of the Republican Period, an evolution in which the sword will be transformed from a symbolic and powerful weapon to a 'democratic' object, possessed by all the soldiers.

The description of some events of Romulus and Remus preluding the foundation of Rome is very interesting. The comparison between two types of stories made by ancient authors allows us to grasp the meaning of the passage towards a new style of combat.

The assault made by Romulus and Remus on King Numitor (unaware that the twins were his grandchildren) turns out to be a very disorganised affair. Indeed, 'Romulus shrunk from a direct attack with his body of shepherds, for he was no match for the king in open fight. They were instructed to approach the palace [of King Numitor] by different routes and meet there at a given time, whilst from Numitor's house Remus his assistance with a second band he had collected.'[61] The weapons used are simple exchanges of punches,[62] 'darts … stones, and … whatever they could lay their hands'[63] as part of a clash that is described to us as a mere tussle: 'without waiting for the others … all rushed upon the first group, … surrounding them'.[64]

On the contrary, the anonymous author of the *Origo Gentis Romanae* relates the release of Remus, who had been captured by his uncle Amulius, with an educational intent based on the organisation of a fight. The author describes how Romulus 'gathered the a gang of shepherds and divided them in groups of a hundred men; he gave them staffs with bundles of hay [*perticae manipolis foeni*] of various size attached to the tip, so that by that sign they could more easily see who was their leader and follow him. Thus they were formed as the later army, who had the same signs, called manipulares.'[65] This quote shows the birth of a structured formation, where the army is divided into units (*manipuli*), each equipped with a sign to move effectively under the command of their centurion. The anonymous author wants to make it clear to the reader that the '*consilium et ratio*', the logic and reason of Romulus, contrasted with the behaviour of Remus who, in the same story, confident in his own strength, therefore with '*audacia et temeritas*', audacity and recklessness, tried in vain to get the better of Amulius's emissaries and was captured.

In reference to the concept of the *manipulus*, Plutarch, in analogy with the anonymous author above, also tells us that '(Romulus) was … leading a large force with him, divided into companies of a hundred men, each company headed by a man who bore aloft a handful of hay and shrubs tied round a pole (the Latin word for handful is "*manipulus*," and hence in their armies they still call the men in such companies "*manipulares*")'.[66] Such a group of armed men was defined by Varro as 'the smallest *manus* troop which has a standard of its own to follow',[67] and last but not least, Ovid explains that from this the soldier took the name '*manipularis*'.[68]

The fact that such an infantry unit was formed by 100 men, as explained by the ancient authors above and by Iohannes Lydus,[69] leads us to believe that the words '*manipuli*' and '*centuria*' were likely synonymous in this ancient period. The structural and functional characteristics of such units would change over time, but in the Romulean Period it had a more administrative role, linked to the provenance of the soldiers, rather than to a specific tactic purpose. As we will see, the military action in this *legio* was linked to the *acies*, the three battle arrays opposing the enemy, formed of various types of infantry according to their age, combat skills and weaponry (Diagram 2 and Plate 1).

The *legio* was formed of 3,000 infantrymen and 300 horsemen, recruited in similar ratios from the three tribes during the Spring levy.[70] Plutarch explains how Romulus distinguished the men-at-arms, calling them *legio* 'because the warlike were selected [*logades*] out of all' by distinguishing them from 'the remainder as a people … and this multitude was called "*populus*"'.[71]

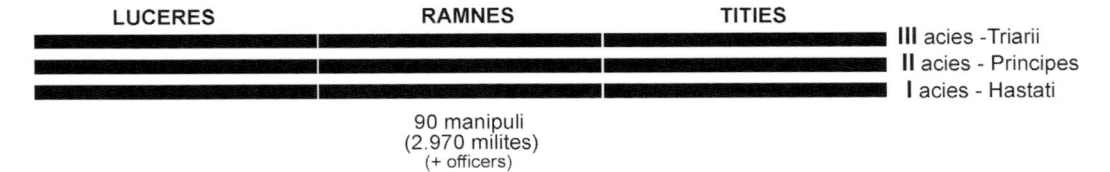

54 The Roman Gladius and the Ancient Fighting Techniques

LUCERES	RAMNES	TITIES	
			III acies - Triarii
			II acies - Principes
			I acies - Hastati

90 manipuli
(2.970 milites)
(+ officers)

Diagram 1: The Romulean legio. (*Author's drawing*)

By studying the political and military organisation of the community structured by Romulus, we wonder about the symbolism of the 'number three'. As emphasised by Battaglia and Ventura, there were three tribes, 30 *curiae*, 3,000 infantrymen and 300 cavalrymen. There were also three *acies* and the theory is that the 100 men forming a *manipulus* were in turn divided into three groups of 33 infantrymen (three ranks of eleven soldiers) including the centurion who probably was also performing the role of *vexillifer*.[72] It was probably Roman superstition that, in order to have good fortune and for an institution to function properly, it should respect the harmony of numbers in its structure, and thus respect the universal order.

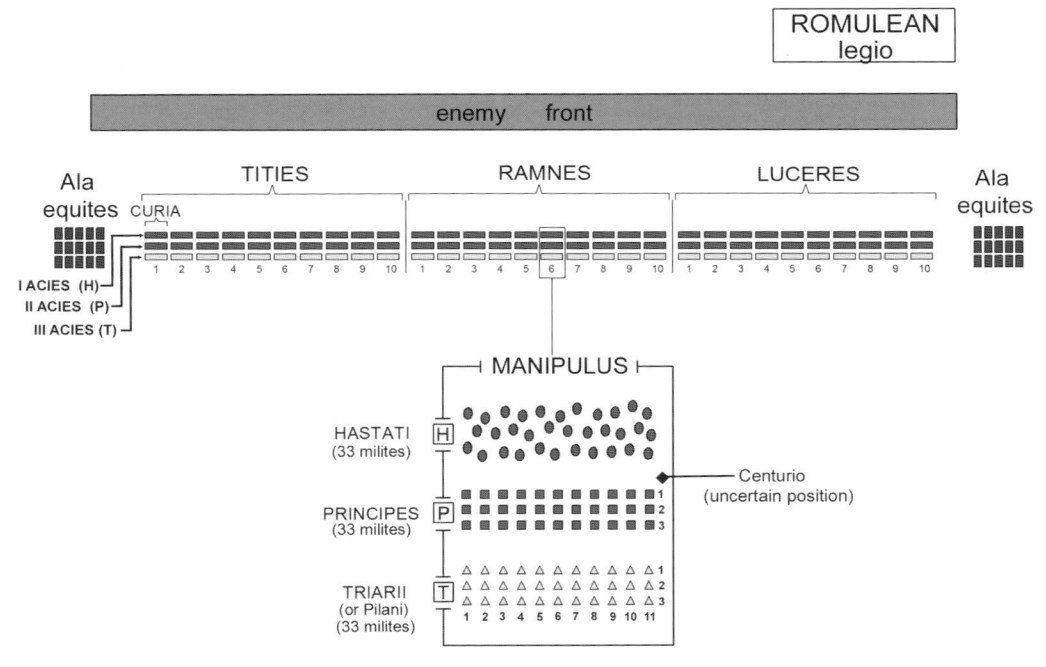

Diagram 2: An army was made up of 3,000 infantry (and 300 cavalry); each of the three tribes supplied 1,000 *milites* and 100 horsemen. While the cavalry formed up on the flanks in two '*alae*', the thirty *manipuli* of which the *legio* was composed (ten from each tribe, i.e. one from each *curia*) made up the infantry formations. The *manipulus* (or *centuria*) was made up of 100 infantrymen, divided into three different types of fighters (*hastati*, *principes* and *triarii*), each of them participating to form one of the three *acies* characterising the Romulean *legio*. The diagram shows the arrayed army with the two wings of cavalry, and the detail explains how a *manipulus* was deployed with the corresponding types of soldiers. (*Author's drawings*)

The proof that the Romulean *legio* was already an effective army and not only a company of individual fighters shown by the circumstance in which Romulus 'is reviewing the army',[73] typical of a general, and by the presence of non-commissioned officers, as when 'the centurions, swords in hand, surrounded Mettius'[74] (the Alban king accused of treachery). Their presence is an indication of a hierarchical organisation, typical of the most complex armies. Paternus, as quoted by Iohannes Lydus, specifies that there were 30 centurions, one for each company of 100 infantrymen, devoted either to military command or to sacred rites.[75]

The standards were already important for the Roman soldier, both for symbolic and signalling functions: they were the sign under which the soldiers coming from different *gentes* of the same tribe (aggregative function) were united. According to the description by Ovid, the standard was the guide for the soldiers on the battlefield, so much so that it was said that 'Heaven's gliding ensigns were beyond their reach, not so their own, which was a great crime'[76] because for the soldiers, losing the standard meant losing their orientation on the battlefield, just like a sailor who has lost the stars for orientation.

We should underline the fact that we are in a phase in which the spontaneity of the tribal fighting is receding in favour of ordered combat, a change linked to the development of the armies of the enemies, always more numerous and with organised battle arrays. The change of the fighting style is reflected in the transformation of the society, abandoning the primitive organisation based upon the *familia* and adopting a system of aggregation that will enable the formation of Rome itself, considered as a congregation of three main tribes formed by the different *gentes*. Indeed, the reader should not be astonished by the description of many battles by the ancient authors as a brawl between men, instead of a true meeting of organised armies. Such a dichotomy is inherent in the slow process of changing the military institutions, in the early phases of which two typologies of fighting certainly coexisted, as it is shown during the early Consular Age at the Battle of Cremera (477 BC), where the Fabii 'not only made raids upon farming lands, and surprise attacks upon raiding parties [the Etruscans of Veii], but at times they fought in the open field and in serried ranks'.[77]

The infantry of the Romulean legio
Ovid says that, within each *manipulus*, the infantrymen were selected according to three different qualities, related to different fighting techniques and weaponry: 'So Romulus … instituted ten companies of men with spears [*hastati*], and as many front-rank and javelin men [*principes* and *pilani*], and also those that officially merited horses …'.[78]

- Hastati

In the battle-array, the first type of troops were the *hastati* who, according to Varro, 'were so called as those who in the first line fought with *hastae* [spears]',[79] while Ennius recalls that 'the line of lancers [*hastati*] scattered its lances: came a shower of iron'.[80] Such definitions, that classified such soldiers as front-rank warriors, are discussed in other ancient sources not only regarding their weaponry, but also the position they had in the battle-array.

Concerning the *hasta*, the classical authors give contradictory definitions of the weapon and therefore also of its employment. Livy[81] says as the *hastati* and *principes* were armed with *hasta*, while the *triarii* (also called *pilani*) had the *pilum*, but Polybius,[82] on the contrary, tells us that the *triarii* were furnished with *hasta*, while the *pilum* was the weapon of the other two categories. If we make a rational distinction, according to which we understand the *hasta* as the weapon wielded overhand or underhand in close combat, by distinguishing it clearly from the *pilum* employed for short-range throwing, we risk concluding that the ancient authors are reporting conflicting and wrong conceptions. The correct solution is offered by Varro himself, who explains that the '*hasta* [spear] is so called because it is usually carried *astans* [standing up]', while 'likewise from its omen was said *pilum* (javelin) by which the enemy *periret*, "might perish", as though '*perilum*'[83] and the *velites* were equipped with the *hasta velitaris* (whose function was, however, that of a *pilum*). We can therefore understand that during this archaic period, the spear had a double function, as also suggested by Maurizio Martinelli and Robert Drews, which is why such 'contradictory' statements can be dismissed because most likely the warrior, after throwing some of his short-range weapons, kept the last one to be employed at close quarters (as a spear).[84]

Another contradictory statement is given about the position of the *hastati* within the battle array. While all the ancient authors write that they fought 'in the front rank', Vegetius, on the contrary, says that 'Those who fought in the first line of their respective legions were called *principes*, in the second *hastati*, and in the third *triarii*'.[85] However, we do not know which time Vegetius, who wrote in the second half of the fourth century AD, is referring to. Moreover, such a contradiction could be overcome by giving the Romulean *hastati* the role of the later *velites*, i.e. that of a mobile body which, originally positioned behind the *principes*, at the moment of the attack, swarmed through the front rank, to return on their previous positions as soon as the skirmishing with the *hastae* came to an end.

The *hastati* of the Romulean *legio* were the light infantry, made up of the younger and less experienced part of the army and operating by skirmishing against the enemy at a distance by throwing one or more *hastae* (see quote from Ennius above) like the later *velites*.

• *Principes*

The second battle line was formed by the *principes*, who represented the veterans and who were, as said by Polybius, 'in the prime of life',[86] or, as defined by Varro, '*principes* "first men" as those who from the beginning [*a principio*] fought with swords [*gladiis*]',[87] although they also carried a *hasta*.[88]

First of all, from the description of the *principes* we can understand the historical flow of the evolving fighting style. A company of troops is equipped with the sword: a weapon that from a symbolic sign of authority has been transformed into an instrument of war, equally distributed among all the soldiers having certain qualities such as the maturity and ability to employ it effectively. Plutarch also confirmed such wider distribution of the sword when, in the abduction of the Sabine women, he explains: 'armed with swords, then, many of his followers kept their eyes intently upon him [Romulus]; and when the signal was given, drew their swords, rushed in with shouts, and ravished away the daughters of the Sabines'.[89]

The word *principes*, which defines such a group of fighters, suggests a position of authority within the army. In fact, if we look at the positions for which this word was used in Roman history, we note that it was used to describe men holding a position of command.[90]

We can therefore say that the *principes* as infantrymen had the authority to use the sword, a position which in the past had belonged to the *pater familias* and his adult male relatives, but during the time period in question and taking into consideration the diffusion of the sword within the army, it now refers more to the age of the fighter than to his aristocratic or economic origins.

Last but not least, we can presumably imagine that many *principes* would have been armed with iron *gladii*, without excluding the presence of bronze ones, as Scardigli advises; 'the army of the times between the monarchy and the Consular Age could not have had a homogeneous aspect. The circumstance by itself that each *miles* should purchase his weapons it is indicative that each one was equipped in different ways and in different garb.'[91] Moreover, the bronze sword was a weapon with great traditional value, for which reason many people could not justify changing the weapon used by their ancestors to fight and to win, and also because both bronze and iron swords were comparably effective as cut-and-thrust weapons.

- *Pilani* (or *Triarii*)

The *pilani* (or *triarii*), represented the third rank of fighters, positioned at the very back; Varro called them '[javelin-men] as being those who fought with *pila* [javelins]'.[92] The name *pilani* can be linked either to the *pilum*, the weapon with which they were equipped in ancient times, to the *piléo*, the conical military headgear made of leather which we see characteristically worn by some warriors of the *Situla della Certosa* or, if we refer to the Latin meaning of *pīlātim*, which in military slang means 'closed ranks, packed lines', meaning the disposition of the soldiers within the battle-array.

This last theory can be supported by the fact that the second name defining them, *triarii*, refers to their position in the third line and not to their armament or headgear. As Varro says, 'the *pilani* were also called *triarii* because they were led as a third rank, reserve in quality, last in the battle array; for the reason that they were "*subsidebant*" [reserve troops] also called "*subsidia*" [*subsidiarii*]'. From the verse of Plautus:

Come now, all of you sit by as troopers in reserve are wanted
[*Agite nunc, subsidite omnes quasi solent triarii*][93]

Diagram 3: Diagram of the Romulean *legio*, presented as three parallel lines (*acies*), where the first was the *hastati*, the second the *principes* and the third the *triarii*. The *legio* was formed of thirty *manipuli*, ten of which came from the Tities tribe, ten from the Ramnes tribe and ten from the Luceres tribe. Its function was to stop and hold the enemy line, without breakthroughs and openings. Victory had a direct relation to the impenetrability of the lines. (*Author's drawing*)

Hastati, *principes* and *triarii* were therefore the three types of soldiers upon which the Romulean *legio* was based, distinguished by their weapons and consequently in their way of fighting. The spear remained the most common weapon as it was present in all three formations, but the most important role was given to the *principes* who were armed with swords as well as the *hasta*.

Such a change is peculiar to the Roman army, because the sword, previously considered as a subsidiary weapon, now begins to play the primary role, present with all elements of the battle array. If we need to present the Romulean legion as a graphic drawing, to comprehend it better especially when comparing it with later formations, we would present it in three horizontal parallel lines, called *acies*, the first for *hastati*, the second for *principes* and finally the rearmost one for the *triarii* (Diagram 3). Such a battle array enabled a containing action, more defensive, acting like a dam and preventing an enemy breakthrough.

Military division linked to age
From an anthropological point of view, age is a very important factor in defining a person's social value, so much so that in all communities, not only ancient but also modern, secular ceremonies and initiatory rites sanctioning the passage of an individual from one status to another exist. Today they exist as school exams (secular tests, for the admission to a higher level of education) and religious ceremonies (initiatory rites like Catholic First Communion and Confirmation) which designate entrance into a new position in the community. In ancient times a distinction between secular and sacred did not exist and the initiatory rite decreed the passage from the 'status of infancy', i.e. a child followed by the mother without civil rights, to 'adult status', a subject integrated into the tribe with the right to bear arms. In Rome, during the festival of '*Liberalia*' on 17 March boys who had reached the age of 16 were dressed in the white *Toga Virilis*,[94] indicating their right to be part of the community, and to enter the Forum[95] (thus participating in civil and political life) and to be ready to fight for it. It is Plutarch himself who, in regard of such subdivision, says that 'at Rome ... *majores* is their name for the elders, *juniores* for the younger men'.[96]

The *Tabulae Iguvinae*, a document written in Latin and Paleo-Umbrian on seven bronze plates in the ancient city of Ikuvium (the modern-day Umbrian city of Gubbio), show how Centro-Italic society presented a subdivision in levels linked to social rank and age, and how that distribution was mirrored within the army. Though some of them are from the third century BC and others from the first century BC, they all describe the description of the lustration and atonement ceremonies of the city relating to a more archaic period,[97] probably around 1000 BC. Such texts should be considered in strict relation to the Latin society because of the interaction with Umbrian society, not only historical but also philological, as we can note in the assonance and meaning of some of the words.[98] A very important sentence for our topic, talking about the age of men-at-arms, appears on the sixth *Tabula Iguvinae*, where in the description regarding the sacrifices and statutes of the sacerdotal confraternity of the 'Brothers Atiedes', which reads:

> '*nerf sihitu ansihitu, iouie hostatu anhostatu.*'[99]
> ('The *seniors* (or veterans) belted (of sword) and not, the *iuvenes* armed (of spear) and not')

The '*ner-*'[100]*iguvini* corresponds to the veterans, the adult soldiers in service because '*sihitu*'[101] i.e. sword-belted (*cinctus*), distinguished by those dismissed as '*ansihitu*' i.e. '*non cincti*', without the sword. The '*iouie*' is instead for the young men, those with less experience in battle, distinguished from those already invested with the *hasta* (note the analogy of the Umbrian word '*hostatu*' and the Roman '*hastati*'[102]) through an initiatory ceremony, and incorporated into the fighting population.

Indeed what we gather is that the possession of a weapon required both being of sufficient age to use it, and being part of the community. Moreover the concept of a veteran underlines the quality of soldiers' experience, understood as being exclusively based upon age. Being deprived of the *cingulum*[103] or of the *hasta*[104] was a military punishment, because when the soldier was deprived of the possibility of being armed, it symbolically meant that he was dismissed by the community (an *ante litteram* excommunication).

Everyone's social life was marked and defined by the sacred rites of initiation, which conferred rights and obligations upon them, including military ones, whilst they were growing. During his growth a young man was only allowed to bear the *hasta* once he had passed an initiatory rite which decreed that he deserved it, and as an adult he would earn the right to carry the sword.

Fighting in close or open formation
It is difficult to determine if the formation adopted by the *Legio Romulea* was open or close, and many hypotheses risk becoming mere speculation, so much so that today no unanimous opinion exists. It is not a mere academic discussion to determine this, but the key point which will allow us to formulate a possible hypothesis on the way in which the fighting developed. Before we can proceed with our analysis, we would like to present the opinions of two Italian historians, both experts in the study of Bronze Age/Early Iron Age Centro-Italic warfare. Their theories are opposed in certain areas, however, if one side expresses confusion on one topic, the other will help to understand some mechanisms in the development of battle in this period.

According to Maurizio Martinelli, the clash proceeded with the fragmentation of the battle array into many small 'Homeric' duels. In this case, the author's hypothesis is that the infantry of the *manipulus*, armed with the *hasta*, after a short run towards the enemy, either threw it or delivered an overhand or underhand blow with it as the first deadly strike. At that point, the soldiers moved on to body-against-body combat, where the battle transformed into a big melee and the fight fragmented into thousands of personal duels where the courage, the physical strength and the personal fighting ability of each warrior was most important.[105]

On the other hand, Armando Cherici emphasises closed-rank fighting, in which the rows of infantrymen were kept united shoulder to shoulder with their comrades, coordinated by the centurions, who decided the moments of attack and retreat, and the *signa* guided the infantrymen in those movements. The author stresses that we should not see the Romans as fighting in hoplitic formation. Differing from the Greek approach, the Italic one was based upon a greater flexibility, demonstrated by the different shield. The most important thing was not to advance with a single front in a packed line, shoulder to shoulder, *clipeus* to *clypeus*, made possible by the fact that the left half of the round, 91cm shield protruded beyond the warrior's profile. For the Roman soldier, the fundamental part of his equipment was the wooden (i.e. wicker, leather or skin) shield, 'covering the armed man only, lighter and more economical which becomes more useful to this kind of more dynamic formation', and more convenient an army now drawn solely from citizens of the lower classes.[106]

Chierici's statement is partially contradicted by the description of Hans van Wees on the fighting between infantry in the eighth century BC. The English author explains that the concept of hoplitism was born in Greece in around 720–700 BC, with the adoption of the bronze panoply and of the large shield with double grip. According to his opinion, the hoplites should have fought in a very open formation, because they continued to use their spears as throwing weapons, which requires a certain space for movement. The vase paintings show that the standard equipment of the hoplites was a pair of spears at least until 640 BC.[107] Indeed an open but ordered battle array could have been adopted also by the Roman *principes* armed with a throwing *hasta*. Moreover, they were also equipped with light armour and a smaller shield, along with a *gladius* of medium size, with a lanceolate shape and elongated point, all characteristics pointing towards an agile way of fighting, based upon a body-to-body clash with thrusting and stabbing (not slashing) blows.

We introduced the concept of the formation of the *principes* as an 'open hoplitic' type, by giving credit to the hypothesis of Hans van Wees, and such an idea of a looser battle-array coincides with the fact that these men-at-arms were not professional warriors, whose military activity took place only during a short period of the year, as their principal activity was essentially subsistence. Further evidence of a compact battle-array, although if more or less translated, is offered by the Umbrian word *katera*,[108] found in the *Iguvinae Tabulae*, with the meaning of 'battle formation host'. This word, dating back to this archaic period, later entered the Latin language as the word *catena* (from *kates-na*) having the meaning of elements united one to another,[109] reinforcing the thesis that already during this time it was diffused to the way of fighting – directly affecting control of the soldiers and the reduction of their personal capacities in favour of collective ones.

The motives which drove the monarchic societies to develop the more complex battle-array is well explained by Ardant du Picq,[110] a nineteenth-century French army officer, who was not only a military tactician but living in an era in which this way of fighting dominated. The French expert advises against the disorganised 'melee', because becoming mixed up with the enemy will only achieve slaughter without victory, while fighting in formation enables smaller armies to defeat larger ones.[111] The French colonel continues by explaining that the men in the first line, who will clash with the enemy front rank, instinctively and forcibly, assured themselves to be in a regular position in relation to their supporters, the companions of the same line near them and those in the second line. The correct position in respect to the others was to avoid offering the flank to the enemy or to leave space for the adversary to penetrate. The front-line battle took place man against man: each one was directed against the enemy in front of him. Each one, therefore, hit his antagonist with the shield, to make him lose his balance and struck him at the same moment in which he tried to recover it. In the rear, the second-rank men, in the intervals necessary for the protection of the front rank, were ready to defend the flanks against advancing enemies, as well as to replace the tired ones; the same applying to the third rank and so on. The description given by the French officer is very compelling but probably referring to Vegetius,[112] the description refers to a later battle array than the Romulean *legio*, although it is of value in describing the basics of organised fighting.

We can make two conclusions from the two initial points of view on the way of fighting of the Romulean soldiers: both open or close formations have a basis in fact and probably express two coexisting ways of fighting. First of all, by reading Livy we learn that many clashes seem to have been fought in a less organised fashion, although in such cases they seem to be small actions, like raiding parties and ambushes. We believe that in the Archaic Age the legacy of the small fighting groups still existed, under the leadership of a *familia*'s hero or more specifically that of a *gens*, which by 'swarming' in small attacks alternating with retreats was trying to cause as much damage as possible to the enemy with as little damage as possible to the family group. Such a deduction is confirmed by the episode of 477 BC, linked to the Battle of Cremera, a small river near Veii, where an army formed only from *Gens Fabia* faced the Etruscan city, as said by the Consul , '… It is our purpose to wage this war as if it were our own family feud, at our private cost …'.[113] The circumstance that, even in the early Consular Age, it was still possible for a *gens* to wage war as 'a family feud, at … private cost',[114] although it was authorised by the Senate, shows us how such an approach could be present in the Monarchical Age, and especially in its more archaic phase. To confirm the two ways of fighting, open formation or closed battle array, it is Livy himself who describes it, as thanks to Fabii, 'yet not only were raids made upon farming lands. and surprise attacks upon raiding parties [incursions by swarming], *but at times they fought in the open field and in serried ranks* [packed formations] …'.[115]

Fighting techniques of the Romulean legio

The development of fighting techniques of the Romulean army occurred in a well-coordinated way. The only thing that allowed numerous groups of *familiae* to fight efficiently was to form armed units distinguished by their age and weapons. This solution was found in the creation of the maniples, that, separated into *hastati*, *principes* and *triarii*, presented, as we know, a division linked to age and fighting experience, which, in turn, implied different weaponry and therefore a specific way of fighting.

Battles fell into three distinct phases, probably between two armies who presented more or less similar weapons and tactics. Indeed the populations the Romans were obliged to fight were close not only geographically, but also as archaeological facies and their weapons were more or less equivalent for breaking, pushing, and causing disorder in the enemy battle line to achieve victory.[116]

- Phase 1, attack of the *hastati* (H)

The clash began with the offensive move of the *hastati* who in a very open formation, ran towards the enemy and threw the *hastae* then rapidly retreated behind the ranks of the *principes* (or *triarii*). Some experimental studies calculated that the time taken by this move was a few minutes, considering that the effective range of the thrown *hastae* was around 40m, with an average running speed of 20km/h.[117]

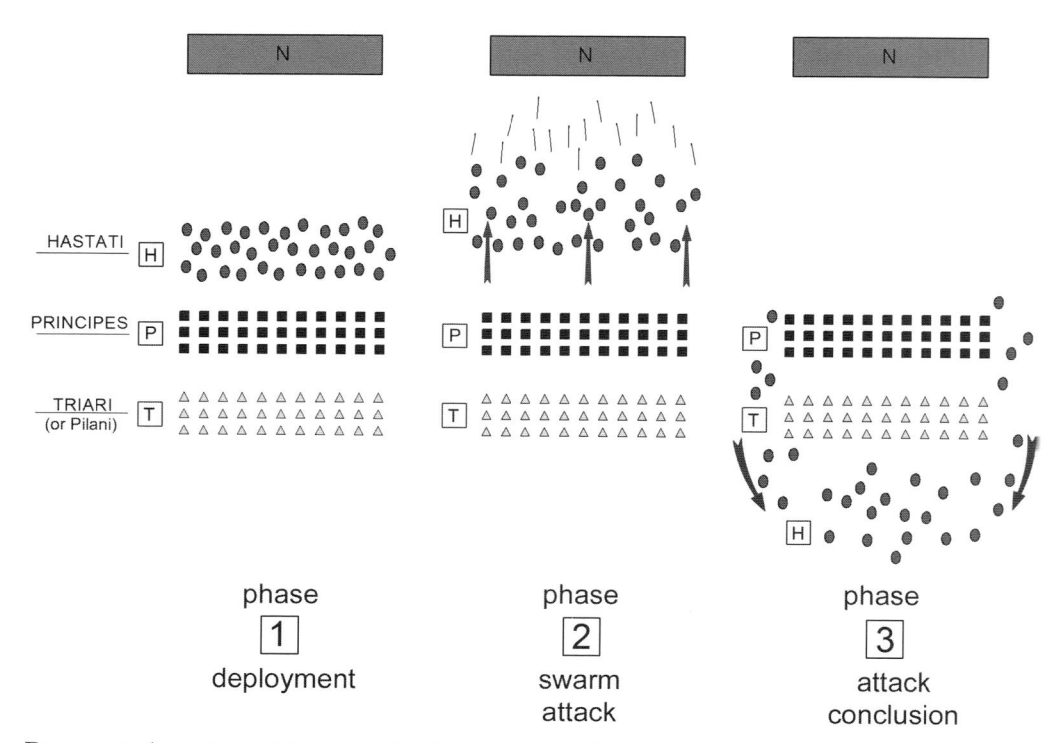

Diagram 4: A single maniple during the phases in which the attack of the *hastati* (H) developed. These light troops began the battle with an attempt to disorganise the enemy's ranks by throwing their own *hastae*. They were young men who, after launching their spears, retired behind the ranks of the *triarii* (T). (*Author's drawing*)

They had many targets but in principle the aim was to trigger the armed confrontation, since battles often remained at a standstill, each side waiting for the other to start the fight. The swarm of young warriors, throwing their spears, served to disorganise the enemy ranks in an action that, in some respects, resembled the disorganised one of the Homeric period and in parallel preceded the role of the *velites*. Rather than inflicting major losses on the rival army, they attempted to create 'psychological fear' from the need for the opponents to protect themselves from a shower of spears and the inevitable appearance of various injured comrades. Such psychological pressure, associated with the prelude to a battle, was often unbearable, especially among the younger infantrymen, whose retreating proved to be the key to the front and therefore achieving a successful outcome of the fight without suffering losses.

Finally, we must not forget that the role of the *hastati* was a good apprenticeship. In fact, these young Roman infantrymen, in their first experience of war, were tempered to combat with a certain security, since the attack took place from such a distance that the enemy would have had to expose himself to fight them effectively and break up their own line, which never happened.

- Phase 2, intervention of the *principes* (P)

After the attack of the *hastati*, these light infantry probably retreated behind the ranks of the *triarii*, allowing the *principes*, infantrymen armed with a *hasta*, a *gladius* and an Argive shield, to enter the action.[118]

They advanced in three orderly ranks and, at a predetermined order, just before contact, they threw the *hasta* and unsheathed the *gladius*. Contact with the enemy meant that the fight was sustained by the front rank of the two opposing sides and, as Ardant du Picq specifies, sword-to-sword combat was the most deadly, offering the most uncertain outcomes, because in it the individual qualities of the soldier – courage, dexterity, calm – fencing skill, in short, was of the greatest and most immediate influence.[119] During the fight, the wounded or killed soldier should have immediately been replaced by one from the rear rank, and any hesitation in this would have had serious consequences, possibly allowing enemy to breach the battle array and cause a defeat. 'The fight took place along the line of contact of the first ranks of the army, a straight line, broken, curved, and bent in different directions according to the various chances of the action at such or such a point, but always restricting and separating the combatants of the two sides.' The French author underlines that in the fight, especially when hard, 'if it gave way tactically before it and availing himself of gaps penetrated it by groups, still there was no melee or mixture of ranks. The wedge entering into a mass does not become intermingled with it'.[120]

Within the Romulean *legio*, the enemy was opposed by a line made up of only three ranks of *principes*, even though it was developed for a very large group of 300 infantrymen. This structure testifies how the 'heart of the fight', based on sword fighting, must have been of rather limited duration, since the killing of a file of only three men would have been enough to break through the front. This 'weakness' reflects the elementary nature of an army in the early stages of its development, which would soon be corrected in the formations of the following centuries.

- Phase 3, the defence of the *triarii* (T)

The efficiency of the *principes* lay in the vigour which enabled such unit to counter the enemy's offensive, in turn avoiding its ranks being thinned, which would have indeed led to a breakthrough and to the collapse and capitulation of the army. When such a risk was felt, the centurions could order a retreat through the ranks of the *triarii*, a compact phalanx formation of soldiers resting on their knees, with *hastae* planted on the ground and pointing towards the enemy. This bastion of soldiers was intended to be a mere passive defence, with the dual purpose of preventing an enemy breakthrough and allowing the *principes* to take a breather and regroup before launching a new attack.

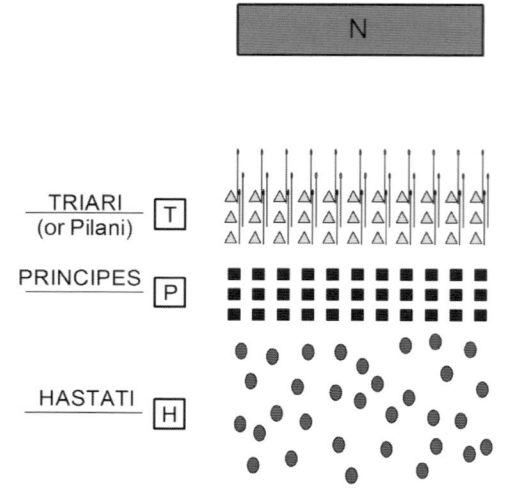

Diagram 5: When the *principes* had exhausted their fighting strength, they retreated behind the ranks of the *triarii* (T), leaving as a last defence a compact phalanx of soldiers who kept their *hastae* pointed towards the enemy. (*Author's drawing*)

Ancient sources do not clarify whether the three phases of combat shown here took place only once or were repeated during the battle, in a context of attacks and retreats by both formations. Probably, like the swarm attacks of the archaic period and those of the indigenous Papuans of New Guinea, the clashes and retreats were repeated several times during the battle, which usually lasted a day. If this was the case, we have to believe that the *hastati* and the *principes* would have retreated behind the *triarii* several times to refresh and reorganise themselves, before returning to the front line in an attempt to defeat the enemy definitively. To summarise this fight, we must remember that the Romulean *legio* deployed essentially in width, useful to prevent encirclement manoeuvres that would have been devastating for the maintenance of the deployment, and at the same time had a narrow depth, since it was a formation designed to support clashes, probably repeated, but individually short-lived. As a metaphor, we can liken this legion to three tight threads, one for each *acies*, each aimed at containing the enemy. Each phase (i.e. each *acies*) during the fight presents a typical movement of a rope, but when the formation projected forward, it acted with a disruptive force that had the purpose of breaking the enemy array. We can imagine the third *acies*, the *triarii* as 'barbed wire', more rigid and with barbs representing the spears of the *pilani* (Fig. 1).

Vestiges of ordeal duels within the Roman combat system

The changes within the military organisation were very slow and linked to tradition. The proof for this can be found in some archaic remainders that persisted over time, not only in the Monarchical Period but also during the Consular one. The ordeal

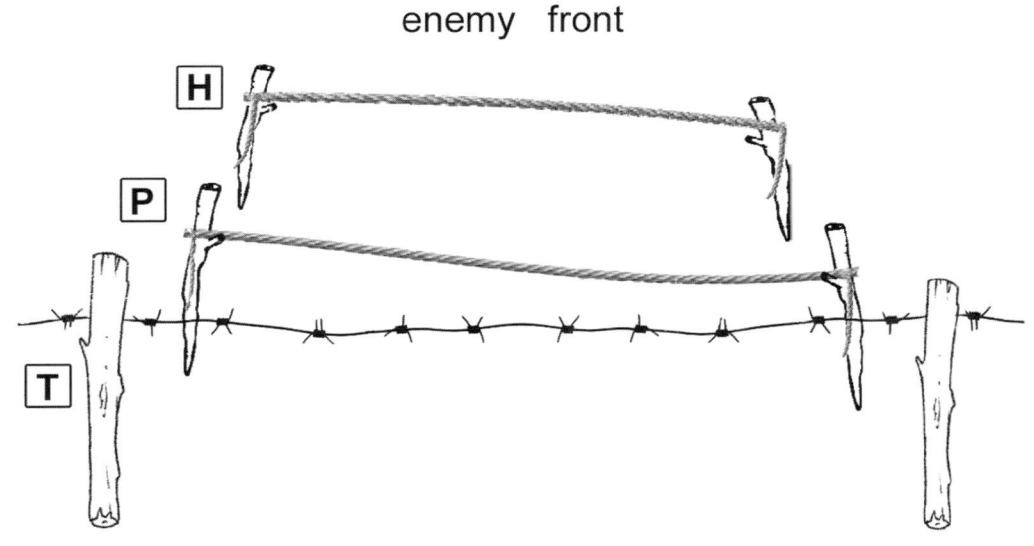

Fig. 1: The Romulean *legio* can be metaphorically related to three taught threads, one for each *acies*. In fact, the fight was not based on the maniple, but on the front that each component of it (the *hastati* (H), the *principes* (P) and the *triarii* (T)) managed to oppose to the enemy. In the clash, the breaking of an *acies* (like the breaking of a thread), especially of the one represented by the *principes* and the *triarii*, could have led to the defeat of the army because it would have led to the disintegration of the whole battle array. The *triarii* (or *pilani*) are depicted as barbed wire to signify their stability and opposing ability linked to their spears (the barbs). (*Author's drawing*)

duel is one of these, where the only judge of the clash was the god who decided the outcome of the duel. There are examples referring to the early Roman period, such as the duel between Acro, the Sabine king of Cenina, and Romulus[121] or the famous clash between the Horatii and the Curiatii, as well as to more recent periods, such as the challenge between Junius Brutus, who overthrew the monarchy, and Aruns, son of Tarquinius Superbus in the sixth century BC,[122] or the story of the heroic soldier L. Siccius Dentatus, who between the sixth and fifth centuries BC overcame his enemies in numerous duels,[123] the fighting that took place in 390 BC between the Roman ambassador and the Gauls,[124] and finally the one between the tribune M. Valerius (later called Corvinus) and a Celtic chief in 349 BC.[125] But perhaps the most significant event is that of Titus Manlius Torquatus in 361 BC, where the typical thematic sequence of duels of the *Iliad* narrative is present, but with typical Roman variants, from which we can hypothesise that it was produced for educational and moralistic purposes.

At the provocation of the 'giant' Gallic warrior ('Let the bravest man that Rome possesses come out and fight me, that we two may decide which people is the superior in war')[126] the Roman answered, but only after having asked permission from the dictator, thus evidencing the first variant from the Homeric canons: 'Without your orders, General,' he said, 'I will never leave my post to fight [i.e. from the battle-array, *extra ordinem*] ...'[127] It follows the description of how the hero carried his weapons and presents the enemy in a typical negative way ('who was exulting in his brute strength, and even ... putting his tongue out in derision'). The Gaul is presented as 'a creature of enormous bulk, resplendent in a many-coloured coat and wearing painted and gilded armour',[128] whereas Titus Manlius was of 'average height, and his arms, useful rather than ornamental, gave him quite an ordinary appearance'.[129] While the two armies remain ordered to witness the duel, typical of those duels described in the *Iliad*, the clash begins:

> the Gaul, like a great overhanging mass, held out his shield on his left arm to meet his adversary's blows and aimed a tremendous cut downwards with his sword. The Roman evaded the blow, and pushing aside the bottom of the Gaul's shield with his own [the first action is a blow with the shield to destabilise the enemy], he slipped under it close up to the Gaul, too near for him to get at him with his sword. Then turning the point of his blade [*mucro*, literally 'the sword's point', in the sense that the Latin infantryman makes the blow with the point of the *gladius* directed towards the Gaul] upwards, he gave two rapid thrusts in succession and stabbed the Gaul in the belly and the groin, laying his enemy prostrate over a large extent of ground.[130]

The spear, the typical weapon of the early stages of archaic combat, no longer appears predominant in these tales and is entirely replaced by the sword, where the thrust was the typical tactic of the Roman soldier, while the slashing blow was typical of the Celtic warrior.

However, the ordeal, although occasionally practised, was always viewed negatively by the Romans as it contradicted their rules of combat based on organisation and on discipline, where the single infantryman, however skilful and strong, could pose a danger if he acted independently. This concept is exalted in the didactic tale of the young Titus Manlius, son of Torquatus, who forgot 'the consul's edict and the obedience due to a father',[131] bravely defeating Geminus Mecius, who was the commander of the Latin cavalry, in single combat. The seriousness of the offence was attributable to disobedience, showing no 'regard for either the authority of a consul or the obedience due to a father' – his father reproached him – 'and defiance of our edict [*adversus edictum nostrum*] have left your post to fight against the enemy [*extra ordinem in hostem pugnasti*], and have done your best to destroy the military discipline [*disciplinam militarem*] through which the Roman State has stood till now unshaken'.[132] The harshness of the extreme punishment, the death sentence, moreover inflicted by the father, should not be seen as an excessive measure for a youthful mistake linked to the ardour of showing one's own valour, but be considered as a punishment for a potentially serious mistake, even to constitute 'a melancholy example, but one that will be profitable to the young men of the future'.[133] Allowing loss of discipline in military training endangered the survival of the training itself.

The persistence of duels until the Republican Period shows that the changes in the way of fighting, where tradition had a very important role, were slow, so much so that certain costumes remained unchanged for over 300 years after the establishment of the Romulean *legio*. As part of a broader reasoning, we must take into account that usually all the changes that we will describe in the Roman army were hardly drastic. In the Roman mentality, the slowness and graduality that characterised any social change were always out of respect for the *Mos Maiorum*, since changing behaviours, which had been accepted and repeated by all generations, would have seemed impious, like breaking with the sacred past.

Cavalry: when the equites became pedites as a last resort
According to Livy, in the seventh century BC at the Aniene river Ancus Marcius fought the Sabines with an army of 3,000 *pedites* (infantrymen), distinguished according to the three tribes, and a cavalry force consisting of 300 *equites*, which was already classically placed on the flanks. The author describes: 'In that battle, the cavalry especially distinguished themselves. They were posted on each wing, and when the infantry in the centre were being forced back, it is said that they made such a desperate charge from both sides that they not only arrested the Sabine legions as they were pressing on the retreating Romans, but immediately put them to flight.'[134]

First of all we must stress that in the Monarchic-Republican Period, the cavalry was always of secondary importance to the infantry. The reasons for this were well defined by Machiavelli, a historian and a politician of the sixteenth century who, although he lived in another historical period, was an expert on this military force, a basic element in the Renaissance. He describes the limits of the Roman cavalry which, unlike the infantrymen, were unable to reach inaccessible places, to respond quickly to an order, to return quickly to formation after an assault, and that the attack can only take place with a reduced impetus given that a brave man may find himself riding on a cowardly horse or vice versa, and that, last but not least, the horse, being a sensible animal, would hardly launch itself against an obstacle which it would have considered dangerous. In fact, knowing the dangers such as 'the pike and the sword', the horse would come to a stop when feeling the sting, and divert its trajectory to avoid them because, as the author says, 'if we push a horse against a wall, we will find few that will crash into it'.[135]

The horsemen were used for scouting, to raid and plunder enemy territory, but above all, during the battle, to protect the formation of the *pedites*. The front ranks of the legions were very effective in countering an attack, but at the same time they were very vulnerable if the formation had been surrounded or taken in the flank. As a result of this weakness, the line was deployed as wide as possible, to prevent the fatal encirclement, and for this purpose the flanks were protected by the cavalry. The horsemen were used to attack and block the opposing cavalry, in an attempt to defend their own infantry and at the same time, try to disrupt the opposing cavalry by taking it from the flanks or attacking it from the rear; when the enemy army was finally routed, the cavalrymen pursed them and cut them down.

As described by Dionysius, Romulus

> chose three hundred men, the most robust of body and from the most illustrious families, whom the curiae named in the same manner that they had named the

senators … and these he kept always about his person. They were all called by one common name, *kelerioi*; according to most writers this was because of the 'celerity' required in the services they were to perform (for those who are ready and quick at their tasks the Romans call Celeres) … these Celeres constantly attended Romulus, armed with spears, and executed his orders; and on campaigns they charged before him and defended his person. And as a rule it was they who gave a favourable issue to the contest, as they were the first to engage in battle and the last of all to desist. They fought on horseback where there was level ground favourable for cavalry manoeuvres and on foot where it was rough and inconvenient for horses.[136]

Therefore the horsemen, called 'Celeres' for their speed of intervention, came from aristocratic families and could fight either as *equites* or as *pedites*.[137]

Their main weapon was the spear, as described in the clash at Lake Regillus in 469 BC, in which the cavalry commanders of the two sides, T. Aebutius and Octavius Mamilius, 'came to blows and in the encounter gave one another grievous wounds, though not mortal, the Master of the Horse driving his spear through the corselet of Mamilius into his breast and Mamilius running the other through the middle of his right arm; and both fell from their horses'. [138] However, it is possible that as they had to fight also as infantrymen, they would have had a sword too, as described in this quotation:

thereupon some of them hurled their spears at the Volscians, and others with their cavalry swords,[139] which are longer than those of the infantry, struck all whom they encountered on the arms and slashed them down to the elbows, cutting off the forearms of many together with the clothing that covered them and their weapons of defence, and by inflicting deep wounds on the knees and ankles of many others, hurled them, no matter how firmly they had stood, half dead upon the ground.[140]

In summary, the ancient authors describe the Romulean *legio* as a well-structured deployment, where cavalry provided protection and dealt with dangerous situations in which the infantry could find themselves. Considered a prestigious part of the battle array, it was drawn from the social elite, since only those belonging to a certain social class could afford a horse and its upkeep. Probably, the danger they faced during a fight were less than that of an infantryman, since in this era, the type of combat for a horseman was mobile and at a distance, compared to that of a *pedes* who fought hand-to-hand. Only if the front threatened to give way, and that the battle was lost, would the aristocrats dismount, 'abandoning their protection privileges' to go to reinforce the melee combat through the use of the sword. The normally secondary role of cavalry became in this situation primary, rising to that of the saviour of the homeland.

II.2,2 The Servian *Legio* (Mid-Sixth Century BC)

A timocratic reform

There was a moment of socio-political change with important consequences on military aspects under Servius Tullius (sixth century BC). We do not know if the civil and social revolution that took place in Rome had been a consequence of a military order already adopted by the Etruscan army (an external influence), or if it was a political reform aimed at affirming the central authority at the expense of the aristocrats (an internal origin). Whatever the reason, Servius Tullius's '*censum instituit*' created a system in which the tasks of peace and war were distributed not by rank, as in the past, but according to the financial status of the individual. While until then individuals' participation in political and military life was connected to being part of a *gens*, favouring the *familiae* who had greater political and economic weight in Roman social life, with this reform the king divided the classes and *centuriae* according to the census.[141] This 'timocratic' reform effectively took away power and political prestige from the clans to which the soldier belonged, since the aristocrats and plebeians now had the same duties within the army and the same political rights in the Curiate Assembly,[142] distributed only by income.[143] In addition, this solution allowed new immigrants to be included in military service who, although numerous, had been excluded under the Romulean system because they did not belong to a tribe.

CLASS	CENSUS	NUMBER OF INFANTRY FOR EACH CENTURIA	SENIORES Defending the city (45–60 years)	IUNIORES For external war (<45 years)
1st CLASS	> 100,000 asses	100 + blacksmiths* and horsemen	Helmet, *clipeus*, breastplate, greaves,** *hasta*, *gladius*	Helmet, *clipeus*, breastplate, greaves, *hasta*, *gladius*
2nd CLASS	100,000–75,000	30	Helmet, *scutum*, greaves, *hasta*, *gladius*	Helmet, *scutum*, greaves, *hasta*, *gladius*
3rd CLASS	75,000–50,000	30	Helmet, *scutum*, *hasta*, *gladius*	Helmet, *scutum*, *hasta*, *gladius*
4th CLASS	50,000–25,000	30	Scutum, *hasta*, javelin (*hasta*, *gladius*)***	Scutum, *hasta*, javelin (*hasta*, *gladius*)***
5th CLASS ****	25,000–11,000	30	Slings and thrown stones *****	
		2	*Tubicines*, *cornicines*	
Exempted	<11,000	1		

Table 2: Composition of a *manipulus* following Servius Tullius' reform, based on the census, as reported by Livy.

* Two unarmed *centuriae* of workers have been joined to the first class, in charge of carrying war machines.
** All the defensive weapons were made of bronze.
*** Dionysius of Halicarnassus reports, unlike Livy, another panoply: *hasta* and *gladius*.
**** Fighting outside the array.
***** Dionysius of Halicarnassus reports, unlike Livy, another panoply: bows and slings;

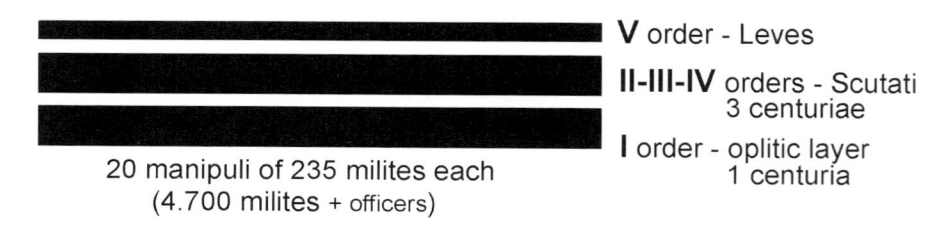

```
■■■■■■■■■■■■■■■■■■■■■■■■     V order - Leves
■■■■■■■■■■■■■■■■■■■■■■■■     II-III-IV orders - Scutati
■■■■■■■■■■■■■■■■■■■■■■■■                     3 centuriae
                             I order - oplitic layer
20 manipuli of 235 milites each          1 centuria
   (4.700 milites + officers)
```

Diagram 6: The *Legio Serviana*. (*Author's drawing*)

From Table 2, which summarises the Servian army reform, various very interesting aspects emerge. First of all, the spread of the *gladius* within the army always involves new types of soldiers, so a weapon initially relegated only to expert adult infantrymen, the *principes*, we now find present in the panoply of almost all soldiers. There are no longer any differences related to the age of the armed, it being present not only among the more experienced, the *seniores*, but also among the majority.[144] We also witness the loss of the elite status of this weapon, with its diffusion even among those not of noble rank. Finally, we have the opportunity to read in the reports of the ancient annalists that the short sword in this period became the main fighting weapon, prevailing over the *hasta*. We can also deduce this important affirmation from an episode narrated by Livy where the Romans prefer not to use the *pila* and instead go directly to fight with the *gladii*, believing the surprise effect and effectiveness of the sword to be greater than that of the spear. This passage narrates a battle that took place against the Volsci, who superior in numbers, attacked the Roman soldiers in a disordered rush. The Romans were commanded

> to stand with their spears [*pilis*] fixed in the ground, and when the enemy came to close quarters, to spring forward and make all possible use of their swords [*gladiis*]. The Volscians, wearied with their running and shouting, threw themselves upon the Romans as upon men benumbed with fear, but when they felt the strength of the counter-attack and saw the swords flashing before them … .[145]

The *pila*, typical elements of the first phase of Roman combat, lost their essential role in the victory, unlike the one assumed by the *gladius*.

One of the most important differences we can see in comparison between the two legions, Romulean and Servian, is first of all the increase in the depth of the maniples but at the expense of their total number, which changed from thirty of the Romulean period, down to twenty under Servius Tullius.

Furthermore, the heavily-armed soldiers, with full panoply, were moved to the front and made more numerous than in the Romulean formation, in which the soldiers who had similar weaponry were the *triarii*, arrayed instead in the third rank.

With regard to the numerical composition of a Servian legion, as for the other successive legions, there is no numerical value reported by the ancient authors that allows us to make a credible reconstruction. The numbers that we will use for the realisation of the schemes are from the reconstructive hypothesis of Battaglia and Ventura[146] with the caveat that, although credible, it still remains such. It defines how each maniple was made up of 235 soldiers thus distributed:

- Hoplitic layer of the *clipeati*: 100 infantrymen (1 *centuria*);
- *Scutati* 2nd, 3rd and 4th class: 90 infantrymen (3 *centuriae*);
- *Leves* (5th class): 45 foot soldiers.

to which must be added the officers and *cornices*.

It should be noted that in this configuration there is no longer the difference between the *centuria* and the maniple that we saw in the previous formation, in fact, a maniple now appears to be composed of four *centuriae* (apart from the *leves*) (Diagram 6 and Plate 2).

The change brought by Servius Tullius was radical, since it involved the *populus*, understood as the whole Roman community, formed by *plebei* and *patricii*. The reform had not only political effects, as the political and civil activities of an ancient society inevitably mixed with the military ones, giving rise to a reform that had very important consequences for the use of the *gladius*, participating in defining the development of a fight which will be increasingly peculiar.

The diversification of the panoply in the Central Italian armies
The presence of various fighting men within a *legio*, armed differently but still in a typical way for each class, suggests a complex and articulated way of combat by the Roman army. We found this aspect in the Romulean *legio*, where there were three orders of troops with different characteristics, and now emphasised in the *Legio Serviana*, consisting of five orders, also characterised by special panoplies. The finding of two different types of shields, the *clypeus*, round in shape and equipping the 1st class warriors, and the *scutum*, rectangular-oblong in shape, carried by soldiers of the 2nd, 3rd and 4th classes, irrefutably implies two completely different combat styles. The simultaneous presence of different shields for different troops is not, however, a prerogative of the Roman army alone, since it is also present in the representations on the *Situla della Certosa* (Archaeological Museum – Bologna, Italy).[147] This large bronze vase belonging to the Venetian-Etruscan culture, which dates back to the end of the sixth century BC, proposes in the cantilevered decoration the real progress of a marching army or a deployment in battle in the Etruscan-Po Etruria of the sixth–fifth century. The individual armed men and especially the individual weapons are reflected in the peninsular area: the individual comparisons can be found in the Etruscan, Picenian or Po areas as well as in the Celtic, Hallstattian and Illyrian areas.[148] The interesting fact is that the scene represented should not be interpreted as a characteristic representation only of the Etruscan-Po Valley people, but more generically as that of a typical central-northern Italian army of this era. The typology of weapons engraved on the *situla* betrays a mixture of facies, suggesting that there was certain homogeneity in the way

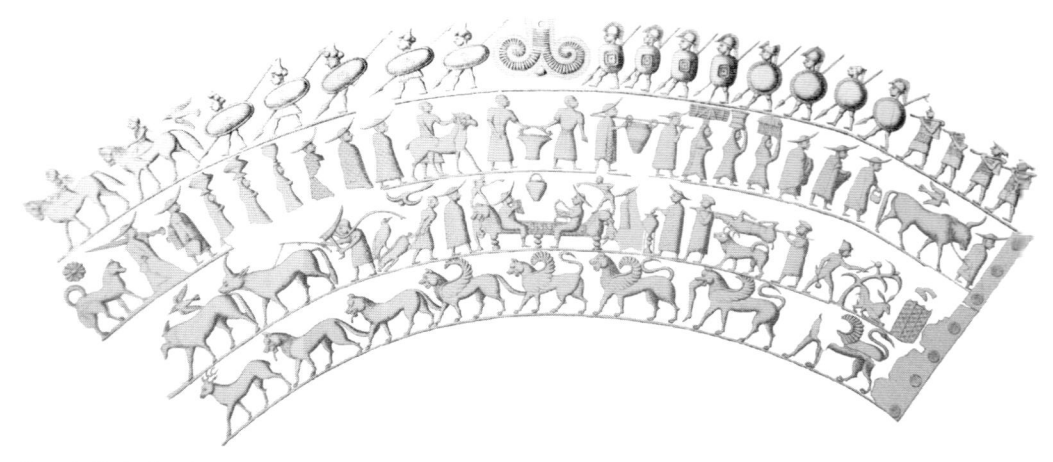

Fig. 2: Reliefs of the *Situla della Certosa* (Civic Archaeological Museum – Bologna, Italy). The first of the four rows portrays a military parade that opens with two horsemen, followed by three types of infantrymen standing out, being armed with different types of shield and with light troops at the rear. (Author's drawing, partially taken from G. Sassatelli, 'L'arte delle situle', in Venetkens, *Viaggio nella terra dei Veneti antichi, Catalogo della Mostra*, Padua 2013.)

of fighting but at the same time a widespread cultural identity. Furthermore, the fact that a similar representation is also found in another *situla* of a later century, called *Arnoaldi*, helps us to conclude that these representations were not an exceptional event, but the reality of an army that could normally have been seen fighting on Italian soil.

However, despite their importance, the represented images cannot be applied simply to the reality of Roman combat, above all because the presence of *gladii* is not highlighted. The important concept that we have to extrapolate from it is that the central-Italian populations had by now developed an articulated fighting style, not limited to the mere clash between two masses of armed men, although each of these people had gained a typical panoply and way of fighting, deriving from its own tradition.

Was the Servian legio a hoplitic one? The concept of hoplitism applied to the Roman army and combat hypothesis of the Servian legio

It is assumed by many modern authors that Roman combat was of hoplitic type, and that the quotations reported as irrefutable proof of this are those of Livy, where he mentions 'the phalanx formation, similar to the Macedonian of the earlier days',[149] as well as the reference in the *Ineditum Vaticanum*, where the author, exalting the Romans over the Greeks, affirms that they were 'very capable of assimilating the methods of others, learned the Phalangitic order from the Etruscans [and] the fighting on horseback from the Samnites',[150] as well as the quote from Atheneus who says that 'from the Tyrrenians they derived the practice of the entire army advancing to battle in close phalanx …'.[151]

Although the quotations seem unequivocal, there are many doubts that the interpretation made by modern literature is the correct one. Initially, it is appropriate to consider the definition of hoplitism and the archaeological evidence for it on Italian soil.

Definition of Hoplitism
According to widespread opinion, hoplite combat is based on 'standing' and 'pushing' and to describe it, the words of Tyrtaeus[152] (a Greek poet who lived in the seventh century BC) are normally referred to, who describes a type of hoplitic attack:

> Let a man learn how to fight by first daring to perform mighty deeds,
> Not where the missiles won't reach, if he is armed with a shield,
> But getting in close where fighting is hand to hand, inflicting a wound
> With his long spear or his sword, taking the enemy's life.

The most emphasised feature is holding position:

> With his foot planted alongside a foot and his shield pressed against shield,
> And his crest up against crest and his helm up against helm
> And breast against breast, embroiled in the action – let him fight man to man,
> Holding secure in his grasp haft of his sword or his spear!

Framing the hoplite concept in a proper way is fundamental in order to understand 'what' and 'how much' was its influence on Roman combat. The question we have to ask ourselves is whether it was only the one described by Tyrtaeus or, in reality, also a wider and more varied way of confronting armies. We believe that all the intellectual misunderstandings and dichotomies are based on this point, from which we must start again to overcome the misunderstandings of the ancient authors. First of all, to condense a way of fighting that has evolved over a few centuries in a few lines of a seventh-century BC poem entails the risk that excessive conciseness misrepresents the reality. If we evaluate in which era the hoplite tactic developed, we note that, according to A.M. Snodgrass, it was introduced progressively from the eighth century BC to meet the military needs of the Greek states, but wasn't fully formed until the seventh century BC; while for H. van Wees the 'mature, but still incomplete' hoplitic system is dated around 600 BC,[153] unlike the Macedonian phalanxes which were introduced by King Philip II of Macedon only in the fourth century BC. So, the first point we want to define is that the evolution of Greek combat runs from the eighth to the fourth century BC, involving political and social phases and types of enemies that are completely different from each other. To outline such a complex picture, we believe fundamentally the study of Bettalli, who manages to frame this type of combat in a very clear way within an admirable synthesis based on three statements:

- phalanx combat has always existed in its fundamental elements and we find it in Homer, if not before. The hoplite and hoplitic phalanx would be merely adaptations of a pre-existing situation and there would therefore be no substantial discontinuity to report;

Fig. 3: Two images of hoplite combat, the first from a Greek vase and the second from an Etruscan one, both showing that the fight was not based on duels between individual soldiers, but between groups of infantrymen who made the compact deployment their strength.
A) Olpe Chigi of the seventh century BC, made in Corinth – Greece, hence it cannot be used as evidence of the hoplite combat in Etruria, as it frequently happens. It represents a typical hoplitic fight to the sound of the *diaulos*.
B) Amphora from Tarquinia attributed to the sixth century BC by the Etruscan painter of Micali, showing a *cornice* that marks the rhythm of a group of *clipeati* infantrymen, all armed in a similar way. The absence of a leader proves that it is not a noble rank, but a hoplite deployment, even if the armament does not appear typical of it. (*Author's drawing*)

- the technological innovations that characterise hoplitism, in particular the shield with the double handle, are the immediate cause of the birth of the phalanx, which alone allows it to develop its potential …;
- the process of adopting a way of fighting definable as hoplitism, characterised by the deployment in phalanx and established in the classical age as an ideological pillar of the community of the *polis*, is much slower and much less clear than as has usually been described. The path cannot in fact be defined completed before the fifth century … .

Bettalli, therefore, dictates the axiom that the hoplite cannot exist without the phalanx and underlines how hoplitism is, to a large extent, an ideologically powerful model, but less defined in the military reality of the *polis*.[154]

We deduce a first important consideration: for the ancients, 'hoplitism' was not exclusively a battle formation but more a type of combat carried out by warriors equipped with heavy armament, such as the metal helmet, the large bronze *hoplon* and the breastplate. For this definition, the offensive weapons used were unimportant, whether it was the spear, on which the Greeks based their offense, or the sword, preferred by the Romans, to which they immediately relied on after throwing the *pila*.[155]

- *The interpretation of the archaeological evidence of hoplitism on Italian soil*

The Greek phalanx, defined as a 'roller', is represented as a block of men who had to maintain their order in the formation, since the individual soldiers operated as a single body, in a fight based on the opposing clash of two compact units. In this type of clash, the damage inflicted by the spears served to reduce the impetus of the opponent and the defensive weapons such as the helmet, the shield and the greaves had to be very protective, even if at the expense of agility which was not required in this type of fighting. But while in Greece there is an admirable quantity of archaeological remains that unquestionably testify for the hoplite deployment, none of this exists in Italy, lacking both an adequate discovery of the Hellenic helmets,[156] useful with their extremely protective form to defend the infantryman from the frontal blows of a spear, as well as the ὅπλα, *òpla*, suitable for combat based on the thrust.

To emphasise the great importance of the type of shields in the role of combat and how they delineate the difference between central Italian and Greek combat, we refer to an analysis dating back to the last years of the twentieth century of all known findings of sheet bronze *clipei* made in central Italy (Villanovian phase – Orientalizing Period), of which there are about hundred specimens, of which fifty are from Etruria, twenty-six from the *Latium Vetus* (one from Rome, eleven from Palestrina, four from Castel di Decima, eight from Laurentina, two from Satricum), five from Cuma, four from Picenus and four from Verucchio, … they only have a central handle, and do not have the 'pair' of bracelet and handle. This indicates an adoption of foreign decorative fashions but, basically, the maintenance of traditional fighting techniques.[157] This study on the different grip of the shields would tend to question the beliefs of the typical hoplitic fight on central Italian soil, probably because the modern analysis is sometimes too tied to excessive and frequently misleading schematizations.

Often the Greek weapons in Italy are considered only as a sign of ostentation and socio-economic power, probably sported during festivities or in the context of agonistic competitions. In this regard, we report the example of the so-called 'Warrior of Lanuvius' (Fig. 4), because it is the evidence that is normally emphasised by those who claim that the Romans used the hoplite combat style. This find from the Alban Hills, dating back to the first decades of the fifth century BC, is characterised by expensive and prestigious weapons consisting of a decorated helmet, a bronze cuirass and a *machaira*,

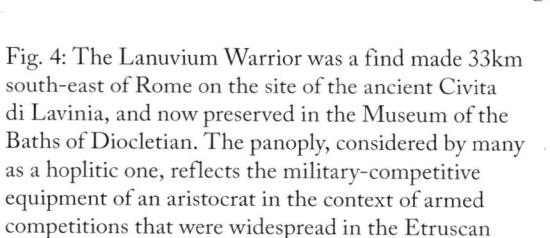

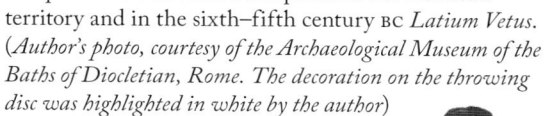

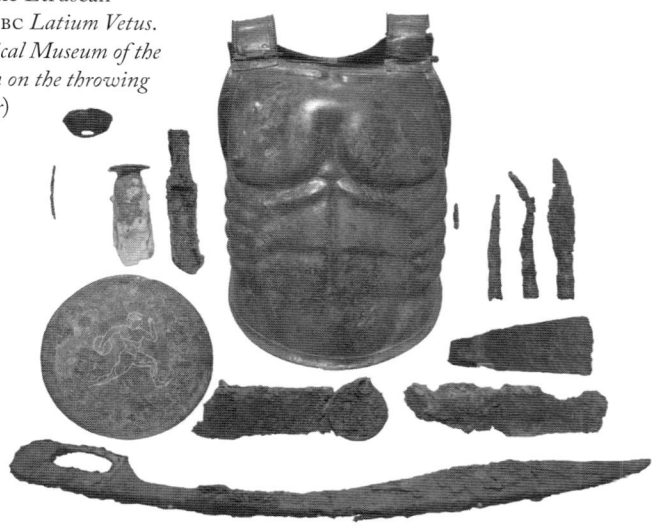

Fig. 4: The Lanuvium Warrior was a find made 33km south-east of Rome on the site of the ancient Civita di Lavinia, and now preserved in the Museum of the Baths of Diocletian. The panoply, considered by many as a hoplitic one, reflects the military-competitive equipment of an aristocrat in the context of armed competitions that were widespread in the Etruscan territory and in the sixth–fifth century BC *Latium Vetus*. (*Author's photo, courtesy of the Archaeological Museum of the Baths of Diocletian, Rome. The decoration on the throwing disc was highlighted in white by the author*)

together with gymnastic equipment such as a bronze discus or *discobolus* (engraved with gymnastic figures on one side and an armed horseman on the other), at least two iron strigils, two alabasters and javelin tips, objects that lean towards a more sporting than military use.[158] This find, which is a part of rare and exceptional discoveries, highlights two concepts: how luxury weapons were a factor of prestige also among the Latin population[159] and how, in athletics, they enhanced the heroic image of the deceased.[160]

Most likely the armour must be considered in the context of armed sports competitions, which also contemplated the use of cavalry armament. This hypothesis is based both on the engraving on the bronze disc (an *eques* equipped with a helmet, armour and spear) and on the *machaira*, whose 90cm length would classify it precisely as a cavalry weapon. This burial is therefore of an athlete-cavalry warrior, which makes it difficult to prove that the weapons found were indications of hoplitic combat.

In summary, on central Italian soil the role of the panoplies was also that of the possession and display of prestigious weapons, which with their Greek character were based on the legendary Trojan War, creating a mythic aura capable of conferring an important level of social distinction upon their owner.

Finally, another proof that derives from archaeology and that we could define as 'visual' is an Italic vase[161] produced by the Falisci (Fig. 5).[162] These people, bordering on the Romans and often at war with them, represented this conflict by referring to the myth of the Trojan War, probably inspired by the *Iliou pèrsis*. The main figure, defined as such by its large size and rich dress, represents a warrior from Faleri, but, referring

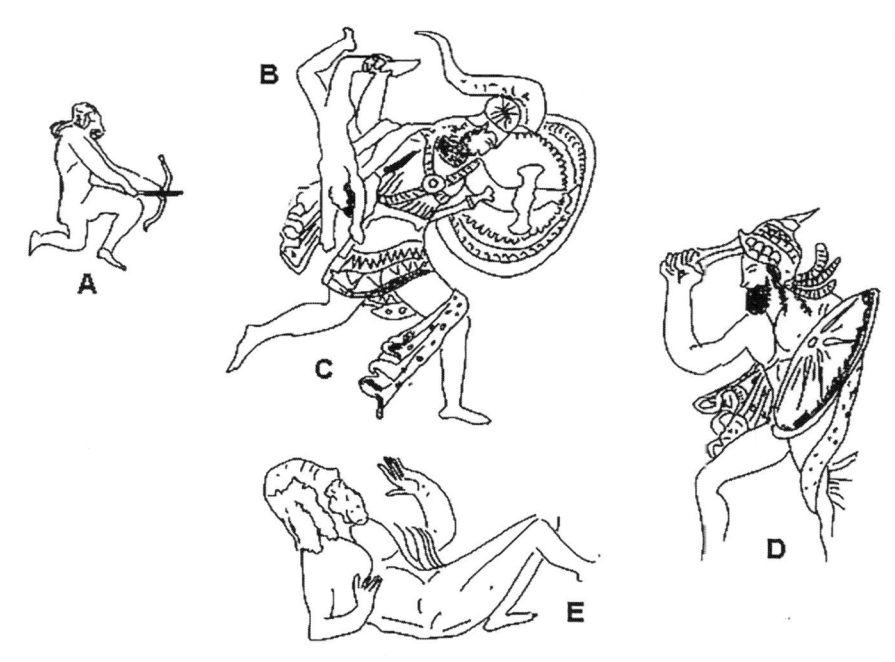

Fig. 5: Vase of the painter of Nazzano, and an artist operating in Faleri in the first half of the fourth century BC (goblet crater from Falerii, preserved in the Museum of Villa Giulia – Rome). It is well known how Neoptolemus (C) holds the double-handled hoplitic shield, while he fights against the 'barbarian' infantryman (D) who defends himself with a small central handle *hoplon* and is in the act of making a blow with his gladiolus sword.
A): Oriental archer (Roman); B) Astianatte (Roman); C) Neoptolemus (Faliscus); D) Eastern infantryman (Roman); E) Priam (Roman). (*Author's drawing*)

to the Trojan myth, identifies himself as Neoptolemus, armed with a Corinthian or Chalcidian helmet and a *hoplon* supported by two handles, while his sword is depicted in the scabbard during the action, indicating that it is a secondary weapon for him. This is opposed by the Trojan warriors, who in the metaphor are the Romans, one of whom we see armed instead with a sword and a round shield which, due to the size and perspective of the representation, would seem to be of the type with a single central handle. This vase therefore gives us, beyond the metaphor, the reality of the different armament of two different Italian cultures of that period, the Greek (of which the Falisci felt the influence through the Etruscans), showing a hoplitic armament in the more classic style, and the Roman, which remains instead attached to the more traditional weapons, including the sword, which owe very little to hoplitism.

The Etruscan influence and combat hypothesis in the Servian Legio
The correct framing of the concept of hoplitism and of what was the difference between the panoply of the Greek soldier and the central Italian one, allows us to approach more correctly the interpretation of the aforementioned quotations that are used today to prove that the Romans had adopted hoplite combat *tout court*. Livy's

testimony in which he declares that the phalanxes were 'similar to the Macedonian of the earlier days'[163] (of the fourth century BC), finds first of all its centrality in the fact that the author used the adjective 'similar' (*similes*), which by definition has a different meaning from 'equal'. Part of the Roman formation could also be traced back to the Macedonian one due to its close order, but the similarity ends here and is very different from believing that they fought in the same way.

The fact that the Etruscans, influenced by Greek culture, had developed compact and deep ranks and fought the enemy with a front that resembled a 'solid wall', forced the Romans to reorganise their deployment. Servius Tullius moved the infantrymen equipped with full armour to the front, so as to oppose the Etruscan hoplites with similar armour, but followed them in the battle-array by others with lighter armour to accommodate the typical Roman combat, based on individual fighting.

Based on this interpretation, we can understand the quote from the *Ineditum Vaticanum*[164] which states how the Roman people changed their way of fighting by adapting it to the Tyrrhenian one so as not to suffer from their superiority: 'For the Tyrrhenians used to make war on us with bronze shields and fighting in phalanx formation, not in maniples; and we, changing our armament and replacing it with theirs, organised our forces against them, and contending thus against men who had long been accustomed to phalanx battles we were victorious.'[165] The text suggests that the Etruscans obtained military supremacy thanks to the development of 'phalanx' combat and the use of the great bronze shield, the *hoplon*, frequently found in central Italy but which often present different characteristics from the Greek ones. These Italian shields, with a single central handle, were also present in Roman culture from archaic times, when they were to protect the *pater familias* or the hero who represented him. This is the reason why Livy informs us that 'The Romans had formerly used small round shields' (*clipeis antea Romani usi sunt*),[166] the defensive element of the *principes* and *hastati* that finally became basic to oppose the Etruscan phalangite combat, as confirmed by the *Ineditum Vaticanum*[167] and from *Athenaeus*.[168] From the archaeological analysis that the Romans possessed a shield that allowed a certain agility in combat, we can assume that even the way of fighting of the front rows, 'the hoplites', was not based only on mere pushing.

We are in a historical context in which the two cultures, Etruscan and Roman, had numerous points of contact and underwent mutual influences, but it was the Tyrrhenian civilisation, culturally more developed, that had the greatest influence on the Roman one, which was still in the full phase of its development. We cannot forget that the Servian *legio* was created by a monarch of Etruscan origin who reorganised the legion according to a mentality that was affected by that of his own people. In fact, of all the Roman formations we know, this is the only one that is closest to the concept of hoplitism, having deployed infantry with hoplitic panoply in the first ranks and having increased the depth of the formation. The Etruscan influence is also present in the numerous symbols or words linked to the military sphere which, in fact, were assimilated by the Latin people. We recall the standards and the symbols of royal power (the lictors with bundles of rods and the axes, the purple robe embroidered with gold, the ivory throne and the sceptre with the eagle[169]), as well as many words such as *Balteum*,[170] *Cassis/cassida*,[171] *Hasta velitaris*[172] and *Subulo*.[173]

Even though we can therefore recognise a certain Etruscan influence, we must not consider this transposition a mere acquisition, but in many respects an interpretation, and to put it in the words of Cherici, Rome acquires – and knows to acquire – techniques and practices from the surrounding world, in particular from Etruria, but it seems to follow, from a social, political, economic and cultural point of view, its own path, in which its birth and persistence as a 'warrior society' allows that solid internal dynamism that accounts summarise in the centuries-old struggle between patricians and plebeians and which focuses precisely on the relationship between military qualification and political capacity.[174]

The *Legio Serviana*, with the adoption of close-formation combat, was a sort of adaptation to the Etruscan armies which, having already absorbed the influence of the Greek hoplite combat, could deploy deeper formations. The previous deployment of the *Legio Romulea* had proved unsuitable because, having removed the line of *hastati* who probably constituted the light infantry in this historical phase (the *ante litteram* of the *velites*), consisted of two *acies* of soldiers, the *principes* and the *triarii*, who opposed only six rows of infantry in total. Therefore, the Roman formation in the Romulean period suffered from the overwhelming superiority of the breakthrough force of the Tyrrhenians. The new Roman *legio*, instituted by Servius Tullius, developed by deploying 'hoplitic' soldiers, armed with helmets, cuirasses, greaves, *clypeus*, *hasta* and *gladius* in the front rank and being capable of opposing the enemy army in an appropriate ' Greek style'. Later on he placed the soldiers belonging to the 2nd, 3rd and 4th class, who were armed with the *scutum*, but not the Argive one like in the 1st class, and with a panoply that was much less defensive (the infantry of the 2nd lacked armour, those of the 3rd class were not protected by armour or greaves and finally, those of the 4th class lacked all protection).

In some respects, it seems that Servius Tullius reversed the positions of the troops of the Romulean *legio*, moving the *triarii* from the rear rank to the front line, to more effectively face the initial confrontation against the Etruscan phalanx, while the *principes* and the *hastati* were distributed in the second and third ranks.

The 1st class probably had to absorb the impact of the Etruscan hoplites, essentially based on the thrust effect of the large shields, and defend themselves from the damage of the spears with adequate protection, such as to justify a complete panoply. But after the initial confrontation, the less well-protected troops went into action in completely different way of fighting, based on agility and attack and less on defence alone.

This interchange of positions, called *recursus*,[175] under the command of the centurions and driven by the *signiferi*, is an evolution deriving from the *Legio Romulea*, where at the critical moment the *principes* withdrew between the ranks of the *pilani*, even if the manoeuvre was more complex because it related to four *acies* of infantry. In the *Legio Serviana*, the formation was renewed three times in the clash, where the most important *recursus* was the passage from the 1st *signum*, which faced the initial clash with the hoplites, probably based on the *hasta*, to the 2nd *signum* based more on the *gladius*. The need for more athletic action, based on fencing, justified less protective equipment, which was reduced more in the 3rd and even more in the 4th *signum*, probably due to a lesser need for protection from enemy spears, in favour of greater vigour in hand-to-hand combat with the *gladius*.

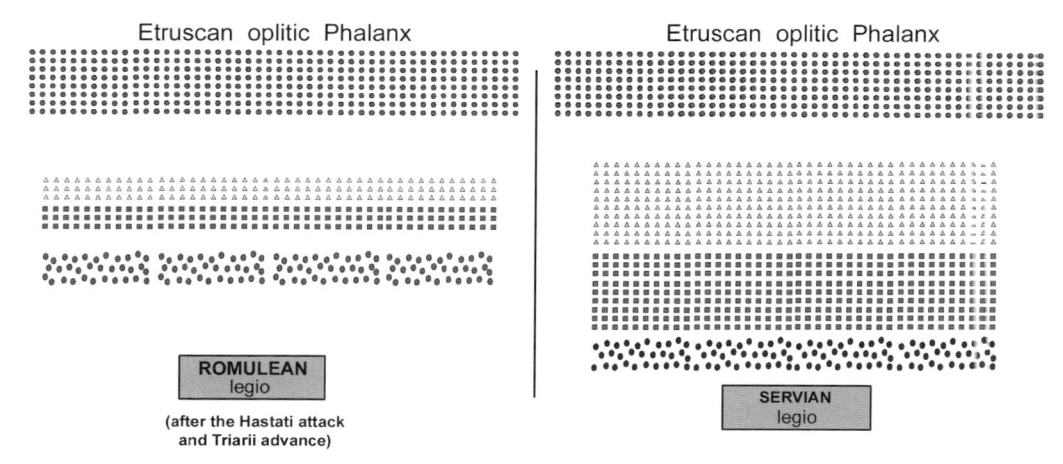

Diagram 7: Visual representation of the difference between the *Legio Romulea* and the Servian one in a clash with the Etruscan hoplitic phalanx (a section of four maniples).

When the Etruscan army adopted hoplitic combat, increasing the ranks of its own formation, it developed a clear military dominance over armies which, like the Roman one, opposed less lines of soldiers. The proposed scheme shows the two Roman formations, that of the Romulean *legio* and that of the Servian legion. The Romulean *legio*, as the *hastati* were light troops (like the later *velites*) and that the *principes* in case of difficulty retreated through the ranks of the *triarii*, was formed by only three rows of heavily-equipped soldiers; on the contrary, the Servian *legio*, with each maniple made up of 100 soldiers of the 1st class on the front line armed as hoplites (with the Argive shield), 90 soldiers of the 2nd, 3rd and 4th class, and 45 *leves* belonging to the 5th class (according to the reconstruction of Battaglia and Ventura), was much deeper and therefore able to receive the impact of the Etruscan hoplite formation. (*Author's drawing*)

In the exposed reconstruction, however, the firm point remains that the Roman combat style was never the same as the Greek one, despite having being subjected to its influence. The Hellenic people always based their combat on the spear and the evolutions and all changes over the centuries of their history revolved around it, up to the introduction of the 6–7m long Macedonian *sarissa*. Roman history, on the contrary, begins with the central-Italic people who preceded them, inheriting the short sword as the basis of their way of fighting interpreting the Greek hoplitic combat, which at this point it would be more appropriate to define as 'Hoplitic-Roman'.

To better understand the essence of the Servian *legio*, we must think of the opposite of the Romulean one which can be described as two ropes stretched to oppose the enemy front, with barbed wire in the third position. We can imagine the barbed wire in the forefront in a helical shape (or concertina), much more efficient in acting as a barrier than a linear one, and behind that the three ropes that portray the *scutati* and one for the *leves* (Fig. 6).

We can ultimately summarise these important concepts by concluding that the Romans used a formation and armament similar to the hoplitic one, not for the entire legion but only for the 1st class of the Servian formation. However, the latter, although probably less mobile than the other ranks, was nevertheless drawn up in a formation that used a combat methodology that had very little to do with the Hellenic one, being on the whole much more dynamic and articulated, based mainly on the *gladius*

enemy front

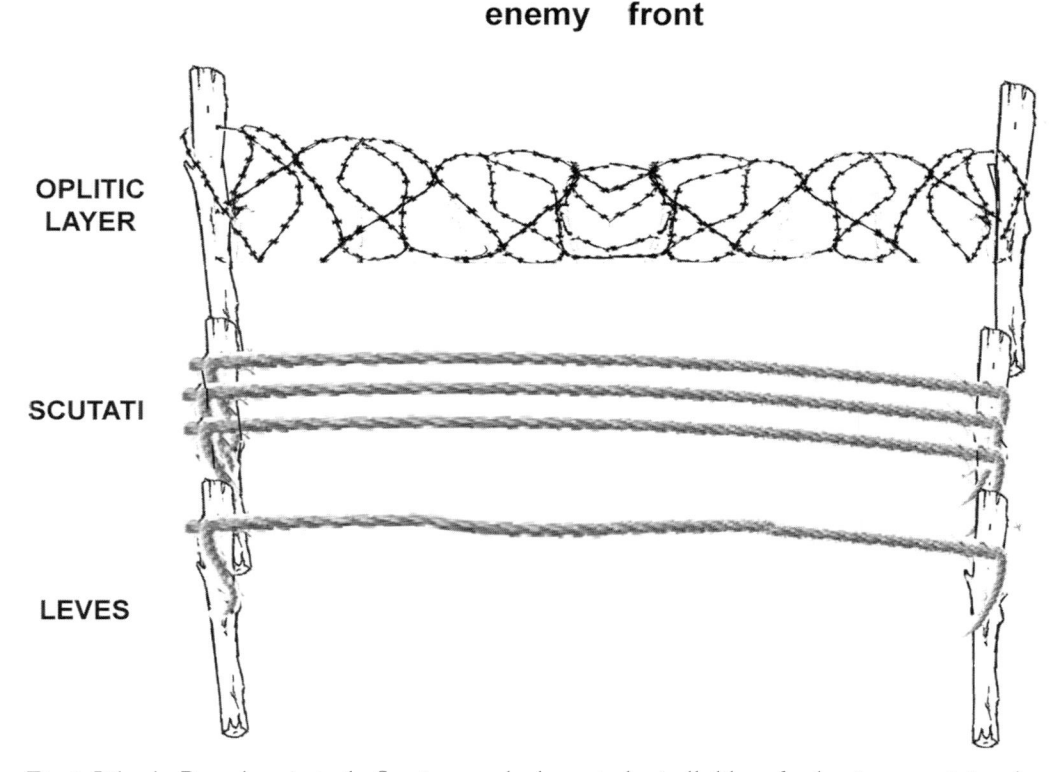

OPLITIC LAYER

SCUTATI

LEVES

Fig. 6: Like the Romulean *legio*, the Servian can also be metaphorically likened to barriers containing the enemy front. The first, that of the hoplites, having to represent a decidedly more robust and impenetrable barrier, can always be shown as barbed wire, not simple, but skein, to make us understand its more effective function. The *acies* behind, three *scutati* and one *leves*, are represented by four ropes that better demonstrated the greater depth of the array. (*Author's drawing*)

and only a little on the spear. Tracing such different weapons and ways of fighting to a single model, as is often done by modern literature, is ultimately as simplistic as it is incongruous.

This important concept is well summarised by Yvon Garlan, who states that the Roman legion is the daughter of the Greek phalanx. But from its birth it was so marked by local traditions, and in its later development so sensitive to the lessons of experience and endowed with such internal strength of improvement, that it should rather be considered the original creation of the Roman genius.[176]

II.2,3 The *Legio Gemina* – Lucius Tarquinius Superbus and the end of the monarchy (end of the sixth century BC)

The succession of Tarquinius Superbus (sixth century BC), the fall of the Monarchy and the establishment of the *Res Publica* (509 BC) led to a succession of social and political changes that inevitably had repercussions on the military level.

The seizure of power by Lucius Tarquinius 'not in accordance with the laws, but by arms'[177] instituted a dictatorship: indeed he 'did not leave even the tables on which the laws were written, but ordered these also to be removed',[178] and created a taxation system similar to the Romulean one ('and whenever he required money, the poorest citizen contributed the same amount as the richest. This measure ruined a large part of the plebeians'[179]), forbade that 'large numbers of people meeting together, should form secret conspiracies to overthrow his power'[180] and scattered observers and spies in all places. With the establishment of this dictatorship he created the discontent that would be the cause of his dethronement, but he would also develop a great innovation represented by the mixed legions of Romans and Latin allies so that they too 'could enjoy a share in the prosperity of the Roman people'.[181] Such a choice will be very important in the future political-military framework of the *Latium Vetus*, since the uniformity of the weapons and the way of fighting of the Romans and Latins would lead to military homogenisation, the germ of a future aggregation between various peoples Livy, writing about the subsequent clashes in which the Roman and Latin populations saw themselves in opposition and no longer as allies, states that (we Romans) 'against the Latins … had to fight, a people resembling them in language, manners, arms, and especially in their military organisation. They had been colleagues and comrades, as soldiers, centurions, and tribunes, often stationed together in the same posts and side by side in the same maniples.'[182]

The legion organised by the tyrant was called the *Legio Gemina* or *Bina* because 'it was composed of one Latin and one Roman century into a maniple, thereby making one unit out of the two, whilst he doubled the strength of the maniples, and placed a centurion over each half'.[183] This maniple was composed of two *acies*, the Roman one in the front and the Latin one at the rear, which apparently could pass through a *mutatio ordinis*, from a double formation to a single one and vice versa.

It is not the task of this study to examine the military tactics of the *Legio Bina*, which the ancient authors do not specify, but which some modern studies explain as 'the ability of the two groups to alternate in the fight thanks to a mechanism of stacking and displacement'.[184]

Apart from the distribution of men and the different panoplies within the maniples and the tactical mechanism of combat development, this deserves a quotation by Dionysius dating back to this historical period, in which the author narrates that the Romans had of the peculiarities that differentiated them from other people, so much so that 'the Sabines, upon seeing them and recognising them by their arms and their standards …'.[185] This makes us reflect on what allowed a clear identification of the Roman army in respect to those of neighbouring people, and in addition to the standards, we must think that the peculiarity was probably linked to the use of the sword as a thrusting weapon, and of the related shield, supported with a central handle, must have appeared in form, materials and use, as a very distinct element for the Sabines, referring to the quotation above.

II.3 THE MONARCHICAL *GLADIUS* OR SWORD WITH CROSS HILT

The deep maturation of the Roman fighting method acquired by the Romulean legion and especially by the Servian one, sees the *gladius* rise to the role of protagonist and to gain a central role in warfare and define itself as a special part of the legionary panoply.

However, the legacy of the central Italian Bronze Age swords also had an effect, providing a solid basis for development and cultural continuity. The phenomenon we are witnessing is that all their special characteristics (with particular reference to the length of the blade and the use of the point) are consolidated and accentuated.

Hence, starting from the end of the seventh century BC, the sword that for centuries will accompany the Roman soldier, with few variations, appears in central Italy until the end of the Late Consular Age. To all intents and purposes we can consider it the first type of *gladius*, in line with the thought of Armando Cherici: 'the blade characteristics [of the Capestrano Warrior's sword], compared to those of the sword represented on a Roman aes signatum, nominate it to be the model of the Roman national weapon, the *Gladius*, the sword shaped like a gladiolum'[186] and for Peter Connolly, 'leaves no doubt that this was also the primary sword used by Rome and the Latin League …'.[187]

To present this sword we will allow ourselves a certain temporal digression, passing in one leap from the seventh to the fourth century BC, the age of a famous archaeological complex very useful for the purpose. Later on we will cover the neglected centuries. The Etruscan pictorial cycle of the 'Saties' tomb,[188] better known as the François Tomb, named after the Royal Commissary of Navy and War Alessandro François who discovered it in 1857 (Fig. 5) will bring this sword back to life, giving us representations that otherwise we could only have deduced. The tomb, which is part of the Etruscan necropolis of Ponte Rotto (Vulci – Viterbo) and datable to 320–310 BC, has its greatest peculiarity in the fact that the seven rooms have walls covered in frescos with a wonderful pictorial cycle.[189]

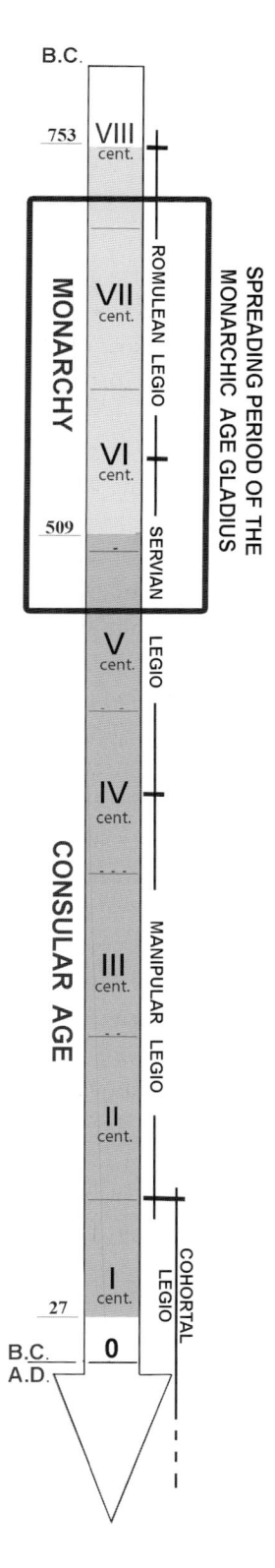

The frescoes depict a probable parallel between the Greek myth of the Seven against Thebes and Etruscan-Roman history shortly before the period of the construction of the tomb. The fact that the grave is located in Etruscan territory could somehow suggest a poor connection with Roman culture, but this is not the case, because in reality, the link is very close. The frescoes describe the contrast between the Etruscans and the Romans in a context in which the Etruscan wars had come to an end and the Roman conquest of Veii had already taken place many decades before, in which we see the exaltation of the city of Vulci and probably of the Saties family, describing the heroic action of some characters closely linked to the history of Rome.[190] In fact, one of the main characters is Macstarna (or Mastarna), who we know to have been among the most important kings of Rome, as, among other things, was attested by the Emperor Claudius in an oration of AD 48: 'Servius Tullius…

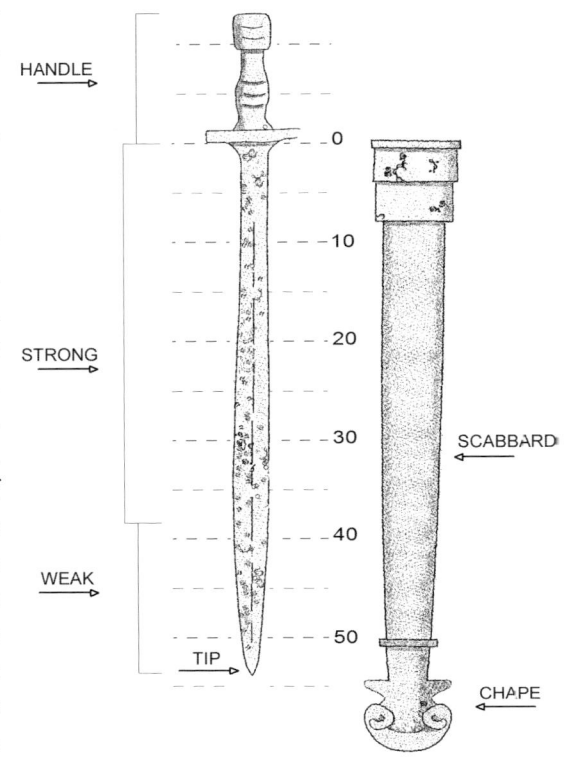

Fig. 1: The Monarchical *gladius* or sword with cross hilt. (*Author's drawing*)

with all the surviving troops of Caelius and seized the Caeliian hill, which thus takes its name from his leader Caelius, and after changing his name (for his Etruscan name was Mastarna) he was given the name I have already mentioned, and became king, to the very great advantage of the state.'[191] Then there is Caelius Vibenna, also closely linked to Roman history and who gave his name to one of the Seven Hills, the Caelian. Massimo Pallottino, one of the most renowned Etruscologists, managed to demonstrate that Mastarna was none other than his servant,[192] 'the commander (who) had been captured by Etruscan warriors … (but Mastarna) his faithful friend, with the help of three other warriors from Vulci, also accompanied by their names, freed him by annihilating his opponents'.[193] This is the only known image of an Etruscan king of Rome (Mastarna-Servius Tullius).[194] The identification of these characters is made certain by the name written in Etruscan next to them.

Therefore, these scenes of fighting between Etruscan and Roman-Latial heroes and events of Trojan history, in which an episode of the archaic history of Rome[195] is to be read, will allow us to understand better the use and characteristics of the sword represented, which, for our studies, is the true protagonist of the pictorial cycle.

For it has been proposed The definitions of 'sword with cross hilt',[196] 'Capestrano type sword'[197] and 'alpha type' have been proposed for it, but more simply you could

Fig. 2: Overall view of the room housing the most interesting part of the pictorial cycle, in which is represented the parallelism between the Trojan War (to the left of the door with Achilles killing a Trojan prisoner) and (to the right of the door) the war of Etruscan factions with the Vulcii warriors who are taking over the Orvietans and manage to free the prisoners. The two representations are pictorial copies committed by the Vatican State to Carlo Ruspi in the pre-photographic era.

call it just by the name of one of the many necropolises where various examples have been found, the 'Campovalano type' sword.[198]

Not wanting to create further unnecessary definitions, we now choose to adopt the one proposed by A. Chierici – the sword with cross hilt – simply because we believe it is more correct not to connect it to a specific place, given its vast geographical spread, and alternatively we will call it the 'monarchic sword' when referring specifically to the Roman army.

II.3,1 Technical characteristics and method of use
From the examination of the scene of the triple killing of the warriors at the hands of the three Etruscan-Roman heroes (Fig. 2) from Volsini (now Orvieto), Sovana and from a third unknown city, all armed with this weapon, we can highlight four fundamental features:

▶ length:
Blade of medium length, slender and light, with a fairly high length/width ratio,[199] around 16;
▶ blade profile:
blade with lanceolate cutting profile and long gladiolus-leaf tip which, together with the features of the previous point, give the weapon a rather elegant appearance. We cannot fail to notice the assonance with the leaf of the gladiolus, from which we know that the name of the weapon derives.
▶ hilt:
a characteristic design, with a cross hilt.
▶ method of use:
almost exclusively thrusting with the point, never slashing, and with high damaging power.

Therefore, all special characteristics of the Roman *gladius* have been introduced, which we will see being present until the end of the Late Consular Age, with the exception of the cross-hilt handle, a feature of the weapon that will disappear in the Early Consular Age.

It is not surprising that the characteristics of this sword are essentially those already seen in central Italian bronze weapons (with particular reference to the E.B.F.[200]). Invariably, as a weapon is the evolutionary result of those that precede it, it is therefore natural and inevitable that the Central Italian people kept what they appreciated and were used to as part of their traditional military culture.

Analysing this weapon in a more technical way, we can define the following characteristics:

- **Length**. By estimating the length of the blades depicted in the François Tomb by the surrounding figures, it was possible to establish with good approximation the real size being about 50–55cm, thus reaching around 63–65cm in total, including the handle. We have seen in the discussion of bronze swords that this feature had already been present for centuries in the central Italic territory. We find precise confirmation of this fact in the archaeological evidence; the numerous specimens found in the central Italian necropolises and preserved in the various museums show that the vast majority of blades are within this range (Fig. 3). However, there are exceptions, such as three specimens kept in the Archaeological Museum of Ascoli Piceno, which measure 74–76cm and 83cm, a length that may suggest more a cavalry than an infantry use.

Fig. 3: Typical examples of cross-hilted swords. From the left – first two examples: from the Campovalano necropolis (courtesy of the Chieti Museum); third example: private collection; fourth example: tomb 69 of the Campovalano necropolis (courtesy of the Campli Museum).

- **The lanceolate blade profile and the damaging power.** The blade almost always shows a lanceolate cut profile (Fig. 1; Fig. 3). We have already seen in the chapter on bronze swords that this feature already had a notable diffusion throughout central Italic culture, and with the beginning of the spread of the iron sword, especially at the end of the eighth and beginning of the seventh century BC, this feature is evident in most of the archaeological finds as well as in their iconographic representations.

    But perhaps the most distinctive feature is the long and tapered tip, up to about 15–17cm long and as previously mentioned, it gives its name to the weapon itself, the *gladius*, taken from the gladiolus leaf.

- **The hilt.** The handle has such a character that it gives its name to the type of sword (cross hilt) but at the same time is the only one that will not survive the evolution of the weapon in the Roman army.

    Of extremely complex manufacture, it is reminiscent of the 'composite technology' of the *pugiones*.[201] As we can see in Fig. 4, it is composed of two symmetrical metal halves (no. '2'), often of iron, shaped in a refined way according to the well-known cross shape and with a terminal knob. These were bound to the underlying fillings with organic material (no. '3'), of similar shape and of which rare traces are preserved on some specimens, all united with the tang of the blade by the means of rivets (no. '4'). The latter has a flat shape, similar to that previously seen for 'grip tongue' swords. Finally, to all this we see sometimes added – but not always – a closing and finishing bridge-like element (no. '5'). In the central part of the handle, a typical swelling is frequently noticed, also very similar to that of the Roman *pugiones*, probably with the aim of giving it a more ergonomic shape.

Obviously the diversity of the ancient world means that this should not be understood as an absolutely unchangeable means of construction solution: there were certainly some similar but not identical variants.

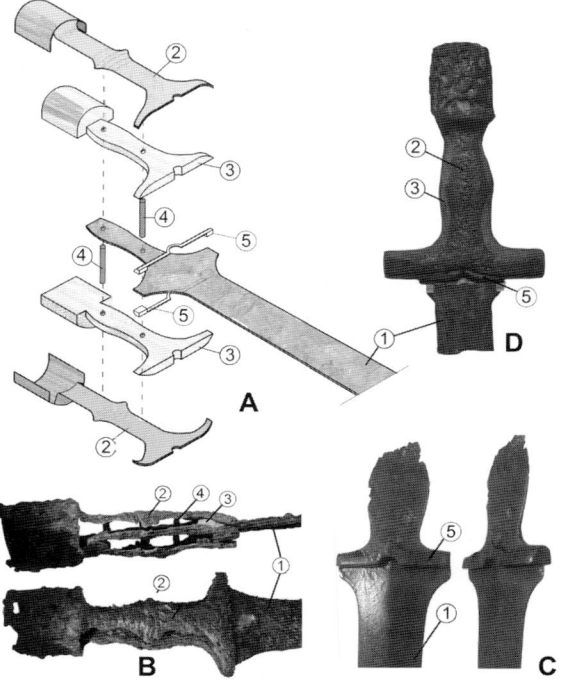

Fig. 4: A- Construction of the cross-hilted sword; B-C-D- same components highlighted in authentic specimens (A- specimen preserved in the Chieti Museum; B- specimen preserved in the Campli Museum; C- specimen in private collection). Drawing: 1) blade, 2) external iron shells, 3) organic filling material, 4) rivets, 5) metal element with closing and finishing bridge. (*Author's drawing*)

However, the final appearance was certainly aesthetically harmonious, structurally strong and a high-performance weapon, but certainly not easy or quick to manufacture, and not at all suitable for mass production. From a military point of view, this is ultimately the only weak point of the weapon, which in fact we will see promptly resolved by the Roman army as soon as the opportunity arose.

- **Use.** Basically with the point and with a high damaging power. In the frescoes of the François Tomb we observe that, in the fratricidal struggle for the throne, the two brothers Eteocles and Polinikes[202] are delivering thrusts: one from top to bottom, entering into the right clavicular fossa and exiting from the left side (after crossing the whole chest), the other, on the other hand, from bottom to top (Fig. 5).

It has great penetrating power, which is even more evident in the other scene in which Avle Vipinas kills his opponent. The latter wears armour but despite this, the blade, entering under the right armpit, crosses the whole chest with such effectiveness that it exits the body by piercing both the breastbone and the armour itself, probably made of leather. The pictorial representation of this feature also finds a correspondence in literature. Livy, in the description of the legendary fight

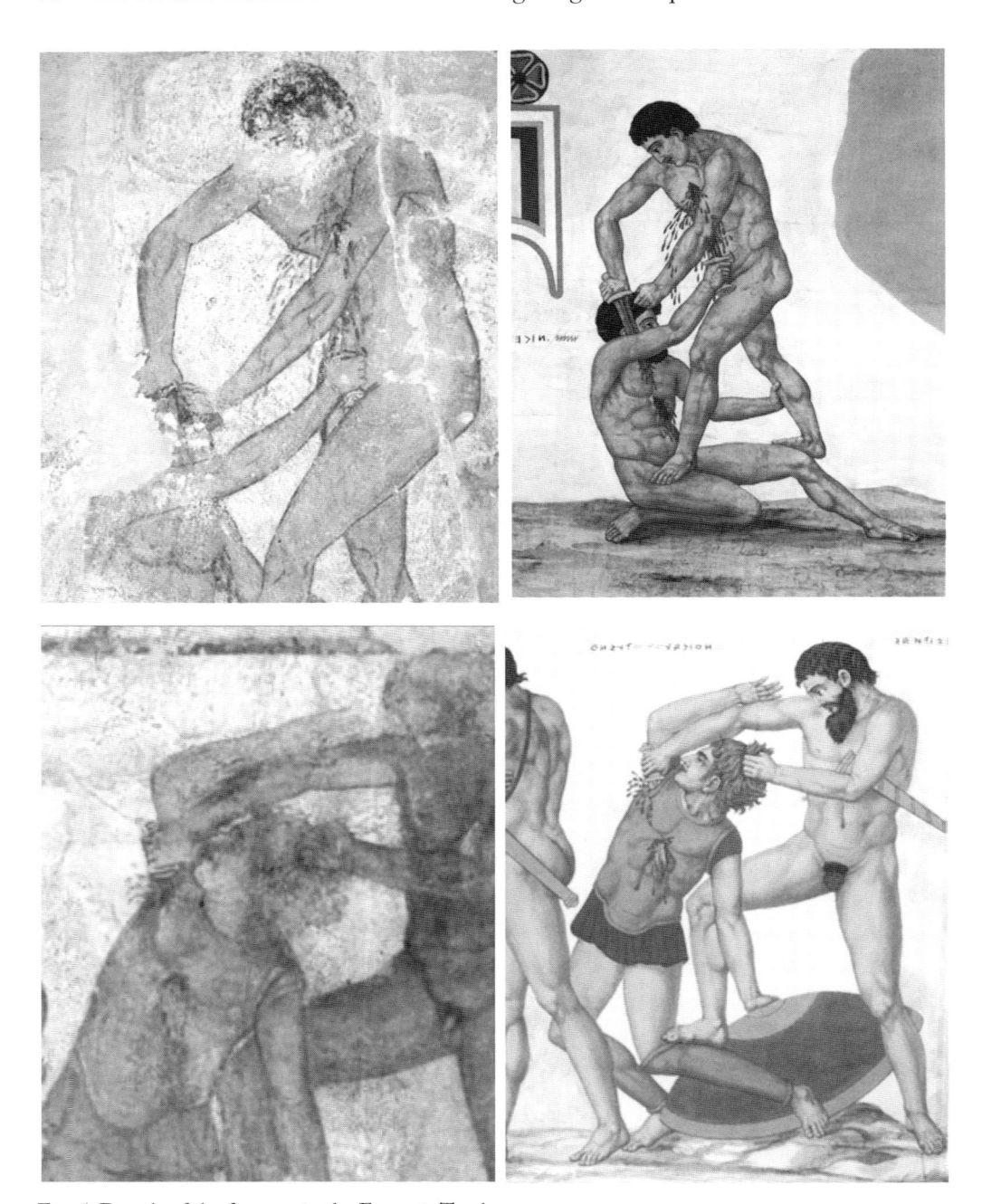

88 The Roman Gladius and the Ancient Fighting Techniques

Fig. 5: Details of the frescoes in the François Tomb.
Above: Duel between Eteocles and Polynikes, the twins who killed each other in the fight for the throne, fulfilling the curse of Oedipus. The fratricidal struggle represents the clash between Etruscan factions for the control of Rome.
Below: Avle Vipinas stabs his opponent, running him through despite his armour.
These images are very interesting for they show the effectiveness of the blows of the Monarchical *gladius*. Beside the original fresco, on the left, we have placed a copy by Carlo Ruspi on the right for a better understanding of the action.

The Monarchical Period (753–509 BC)   89

between the Horatii and the Curiatii in the seventh century BC, says that the clash was resolved by the Roman victor Horatius with a sharp blow, 'Horace … , thrust his sword downward into the neck of his opponent',[203] the same blow that we see represented in the François Tomb. A few lines later it is Horatius himself who, outraged by his sister's cry for one of the dead Curiatii, to whom she had been betrothed, 'drew his sword and stabbed the girl … '.[204] The verb *'transfigit'* leaves no room for dubious interpretations.

Returning to the aforementioned fight of Torquatus Manlius, which took place in 361 BC, the Roman hero emerged victorious thanks to the lethal use of his weapon.

The Roman evaded the blow, and pushing aside the bottom of the Gaul's shield with his own, he slipped under it close up to the Gaul, too near for him to get at him with his sword. Then turning the point of his blade upwards, he gave two rapid thrusts in succession and stabbed the Gaul in the belly and the groin, laying his enemy prostrate over a large extent of ground.[205]

In this case not a *coup de grâce*, like at the end of a real fight as in the story of Horatius or in the François Tomb, but a rapier stroke carried out in a precise fighting style.

A text by Polybius, despite apparently seeming to contradict what has just been stated, instead introduces us to a collaborative and complementary action to this primary stroke of the rapier: '(the Roman sword) has an excellent point and a strong cutting edge on both sides, as its blade is firm and reliable'. The observation of the Greek historian does not indicate a cutting blow with a trajectory from top to bottom, similar to that of a Celtic sword (Fig. 6, left), but rather longitudinal, generated by the movement of the blade parallel to its axis (Fig. 6, right), pushing the tip towards the front and then suddenly drawing it backwards (cutting blow). In a nutshell, the warrior who tries to sink the tip of his blade into the opponent's body, as a backup plan (and probably in the alternative), can also count on the cutting action of the blade's edges.

This would potentially cause very serious damage, as clearly highlighted in the scene of the clash between Eteocles and Polynikes. In fact, we see how because of

VERTICAL CUTTING ACTION

LONGITUDINAL CUTTING (THRUSTING) ACTION

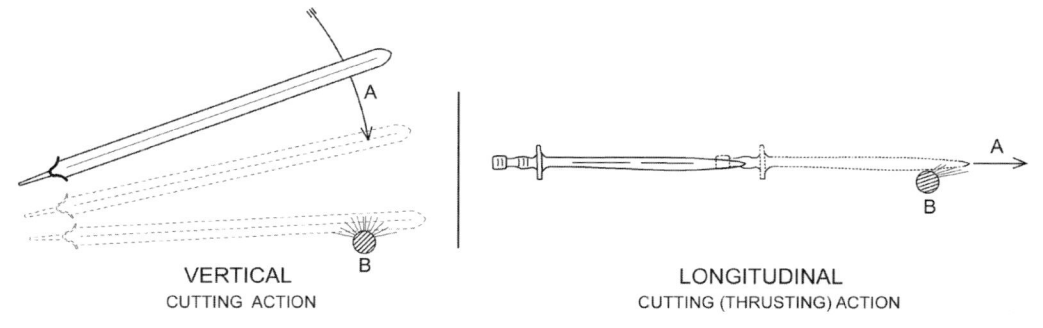

Fig. 6: Difference in blade movement between the VERTICAL cutting action (Celtic sword type) and the LONGITUDINAL (used in the cross-hilt sword). (*Author's drawing*)
A = direction of blade movement; B = target.

this action one of the two fighters causes a fatal wound to the opponent through the severing of the brachial artery (Fig. 5, top). The lanceolate profile of the blade lends itself well to this and without this a large part of its offensive potential would be lost. The Romans were well aware of this, as Vegetius attests when he tells us that the recruits trained at the pole to hit the back of the legs, i.e. the calves, among other things,[206] a very vulnerable area due to the presence of muscle-tendon structures, the severing of which would prevent one's opponent from maintaining an upright position, immediately putting him out of action.

Unlike what one might think, the amplification of the damaging power of the lance-shaped blade is much less relevant when it exits the wound. The tip of these weapons was particularly long (16–17cm in the case of the first two specimens from the left in Fig. 3), and therefore the penetration could hardly be so deep as to affect the tapered rear part of the blade, located about halfway along, which would therefore remain without any function in the majority of cases.

Finally, it is worth mentioning that the fracturing action of the vertical cutting blow is negligible despite most authors considering it predominant (Fig. 6, left). Although the tapering of the blade generates a certain increase of the weight towards the tip and consequently a shift of the centre of gravity forward, this is very modest, virtually irrelevant and in any case not such as to make any difference. The widening of the blade, in fact, is only a few millimetres, sometimes no more than three, and therefore the weight increase is negligible.[207] It is easier to understand if we consider that the total weight of these blades was very low, around 300–400g, which in itself is inadequate for a fracturing blow.

The misunderstanding probably arises from the fact that the vast majority of scholars curiously focus their attention only on one of the numerous specimens found, namely the one exhibited in the Campli Museum from tomb no. 69 of the necropolis of Campovalano, believing that it is the standard for these weapons, when instead it is far from it.[208]

- **The scabbard**. It should be noted that we can only refer to the iconographic evidence and the few surviving specimens, which however are almost certainly among the most prestigious and, as such, probably meant for social display by their owners and not necessarily for battlefield use (which, however, they should not be entirely excluded from). It is reasonable to assume that scabbards made purely for military use were similar but less sophisticated, although perhaps the more decorated ones, the prerogative of the most eminent personalities, were precisely to be flaunted in battle before the enemy as a sign of military power and strength. In any case, they suffered the same fate as the handle, which was originally a characteristic part but was later abandoned by the Romans, even if only partially.[209] There is no doubt that its most striking feature was the spectacular and wide closing chape, which could be more or less elaborate but often decorated to such a level as to be a work of art, worked in bone or ivory with animal or foliage motifs (Fig. 7).

The Monarchical Period (753–509 BC)   91

Fig. 7: Specimens of scabbard shapes. A) Detail of the statue of the Warrior of Capestrano. B) Authentic iron specimen, still preserving a good part of the organic material it was composed of. (*Courtesy of the Archaeological Museum of Chieti, author's photo*)

There were mainly two construction techniques: the first, very common in Villanovan/Etruscan craftsmanship, consisted of the union of two metal halves, almost always in bronze; the second, used by numerous other central Italic populations (the Picentes, Vestini, Aequi, Samnites, Paeligni, Frentani, Marsi, Marrucini …) consisted of an edged metal frame, with a 'U' section, intended to accommodate closure of two halves of organic material, sometimes finished with a metal sheet

Fig. 8: Bronze statue of Germanicus who carries a cross-hilted sword tied to the *balteus*, easily recognisable by the hilt and the broad, rounded shape of the scabbard. In the first century AD, the period in which the statue was made, the *gladius* had lost the typical characteristics of the Monarchical *gladius*. Amelia (Terni) Archaeological Museum. (*Author's photo*)

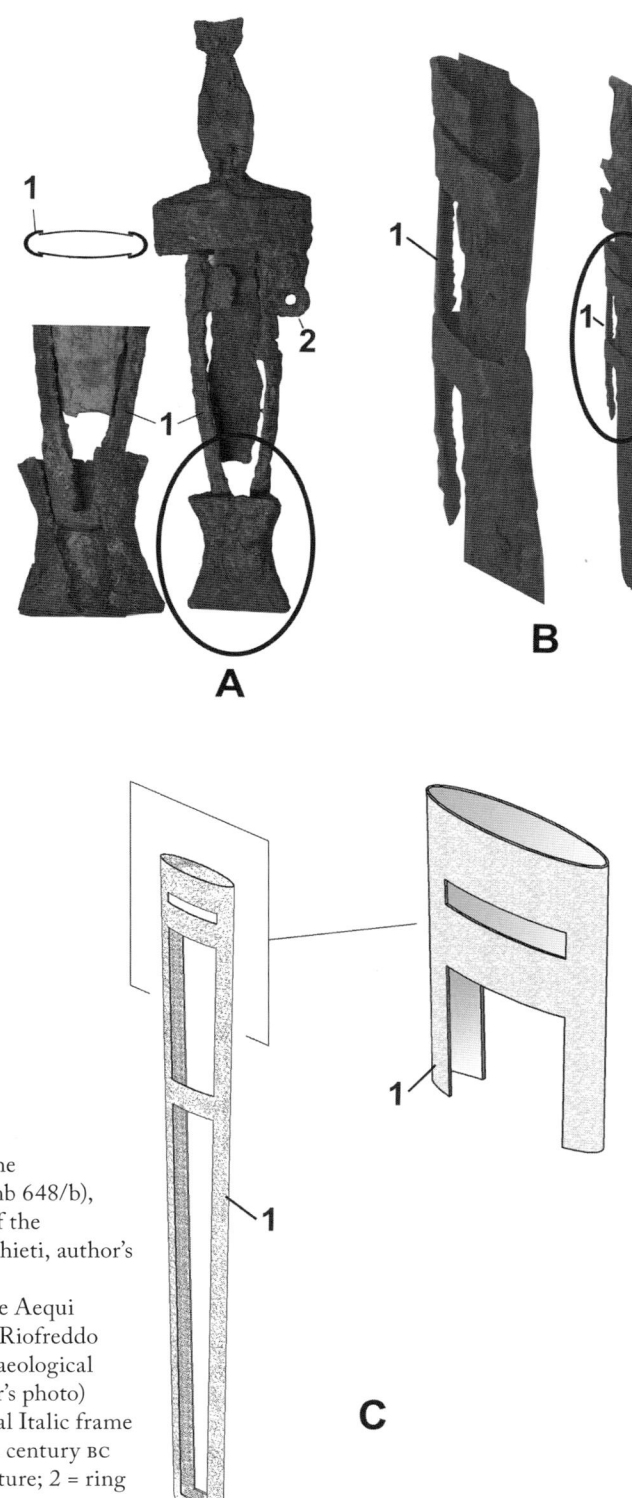

Fig. 9:
A) Dagger with scabbard from the Campovalano necropolis (tomb 648/b), sixth century BC. (Courtesy of the Archaeological Museum of Chieti, author's photo)
B) Sword with cross hilt from the Aequi necropolis of Casal Civitella, Riofreddo (RM). (Courtesy of the Archaeological Museum of Riofreddo, author's photo)
C) Graphic restitution of a central Italic frame scabbard of the seventh–sixth century BC

Key 1 = edged metal frame structure; 2 = ring for suspension; (*Author's drawing*)

placed transversely (Fig. 9). This last scabbard featured a ring placed on one side only, and could be suspended from a belt or with a chain or more simply with a fabric or leather binding, as is clearly visible in some scenes in the François Tomb. The number of specimens found is very significant and, as an excellent example of this technology, we report a specimen intended to accommodate a dagger, from the necropolis of Campovalano[210] (Abruzzo), which clearly shows both the edged frame and the related ring for suspension (Fig. 9-A) and the scabbard of a sword from the necropolis of Casal Civitella, Riofreddo (Rome, Fig. 9-B).[211]

The interesting thing about the frame scabbard technology is that, unlike the first, it was widely used in Roman culture, used for both *pugiones*[212] and the *gladius*. We should recall here the sheaths of the *gladii* from Giubiasco (Switzerland, tomb 471, second–first century BC), from Delos (Greece, 69–75 BC), Berry Bouy (France, 20 BC) and from the Ljublijanica river (Slovenia, 20 BC), all from the Late Consular Age and all made with this technique, which has its origins in central Italy in remote times, although many scholars make the mistake of considering it a more recent Celtiberian technology by several centuries.[213]

The paradox is that the most typical elements of the Monarchical *gladius*, the cross hilt and the spectacular chape of the scabbard, although they were the only two abandoned by the legionaries in the war, are on the other hand so characteristic that not only they survive for centuries in Roman iconography, but they assumed an even greater symbolic importance (see Chapter V).

II.3,2 History and evolution

The Monarchical *gladius* (or cross-hilted sword) is substantially unknown by modern scholars, especially non-Italians, to the point that some misunderstand its origins believing that it is of Greek origin (so-called 'Xiphos'; to understand this problem better, we have dedicated Chapter IV 'De falsis originibus, on the erroneous derivation of the *gladius* from non-Italic people' to it), used only by the Romans, generically, during the Consular Age, thus neglecting a long period of Italic history and not posing the problem of the *gladius* type used in the Monarchical and early Consular times.[214] The first important preliminary work regarding these weapons by P.F. Stary[215] was published in 1981, and followed only by a few others.[216] Furthermore the excavation reports are often difficult to find, which makes it difficult to study its origins and its evolution. However, they are to be considered typical and characteristic of central Apennine and Picenian Italy, up to the Faliscan-Capenate countryside and the Sabina Tiberina, near Rome.[217]

First appearances in Italic territory
The earliest origins seem to be in the last decades of the seventh century BC in Sabina.[218] In the necropolis of Colle del Forno, funerary goods containing this type of sword were first recorded, often replacing the stami daggers,[219] but also other specimens, testifying of such archaic origins, like that from the necropolis of Monte Cerreto in Narce, tomb 73.[220]

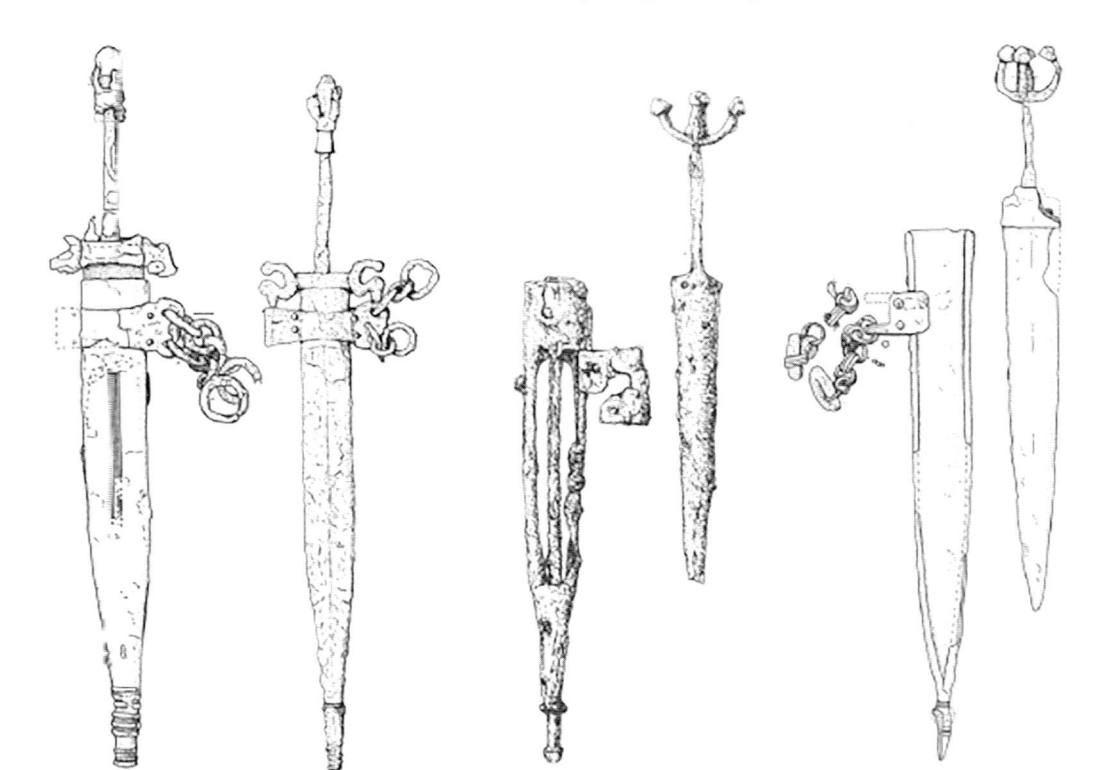

Fig. 10: Samples of Stami daggers, from left: Bazzano, Pennadimonte, Numana and again Pennadimonte (From J. Weidig 'I pugnali a stami, considerazioni su aspetti tecnici, tipologici, cronologici e distribuzione in area abruzzese').

At the end of the seventh century BC, the traces of our sword are still modest, but a few decades later we witness a rapid and widespread accentuation of the aforementioned phenomenon of substitution between the two weapons. This effect can be seen in most of the funerary sites of Abruzzo and Piceno towards the middle of the sixth century BC.[221]

Opposite: Fig. 11: Distribution chart of stamen daggers and cross-hilted swords.
1) Bazzani. 2) Fossa. 3) Caporciano. 4) Capestrano. 5) San Benedetto in Perillis. 6) Loreto Aprutino. 7) Atri. 8) Campovalano. 9) Castelvecchio. 10) Scurcola Marsicana. 11) Lecce nei Marsi. 12) Sulmona. 13) Opi. 14) Alfedena. 15) Barrea. 16) Pennapiedimonte. 17) Collarmele. 18) Trasacco. 19) Collelongo. 20) Villavallelonga. 21) Tornareccio. 22) Pettino. 23) Pescina. 24) Basciano. 25) Ortona dei Marsi. 26) Castel Trosino. 27) Colli del Tronto. 28) Montedinove. 29) Grottazzolina. 30) Montegiorgio. 31) Pitino di San Severino Marche. 32) Numana. 33) Novilara. 34) Colfiorito di Foligno. 35) Monteleone di Spoleto. 36) Assisi. 37) Nocera Umbra. 38) Perugia. 39) Terni. 40) Corvaro di Borgorose. 41) Tivoli. 42) Riofreddo. 43) Colle del Forno/Eretum. 44) Poggio Sommavilla. 45) Capena. 46) Narce. 47) Falerii Veteres. 48) Capracotta. 49) Colli a Volturno. 50) Presenzano. 51) Capua. 52) Rocchetta e Croce. 53) Cales. 54) Frosinone. 55) Montereale. 56) San Biagio Saracinisco. 57) Cupello. 58) Poggio Picenze. 59) Cartone di Borgorose. 60) Vallesanta di Collecroce. 61) San Pio delle Camere. 62) Montebello di Bertona. 63) Belmonte Piceno. 64) San Vincenzo Valle Roveto. 65) Balsorano. 66) Spinetoli. 67) Mozzano. 68) Barisciano. 69) San Giovanni al Mavone. 70) Sant'Egidio alla Vibrata. 71) Montesarchio/Caudium. 72) Gualdo Tadino. 73) Alife. 74) Stabie. 75–79) Unknown origin. 80) Albano. (From J. Weidig,'I pugnali a stami, considerazioni su aspetti tecnici, tipologici, cronologici e distribuzione in area abruzzese')

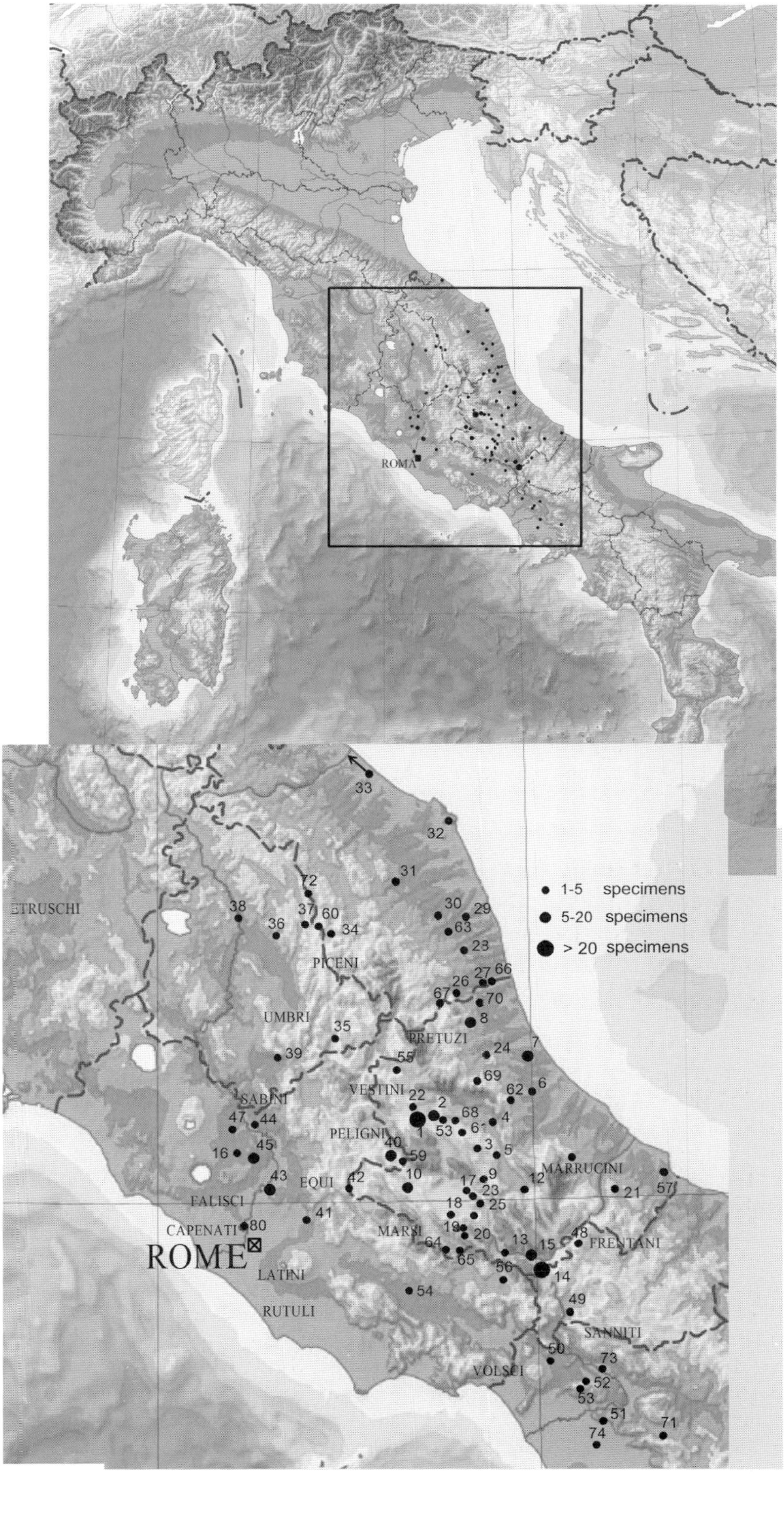
ROMA
1-5 specimens
5-20 specimens
> 20 specimens
ETRUSCHI
PICENI
UMBRI
PRETUZI
VESTINI
SABINI
PELIGNI
EQUI
FALISCI
CAPENATI
ROME
LATINI
RUTULI
MARSI
MARRUCINI
FRENTANI
SANNITI
VOLSCI

96   The Roman Gladius and the Ancient Fighting Techniques

From this point on, their presence in the archaeological finds in the central Italic areas becomes very significant, a massive presence in numerous necropolises being recorded.[222]

To understand the extent of its diffusion, we can rely on the testimonies of the various authors who were involved in the excavation of these funerary sites. The number of tombs excavated in the numerous central Italic necropolises (Fig. 11) adds up to several thousands and in them 'unarmed burials are very rare ... and usually consist of a sword and dagger, associated with one or more spears ... The sword is a cross-hilt type,'[223] the

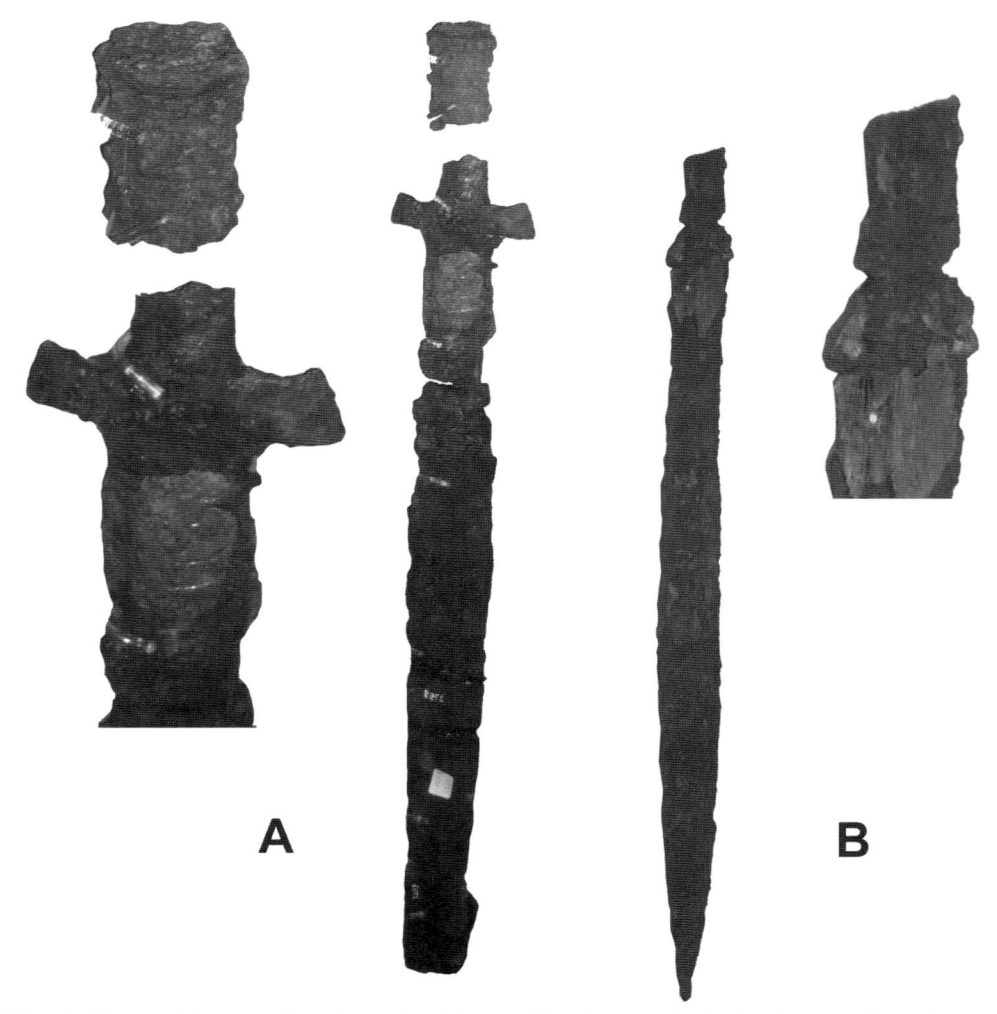

Fig. 12: Very archaic examples of swords with cross hilts from territories in the immediate vicinity of Rome:
A) From the Alban Hills, end of the seventh century BC. (*Author's photo, courtesy of the Archaeological Museum of Albano – Villa Ferrajoli*)
B) Tomb 239 of the necropolis of Castel di Decima, dated by the Museum to the IIIB period (eighth–seventh century BC). (*Author's photo, courtesy of the Museum of the Baths of Diocletian, Rome*)

sword that can be classified "alpha" type of the Paribeni classification [remember that this is another definition of the same weapon] is widely attested in the necropolis of Capena, Narce, Veio, Colle del Forno, Campovalano, etc.',[224] and still '[in the Abruzzo and Molise Necropolis, in particular with reference to that of Campovalano] iron and bronze weapons abound: bladed swords with cross hilt, "stamen" daggers, solid iron mace heads with a central hole for inserting the wooden handle, willow leaf ribbed and triangular spear points, elements of war chariots and bits for horses, a helmet with closed cheeks and found together with a bronze-sheet greave'.[225]

When talking about this historical period, we cannot ignore one of the most beautiful examples of a cross-hilted sword, namely the so-called Warrior of Capestrano, because 'the type of swords depicted on the statue of the warrior of Capestrano finds innumerable confirmations in the archaeological reality …'.[226]

Discovered by chance, near ancient Aufinum (modern-day Ofena), a Piceno settlement of the sixth century BC, in 1934 during agricultural works and datable to the archaic period, the statue of Capestrano represents a Picene warrior on a scale slightly larger than life-size, and it is characterised by the presence of different elements typical of the panoply of this age.[227] It has a pair of javelins with foliate points[228] placed either side of the warrior and, on the chest, a splendid sword with a cross hilt, perfectly detailed. The handle is embellished with anthropomorphic and zoomorphic frieze decorations. On the scabbard, which shows the typical spectacular semi-circular chape, a knife is present, perhaps serving as a whetstone for sharpening the blade.

Although it is undoubtedly the best-known sculptural representation of a central Italic warrior, it is not the only one. In 1992, a similar find, smaller in size and of which only the torso remained, was sold at auction in New York, also showing the same sword on the chest, although without the knife on the sheath. Also worth mentioning is the *stele* of Guardiagrele, with great similarities with the Warrior of Capestrano even if it does not show a sword on his chest, as well as the discovery in 1937 of two bases of statues, one of which was very similar to that of the Warrior.

First appearances in the Roman military world
The tumultuous evolution of the Roman military world in this period determined the deep rooting of this weapon within it, there now being a very clear and close ethnic-social relationship between the Romans and the other Central Italic people, with whom they shared their roots.

However, such archaic finds in the area of Rome are very rare due to the custom of cremation as the funeral rite instead of entombment, but precious testimony is provided by two iron swords dating back to the end of the seventh century BC, coming from the territories of the Alban Hills, a few kilometres east of Rome, and currently housed in the museum of Villa Ferrajoli in Albano (Rome, Fig. 12-A).[229] Both have a lanceolate blade, even if scarcely evident due to the residues of the wooden sheath and the poor state of conservation, but while one shows a clearly fragmented tongue grip, still retaining part of a piece of bone, the other is equipped with a refined cross hilt,[230] largely preserved, in which the construction technology previously described is clearly visible. Even the cylindrical bronze pommel is in good condition.

Obviously, the problem arises that the populations settled in those areas, of Latin stock and concentrated mainly in the cities of Alba Longa, Tusculum, Aricia and Lavinum, were not Romans but rather their fierce adversaries for centuries, but in the historical period to which this specimen belongs, especially from the socio-cultural as well as the military point of view, Rome and Alba Longa were exactly the same. The praetor Lucius Annius, in his speech in the Latin assembly, convened to decide the answers to be given to the Senate of Rome on the occasion of the insurgent conflicts following the first Samnite War, which would then lead to the Latin War, defines Latins and Romans as consanguineous[231] probably from a socio-cultural point of view. Much more explicit in underlining their being virtually identical from a military point of view, is Livy who, in describing a phase of the Battle of Vesuvius with the Latins in 340 BC, attests that 'their anxiety was sharpened by the fact that they must fight against the Latins, who were like themselves in language, customs, fashion of arms, and above all in military institutions',[232] and still 'now the battle was exceedingly like the battles in a civil war, so little did the Latins differ from the Romans in anything but courage',[233] 'the Latins, who were now the enemies of the Romans and had drawn up their battle-line in the same formation; and they knew that not only must section meet in battle with section, *hastati* with *hastati*, *principes* with *principes*, but even – if the companies were not disordered – centurion with centurion'.[234]

To these examples another contemporary should be added, if not even an earlier example (preserved in the Museum of the Baths of Diocletian in Rome and dated to the Latial phase IIIB, eighth century BC), from the necropolis of Castel di Decima (south of Rome, Fig. 12-B), still with traces of wood from the scabbard, in which the typical blade with a long and tapered gladiolus leaf tip is perfectly evident.

In conclusion, these archaic specimens, substantially contemporary with the first appearances in Abruzzo, can be considered as archaeological evidence of the presence of this weapon in Roman military culture since the seventh century BC, if not before.

Diffusion in the Roman military world
From the iconographic point of view, we have countless evidence and confirmation of the great diffusion of the *gladius* with a cross hilt in Roman culture. Although many of them go beyond the Monarchical era, affecting the Early Consular Age, their testimonial value in this regard remains unchanged. Among them is a splendid cist from Palestrina (circa fifth century BC). In one scene we see a Latin horseman, on foot and fighting as an infantryman, wielding a lanceolate and long-pointed dagger while another, even more clear in detail, is placed at his feet, perhaps fallen in the fight. The classic scabbard with the typical chape appears under the left armpit. Very similar is a second scene in which another horseman, still fighting on foot, holds our sword with the scabbard hanging from his left arm (Fig. 13).

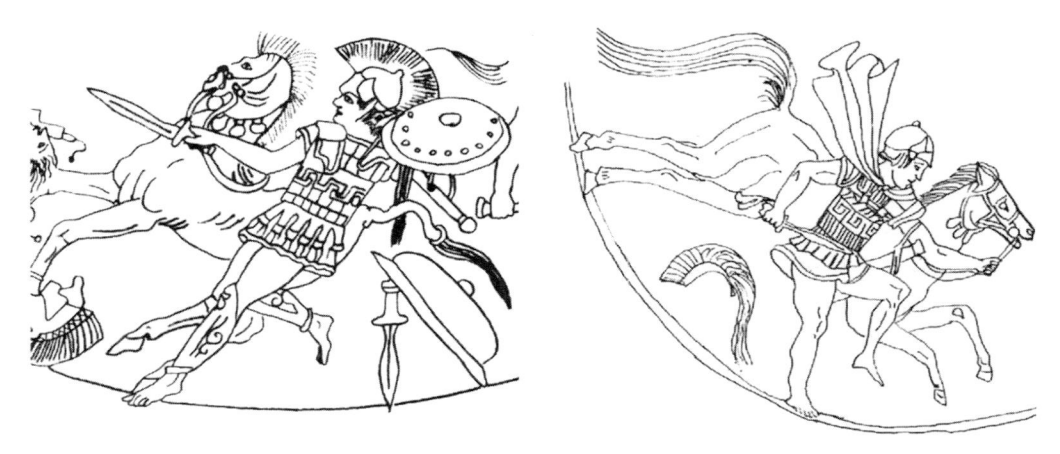

Fig. 13: Cista details from Palestrina, fifth century BC. (From D. Battaglia and L. Ventura, *De Rebus Militum*, Vol. 1)

We have already spoken extensively about the François Tomb (late fourth century BC) and therefore we do not need to mention it again despite it being rich in information. Dated to the fourth–third century BC are a number of examples of *aes signatum*[235] that clearly show our sword on one side and its scabbard with the characteristic chape on the other. The profile of the lanceolate blade is always emphasised, as are the characteristics of the scabbard and in some cases the lace used for the suspension (Fig. 14,1).

A Volterra funerary urn, also from the fourth–third century BC, depicts an Etruscan-Roman centurion[236] of the Early Consular Age, who has his helmet fitted with a transverse crest, and the sword we are describing is visible in his right hand (Fig. 14,2).

Given the enormous abundance of iconographic finds bearing the image of this weapon, it is not possible to quote them all, so we will limit ourselves to a few further examples. A Roman gold stater[237] from 218 BC, in the lower part of the reverse shows the name ROMA and two generals, one Italic and one Roman, officiating at the ceremony of an oath of alliance. The latter wears a muscular armour and holds a sword with a cross hilt in his right hand, recognisable by the classic scabbard worn as usual under the left armpit (Fig. 14, 3).

In a fresco from Pompeii, from the first century AD, it is evident how the memory of this archaic sword remained with the Roman people, now having been transformed into a parazonium for commanders. The artist, drawing inspiration from an episode narrated by Virgil in the last book of the *Aeneid*,[238] depicts Aeneas wounded by an arrow receiving treatment from the doctor Japix, immediately after a battle on Italic soil against the Rutuli.[239] The hero appears to be leaning on a spear held in his right hand and clearly shows his sword with a cross hilt under his left armpit (Fig. 15, left). The choice of the subject, represented inside a *triclinium*, and therefore in a room intended to receive guests, undoubtedly represents a tribute to the mythological tale of the origins of Rome, testifying to its importance in a historical period in which his memory was now entrusted to the swords reserved for senior officers.[240]

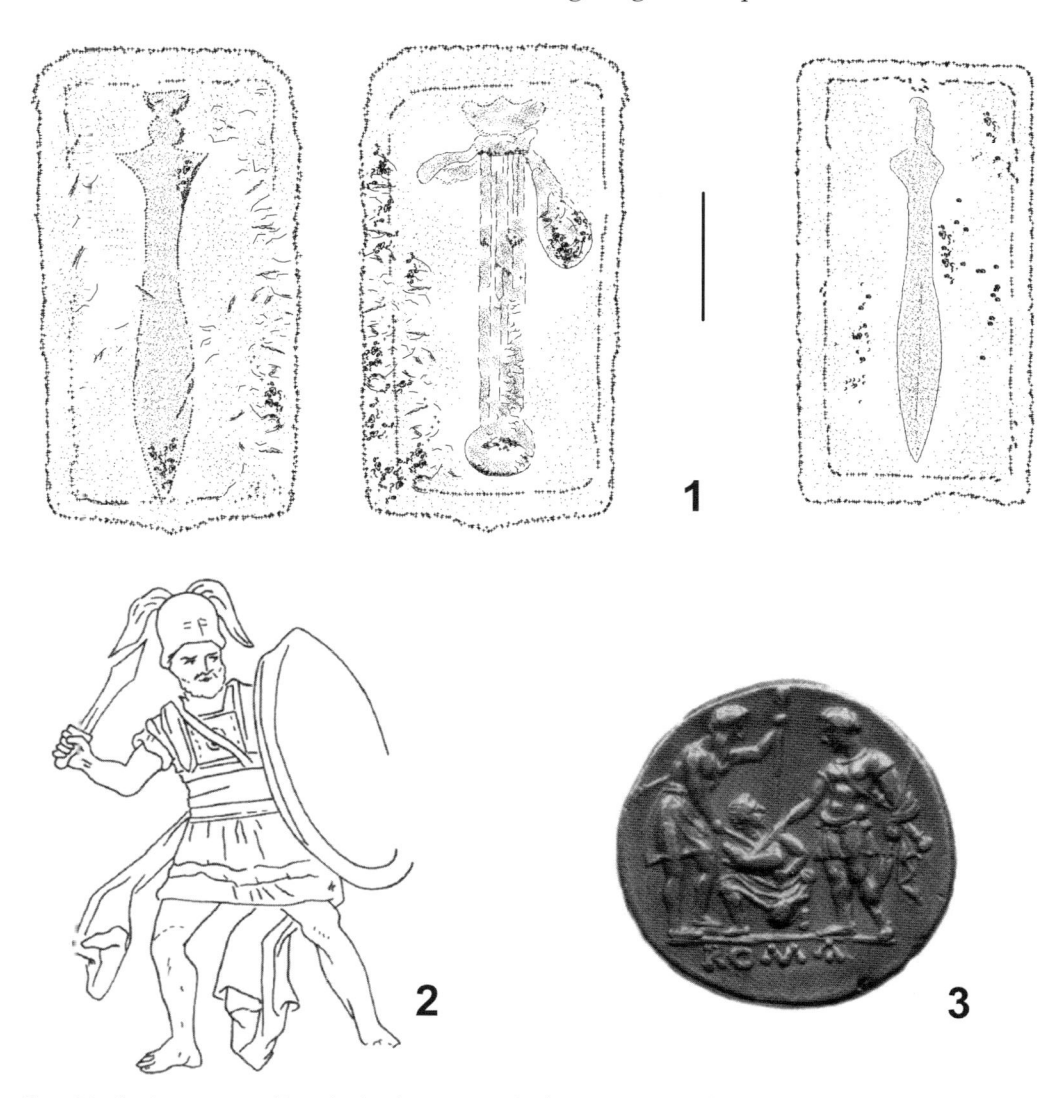

Fig. 14: 1) *Aes signatum* (fourth–third century BC). (*Author's drawing*); 2) Etruscan-Roman centurion depicted on a Volterra funerary urn of the fourth–third century BC, of which, unfortunately, traces have been lost today. (Drawing from R. D'Amato '*I centurioni Romani*'); 3) Roman gold stater from 218 BC. (*Photo: Munich, Hirmer photographic archive*)

Countless further images can be seen in Romanised Etruria, among which is an example of a beautiful sarcophagus from the fourth century BC, today in the archaeological museum of Orvieto, in which we see Ulysses threatening Circe, holding a sword with a clear gladiolus blade (Fig. 15, right). The handle is a little rough in detail, but it can definitively be classified as a cross-hilt type, both from the blade and from the typical suspension of the shoulder sheath. Finally, we mention a large number of cinerary urns, extremely widespread in the Etruscan necropolis, representing scenes of heroic battles, where inevitably all the warriors wield this weapon.

Fig. 15: On the left, Aeneas wounded by an arrow, fresco from Pompeii from the first century AD. Right, scene on the sarcophagus of San Severo (Orvieto), designed by G. Gatti, depicting Ulysses threatening Circe with a sword. (*Author's photo*)

II.3,3 Suspension and Wearing of the Weapon in the Monarchical Period

In the Monarchical Period, and therefore starting from the beginning of the Iron Age, the evidence of the various ways of suspending the weapon from the body of the soldier (or of the warrior) began to become more abundant than in previous centuries. Bear in mind that we are not yet in a period in which it is possible to make a clear distinction between the Roman and non-Roman modes, for which we will have to wait many more centuries. We will therefore review the more generically Italic suspension types, trying however to give precedence to those related to our subject. Generally speaking, the load-bearing strand always remains the same, which includes two main types of suspension, the *balteus* and the belt.

Suspension with Italic archaic baldric
• First variant – weapon under the armpit:
The iconography gives us countless testimonies with a simple morphology: a shoulder strap (*balteus*), probably fabric but also possibly of leather, was connected to the sheath through a simple binding, which was worn over the shoulder so that the scabbard was positioned under the opposite armpit (Fig. 16). In the François Tomb, as in many other sources, one can see excellent representations, which clearly show this.

More archaic, since most of the Villanovan-Etruscan edged weapons were kept and transported in scabbards suspended by this system,[241] were scabbards that could be either in bronze, especially in more ancient times, or in leather and wood.[242]

In this regard, it is necessary to make a conclusion. While it is true that the iconography gives us countless examples of this suspension type, we must ask ourselves what their real value and effectiveness was in the context of a fight. In fact, these scabbards, being simply hung on the shoulder with the aid of the aforementioned baldric without any other constraint, had considerable mobility, being able to move on the warrior's torso almost freely and potentially creating a serious obstacle. We can imagine how dangerous this could be during an armed confrontation; moreover, the drawing of the sword from the sheath with the use of only one hand in an upward movement would uncomfortable since the sheath could on certain occasions suffer the drag effect of the blade itself. An excellent image of this mobility is visible in the aforementioned cist from Palestrina from the fifth century BC, where it is evident that the scabbard is not resting against the warrior's body but waving around, almost close to being lost. Another scene shows us two horsemen engaged in a fight on foot, both without scabbards (Fig. 17).

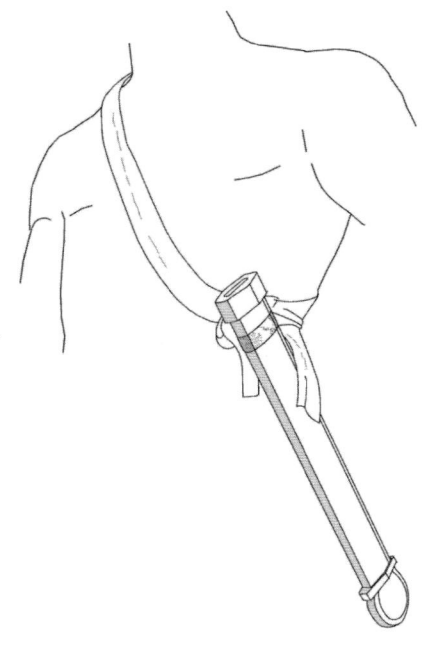

Fig. 16: Archaic period scabbard worn across the shoulder suspended from a fabric baldric. (*Author's drawing*)

Fig. 17: Fighting scenes of dismounted Latin horsemen on a cista from Palestrina, fifth century BC. It is to be noted how on n. 1 (detail of the image in Fig. 13) the scabbard is simply placed over the left arm, in a decidedly unstable way. In n. 2, on the other hand, both are entirely without scabbards. (Drawings taken from Battaglia and Ventura, *De Rebus Militum* – Vol. 1).

The Monarchical Period (753–509 BC) 103

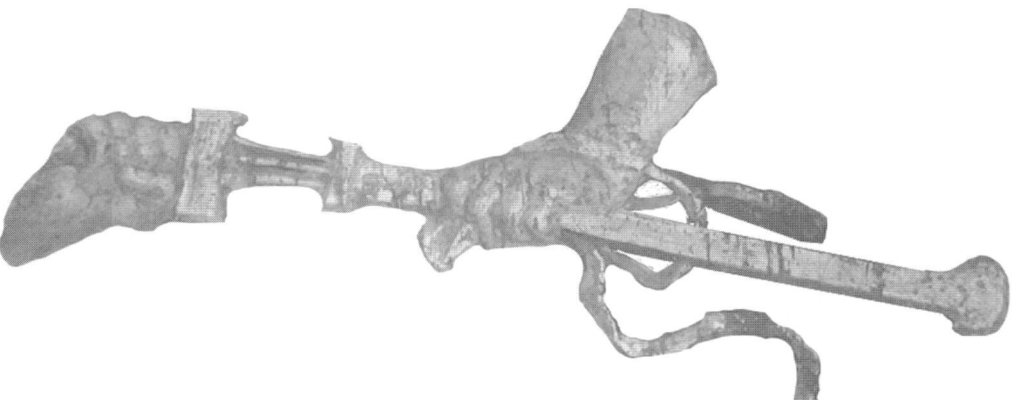

Fig. 18: Achilles unsheathing his sword, simply holding the scabbard with his left hand, while the baldric is now not used. Below: a detail of the sword and baldric. (*From the 'Casa dei Dioscuri', Pompeii, photo by the author*)

Similarly, the 'House of the Dioscuri' in Pompeii has a splendid representation of Achilles who, assisted by Athena, is preparing to attack Agamemnon, drawing his sword from the scabbard held in his left hand, with the baldric now removed from his shoulder (Fig. 18).[243]

And perhaps the latter is the correct interpretation: it is possible that the scabbard was abandoned immediately before the fight. The warrior, after throwing his javelins and needing his sword, could (and should) have freed himself easily, in order to have unrestrained movement without any hindrance. This fits well with the typical representation of an archaic warrior (the *pater familias* or the *princeps gentis*) and his circle of warriors, especially as a horseman who used his mount to move around the battlefield, only to then dismount to fight on foot. Such a shoulder strap enabled the sword to be carried in a suitable way for this character: it would not have hindered him while he was on his horse, after which he would have had all the time he needed to get rid of it as soon as he was on foot, preparing to fight.

This type of suspension, although certainly present in archaic times, shows characteristics making it suitable exclusively for Homeric-type monomachy combat, carried out by high-ranking horsemen–foot soldiers. On the other hand, it seems completely unsuitable for fighters in denser and more ordered ranks, especially if they needed to run, perhaps carrying other weapons at the same time.

- Second variant – weapon on the breast:

The *balteus* allowed the weapon to be placed on the chest, rather than under the armpit, as a variant of the previously-seen suspension system. The remarkable resemblance with the one of the Sardinian tribal chiefs is very interesting, so much so that we can hypothesise that its origin may be Sardinian. In this culture, these representations are more archaic and we have also learnt from Strabo that Sardinia was subjected to the Etruscans before the (better known) Carthaginian colonisation,[244] which allowed an easy intercultural exchange with all of central Italy and therefore the assimilation of this tradition.

Fig. 19: Detail of the sword and scabbard of the Warrior of Capestrano, sixth century BC. (*Author's photo, courtesy of Museo Archeologico of Chieti*)

The best example can be seen on the aforementioned Warrior of Capestrano. It certainly seems to rest more firmly against the warrior's body compared to the *balteus* hung under the armpit, with the scabbard secured on the chest 'from a protection of ribbed baldrics and corselets that prevents it from falling under the arm and bouncing on the chest'.[245] However, what the author stated immediately afterwards seems less acceptable, namely that '[the sword] can be easily held with the right hand upside down [with the back of the hand facing the chest]: extending upwards the arm bent at the elbow to draw the blade; the blow is already set up.' On closer inspection, this movement leads the blade and its cutting edge to pass only a few centimetres from the face, which would result in the fighter injuring himself sooner or later, especially in combat.

A key to understanding this apparent inconsistency could be the fact that, strictly speaking, this type of suspension was more representative of the warrior's social status than military utility, as seen with the Sardinian tribal chiefs. From this perspective, the lack of practicality and the risk of injury at the time of drawing the sword would not have represented a particular inconvenience.

Belt suspension: technology with rings and chains
The type of suspension that we will call 'rings' was based on these elements and the main feature was that this was used exclusively to attach the weapon to the waist, and not to the chest or under the armpit.

Contemporary with the archaic baldric, the ring suspension was in use among the central Italic population as early as the second half of the seventh century BC, useful for both daggers and swords with cross hilt. This system has a special position in characterising and as a unique element of the weapons of these populations. With the short weapons, the support for the suspension is usually made with a single rectangular iron sheet, wrapped around the scabbard near the upper part (Fig. 20-A, 3), and with a pronounced projection on one side (Fig. 20- A, 4). Two chains of equal length[246] were attached to this projection (Fig. 20-A, 2 and B), both ending with a ring (Fig. 20-A1 and B), through which the warrior's belt passed, so as to complete the suspension. However, these were not of standardised length, varying from a few centimetres (as

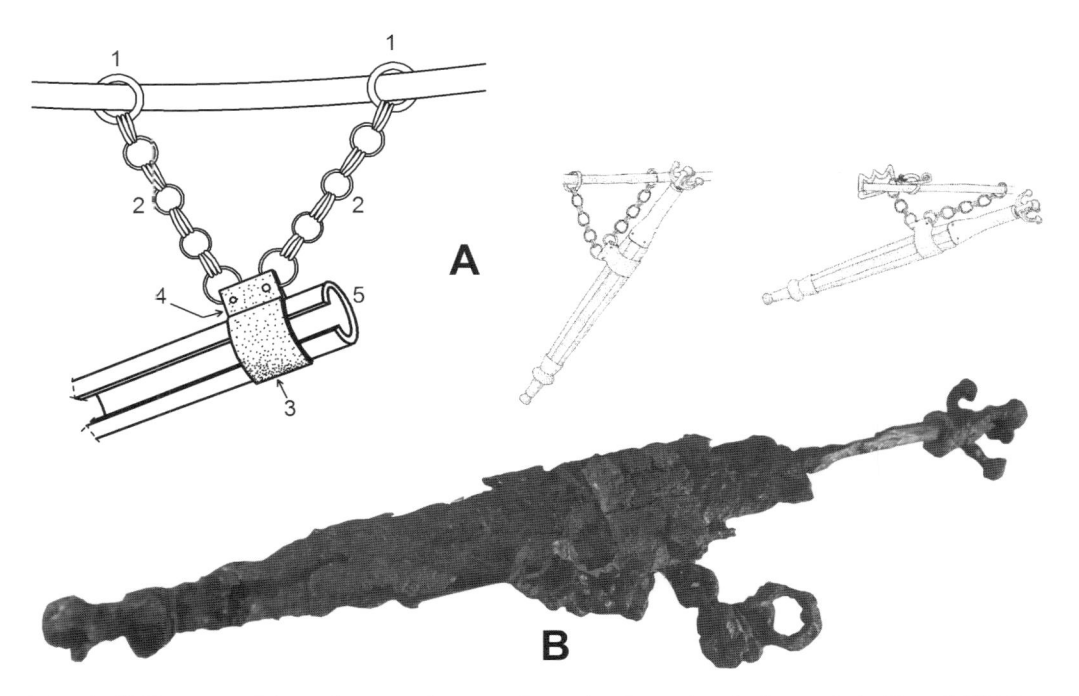

Fig. 20: A) Variation of the inclination of a stami dagger by shortening the lower chain (from J. Weidig, 'I pugnali a stami, considerazioni su aspetti tecnici, tipologici, cronologici e distribuzione in area abruzzese'). Key: 1= Big rings; 2= Small sheet; 3= Metallic sheet; 4= Fastening element of the small chains; 5= Scabbard; B) Sample of a stami dagger from the end of seventh century from Campovalano necropolis. (*Author's photo, courtesy of Chieti Archaeological Museum*)

in the example in Fig. 20-B, necropolis of Campovalano, Archaeological Museum of Chieti) to 16cm (necropolis of Fossa, tomb 320), both composed of a row of seven rings plus the final ring

In this technology, the equal length of the two chains made the sheath slightly inclined in respect to the belt, an easy position for carrying the weapon without hindrance. However, this inclination could be increased simply by shortening the lower chain (Fig. 20-B), which was done through the use of a special fibula passing through one of the links of the chain. We can deduce this from the archaeological evidence showing an abundance of these elements, made in a way 'as to be able to attach a strap in perishable material, in turn joined to the belt',[247] in addition to the two chains, making it quick and easy to increase the inclination of the weapon.

Arranging the weapon in a more horizontal position allows freer movement of the leg, which is likely to be of great importance in the event of an agitated action such as combat. This observation has a great value and we will see it later used in the suspension systems for the Roman *gladius*.

Ultimately, perhaps the most important unusual characteristic of this innovative suspension technology is the possibility of varying the angle of the sheath at will and quickly, so as to ensure adjustment to various situations.

Alongside this technology, the simpler systems of the archaic period certainly coexisted, made up only with ligatures, because the Etruscan-type daggers, for which they were mostly used, were still widespread in the high Monarchical Period.

If this is ultimately the case in the Italic territory, with current knowledge it is impossible to say precisely which of these suspension types were most used in the Roman army, until more archaeological evidence is discovered.

II.3,4 Defensive weapons

To support our dissertation on the Monarchical *gladius* and combat techniques, we believe it is essential to briefly investigate some contemporary defence weapons, that will indirectly confirm what has been reported so far.

In the central Italic territories, the fighting was based more and more on the sword, which consequently enabled progressive modification of the defence weapons that had to fit into the new way of fighting. The helmets, which were most affected by this change, thus passed from a primary protective function against the 'blows', essentially given by axes,[248] by spears, by the slashing of swords, as well as from missiles like stones, to protection from thrusts. In the Monarchical Period, it became increasingly important to protect the infantryman not only from *hastae* and arrows shot by the enemy, but also from the thrusts of swords which, in hand-to-hand combat, became increasingly lethal.

The characteristics of the two types of helmets, designed to mainly counteract either blunt or pointed weapons, are described below and distinguished mostly for educational purposes, since both these requirements always tend to be present, with a certain variability, in the same helmet.

The 'blow' helmets

The blunt weapon has its damaging power in the kinetic energy caused by the action of the warrior, enhanced by the weight (in the case of heavy weapons, such as clubs), by the cutting effect (in the case of swords) or by both (in the case of axes). Consequently, to counteract this effect it is of fundamental importance that this energy is discharged in as much space/time as possible,[249] therefore the purpose of the helmet is not to hold back and absorb the blow, which in any case would be equally devastating on the skull and neck of the subject wearing it, but the opposite, which is to deflect the blow, causing the most of the kinetic energy to be discharged either on the upper edge of the shield or on the suitably-protected shoulders.

The characteristics that a helmet must have to achieve this result are very intuitive, with the sloping cap being as smooth as possible, devoid of any element that can hold back the blow (Fig. 21).

Excellent examples are some Villanovan types (eighth century BC – Fig. 21-2), from the Italic lands, and those from Urartu[250] (eighth–seventh century BC, Fig. 21-1a and 1b). The warriors who wore them faced their fellow men, who made great use of axes and maces, weapons that had to be met with particularly suitable helmets. As can be

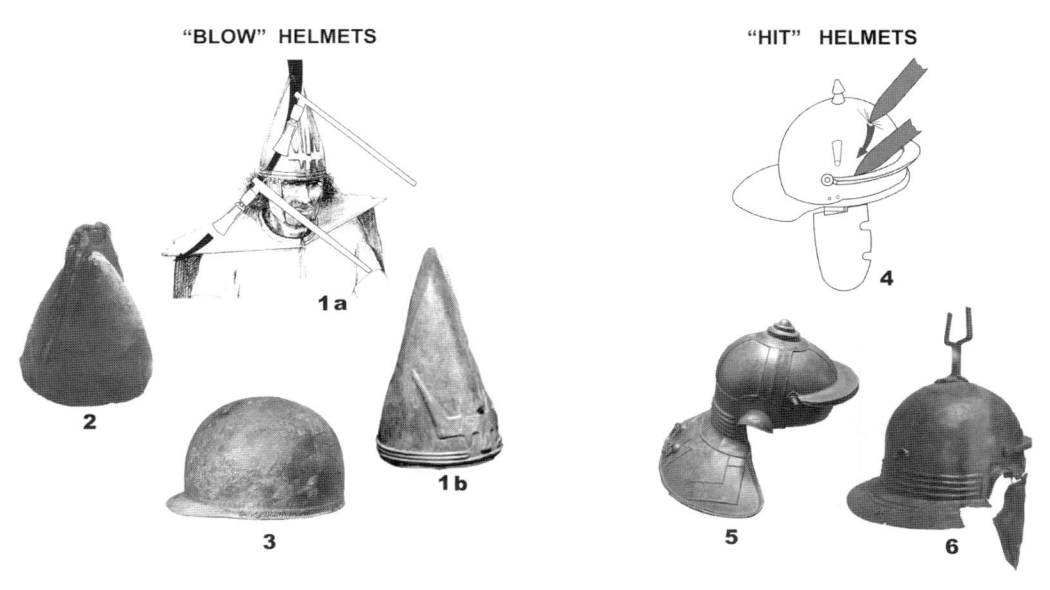

Fig. 21: 'Blow' helmets: 1a) Example of the sliding action caused by an Urartu helmet on an axe hitting it from above. 1b) Original Urartu helmet, eighth century BC. (Courtesy Christie's auction house); 2) Italic crested helmet from Verrucchio. (*Author's photo, Rimini, courtesy of the Civic Archaeological Museum of Bologna*); 3) Roman 'Mannheim' helmet ', from the Caesarian period.
'Hit' helmets: 4) Example of the holding action induced by a sword hit that could strike the helmet. This, at close range, would be blocked by the bar above the forehead, protecting the soldier's face; 5) Roman helmet, late second – early third century AD. (Courtesy Rheinisches Landesmuseum, Bonn); 6) Roman helmet, late first century AD (Courtesy Vindonissa Museum, Brugg). Note that in these two specimens, the wide front bar, the protrusions above the ears and the large neck piece leave no gap available for the tip of a weapon to slide into. (*Drawing and photo by the author*)

easily guessed, the wide crest or rounded shape deflects the vast majority of the blows from above, safeguarding the skull and neck, and possibly causing less damage on the shoulders which were protected by special armour. Equally interesting, if we want to make a chronological jump and refer to the Roman culture, is the typical helmet that Caesar often gave to his legions, the so-called Mannheim (Fig. 21-3), which is completely smooth and simple, practically a hemisphere in shape. In this case his legionaries had to face the Celts, at that time equipped with the long La Tène III type swords, without a point and used exclusively for slashing. This helmet is suitable to let these large blades slip away, leaving the upper edge of the shield to intercept them.

Plutarch gives us a colourful confirmation of this:

> [Camillus] knowing that the prowess of the barbarians lay chiefly in their swords, which they plied in true barbaric fashion, and with no skill at all, in mere slashing blows at head and shoulders, … had helmets forged for most of his men which were all iron and smooth of surface, that the enemy's swords might slip off from them or be shattered by them. He also had the long shields of his men rimmed round with bronze, since their wood could not of itself ward off the enemy's blows. The soldiers themselves he trained to use their long javelins like spears, — to thrust them under the enemy's swords and catch the downward strokes upon them.[251]

Therefore, in a few lines, the author confirms the real function of the helmet, in close relation with the shield.

The 'hit' helmets
The situation completely changes in the case of 'hit' helmets, designed to protect from hits from swords, spears, daggers and the like. The kinetic force was not a problem, being very modest thanks to both the lightness and the low speed of the weapon,[252] so much so that the structure of the skull and the upper muscles of the body and neck could have absorbed it without any problems. On the other hand, what was absolutely necessary was that the blade did not come into contact with the body. The helmet that allowed this type of blow to slip away would have proved very dangerous, as it would have deflected it towards the face, neck and shoulders, where it could create serious damage.

The characteristic required for the 'hit' helmet is ultimately exactly opposite to that of the blow helmets, i.e. that they were not just required to hold back the blow, absorbing its modest and non-dangerous kinetic energy, but to stop the lethal path of the tip of the enemy weapon. The constructive elements that serve this purpose are all horizontal projections, located in the theoretical path of the weapon. The most important improvements to protect the soldier from hits were made in the Roman helmets of the late Republic–early Empire, were a prominent horizontal bar on the forehead, two smaller elements above the ears (the latter appear in the Imperial era) and a pronounced neck piece. The tip of a sword impacting with the helmet bowl would have no way of slipping away because of these obstacles, thus nullifying the potential action of secondary wounding of the face and the neck of the infantryman (Fig. 21-4, 5, 6).

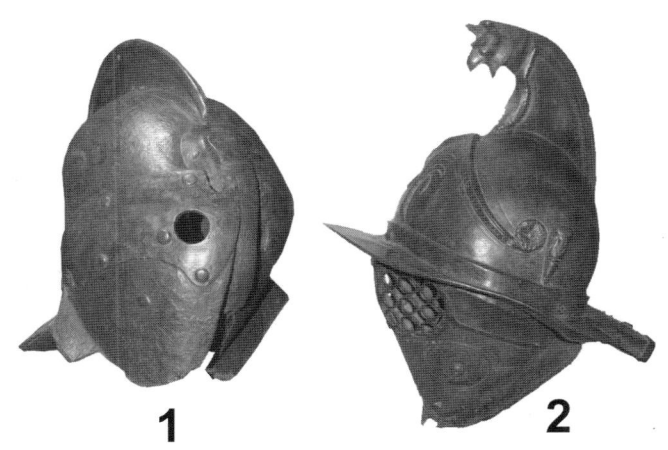

Fig. 22: These gladiator helmets from Pompeii represent well the stereotype of the types of blows and hits: 1) 'blows': helmet of the Counter-Raetiarius, with the rounded shape and the upper crest, equally rounded, ideal for deflecting the trident blows of his typical opponent, the Raetiarius; 2) 'hits': helmet of the Thracian, with a wide brim over the entire edge of the helmet, ideal for stopping the path of the *gladius* tip of his typical opponent, the Murmillo. (*Author's photo*)

The kardiophylax
In addition to the protection of the head, great importance was given to the protection of the chest. In the central Italic area we find numerous examples of a rather simple type of armour, called the *kardiophylax*, which goes back to the Bronze Age and extends into the Iron Age. It is made up of two bronze plaques, one on the chest and another, similar, on the back. Their shape is 'generally rectangular or sub-rectangular, with symmetrically curved borders'[253] which De Marinis divides into two main types: Type A, with an elliptical shape and maximum length of 27cm, and Type B, with a quadrangular shape and maximum length of 25cm.[254] However, there are also examples of perfectly circular or oval plates.

The first appearances are recorded in the Villanovan Etruscan area, but most of the specimens come from Latium, southern Etruria and Abruzzo,[255] also spreading to all other areas of central Italy and Sardinia. We also have evidence from Rome itself, with two Type B specimens (according to the De Marinis classification), from tombs 14 and 86 of the Esquiline necropolis,[256] where swords with antennae were also discovered. Particular mention should be made of Campovalano and Alfedena, important metalworking centres in the Abruzzo and Molise area (and therefore of the Middle Adriatic and Samnite culture), whose necropolises abound with weapons, and among them these armour discs stand out.[257]

The most archaic specimens appear between 760 and 720 BC, and archaeological traces can be found until at least the fourth century BC, always in a purely Italic context. This breastplate also appears to have been used in the Roman military culture of the Consular Age, as Polybius attests it being used alongside the ring mail armour, better known in modern terms as *lorica hamata*: 'The common soldiers wear in addition a breastplate of brass a span square, which they place in front of the heart and call the heart-protector (pectorale), this completing their accoutrements; but those who are rated above ten thousand drachmas wear instead of this a coat of chain-mail.'[258]

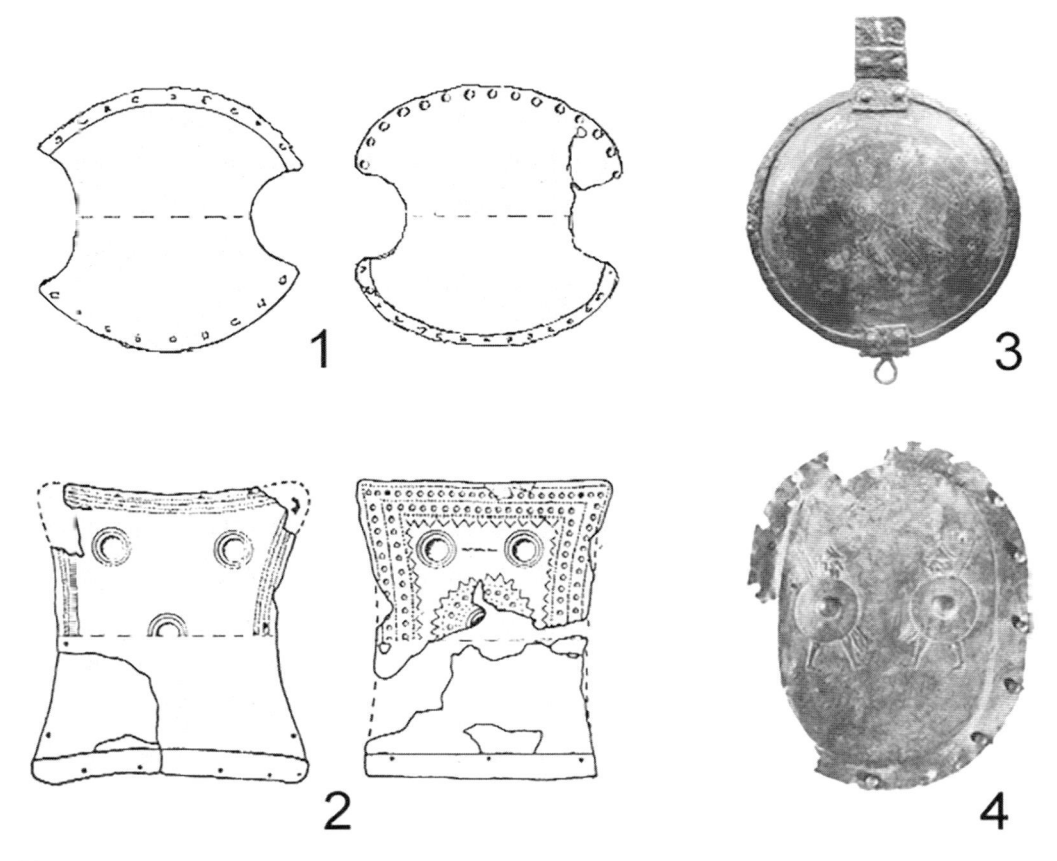

Fig. 23:
1) Pair of Type A pectoral plates of (n De Marinisclassificatio), respectively – on the left unknown provenance, and – on the right – from tomb 25 of Bolsena La Capriola – Rome, Museo di Villa Giulia.
2) Pair of Type B pectoral plates (De Marinis classification), respectively – on the left – from tomb XIV in Via Lanza in Rome, and – on the right – from tomb LXXXVI of the same necropolis – Rome, Antiquarium Comunale.
3) Circular chest plate, from Alfedena (AQ).
4) Breastplate from Rio Carpena (Forlì).
(*1 and 2: drawings from Martinelli*)

We can see how the diffusion of a simple and light chest protection system such as the *kardiophylax*, widespread in the central-Italic area, clearly contrasts with that of the Greek bronze corselet, which in Italy was confined to areas of Etruscan and Greek cultural influence (Magna Graecia). The plate protection, of modest size placed only on the chest and back, clearly speaks to us of the need to protect oneself from blows with a more or less horizontal trajectory, but also of an agile combat such as fencing, while a heavy bronze corselet, was aimed to protect from vigorous blunt blows, although at the same time it limited the agility of the wearer.

Martinelli confirms our findings. In fact, 'the light armour ... of protohistoric central Italy appears as a practical tool, the best possible pact between the need for protection, lightness and wearability in the context of the tactics in use. Its use was on the other hand a legacy within the tradition of clashing with other armed groups lightly in ambush or in any case not deployed in closed and complex formations ... [this type of armour aims] to protect the individual and not the complex of an organised host [as hoplitic shields will do later], respecting a need for agility that basically refers to warriors-duellists.'[259]

Although our concise discussion leaves room for future studies, it is clear that defence weapons provide us with the proof that in the central-Italian area fencing was an important type of combat and that this is clearly distinctive from other geographic areas, with a different political, social and military culture.

II.4 THE MONARCHICAL PERIOD: CONCLUSIONS

The Roman people were born in the context of a joining-together, mainly with the Latin people, but also with the neighbouring ones such as the Sabines and the Etruscans, whose *primum movens* was the River Tiber [260] and its easy ford near the Tiber island.[261] Here Rome was born, because it was the obligatory crossroads for the north–south trade between Etruria and Campania, and the east–west one, also because of transhumance between the Apennine peoples and the coasts. In addition to this, it became a religious centre (replacing Mons Albanus) and was the aggregation point of the rural population who lived in the surrounding areas with the creation of a market (the *Olitorium Forum*) and a field for the cattle fair (the *Boarium Forum*).

The society that was born was of an open type, in the sense that merchants, brigands, priests[262] and foreign princes found refuge and integration, making it a melting pot for the synthesis of various cultures.[263] Livy tells us that 'It had been the ancient policy of the founders of cities to get together a multitude of people of obscure and low origin and then to spread the fiction that they were the children of the soil … A promiscuous crowd of freemen and slaves, eager for change, fled thither from the neighbouring states. This was the first accession of strength to the nascent greatness of the city.'[264] We can affirm that the great novelty and strength of Rome, compared to that of other contemporary peoples, was its multi-ethnicity and openness to merit, rather than to lineage and family descent, concepts that we can find in the speech that the Emperor Claudius made in 48 AD to propose the admission of the elders of Gaul to the Senate.[265]

The Roman polity was therefore characterised by a social openness that we find surprising even today, aimed at increasing the power of Rome regardless of who took part in it, and as a demonstration of this we have the Romulean asylum[266] (the ancient custom of preserving the defeated enemy by guaranteeing them the same rights as the winners – *vetustissimus mos victis parcendi*[267]), the granting of citizenship to freed slaves,[268] a policy based on integration (the Greek one was more restrictive[269]) and above all on being 'ready to adopt new fashions and imitate what they see is better in others'.[270]

This availability of hospitality and the fusion of the people was perhaps more a choice forced by circumstances rather than a desire, but in short it was a determining reason for its development, certainly a factor of civilisation highlighted and exalted not only by modern historians, but also by contemporaries themselves, as was written by Philip V of Macedon in the letter he sent to the Thessalian city of Larissa.[271]

The Roman people did not suddenly appear, but their greatness took shape gradually, bargaining–comparing–clashing–learning against and from neighbouring people, who presented divergences and also many cultural analogies, language, tactics and war technology, each becoming stimulus of survival, development and making a cultural contribution.

All this had close repercussions on the military sphere, giving rise to the *Legio Romulea*. Citizens of the three tribes of which Rome was composed of were enrolled distinguished according to age and wealth, thus allowing the definition of the armament and combat prerogatives of each *cives*, as well as his assignment to the infantry or cavalry (young aristocrats). In this first formation, the battle-array, spread out in width with the cavalry on the wings, was divided into three orders of soldiers the *hastati* represented the light troops who first swarmed the opposing formation through throwing of *hastae*, creating both disrupting effects, like the future *velites*, and opposing the armed men who fought in a similar way; the *principes* were the heart of the formation who, after throwing javelins, fought the enemy with the *gladius* and the shield, maintaining their position within the array; behind all of them were the *triarii*, the heavy infantry, who were armed with long spears and formed a wall against the enemy's penetration, in case they overwhelmed the *principes*.

The Romulean deployment was the answer to the armies that fought in a 'swarm', for whose containment this deployment was more than sufficient, despite its modest depth. It was during this period when the idea that an ordered combat was clearly superior to a loose or a single warrior-hero one started to emerge. One of the consequences was that the ordeal was contrasted, to prevent individual initiative from taking over a group-based confrontation.

The thin line of only three orders, however, became inadequate to counter the power of the Etruscan phalanx and the answer was the birth of the Servian legion, whose main innovation was the depth of the ranks and the displacement of the heavily-armed soldiers (the *triarii* of the *Legio Romulea*) from the third to the first line. The Monarchical Period ended with Tarquinius Superbus, who developed the *Legio Gemina*, a group made up of Romans and Latins, due to which the weapons and the way of fighting of the entire *Latium Vetus* became standardised.

This period, in which the maturation of fighting techniques took place, changing from an instinctive to an organised system, a similar maturity of the *gladius* and its use was decreed. The Roman weapon, which is identified as the sword with a cross hilt of the central Italic culture of which Rome was an integral and indistinguishable part, is presented in continuity with the tradition of the previous centuries of the Bronze Age, whose main characteristics survived unchanged. It was consolidated more and more as a fairly short weapon, with an often lanceolate profile and extremely effective in thrusting use, the latter being so typical in its long and tapered shape that it gives its name to the weapon itself. The handle and the scabbard are characteristic and very elaborate, but for this reason they are not very suitable for mass production, which is why these two elements did not survive into the following centuries. The history of Rome proceeds impetuously, bringing the city and its culture to an ever greater maturity, passing however through continuous battles and wars against countless people such as the Latins, the Sabines, the Etruscans, the Lavinii, the Aedui, the Tusculi, the Volsci, the Veientani and many others. Centuries of continuous conflict in which, although the spear was still the quantitatively most widespread weapon among soldiers, the basis of combat now turned to fencing in which the *gladius* was the protagonist, no longer the prerogative of the soldier-hero but available to all of the more experienced infantrymen, the *ordines*, in the context of deployed and organised training.

However, after two and a half centuries of monarchy, one of the rare moments of clear break comes, even if only on a political level, namely the advent of the *Res Publica*. From here and through other tumultuous events begins a new evolutionary process that will lead to new fighting techniques and, after about another hundred years, to an important evolution of the *gladius* itself, as we will see in the next chapters.

Chapter III

The Consular Age

III (A) THE HIGH AND MIDDLE CONSULAR AGE (END SIXTH – EARLY FIRST CENTURY BC)

III (A).1 HISTORICAL FRAMEWORK

III (A).1,1 The birth of the Res Publica

With the deposition of Tarquinius Superbus (509 BC), who held all the power (legislative, executive and judicial, as well as religious and military), the Roman state was established as a *Res Publica*, which, synthetically, meant the restoration of power in the hands of the patricians, and established the basis for their historical contrast with the plebeians. In truth, the imbalance between patricians and plebeians had already increased during the Monarchy, but in this phase it became unsustainable because the majority of citizens (the plebeians), rich and poor, had been completely excluded from political activity and from military command. In fact, the new Republican political order could not accept the army being in the hands of the rich plebeians, such as that established by King Servius Tullius with the reform of the centuriation based on wealth.

The patricians, as explained by Livy,[1] were the descendants of the 199 senators who Romulus chose for their dignity to establish the *Consilium*, the first Roman senate; Dionysius of Halicarnassus explains that they 'were eminent for their birth, approved for their virtue and wealthy for those times, provided they already had children …' distinguished 'from the obscure, the lowly and the poor'.[2] The patricians, with the creation of the *Res Publica*, appropriated all the power, creating a government that we can define as aristocratic: they parcelled it out to reduce the risk of a new dictatorship, and created various political positions where the main offices became elective and temporary (they were renewed periodically) and provided for mutual control. The heart of the political system became the 'Senate', which elected and controlled the magistrates, who in turn had to govern the various aspects of Roman life, among whom the most important were the 'consuls', from the Latin *'consulere'* which means to provide. The latter had full powers, similar to those of kings, even if provisional, since their term of office lasted one year and power was shared between two of them. They commanded the army (*imperium militia*), convened the Senate and the *Comitia*, and also judged the most serious crimes. In case of serious danger to the Republic, a '*dictator*' could be appointed, who replaced the consuls for a maximum period of six months.

While the nobles could wield power and were put in a position to get richer, the plebeians on the other hand were forced into military service, without being able to benefit from a salary or the distribution of loot, and were laden with the burden of having to temporarily neglect their livelihoods. Politically, the plebeians were excluded from access to the judiciary and, from the civilian point of view, banned from marriage with patricians. In short, they were destined to become poorer and many families found themselves falling into debt: failure to settle these debts was punished severely, possibly leading to slavery and even death.

The great economic and political tensions that set the patricians, who ruled with arrogance and abuse, against the plebeian class (which we must remember was not only formed of the poor, but also rich artisans, traders, etc.), caused bitter struggles that in history recall the French Revolution at the end of the eighteenth century. Since military strength depended on the response of the plebeians to recruitment, each year they 'bargained' their availability to obtain benefits, and the negotiations were so demanding that a specific magistrature of the 'Tribune of the Plebs' was created. The negotiations involved reforms that were reflected in military and civilian life, and each year the bargaining was increasingly tough because the Tribunes of the Plebs tended to get the maximum demand. After the oath, the plebeians became soldiers, effectively being under the management of the commanders and therefore of the patricians, contractually losing their bargaining strength and all rights.

What drove the patricians to such concessions was the progressive awareness that the plebeians had become irreplaceable within the army and without them Rome would not have been able to survive the pressure of war with neighbouring people. In the fourth century BC, a progressive reduction of the patrician *gentes* was underway, so much so that of the initial forty-six noble clans who supplied magistrates to the Republic, sixteen disappeared from the list of consular *fasti* after 445 BC, and after 367 BC, they were reduced by another ten, limiting themselves to a total of twenty *gentes*.

Among the concessions that had the greatest impact in the military was that of 407 BC, when the 'senate decreed that the soldiery should receive pay[3] from the public treasury. Previously, each man had served at his own expense.'[4] This initiative aroused such enthusiasm that 'the plebs ... crowded round the Senate-house ... and declared that after what they had done no one would ever spare his person or his blood, as long as any strength remained, for so generous a country'.[5] This transformed the army from a citizen militia into a professional one. Furthermore, 367 BC was the year in which, due to the approval of the *Liciniae Sextiae* Laws, a policy of integration was initiated: the *nexum*, the debt slavery that oppressed the plebeians, was regulated in such a way as to reduce its applicability,[6] the division of the spoils of war was changed, which until then had been at the discretion of the consuls,[7] and finally the plebeians were allowed to have access to political power, since from this period at least one of the two consuls had to be a plebeian.[8]

A military career increasingly became the only possible employment for the plebeians, since territorial expansion had led to an increase in prisoners of war, consequently giving easy access to unpaid labour, depriving the common people of work and making them increasingly poor.

III (A).1,2 The Great Changes of the Fourth Century BC

The fourth century BC was time of great transformation, seeing the abandonment of military organisation based on social class in favour of putting the state first, a change which coincided with confrontations with new enemies, whose different ways of fighting contributed towards the resurrection of the *legio*. The changes that we will find in the nascent Consular *legio* were the result of variations that occurred progressively over time, where a single event was not always the direct cause of a change, even if we tend towards this for simplicity. The basis of our dissertation, where we try to explain the revolution that acted as a basis for the military changes in this era, will be the description of the *stipendium* and a description of the new way of fighting new enemies such as the Gauls, the Samnites and the Carthaginians under Hannibal.

The establishment of the *stipendium*

The establishment of the *stipendium*, which according to tradition, took place with the capture of Veii in 396 BC, was the moment that allowed the army, now supported by the institutions of the state and no longer bound to the wealthiest citizens, to become professional.

The reason this remuneration was introduced is to be found in the situation of the plebeians who, due to their economic difficulties, were increasingly reluctant to enlist. The small landowners had to interrupt their farming and if the wars lasted for a long time, risked the drying-up of the fields with the consequence that families easily fell into debt. A good example is the figure of a centurion who fell into poverty because his properties were devastated during the war against the Sabines (not because of the absence of the soldier from his land), portraying the precariousness of the times and how debts easily carried to the misfortune the families who could no longer have the support of the harvest of their fields, despite the fact that the head of the family had served the state with honour:

> His clothing was covered with filth, his personal appearance was made still more loathsome by a corpse-like pallor and emaciation, his unkempt beard and hair made him look like a savage … they said that he had been a centurion, and mentioned other military distinctions he possessed. He bared his breast and showed the scars which witnessed to many fights in which he had borne an honourable part … He stated that whilst serving in the Sabine war he had not only lost the produce of his land through the depredations of the enemy, but his farm had been burnt, all his property plundered, his cattle driven away, the war-tax demanded when he was least able to pay it, and he had got into debt. This debt had been vastly increased through usury and had stripped him first of his father's and grandfather's farm, then of his other property.[9]

This precariousness and being burdened by taxes favoured the secession of the plebians in 494 BC.

The only benefit for the soldiers, before salaries were established, was the possibility of participating in the division of the spoils. However, their distribution was decided by the army commander, the consul, who usually was never generous towards the soldiers and above all, it was not a consistent income because it was linked to the course of the war. The proposal of the consul Appius Claudius, which was not accepted by the Senate at the time it was put forward, explains well the opposition of the individual citizen to giving 'his services to the State at his own cost, [because] he had the satisfaction [or better, it was essential for him], however, of cultivating his land for a part of the year, and acquiring the means of supporting himself and his family whether he were at home or on service. Now he has the pleasure of knowing that the State is a source of income to him, and he is glad to receive his pay.' The solution, according the consul, was that 'he has the pleasure of knowing that the State is a source of income to him, and he is glad to receive his pay. Let him therefore take it patiently that he is a little longer absent from his home and his property, on which no heavy expense now falls.'[10]

Tensions with the plebeians grew until the consuls, to prevent the rebellion of the soldiers, let them plunder the city of Anxur (406 BC), modern Terracina, which was in the hands of the Volsci, a further front opened during the war against Veii:

> This generosity on the part of the generals was the first step towards the reconciliation of the plebs and the senate. This was followed by a boon which the senate, at a most opportune moment, conferred on the plebeians. Before the question was mooted either by the plebs or their tribunes, the senate decreed that the soldiery should receive pay from the public treasury. Previously, each man had served at his own expense.[11]

The salary of the soldiers did not solve all the problems, however, because the tax for military expenditure, the *tributum*, was increased, so although it was distributed proportionally over the different classes, and therefore had more impact on those with higher wealth, the tax also affected the lower orders:

> ... the wretched plebeians might never have any respite. And now, to crown all, they even had to pay a war-tax, so that when they returned, worn out by toil and wounds, and last of all by age, and found all their land untilled through want of the owner's care, they had to meet this demand out of their wasted property and return to the State their pay as soldiers many times over, as though they had borrowed it on usury.[12]

However, the establishment of the *stipendium*, together with the *tributum*,[13] was a great revolution as the army evolved from a seasonal one to a professional one, allowing military campaigns to take place far from Rome, and therefore be prolonged. The great change was that the power was no longer wielded by the wealthiest classes and the individual infantrymen paid for his armaments himself, but these were supplied by the state, so that the institution supplied the armament based on the age of the soldiers, and no longer according to their rank. This is one of the much-debated points among modern historians, since it is not well defined whether state supply was already well developed during this period or, as others argue, was a much later planning, attributing to the Consular Age a considerable variability of armaments within each legion. We can certainly say that a greater coordination in offensive and defensive equipment developed, since these were no longer dictated by the individual's financial resources. Initially, state planning probably had a more elementary form than later on, but the supply, as Polybius[14] reminds us, was basically paid by the soldier himself through a deduction from the *stipendium*, affirming good coordination in the possession of military equipment from this period onwards.

The new enemies: Celts, Samnites and Carthaginians

Polybius, in his work, says that compared to those of his contemporaries, 'the fighting way of the ancients' had changed, because wars far from Rome had changed the types of territories in which battles were taking place and especially the enemies they fought. The neighbouring peoples presented, despite their diversity, a homogeneity of weapons and customs that were based on the acceptance of common rules such as establishing a battlefield by 'mutual agreement' and weakening the spirit of the adversaries with an open battle, without deception and without long-range weapons, where 'only a hand-to-hand battle at close quarters … was truly decisive. Hence they preceded war by a declaration, and when they intended to do battle gave notice of the fact and of the spot to which they would proceed and array their army. But at the present they say it is a sign of poor generalship to do anything openly in war.'[15] This comment sums up well how the concept of waging war evolved from the end of the Monarchy to the Middle Consular Age, and we can see the strength of the Romans who knew how to adjust both strategy and armament to different situations in

The Battle of the Allia (390 BC) represented the first major event that subverted the traditional way of setting up a battle, during which the Romans ran into 'a horde of Gauls', a large crowd of men armed with long swords, who attacked violently, with neither order nor discipline. The Capitoline army, tied to its rigid strategy of deployment, was in difficulty, highlighting the serious limits in its tactics. The battle against the Senonian Gauls, led by Brennus, took place a few years after the fall of Veii, surprising the Romans who opposed an almost improvised army '… already overwhelmed by fear since … the whole country in front and around was now swarming with the enemy, who, being as a nation given to wild outbreaks, had by their hideous howls and discordant clamour filled everything with dreadful noise'.[16] The great multitude of enemies forced the Romans, in the deployment of their army, to extend 'their line on either wing to prevent their being outflanked, but even so they could not make their front equal to the enemy's, whilst by thus thinning their line they weakened the centre so that it could hardly keep in touch'.[17] Livy's bitter comment was that 'there was nothing to remind one of Romans either amongst the generals or the private soldiers', leading to the disintegration of the ranks, and therefore to the rout of the formation as soon as 'the Celtic battle-shout was heard'.[18]

What emerges from the reading of the description of the battle on the Allia, the first encounter that the Romans had with the Gauls, is that that the way of fighting of the barbarians was completely different from what the Romans were used to. Livy defines them as 'trained to arms from the cradle, naturally courageous'[19] but 'their whole strength both of mind and body depended upon rapid movements, and even a short delay told upon their vigour'.[20] Dionysius of Halicarnassus explains that

> the barbarians' manner of fighting, being in large measure that of wild beasts and frenzied, was an erratic procedure, quite lacking in military science. Thus, at one moment they would raise their swords aloft and smite after the manner of wild boars, throwing the whole weight of their bodies into the blow like hewers of wood or men digging with mattocks, and again they would deliver crosswise blows aimed at no target, as if they intended to cut to pieces the entire bodies of their adversaries, protective armour and all; then they would turn the edges of their swords away from the foe.[21]

Mommsen's comment is enlightening. He declared that the struggle of the Gauls and the Romans, different from that between Rome and Etruria or between Rome and Samnium, was not a collision of two political powers that agree and stipulate between them, but is rather comparable to a natural disaster, after which the organism, if it is not destroyed, immediately regains its balance.[22] The rigid approach of the Servian *legio* was undermined by the difficulty of contain a chaotic fury, with an enemy occupying a very extensive front, so much so that the Roman one which was well organised, and with well-defined limits because it was developed in depth, was overwhelmed. For four centuries the Romans had been used to fighting against enemies who, within certain limits, based their combat on similar approaches, following the same rules and presenting a similar array, but the Gauls put this way of understanding war into crisis.

The Romans adapted their military capabilities to this new way of fighting. Plutarch describes to us that Camillus,

> knowing that the prowess of the barbarians lay chiefly in their swords, which they plied in true barbaric fashion, and with no skill at all, in mere slashing blows at head and shoulders, he had helmets forged for most of his men which were all

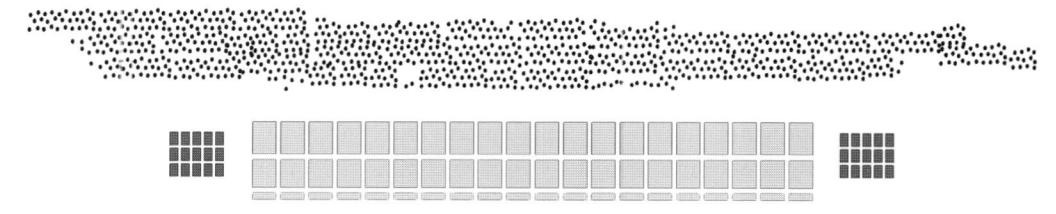

Fig. 1: Schematic representation of a Gallic assault on a Roman Servian *legio*. The *legio* reformed by Servius Tullius was useful in countering Etruscan armies that fought in hoplite fashion, for which it was necessary to deepen the formation rather than extend the battle array. But, faced with a tumultuous and chaotic attack like the Celtic one, with a very vast array, this formation soon proved ineffective.

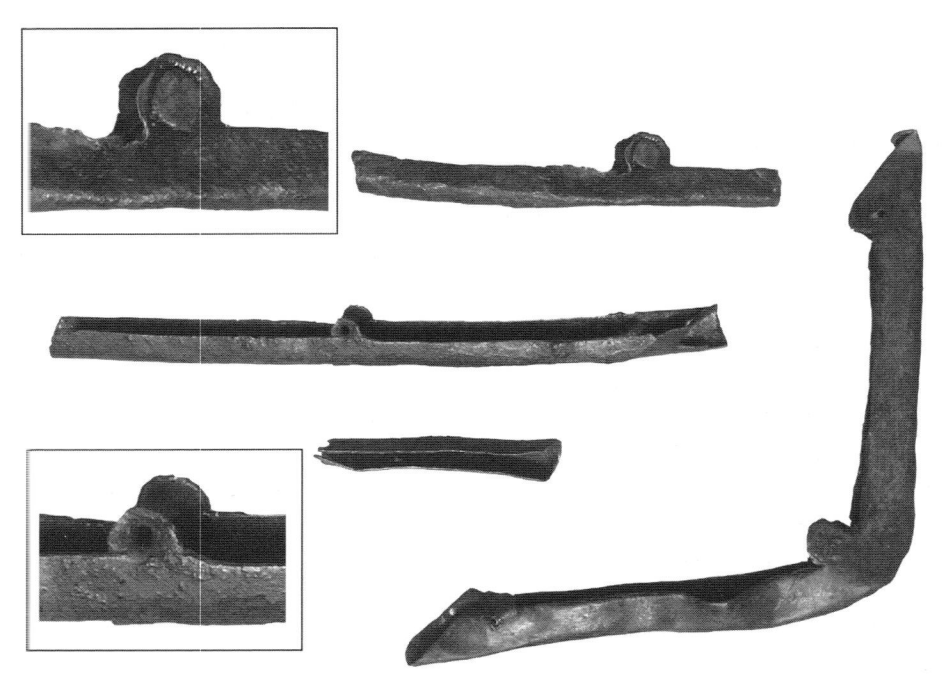

Fig. 2: Bronze elements of a shield edge that were fixed to the wooden structure by means of small nails, for which the holes remain and in one case also the rivet (see boxes with two details highlighted). Their introduction was in order to avoid the shield from being split, in case of blows, thus making it unusable in combat. (*Author's photo*)

> iron and smooth of surface, that the enemy's swords might slip off from them or be shattered by them. He also had the long shields of his men rimmed round with bronze, since their wood could not of itself ward off the enemy's blows. The soldiers themselves he trained to use their long javelins like spears, — to thrust them under the enemy's swords and catch the downward strokes upon them.[23]

It is interesting to see in this quotation how the Romans were able to adapt to new military situations and to develop a response with homogeneous weapons supplied by the state. Since the helmets worn by the infantrymen were not adequate to protect against the violent blows of the Celtic swords, they were replaced with iron ones with characteristics to classify them as 'hit' helmets (see Chapter II.3,4); furthermore, to ward off the dangerous blows of the long Celtic blades, they chose to use spears, which 'the Latins brandished as swords'.

After this first defensive solution, Dionysius of Halicarnassus tells that an active style of combat was adopted, based on good protection of the soldier associated with the high degree of injury inflicted by the *gladius*. The Greek author describes how:

> on the other hand, the Romans' defence and counter-manoeuvring against the barbarians was steadfast and afforded great safety. For while their foes were still raising their swords aloft, they would duck under their arms, holding up

their shields, and then, stooping and crouching low, they would render vain and useless the blows of the others, which were aimed too high, while for their own part, holding their swords straight out, they would strike their opponents in the groins, pierce their sides, and drive their blows through their breasts into their vitals. And if they saw any of them keeping these parts of their bodies protected, they would cut the tendons of their knees or ankles and topple them to the ground roaring and biting their shields and uttering cries resembling the howling of wild beasts.[24]

The Romans again realised the limits of their legions when they faced the Samnites, 'living at that day in open hamlets among the mountains, and that were in the habit of making marauding incursions into the low country and the coastal districts',[25] who engaged them for about half a century, in three wars: the first from 343 to 341 BC; the second from 326 to 304 BC; the third from 298 to 290 BC. The Samnites were a group of very warlike and stubborn populations, whose characteristics were typical of mountaineers accustomed to the sacrifices of a hard life. They lived in a mountainous environment, the Apennines, characterised by rugged rocky reliefs and narrow valleys, easily defensible with numerous fortifications (*oppida*), connected to each other by mule tracks that allowed easy control of a vast territory, but difficult to attack without risking serious losses. The battles that the Romans had to fight were different from those they had fought up until that time, because they were mostly operations that consisted, as Brizzi explains, '*de marches, de contremarches, d'embuscades, d'assauts contre des villesou des forteresses*' (quotation from Saulnier, translating as 'of feints, attacks, retreats and above all of offensive returns, of poliorcetic operations, often repeated against the same objectives, which were conquered – and evidently lost – several times by Rome in the space of only a few years').[26] Furthermore, the Roman victories were of limited scope because the population was scattered over the vast territory, without forming towns that could be identified as nerve centres.

The new military context that the Roman soldiers had to face was characterised by guerrilla warfare. Livy reports a description of a Samnite assault on a Capitoline army on the march, in which

> the suddenness of the affair at first created some confusion, while the men were piling their kits in the centre of the column and getting at their weapons, but as soon as they had each freed themselves from their burdens and put themselves in fighting trim, they began to assemble round the standards. From their old discipline and long experience they knew their places in the ranks, and the line was formed without any orders being needed, each man acting on his own initiative.[27]

This shows us how the new type of warfare, no longer based on opposing battle lines but on ambushes, had induced the Roman soldiers to rework a new tactic, which in the context of professional preparation, made it possible to quickly organise an efficient defensive formation.

The Capitoline army, therefore, had made a further qualitative leap to match the tenacious and strong Apennine people who committed them to three long wars until their final defeat. But the challenges that had to be faced by the Romans were far from over, since the confrontation with the Carthaginians, which took place between the third and second centuries BC, was disruptive. The main reason behind the Romans revolutionising their approach to war was Hannibal and his ability to manage an army varied in language and customs as well as in ways of fighting, composed of Libyan, Numidian, Iberian, Gallic, Greek, Italic troops, etc. While for some ethnic groups of infantrymen, such as the Greeks, he maintained the way of fighting based on the spear, useful for the clash against the Roman *triarii*, he put his trust in the sword already in use among the Iberians and the Gauls to strengthen the success in close combat, teaching it to the Libyans, accustomed to fighting in another way, supplying them with the weapons and armour captured from the Romans after the victories in Italy. His great ability to manage resources was associated with the ability to use the *stratégema* (stratagem) and *mètis* (cunning), which the Romans however called *fraus* (deception), *dolus* (fraud) and *calliditas* (cunning) and, as Brizzi reports, 'such unscrupulous behaviour … some members of the Senate were still condemning half a century later, at the time of the last war against Macedonia'.[28]

The Samnitic *scutum*
However, the Romans' new way of fighting was incompatible with the large *clipeati* shields, which certainly protected the infantryman, but at the same time restricted the movements of those who carried them. Livy explains that 'when the soldiers received pay, the smaller oblong shield called the *scutum* was adopted. The phalanx formation, similar to the Macedonian of the earlier days, was abandoned in favour of the distribution into companies [*manipulatim structaacies*]'.[29]

The change of the shields, from *clypei* to oblong *scuta*, and the transformation of the *Legio Serviana*, with hoplite characteristics, into the more dynamic manipular form, is further confirmed by the *Ineditum Vaticanum*, which explains how

> the Samnite [oblong] shield (*scutum*) was not part of our [Roman] national equipment, nor did we have javelins, but fought with round shields and spears … But when we found ourselves at war with the Samnites we armed ourselves with their oblong shields and javelins, and fought against them on horseback, and by copying foreign arms we became masters of those who thought so highly of themselves.[30]

The Samnites, therefore, were the people from whom the oblong shield was adopted, as is also remembered by Julius Caesar who stated that they 'took their offensive and defensive weapons from the Samnites',[31] and from Atheneus of Naukratis who wrote that as the

Romans at the same time ... retained their ancestral customs, they took over from their subjects whatever remnant of noble discipline they could find, leaving to them that which was useless, in order that they might never become capable of attaining to the recovery of what was lost ... From the Etruscans, also, who attacked in close formation, they took over the close battle; from the Samnites they learned the use of the oblong shield, from the Spaniards, the use of the javelin, and so on, learning different things from different peoples, and bringing them to greater perfection.[32]

While these quotations state that the oblong shield was introduced to the Roman army in the fourth century BC, there are others that contradict this. Plutarch writes that this oval shield was already in use by the Sabines, and that Romulus 'made use of their oblong shields'.[33] Livy and Dionysius of Halicarnassus argue that the *scutum* was already used by some classes of the *Legio Serviana* in the sixth century BC (in this case Livy seems to contradict himself), and we can also find it borne by the infantrymen depicted in the *Situla della Certosa*, testifying towards an earlier use.

Fig. 3: Samnite warrior with oblong *scutum*, Capua, fourth century BC. (*Author's photo*)

Table 1: The appearance of the *scutum* in the Roman legion according to various authors.

Period	Author or Artefact	Legion	People From Which It Was Adopted
Eighth cent. BC	Plutarch, *Romulus*, 21, 1.	*Legio Romulea*	Sabines
Sixth cent. BC	Livy, I, 43	*Legio Serviana*	
Sixth cent. BC	Dionysius of Halicarnassus, IV, 16-17		
Sixth cent. BC	*Situla della Certosa*		
Fourth cent. BC	Livy, VIII, 8, 3	Livian *legio*	Samnites
Fourth cent. BC	*Ineditum Vaticanum*, H. Von Arnim (1892), Hermes' 27, 1892, p. 118.		
Fourth cent. BC	Sallust *De coniuratione Catilinae*, 51		
Fourth cent. BC	Atheneus of Naucratis, *Deiphnosophistes*, VI, 106.		

The inconsistency of the ethnographic (from whom it was adopted) and chronological (when it came into use) provenance of the Roman *scutum* has been highlighted since ancient times. Guattani, an Italian archaeologist of the late 1700s, tried to solve this by elaborating the hypothesis that the Romans had abandoned the use of the Argolic round shield in order to initially adopt the oval one from the Sabines, and then moved on to that of the Samnites, which was square-shaped like a tile.[34]

We personally consider this contradiction as a false problem since, first of all, the Sabines and the Samnites were two groups of people who belonged to the same Osco-Umbrian stock. Starting from this statement, we deduce that, while the classical authors were trying to indicate the precise ethnicity of those who had given rise to the oval shield, the overall view was lost, making those who had developed it first only of academic significance.

But if we can assume that we have solved the question regarding the origin, that is that the oblong shield, as indeed the cross-hilted sword, had an Apennine derivation, the difficult explanation of the chronological classification remains, i.e. when was this shield adopted by the Romans?

Fig. 4: Soldiers holding oblong *scuta*, represented in the Ara di Domitius Aenobarbus, late second–early first century BC. (*Author's photo*)

Livy's contradiction, which states that the introduction of the *scutum* took place in the Servian *Legio* in the sixth century BC (I, 43) as well as in the Livian *legio* of the fourth century BC, can be solved by interpreting the phrase 'they replaced the *clypei* with the shields (*scuta*)' not so much in the sense of 'introduction of the oblong shields' but more probably the abandonment of the Argolic shields when the formation in maniples was adopted. These citations, therefore, would be due to the fact that the fourth century BC was a time of great change, in which the aspects of hoplitism of the Servian *legio* were completely eliminated in favour of an active combat, based on fencing, present in all orders of the formation. If we accept this interpretation, the only inconsistency remaining between the citations is what is stated by the *Ineditum Vaticanum*, which denies the use of the *scutum* in a period prior to the fourth century BC, a claim that, due to the representation on the Situla of the Certosa, is difficult to accept.

Fig. 5: Finds from two distinct sites, but clearly framing what were the characteristics of a Consular Age *scutum*.
A) *Umbo* made of iron that covered the central part of the 'spine', the wooden reinforcement of the shield. The metal of which this central element of the shield was made, underlines the stresses to which this defensive weapon was subjected to. Dated to the second and first century BC, it was found in La Caridad, Caminreal, Spain (Photo by Cesare Rusalem from the site https://www.roma-victrix.com).
B) Republican shield found in El Fayum, Egypt, the wooden part still in perfect condition. It should be noted that the *scutum* was made up of numerous small juxtaposed elements, the structure of which accentuated its elasticity, a fundamental characteristic for cushioning enemy blows while preventing it from breaking. (*Photo by Raffaele D'Amato*)

The description of how the Samnite shield was introduced in the Roman legion is found in Polybius, who uses the Greek word θυρεος to define it, which literally means 'door'. The Greek historian informs us that it had a convex surface (with a width of about 120cm by 75cm and a thickness, including the *umbo* [boss], of 7.4cm).

> The shield [he writes] is made of two planks glued together, the outer surface being then covered first with canvas and then with calf-skin. Its upper and lower rims are strengthened by an iron edging which protects it from descending blows and from injury when rested on the ground. It also has an iron boss [*umbo*] fixed to it which turns aside the most formidable blows of stones, pikes, and heavy missiles in general.[35]

Comparing the characteristics of the Samnite shield with the Greek *clypeus*, we note that the oblong shape of the Italic shield allowed a better protection of the infantryman,[36] since he was able to cover himself entirely, in addition to the fact that due to its smaller size, it allowed greater freedom of movement and consequently enabled the practice of individual combat. In addition, the elasticity of the materials used made the shield flexible and therefore capable of cushioning blows without breaking, while the metal reinforcements of the edges and the *umbo* were useful to provide protection from sword and spear.

In contrast, the *clypeus*, with a diameter of about 90–100cm (measurements from some finds from Verrucchio, Rimini)[37] did not cover the legs, which were for this reason protected with greaves; at the same time, being round, its greater width was such that it was also used to defend the fellow soldier who was on the left of the wearer. This characteristic, in the battle array, induced the soldiers to defend themselves behind the shield of the infantryman on the right, thus favouring greater compactness of the formation, but at the same time restricted the manoeuvrability of the individual soldier. We also remember that the *oplon*, with a weight of 8kg,[38] was for combat based above all on the thrust and the spear and less upon dynamic movements.

We can therefore argue that the delineation of two models of shields, an oblong one that protected a single infantryman and a round one that also partially favoured the protection of the adjacent comrade-in-arms, were configured for two different styles of combat.

Despite this clear differentiation of use, we find a contradiction in the numerous Etruscan urns of the Hellenistic period that depict a swordfight between heroes who hold large two-handled *oplons*. We will never know if these representations are an idealisation of Homeric heroism or a real representation of the Etruscan armed forces or, much more likely, a mixture of elements typical of the Greek and contemporary Etruscan panoply. But beyond these findings, the agility and movements required for the fight with the *gladius* led the Romans to choose a lighter shield that did not hinder the movement of legs and arms, but at the same time effectively protected from an enemy's blows. This choice led to the abandonment of the *oplon*, developing an armament and a way of fighting that became an identifying feature of the Roman army. It should also be remembered that the Etruscan urns have different dates and that in any case in the Etruscan noble tombs of the fourth–third century BC old *opla* were found, a sign of a continuation of use of this defensive element in the aristocratic context, even if not used in the Roman army. Many warriors represented in the Etruscan urns are also cavalrymen, and with oblong shields, especially in the urns of the second–first century BC.

III(A).1,3 The gladius replaces the hasta as the main weapon
The early Consular Age was the moment in which the clear predominance of the *gladius* over the spear was assured, not so much because the ancient authors report particular events or considerations, but due to the fact that in several stories witness how the Roman army managed to defeat the enemy without the *hasta*. The first incident that demonstrated this change of importance was a clash against the Volsci, a people of Osco-Umbrian origin, who during the fourth century BC were one of the fiercest opponents of Rome. Livy says that while the armies were facing each other,

> the Roman consul … ordered them to stand with their spears fixed in the ground, and when the enemy came to close quarters, to spring forward and make all possible use of their swords. The Volscians, wearied with their running and shouting, threw themselves upon the Romans as upon men benumbed with fear, but when they felt the strength of the counter-attack and saw the swords flashing before them … retreated in confusion.[39]

It should be noted that the Volsci expected the classic sequence of attack by the Romans, represented by the throwing of the *hastae* and then hand-to-hand combat, but this change in the combat was the cause of their disorientation and defeat. The *gladius* had now become the main weapon to such an extent that it could be used alone to achieve victory. There are other narratives confirming the ennobling of the *gladius*, including the *adlocutio* given in 385 BC by the *dictator* Aulus Cornelius Cossus to the soldiers during the war against the Volsci Latins, Ernici and Circei. In this speech the *dux* encouraged his men by stating that the 'enemies [were] no match for us', and said they should

> lay our javelins at our feet and arm ourselves only with our swords. I would not even have any running forward from the line; stand firm and receive the enemy's charge without stirring a foot. When they have hurled their ineffective missiles and their disordered ranks fling themselves upon you, then let your swords flash and let every man remember that it is the gods who are helping the Romans, it is the gods who have sent you into battle with favourable omens.[40]

Even during the war against the Privernates, circa 350 BC, we find a similar situation cited, in which Sextus Tullius relied completely on his sword: '"See, General, how your army is fulfilling its promise to you," and with the word he dropped his javelin and drawing his sword charged the enemy.'[41]

But if the ancient authors suggest the widespread use of the sword, studying the paintings of the previously mentioned François Tomb of Vulci, we note an exaltation of the distinction of the use of weapons between Greeks and Etruscans/Romans. In fact, the pictorial cycle is used as a parallel between the exploits sung by Homer and the Etruscan ones, for which the sacrifice of the Trojan heroes by Achilles, to avenge the killing of Patroclus, is compared to the heroic enterprise of the Vulcii fighters, who managed to prevail over other powerful Etruscan communities in the Tiber valley, including Volsinii (modern Orvieto) and Rome, at the time dominated by the Tarquinii. Analysing the weapons of the Homeric fighters, out of four armed warriors, only Achilles possesses the *gladius* as his only weapon, with which he kills the Trojan; Agamemnon only has the spear, while the two Ajaxes have both the spear and the *gladius*. On the contrary, in the fresco that describes the Etruscan exploits 'contemporary at the time of the creation of the fresco', the four Vulcenti fighters are all only armed with the *gladius*. As Roncalli says,[42] the Greeks are 'lightly armed and expert in ranged combat, they shine through the painting with a precision that reveals this knowledge in the painter's culture'. In our view, the attribution of the two different types of weapons to the Greek and Etruscan warriors is not accidental (weapons that imply throwing combat for the former and hand-to-hand combat for the latter), being weapons that the artist knew very well, and which allow us to confirm the hypothesis of a combat centred around the *gladius* for the Central Italic people.

III (A).2 THE FIGHTING IN THE EARLY–MIDDLE CONSULAR AGE

III (A).2,1 The Livian manipular legio of the fourth–third century BC
The early Consular Age battle: Lake Regillus and the Dioscuri (fifth century BC)
Once the *Res Publica* was established, Rome immediately had to face a series of wars, not only to counter the attempts at reconquest by the deposed king Tarquinius Superbus, but also to fight the Latin cities which, united in a league, tried to prevent the dominance of the city in the *Latium Vetus*. The Battle of Lake Regillus in 496 BC marked the climax of that clash, which saw the defeat of the Latin League. This event appears very interesting because it is admirably described in its developments, in such a way that the dynamics can be analysed and understood.

At the beginning of the battle 'when they had received the watchword from their commanders and the trumpets had sounded the charge, they gave a shout and fell to, first, the light-armed men and the horse on each side, then the solid ranks of foot, who were armed and drawn up alike; and all mingling, a severe battle ensued in which every man fought hand to hand'.[43]

The clash began with the charge of the respective cavalry *alae* to prevent the opposing *equites* from disrupting the deployment of the *pedites* through an attack on the flanks, the weak point of every army. While the cavalry neutralised each other through a direct confrontation, the light infantry, by throwing the *hastae*, tried to disrupt the enemy line by wounding the men in the front ranks.

The second phase of the battle developed with the attack of the Roman infantry against the Latins, from which two very important pieces of information emerge: the first is that the ranks were 'compact' and the second is that the armies were 'superimposable both in terms of weapons and in the deployments'. The initial statement implies a clash between the two armies in close formation (a passive clash, of the hoplitic type), but it seems that after the collision a 'melee' and therefore 'hand-to-hand' fighting was generated so that the armies 'fought all confusedly' (an active conflict). Unfortunately, the generic description does not allow us to individuate the military battle array of the legions in the best possible way, or to understand whether this situation of 'confrontation outside the lines' was exceptional or the normal way of fighting. Certainly the maturity of maintaining the coordination of the various soldiers during combat, so that the ranks remained compact even during the development of the fighting, was not acquired at once, but was part of an evolutionary process that progressively asserted itself over time, such that a specific date or event cannot be assigned to it. Probably, even in subsequent eras, when this well-framed combat approach was used, it would have been very difficult, depending on how the battle evolved, to regulate it.

In any case, for the author it was important to emphasise that the fighters showed themselves to be brave and going beyond their own strength. The fate of the battle was uncertain, since the value of the soldiers prevailed over the type of combat.

The second piece of information we are given, is that of an identical military organisation between the Roman army and that of the Latin League. This is due to their assimilation/integration introduced at the time of Tarquinius Superbus, when he established the *Legio Bina*, an event that, however, did not interest the other central-Italic people, allowing the differences in the way of fighting to persist in other neighbouring peoples, such as the Sabines and the Etruscans. The Battle of Lake Regillus is the exemplification of an organised battle, in which the Romans spread their way of fighting among the Latins, the first step towards its extra-regional extension. In fact, the sword was already considered as the main weapon, as can be noted in the description of the killing of the Roman vice-commander Herminius who 'having rallied from their rout those of his men who had been put to flight, brought them up and attacked the troops arrayed under Mamilius; and encountering this general, who both for stature and strength was the best man of his time, he not only killed him, but was slain himself while he was despoiling the body, someone having pierced his flank with a sword'.[44] He was killed by an anonymous soldier, armed with an ordinary *gladius*, a weapon that had now become as important as the spear.

However, the Roman victory over the Latin League did not have great effects, so much so that the treaty ending the war, the *Foedus Cassianum* of 493 BC, recognised the positions of both sides: the Roman power was considered equivalent to that of the entire Latin League.

The Battle of Lake Regillus was also the occasion of the myth of the Dioscuri, the twin sons of Zeus, who led the Roman soldiers to victory, when the battle had taken an unfavourable turn. Castor and Pollux are connected to the *gladius* as they became a symbol and political message. The twins were considered to represent the Roman and Latin people, united in destiny, each carrying the *gladius* on the forearm with the tip pointing upwards to spread a message of harmony (see Chapter V 'The Symbolic Value of the *Gladius*').

Structure of the Livian manipular *legio*

The description of the fourth-century *legio* by Livy[45] is very significant, since hardly anywhere in the annals is such great importance given to technical military issues, described in detail. As the author tells us, this great change in the disposition of the infantry and their way of fighting, the explanation of which is preceded by an ethical and formative framework, was a brilliant event that allowed the legions to prevail over other armies.[46] Combat, like all Roman social life, was based on discipline and organisation, which required a mental acceptance that was taught from early on. The fable of Titus Manlius Torquatus, who punished his disobedient son Titus with death, is a useful example that falls within this idea, in which the rational Roman mentality condemns the young man who was victorious over a champion of the Latin League, because his digression could have been an example for further individual behaviour, favouring the subversion of order. Combat was not just technique, but accompanied by the *animus*[47] (from Greek ανεμος 'wind, souffle'), intended as a positive disposition for

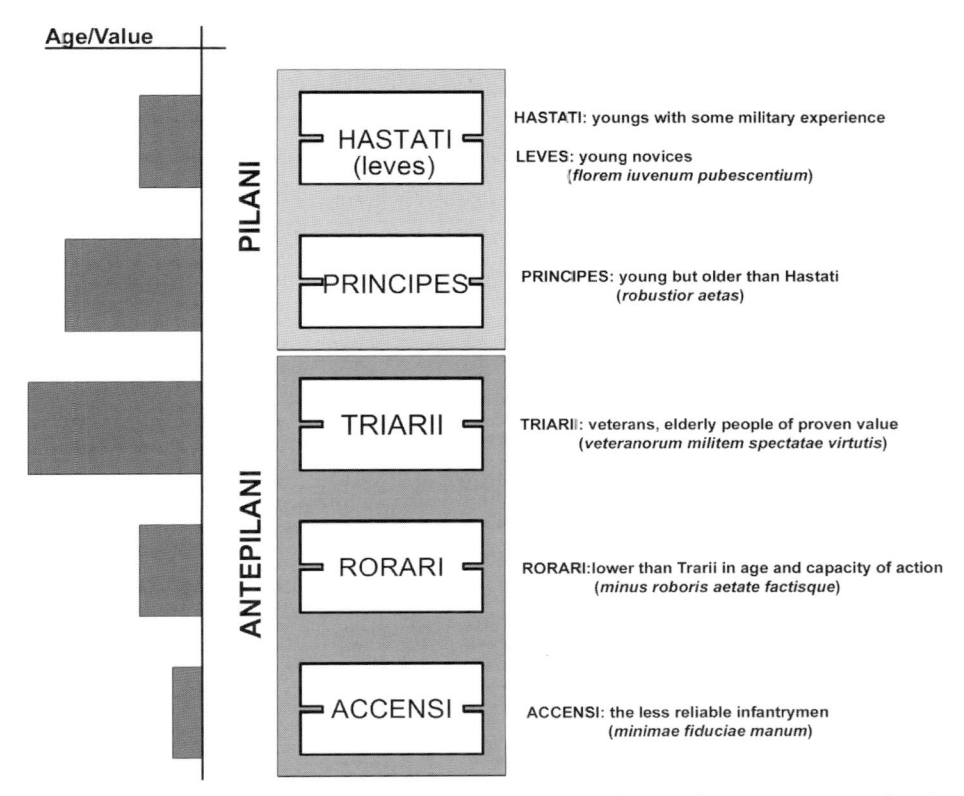

Fig.1: An *ordo*, which shows how the line-up was made up of infantry of increasing age and military value from the *hastati* to the *triarii*, and then decreasing again in the *rorari*. The *accensi* were the least reliable troops and therefore positioned behind all the rest. (*Author's drawing*)

more effective action, and from the *consilium*,[48] where prudence had to imply reason, but never turn into fury, as individual fury would have affected the common coordination.

After revealing the reason why the Roman soldiers were superior over others, Livy moves on to the technical description of the new army, comparing it to the formation of the Monarchical Period which appeared as a compact mass, in which the *pedites* of the first class were armed and set up to counter the Etruscan hoplite army (*Legio Serviana*). In this context, the term 'Macedonian-like phalanxes' is used, since the previous arrangement recalled the Macedonian formations, but in the new formation of the early Consular Age the soldiers, within the maniple, went back to being distinguished as *hastati*, *principes* and *triarii*, like in the *Legio Romulea*. The fall of the monarchy had defined a change in the criteria on which the military levy was based. Age, which had always been a discriminating factor in defining the roles of individual soldiers, became secondary to wealth in the *Legio Serviana*, a change justified by the fact that it became the factor determining the armament capabilities of the infantry. With the Consular Age, the criteria of distinction is described by Polybius, who reports that 'when they come to the rendezvous, they choose the youngest and poorest to form the *velites*; the next to them are made *hastati*; those in the prime of life *principes*; and the oldest

Diagram 1: The Livean *legio*. (*Author's drawing*)

of all *triarii*.⁴⁹ The census, therefore, maintains a weight in the selection criteria, but age, to which the concept of military valour was linked, as well as experience and combat skills, tends to prevail again in the Livian manipular legion. If we look at Fig. 1, we note that the more we delve into the heart of the legion, starting with the *hastati* and moving on to the *triarii* (the third line of soldiers), the value of the soldier increases, as does their age. Behind the *triarii* we witness an analogous but inverse process, with the progressive reduction in age and skill requirements. The disposition of the various soldiers in this *legio* is very important because it defines the peculiarity of its functioning mechanism of the legion, a procedure that was already present in the Romulean one and that in the Livian one we will find being exalted and more complex.

In fact, despite the fact that the name of the types of infantrymen forming the maniple remaining unchanged, the way of conceiving combat was changed, creating a break between what had been the Monarchical one and that of the Consular Age. The Romulean and Servian legions were based on deployments developed on the horizontal axis (although the formation of Servius Tullius was much deeper than the one conceived by Romulus), designed to stem the enemy front like a dam. However, in the early Consular Age, the development of the array changed from horizontal to vertical. The combat started to be based on the *ordines* (columns) and no longer on the *acies* as described by Livy,⁵⁰ fifteen units for each legion, divided into two groups called '*antepilani*' and '*pilani*', which appear as an evolution of the compact mass of the Servian formation. Ultimately we can note, that while in the *Legio Romulea* the single maniple, which included the three types of infantrymen (*hastati*, *principes* and *triarii*), represented the depth of the deployment, in the *Legio Liviana* it was the *ordo*, consisting of five *manipuli* (one of *hastati*, one of *principes*, one of *triarii*, one of *rorarii* and one of *accensi*) to determine the depth of the legion. The unity of the legion, from manipular in the Romulean one, had become 'ordal' in the Livian one.

Antepilani

The *antepilani* (literally 'those who are placed before the *pilani*'), were the soldiers who made up the front lines of the *manipulum*, among which we note the young *leves*, the *hastati* and the *principes*.

a) *Hastati* (and *leves*): Livy explains that the 'fifteen companies [*manipuli*]' were drawn up 'at a short distance from each other', thus informing us that the formation was compact with no spaces allowing the enemy to penetrate, and he continues by explaining that each maniple (of *hastati*) 'had light armed companies [*leves*], as whilst one-third carried a long spear [*hasta*] and short iron javelins, the remainder carried shields. This front line consisted of youths in the first bloom of manhood just old enough for service [*florem iuvenum pubescentium*]'.

The observation of J. Marquardt[51] is very interesting, connecting in this context young adolescents who possess the *hasta quiris* (free citizens), who have the right to be part of the state and its defence, and for this reason they were called *hastati*, while the withdrawal of the spear sanctioned their exclusion. Niebuhr hypothesises that the unit of *leves* was an organised body of *hastae* throwers, quite distinct from the *hastati* and *principes*, who opened the fight for the aforementioned maniples. This definition would place the *leves* in the position of the future *velites*, even if in some ways they would appear to be analogous to the *rorari*, infantrymen belonging to the *pilani* group. According to Livy, the *leves* were 'in the first bloom of manhood', and therefore would not have had the experience, nor the technical capacity and not even the armament suitable to support a melee, compared to the remaining body of *hastati* who, although also made up of young soldiers, had more experience and possessed a *gladius* and two *pila*.

The armament of the Livian *hastati* is well described by Polybius,[52] who specifies how they were protected by a wooden shield, a plumed bronze helmet, the *cardiophylax* and greaves, while as offensive weapons they possessed the *gladius*, which was carried on the right side and two javelins (*pila*). What we can see is that these infantrymen were an evolved form of the *hastati* of the *Legio Romulea*, but while the latter had only the possibility of throwing the *pila*, like the *leves*, these *hastati* were armed with a *gladius* and were able to support a fight with the enemy light infantry. In the Early Consular Age, therefore, the *hastati*, had acquired an intermediate combat capacity, such as to classify them as fighters positioned between the young *leves* and the mature *principes*. The role of these infantrymen, although not decisive to the outcome of a battle, had now assumed increased importance, as can be seen from the account of Frontinus, who explains how Fabius Rullus Maximus '... having vainly essayed in every way to break through the line of enemy, finally withdrew the *hastati* from the ranks ...',[53] or when the author describes the Battle of Palermo in 251 BC (in the First Punic War), where the consul, 'observing Hasdrubal's army, with the elephants in the front rank, ... ordered the *hastati* to hurl their javelins at the beasts and straightway to retire within their defence ...'.[54]

b) *Principes:* Livy's account continues with the description of the second line of *antepilani*: 'behind them [the *hastati*] were stationed an equal number of companies, called *principes*, made up of men in the full vigour of life, all carrying shields and furnished with superior weapons [*insignibus maxime armis*].'[55] Therefore, behind the fifteen maniples of *hastati*, there were an equal number of *principes*, who were of more mature age, similar to the *Legio Romulea*, and with armament similar to that described for the *hastati* but characterised by greater protection given by a *lorica conserta hamis* (ring mail armour) instead of the *cardiophylax*. This type of infantryman constituted the core of the legion, the fulcrum on which the hand-to-hand combat based on the *gladius* developed, even if, unlike in the *Legio Romulea*, they were no longer the only bearers of this weapon.

Pilani
Livy states that

> this body of thirty companies [in the front] were called the *antepilani*. Behind them were the standards under which were stationed [in the rear] fifteen companies, which were divided into three sections called *vexillae*, the first section in each was called the *pilus*, and they consisted of 180 men to every standard [*vexillum*]. Each *vexillum* had 60 soldiers, 2 *centuriones* and one *vexillarius*, for a total of 186 men.[56] The first *vexillum* was made up of the *triarii*, veterans of proved courage; the second by the *rorarii*, or 'skirmishers,' younger and less distinguished men; the third by the *accensi*, who were least to be depended upon, and were therefore placed in the rearmost line.'[57]

Behind the *antepilani* (which, we recall, consisted of a first row of fifteen maniples of *hastati* and a second of fifteen of *principes*), a further fifteen formations of *pilani* were lined up. Each *ordo* of *pilani* was divided into three maniples, which on this occasion Livy called *vexillae*, sixty *pedites* strong: the first was the *triarii*, made up of veterans, and behind them two banners of *ferentarii* were drawn up, the troops comprising the youngest and the least experienced, and lightly equipped,[58] divided into *rorarii* and *accensi* (both also sixty in number).

a) *Triarii*
As in the *Legio Romulea*, the *triarii* (or *pilani*) were made up of veterans and represented the last bastion of the battle array. Their armament, consisting of a spear and shield, suggests a static combat style, unlike that of the *hastati* and the *principes*, based mainly on the *pila* (the former) and on the *gladius* (the latter). These infantrymen had many similarities with the phalangites, as confirmed by both Livy and Vegetius. Livy explains that the *triarii*, in the meantime, 'were resting on one knee under their standards, their shields over their shoulders [*innixa umeris*: to be understood literally as 'positioned on the humerus, i.e. on the arm'] and their spears planted on the ground with the points upwards, giving them the appearance of a bristling palisade'.[59] Vegetius completes the description by saying that

> the *triarii* would wait in reserve behind their shields on bended knees, lest they be wounded while standing by oncoming missiles and, when circumstances required, would attack the enemy with more violence for having rested. They often gained the victory, it is said, after the *hastati* and those who stood at the front had fallen. However, in ancient times there were also men among the infantry called 'light armament', slingers, and light-armed troops.[60]

Fig. 2: Depiction of warriors in hoplitic armour from Praeneste (modern Palestrina, located 35km east of Rome), dating back to the fourth century BC. These infantrymen, with helmet, cuirass and greaves, equipped with spears, represent what must have been the characteristics of the *triarii* of the Livian *legio* of the fourth century BC. Cist lid from the necropolis of Colombella Preneste, depicting two warriors in hoplitic armour, carrying a wounded one. (*Courtesy of the National Etruscan Museum of Villa Giulia, Rome. Author's photo*)

Livy also underlines their decisive function by describing, in the words of the Latin commander Numisius, that 'their whole army was massacred, their *hastati* and *principes* killed; the companies both in front of and behind the standards had suffered enormous losses; the *triarii* in the end saved the situation'.[61] The *triarii* were the last resort to prevent the defeat of the army.

b) *Ferentarii*: *Rorarii* and *Accensi*

The body of the *ferentarii*, even if they did not constitute a real armed force and did not possess the *gladius*, deserves to be analysed for a more complete image of the entire military structure. This body is well described by Vegetius, who specifies that

> there were also in ancient times men among the infantry called 'light armament' [*ferentarii*] slingers, and light-armed troops. They were mainly located on the wings, and undertook the opening phase of the fighting. They were chosen for their great speed and fitness; they were not very numerous. If the course of battle compelled it, they would retire and be received between the front ranks of the legions, in such a way that the line remained unmoved.[62]

Plautus calls this type of soldier '*ferentarius amicus*'[63] in the meaning of 'loyal friend, of certain help if necessity arises', as specified by Varro when he describes them as '"third-line-men," because in the battle arrangement they were set in the rear, in the third line, as reserves; because these men habitually "sat" [*subsidebant*] while waiting, from this fact the *subsidia* "reserve force" got its name', whence Plautus says 'Come now, all of you sit by as troopers in reserve are wont'.[64]

Livy, mentioning the *rorarii* first, seems to give them greater importance, as can also be deduced from Plautus' comedy in which the appeal to a company is made: 'Where are you, *rorarii*? Behold, they're here. Where are the *accensi*? See, they're here.'[65] This was probably due to the fact that, as Varro explains, '*Rorarii* "skirmishers" were those who started the battle, named from the *ros* "dew-drop" because it *rorat* "sprinkles" before it really rains'.[66] This explains to us his affirmation that their role was similar to that of the later *velites*, which at this time did not yet exist, but who were integrated with the *leves*. These troops had been set up not to engage in hand-to-hand combat with the enemy, but to run in front of the array to launch javelins, creating skirmishes, and then retreat behind the *triarii*, as Livy also confirms: they 'rushed forward between the companies of *antepilani* and added strength to the *hastati* and *principes*, whilst the *triarii*, kneeling on their right knee, waited for the consul's signal to rise'.[67] However, this quote can also be interpreted in another way, that the *rorari* brought 'vigour' to the *antepilani* not so much by the support of thrown *pila*, but by replacing casualties in their ranks so that no gaps were created in the battle formation. Thanks to Nonius Marcellus, we know that they were dressed in a *paludamentum*, the military cloak, and armed with five javelins, held together in a gilded belt.[68]

The *accensi*, a term which Varro uses to mean 'auxiliary',[69] were instead placed in the rearmost ranks, probably used for 'support' functions, as Nonius confirms, describing that they brought the soldiers what they needed, for example weapons when broken and drinks when they were thirsty.[70] There is a quote from Livy where, describing a critical phase of a battle against the Latins, he emphasises the importance of the *accensi*, used in battle after the intervention of the *rorarii*, to which the consul 'gave orders for the *accensi* at the extreme rear to advance to the front. When they came up, the Latins, taking them for the opposing *triarii*, instantly called up their own.'[71]

According to Festus these soldiers were defined as '*accensi*' because they were surplus, in the sense that they replaced the soldiers who fell in battle: *ad censum legionis adscripti*. For this reason they were also called '*adscriptivi*', and Varro, quoting Plautus, confirms such usage: 'the *adscriptivi* enrolled as extras were so called because in the past men who did not receive arms used to be enrolled as extras, to take the place of the regularly armed soldiers if any of them should be killed'.[72]

In conclusion, even if there are some small discrepancies between the ancient authors on the function of the *ferentari*, in principle we can classify the *rorarii* as the precursors of the *velites*, and in the *accensi* we recognise those who brought logistical support to the soldiers during battle and replaced them when they fell to the blows of the enemy.

The numbers of the Livian *legio*

A correct reconstruction of the numbers of the various components of the *Legio Liviana* still remains very complex, since the ancient sources are not always easy to interpret. The biggest problems arise from Livy's text,[73] where the inconsistency of information has given rise over time to numerous interpretations, especially in the estimation of the last three *vexillae*. At the time of the Latin War (340–338 BC) the levy comprised two armies, one for each consul, each made up of two legions of 4,200–5,000 soldiers and 300 horsemen, for a total therefore of 16,800–20,000 infantry and 1,200 cavalrymen (i.e. 4 legions).

Analysing the numbers more carefully, the two *acies* of foot soldiers who were in front of the *triarii* (the *antepilani*) were made up of 15 maniples of 60 *hastati* and 15 of 60 *principes* each, for a total of 1,800 men (Diagram 1 and Plate 3). If we consider the 300 *leves* included in the calculation, the number of *antepilani* rises in this case to 2,100, while we know that there were two centurions per maniple (one per *centuria*), while there was only one standard bearer, but in this regard it should be noted that the historical sources tell us nothing about their exact position within the formation.

The Danish historian Niebhur,[74] considering that each of the thirty *curiae* (in which the three tribes of Rome were distinguished) served as the basis for conscription, hypothesised that each maniple was made up of sixty soldiers drawn from all the *curiae* and thus ultimately represented Rome itself.

While there are estimates for the number of *antepilani*, there are inconsistencies in the calculations of the number of *pilani*, since the various attempts by modern authors haven't produced unanimous results.

According to Niebuhr's interpretation of Livy's passage,[75] an *ordo* was made up of 1,620 men, for a total of 24,300 *pilani* (15 *ordo* of 1,620), a number that he himself considers to be excessive, while Marquardt,[76] considering that the total of a legion at the most was 5,200 men, believed that the *triarii* consisted of no more than 600 men, while the *rorarii* and *accensi* were no more than 1,000.

Delbrück,[77] like Fraccaro[78] and De Sanctis,[79] decided to completely reject Livy's idea relating to the last three groups, considering it corrupted; Conway managed to interpret correctly Livy's final step by moving the phrase '*ordo; sexagenos milites, duos centuriones, vexillarium unum habebat*' from the beginning of the passage to the end, making it possible to obtain the total of 2,790 men for the last three groups. Therefore, accepting the possibility of error, we can deduce that Livy attributes each formation of *pilani* being composed of 186 men, divided into 60 *triarii*, 60 *rorarii* and 60 *accensi* plus centurions, deducing that the three missing men, to reach the total of 186, are the *vexilliferi*. Finally, by multiplying 186 by the 15 *ordines*, we obtain a total number of 2,790, which were the infantrymen who made up the *pilani* of a legion.

We have reported a summary of what is still an ongoing discussion on the numbers of the Livian manipular legion, as we consider it correct to help the reader to understand how, in the absence of certain data, the hypotheses are innumerable and sometimes contradict each other. We prefer not to go deeper into the subject because, for our purposes, it is of little value, and it would remain pure speculation, not adding to the knowledge of the *gladius*.

	Age	No. Infantrymen for Legion	No. Infantrymen each Maniple	Officers and Non-commissioned Officers	Defensive Weapons	Offensive Weapons
LEVES	Youths in the first bloom of manhood	300	20			*Hasta* and javelins
HASTATI	Youths with some military experience	900	60	15 centurions, 15 *signiferi*	Helmet, shield, *kardiophylax*, greaves	2 *pila*, *gladius*
PRINCIPES	Mature men	900	60	15 centurions	Helmet, oblong shield, *lorica consertis hamis*	2 *pila*, *gladius*
TRIARII	Veterans	900	60	60 centurions, 30 *signiferi*	Helmet, round shield, *lorica*	Spear
RORARII	Young and the poor	900	60		*Paludamentum*	5 light spears
ACCENSI	Least to be depended upon	900	60			

Table 2: Summary of the characteristics of the various units (age, numerical composition and weapons they were equipped with) according to Conway's hypothesis, which is based on a hypothetical incorrect transcription of Livy's final passage.

III (A).2,2 The Maniple of Livian Battle
The *recursus*[80] (or *mutatio ordinis*)
The defeat on the Allia by the Gauls of Brennus and the failures against the Samnites, which culminated in the defeat at Caudium in 321 BC and in the humiliation of the Caudine Forks, forced the Romans to review their way of fighting. The need to confront enemies who used different tactics from those faced until now, such as deployment in larger battle arrays, dynamic fighting and guerrilla activity in harsh and mountainous terrain, led the Romans to reconsider both the formation of the army on the battlefield as well as its armament, in the context of a revolution that had also repercussions on a social level through the introduction of the *stipendium* and the ending of the system based on the census.

But if in this new historical context the combat intended as a simple clash between two forces, as in the *Legio Serviana*, had lost its effectiveness, the evolution that led to the adoption of a dynamic combat, represented by the *recursus*, was no more than the development of a mechanism already present since the time of the archaic *Legio Romulea*. We remember that when the *principes* of this *legio* were exhausted or overwhelmed, they retreated behind the ranks of the *triarii*. We do not know if this action was the end of the battle or if it was just a pause aimed at letting the infantrymen recover and to reorganise the *acies* before resuming combat, but it testifies how these dynamics already existed within the battle array.

Although the precise mechanism is not known, Livy's account is very explicit on its existence, explaining that when the battle formation of the army was completed, the *hastati* were the first to engage. If they failed to repulse the enemy, they slowly retired through the intervals between the companies of the *principes* who then took up the fight, the *hastati* following in their rear [*pede presso eos retro cedentes in intervalla ordinum principes recipiebant*].[81]

It is Livy himself who explains how this terrifying tactic worked: 'the enemy who had followed up the others as though they had defeated them, saw with dread a new and larger army rising apparently out of the earth.'[82] The fact that this change developed via the movement towards the rear of infantry ranks who had fought up until that moment explains why the enemy mistook it for a retreat when instead in reality it was an alternation of maniples.

During the battle, the clash could frequently remain uncertain to such an extent that, in the description of a fight against the Samnites, Livy narrates that 'the standards neither advanced nor retreated [*recursum*: this is the passage from which the Latin name of the alternation of infantry in combat is derived] in no direction was there any giving way. They fought, each man keeping his ground, pressing forward with their shields, neither looking back nor pausing for breath.'[83] This quote shows us how during a decisive fight, the insignia remained stationary to signal the soldiers that they had to continue to fight and how they did not 'look back' because this was the typical action in performing a retreat.

We have two examples of the *recursus* (or *mutatio ordinis*) from the war against the Etruscans that took place near Lake Vadimone in the years 311–309 BC. The first is from the battle for the liberation of the allied city of Sutri: the Etruscans and the Romans

> rushed to the fight with violent animosity; the enemy were superior in numbers, the Romans in valour. The battle being doubtful, carried off great numbers on both sides, particularly the men of greatest courage; nor did victory declare itself, until the second line [*secunda acies*] of the Romans came up fresh to the front, in the place of the first [*prima signa*], who were much fatigued. The Etrurians, because their front line was not supported by any fresh reserves, fell all before and round the standards.[84]

The decisive turning point was the replacement of the first *acies*, whose men were exhausted by having fought up until then, by the unengaged second *acies*. Since there was no possibility of such change in the Etruscan front, the latter, tired, found themselves fighting against fresh troops who overwhelmed them.

The second example comes from the final battle:

> the battle began with swords [*gladii*], and, furious at the outset, waxed hotter as the struggle continued, for the victory was long undecided. It seemed as though the Romans were contending, not with the so oft defeated Etruscans, but with some new race. No sign of flight was visible in any quarter. As the front-rankers

fell, the second line moved up to replace the first, that the standards might not want defenders. After that the last reserves were called upon; and to such extremity of distress and danger did the Romans come that their cavalry dismounted, and made their way over arms and over bodies to the front ranks of the infantry. Like a fresh line springing up amongst the exhausted combatants, they wrought havoc in the companies of the Etruscans. Then the rest of the soldiers, following up their charge, despite their weariness, at last broke through the enemy's ranks.[85]

In summary, with the defeat of the maniples of *hastati* and *principes* (the *antesignani*), the *triarii* became the first group to be joined by the horsemen who, dismounting, began to fight in the front rank, claiming a victory over the enemy.

As we have already learned from the most archaic formation, the function of the *triarii* was to be the last resource. Livy helps us to understand this by explaining that,

if the *principes*, too, were unsuccessful in their fight, they fell back slowly from the battle-line on the *triarii*. (From this arose the adage, 'to have come to the *triarii*' [*ad triarios redisse*], when things are going badly.) The *triarii*, rising up after they had received the *principes* and *hastati* into the intervals between their companies, would at once draw their companies together [*compressis ordinibus*] and close the lanes, as it were; then, with no more reserves behind to count on, they would charge the enemy in one compact array [*continenti agmine*]. This was a thing exceedingly disheartening to the enemy, who, pursuing those whom they supposed they had conquered, all at once beheld a new line rising up, with augmented numbers.[86]

A further explanation of the function of the *triarii* comes from a quote by Marcus Servius Honoratus, a grammarian of the end of the fourth century AD:

The Ausonian Legion advances, and the armed squadron [*pilata plenis*] pour forth at the crowded gates.
   On the other side the full Trojan and Tuscan army with various arms rush to the field,
   No otherwise arranged in battle array, with sword in hand, than if he summoned to the fierce combat of Mars.
   … and as soon as, upon the signal given, each man to his station retired, they fix down their spears [*hastae*] in the ground.[87]

In this description, the Italic legion (defined as *ausònia*) is compared to a building from whose doors soldiers armed with *hastae* emerge from the body of the *triarii*. The opposing side, ready to fight, is equipped with various Trojan-type weapons (it is doubtful whether we must understand them as a certain type of spears or as *gladii*, referring to the metaphor that the Romans were descendants of Aeneas and in this case the Tyrrhenian weapons would refer to the Etruscan ones). But as soon as the signal was given 'everyone returned to his space' in the sense that the *triarii* redistributed themselves by closing up the individual spaces through which the *principes* had passed to the rear. At this point the *pilani*, kneeling, planted the long spears on the ground and, leaning them on their shield, created a solid barrier bristling with *hastae* that prevented the breakthrough of the front.[88] After explaining the complex mechanism of alternating troops within the formation by the Roman army, the doubt that arises in the opponent is useful in carrying out a series of such complex manoeuvres, movements that involved a well-coordinated army, where it was easy for the benefits to turn into disadvantages in the chaos of battle. The answer is probably inherent in the question, in the sense that the *recursus* was adopted to avoid the disruption of the formation caused by attacks, retreats and deaths that normally occurred in a fight. We must understand that during a battle, in order to keep the front intact, the empty spaces in the front ranks left by casualties were filled by the soldiers from the rear ranks. This entailed a progressive slipping forward of the soldiers so, in theory, the front always remained straight while the rear ranks assumed an irregular appearance, causing their depth to diminish (Fig. 4).

In a deployment where the *recursus* was not practised, as in the Etruscan army, it was essential that the formation had greater depth, consisting of numerous ranks of soldiers. The *milites* in the front ranks fought to the point of exhaustion, as long as they were not killed or forced to leave the fight, and were then replaced by the soldiers from the rear ranks. The greatest effort was therefore focused on the front half of the formation, while the soldiers in the last ranks would fight only in cases of extreme danger (therefore they mostly remained unused). Furthermore, with this approach, soldiers who were already tired would have been present in the front line, together with fresh *milites*. This was less effective for obvious reasons and tended to be less resistant. On the contrary, the Roman army appeared much more efficient because it was divided into small formations that could alternate with each other, so that it could repeatedly present the enemy with a completely fresh and intact formation. Machiavelli, in commenting on the *mutatio*, exalted its validity by affirming that it was 'difficult for

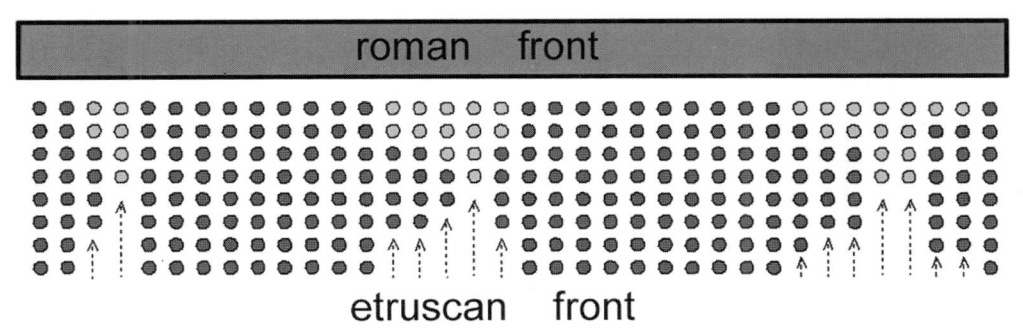

Fig. 3: Theoretical representation of a compact array, not divided into separate orders, such as the Etruscan one might have been. During a battle, in this type of formation, the soldiers in the front ranks were directly engaged in combat, while those in the rear remained inactive, waiting to move forward to replace their killed comrades and start fighting. In all the ancient armies, which fought in formation, to avoid defeat it was essential to keep the front line intact, so casualties had to be replaced by the soldiers from the rear ranks (gray dots). Replacing the front-rank casualties involved the rear-rank soldiers sliding forward, causing a progressive reduction in the thickness of the deployment. (*Author's drawing*)

142   The Roman Gladius and the Ancient Fighting Techniques

luck to abandon you three times and that the enemy has so much virtue that it beats you three times',[89] allowing the reader to understand how Roman army engaged against the same enemy with three different formations, therefore an eventual defeat was only possible in truly extreme situations.

The actual way the *recursus* happened is an endless source of hypotheses amongst scholars and of reconstructive conjectures among the various groups of re-enactors. The observation of Battaglia and Ventura is interesting, who tried to explain the manoeuvre of the maniples beginning with the statement of Vegetius.[90] The Latin writer says that 'the centuries were themselves subdivided into 10-man sections. For every ten soldiers living under one tent, there was one in charge as "dean", now called "section-captain". The 10-man section used to be called a "maniple" because they fought in groups joined together [*quod coniunctis manibus partier*, literally 'as a pair of joined hands'].'[91] Even if the numbers of the unit (synonymous with the *contubernium*) do not correspond with Livy and Vegetius,[92] the metaphor of the 'fingers of two hands joined' (Fig. 5) is fundamental for understanding the *recursus*. The soldiers of two units, like the fingers of two joined hands, could form a tight array and separate again, without losing their cohesion.

To explain this 'mutation' in detail, Battaglia and Ventura focused on the basic mechanism of the unit, the alternation of the two centuries of a maniple. Based on experimental archaeology, the two authors hypothesise that the soldiers of the 'paired' rows, belonging to the *acies* of the *hastati*, for example, performed the *recursus* by taking

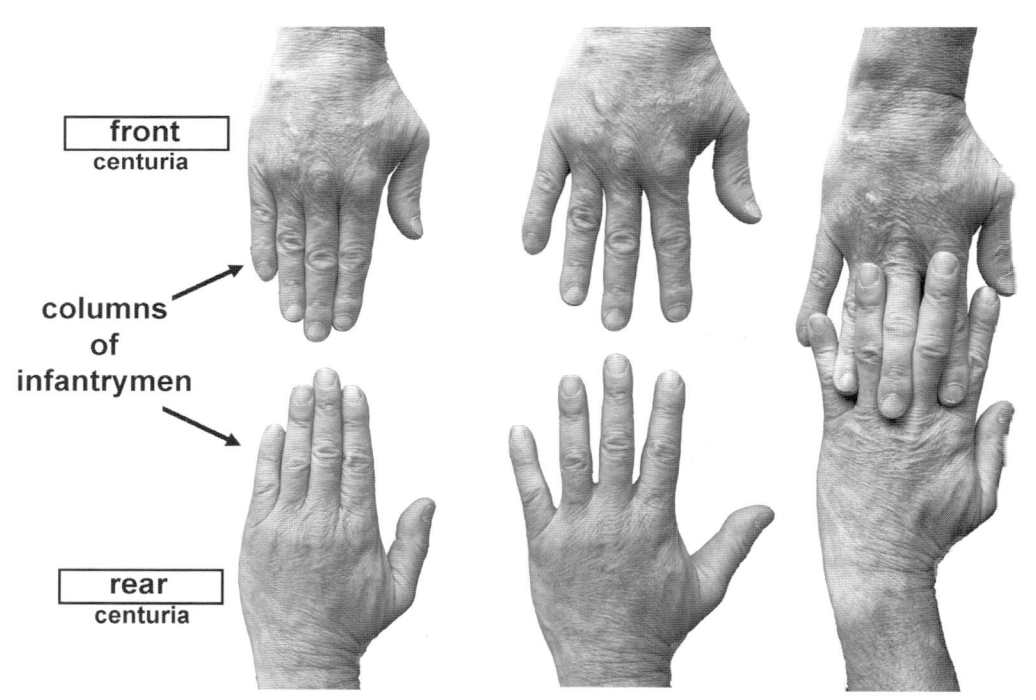

Fig. 4: Representation through the use of the fingers of the *mutatio ordinis* (or *recursus*). The hands have both fingers joined together (which metaphorically are the rows of close-order soldiers), and when joined together, the latter can intertwine without losing cohesion. (*Author's photo*)

a step backwards and to their right (therefore oblique), so that, entering inside the column of soldiers on the right (Fig. 6) they transformed the century from ten columns to five.

Therefore, as can be seen from the drawing, the continuous front of ten columns of infantry thinned out into five columns and five empty lanes; at the same time the columns of soldiers doubled in number of fighters so that one made up of three soldiers became one of six. The two centuries, became like the fingers of two hands, ready to intersect, allowing the column of soldiers of the front century to pass through the lanes

STEP 1) - starting position

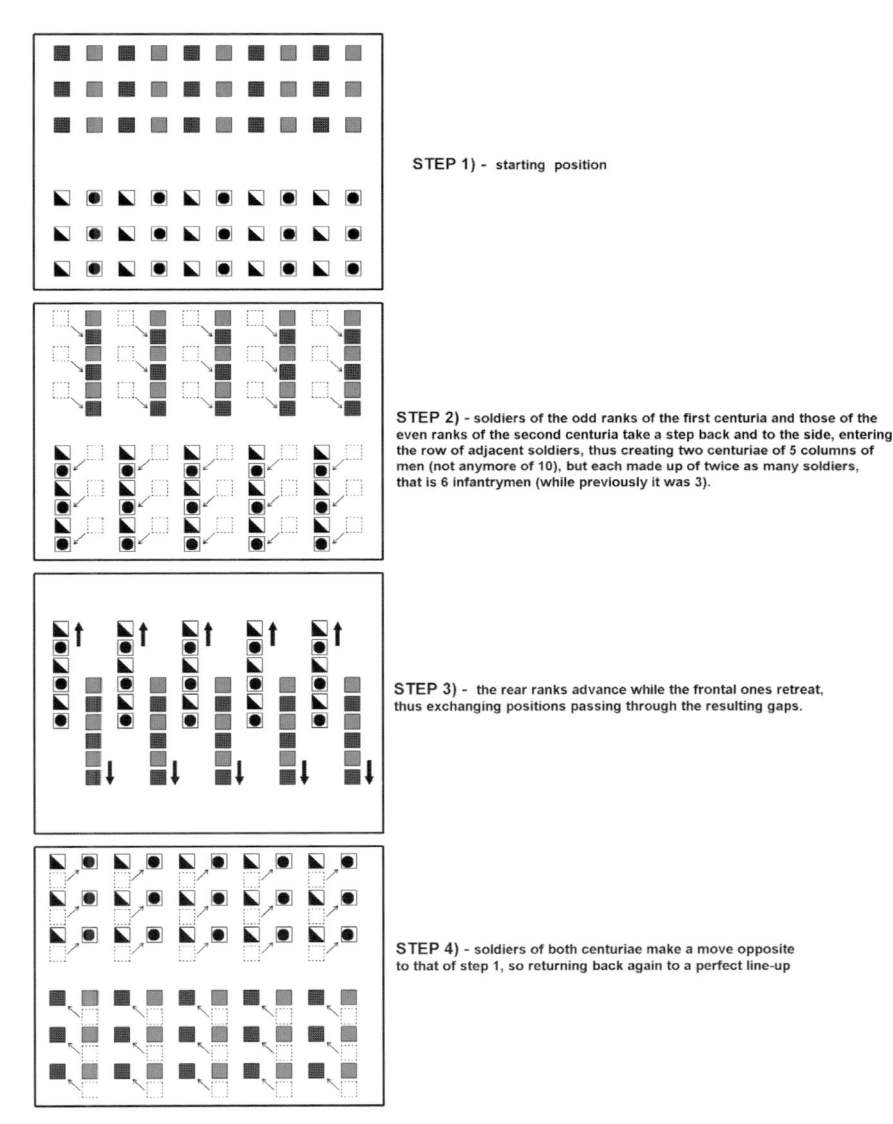

STEP 2) - soldiers of the odd ranks of the first centuria and those of the even ranks of the second centuria take a step back and to the side, entering the row of adjacent soldiers, thus creating two centuriae of 5 columns of men (not anymore of 10), but each made up of twice as many soldiers, that is 6 infantrymen (while previously it was 3).

STEP 3) - the rear ranks advance while the frontal ones retreat, thus exchanging positions passing through the resulting gaps.

STEP 4) - soldiers of both centuriae make a move opposite to that of step 1, so returning back again to a perfect line-up

Fig. 5: The *recursus* or *mutatio ordinis* (exchange of position among two centuries). At the end of phase 4 we see all of the infantry in the starting position, but the position of the centuries has been reversed. With proper training, the manoeuvre takes only a few seconds. (*Author's drawing*)

in the rear one. This hypothesis, given the simplicity of its execution, appears very credible, so much so that we prefer to quote the authors' words:

> we can understand how a maniple in *prima acies* could instantly open intervals with a single step, halving the number of soldiers on the front. And if the arrangement at open intervals was also assumed by the maniple behind, it can be understood how one could move backwards, being absorbed in the intervals of the other and finally 'parked' behind it, with a simple vertical movement. Closing the front after the change was then simply a matter of one diagonal step …[93]

From the enemy's point of view, a *mutatio* took place through a cession of ground, so that the opponents 'who, pursuing those whom they supposed they had conquered, all at once beheld a new line rising up, with augmented number'.[94] The Romans, therefore, performed the movement by retreating, being the safest way to do it, like a Renaissance swordsman in difficulty during a duel, who moves backwards and then leaves the fight (but in this case the retreat was only to replace the tired fighter with a fresh one in the front rank).

Like in the *Legio Romulea*, we do not know if the phenomenon occurred in just one direction, only to the rear, allowing each maniple only to fight once, or if the *recursus* could take place in both directions. In the latter case, during a lull in the fighting, the *hastati* who had already fought and had retreated behind the *principes*, could move back to the front through a forward *mutatio*, after having rested and the killed and/or wounded infantry quickly replaced by the *ferentarii*. When the troops of the *antepilani* were exhausted or the losses were very high, the *recursus* with the *triarii* took place.

We can summarise that the Romans perfected the system of the 'retreat' of the *principes* behind the *triarii*, present since the Romulean legion, developing a more articulated and efficient mechanism, enabling them to face the enemy front always with fresh infantry. From this point of view, the *Mutatio Ordinis* was a revolution in the way of conceiving combat as it quickly allowed them to prevail over all other forces, which continued to fight with static troops in their battle-array.

The development of the battle

The troops of the *Legio Romulea* and of the early Consular one shared the same names and, albeit in a different way, replicated their arrangement. In fact, in both of the legions, the *hastati* formed the first front (*acies*), the *principes* the middle one and the *triarii* the rear. The main change introduced was represented by the deployment, which evolved from a continuous and compact one, into separate maniples, revealing a certain autonomy in combat. Even more important was that the *hastati* ceased to be light troops, leaving that task to the *leves* and *rorarii*, the latter representing the embryo of the future *velites*. This statement is reasonable because in the fifth century BC Livy arms the *hastati* with the *pilum* and *gladius*, like the *principes*, becoming front-line fighters, even if with lower technical skills. Thus from a single fighting body, limited only to the *principes* of the Monarchical era, it changed to two in the Republican era, while the *triarii* remained the final line, as can also be understood from the Polybian statement 'armed with spear instead of *pila*',[95] in addition to also having, as described by Dionysius of Halicarnassus, the function of protecting the *castrum* from attack:

> when [the Volscii], after attacking the hill and surrounding the camp, endeavoured to pull down the palisades, first the Roman horse, obliged, from the nature of the ground, to fight on foot, sallied out against them, and, behind the horse, those they call the *triarii*, with their ranks closed. These are the oldest soldiers, to whom they commit the guarding of the camp when they go out to give battle, and they fall back of necessity upon these as their last hope when there has been a general slaughter of the younger men and they lack other reinforcements.[96]

When imagining a Livian legion in battle, we should think that the first action was conducted by the *leves*, inexperienced young men, probably supported by the *rorarii*, who swarmed in the neutral ground between the two sides, throwing javelins like the future *velites*. This would not have caused much damage to the enemy lines, so this was probably aimed more at provoking the enemy into a premature and disorderly attack. However, when the enemy ranks began to advance, the action passed to the *hastati* armed with two *pila* each. These were throw to disrupt the enemy front ranks, as soon as the enemy soldiers were at a close enough distance: we should imagine 120 *pila* per maniple, for a total of 1,800 missiles (after those launched by 300 *leves* and 900 *rorarii*) being thrown against the opposing front, forming a rain of death. At the same time, thanks to their elongated shield, the *scutum*, the *hastati* could protect themselves from the javelins that were thrown by the enemy. At this point the infantrymen drew the *gladius*, ready to meet the first enemy attack in close combat, the duration and effectiveness of which had to be limited due to the youth and relative inexperience of the fighters.

The clash with the enemy lasted until the centurions judged that the maniple they commanded was no longer able to withstand the enemy attack, so, with the movement of the *signum*, the *recursus* was ordered and carried out. At this point, the *hastati*, following the signal, retreated behind the ranks of the *principes*, so that these swordsmen, younger and by now exhausted, were replaced by more mature and skilled fighters. The *principes*, protected by armour, regardless of whether it was a *cardiophylax* or a *lorica consertis hamis*, continued to fight the enemy in close combat, keeping the ranks in close order (but without overlapping shields as for hoplites), to prevent the enemy breaking the line.

In the meantime the *accensi* reached the tired *hastati* to bring water or replace the lost or damaged *gladius*, or to take the place of those who had been killed, in order to restore the maniple's strength for a resumed fight (without leaving gaps in the battle-array).

The *principes* continued to fight as long as they were able to. At this point, two possibilities opened up: during a lull in the fighting, the *hastati* could, thanks to a new *mutatio*, return to the front ready to fight again, or the *principes* could retreat behind the *triarii*, the last hope for the Romans. The ancient authors do not elucidate if the *recursus* took place only with the alternation of the maniple, or also to determine the rotation of the Centuries so that the front was replaced by the second line.

146 The Roman Gladius and the Ancient Fighting Techniques

Furthermore, it is a subject of discussion whether the *mutatio* was 'unidirectional', where the units that had already fought could not return to the front, or 'bidirectional', introducing the possibility that those centuries and maniples could reappear at the front through a reverse movement to fight. This scenario would involve a forward movement by the troops, that could only take place during a lull in the battle, when the front was not under the pressure of enemy attack. The *triarii*, after having allowed the *principes* to pass through, would have risen from the kneeling position, closing their ranks, and after having uttered a war cry, would have advanced with bristling spears to block and/or unhinge the enemy troops with an effectiveness equal to that of a porcupine.

We are far from the 'hammer' effect of a hoplitic thrust, the purpose of which was to stop the enemy lines in a passive way. The Roman army had developed a combat

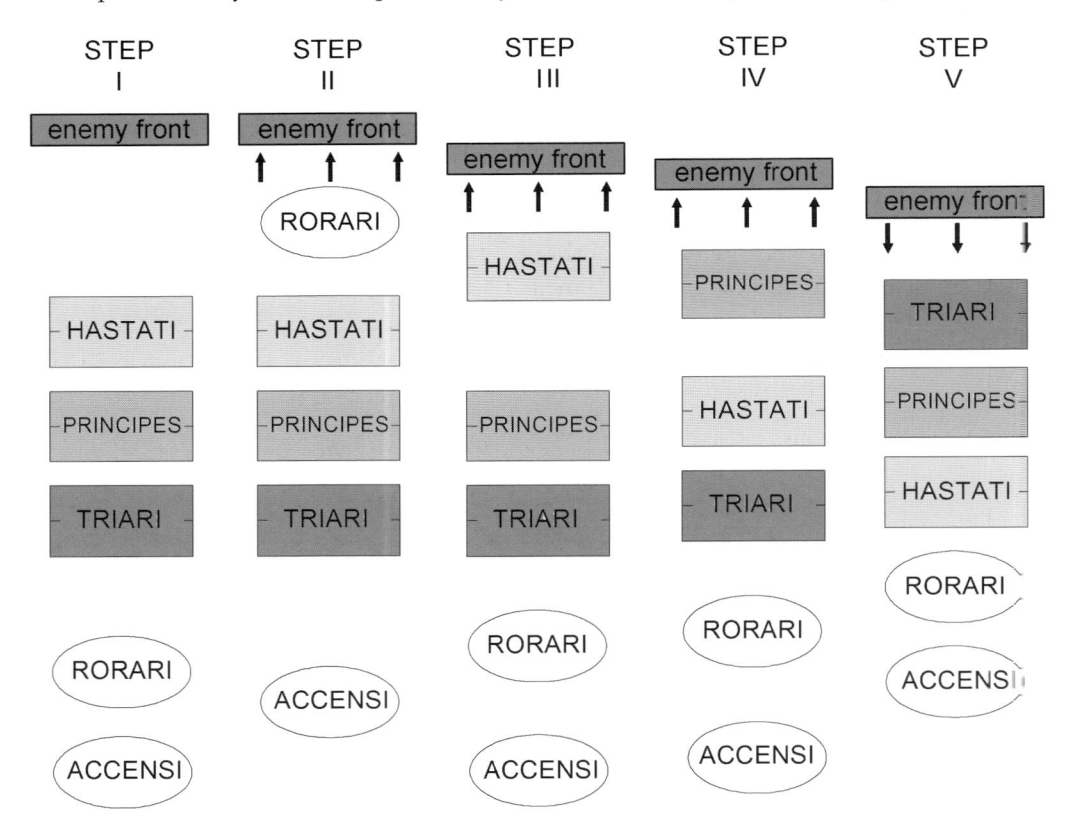

Fig. 6: Dynamics of the battle of the Livian *legio*.
- Phase 1: the armies oppose each other;
- Phase 2: the disruption by the *rorarii* begins;
- Phase 3: immediately afterwards the combat begins, carried out by the *hastati*;
- Phase 4: *recursus*: the *principes* enter combat replacing the *hastati*. We can hypothesise that through repeated *mutatio*, the *hastati* and *principes* could repeat this phase of the fight after being supported by the *ferentari*;
- Phase 5: Now the protagonists are the *triarii*. When both *hastati* and *principes* are exhausted, the order is given to retreat behind the *triarii* which, with a pseudo-phalangitic deployment, are the last chance to obstruct the enemy assault and protect the other troops. (*Author's drawing*)

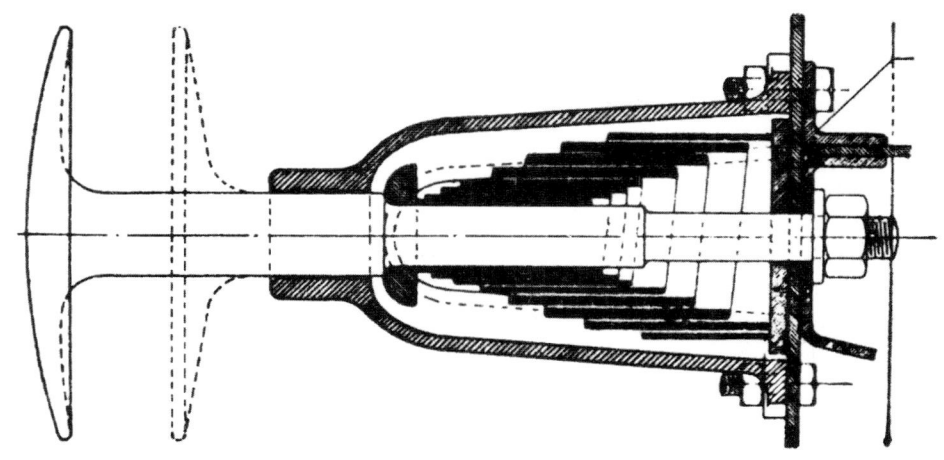

Fig. 7: Buffer of a train that metaphorically illustrates the mechanism to which the Roman army was based on. Subjected to an enemy attack, the Roman maniples withdrew and alternated increasing resistance until they reached the blocking point represented by the *triarii*, functioning similarly to a buffer. (*Author's drawing*)

system where the 'monomachy' was multiplied by all the infantrymen that formed the front, defined as *acies* by the ancient authors. The use of this word is effective because it shows us what function it had. *Acies* means 'host', but also has the meaning of 'tip', 'cutting edge', 'sharp cut', for which, by metonymy, it acquires the meaning of a sword, the task possessed by the front, to hit the enemy with the blade. Consequently, while

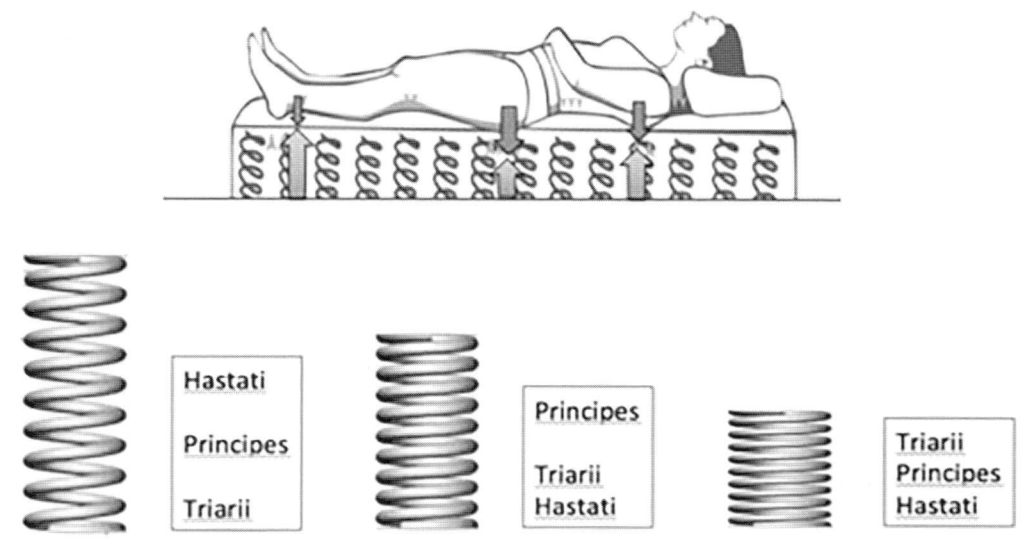

Fig. 8: Schematic and metaphorical representation of the functioning of the Livian manipular legion of the Early Consular Age. The springs of a mattress represent the column of *antepilani* and *pilani*, which in the case of a bed must support the sleeper by adapting to the different weight of the individual anatomical parts, just as the Roman army had to adapt to the enemy thrust which invariably was different in various points of the clash. The adaptability of the Roman army made it easier to hold the front line. (*Author's drawing*)

the *pedites* of the first row fought as if to sustain a duel against an enemy infantryman, by definition the front assumed the idealised figure of a *gladius* who was figuratively going to defeat the enemy.

It is important to understand the concept of Roman soldiers' fencing in this context, which must not be understood as the archaic duels with the 'buckler' (see Chapter I, 2.4) – where the contenders studied each other by turning around a theoretical axis to find the enemy's weak point – nor as the medieval ones where the soldiers fought in a confused scuffle. The *milites* fought holding their position and maintaining a united front, because it was essential to avoid creating a melee, even if sometimes it was inevitable.[97] In fact, the victory for the battle array was based on the united front, which had to be impenetrable to the enemy, and on maintaining the compactness of the maniples and the order of the ranks of soldiers, which allowed the replacement of exhausted troops with fresh and stronger reinforcements from the rear.

Metaphorically, a unit of *antepilani* and *pilani* behaved like the 'buffers of a train', which, when subjected to pressure, retracts, gradually increasing its rigidity (Fig. 7). This retraction and the progressive increase in combat strength decreased the damage caused by the attack of the enemy army, because its vehemence was weakened by fresh and progressively more capable troops, up to the blocking point represented by the *triarii*.

Continuing with the metaphors, the Roman legion of the early-middle Consular Age can be described as the profile of a spring mattress, where each spring represents a schematic column of *antepilani* and *pilani*. The mattress (the legion), despite being a single object, is formed by numerous springs, some of which will be more compressed because they will have to support a greater weight (such as the shoulders and buttocks of the sleeper) while others will be more extended, where the weight supported is less (such as the legs) (Fig. 8).

Similarly, the legion adapted to the various attacks of the enemy front, so in the points where the enemy attacks were more aggressive, the *antepilani* retreated until they reached the *pilani*, simulating compressed springs, while, where the enemy was less impetuous, the fight could be continued by the *hastati* or the *principes*, simulating the extended or partially-compressed springs respectively.

Despite the great advantage of the army of this period had in being able to adapt according to the enemy force, it remained, like the Monarchical one, a single, cumbersome formation, and for this reason, as well as certain advantages, limitations began to emerge.

III (A).2,3 The limits of the Livian legio
The Livian manipular legion was successful until the fourth century BC, when the Romans clashed with new enemies against whom this military approach was ineffective.

The confrontation against the Gallic hordes was a completely new situation because the Romans had to face an army that often presented a very vast front, far more extensive than the Capitoline one, and attacked in a disorderly mass with great speed and aggression. The orderly Roman ranks were often in difficulty in sustaining such pressure, especially at the concentrated points of attack at the front, as well as on the flanks of the formation, because of the fact that the maniples were set up to sustain a frontal attack, not one from the side.

The Samnites, on the other hand, waged a guerrilla war in mountainous terrain. Military actions were never a clash of two organised formations, structured in a similar way, as the Roman legion was used to up until this time. In isolated skirmishes, very small and mobile units attacked the large Roman formations which found themselves totally inadequate both in defence and in attack. Finally, the Hellenistic and Carthaginian armies, even more so than the previous ones, highlighted the great limitation of the Roman system of attack which, as Giovanni Brizzi affirms, was devoted to a frontal collision only, but was immediately in difficulty against the enveloping manoeuvre of the Hellenistic school. The basic movements were still extremely repetitive and mechanical; the legion could oppose the action of the *pezeteri*[98] only by repeated direct attacks by its units, courageous suicidal attacks, destined to break like waves on the rocks against a massive block of men which, at least from the front, was completely impenetrable. The way of fighting of first Pyrrhus and later of the Macedonian armies, was aimed at neutralising the Roman frontal attack through an 'impenetrable wall';[99] but the great evolution came with Hannibal's strategy, which understood how victory could be achieved not through a frontal fight, for which Roman effectiveness was developed for, but aiming at the weak point represented by the flanks.

For a better understanding of the problems that the Romans had to face, starting from a certain historical moment, we highlight the peculiarities of the Macedonian army and Hannibal's tactics, which had a great influence on the military changes that led to the transition from the Livian legion to the Polybian one.

The Macedonian phalanx

In 280 BC, the new military reality the Romans had to face was the invasion of Pyrrhus, ruler of Epirus, called in by the city of Taranto to counter the advance of Rome in Magna Graecia. The Epirote army was strongly influenced by the Greek, Macedonian and Thracian military traditions, assisted by a cavalry developed on the Alexandrian model and, above all, characterised by the support of elephants, against which among the Romans, panic overcame the military virtues. The big technical innovation with which the Romans clashed were the *sarissas*, pikes 5–7m long, which prevented the Roman infantry from reaching hand-to-hand combat against the Epirote infantry, effectively hindering the military action that was based on the blows of the *gladius*. Polybius says that against a Macedonian phalanx,

> one Roman must stand opposite two men in the first rank of the phalanx, so that he has to face and encounter ten pikes, and it is both impossible for a single man to cut through them all in time once they are at close quarters and by no means easy to force their points away, as the rear ranks can be of no help to the front rank either in thus forcing the pikes away or in the use of the sword.[100]

The major limitation on the effectiveness of the Macedonian phalanx was that it had to maintain the compactness of the array, since the slightest disorder could lead to its

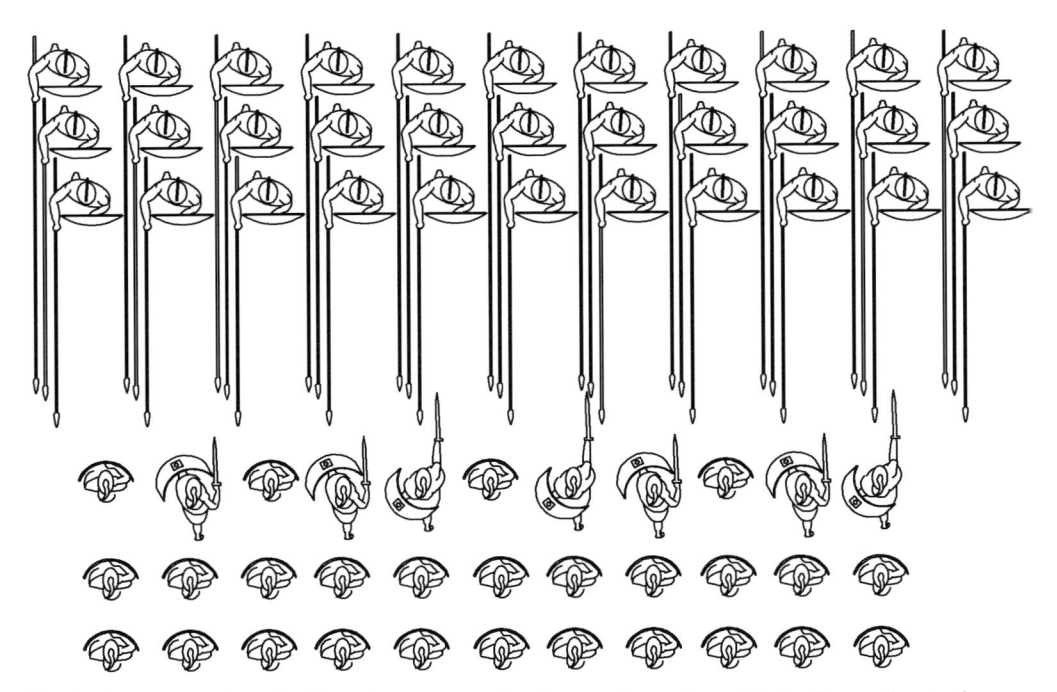

Fig. 9: An army equipped with *sarissae* prevented a close confrontation with the Roman host, who were unable to come into contact with the enemy and therefore to carry out their combat based on the *gladius*. (*Author's drawing*)

total disintegration. For this reason, 'the phalanx requires level and clear ground with no obstacles such as ditches, clefts, and clumps of trees, ridges and water courses, all of which are sufficient to impede and break up such a formation'.[101] Based on this weakness, the Romans tried to break up the Macedonian formation by noting that 'the phalanx drives back by its charge the force opposed to it or is repulsed by this force, its own peculiar formation is broken up. For either in following up a retreating foe or in flying before an attacking foe, they leave behind the other parts of their own army, upon which the enemy's reserve [the Romans of course had a reserve line] have room enough in the space formerly held by the phalanx to attack no longer in front but appearing by a lateral movement on the flank and rear of the phalanx.'[102]

As Polybius tells us, the Romans understood that the fight could no longer be based only on a head-on collision, but had to evolve to manage a multidirectional attack: this lesson was only fully understood after the various defeats suffered at the hands of Hannibal.

Hannibal

The Punic Wars were fought between the third and second century BC (the first between 264 and 241 BC, the second between 218 and 202 BC and the third between 149 and 146 BC), and it is precisely on these occasions that the Romans were able to ascertain the limits of their own legion. While the Romans relied 'in the victories that had been won … on the numbers and the bravery of their men … [Hannibal] on the contrary, preferred to manœuvre; to conduct the affair by strategy, not by force, and to make it a contest'.[103] Hannibal always managed to conduct the clashes in favour of his strengths, such as the cavalry,[104] that Livy remembers being predominant, and shrewdly avoiding the frontal attack of the Roman army. Thus he overwhelmed the Capitoline forces, using enveloping manoeuvres both in the battles of the Ticinum and Trebbia, but above all at the Battle of Cannae, where he used 'the circumvention' of both wings of the Roman army, in order to attack it from the flanks and behind, overwhelming it.

Like Pyrrhus, the Carthaginians also made use of elephants in order to fortify the weakest part of their array, to support the attack of the horsemen as well as to reduce the vehemence of the Roman attack. To metaphorically describe their effect, the pachyderms were like bowling balls thrown against the pins, which with their size, associated with physical strength and terror, managed to disorder the ranks, condemning them to defeat.

Finally we must consider that the Carthaginians fought with no respect for the rules and rituals of combat to which the Romans were used to operate under, so much so that Livy, although he praised the Barcids as generals of quality and value (*tantas viri virtutes ingentia*), despised them for the immense cruelty and typically Carthaginian treachery (*inhumana crudelitas, perfidia plus quam Punica*). The Roman claimed that the Punics, by their behaviour, held the most sacred things, the gods and the oaths, in contempt,[105] but the real problem was that they did not respect the rituals of battle that the Romans were used to when they fought with neighbouring peoples.

Polybius comments that the Romans 'met with defeat not owing to their equipment and formation but owing to Hannibal's skill … when the Romans had the advantage of the services of a general of like capacity with Hannibal then victory was an immediate consequence of this'.[106] Probably, the most correct analysis is the Carthaginian general had understood the limits of the Roman battle-array and took advantage of it to inflict repeated defeats, and only when the Romans were able to field an array that overcame these inadequacies, could regain military supremacy.

III (A).2,4 The Polybian legio (proto-cohortal) of the second century BC
The Polybian *legio* must be understood as a transitional formation between the Livian legion to the cohortal one. It was described by the Greek author in the second century BC, but there are sources suggesting it had already been adopted before this. For example, in 504 BC the Battle of Fidene took place, against a coalition of Sabines and Fidenates, led by the son of Tarquinius Superbus, Sextus Tarquinius. Here, 'the Romans were lying in wait by cohorts [*speirai*] between the ditches and the palisades, being unperceived by reason of the darkness; and they kept killing those of the enemy who crossed over, as soon as they came within reach …'.[107] From this reference, apart from the real meaning of the Greek terms '*lochos*' and '*speira*' which Dionysius of Halicarnassus does not always use consistently for the respective meaning of *manipulus*

Triarii (+ Velites)
(20 centuriae)

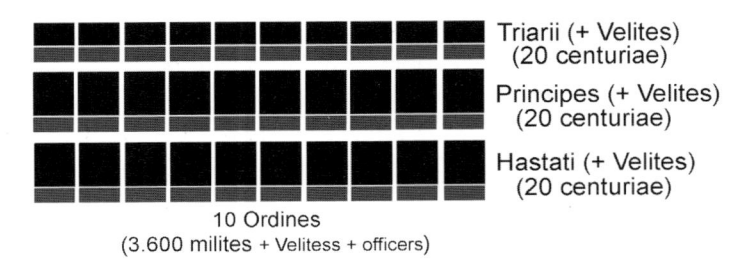

Principes (+ Velites)
(20 centuriae)

Hastati (+ Velites)
(20 centuriae)

10 Ordines
(3.600 milites + Velitess + officers)

Diagram 2: The Polybian *legio*. (*Author's drawing*)

and *centuria* or cohort, it seems possible that already in the Early Consular Age parts of a legion could carry out attacks. This was in contrast with the Livian manipular system, organised in fifteen *ordines* of five *manipuli* each, which were optimised as a whole within the *ordo*, but structurally weak individually. This led to the development of a stronger and at the same time more agile structure.

Furthermore, we must remember that changes in the Roman world always occurred slowly, and were linked to traditions. This mind-set led to the coexistence of novelties with old approaches, so that defining a precise date for the appearance of a certain innovation is almost impossible, and all modern attempts risk becoming mere dissertations for their own sake.

If we were to schematically present the Polybian legion, unlike the Livian one drawn up in fifteen parallel vertical lines anchored on a horizontal one (the latter representing the *triarii*), it would be represented by ten vertical lines divided into three segments, thus defining the autonomy of each maniple (Diagram 2-B).

In the following paragraphs we will review the description of the individual bodies, both to understand them better and above all to contextualise the changes in the light of the conditions that the Romans faced.

Velites

The establishment of the *velites* is described by Livy in the context of the siege of the city of Capua in 210 BC, during the Second Punic War. After two years of fruitless attempts to make the Campanian town capitulate, which resisted due to the Carthaginian cavalry, the Paduan historian says that 'at length a method was devised [by the Romans], so that what was lacking to their strength might be compensated by skilful tactics'. He continues:

> Out of all the legions were picked young men who by reason of strength and lightness of build were the swiftest. These were furnished with round shields of smaller size than those used by cavalry, and seven javelins apiece four feet [118.6cm] long and having iron heads such as are on the spears of the light-armed troops. The horsemen would each of them take one of these men on to their own horses, and they trained them both to ride behind and to leap down nimbly when the signal was given.

The Capuans were put to flight by the 'infantry line suddenly dashing out from the cavalry at the enemy's horsemen, and while attacking they hurl one javelin after another; by throwing a great number of these against horses and men in all directions, they wounded very many. But more consternation was created by the strange and the unexpected, and the cavalry charging into the frightened enemy caused them to flee with slaughter all the way to the gates.'[108] These soldiers succeeded the *rorarii* and the *accensi*, and differed from them by not being divided into companies, nor being deployed behind the *triarii*. As can be deduced from Livy's description, during the war against the Gauls of Asia, such a light infantryman 'carries a three-foot shield and, in his right hand, javelins which he uses at long range; he is also equipped with a Spanish sword [*gladio Hispaniensi est cinctus*].'[109]

Polybius shares many points with Livy in describing them, classifying them first of all as drawn from among the youngest and poorest and attributing the same armament to them, defining the sword as μάχαιρα, but his detailed description of their javelin suggests that the latter was the main weapon: 'The wooden shaft of the javelin measures about two cubits [88.9cm] in length and is about a finger's breadth [1.85cm] in thickness; its head is a span [20cm] long hammered out to such a fine edge that it is necessarily bent by the first impact, and the enemy is unable to return it. If this were not so, the missile would be available for both sides.' In describing them, the Greek author highlights how they wore particular clothing, namely a 'plain helmet, and sometimes cover it with a wolf's skin or something similar both to protect and to act as a distinguishing mark by which their officers can recognise them and judge if they fight pluckily or not'.[110]

Their action was not only to wreak havoc, but to carry out actual attacks, because they were armed 'alike for defence or offence'.[111] Being an additional flexible force, outside the main battle-array, they had the function of opening the battle by damaging the cohesion of the enemy army, thus exposing it to the counter-attack of the Roman heavy infantry, in addition to protecting the flanks of their own army. Based on various battles narrated by Livy the 'Velites after hurling their spears, came to a hand-to-hand combat with their swords'.[112] Polybius's description of the Battle of Talamone in 225 BC against the Insubrian Gauls, whose ardour was miserably extinguished by the action of the *velites*, is very exhaustive. The Greek author describes that 'when the javelineers advanced, as is their usage, from the ranks of the Roman legions and began to hurl their javelins in well-aimed volleys …' suggesting that they were not a deployed body but a force within the legionary array that, attacking, came out from the formation itself without disorganising or weakening it. The account continues by highlighting how the prowess of the Celts, manifested with their own nakedness, turned out to be a weakness and cause of the breakdown of their array: in the face of the rain of javelins thrown by the *velites* 'the Celts in the rear ranks indeed were well protected by their trousers and cloaks, but it fell out far otherwise than they had expected with the naked men in front …'. The reason for these unexpected casualties was that '… the Gaulish shield does not cover the whole body; so that their nakedness was a disadvantage, and the bigger they were the better chance had the missiles of going home'. This observation is essential for understanding the evolution of the Roman shield, adopted by the *hastati* and *principes*, which changed from round [*oplon*] to oblong, to better protect the warrior from missile weapons. Polybius goes on to testify that the attack by the *velites* was so effective that the Celts were 'unable to drive off the javelineers owing to the distance and the hail of javelins, and reduced to the utmost distress and perplexity, some of them, in their impotent rage, rushed wildly on the enemy and sacrificed their lives, while others, retreating step by step on the ranks of their comrades, threw them into disorder by their display of faint-heartedness'.[113]

In other battles, the action of the *velites* is described as a direct confrontation, suggesting that this body had the capacity and training suitable for close combat. The *velites*' ability to use a sword can be seen in an episode of the Battle of Mount Olympus, fought in 189 BC against the Galatians, where the 'veles compelled to fight hand to hand... shifts his javelins to his left hand and draws his sword [*gladius*]', which is confirmed by Livy who writes that the Galatians 'were slain by the swords of the skirmishers';[114] another example is the ambush hatched on the Ebrum Rive during the Second Punic War: 'The Spaniards, catching sight of cattle in the distance [a trap prepared by the Romans], dashed upon them, and the light-armed fell upon the Spaniards busy with their plunder; first they inspired alarm by their missiles; then abandoning their light weapons, which could provoke rather than decide the battle, they drew their swords [*gladii*] and began fighting at close quarters.'[115]

The *velites* did not last for long and by the time of Caesar, they must have already been abolished because he never mentions them in his commentaries. Already at the time when Livy was writing, the *velites* no longer existed as a military body, so much so that the historian, in describing them in the context of the Battle of Zama, calls them '*ea tunc levis armatura erat* [*velites*, the light-armed of that day]'.[116]

There is no agreement among the ancient authors regarding the derivation of the name '*velites*'. Ovid reports that the name had been applied to a certain type of gladiator who made use of the *hasta*, '*utque petit primo plenum flaventis arenae nondum calfacti velitis hasta solum*',[117] while Festus and Vegetius derive the name from the speed of these soldiers, as if they were almost flying (*Expeditos velites quasi volitantes nominabant*),[118] unlike Pliny and Isidorus who made it derive from a people of Etruria called the '*velete*'; finally Cicero, in *Epistulae ad familiars*, uses the definition of 'provocative joker' (*scurram velitem*), one who makes jokes at the risk that they may turn against him.[119] Probably this was the real meaning, that of 'provocateurs', in that they could engage in battle and, perhaps, disrupt the front ranks of the enemy.

Hastati, principes and triarii

The reorganisation of the army led to the loss of the *rorarii* and *accensi* as well as of the *leves*, but to keep the number of infantry in a legion unchanged, the number of remaining fighters had to be doubled. Polybius says that 'they divide them so that the senior men known as *triarii* number six hundred, the *principes* twelve hundred, the *hastati* twelve hundred, the rest, consisting of the youngest, being *velites*'.[120] The Greek author continues his description by saying that the infantrymen of each class were divided into ten companies, except the *velites*, and two centurions and two optios from among the elected officers were assigned to each company. 'The velites are divided equally among all the companies.'[121] As we can see, the number of *ordines* (columns) was reduced, from fifteen to ten, but in practice the infantrymen that made up the individual maniples were doubled, increasing from 60 to 120, and this was the solution to make these bodies autonomous in combat without the risk of exposing them to being overwhelmed. The Greek historian does not specifically mention the centuries, but the presence of two centurions per maniple suggests that they still existed.

	Age	No. Infantrymen per *Legio*	No. Infantrymen per Maniple	Defensive Weapons	Offensive Weapons
VELITES	Young (and poor)	1,200	40	Wolf skin *Parma* (shield)	Javelins *Gladius*
HASTATI	Adults	1,200	120 (60 per *centuria*)	Helmet Oblong shield *Kardiophylax* or *lorica conserta hamis*	2 *Pila* *Gladius*
PRINCIPES	Mature	1,200	120 (60 per *centuria*)	Helmet Oblong shield *Lorica conserta hamis*	2 *Pila* *Gladius*
TRIARI	Veterans	600	60 (30 per *centuria*)	Helmet Oblong shield *Lorica conserta hamis*	Spear *Gladius*

Table 3: Characteristics of the various bodies of the new manipular *legio* of the second century BC as described by Polybius. The most evident changes are represented by the disappearance of the *rorarii* and *accensi* and the presence of the new body of light infantry, the *velites*, in addition to the reduction in the number of *ordines*, from fifteen to ten but at the same time doubling the number of soldiers within them. All the infantrymen are armed with the *gladius*.

	LIVIAN *LEGIO*		POLYBIAN *LEGIO*	
	No. infantrymen for *Legio*	No. infantrymen for maniple (15 maniples)	No. infantrymen for *Legio*	No. infantrymen per *ordo* (10 *ordines* each 3 maniples strong)
VELITES (or *Leves*)	300	20	1,200	120 (40x3)
HASTATI	900	60 (30 per *centuria*)	1,200	120 (60 per *centuria*)
PRINCIPES	900	60 (30 per *centuria*)	1,200	120 (60 per *centuria*)
TRIARII	900	60 (30 per *centuria*)	600	60 (30 per *centuria*)
RORARII	900	60	/	/
ACCENSI	900	60	/	/
TOTAL	4,800	320	4,200	420

Table 4: Numerical comparison between the various corps of the manipular *legio* described by Livy, dating back to the Early Consular Age, and the Polybian *legio* of the second century BC

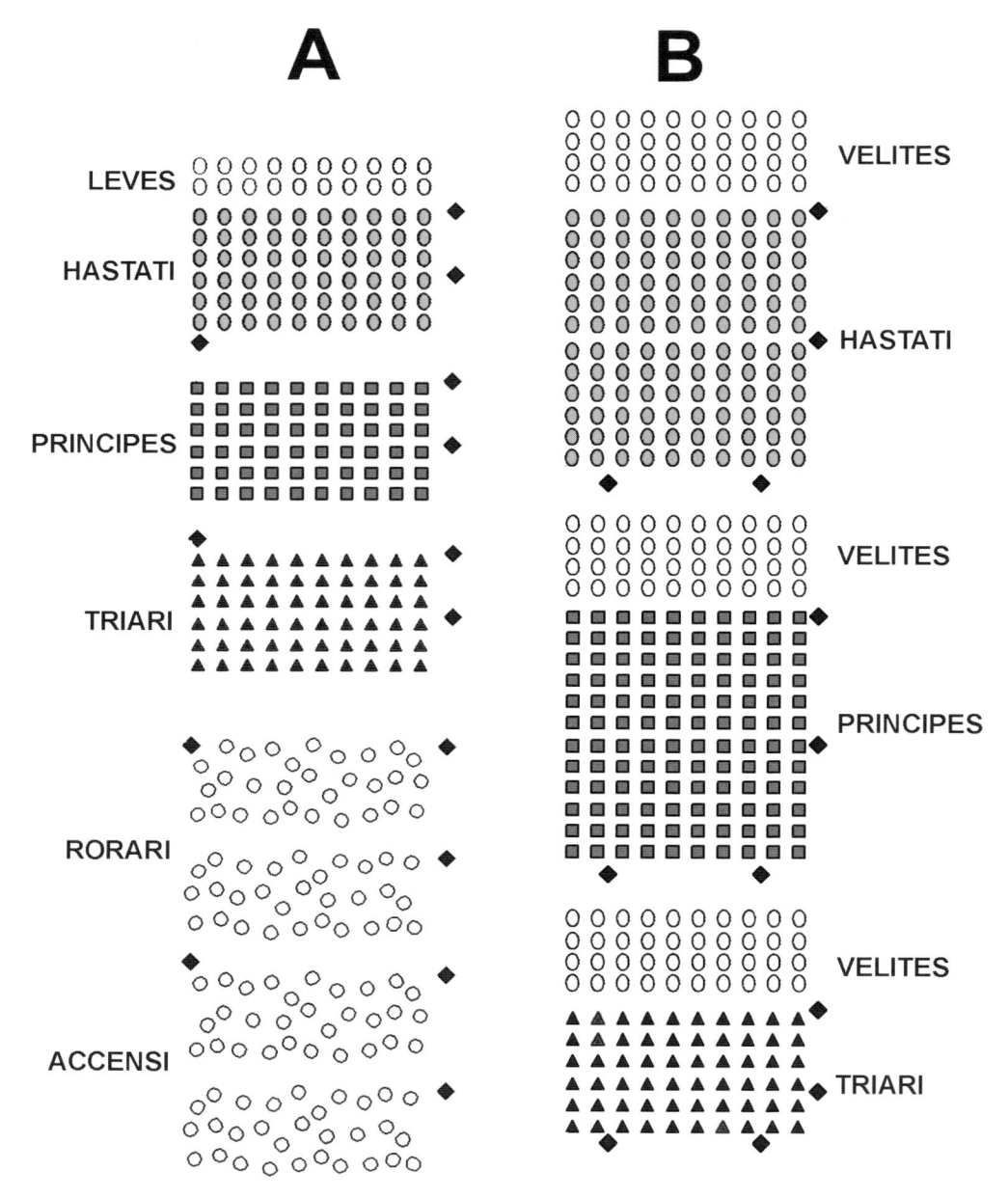

156 The Roman Gladius and the Ancient Fighting Techniques

A **B**

(diagram showing formations: A - LEVES, HASTATI, PRINCIPES, TRIARI, RORARI, ACCENSI; B - VELITES, HASTATI, VELITES, PRINCIPES, VELITES, TRIARI)

Fig.10: Comparison between an *ordo* of the Livian *legio* (A), made up of five maniples and a Polybian *ordo* (B), made up of three maniples, plus *velites*. It can be noted that in the latter the number of infantry making up the *hastati* and *principes* groups has increased and therefore have a consistency such that each maniple can sustain an autonomous combat. However, the total number of infantrymen per legion remains unchanged: indeed in the Polybian *legio* it is slightly reduced, for the simple fact that the *ordines* change from fifteen (Livian *legio*) to ten (Polybian *legio*).

The *hastati*, older and wealthier than the *velites*, totalled 1,200, divided into 120 per maniple. Their armament consisted of an oblong shield with a convex surface (2.5ft wide and 4ft high, i.e. about 75cm x 120cm), reinforced by a boss and an iron frame along the upper and lower edge to protect 'it from descending blows and from injury when rested on the ground … Besides the shield they also carry a sword [μάχαιρα], hanging on the right thigh and called a Spanish sword [Ιβηρική]. This is excellent for thrusting, and both of its edges cut effectually, as the blade is very strong and firm. In addition they have two *pila*, a brass helmet, and greaves.' Polybius gives a long dissertation about the *pila*, explaining that the two carried by the soldiers, about 138cm long, could be of two types, the first being larger, round or square, with a diameter of a palm (about 77mm), the latter thin, like 'moderate-sized hunting-spears'. They were composed partly of iron, the tip, the length of which was similar to the wooden shaft, and great attention was given to their union. The reason for the two types of *pila* is probably due to the characteristics of the enemy with whom they would fight.

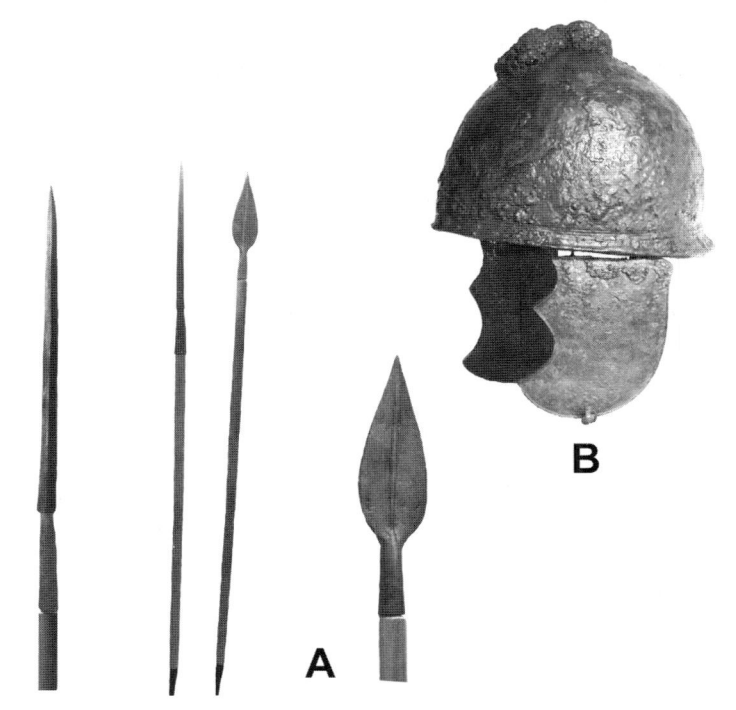

Fig. 11:
A): A votive deposit was discovered on the site of Talamone, that can be dated to between the middle of the third and the end of the second century BC. The weapons discovered could have been related to (but this is not certain) the victory achieved in Talamone by the Roman army over the Gauls in 225 BC. This find includes eleven laurel-leaf spearheads (23cm long and about 5cm wide) and eleven pyramid-shaped spearheads 40cm in length. (*Archaeological Museum of Orbetello*, Catalogue 'The collections' edited by Gabriella Poggesi, p. 177. Two spears with the detail of the tips. Author's photo).
B): Bronze Montefortino helmet, with remains of the iron crest and complete cheek-guards. (*Private collection, author's photo*)

They wear a crested helmet with three upright purple or black feathers, 'a breastplate of brass a span square, which they place in front of the heart and call the heart-protector [καρδιοφύλαξ] or those who are rated above ten thousand drachmas wear a ring mail armour instead'.[122]

Also in this formation, the *principes* were again older than the *hastati*, and this was the characteristic that differentiated them the most, being a sign of greater combat experience; they shared the same panoply and were equal in number (1,200 infantry), but they were positioned behind the *hastati* in the second line.

Finally, the *triarii*, which formed the last line of soldiers comprising 600 infantry, were the oldest and 'are armed in the same manner except that instead of the *pila* [they] carry long spears [*hastae*] …'. We deduce that these spears must have been long and sturdy from an episode of combat against the Celts. Polybius writes that the Gauls in general were most formidable and spirited in their first onslaught, '… and that, from the way their swords are made, as has been already explained, only the first cut takes effect; after this they at once assume the shape of a strigil, being so much bent both length-wise and side-wise …'. But the Romans distributed 'among the front lines the spears of the *triarii* who were stationed behind them, ordering them to use their swords instead only after the spears were done with. They then drew up opposite the Celts in order of battle and engaged.' This solution allowed the attack of the Gauls to be neutralised ('by depriving them of the power of raising their hands and cutting, which is the peculiar and only stroke of the Gauls, as their swords have no points') and their swords were 'made unserviceable'.[123] The Romans had learned from Pyrrhus that keeping a fearsome enemy at a safe distance with long spears made them harmless and easy to overpower.

A final consideration is that the division into '*classes*', typical of the Servian reform, has now completely disappeared. Belonging to various *acies* was dictated exclusively by age, and consequently by the professional skills that the infantryman had acquired in battle. Probably economic factors allowed better armament, such as being able to equip oneself with a *lorica hamis conserta* instead of a *kardiophylax*, as described by Polybius for the *hastati*, but they did not carry any additional weight in the distinction of individual infantrymen.

Cavalry

Cavalry was a fundamental element of the legion because, in addition to carrying out protective functions through scouting and as the vanguard, it completed the structure of the array by giving it support in both defence and attack. As the infantrymen were set up for direct combat to the front, the weak points of the formation were its flanks and rear, which, if attacked by the opposing cavalry, could cause an easy defeat.[124] Furthermore when the enemy army was routed, the main function of the horsemen was to pursue and kill the fleeing soldiers.

The practice of cavalrymen dismounting and fighting as infantry at critical moments, a typical characteristic of most ancient periods, tended to stop in this period according to Polybius. The Greek author explains that the horsemen, to be agile, do not wear armour, ready to get on and off their horse, and 'were exposed to great danger in close combat', enough to induce a change their armament during this period, adopting a more robust spear and shield that had a 'solid and firm texture do good service both in defence and attack'.[125] The change turned out to be fundamental in battle, so much so that Polybius describes 'that in times of war it is better to give battle with half as many infantry as the enemy and an overwhelming force of cavalry than to be in all respects his equal'.[126] However, during the Battle of Cannae the horsemen had a dual role, probably resulting from the critical situation that arose there: 'the struggle that ensued was truly barbaric; for there were none of the normal wheeling evolutions, but having once met they [i.e. the Roman cavalrymen] dismounted and fought man to man.'[127]

Ultimately, the end of the double function of the horsemen, as both *equites* and *pedites*, favoured the abandonment of the *gladius* in favour of a longer sword, which would acquire the name of *spatha*, as well as of the spear, relegating our weapon to the infantry.

III (A).2,5 The structure of the Polybian legio

In the Middle Consular Age 'four legions' were always enlisted, wrote Polybius, 'each numbering about four thousand foot and two hundred horse, but on occasions of exceptional gravity they raise the number of foot in each legion to five thousand and that of the cavalry to three hundred. They make the number of the allied infantry equal to that of the Roman legions, but, as a rule, the allied cavalry are three times as numerous as the Romans.'[128] The peculiarity is that, according to need and the enemies to be faced, larger numbers were enlisted, up to 6,200 infantry,[129] and, as the Greek historian explains: 'when they have chosen the number determined on – that is when the strength of each legion is brought up to four thousand two hundred, or in times of exceptional danger to five thousand'.[130]

Beyond the numbers, conflicting opinions still exist in the various modern reconstructions. In the nineteenth century, the great innovation of the Middle Consular manipular legion was not understood because the stereotype of the hoplitic army remained, so much so that Napoleon, in describing an ancient military army, 'which based its fighting strength on the sword and spear', explained that their usual order of battle had to be deep.[131] For the French general, effectiveness lay in the depth of the deployment, where the thrusting action was prevalent over that of individual fighting, and this idea was so deeply rooted that even Zambelli,[132] another nineteenth-century historian, confirms this belief. In fact, he wrote that the ancients had discovered the principle of concentrating a greater force against a given point of the enemy front, to overwhelm it in one part, and therefore with unequal forces to push victory over the entire line from point to point. Therefore, the strongest ones thickened into a wedge, to break the enemy line in the middle. On the contrary, the main characteristic of the Roman army was its dynamic capacity, a disposition present in an embryonic state already since the *Legio Romulea*, the characteristics of which were accentuated over time during its evolutionary process. In the manipular Polybian *legio* of the second century BC, the individual maniples could move autonomously in the battle to carry out attacks on the weak points of the enemy army, perform an encirclement or reinforce sections of the line that were yielding under attack.

Zambelli described the static nature of an ancient army in order to extoll the qualities of those of his own time, the latter capable of performing 'manoeuvres' and adapting to various situations, even if in this description the author seems instead illustrate the Roman '*mutatio*' of a manipular army. In fact, referring to his contemporary army, he explains that the infantry had the ability to change order, easily pass from the battle line to the column of march, and get back in line at whatever point was best suited, combining mobility with solidity, under the agile support of artillery, so that distances and impetus are measured almost with compass and pendulum; and the captain can calculate the speed of the mass, as if it were a mechanical effort, or a current of water.

But these characteristics were precisely those of the manipular *legio* of the Middle Consular Age, since

> every Roman soldier, once he is armed and sets about his business, can adapt himself equally well to every place and time and can meet attack from every quarter. He is likewise equally prepared and equally in condition whether he has to fight together with the whole army or with a part of it or in maniples or singly. So since in all particulars the Romans are much more serviceable, Roman plans are much more apt to result in success than those of others.[133]

Therefore, the Roman Polybian formation had a great adaptability, since its efficiency remained unchanged whether a complete legion was used or only a part of, i.e. the individual maniples.

In summary, 2,000 years before the Napoleonic armies, the Roman legion had acquired the ability to develop an attack power that could be easily altered according to the needs and contingent situations, without risking the weakening of the legion as a whole, where individual parts (the maniples) became autonomous and could be deployed as solo combat units. Even if the classic deployment was that of a united front, a particular arrangement put in place by Scipio to fight the Battle of Zama (202 BC) should be described. Polybius tells us that

> Scipio drew up his army in the following fashion. In front he placed the *hastati* with certain intervals between the maniples and behind them the *principes*, not placing their maniples, as is the usual Roman custom, opposite to the intervals separating those of the first line, but directly behind these latter at a certain distance owing to the large number of the enemy's elephants. Last of all he placed the *triarii*. On his left wing he posted Gaius Laelius with the Italian horse, and on the right wing Massanissa with the whole of his Numidians. The intervals of the first maniples he filled up with the cohorts of *velites*, ordering them to open the action, and if they were forced back by the charge of the elephants to retire, those who had time

Triarii (+ Velites)
(20 centuriae)

Principes (+ Velites)
(20 centuriae)

Hastati (+ Velites)
(20 centuriae)

10 Ordines
(3.600 milites + Velitess + officers)

Diagram 3: The Polybian *legio* in '*quincunx*'. (*Author's drawing*)

to do so by the straight passages as far as the rear of the whole army, and those who were overtaken to right or left along the intervals between the lines.[134]

This arrangement, in which the *ordines* were separated by open intervals, was designed to manage the charges of Hannibal's elephants, an anomaly in the Roman strategic conception and more generally in ancient warfare, since this discontinuity of the front would have favoured the penetration of the enemy forces and therefore the collapse of the array. It is for this reason that it is perplexing to learn from Polybius how the Roman custom ('as they usually do' writes the Greek author) was to arrange the *manipuli* separated by spaces so that they formed a sort of chessboard: the *manipuli* of the *principes* were positioned 'at the intervals' formed by the *hastati* maniples.

Furthermore, the fact that this '*quincunx*' formation (a modern definition of such an array that recalls the position of the five points on a dice – Diagram 3) is not mentioned by any other classical source, and indeed it would seem to be disproved by Livy who, in reference to a battle in 210 BC, reports that the Romans 'were in their usual close order …'.[135] This has induced some modern authors to express doubts as to its real existence or in any case on the correct interpretation of the words of Polybius.

In any case, a commander, once having prepared the battle-array on the basis of how the enemy had arranged his own, could continue to maintain control of the fight even once the battle was already underway. With previous battle-arrays it was not possible to adapt to the course of the battle after it had begun, since the initial deployment was unchangeable, while with the proto-cohortal legion, because of the possibility of moving individual maniples, one had the opportunity to take advantage of weaknesses of the enemy or, at the same time, to strengthen deficiencies that could have occurred among the ranks of the army.

If we wanted to find an allegory for this legion, as for the previous ones, we could refer it to concrete blocks used as road bollards. They can be placed against each other, thus creating a formidable barrier, but they can also be used individually, when a particular need arises (Fig. 12).

How the movement of the centuries of each maniple took place and how they moved within the deployment of the entire legion was not explained by the ancient authors and the modern reconstructions all remain hypotheses, which we preferred not to report. However, the concept of dynamism that was completely absent in previous formations was certainly introduced with the Polybian *legio*.

The autonomy of the maniples

The independence of the individual maniples was possible due to the fact that each of them was doubled in numbers, so that the single maniples of *hastati* and *principes* increased from the 60 infantry of the Livian *legio* to 120 (Diagrams 2 and 3). In this way, the Roman army became very versatile and 'the order of a Roman force in battle makes it very difficult to break through, for without any change it enables every man individually and in common with his fellows to present a front in any direction, the maniples which are nearest to the danger turning themselves by a single movement to face it'.[136]

Livy tells how the Romans managed to overcome the strength of the Macedonian phalanx, impenetrable because of the length of the *sarissa* and its ability to fight on the same footing as the Romans, because 'the Macedonian phalanx lacked mobility and formed a single unit; the Roman army was more elastic, made up of numerous divisions, which could easily act separately or in combination as required'.[137] The individual maniples could be moved and used to carry out autonomous attacks by hitting the vulnerable points of a Macedonian phalanx, represented by the flanks and the rear, parts that were not defended by long spears and therefore likely to collapse into disorder when they were attacked.

Another example of this autonomy is described in a battle of 297 BC against the Samnites conducted by the Consul Fabio who ordered Scipio, his lieutenant, '… to draw off the *hastati* of the first legion and, attracting as little observation as possible, take them to the nearest hills. Then climbing up where they could not be seen, they were suddenly to show themselves in the enemy's rear.' In this action, which was interpreted by the Samnites as a retreat, we also highlight a *mutatio ordinis*, in which the forces exhausted by combat were replaced with fresh ones. In fact, Livy tells us that 'the Roman front could not have sustained the prolonged contest, met as they were by

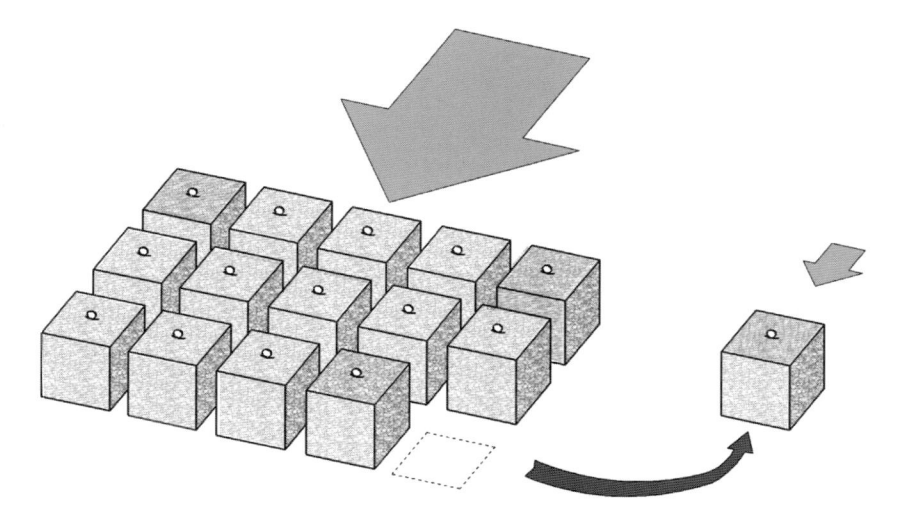

Fig. 12: The Polyibian *legio* can been seen as akin to concrete blocks used as road bollards (or in any case, generically, as a barrier). Together they constitute a powerful and impenetrable obstacle, but if necessary they can also be used individually.

a resistance [of the Samnites] which was becoming more stubborn as its confidence rose, had not the consul ordered the second line to relieve the first. These fresh troops checked the advance of the Samnites, who were now pressing forward …'.[138] The confirmation of this way of fighting is also reported by Polybius when he describes that during the Celtic attack at Cannae, the Romans 'were caught between the two divisions of the enemy, and they now no longer kept their compact formation but turned singly or in companies to deal with the enemy who was falling on their flanks'.[139]

The manipular formations were numerically smaller, making them capable of movements and changes at the front, as in the quotation from Polybius above, actions that would have been impossible for the unified front lines of previous eras. Above all, we must imagine that a battleground is far from an ideal situation as we often imagine, because where there are no natural obstacles, as the battle developed, impediments due to the results of the fighting are formed, as Livy reminds us in this very harsh description 'accordingly the men of the front line, the *hastati*, pursuing the enemy wherever they could over heaps of bodies and arms and through pools of blood, broke up both their own maniples and their ranks …'.[140] In this situation, the fact that the ranks could not be kept compact and united because of the piles of corpses and scattered weapons, and that the soldiers might slip in pools of blood, left them dangerously exposed to enemy attack. Had such a situation arisen in an army with a united, inflexible front, such as the Servian one, the loss of units in the front line would have exposed the army to enemy penetration and the entire array would have disintegrated. The manipular system, on the other hand, being more flexible, made it possible to recover critical situations more effectively. Polybius, describing the same episode as Livy that we have reported, shows us how easy such a reorganisation of the army was. Indeed, 'recalling by bugle those of the *hastati* who were still pursuing the enemy, he stationed the latter in the fore part of the field of battle, opposite the enemy's centre, and making the *principes* and *triarii* close up on both wings ordered them to advance over the dead. When these troops had surmounted the obstacles and found themselves in a line with the *hastati* the two phalanxes closed with the greatest eagerness and ardour.'[141]

The organisation of the Polybian manipular army therefore allowed it to acquire a high level of plasticity, managing to adapt not only to varied battlefields and to various combat situations, but above all to prevail over their new enemies, including Hannibal, known for his intelligence, cunning and his multi-ethnic army that almost brought Rome to its knees.

III (A).2,6 *The Polybian manipular battle*
The light infantry

The way in which battles developed was very flexible but certain paradigms were characteristically respected, such as emitting shouts and war cries before the start. This ritual served to charge the Roman soldiers emotionally as well as to create group spirit, but at the same time it was useful to affect the psychology of the opponents, provoking fear. This can be compared to two wild animals fighting for the role of the pack leader, where the real fight is always preceded by a manifestation of signs of strength, such as growls and gnashing of teeth, arching of the back with bristling fur etc., all suitable to encourage the rival to avoid a fight and its inevitable damage. This attitude was typical of ancient armies, and the Romans were not excluded from it. When the two formations were close 'the Romans fell upon their foes, raising their war-cry and clashing their shields with their spears as is their practice, while there was a strange confusion of shouts raised by the Carthaginian mercenaries, for, as Homer says, their voice was not one, but "Mixed was the murmur, and confused the sound, Their names all various"'.[142] Even in the description of the war cry, Polybius seems to contrast the two armies, praising the cohesion, a sign of strength, of the Capitoline people while disparaging the ethnically-mixed Carthaginians.

First contact was made by the *velites*, who, swarming through the maniples, threw their javelins, but not in a secondary role, indeed to the extent that during the Battle of Zama (202 BC) they played a decisive role in the neutralisation of Hannibal's elephants. Scipio based the attack on the pachyderms on such light infantry which, as it was not in close formation and had thrown weapons, could more easily get the better of the large, slow animals. The intention of the Roman general was to kill as many of the animals as possible or, if the *velites* were overwhelmed by them, to draw them into the corridors left between the maniples, leading them in the right direction to do as little damage as possible to the ranks of soldiers: 'The intervals of the first maniples he (Publius)

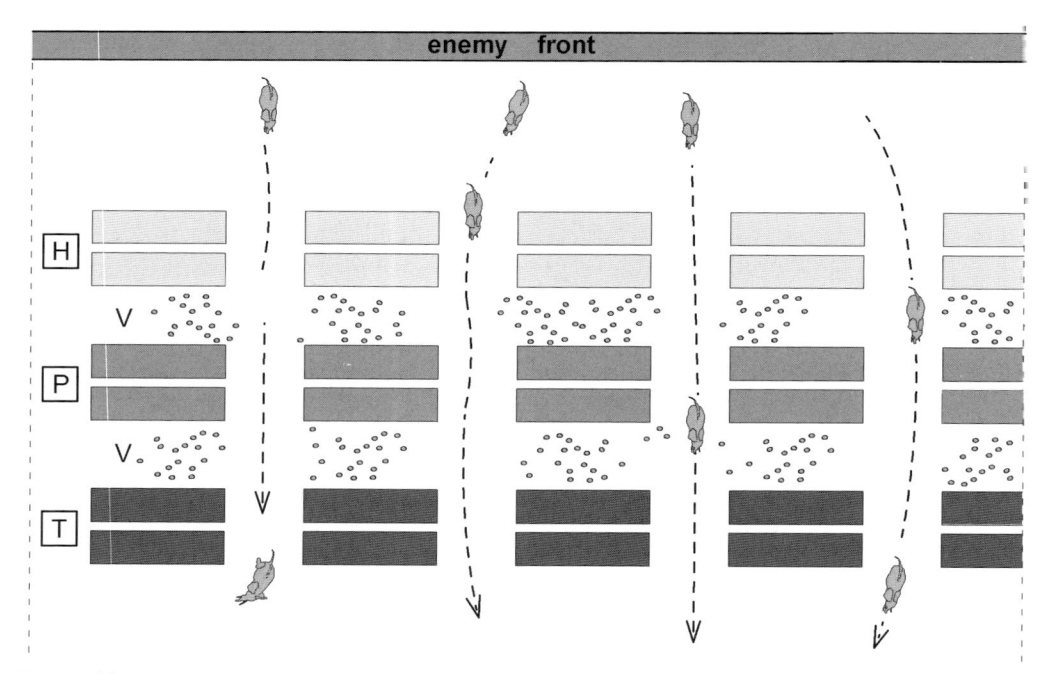

Fig. 13: The formation chosen by Scipio Africanus in the Battle of Zama was that of 'column of maniples' with particularly large spaces between them, so that the elephants, in their charge, could pass through them, causing as little damage as possible.

filled up with the cohorts of velites, ordering them to open the action, and if they were forced back by the charge of the elephants to retire, those who had time to do so by the straight passages as far as the rear of the whole army, and those who were overtaken to right or left along the intervals between the lines.'[143]

It is interesting to note, as already highlighted in other points of this chapter, that the military ability of the *velites*, despite being made up of the young and the poor, was not of low quality, as shown by the courageous way in which they attacked the pachyderms, implementing precise tactical schemes, through arranged attacks, using javelins but also close combat: '[the Roman soldiers] who had learned by experience in the African wars, both to evade the onset of the animal [the elephant], and, getting at one side of it, either to ply it with darts, or, if they could come near enough, to wound its sinews with their swords [*gladii*]'.[144]

The heavy infantry

While the *velites* represented a dynamic force based on swarm combat, not subjected to the rigid framework of the battle array, on the contrary the heavy infantry, represented by the *hastati*, *principes* and *triarii*, based their power on the closed pack of soldiers and on the organised combat, which involved keeping the ranks and fighting fearlessly.

The heavy infantry battle typically began with an exchange of thrown weapons between the two formations. As Livy tells us, in a clash in 210 BC between Marcus Junius Silanus, a lieutenant of Scipio, and a contingent of Celtiberi, who were part of a Carthaginian army, 'the Romans hurled their javelins at them. The Spaniards [*Hispanici*] squatted down to meet the enemy's volley; then they in turn rose to hurl their weapons. After the Romans in dense array, as usual, had received these on their shields held close together, men fought at close quarters and began to use swords [*gladii*].'[145] From this quote it is clear that the Roman formations were adjacent, one next to the other, to form a wall of shields against the Celtic attack 'whose custom it is to be skirmishers in battle'. But a battlefield is never flat and unobstructed, and that the 'restricted spaces and intervening thickets broke up their ranks, and they were forced to engage now singly, now in couples, as though with men paired against them'.[146] Although the deployment could be disrupted by the terrain, the soldiers had to try to maintain their position, because holding formation was the strong point allowing the full potential of Roman combat to be exploited.

When the first ranks of *hastati* fought, 'the rear ranks of the Romans followed close on their comrades, cheering them on ...',[147] creating support behind the fighters stimulating fervour and at the same time a sense of protection that certainly increased the efficiency of the fight.

In this period, what had already been seen in the Monarchical Period, the condemnation of individualism in the Roman way of fighting, became consolidated and this reprobation became all the more important as the combat evolved into being based on a complex mechanism of coordination. Losing the compactness of the array implied exposing the formation to enemy attack and therefore to its collapse, causing defeat. The Roman infantrymen had to fight while maintaining their position, in the context of their own line of their own maniple, and, as Livy states, 'pressed on into the enemy by their own weight and that of their arms'.[148] The loss of formation transformed the combat from organised to individualistic, as happened during the ambush carried out by Hannibal at Lake Trasimeno against Flaminius's troops. Since the Romans were

> surrounded; and they were already engaged on their front and flank before they could properly form up or get out their arms and draw their swords [*gladii*] ... when it became apparent that their only hope of safety lay in their right arms and their swords; then every man became his own commander and urged himself to action, and the battle began all over again. It was no ordered battle, with the troops marshalled in triple line, nor did the vanguard fight before the standards and the rest of the army behind them, neither did each soldier keep to his proper legion cohort and maniple: it was chance that grouped them, and every man's own valour assigned him his post in van or rear.[149]

Vegetius[150] explains that by 'dint of their constant exercises soldiers should keep their appointed ranks in the line, and not mass together or thin out the formation at any point inconveniently. For when densely packed they lose room to fight and impede one another, and when too thinly spread and showing the light between them they provide the enemy with an opening to breach.' But in addition 'recruits should be led out constantly to the exercise-field and drawn up in line following the order of the roll, in such a way that at first the line should be single and extended, having no bends or curvatures, and there should be an equal and regular space between soldier and soldier'. But, as we can guess, a battle did not take place in a static way; on the contrary it was a phenomenon where thrusts and counter-thrusts alternated with each other, with enemy fronts that yielded, front lines that advanced alternately, sometimes too far compared to the remaining maniples, making it very complicated to practise what had been taught and which was the basis of the strength of the army itself.

'During an assault, panic and chaos could not possibly take over but, on the contrary', the infantrymen had to maintain control to

> double the line, so that in an actual assault that arrangement to which they are used to conform may be preserved. Thirdly the command should be given suddenly to adopt a square formation, and after this the line itself should be changed to triangular formation, which they call a 'wedge'. This formation is usually of great advantage in battle. Next they are commanded to form circles, which is the formation commonly adopted by trained soldiers to resist a hostile force that has breached the line, to prevent the whole army being turned to flight and grave peril ensuing.

We do not know if these 'complex military figures' already existed in the Early Consular Age or were typical only of the Imperial period, but the basic concept remains that a formation of soldiers had the ability to modify their deployment according to various needs, assuming a defensive or attacking disposition, independently from what the other maniples might do, making this legion much more adaptable to the various developments of a battle. These manoeuvres, more or less difficult to carry out, had to be taught and repeated through continuous exercise because, as the author says, 'If recruits learn these manoeuvres by continual practice they will observe them more easily in actual battle'. A reference to training for the learning of these 'military figures' is also made by Livy,[151] who relates how the king of the Numidians, Siface, asked the Roman ambassadors, centurions, to teach him 'the military strength' because, while he had skilled horsemen, his infantry were very inexperienced, untrained and poorly armed, so much so as to define his own army as 'formless and unmethodical, as if a mob had been gathered by chance'. Quintus Statorius, the deputed 'Centurion, enrolled infantry for the king, organised them almost in the Roman manner, taught them in formation and evolution to follow standards and keep their ranks'.

A Roman soldier did not go to fight without adequate preparation since a linear battle needed careful training so that the movements became almost instinctive, performed correctly even in difficult moments under fear of death. Since the flight of soldiers overwhelmed by terror was the most terrible event, because it exposed the array to disintegration and defeat, the Romans countered the feeling of fear through military training, the exaltation of *virtus* and physical punishment.

Combat exercises, the first of the three points, was based on the standardisation of military activities, to favour planned and well-controlled behaviour even in battle, an event in itself random and unpredictable. The actions and movements were repeated until such actions became instinctive, which on the one hand increased their efficiency and on the other reduced the risk of panic. The second point, which the *milites* were educated in, was *virtus*, a value in which death in battle was more honourable than a dishonoured life stained by cowardice, as Cicero claimed, affirming that happy is he who he is not afraid and life is never too short if the duty of virtue has been fulfilled.[152] Finally, force and punishment were applied against those who panicked, such as the tribune Marcus Aemilius who, when some of his infantry sought to flee, 'gave orders to his own men to kill the foremost of the runaways, and with sword-wounds to drive the crowd of fugitives back against the enemy. The greater fear now overcame the less. Compelled by the danger on either side, they first halted, and then returned to the encounter …' [153]

When the Roman soldier fought, he did it for Rome, his own legion, to defend the comrades of his *contubernium*[154] and for the honour of his own family.

III (A).3 THE *GLADIUS* OF THE EARLY AND MIDDLE CONSULAR AGE

In modern literature it is often argued that the oldest known Roman *gladii* date back to no later than the first century BC (with very few exceptions dateable to the second century BC, Fig. 1 of Chapter III (B).3 'The Late Consular *gladius*'), and that there are no finds of earlier ones. Explanations with questionable historical basis are provided for this anomalous and surprising lacuna, such as the fact that the Romans fought as hoplites, and that they only used the spear.[155] In reality, the problem – and the mistake we should avoid – is that the Italic cultural miscellany previously described is not taken into account, which introduces a fundamental concept: in the Early–Middle Consular Age (which for our purposes we have identified from the beginning of the fourth to the first part of the first century BC) it is certainly possible to speak of a Roman *gladius*, but not yet of an 'exclusively' Roman *gladius*. The specimens appear numerous in the archaeological panorama, but they are also common weapons to the other central Italic cultural facies, which make them difficult to be recognised as Roman, when we consider the various cultures being clearly separated from each other.[156] We can only note that the known finds seem more abundant among the central-Italic people than in purely Roman territory. This is simply due to different burial rites, since among the central-Italic people the panoply of the deceased warrior was buried with him, whilst this did not happen with the Romans.

To properly understand the Roman *gladii* of this period, it is necessary to look further into this social and military situation. The reason which led the Monarchical *gladius* to become the 'Consular' type from the beginning of the fourth century BC[157] can be found in the influence of Celtic culture, starting a long evolutionary process, so much so that '… in 187 BC. the Roman legion had long since gradually incorporated many elements of Celtic armament'.[158]

The influence was so important that it would be impossible to understand the development of the *gladius* and the advent of the new type, if we did not fully understand it from a historical, sociological and technological point of view, from which we will begin our study. Furthermore, taking the above into consideration, in this chapter the weapon will

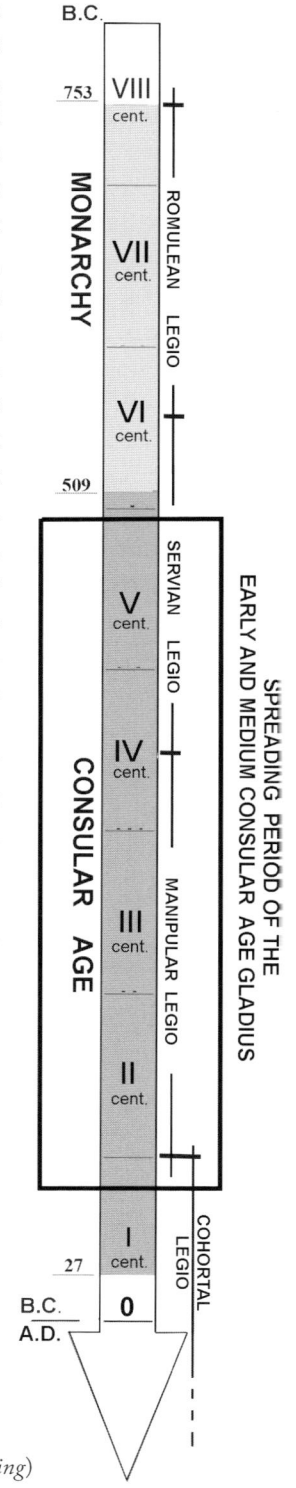

Timeline of the period of use of the Early Consular *gladius*. (*Author's drawing*)

be referred to as the 'Italo-Celtic sword' when referring to it in a generically Italic context and as the 'Early–Middle Consular *gladius*' when referring to a more purely Roman context.

III (A).3,1 Celtic influence in Italic territory
The Celtic presence in Italian territory was certainly not sporadic and/or limited to raids and invasions, however frequent and bloody. On the contrary, Italy has a strong Celtic past, like the rest of continental Europe.

The conquest of Rome in 390 BC, with Brennus humiliating the rising superpower of the Western World by throwing his sword on the balance where the booty was being weighed, is closely linked to our scholastic reminiscence, but it is nothing but an episode like many others of which there is no memory.[159]

From an ethnic, linguistic,[160] cultural and political point of view, the Celtic influence was undoubtedly great in pre-Roman Italy, as is also testified by the efforts of Greek and Roman historians to try, with the means at their disposal, to look clearly for the past of these *recentissimi advenarum*[161] among the people of the peninsula and the reasons for their movement south of the Alps.

The identification of the moment when the first Celtic penetration into Italy took place is not easy, to the extent that the ancient authors themselves do not agree. Livy refers to it three times in relation to the sixth century BC, during the reign of Tarquinius Priscus (616–578 BC), at the foundation of Marseilles (600 BC) and finally 200 years before the sacking of Rome, therefore around 590 BC,[162] even if in other passages in his work he seems to contradict himself.[163] Dionysius of Halicarnassus and Appianus instead place it in 390 BC, and therefore the sacking of Rome would have been the work of the first Celts appearing in Italian territory. Finally, Polybius and Plutarch remain generic, the first claiming that their arrival in Italy preceded the capture of Rome 'for some time', the latter that it happened 'a long time before'. A curious version, perhaps more a legend than anything else, but reported by both Livy[164] and Pliny,[165] is that the Celts came to Italy attracted above all by wine, of which until then they knew neither the existence of nor its production methods.

However, the archaeological and historical evidence leads to confirmation of the Livian thesis of the 'long term',[166] and it is now accepted that there were three main waves of penetration into Italy, the first happening towards the sixth century BC, during which many tribes[167] led by Bellovesus, king of the Biturges, clashed with the Etruscans on the Ticinum and later founded Mediolanum.[168] The second wave followed a few decades later and saw the Cenomani[169] and various other ethnic groups[170] settling further east, in the territory of Brescia and Verona. The third and the last occurred in the fourth century BC when the Senones, in the search for new lands, were forced to advance down to Chiusi.

In any case, the study of the archaeological evidence and the uses and customs of the various populations affected by these movements suggests that some form of contact with the Mediterranean must have existed before the sixth century BC, which may have been linked to mercenary service,[171] an economic activity that was of primary importance for the Celtic world: 'I am rich thanks to my great spear, my sword and my great shield that protects me. With them I am working, with them I reaping, with them I am crushing the sweet grapes of the vineyard, thanks to them I am hailed as lord.'[172] Strabo even considers infantrymen and horsemen as a natural resource, typical of the area close to the province of Narbonensis[173] and Polybius tells us how two powerful lords of the Rhone valley, Concolitanus and Aneroestos, sold the military services of their people, the Gaesati, not so called because of the weapon they used but most probably because they fought as mercenaries.[174] The phenomenon of mercenaries was so influential that from the fourth century BC, there was not a Mediterranean power able to act without Celtic mercenaries, Herodotus tracing them back to fifth century BC Greece.[175]

It is reasonable to believe that the aforementioned Celtic penetrations into Italy may have followed the stimulus and the trail of these mercenaries, who already had travelled those roads and were already known in this world. Ultimately, their military skills were the best commercial counterpart that the Celts could offer for the import of highly valued consumer goods from Italy and other Mediterranean countries, and in this the mercenaries were involuntary pioneers.[176]

The most important consequence of this particular social phenomenon was a conspicuous mixing of uses and customs, often wide-ranging and not limited to the military. The departure and return of a mercenary was not only an economic event, but also and above all a cultural fact involving fashions, social behaviour and ideological models, which the hired warrior knew, experienced and lived in whilst being in other locations, bringing these back home, becoming richer and more evolved. This phenomenon had an impact amplified by the circumstance that the mercenaries operated often in very numerous groups of the same origin and that therefore, upon their return, they brought with them the experience of many and not just one to their native community.[177]

However, it would be a mistake to consider this as a one-way traffic, since all the cultures mutually created customs with the people they came into contact with, creating a real social osmosis, which, among other things, did not only concern the Celtic and Italic world but the entire Mediterranean basin. This is perhaps one of the main reasons why we should not consider the Celtic culture as unique and homogeneous, but on the contrary the tribes of the Italian peninsula exhibit customs and traditions often very different from those of the more isolated Alpine and continental Europe over time, which in turn differ from those of Britain and the Iberian Peninsula.

The archaeological evidence documents such a deeply-rooted adhesion of the Celts of the Italic peninsular to Mediterranean models, that at times we witness the almost complete abandonment of traditional customs, to the extent that we can speak of the birth of a new culture, definable as Celtic-Italic for the Senones and Boi and Gallo-Roman for the Cenomani and Insubrians, the latter two strongly linked to the Roman world.[178]

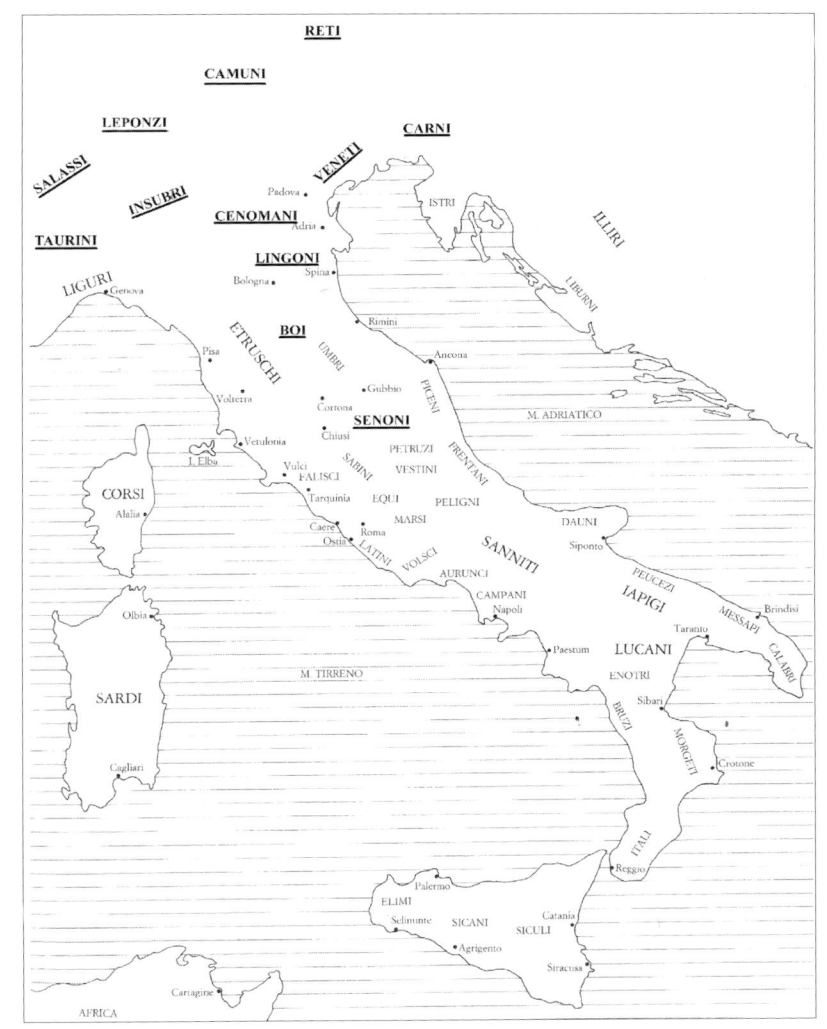

Fig. 1: Map of the main Celtic populations in the Italian peninsula and neighbouring areas in the fourth century BC (names underlined). (*Drawing from* Gli Italici – l'arte *by Sabatino Moscati*)

The military context was certainly not immune to this cultural interchange – on the contrary, it was greatly influenced by it, generating a profound mutation in their mutual armament. To confirm this, G. Bergonzi points out, that 'recently the influence exercised by Italic societies on Celtic communities has been highlighted again by various authors. Peter Stary traced in Italy the origin of the oval shield with elongated umbo, which will become the typically Celtic shield during the middle and late La Tène.'[179]

In the context of this interaction, during the century and a half separating the sacking of Rome from the events of Talamon[180] and Clastidium,[181] the historical sources suggest a substantial change in Roman military organisation, with an assimilation of parts of the panoply of the Celts,[182] who, however, were themselves forced to adapt to the changed military and social conditions. Towards the end of the fourth century BC, they had settled in what was now the *Ager Gallicus*, corresponding to a large part of the modern regions of Marche and Romagna and what was once Etruria Padana, taking the name of Gallia Cisalpina. However, they were forced by this densely populated territory to change from a semi-nomadic society to a more settled one, participating in the conflicts of the Mediterranean world no longer only as mercenaries, but as a proto-state entity, which required them to make an effort of great intensity and completely new in the annals of war.

The Volterran or Faliscan[183] Etruscan vascular painting provides us with a good reference for understanding how important the phenomenon of social and military exchange between the Celtic world and the Middle-Italic world was. There are numerous examples of iconographic finds that show images of Celtic warriors, which upon closer examination show a mixture of elements that make it difficult to contextualise them only within this culture.

Good evidence can also be found on a Faliscan chalice crater, dating back to about 340 BC, currently in the Louvre Museum in Paris (Fig. 2-1).[184] In the depiction, we see a pair of warriors, the first on the left with a sheathed sword and shield, the second, naked and bearded, in the act of advancing with a determined expression, wearing a helmet with a crest, shield and sword held firmly in his hand. A fallen naked warrior lies in front of them, pierced in the neck by a javelin thrown by the first character. The first character (which we have reproduced as a drawing) presents characteristics that point decisively towards a Celtic character, such as nudity and the helmet, having specific archaeological evidence from this area, and the sword hilt with three lower and two upper globes.[185] However, other features are strongly linked to the Italic world, such as the oval shield with a long central spine and metal *umbo*, which despite being in use by the Gauls since the beginning of the Latenian era, shows in the fourth century BC a widespread diffusion among the Italic populations.[186] The same can be said of the blade of the sword, being of medium length, lanceolate, with a gladiolus-leaf tip and a central rib, which in the Faliscan iconographic tradition is normally assigned to Etruscan-Italic characters, and finally, the typically Italic suspension of the scabbard (barely visible due to the degradation of the image), fixed to the side by a leather strap passing several times around the waist.

This ambiguity of cultural attribution continues in the dying character, placed on the right of the foot of the soldier described above. His nudity would place him in the Celtic context, but not his shoes, which are almost never present in this iconographic context. Similar findings are frequent in central Italic culture, as we can see from a slightly less archaic Volterra skyphos (late fourth–early third century BC, Fig. 2-2) [187] and from the crater T 952 of Leipzig, in the Antiken Museum, from Vulci (Fig. 2-3).[188]

What emerges from all of the above is ultimately the intriguing interaction between Celtic and Central-Italic cultures, with blurred borders, where one gradually merges with the other. Even though it is always possible to characterise these people as 'mostly' Celtic, rather than Etruscan, Umbrian, Sabelle, Picene etc., it would be a mistake to consider them 'completely' as such. A clear distinction between the various *gentes* would be an error that would prevent us from fully understanding the complex multi-ethnic reality and ultimately all the effects that Celtic culture had on the *gladius*.[139]

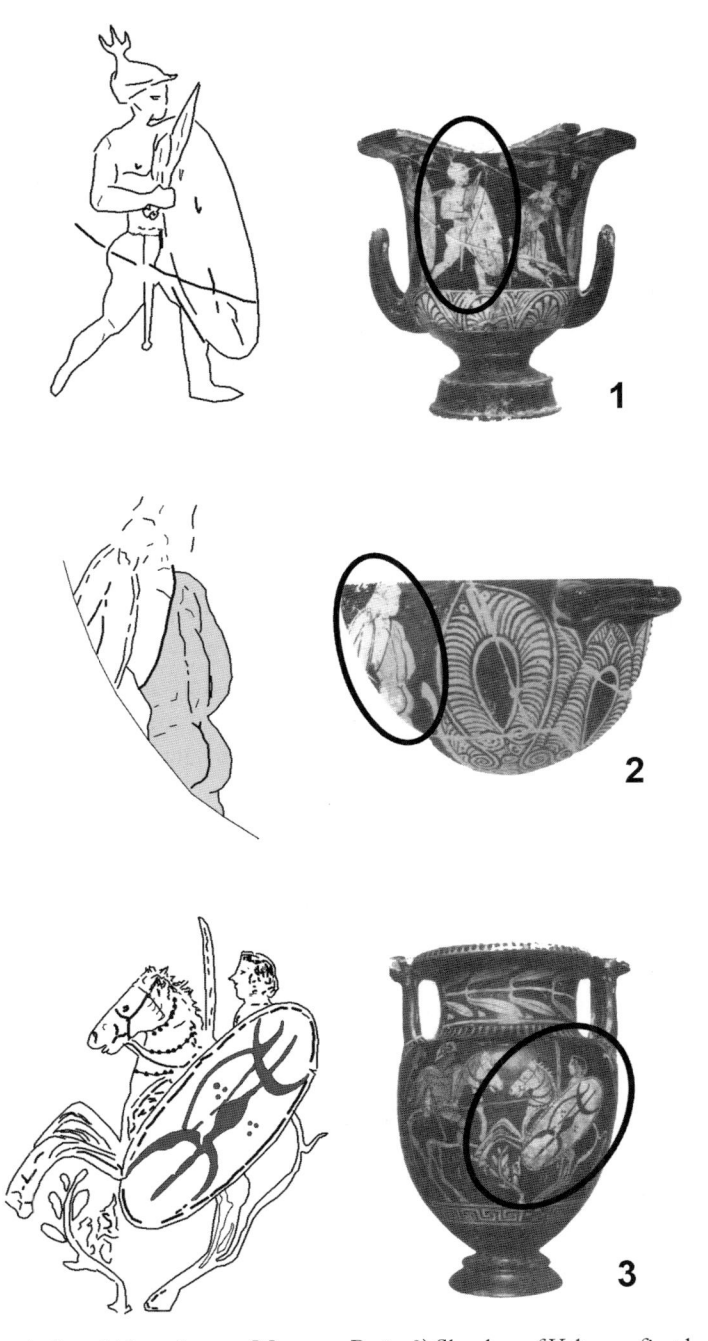

Fig. 2: 1) Faliscan chalice, 340 BC, Louvre Museum, Paris; 2) Skyphos of Volterra, first half of the fourth century BC; 3) Vulci crater, Antiken Museum, Leipzig. In these works, alongside Celtic characteristics, appear other typical of Italic armaments such as the oval shield, the sword with a medium-length blade with a central and lanceolate rib, usually combined with Etruscan-Italic characters in Faliscan iconography, and finally, the suspension of the scabbard at the side by means of a leather strap (although not very visible due to the deterioration of the find in this part). Note also the harness around the horse's neck with disc-shaped studs, typically Etruscan.

III (A).3,2 First appearances of the Italo-Celtic sword and its spread in the Italian peninsula
One of the outcomes of this intriguing cultural interaction was that the Latenian sword (see specimen in Fig. 9-A), understood as being an evolved version of the Halstatt one, had a great influence on the central Italic populations. The first examples of this weapon begin to be present in burials beyond the Alps from the fifth century BC.

The epicentre of the presence of the contemporary traditional central Italic swords (with cross hilt) seems once again to be in Romagna; 'border area between Senoni and Boi, settled in central-eastern Emilia, has a rather complex population pattern, with a differentiated ethnic base, in which Greek, Etruscan, Umbrian and Gallic elements converge.'[190] In this area the inevitable process of mutual influence and evolution began, which lead to the birth of the Italo-Celtic sword, which we see being widespread in the Middle Consular Age (substantially beginning from the fourth century BC), as well as in Sabelli contexts, in the Marsa, Vestina, Peligna, Marrucina and Pentra areas.[191] It can be said that swords of this type come from all over central Italy, from areas such as Bazzano (Vestino territory), Manoppello and Chieti (Marrucino territory), Secinaro, Castelvecchio Subequo and Sulmona (Pelign territory), Fucino and Amplero (Marso territory), San Biagio Saracinisco, Presenzano, Pietrabbondante (Pentro territory), Monteluce (Umbrian-Etruscan territory), Moscano di Fabriano and S. Paolina di Filottrano (Piceno territory), as well as Rome itself and other areas. In Sannio Pentro, including in the sanctuary area, their presence is well documented, as demonstrated by various specimens found in Pietrabbondante, both from nineteenth-century excavations and from more recent ones[192] and at the same time also attested on the Etruscan, Umbrian and Faliscan Tyrrhenian side.[193]

These are not purely Celtic weapons, but what we can call the result of the encounter and fusion between the traditional Italic and Latenian ones. In fact, alongside the characteristics of the latter, we see various other typical local ones: often missing, for example, are the ritual folding of the blade[194] and the suspension of the chain sheath; on the other hand there is a small knob at the end of the scabbard, typical of later Imperial Rome, and Samnite-type belts (Manoppello, Bazzano and others) are often found in the graves, testifying their direct use by Sabellian warriors. A particular reference should be made to the tips of these weapons, which have a focal and distinctive long and sharp point, like a gladiolus petal. In general, the burials in these areas normally have all the typical Italic connotations and it is only the presence of this particular weapon that constitutes their distinctive feature.[195]

However, it should be noted that this type of sword can also be found in more purely Celtic contexts, which at first sight can certainly create some confusion. Bearing in mind the intense intercultural exchange mentioned

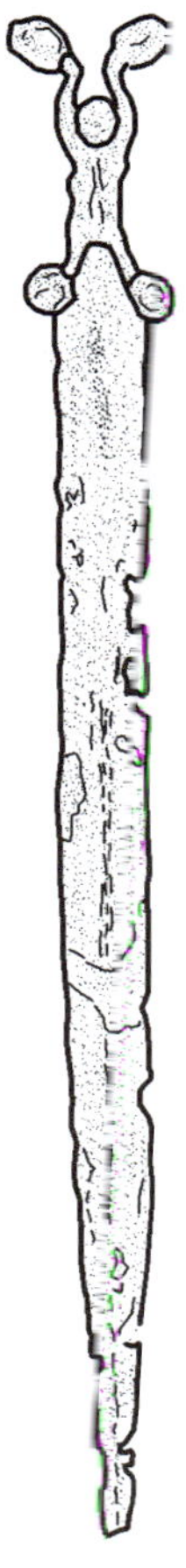

Fig. 3: Halstatt sword from Como, fifth century BC. (*Giovio Archaeological Museum, Como. Author's drawing*)

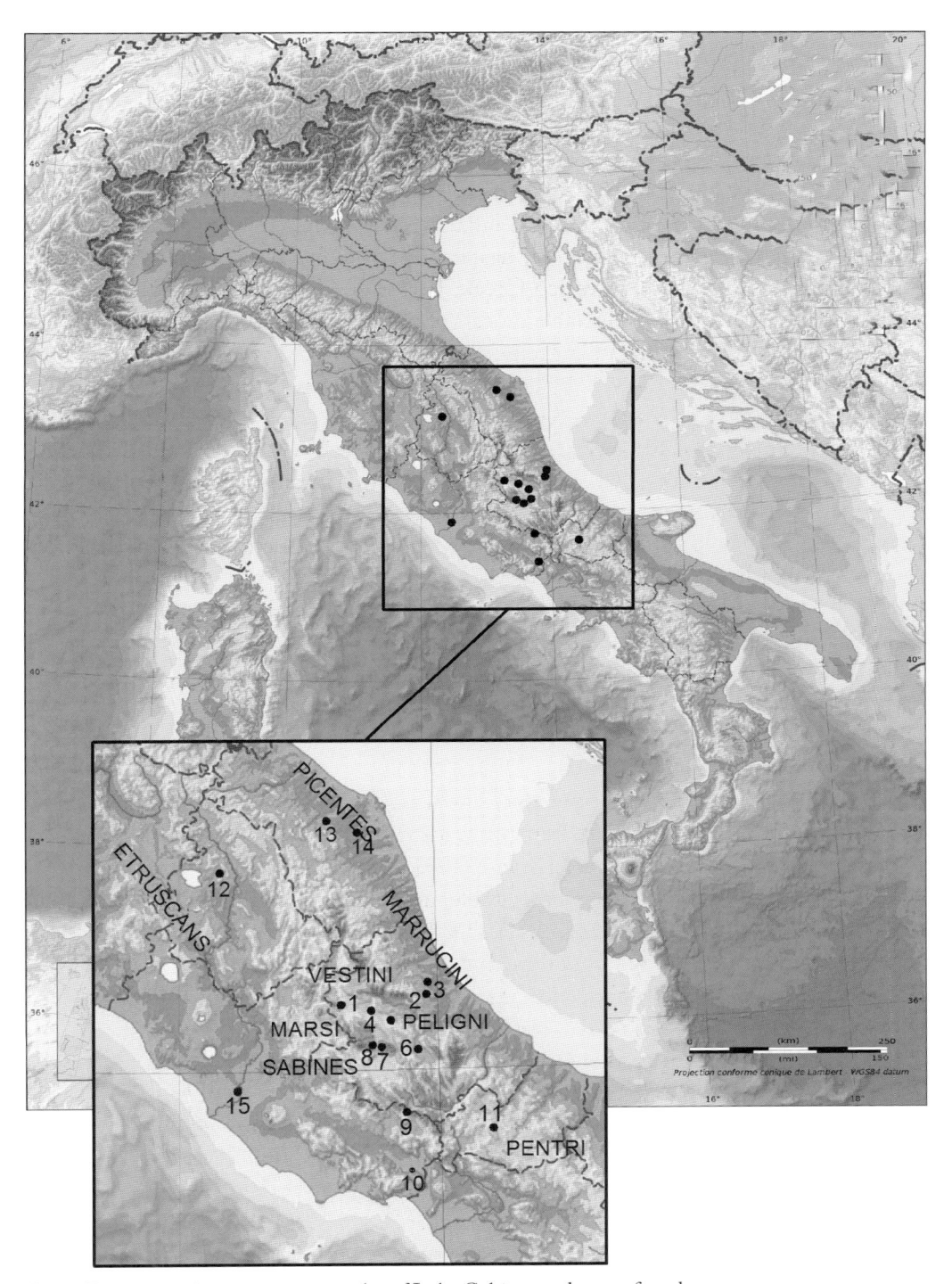

Fig. 4: Locations where various examples of Italo-Celtic swords were found:
1 = Bazzano; 2 = Manoppello; 3 = Chieti; 4 = Secinaro; 5 = Castelvecchio Subequo; 6 = Sulmona; 7 = Fucino; 8 = Amplero; 9 = San Biagio Saracinisco; 10 = Presenzano; 11 = Pietrabbondante; 12 = Monteluce; 13 = Moscano di Fabriano; 14 = San Paolina di Filottrano; 15 = Rome.

above, it is reasonable to assume that, when the native weapons had to be replaced by new ones, the influence of the peninsular armament inevitably had an impact.[196] This phenomenon is proven and evidenced to a certain extent by the fact that it is widespread above all in the burials of the Senones, Boi and Cenomani, which were the tribes most in contact with the Italics and the Romans, but less among the Alpine ones, which we know being less interested in intercultural exchange.

On closer inspection, there was no longer a clear distinction between the many Middle Italic facies, and from approximately fourth century BC onwards, the distinction wasn't even present among their weapons.

III (A).3,3 Description and characteristics of the early Consular gladius (or Italo-Celtic sword)
To introduce the weapon, we will use a specimen known as the 'Trebius Pomponius' sword (Fig. 6-A). It was found in 1962, near San Vittore in Latium, about 120km south-east of Rome, in the Samnite sanctuary of Fondo Decina, datable to the last quarter of the fourth century BC.[197] It has two exceptional characteristics that prevent it being confused with the many contemporary specimens: the first is a decoration in agemina made with two eight-pointed stars inspired by the Macedonian model; the

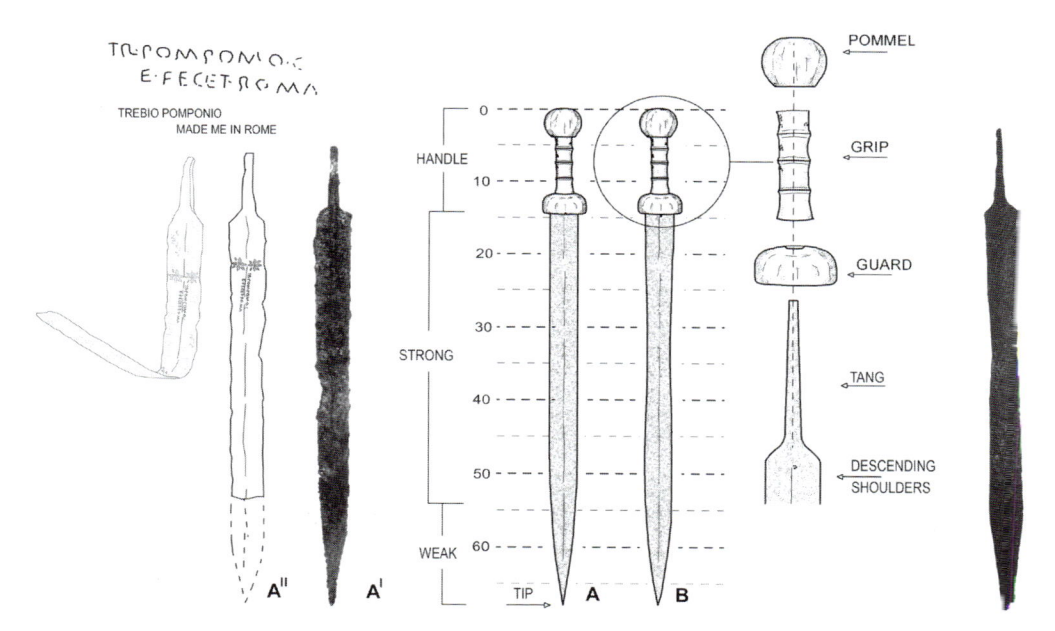

Fig. 5: The High Republican *gladius* (or Italo-Celtic sword) in its two variants:
A) Variant with parallel cutting blade (A^I: Specimen from tomb no. 214 of the necropolis of Numana (province of Ancona, Marche, in the Picenum territory). The funerary equipment also includes fragments of a bronze helmet, a spearhead and personal ornaments (sword data: blade length = 62.5cm, max width = 5.5cm, tang length = 9cm.) From Zuffa, *I Galli e L'Italia*, pp. 185–6).
A^II: Trebius Pomponius's sword from S. Victor, with enlarged inscription.
B) Variant with lanceolate cutting blade.
B': example of Italic origin, in a private collection with ritually destroyed point (blade data: length = 60cm, Max. width = 4.9cm, Min. width = 3.7cm, Tang length = 1.2cm). (*Author's drawing*)

second, much more significant for our purposes, is the fact that its maker, of Oscan origin, signed it with the archaic Latin engraving Tr [ebios] • Pomponio [s] • C. • [f?] [m] e • fecet • Roma [i], or 'Trebius Pomponius made me in Rome'.

In other words, we are faced with a discovery of exceptional historical value, being the only example of an ancient sword with the place name where it was made inscribed on it which, being Rome, unequivocally certifies the presence of the long type of Consular *gladius* in Roman culture since the fourth century BC. Its discovery within a Samnite sanctuary could easily be explained by the fact that, in the years between the second and third Samnite wars, the weapons taken from the Romans or their associates were often dedicated to the divinity as *spolia hostium*, spoils of war.

The blade has been ritually destroyed, both by bending and by removing its salient element, the point. Trebius Pomponius, who made the sword in Rome, most likely conceived it as a thrusting sword, primarily in the central Italic style and secondarily in the Roman style.

Based on some examples of grave goods from tombs 214 and 502 of the necropolis of Numana[198] (province of Ancona, Marche, in the Picenum territory, Fig. 5-A), as well as on various others examples, we can introduce the characteristics of the early Consular *gladius*.

Generally speaking, they are iron weapons, on average 60–70cm long, with a double-edged blade and a long and sharp point, sometimes with a central rib. The shoulders are the oblique convex type (Fig. 6-B) and with a tanged hilt.[199] The blade can have parallel (Fig. 5-A) or lanceolate cutting sides (Fig. 6B, specimen showing the ritually-damaged point).

These characteristics can be better understood by analysing them individually.

▶ The tanged (or spiked) hilt and the oblique 'shoulders' of the blade.
The tang is the most important innovation of this period, a remarkable technological advance, comparable with that of the 'grip tongue' sword from six centuries before.

From now on, we will see it as the type usually called 'spiked' (tanged, Fig. 6) with the definitive abandonment of the 'composite' construction technology used for the Monarchical sword. It is joined with the blade through shoulders with a descending profile. It is so important, that from this time on we will see it present in the Roman army until the end of the Empire.

The Latenian influence is undeniable, being constant in the swords of this culture since the earliest times,[200] even if the technology was not entirely unknown to the Italic populations. In fact, we have some archaic evidence of this type of tang, well before the first contact with the Celts,[201] but only a few isolated examples.

It seems that in the time before the advent of the Italo-Celtic sword, this technology was not sufficiently appreciated by the central Italic populations, who reserved it to merely a marginal use, contrary to the Celts. It should be noted, however, that this technological complex was not taken up completely by the Italics, but partially interpreted to adapt it to their main requirements. While the swords

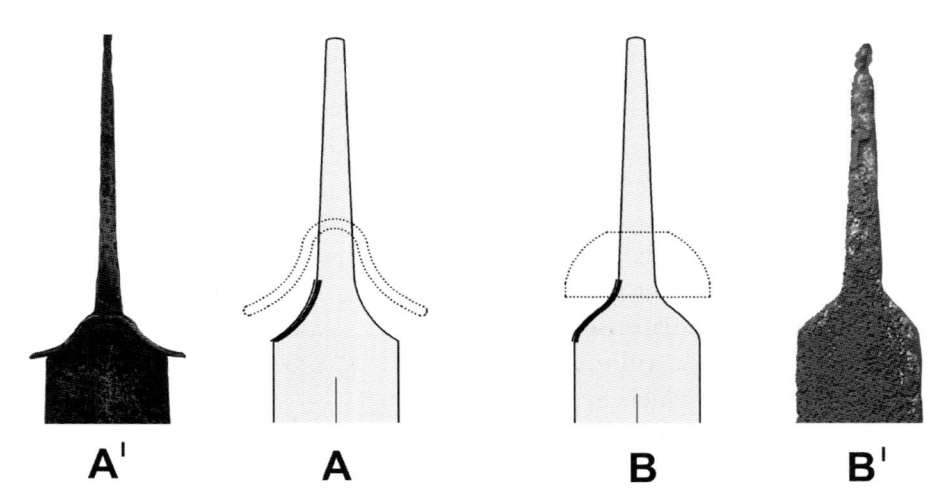

178   The Roman Gladius and the Ancient Fighting Techniques

Fig. 6: Tanged hilt and shoulder of the blade of type: A) concave, typical of the Celtic culture; B) convex more typical of Italic territory. A¹ and B¹: Same type of shoulders but in archaeological specimens. (*Author's drawing*)

of the continental or British Celts have more (but not always) concave oblique shoulders (Fig. 6-A and 6-A¹), the Italic ones, whether they are Italo-Celtic or later more purely Roman, have most often oblique convex shoulders (Fig. 6-B and 6-B¹).[202] This solution is ideal for optimising the solid insertion inside the guard, a stabilising factor that would have been lost with concave shoulders.

The fundamental strength of this type of weapon remains in its simplicity, meaning speed and economy in construction. In comparison with that of the cross-hilted sword, it is possible to see how much easier and faster it was to make, even by an unskilled blacksmith, and it is likely that it took more effort to make one Monarchical type, than making one of the early Consular type.

▶ The three-part handle.
In a very close relationship with the tanged hilt, the handle is greatly modified compared to the most archaic times. The typical tripartite handle consists of a pommel, a grip and a guard, which will accompany the *gladius* (and later the *spatha*) from here on (Fig. 5 and 7-B). Usually, the pommel is spherical (or semi-spherical), the handle being shaped as a cylinder with four (on average) grooves, made of bone, ivory or wood, and can be considered peculiar to the Roman world, not being adopted by other cultures either before or since. Finally, the guard is usually hemispherical.

Also in this case there seems to be a connection with the La Tène culture, whose swords, since the beginning of the Iron Age, were made in this way, even if the individual pieces usually appear much more elaborate and complex to make (Fig. 7-A).

In the Roman context, everything was characterised by an extreme simplicity of construction which made it ideal for satisfying the needs of the Roman army with semi-industrialised mass production.

It is not possible to say with certainty when the tripartite handle was definitively adopted for the *gladii*, because no example of the Early Consular Age has been found complete; however, the prototypes of the individual elements were used in Italy already in archaic times. We have evidence of the use of such a pommel in central Italy in some bronze swords found in necropolis dating back to the eighth century BC (Fig. 8-A and 8-B), which despite having all the characteristics of the 'full handle' type (see Chapter I.3 'Bronze swords in the Italian territory'), are equipped with a pommel made of wood in this case.[203] As for the grooved handle, we have an example of a miniaturised votive dagger belonging to the Nuragic culture (tenth–eighth century BC, Fig. 8-C[204]), which, although isolated, testifies that it was native to the Italic culture.

From a technological point of view, it is very important to note that these three pieces (pommel, grip and guard), which although at first glance do not constitute anything exceptional, are in fact a real revolution because they can be made on a lathe, making production extremely fast, easy and cheap. After their construction and drilling them with a normal drill, they were inserted onto the blade with the new tanged hilt, perfectly fitting for this purpose, the end product being extremely solid and able to withstand the blows of other blades.[205]

If we once again compare the work to create the handle with the previous Monarchical sword, we realise how much the production has been simplified since then. After having shaped the various metal parts of the weapon, it was necessary to do the same with the elaborate shoulder piece and all the other equally elaborate pieces, and then assemble everything with rivets and other attachments, a challenging job largely done by hand, without the use of special tools. The real extent of this innovation can be understood by examining the time required for making of the various weapons, as highlighted by the studies of D. Sim and J. Kaminski, from which it is clear how the *gladius*, even in its new and simpler Early Consular technology, still took a long time to make, suggesting how problematic it would have been to forge large quantities of the much more complex Monarchical types.

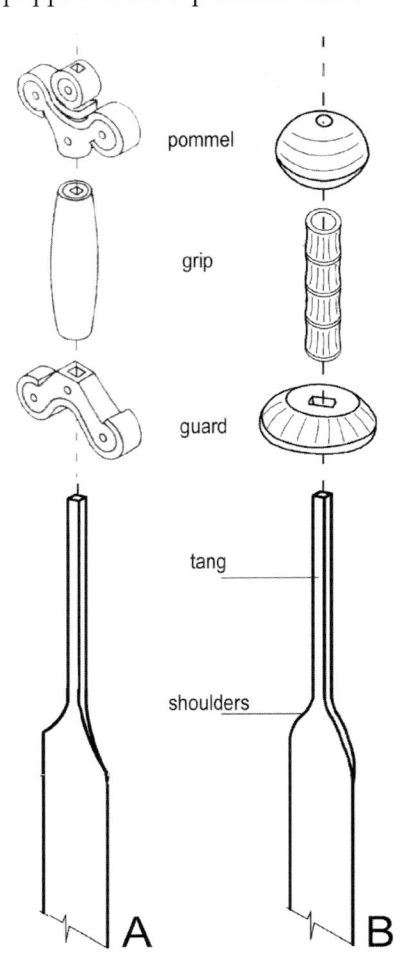

Fig. 7: Examples of tripartite handles, with elements to be inserted in the tang of the blade.
A) Celtic sword in vogue since the first La Tène.
B) Roman Republican sword.
(*Drawing by the author, partially taken from Cartwright and Lang,* British Iron Age Swords and Scabbards *regarding the Celtic handle*)

Fig. 8: A and B: Examples of bronze swords with wooden pommels, eighth century BC (A: Necropolis of Sotto la Rocca, tomb 17, loc. Verucchio; B. Necropolis of Lavatoio, tomb 55. Perugia Archaeological Museum. C: Example of a 'shaped cylinder' handle (votive dagger from the Nuragic age, tenth–eighth century BC. Sassari Archaeological Museum). (*Author's photo*)

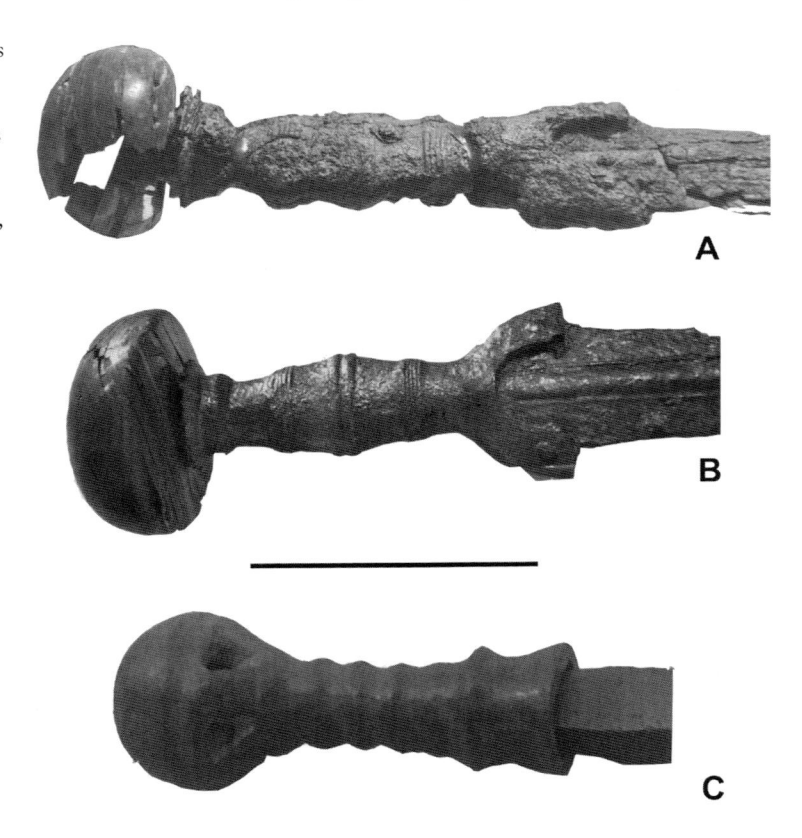

	Coarse Shape Forged	Final Shape Forged	Cleaning and Defining	Total
Gladius	1h	2h	31h	34h
Pilum	4h+38min	2h+7min	3h+41min	10h+26min
Artillery bolt	31min	5min	0	36min
Spearhead	54min	46min	1h+20min	3h
Incendiary arrow	2h+29min	23min	7min	3h
Flat arrow	30min	5min	2min	37min

Table 5: Number of hours of work for the production of the principal weapons (from D. Sim and J. Kaminski, *Roman Imperial Armour*).

We have therefore witnessed an extremely innovative and modern construction technique taking shape. Although this probably derived originally from the Celts, it was the main difference between these two groups. These warriors had a fighting tradition that held the value of the individual in high regard, who bought his own weapons and had a personal relationship with them. Consequently, a Celtic warrior aspired to the possession of a sword with a personalised and refined handle, in which two out of three elements (guard and pommel), took on a more complex shape, not executable on the lathe and unsuitable for mass production (Fig. 7-A). In this context, the cost and difficulty of construction was not relevant, but rather the prestige that the weapon conferred on its owner. The Roman army, on the other hand, was state-owned and the supply of weapons was not a choice entrusted to the individual, 'This booty having been sold at public auction, all the citizens received back the amount of the contributions which they had severally paid for the equipment of the expedition.'[206] The great benefit of the Roman *gladius* was its ability to be produced relatively uniformly, quickly, economically and in large quantities.

On the other hand, standardised weapons and armour are essential when the soldiers of an army fight in units and not as individuals.[207] Every army that employed regular deployments and unit manoeuvres, from the Greeks to the Macedonians, from the Sumerians to the Persians, had to have standardised and mutually compatible armament.[208]

▶ The profile of the blade:
During this period there is a coexistence of two styles of blade, the most proper Italic one, lanceolate (Fig. 5-B), which we have already seen for the Monarchical *gladius*, and the one closest to the Celtic tradition, with parallel or almost parallel cutting edges (Fig. 5-A). The archaeological finds do not seem to suggest a precise rule in the diffusion and distribution in the various Italic cultures of one or the other type, although in the purely Celtic burials the type with parallel cutting edges appears as widespread as the lanceolate is rare, evidently in deference to the main atavistic traditions.

▶ The point:
This element is in continuity with the Italic tradition and therefore with the Monarchical sword, being the long and sharp gladiolus-leaf tip. In this case, the Celtic

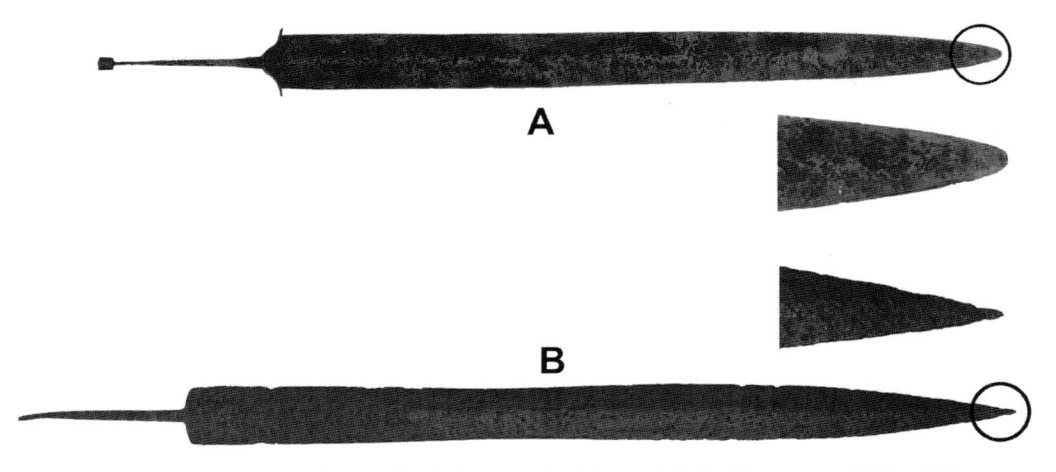

Fig. 9: Comparison between the tip of a Celtic sword of the middle La Tène period (A), which seems only slightly sharp, and that of a long Republican specimen (type B). The first is ineffective, the second, on the contrary, is sharp and more effective. (*Author's photo*)

influence is not strong since it has instead always shown a strong tendency to endow the swords with a rounded point. If this is very evident in the final period (second and first century BC), a careful examination confirms this also being present in previous centuries, albeit in a less evident way. Judging from images and/or drawings, it is often believed that during the middle La Tène period,[209] Celtic swords were equipped with an effective point: in reality we see that instead it is very often rounded and not very effective (Fig. 9-A), when compared to that of an Italic weapon (Fig. 9-B)

It is no coincidence that the ritual destruction of swords in the Celtic context took place only by bending the blade, not giving any particular attention to the point, while in the Italic context we often witness its removal (sword of San Vittore).

▶ Length and use:

These two characteristics, dimensional (the weapon is never excessively long) and functional (weapon designed to hit with the point), remain unchanged compared to the Monarchical *gladius*, to which we therefore refer for a more precise description.

We can say, that just as Rome itself was born from the political synoecism among local populations and more generally among those in central Italy, the Early Consular *gladius* was born from the union between the technological characteristics belonging to cultures that had found their own union in Italy, and that Rome knew how to improve them, expanding their potential and finally adapting them to their own needs. We can schematically summarise this as follows (the numbers that follow in '[ ]' refer to Fig. 10):

from the generic centro-Italic culture:

- Lanceolate blade [6], which has existed since the Bronze Age and has remained a constant even in the Monarchical *gladii*, the shape and proportions remaining almost unchanged;
- The pommel [1] and the guard [3], with shapes suitable to be made on a lathe, tending to the hemispherical shape, of organic material; the cylindrical hilt [2] with grooves, also fashioned with the lathe;
- The long and tapering point [7];

from the Celtic culture:

- The spiked tang and descending shoulders [4];
- In the observed limits, the parallel cutting profiles [5];

from the proper Roman culture:

- The understanding, improvement and enhancement of these features and the manufacturing of the handle with semi-industrial methods.

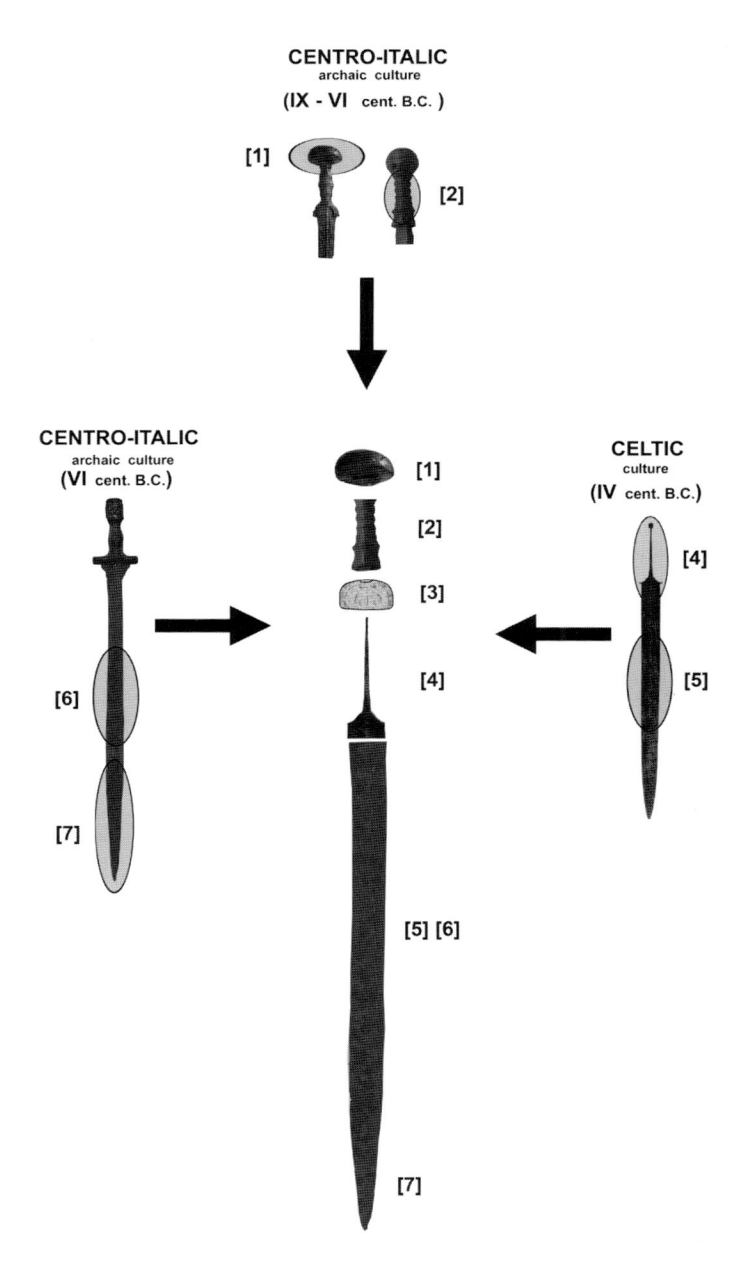

Fig. 10: Schematization of the syncretism between the various technological components from which the early Consular *gladius* derives:
From the archaic Centro-Italic culture:
[1] and [3] Pommel and guard tending to a hemispherical shape.
[2] Cylindrical handle with grooves.
[6] Lanceolate cutting blade.
[7] Long and tapering point, gladiolus-shaped
From the Celtic culture of the fourth century BC:
[4] Spiked tang and descending shoulders.
[5] Parallel cutting edges of the blade. (*Author's drawing*)

This new type of weapon, with all its distinctive features, was important with its performance making it remain in use of the Roman army longer and with greater possible diffusion, practically for the entire Consular Age (and partly for the Imperial one), although, as we will see, in the first century BC it will be accompanied by new models to meet specific military needs.

To explain this concept, in Fig. 11 we present two specimens several centuries apart: on the left (A) an Italo-Celtic sword, preserved in the archaeological museum of Cassino (fourth–third century BC), from the Samnite territory (near San Biagio Saracinisco, some kilometres from San Vittore), with a scabbard that has Celtic influences alongside some Italic characteristics; on the right (B) a Late Republican Roman *gladius*, with a scabbard that allows us to date it to the Augustan period by analogy with that from Vrhnika (Ljubljanica river).[210]

We can see that they are practically identical, with similar long and sharp points, parallel cutting edges (if the Augustan specimen at first sight appears to have a slightly lanceolate profile, in reality it is only an effect given by the widening of the blade near the shoulders), spiked tangs, and the same proportions and dimensions. A legionary using this *gladius* in the first century BC could have found the other sword, two or three centuries older, in his hand probably without noticing the difference. It certainly isn't the only example: if we take into consideration the specimen in Fig. 12, from the site of the Battle of Numantia, probably datable to the third Celtiberian war (143–133 BC), as well as Fig. 1 in Chapter III (B).3 'The Early Consular *Gladius*', showing some of the specimens that modern literature normally considers to be the most archaic type of Roman *gladius*, it makes us realise that in reality they

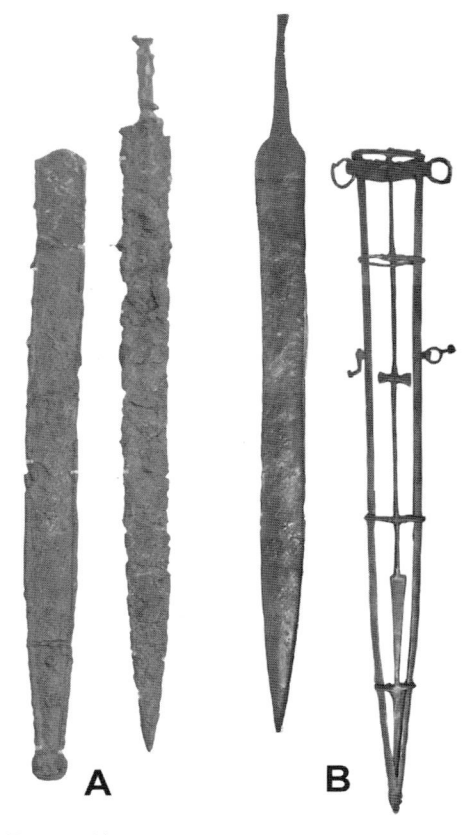

Fig. 11: A) Italo-Celtic sword from Samnite territory, fourth–third century BC (courtesy of the Archaeological Museum of Cassino); B) Roman *gladius* of the Augustan period. Note the great similarity of the two blades. (*Private collection, author's photo*)

Fig. 12: Example of an Early Consular *gladius* from the Roman camp of Numantia, probably dating back to the third Celtiberian war (143–133 BC). (Author's drawing)

fit perfectly into the category of Italian Celtic swords.[211] All are specimens that we can define as *gladii* since they are part of the Roman world, but which are nothing more than Italo-Celtic swords, present in Italic territory since the fourth century BC.

III (A).3,4 Suspension and transportation of the weapon in the high and middle Republican period

In these centuries we cannot yet speak of typical Roman suspension systems, or at least historical sources do not allow this, since they do not provide additional data compared to what was seen during the Monarchical Period. It is therefore legitimate to think that the various traditions and suspension systems of the Italic people, as previously seen, were still alive and in use. This was above all because the political, social and military situation of the peninsula was not yet completely Romanised. In parallel with them we see a salient novelty appear, closely linked to the aforementioned Celtic influence. As for the *gladius*, the transport and suspension of the weapon was an important feature and therefore it is essential to analyse it with due care.

Celtic suspensions with chains and rings

Towards the end of the fourth century–beginning of the third century BC, we see the archaic 'rings and chains' technology of central Italic origin (see Chapter II.3 'The Monarchical *Gladius*') appearing among Celtic warriors. At present we cannot know if they were directly inspired by it or created the technique independently, but the considerable time between the Italic and Celtic suspension, together with the close cultural exchanges already seen, allows us to incline towards the first hypothesis.

What is certain, however, is that the Celts made every effort to optimise it, improving the Italic tradition and adapting it to their own needs. The problem was essentially related to the greater length of their sword compared to the Italic ones,[212] which produced two challenges: the first was the great tendency to swing, the second an equally marked propensity to assume a vertical position. This involved great hindrance to the warrior's leg while running, caused by the rebound against the thigh, which became an even more difficult problem during a sideways movement, with the possibility that the scabbard got between the legs. It would have been just as difficult to overcome an obstacle, even a modest one, since it would have been necessary to take the scabbard in one hand to prevent it from colliding or entangling with something. Furthermore, in drawing the blade from the sheath in this excessively vertical position, whatever the way in which it was held, one would have instinctively pushed the handle towards the front of the sheath which, over time, would have inevitably caused a crack in the scabbard's mouth.[213]

If all of this was not very important for the Italic weapons, given their modest size, on the contrary it was particularly felt by the Celts, who were characterised by a tendency to use long swords and a fast and mobile type of combat (at least until they were forced to adapt to the tactics of their Roman and Italic enemies in general).

At the end of the fourth–beginning of the third century BC, the problem was solved with the introduction of chains to replace the more archaic leather belts, which had proven to be too elastic and mobile. They were nothing more than an excellent expedient to ensure good rigidity of the entire suspension system and an oblique position of the sheath, which ultimately is perhaps the real goal of all the efforts made to improve the suspension system. The systems adopted by the Celts in this period were various, and all based on the use of various types of chain rings, sometimes in combination with leather elements. Without going into too much detail, it is still useful to note that they all have two characteristics:

- they are quite elaborate and not easy to make;
- they have the sheath joined to the chain by means of a single element, consisting of a simple bridge placed on the rear part of the sheath itself (Fig. 13).

Exploring the first characteristic further, the logistical-social aspect of a purely technological matter is highlighted. In fact, the circumstance that this technology, in each of its variants, was so articulated and complex, it could be compatible with the military organisation and Celtic culture, given the particular relationship that existed between the weapon and the warrior. We should remember that for these people, the sword was an object of private property, responding to the aesthetic tastes and characteristics of the warrior with a function not only of a mere weapon but also a status symbol. The complexity of the suspension system enhanced the military aspect of the warrior by defining his status. From the technological point of view, we can note that to keep the sheath in an oblique position, it is necessary to generate a constant torsion.[214] In this case, torsion occurs with the application of the pair of forces[215] constituted by the two chains (or belts) acting on a small bridge (Fig. 13), sometimes assisted by large rings.

The limitation of the Celtic suspension is given by the inevitable modest dimensions of the bridge, which create a contained arm[216] and a consequent need to increase the strength of torque to be applied to obtain a greater inclination of the scabbard. This drawback subjected the structure to considerable stress, with consequent possible deformation and breakage of both the bridge itself and the metal sheet on which it was fixed.

Finally, it is useful to underline that once the chains were tied and positioned in a certain way, and therefore the sword was more or less inclined,

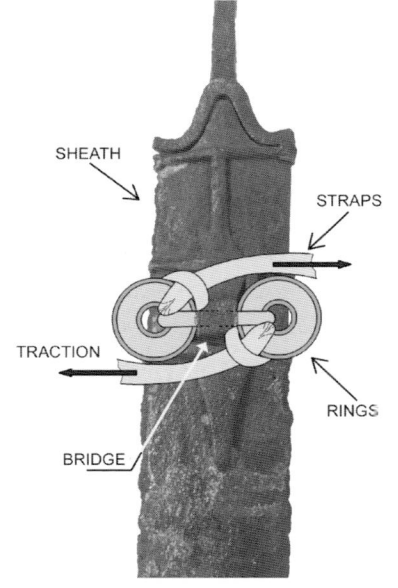

Fig. 13: Examples of ligatures adopted by the Celts to allow the scabbard to assume an oblique position. (*Author's drawing*)

it was basically the only possible position, unless a rather complex effort was made to modify it.

For completeness, we will say that towards the second century BC, the Celts partially return to the leather suspension system, perhaps due to the increasing role of cavalry, since unlike the infantry, horsemen had to worry less about the hindrance of the sword hanging by their side. Although this technology can certainly be considered more efficient and suitable for purely military use than the archaic Italic ones previously seen, its limitations did not yet make it completely adequate for Roman needs, although some valuable elements were received by Roman culture in the following period, if not tout court, at least as an inspiration.

Italo-Roman belt suspensions

If this was the situation in the Celtic culture, significant evidence shows that already in the fourth century BC, even in central Italy, the weapon could hang from a belt around the waist, although almost certainly one made of leather (or in any case organic material) and not a metal chain. Among these, the aforementioned Faliscan crater n. 9830001 AGR, dated 340 BC, in which this detail is evident in the Italic (or Italo-Celtic) warrior in the foreground (Fig. 2-1).

Slightly more recent are two bronze statuettes currently in Rome (Villa Giulia museum), which show two fighters both with shields, helmets and swords hanging from a belt on the left side (Fig. 14-1). Although various interpretations have been given for them in modern literature, the most accepted is that they are Roman legionaries (*velites* or *principes*). They are certainly attributable to central Italic production in the third century BC and are very interesting because they are perhaps the most archaic evidence known to date of the suspension of the sword from a belt tied around the waist in a purely Roman context.

It is reasonable to hypothesise that this custom continued unaltered over time, since we find evidence of it both in the monument of Aemilius Paulus[217] (Fig. 14-2), erected in Delphi to commemorate the victory of Pydna in 168 BC, and in the well-known altar of Domitius Aenobarbus (end of the second – beginning of the first century BC (Fig. 14-3)).

Although the detail in these finds is of a good standard, especially in the Faliscan crater, sufficient to allow A.M. Adam and V. Jolivet[218] to trace the weapons represented to precise archaeological finds, it is unfortunately not enough to allow us to understand how the connection between the belt and the weapon's scabbard was made.

In any case, we can definitively state that throughout the Early Consular Age the transport of the *gladius* with a belt tightened around the waist was in use and that this was most likely made from organic material.

188 The Roman Gladius and the Ancient Fighting Techniques

Fig. 14: Examples of Italic warriors with the sword hanging from a belt tied around the waist:
1) Figurines most likely depicting Roman legionaries of the third century BC. (*Author's photo, courtesy of the Museum of Villa Giulia, Rome*)
2) Detail from the altar of Aemilius Paulus. (*Photo by Raffaele D'Amato*)
3) Excerpt from the altar of Domitius Aenobarbus. (*Author's photo*)

III (B) THE LATE CONSULAR AGE (FIRST CENTURY BC)

III (B).1 HISTORICAL FRAMEWORK

The historical-political framework of the first century BC is very important since numerous events occurred in this era which had significant repercussions for Roman society and consequently for military organisation. The *gladius*, as an expression of the way of fighting, was not unaffected and underwent technical transformations as a result of adaption to the new enemies that the Roman legions had to face. To remind the reader of what happened, we report the *Res Gestae*[219] of Gaius Marius, the leader who was key to many of the political-military innovations:

> Gaius Marius C.f., seven times consul, praetor, tribune of the plebs, quaestor, augur, military tribune, contrary to the rule governing provincial assignments, waged war as consul against Jugurtha, the king of Numidia, and captured him, and celebrating a triumph in his second consulship ordered that the monarch be led before his chariot. In his absence he was declared consul for a third time, and in his fourth consulship annihilated an army of the Teutones and in his fifth routed the Cimbri. He again celebrated a triumph [this time] over the Cimbri and Teutones. In his sixth consulship he liberated the state when it had been thrown into chaos by the seditions of a tribune of the plebs and a praetor who had armed themselves and occupied the Capitoline hill. When he was aged more than seventy years he was expelled from his country through civil strife and was restored through force, and made consul for a seventh time. From the spoils of the Cimbri and Teutones as victor he dedicated a shrine to Honour and Virtue.[220]

In this document we see the events of the life of Gaius Marius, born in 157 BC in Arpinum (or most probably *Cereatae Marianae*) and died in 86 BC in Rome. We can define him as one of the most important characters since the birth of the Roman *Res Publica*, a skilled leader (seven times consul) who led the Romans to victory over non-Italic peoples (Africans and Germans). He was also the catalyst that through war favoured the creation of Roman Italy, laying the foundations for the future Imperial period. At the heart of the great military and cultural revolution, there was a very important aspect of Gaius Marius, represented not only by his qualities, but above all by the fact that 'he had neither wealth nor eloquence, with which the magnates of the time used to influence the people. Still, the very intensity of his assurance, his indefatigable labours, and his plain and simple way of living, won him a certain popularity among his fellow citizens.'[221] In fact, as Sallust tells us, Marius was of plebeian origin, and his fortune was built on the basis of his own military sacrifices and victories, as opposed to aristocratic privileges, making him a hero of the people: 'I cannot, to justify your confidence, display family portraits or the triumphs and consulships of my forefathers; but if occasion requires, I can show spears, a banner, trappings and other military prizes, as well scars on my breast. These are my portraits, these my patent of nobility, not left me by inheritance as theirs were, but won by my own innumerable efforts and perils …' The author continues, having the Arpinian hero say that his strength came from living like his soldiers and sharing the same sacrifices with them.

> Nor have I learned Greek; for I had no wish to acquire a tongue that adds nothing to the valour of those who teach it. But I have gained other accomplishments, such as are of the utmost benefit to a state; I have learned to strike down an enemy; to be vigilant at my post; to fear nothing but dishonour; to bear cold and heat with equal endurance; to sleep on the ground; and to sustain at the same time hunger and fatigue. And with such rules of conduct I shall stimulate my soldiers, not treating them with rigor and myself with indulgence, nor making their toils my glory. Such a mode of commanding is at once useful to the state, and becoming to a citizen. For to coerce your troops with severity, while you yourself live at ease, is to be a tyrant, not a general.[222]

Gaius Marius was a military man, not a politician, and this allowed him to restructure the army from within, organising a revolution that reflected the needs of that particular historical moment. The development of the *dilectus* based on the poor and the creation of an army of professional soldiers, were the foundations of his military revolution which took place at a very particular time, a *pabulum* of new combat strategies and of the armament itself: the war against the barbarian Cimbri and Teutones and the civil wars.

III (B).1,1 *The dilectus spread to the poor*

Marius's hostility to the aristocratic class made him their fierce[223] opponent and on this basis, or probably as a consequence, he instigated one of the most important changes in military conscription, making it no longer based on wealth. It should be noted that, even with the establishment of the *Res Publica*, the organisation of the infantry based on economic availability by Servius Tullius had failed: there was still a minimum income limit for a person to be able to participate in military and political life. Marius, by completely eliminating the income limits, opened to *capita censi* ('counted per head', that is, those who had nothing but their own person) the possibility of enlisting in the army, regardless of their possessions, since they would be armed at the expense of the state. So, as Plutarch tells us, Gaius Marius

> was triumphantly elected, and at once began to levy troops. Contrary to law and custom he enlisted many a poor and insignificant man, although former commanders had not accepted such persons, but bestowed arms, just as they would any other honour, only on those whose property assessment made them worthy to receive these, each soldier being supposed to put his substance in pledge to the state.[224]

This change was perceived as a real 'revolution' because it went against the *Mos Maiorum*, and above all it destroyed the relationship with the aristocrats, part of their power being eroded. Furthermore, Sallust explains that Marius's true intentions were questioned, he writes that while this was done from a scarcity of better men, and others from the consul's desire to pay court to the poorer class, because it was by that order of men that he had been honoured and promoted; and, indeed, to a man grasping at power, the most needy are the most serviceable, persons to whom their property (as they have none) is not an object of care, and to whom everything lucrative appears honourable ... .[225]

However, we can see from Table 6 that this event was not a real innovation since, already in previous centuries, the *dilectus*, the annual levy, had shown a progressive difficulty in recruiting a sufficient number of soldiers to meet the needs of the various wars. The economic limits of the census had been reduced over time, so the innovation of Gaius Marius was probably nothing more than the formalisation of an already-established practice, and in this period made compulsory because of the difficulty in finding soldiers for the war in Numidia.

Historical Period	Economic Limit of the Caput Censi	Quotes
Servius Tullius, sixth century BC	11,000 asses	Livy, I, 43
End third century BC	400 dracmes (4,000 asses)	Polybius, *The Histories*, VI, 19, 2
133–123 BC	1,500 asses[226]	Cicero, *De Re Publica*, II, 22, 40
Marius, 107–04 BC	Abolition of conscription for census	Plutarch, *Parallel Lives*, IX 9,1; Sallust, *The Jugurthine War*, 86, 1-2; Valerius Maximus, *Memorabilia*, II, 3, 1

Table 6: Summary of the progressive reduction over time of the census, understood as an economic limit for accessing military obligations. Already at the end of the second century BC it had reached 1,500 asses, an amount for which a medium-sized family would have experienced economic difficulties, suggesting that Gaius Marius's solution was nothing more than a natural evolution begun long before.

The Marian revolution also affected the identity of the armed forces, which from being a 'state army' became linked to the general who led them, soon establishing a personal relationship, in which the commander promised, in addition to the *stipendium* and booty, grants of land for veterans on retirement. When Gaius Marius embarked for the war in Numidia, he 'immediately freighted vessels with provisions, pay, arms, and other necessaries',[227] confirming how the ancient seasonal city army, armed at its own expense, had become in all respects a professional army, made up of volunteers, paid to fight and armed at the expense of the state. Furthermore, the loyalty of the soldier to his *dux*, on which his life depended entirely, created the conditions for the political clash between plebeians and aristocrats to become an armed one, the basis for civil wars. The practice of handing over 'arable land' to the retired soldiers led to their requisitioning it from private farms, in which veterans often found themselves driving out the old owners to take over the assigned land, creating conflict and a period of serious political instability. Evidence of this practice is given by the poet Virgil, who in the *Eclogues* poetically described the requisitions ordered by the young Octavian (the future Augustus) to meet the grants of his adoptive father Julius Caesar, of which he himself was an illustrious victim of. In the first *Eclogue*, the fictional character Melibeus is forced to leave for exile after the confiscation of his land: 'We are leaving the sweet fields and the frontiers of our country; we are fleeing … An impious soldier will own these well-tilled fields, a barbarian these crops. See to what war had led our unlucky citizens … I'll no longer see you … '[228]

III (B).1,2 A professional army

It is obvious that a professional army made up of men without property was in the beginning composed of untrained troops who had never participated in the previous seasonal wars. 'Take a courageous but untrained soldier,' Cicero wrote, and the answer given is that 'he will seem like a woman.'[229] Therefore, Gaius Marius had to create soldiers from scratch and this general of non-aristocratic origins, with a determined and inflexible character, who knew the soldiers and the various aspects of their life well, was the most suitable for this job. He subjected the soldiers to hard training and, as we are told, 'practising the men in all kinds of running and in long marches, and compelling them to carry their own baggage and to prepare their own food. Hence, in after times, men who were fond of toil and did whatever was enjoined upon them contentedly and without a murmur, were called "Marian mules".'[230]

The classical authors had never before placed such emphasis on training as an indispensable practice for the constitution of a good soldier and a strong army, so much so that Valerius Maximus tell how the consul Gnaeus Mallius, who participated in fighting with the Germans, 'for not following the example of any Commander before him, calling together the teachers of the Gladiators, from the games of C. Aurelius Scaurus, first began to have the Soldier learn the way of shunning and giving blows, according to the reasons of Art; mixing virtue with art, and art with virtue; strengthening virtue with the force of art, and encouraging art with the force of strength'.[231] Technical preparation was the basis of a more efficient army, so much so that from this moment on it became a basic element of training. Indeed, a well-formed and disciplined army, even if numerically small, was superior, so much that 'when Gaius Marius had the option of choosing a force from two armies, one of which had served under Rutilius, the other under Metellus and later under himself, he preferred the troops of Rutilius, though fewer in number, because he deemed them of trustier discipline'.[232] Discipline and skill were the basis of the training of a good Roman soldier, against whom the instinctive and furious hordes of the Cimbri and Teutons could do nothing.

III (B).1,3 The clash against the Cimbri and the Teutones (113–101 BC)

The war against the barbarian Cimbri and Teutones, could have been the spark that led Marius to reform the tactical organisation by transforming the manipular legion into a cohortal one. During the Jugurthine War, the general still used the old battle array and this is mentioned for the last time in the passage of Sallust describing it:

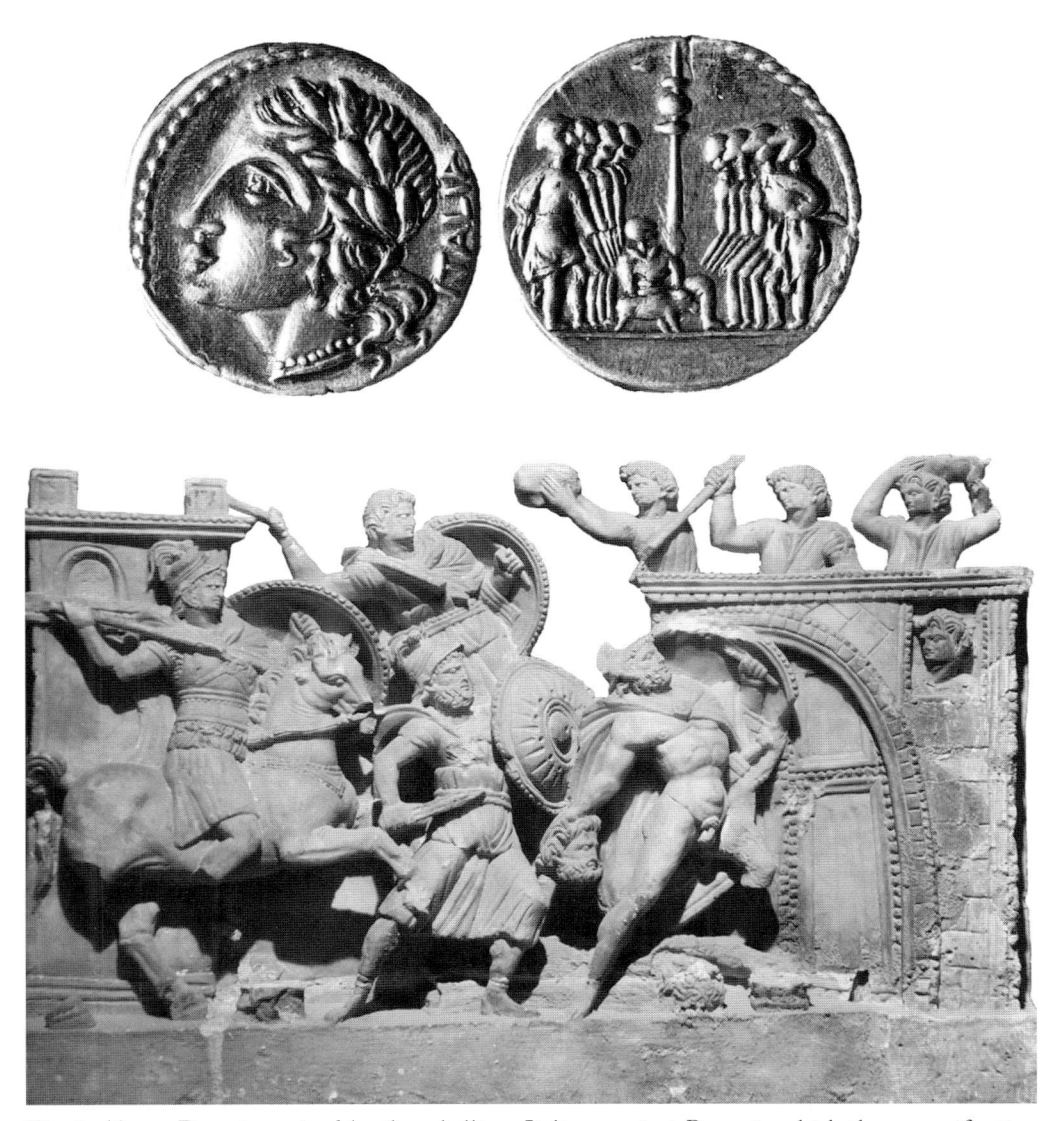

Fig. 1: Above: Denarius coined by the rebellious Italians against Rome in which the personification of Italy is reproduced on the obverse in the form of a laureate head and the inscription ITALIA, while on the reverse the ceremony of the oath of allegiance of the Italians against Rome is illustrated by four warriors on each side who draw swords to a sacrificial pig held by a young man; in the background there is a banner.
Below: The Social War. According to Fabrizio Burchianti, Director of the Volterra Museum, this Etruscan cinerary urn, which represents the mythological siege of Thebes, could be a metaphor for Sulla's siege of Volterra in 82–80 BC. The besieged city seems to be Volterra exactly, with the Porta all'Arco sculpted with its typical three decorated heads, while the besiegers seem to be Roman soldiers, with a horseman armed with a spear and three infantrymen, of which two are in tunics with *gladius* in hand and one depicted in heroic nakedness with his sword in its scabbard. Volterra, Guarnacci Museum. (*Author's photo*)

'having altered the arrangement of his troops, he drew up those in the right wing, which was nearest to the enemy, in three lines; he distributed the slingers and archers among the infantry, posted all the cavalry on the flanks, and having made a brief address, such as time permitted, to his men, he led them down, with the front changed into a flank, toward the plain'.[233]

The impossibility of defining with certainty when and why the cohortal battle array was born, has led modern authors to theorise that it was an innovation necessary to face the new enemy. The Germanic populations of the Cimbri and Teutons created great fear among the Romans, bringing back the memory of the Celtic invasions[234] at the time of the sack of Rome by the Senonian Gauls in the fourth century BC.

In fighting 'their courage and daring made them irresistible, and when they engaged in battle they came on with the swiftness and force of fire …'.[235] Marius managed to get the better of these barbarian hordes because on the one hand he prevented any reckless attitude of his soldiers, while on the other he 'accustomed them not to fear their shape or dread their cries, which were altogether strange and ferocious; and to make themselves acquainted with their equipment and movements, thus in the course of time rendering what was only apparently formidable familiar to their minds from observation. For he considered that their novelty falsely imparts to terrifying objects many qualities which they do not possess, but that with familiarity even those things which are really dreadful lose their power to affright.'[236]

Precisely how the Germanic attacks were carried out at the time of Marius is not very clear, as Plutarch does not go into much detail. It was certainly a violent horde, poorly organised, prone to fury and the desire to fight, so much so that it attacked in a complete tactical disadvantage with the Roman army deployed on a hill. While the Teutons 'wrathfully' attacked the hill, Marius ordered his men to hurl the javelins only when they were within their reach, 'then take to their swords and crowd the Barbarians back with their shields; for since the enemy were on precarious ground their blows would have no force and the locking of their shields no strength, but the unevenness of the ground would keep them turning and tossing about'.[237] Probably the cohort was created to meet this type of attack, to overcome the limits of the manipular deployment, the small size of which made it weak in the face of a brutal mass attack.

The cohort was, therefore, a formation that had the characteristics of autonomy from the rest of the army but also of size; necessities that were created to face enemies that attacked on a very wide front, in an impetuous, even if not organised, way.

III (B).1,4 The Social and Civil Wars (90-40 BC)

The first century BC was a period of great political instability, marked first by the Social War, in which the Romans fought against their Italic allies who claimed Roman citizenship, followed by the Civil Wars in which the Roman legions faced each other. In the end, after its first seven centuries of existence, Rome, which had always fought against external enemies, found itself fighting against itself, against armed men who had a military organisation and equal (or largely comparable) armament. We find a similar phenomenon, as the only exception, in the wars against the Latins who fought and were armed like the Romans, after Tarquinius Superbus placed them in the *Legio Gemina*, that is, made up of mixed groups of Romans and Latins. But this ancient incident was not disruptive, in the sense that there were no particular repercussions on the type of armament, such as happened in the Late Consular Age, probably because the combat was seasonal (not professional) and the result that each army sought to obtain was victory and not the definitive defeat of the opponent, a fact that did not emphasise the technical skills of the fight. Above all, we must consider that the ancient clash against the Latins lasted only a limited time and employed much smaller number of fighters than the Civil Wars, to the extent that it did not leave any tangible signs in the historiography and had even less influence on weaponry.

After the historic reforms of Marius, the Roman army became professional and above all bound to its commanding general, transforming the political conflict between plebeians and aristocrats into a military one, with Gaius Marius representing the faction of *populares* and Lucius Cornelius Sulla the nobles. Appian tells us that 'while they were thus occupied the so-called Social War, in which many Italian peoples were engaged, broke out. It began unexpectedly, grew rapidly to great proportions and extinguished the Roman sedition for a long time by a new terror. When it was ended it also gave rise to new seditions under more powerful leaders, who did not work by introducing new laws, or by the tricks of the demagogue, but by matching whole armies against each other …'[238] To understand how the political climate had changed, see the statement of Julius Caesar, who said how '… arms and laws had not the same season',[239] responding to Metellus who had demanded he respect them. In many aspects the first century BC was a period of civil regression, but also one of great development in fighting technique. The society increasingly based its political choices on acts of force, where power was represented by the *gladius*, so much so that Julius Caesar 'slapped the handle of his sword' when the Senate denied him the extension of his command in his province and declared 'But this will give it!'[240] The *gladius* had now become the weapon par excellence, not only for the general and his bodyguard ('one soldier standing behind him with a sword'[241]), but also for all the soldiers, so much so that during the Battle of Pharsalus, Lucanus stated: 'Winged forth their shafts unaimed, till all the sky grew dark with missiles hurled; and from the night brooding above, Death struck his victims down … By civil war suffices spear nor lance, urged on their flight afar: the hand must grip the sword and drive it to the foeman's heart.'[242]

The clashes and battles that followed one another during the first century involved numerous regular armies loyal to one or the other faction, which fought not only in Italy, but also on foreign soil. Lucanus described civil wars as '… worse than civil on Emathian plains, And crime let loose we sing: how Rome's high race plunged in her vitals her victorious sword; Armies akin embattled, … Of all the shaken earth bent on the fray; and burst asunder, to the common guilt, A kingdom's compact; eagle with eagle met, Standard to standard, spear opposed to spear.'[243]

Horace showed the indelible marks that these wars left on Roman history with the allegory of the murder of Remus committed by Romulus, of which we quote some verses, since it is the poem that is most easily able to describe the drama that took place in that period:

> Villains where are you rushing to? Why are your hands
> Grasping those swords that were sheathed?
> Hasn't enough Roman blood been shed over
> The fields, and Neptune's waves?…
> That's it: a cruel fate and a crime
> of a brother's murder have driven the Romans on,
> even since the innocent's Remus blood
> was spilt on the ground,
> blood that has brought a curse on her descendants.[244]

> Now another generation is crushed by civil war
> And Rome collapsed under its own power.
> The city that neither its Marsian neighbours managed to destroy,
> not the threat of Porsenna's Etruscan troops,
> nor the valour of its rival Capua, no fierce Spartacus
> not the rebellious and disloyal Allòbroges,
> which wild Germany with its blue-eyed youth never mastered
> nor Hannibal, the dread of parents,
> that city will be destroyed by use, un unholy generation whose blood is accursed, and
> the ground will be taken over once again by savage beasts.[245]

Armitage calculated that in the culminating phase of the civil wars of the first century BC, probably about a quarter of the male citizens in Rome between 17 and 46 years of age were under arms.[246] But probably the only way to understand the true scale of these conflicts is to see the numerical strength of the armies that faced each other, which, while analysing only the most relevant events, is impressive:

First Civil War 88–81 BC: Marius against Sulla

Eutropius tells us that the celebration of the victories of Pompey in Africa and Sulla over Mithridates '… was the termination of two most lamentable wars, the Italian, also called the Social, and the Civil, which lasted for ten years, and occasioned the destruction of more than a hundred and fifty thousand men; twenty-four of consular rank, seven of praetorian, sixty of that of aedile, and nearly three hundred senators'.[247]

Historical Event	Troops	Sources
83 BC, Sulla returns to Italy after the First Mithridatic War	Army of 30,000 experienced soldiers	Velleius Paterculus, *Roman History*, II, 24.
The Marian army is waiting for Sulla	15 generals 450 cohorts of inexperienced soldiers	Plutarch, *Parallel Lives*, 'Sulla', 27.
Gnaeus Pompeius Magnus recruits his father's veterans	3 legions	Plutarch, *Parallel Lives*, 'Pompey', 7.
Sulla defeats the army of Gaius Norbanus	The Democratic army lost 7,000 soldiers	Plutarch, *Parallel Lives*, 'Sulla', 27.
Sulla opposes Cornelius Scipio	40 Marian cohorts joined the Sullan army	Plutarch, *Parallel Lives*, 'Sulla', 28.
Clash between Sulla and the Consul Marius, son of Gaius Marius	Sulla lost 400 men, Marius lost 15,000 men	Eutropius, *Roman History*, V, 8, 1.
Clash between Sulla and the Marians Lamponius and Carinate	Of Marius' 70,000 men, 12,000 surrendered to Sulla, the others were killed	Eutropius, *Roman History*, V, 8, 1.

The Sertorian Wars 82–72 BC

Quintus Sertorius, a Marian general, united the Iberian tribes with his three original legions, which he armed and instructed in Roman tactics against the Sullan armies of Metellus Pius and Pompeius Magnus. Frontinus tells us that

> Sertorius was admired and loved by the Barbarians, and especially because by introducing Roman arms and formations and signals [*tesserae*][248] he did away with their frenzied and furious displays of courage, and converted their forces into an army, instead of a huge band of robbers. Still further, he used gold and silver without stint for the decoration of their helmets and the ornamentation of their shields, and by teaching them to wear flowered cloaks and tunics, and furnishing them with the means to do this, and sharing their love of beautiful array, he won the hearts of all.[249]

He developed tactics that 'evaded every kind of open fighting, and who made all manner of shifts and changes, owing to the light equipment and agility of his Iberian soldiers' putting the troops of Metellus Pius in difficulty, who adopted a phalanx-like battle array, 'ponderous and immobile, which, for repelling and overpowering an enemy at close quarters, was most excellently trained, but for climbing mountains, for dealing with the incessant pursuits and flights of men as light as the winds, and for enduring hunger and a life without fire or tent, as their enemies did, it was worthless'.[250]

Historical Event	Troops	Sources
The consul Octavius, supporting Sulla, defeats the Marian consul Cinna, supported by Sertorius.	The Marians loose about 10,000 men	Plutarch, *Parallel Lives*, 'Sertorius', IV, 8.
Sertorius has the Pyrenees garrisoned against a possible Sullan attack	He garrisoned the Pyrenees with 6,000 infantry	Plutarch, *Parallel Lives*, 'Sertorius'. VII, 1.
Composition of the Sertorian army	2,600 Romans 700 Libyans 4,000 Lusitan peltasts 700 horsemen	Plutarch, *Parallel Lives*, 'Sertorius', XII, 2.
Composition of the Roman army	120,000 infantrymen 6,000 horsemen 2,000 archers/slingers	Plutarch, *Parallel Lives*, 'Sertorius', XII, 2.
Army of Perpenna Vento, Marian, who supports Sertorius	53 cohorts	Plutarch, *Parallel Lives*, 'Sertorius', XV, 5.

Second Civil War 49–45 BC: Caesar against Pompey

Adlocutio of Caesar before the Battle of Pharsalus against Pompey the Great:

> This the day … which gives you back Your homes and kindred, and the peaceful farm … And by the fates' command this day shall prove whose quarrel juster: for defeat is guilt to him on whom it falls. If in my cause with fire and sword ye did your country wrong, strike for acquittal! Should another judge This war, not Caesar, none were blameless found … . But you, I pray, ' Touch not the foe who turns him from the fight,' A fellow citizen, a foe no more.' But while the gleaming weapons threaten still,' Let no fond memories unnerve the arm,' No pious thought of father or of kin;' But full in face of brother or of sire,' Drive home the blade …[251]

Historical Event	Troops	Sources
Spain 49 BC Army of Afranius and Petreus (Pompey's representatives)	5 legions Cavalry	Caesar, *De Bello Civili*, I, 83.
Spain 49 BC Caesar's Army	5 legions Cavalry	Caesar, *De Bello Civili*, I, 83.
Army of Isauricus in support of Caesar (early 49 BC)	600 elite cavalrymen 5 legions	Plutarch, *Parallel Lives* 'Caesar', XXXVII, 3.
Battle of Pharsalus: Pompey's army	7,000 horsemen 45,000 Infantrymen	Plutarch, *Parallel Lives* 'Caesar', XLII, 3-4
Battle of Pharsalus: Caesar's army[252]	1000 Horsemen 22,000 Infantrymen	Plutarch, *Parallel Lives* 'Caesar', XLII, 3-4

Historical Event	Troops	Sources
War of Africa:	'*Infinitus*' number of horsemen 4 legions of King Juba Many light troops 10 legions of Scipio 120 elephants Many naval squadrons	Pseudo-Caesar, *La lunga guerra civile*. Rizzoli, *La guerra d'Africa*, I, 4.
Republican army	2,000 horsemen 6 legions	Pseudo-Cesare, *La lunga guerra civile*. Rizzoli, *La guerra d'Africa*, II, 1.

Third Civil War 44–43 BC: Modena war between Marcus Antonius and Decimus Brutus

Historical event	Troops	Sources
Army of Antonius and Publius Ventidius Bassus	3 veteran legions (II Gallica and XXXV) 1 *evocati* legion (M. Antonius) 3 *evocati* legions (P. Ventidius Bassus)	Appian, *The Civil Wars*, III, 46-49.
Army of Octavianus, Aulus Irtius, Gaius Vibio Pansa and Decimus Brutus	2 veteran legions (III Macedonica and Martia) 1 legion of recruits 2 *evocati* legions commanded by A. Irtius and Octavianus 4 legions of recruits (commanded by Vibius Pansa) 2 veteran legions 1 legion of recruits (commanded by Decimus Brutus)	Appian, *The Civil Wars*, III, 46-49.

42 BC: Victory over Caesar's Murderers

Army of Marcus Junius Brutus and Caius Cassius Longinus	17 legions (2 complete, the others understrength)	Appian, *The Civil Wars*, IV, 112.
Army of Marcus Antonius and Caesar Octavianus	19 complete legions 13,000 horsemen (Octavianus) 20,000 horsemen (Antonius)	Appian, *The Civil Wars*, IV, 112.

41–40 BC: Octavianus besieges Perugia defended by Lucius Antonius and Fulvia, wife of Marcus Antonius.

Octavianus	4 legions	Appian, *The Civil Wars*, V, 32.

The value of these lists, albeit incomplete, consists the message we can see, represented by the enormous number of soldiers involved in this conflict, all of Roman origin, who in the effort to prevail over the other faction determined changes both in tactics and in armament, including the *gladius*.

III (B).2 THE FIGHTING IN THE FIRST CENTURY BC

III (B).2,1 The cohortal legio

According to Varro, the *cohors* is called '"cohort," because, just as on the farm the *cohors* [yard] "is joined together" [*coniungitur*] of several buildings and becomes a certain type of unity, so in the army it "is coupled together" by several maniples'.[253] In other words, the cohort was the result of the union of three maniples: one from the *hastati*, one from the *principes* and one from the *triarii*. Polybius also confirms this approach, stating that 'the usual number of velites and three maniples (this body of infantry the Romans call a cohort)'[254] were placed in front of the cavalry squadrons.

The maniples, which we remember were 'the smallest *manus* [troop] which has a standard of its own to follow,'[255] in the previous legions were distinguished by age, military value and armament, such that the classification into *hastati*, *principes* or *triarii* conditioned tactics. In the Late Consular Age, this difference disappears although the previous names remained, so the maniple survived only as an administrative unit. We can deduce this concept very well from the episode narrated by Julius Caesar, to which we will return later, in which to counter encirclement by the cavalry of Labienus, he changed the front of some of his cohorts, without modifying the arrangement of the maniples, allowing us to understand how their roles were superimposable.[256]

From the information of Aulus Gellius, who wrote in the first half of the second century AD how 'in a legion there are sixty centuries, thirty maniples, and ten cohorts',[257] we understand the military structure, where each maniple was made up of two centuries and how each of the ten cohorts had three maniples. Furthermore, we can conclude how the military organisation developed vertically, similarly to the Polybian one from which it derived, thus understanding that an *ordo* corresponds to a cohort.

The historical moment in which the cohort was formed is universally attributed to that of Gaius Marius, but this approach is questionable as there are some mentions which, as described in the previous chapters, could confirm the hypothesis that it existed before this. The most important question is not by whom and when it was created, but the reason why it was. The war conditions and the enemies they faced gave rise to the need for formations that were endowed with greater autonomy and flexibility in combat, therefore able to fit the various war requirements. We know that the enemies in this historical period were mainly Romans themselves, and their way of fighting and deployments made the previous formations inefficient.

We can understand this concept by analysing the limits of a legion commanded by Quintus Cecilius Metellus Pius, who, 'now getting on in years'[258] (and for this reason perhaps less open to more innovative types of combat) did not know how to deal

> with a man of daring [Sertorius] who evaded every kind of open fighting, and who made all manner of shifts and changes, owing to the light equipment and agility of his Iberian soldiers; whereas he himself had been trained in regular contests of heavy-armed troops, and was wont to command a ponderous and immobile phalanx, which, for repelling and overpowering an enemy at close quarters, was

Triarii   (20 centuriae)
Principes (20 centuriae)
Hastati   (20 centuriae)

10 Cohortes
(4.800 milites + officers)

Diagram 1:
The cohortal legion. (*Author's drawing*)

most excellently trained, but for climbing mountains, for dealing with the incessant pursuits and flights of men as light as the winds, and for enduring hunger and a life without fire or tent, as their enemies did, it was worthless.[259]

The legion, understood as a compact, 'phalangitic' formation, was not suitable for a mountainous environment, in the context of a guerrilla war, nor to perform rapid actions such as in the capture of favourable positions. As Caesar explains, when he had to attack an enemy such as the Eburons,[260] who did

not have any definite body of troops, any stronghold, any garrison to defend itself in arms, but the population was scattered in all directions. Each man had settled where a hidden valley or a wooden locality or an entangled morass offered some hope of defence or security, … [therefore] if Caesar wanted to finish off the business and to make away with a brood of malefactors, he must needs send several cohorts in different directions and move his troops at wide intervals; if he wished to keep the companies with the standards, as the established rule and custom of the Roman army required, the locality itself gave protection to the natives, and individuals among them lacked not to daring to lay secret ambush and surround scattered detachments.[261]

In summary, the condition of the terrain and of the enemies to be faced, led the Romans to develop an array of characteristics of extreme flexibility, where the cohorts became the unit carrying out military actions, of which various examples are given below.

Afranius, legate of Pompey the Great, noticing Caesar intending to storm a small hill, promptly sent 'the cohorts … which were stationed in front of the camp … by a shorter route to occupy the same position'.[262] Even Lucius Licinius Lucullus, on Sulla's side in the Social War, found himself in a position to seize a favourable position on top of a hill so 'he himself, with two cohorts, hastened eagerly towards the hill … he led his men against the mail-clad horsemen, ordering them not to hurl their javelins yet, but taking each his own man, to smite the enemy's legs and thighs, which are the only parts of these mail-clad horsemen [cataphracts] left exposed'.[263]

Using autonomous combat units allowed reinforcements to be sent to the points in the battle where they were required: when the Britons carried out a sudden assault on Caesar's outposts by engaging in a fierce fight, 'Caesar sent up two cohorts in support';[264] or they were useful in cases where it was necessary to increase offensive pressure at critical moments such as when 'the cohorts [of Caesar)] surrounded the left wing, the Pompeians still fighting and continuing their resistance in their lines'.[265]

At the same time, in the context of the Civil War, the armies used the same fighting methods and the cohorts were used by both sides to reinforce the fighting line, so that 'the forces of the foe were increasing and cohorts were continually being sent up to them from the camp through the town so that the unexhausted were always taking the place of the exhausted. Caesar was obliged to adopt the same course of withdrawing the exhausted and sending up supporting cohorts to the same place.'[266]

Up until now, we have emphasised the cohort as a single unit of action. In reality, the commander, because of this new legion, could rely on various combinations to obtain the most effective conduct for military requirements. For example, when a river had to be crossed '… the cohorts were seen forming in maniples with a view to crossing';[267] while, during the fight with Afranius, Caesar 'leads three legions out of the camp, and having drawn up the line in a suitable position, he orders a picked advance guard [the *antesignani*] from one legion to charge and occupy the mound'.[268] We therefore see that the individual military units making up a cohort could be used like pieces on a chessboard to achieve the best outcome.

At the same time the *dux* could act on the dynamics of the formations and when situations of encirclement occurred, in this regard Caesar explains that 'some of these proposed to form a wedge and break through speedily, as the camp was so near at hand, feeling confident that if some part were surrounded and slain, yet the remainder could be saved'.[269] In another situation, Caesar's troops 'were surrounded by the enemy cavalry [Numidians], and compelled [to fight] penned behind bars as it were'.[270]

Julius Caesar narrates that a formation was initially assumed in which the front of the cohorts was arranged on all four sides so as to always expose the first line to the enemy, and the cohorts were 'compact', so that the individual infantrymen occupied a minimum space ('penned behind bars') better to face the cavalry.

> Meanwhile Caesar, aware of the enemy's tactics, gave orders for the line to be extended to its maximum length, and for every other cohort to turn about, so that one was facing to the rear of the standards, while the next one faced to their front. By this means with his right and left wing he split in half the encircling enemy force; and having isolated one half from the other with his cavalry, proceeded to attack it from inside with his infantry, turning it to flight with volleys of missiles: then, after advancing no great distance for fear of ambush, he retired to his own lines.[271] (Fig. 1).

The general, thanks to his intelligence and the ability to move his army in a flexible way, was able to prevail over a superior force.

But if agility and flexibility were the qualities that characterised the cohortal legions, these characteristics were at the expense of the power that these sub-units could oppose. As Caesar tells us, when his soldiers were attacked by the Numidian cavalry of Afranius's array, 'if the cohorts advanced against them, they fell back, and

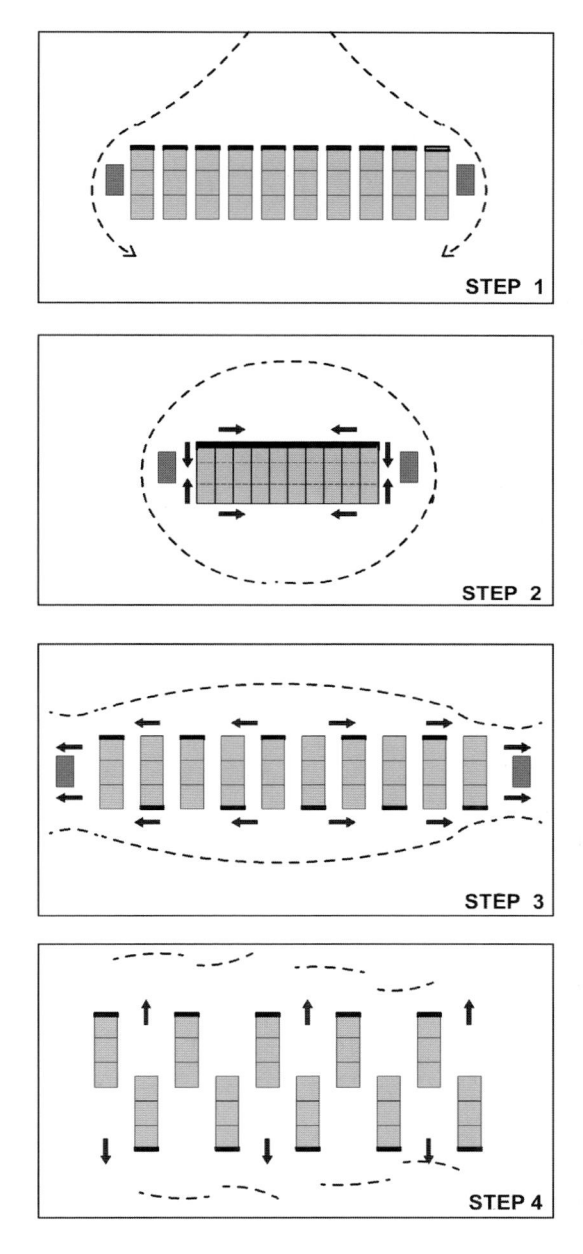

Fig. 1: Representation of the movements of the cohorts of a legion in a battle described by Caesar:
Phase 1: the Roman hosts are surrounded by the Numidian cavalry;
Phase 2: the cohorts are compelled to close up into a square;
Phase 3: Caesar widens the line as much as possible and at the same time deploys them on alternating sides. The cavalry attacks and breaks through the Numidian encirclement;
Phase 4: the cohorts, now with alternated front, start to attack on both fronts and disperse the enemy.
It should therefore be noted how the great flexibility and manoeuvrability of the cohorts themselves should therefore be noted, as well as how the behaviour of the maniples is indifferent to the position they occupy within the cohort, testifying how the distinction of *hastati*, *principes* and *triarii* is now merely administrative. (*Author's drawing*)

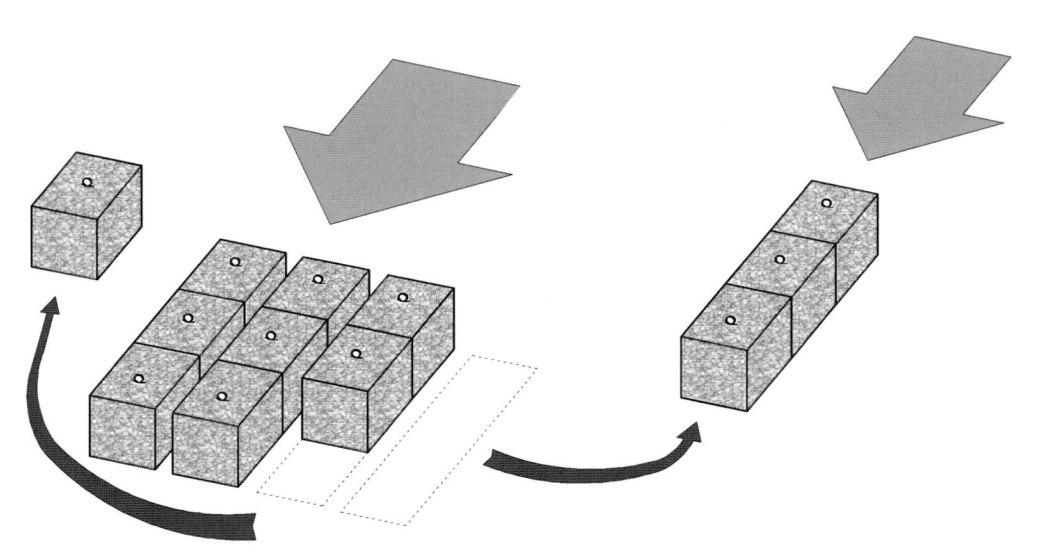

Fig. 2: As for the Polybian legion, we can use the allegory of concrete blocks (the maniples) having a barrier function for the cohortal legion, but whilst the Polybian were collaborating but always separated, in this case they can virtually merge with each other to create a single body of great strength (the cohort), which can be used both in collaboration with the others or separately and, if necessary, again subdivided into the three original blocks. All this to show the great flexibility of use and variety of configurations. (*Author's drawing*)

by the quickness of their retreat, eluded the charge, but immediately returning, they got behind our men, and cut them off from the rest of the army. Thus it was equally dangerous for them to maintain their ranks, or advance to battle.'[272]

We can finish our description of the cohorts and their autonomous formations, by observing that such units could behave in a heroic way, but also disappoint the expectations of their commander, as when 'Sulla ordered a cohort and its centurions, though whose defences the enemy had broken, to stand continuously at headquarters, wearing helmets and without uniforms',[273] confirming the independent identity of these formations. We should also remember how the *velites* were dismissed with the establishment of the cohortal *legio*,[274] a topic already dealt with in the section on the pre-cohortal legion.

As for the armament of the infantrymen, we must say that the ancient sources do not provide us with information regarding this. We can deduce that the armament was now standardised and same for all soldiers including the *gladius*, from the fact that the differences between *hastati*, *principes* and *triarii* were, as previously mentioned, no longer tactical but only administrative and that therefore the units could be considered as equivalent and interchangeable with each other.

To conclude, as for the previous ones, we would like to introduce an explanatory metaphor of its essence, which being very similar to the Polybian, will also be so in the allegory itself. So let us think once again of barriers made of concrete blocks, with units of varying size and of various shapes, to adapt to the needs of the terrain or the enemy they are facing.

III (B).2,2 The numbers of the cohortal legio
The numerical definition of the cohortal legion is a complex subject to deal with, based on many respects on pure speculation, since there are no ancient sources that give us precise numbers. First of all, as for the previous legions, we must not think that the number of infantry making up a single legion was always the same, since there were many factors that could vary its size. It is sufficient to think that in the Marian period, the first cohort was not double in numbers, but this begins to appear in the Caesarian period; moreover, according to the requirements of war, the legions could be larger, while, on the contrary, in case of losses, they could be smaller.

Following the definition given by Vegetius, we know that the

> first cohort exceeds the remainder in the number of soldiers and in rank, for it seeks out the most select men as regards birth and instruction in letters. It protects the eagle, which was always the especial and distinctive sign in the Roman army of a whole legion … it has 1,105 infantry, 132 armoured cavalry and it is called military cohort [*cohors militaria*].[275]

The author continues with the explanation that the other cohorts are made up of 555 infantry and 66 horsemen each, and that 'with these ten cohorts the full legion is formed, having 6,100 infantry, 730 cavalry'.[276] Although the author lived in the fourth century AD, we have a confirmation of the validity of these numbers from a quotation from Appian, who states how the consuls Gaius Norbanus and Lucius Scipio, together with the former consul Carbo, 'marched against Sulla in detachments. They had 200 cohorts of 500 men at first, and their forces were considerably augmented afterward.'[277]

Therefore, we have an indicative value of what the size of a cohort should have been (500–555 men), even if this data does not correspond to that reported by Hyginus, according to whom a complete *centuria* was composed of 80 soldiers,[278] so that we would get a legion with smaller numbers, precisely of 4,800 men (with each cohort of 480 infantry), excluding the officers (Diagram 1). The number of men in a legion according to Hyginus, could rise to 5,280 infantry, again without considering the officers, in the event that the first cohort was considered 'military', that is double strength.

Also in this case, as for the previous legions, we are not interested in investigating the numerical problem in depth, especially when this dissertation is exclusively based on personal speculations or hypotheses of other modern authors. In fact, the real objective is not so much to understand the size of a formation, but instead the *gladius* and the Roman combat, trying to understand the meaning and reasons for its evolution.

III (B) 2,3 First-century BC combat – techniques and training
The first century BC was a turning point for the adopted fighting techniques, since the Civil Wars were a historical event in which the enemy was Romans themselves. The infantrymen of the opposite sides, fighting with identical tactical schemes and using the same attack and defence weapons, pushed the army to make changes that would increase their mutual effectiveness. The evolution was sudden and truly innovative,

especially when compared with that of the previous six centuries, and concerned both technology and armaments.

Over time, Roman fighting techniques had progressively evolved, becoming more and more complex, to the point that the infantry had become professional men-at-arms. The movements had to be coordinated, the adopted manoeuvres were varied and had to be carried out without hesitation, and the combat that the infantrymen sustained had to follow specific criteria, based on preparation and not on improvisation. These principles, compared to the past, were emphasised to such an extent that to make it clear, we report the teachings of Sertorius (126–72 BC), when he had to make this understood by the Iberians, who formed a large part of his army. The Marian general

> introduced before it two horses, one utterly weak and already quite old, the other large-sized and strong, with a tail that was astonishing for the thickness and beauty of its hair. By the side of the feeble horse stood a man who was tall and robust, and by the side of the powerful horse another man, small and of a contemptible appearance. At a signal given them, the strong man seized the tail of his horse with both hands and tried to pull it towards him with all his might, as though he would tear it off; but the weak man began to pluck out the hairs in the tail of the strong horse one by one. The strong man gave himself no end of trouble to no purpose, made the spectators laugh a good deal, and then gave up his attempt; but the weak man, in a trice and with no trouble, stripped his horse's tail of its hair.[279]

According to Sertorius, violence and unexpected haste were not effective against an organised way of fighting, based on perseverance and the exploitation of opportunities, to the extent that when he trained an army of barbarians, he managed to beat the Roman legions of Metellus, by ambushing them.

It is possible to understand the statement of Dionysius of Halicarnassus in this context, who wrote: 'a smaller army which understands what must be done is superior to a large army that is uninstructed'.[280] Marius, on the basis of such principles, created a professional army, preparing training no longer based on roles related to age and military maturity, but aimed at giving them all the technical skills to fight in an adequate way right from the beginning. Polybius tells us that Scipio, after the conquest of Cartago Nova (209 BC), organised the training of the infantry in a way that suggests the great planning ability of the Roman:

> [he] instructed the tribunes to train the land forces in the following manner. He ordered the soldiers on the first day to go at the double for thirty stades in their armour. On the second day they were all to polish up, repair, and examine their arms in full view, and the third day to rest and remain idle. On the following day they were to practise, some of them sword-fighting with wooden swords [μαχαιρομαχεῖνξυλίναις] covered with leather and with a button on the point, while others practised casting with javelins also having a button at the point. On the fifth day they were to begin the same course of exercise again.[281]

Vegetius[282] confirms to us, like Dionysius of Halicarnassus, that weapons training became the starting point for the military preparation of soldiers, because 'neither the arena nor the battle-field ever proved a man invincible in armed combat, unless he was judged to have been thoroughly trained at the post'. The training of the recruits was based on harmless weapons ('wooden foils likewise of double weight, instead of swords'), having 'a double weight' to better condition them for actual combat. The training of the recruits took place against a 'single post in the ground' against which he 'fought' by repeating a well-defined sequence of moves, as if fighting 'against an enemy'. The recruit 'trained himself using the foil and hurdle like a sword [*gladius*] and shield [*scutum*], so that now he aimed at as it were the head and face, now threatened the flanks, then tried to cut the hamstrings and legs, backed off, came on, sprang, and aimed at the post with every method of attack and art of combat, as though it were an actual opponent'.

The comparison of military training to gladiatorial training by Vegetius is indicative of a notable evolution of combat, which in this period becomes very technical, losing any characteristic of instinct and strength. Caesar too emphasises this phenomenon, so much so that he

Fig. 3: Examples of wooden weapons found in the context of legionary fortresses and probably related to training equipment. A) *gladius* from the fort of Saalburg (Germany); B) and C) specimens from the fort of Vindolanda, near Hadrian's Wall (England). (*Author's photo*)

> proceeded to train his forces, not as a commander trains a veteran army with a magnificent record of victorious achievements, but as a gladiatorial instructor trains his recruits. How many feet they were to retreat from the enemy; the manner in which they must wheel round upon their adversary; the restricted space in which they must offer resistance – now doubling forward, now retiring and making feint attacks; and almost the spot from which, and the manner in which they must discharge their missiles – these were the lessons he taught them.[283]

Therefore, just as in the fencing treatises of later centuries, we find for the Roman infantrymen a precise framing of what must have been the position of the body, the movement of the legs and of the various types of blow which, as Vegetius points out, took place 'under the drillmaster: but by all ordinary soldiers alike in daily practice. For speed is acquired through bodily exercise itself, and also the skill to strike the enemy whilst covering oneself, especially in close-quarters sword fighting. What is more, they learn how to keep ranks and follow their ensign through such complicated evolutions in the mock-battle itself.'[284] Positions and movements were learnt through a mechanical repetition of exercises, so that they became second nature and could be carried out instinctively. Thinking during a battle could easily enable one to become a victim of fear or even cause a panic, while instinctive movements allowed the maintenance of calm, essential for one's own salvation and that of the entire legion.

To better understand what some of these codified behaviours might be, we examined various representations of archaeological finds, including some military scenes and various gladiatorial figures. The latter should not be considered out of place, since we know how the consul Gnaeus Mallius Maximus, and also Julius Caesar, hired gladiator instructors as trainers, and Vegetius himself exalted gladiatorial techniques to make legionary combat more effective.

For a better understanding of the basic techniques used by a Roman soldier, we focused on the actions of an infantryman, as if he were facing a single enemy attacking head on. This didactic simplification, multiplied for the whole legionary front, formed the basis of how the overall combat could develop, which in a sense was the sum of many single duels. We must not forget that the posture of the infantryman and all his actions were intended to fight within a formation, aimed at maintaining the compactness of the front (*acies*). The general analysis for this will be addressed at the end of the paragraph, after looking further into the actions of the individual fighter.

First of all, the infantryman had an upright guard and this posture will change in the Imperial period, to assume a more aggressive and effective guard position in protecting himself from enemy blows. This different type of weight bearing can be understood by comparing two reliefs which, although both belonging to the first century AD, are good examples of this evolution of combat. The terracotta relief of the gladiator preserved in the National Roman Museum of Termae in Rome shows an upright position, where the guard is justified by the type of helmet that has a small neck guard, an indication that it would not have protected from direct hits in this area; the torso is straight and the weight of the body is mainly supported by the rear leg. It can be deduced that this attitude is aimed at better protecting himself from frontal blows and those struck from top to bottom. On the contrary, the infantryman of the stone relief of the Landen museum of Mainz is leaning forward, with the weight of the body on the forward left leg, thus assuming a more aggressive position, but at the same time giving more attention to protection, a fact testified by the large neck guard of the helmet, which is useful in this context for a better defence of the neck and the upper part of the shoulders. This guard is designed to prevent sword blows from hitting the neck and nape, the weak points of the previous type of guard (Fig. 4).

All the representations confirm that the Roman infantryman approached the enemy while maintaining a low guard, with holding the *gladius* unsheathed at waist level. The sword was held on the horizontal axis (or slightly oblique at the top), directed towards the opponent, with the blade held flat to the body and its shield (Fig. 5).

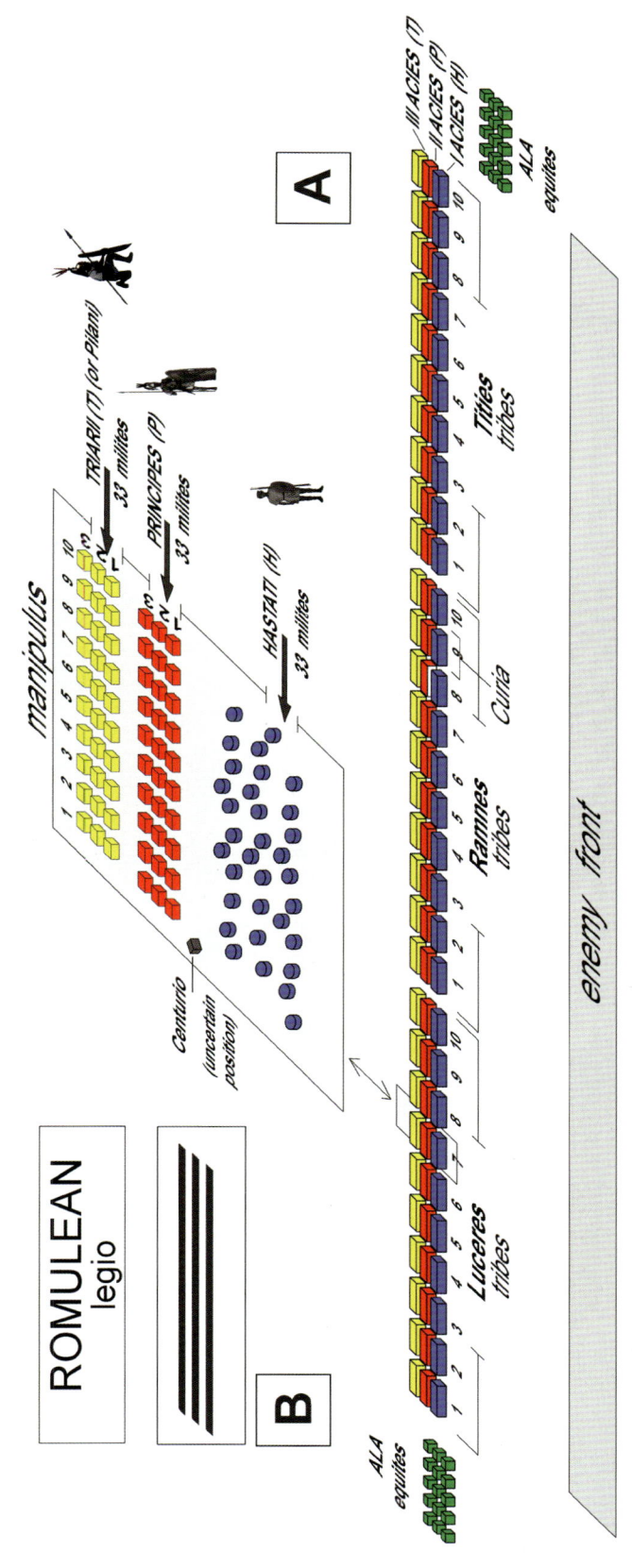

Plate 1: The Romulean *legio* was made up of 3,000 infantry (and 300 cavalry); each of the three tribes supplied 1,000 *milites* and 100 horsemen. While the cavalry formed up on the flanks in two 'alae', the thirty *manipuli* of which the *legio* was composed (ten from each tribe, i.e. one from each *curia*) made up the infantry formations. The *manipulus* (or *centuria*) was made up of 100 infantrymen, divided into three different types of fighters (*hastati*, *principes* and *triarii*), each of them participating to form one of the three *acies* characterising the Romulean *legio*. The diagram shows the arrayed army with the two wings of cavalry, and the detail explains how a *manipulus* was deployed with the corresponding types of soldiers. (*Author's drawing*)

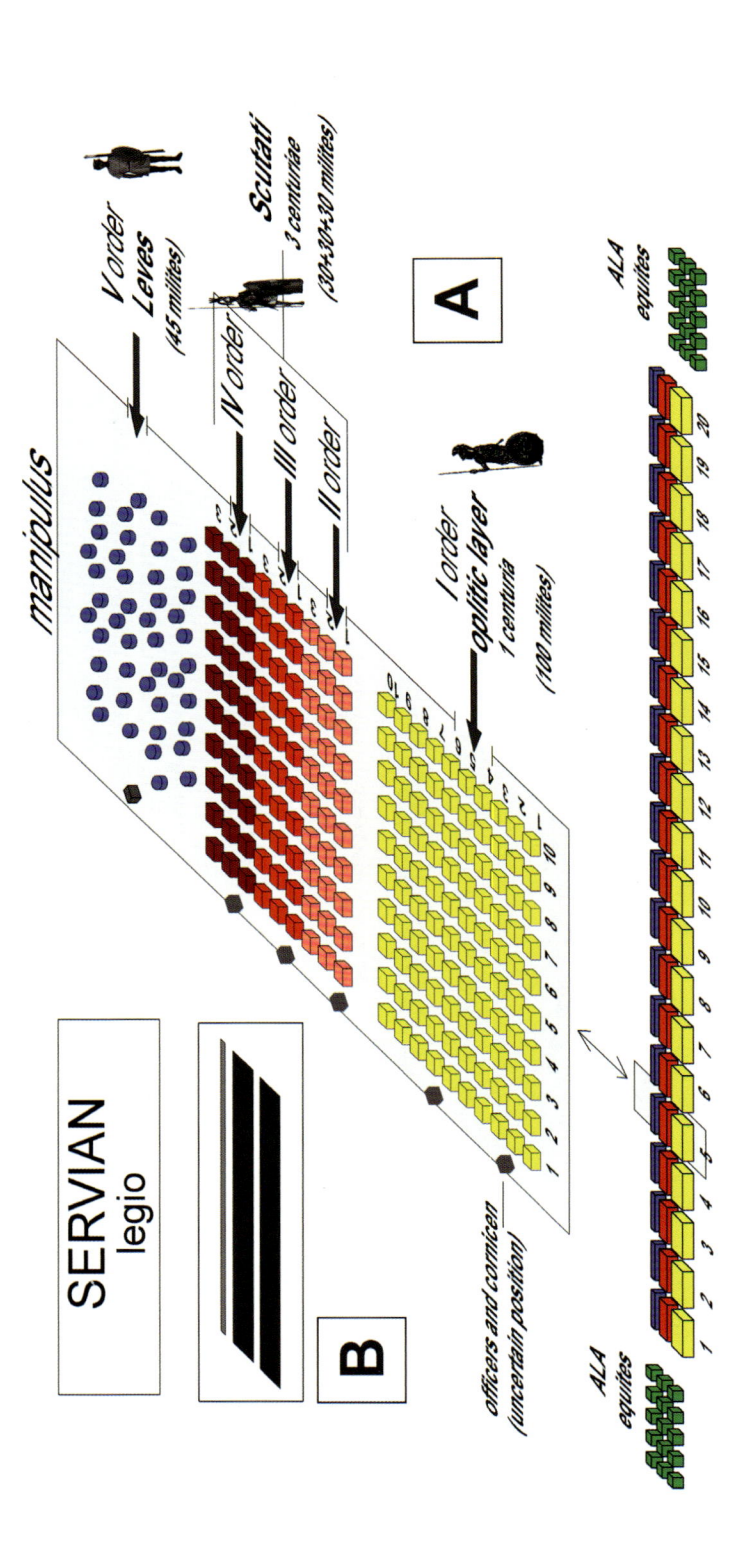

Plate 2: The *Legio Serviana*. This formation derives from the Romulean one from which it differs due to a reduction in the length of the front (from thirty to twenty maniples), with a consequent increase in the depth of the formation. Furthermore, the Servian soldiers armed with the entire panoply (of hoplite type) are placed in the front, to withstand an attack of greater strength such as that perpetrated by the Etruscan armies, and not in the third row like the *triarii* of the Romulean *legio*. The impression is therefore that with the Servian military reform, the entire Romulean formation was overturned, placing light troops at the back and heavy troops in the front. However, the real number of soldiers who made up the twenty *ordines* of the Servian front is still the subject of discussion among modern authors. A) Graphic representation of a legion with detail of a maniple. B) Diagram of the same. (*Author's drawing*)

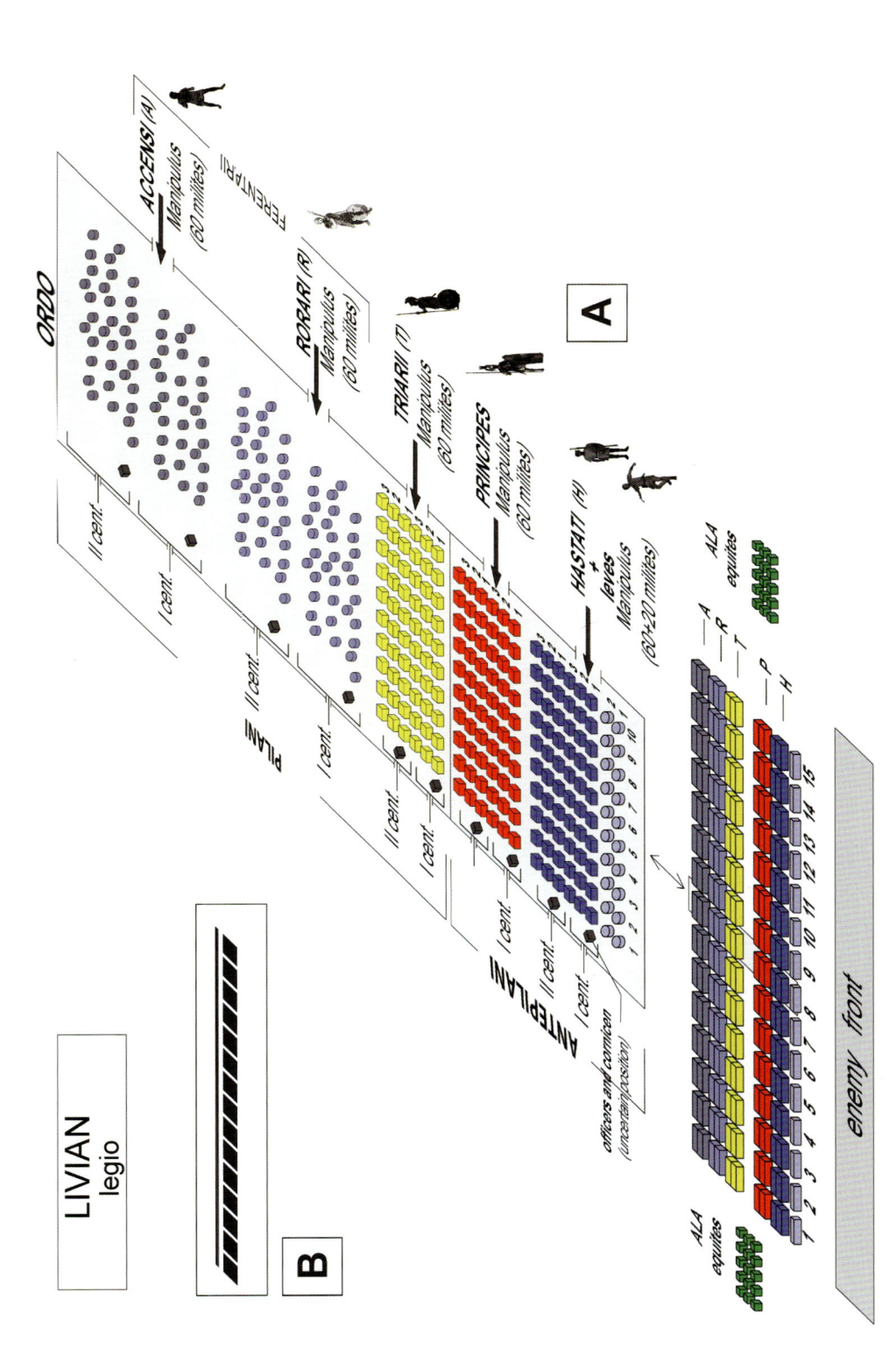

Plate 3: Graphic representation (A) of the Livian *legio* with enlarged detail of a single column (*ordo*), and schematic representation (B). It can be easily seen that this formation had a mainly vertical structure, where the maniples, drawn from administrative entities (representatives of the tribes and *curia*), became effective combat units.
The Livian *legio* can be schematically arranged in fifteen parallel and vertical rectangles (*ordines* of the *hastati* and *principes*), autonomous from each other in combat, but anchored on the unified body of the *triarii*, indicated by a single long horizontal line. The *ferentari*, as a support body, have not been represented here. (*Author's drawing*)

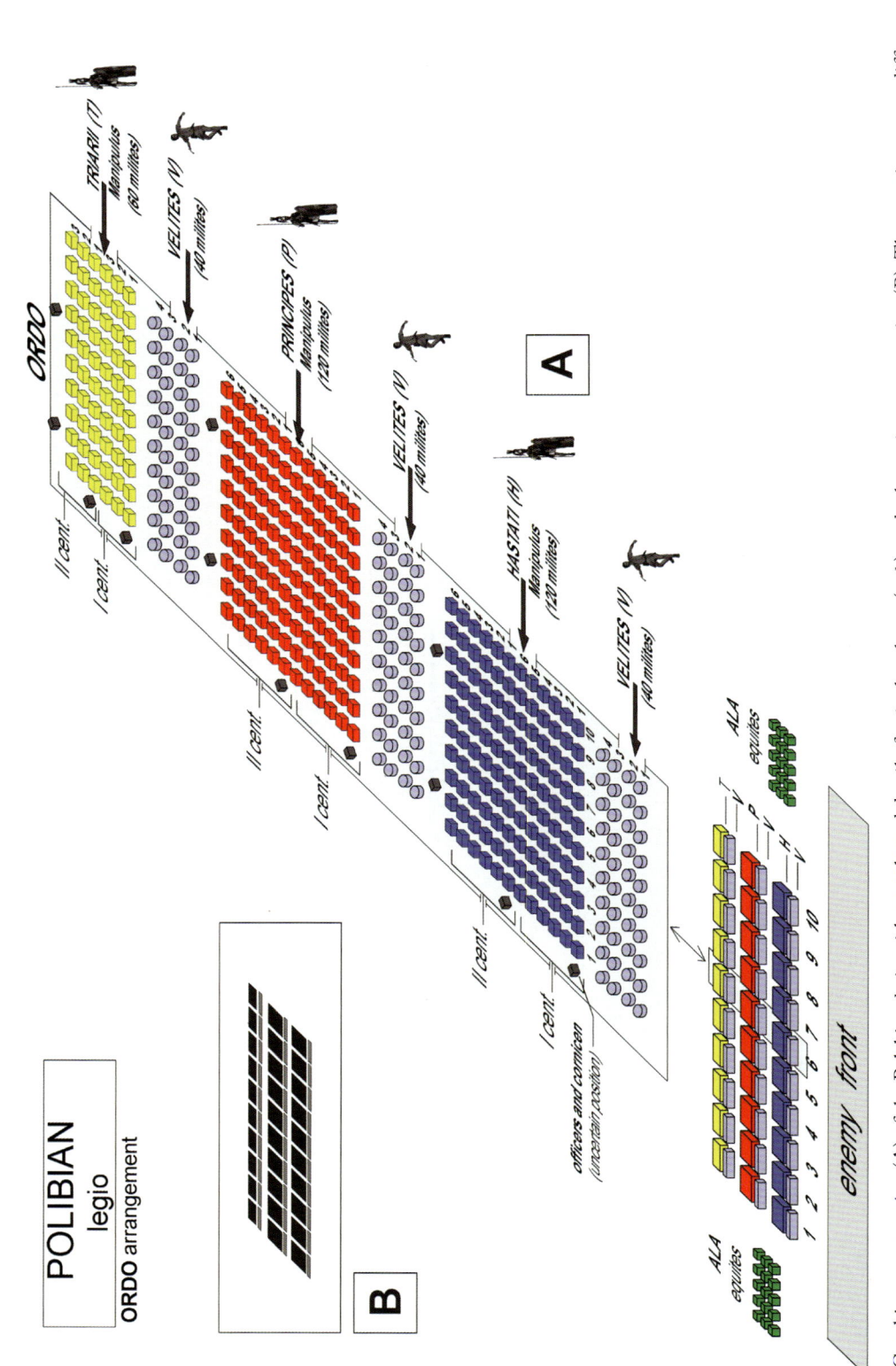

Plate 4: Graphic representation (A) of the Polybian *legio*, with an enlarged detail of a single column (*ordo*), and schematic representation (B). The most important difference from the Livian formation emerges from the analysis of the two schematic representations, where the Livian one which we have seen to be similar to fifteen parallel vertical *ordines* (*hastati* and *principes*) and a long horizontal one (the *triarii*) (see Diagram 1-B), while the Polybian one is thought of as made up only of ten parallel rectangles, each divided into three segments, thus resulting in each *ordo* (composed of a maniple of *hastati*, *principes* and *triarii*), each independent from the others. (*Author's drawing*)

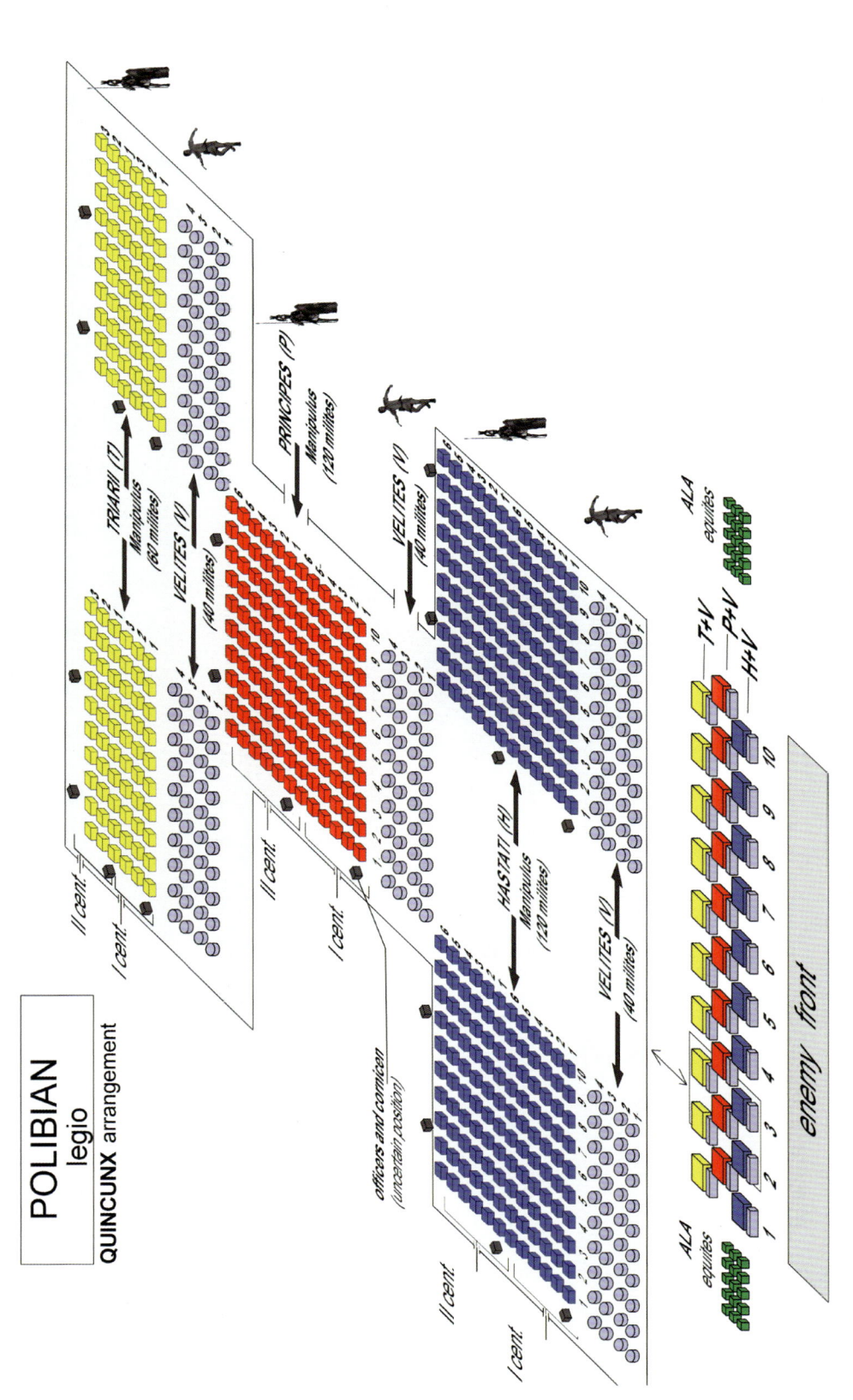

Plate 5: The battle array of the manipular legion in 'quincunx', from the name in which the number five was depicted on the face of a dice, the typical one according to the testimony of Polybius. The three maniples of each *ordo* were staggered, so that the *hastati* were aligned with the maniple of the *triarii* while the maniple of the *principes* was offset from them. The legion assumed a checkerboard layout which, intuitively, thanks to the movement of the centuries and maniples, could easily adapt to the individual needs of the battle. By doing so, however, a problem arises – which has not yet been given an explanation – that empty spaces were created into which enemies could infiltrate, aggravated by the fact that the maniples of the *principes* were not supported by the *hastati* in front nor by the *triarii* behind.

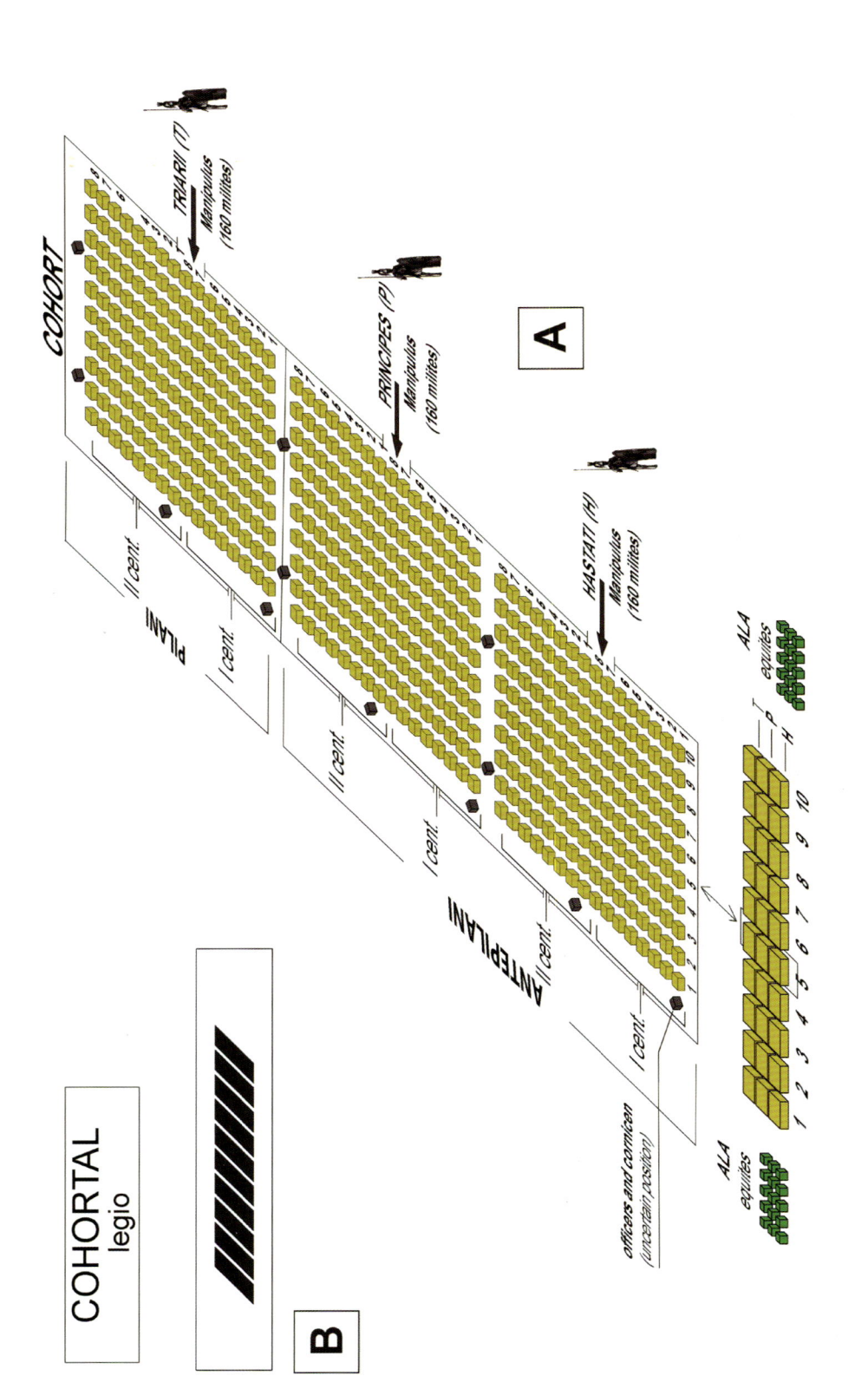

Plate 6: A: Representation of a cohortal legion of the first century BC, according to the description of Hyginus, with detail of a cohort. It was divided into ten cohorts, each of which in turn was formed by a maniple of *hastati*, one of *principes* and one of *triarii* (the *velites* have now disappeared), for which, however, the difference was only administrative and no longer linked to age, wealth, tactics and armament. To emphasise this lack of clear distinction, all infantry are represented in the same colour unlike the previous

Plate 7: Mars and Venus, fresco from the homonymous House of Pompeii, VII, 9, 47 (National Archaeological Museum of Naples). We can see represented the metaphor of the deposition of weapons in favour of love. Note how those, military symbols of Mars, are held by Venus, who holds the spear with the tip lowered as a sign of non-belligerence, and by the Putti, playing with the helmet and the Monarchical *gladius*.

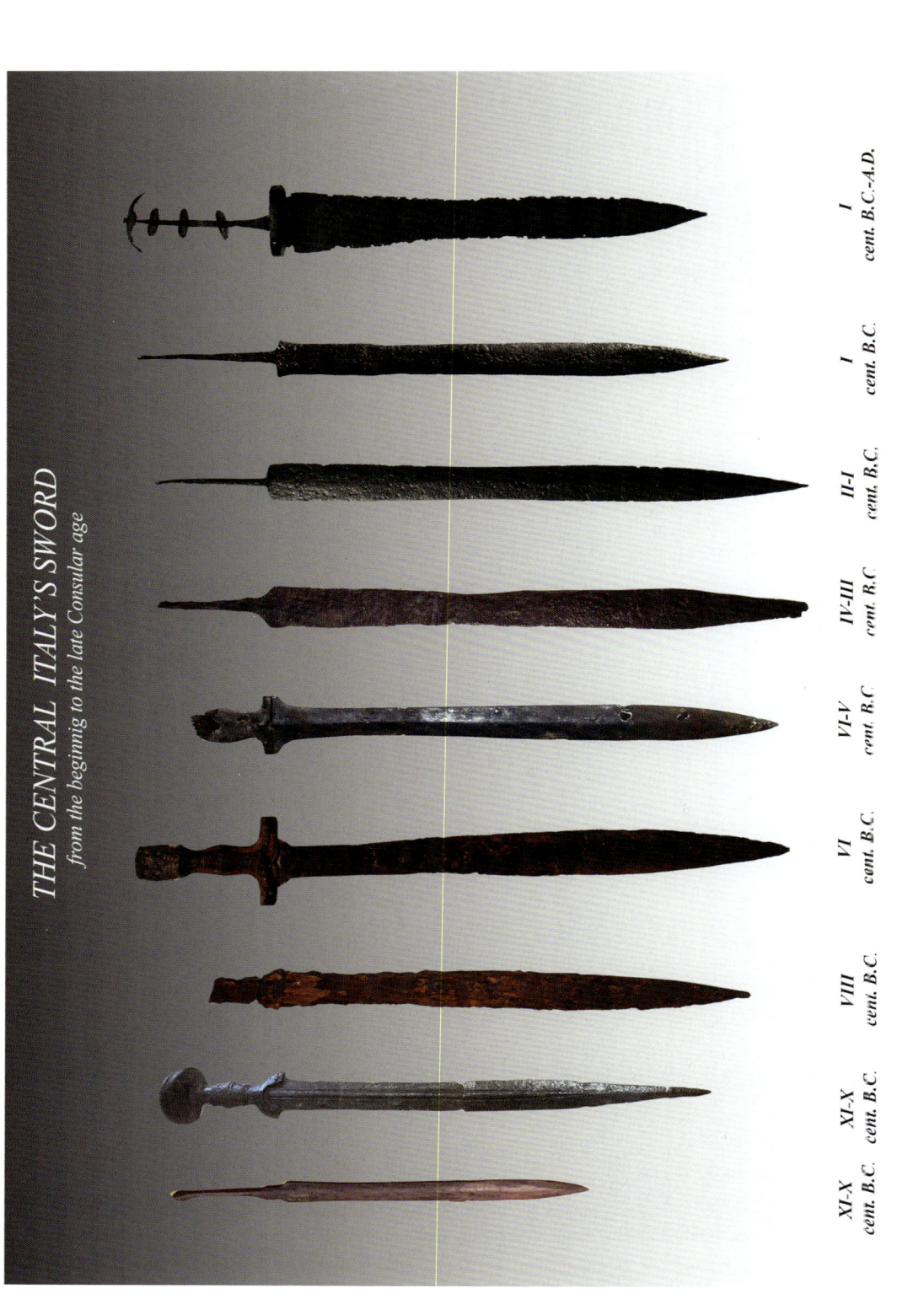

THE CENTRAL ITALY'S SWORD
from the beginning to the late Consular age

| XI-X cent. B.C. | XI-X cent. B.C. | VIII cent. B.C. | VI cent. B.C. | VI-V cent. B.C. | IV-III cent. B.C. | II-I cent. B.C. | I cent. B.C. | I cent. B.C.-A.D. |

Plate 8: Various swords present in Central Italic territory from the Bronze Age to the Late Consular one. It should be noted that the blade, despite varying in size, especially in

Fig. 4:
A) Gladiator forming part of a terracotta relief depicting a fight in the circus against wild animals. The fighter is standing erect, with the weight of the body resting mainly on the right, rear, leg, while this guard justifies the use of a helmet with a not very prominent neck roll. First century AD, Museo Nazionale delle Terme, Rome.
B) In the stone relief of the Landesmuseum of Mainz, the Roman infantryman has a more forward-leaning position, indicating a more aggressive attitude of the soldier, but at the same time seeking greater protection of the body, also exploiting the defence given him by the large neck guard of the helmet. First century AD, Landes Museum of Mainz (Germany). (*Author's photo*)

The legionnaire's torso was slightly rotated to his right side, facing the fellow soldier on his flank, so that his left side was exposed to the enemy, although completely protected by the *scutum*. The shield, large in size and semi-cylindrical in shape, was held with the left hand, resting on the body to better cushion the impact of the enemy attack. The part of the soldier that remained uncovered was the portion of the face from the lower part of the forehead, delimited by the lower edge of the helmet, to the tip of the nose, demarcated by the upper edge of the shield, thus allowing almost total protection. This approach suggests that, waiting for the first blow from the enemy, the sustained action was mostly defensive, as if the Roman soldier were waiting for action

Fig. 5: The attack position of the two gladiators, the shield held with the left hand to protect the body and the *gladius*, gripped with the right, held horizontally at waist height. Sarcophagus from Perugia, National Archaeological Museum. (*Author's photo*)

from the opponent, and therefore for him to expose himself, before carrying out an effective counter-attack.

Highly relevant in this context is the different protective approach adopted by a Greek hoplite compared to a Roman infantryman. The Hellenic soldier wore a helmet that only left the eyes uncovered, rigid armour and a large hoplon. The latter was used for an 'embrication' with the other adjacent

Fig. 6: In this fragment of a relief we can see a portrait of a *hoplomacus* in profile. The gladiator protects himself by barely uncovering his face due to the helmet equipped with a visor and wide cheek pads and the large semi-cylindrical shield held in the left hand. First century AD, Amphitheatre of Benevento, Sannio Museum. (*Author's photo*)

shields, revealing a static defensive approach, completely opposite to that sought after by the Capitoline soldier, whose protection was based on a more dynamic one. For the Romans, the shield was a weapon which, depending on how it was held, allowed an almost total defence, or became an active resource for destabilising the enemy, as we will see later. Furthermore, the helmet was designed to allow wide vision, essential for combat control based on fencing and shield moves, excellent mobility of the head, fundamental in the 'athletic' movements of the soldier and finally having uncovered ears, aimed at understanding the sound signals that were given during the battle.

The infantryman therefore were engaged in an active combat and, as explained by the Renaissance fencing manuals, including that of Maestro Manciolino, the fencer had to acquire a synchronisation between the movements of the upper limbs, capable of delivering lethal blows and parrying them with the help of the shield held in the left hand, with those of the legs. This setting allowed a greater efficiency of the blows delivered and at the same time a more effective defence from blows of the enemy. In addition, the Master of the Opera Nova shows us which were the steps taken by the soldier during a skirmish, showing a complete similarity between what was done in the middle of the Renaissance and what the archaeological findings show us: 'you swordsman must keep the left foot in front and [to advance] you will have to bring the right foot close to the left one and slide the latter forward without pulling any blows. Finding the enemy at close range, he will be able to do two things, either

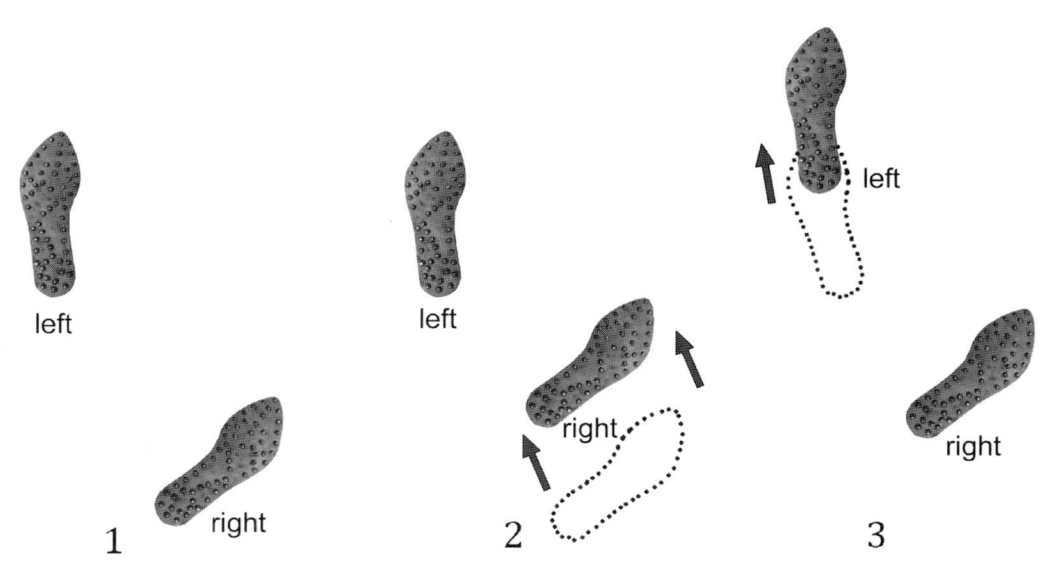

Fig. 7: Representation of the position of the legs and steps of the Roman soldier during combat. In the starting position (1), the left leg was placed forward with the foot directed towards the enemy while the right one was positioned backwards with the foot obliquely oriented. This arrangement was aimed at giving greater stability to the body. While advancing towards the enemy, the right foot was first brought closer to the left (2) and only afterwards, the infantryman made the step forward with his left leg (3). In this way the stability of the body was maintained without losing the ability to carry out an attack during the advancement phase. (*Author's drawing*)

throw a sword blow or flee backwards. If he throws a blow, the more actions you can counter.'[285] It can be concluded that the Roman soldier advanced towards the enemy by bringing his right foot forward first and, only after this action, did he advance the left leg, so that the body remained stable and always ready for an attack. The advance took place, step by step, without throwing any blows, with the left foot aligned with the body (which we remember being on the side) and the right foot perpendicular to the direction of the fighter.

Regarding what might have been the ways of handling the *gladius*, we have analysed the medieval fencing treaties that have been passed on to us. The medieval weapon, probably closer to the characteristics of the *gladius*, was the half-length sword. Francesco Altoni, a Florentine master of fencing who lived in the first half of the 1500s, specifies that 'A sword which is smaller and does not wound at a distance would be a half-length sword, rather than a sword, as it lacks the sword's characteristics of wounding at distance',[286] indicating that it was two-thirds of the length of a Renaissance sword. By adopting this comparison, we have tried to extrapolate the technical use of the *gladius* from the Renaissance treatises and infer what hypothetically could be the basis of the strikes adopted in Roman times. In fact, although there are divergent conceptual bases between the Roman combat approach, based on coordination between multiple individuals deployed and the small size of the *gladius*, and the Renaissance one, based on single combat and longer weapons, the techniques presented important meeting points. These convergences are explicitly declared by the same Renaissance fencing masters Altoni and Di Grassi, who claim to refer to the treatise of Vegetius in their works. Altoni[287] says that 'the point is the main of all blows because it is the fastest, easiest and safest'; the first two qualities, 'faster' and 'easier', are due to the fact that in every act the infantryman pushes the blade forward; 'safest' is because it never lets his guard down too much. The Renaissance teaching is confirmed by Vegetius, i.e. that the soldiers

> learned to strike not with the edge, but with the point. For the Romans not only easily beat those fighting with the edge, but even made mock of them, as a cut, whatever its force, seldom kills, because the vitals are protected by both armour and bones. But a stab driven two inches in is fatal; for necessarily whatever goes in penetrates the vitals. Secondly while a cut is being delivered the right arm and flank are exposed; whereas a stab is inflicted with the body remaining covered, and the enemy is wounded before he realises it. That is why, it is agreed the Romans used chiefly this method for fighting.[288]

Returning to the explanation of the Florentine master, he teaches us that

> the fencer, when he holds the sword, always keeps it under control and can always strike where he wants, and when he pulls back the sword or returns to the guard position, he does so comfortably, always ready to be able to strike all parts of the body much smoother than any other shot. The effect is also much faster as its force is focused on the tip of the sword and this power can be transferred to all blows with a small movement unlike cutting blows.

Fig. 8: Painting from Pompeii depicting the final clash between two gladiators. Note the attack style of the right fighter who, in the act of lunging with the *gladius*, rotates his torso frontally advancing with his right foot. The gladiator on the left, on the other hand, defends himself by showing his rival his left side and parrying the blow with his shield. External facade of the Caupona di Purpurius in Pompeii (Luciana Jacobelli, *Gladiatori a Pompei, Protagonisti, Luoghi, Immagini* (L'Erma di Bretschneider, 2003), p. 85, image from Vittorio Spinazzola, *Pompei alla luce dei nuovi scavi – 1953* (La Libreria dello Stato, Rome, 1953). (*Author's photo*)

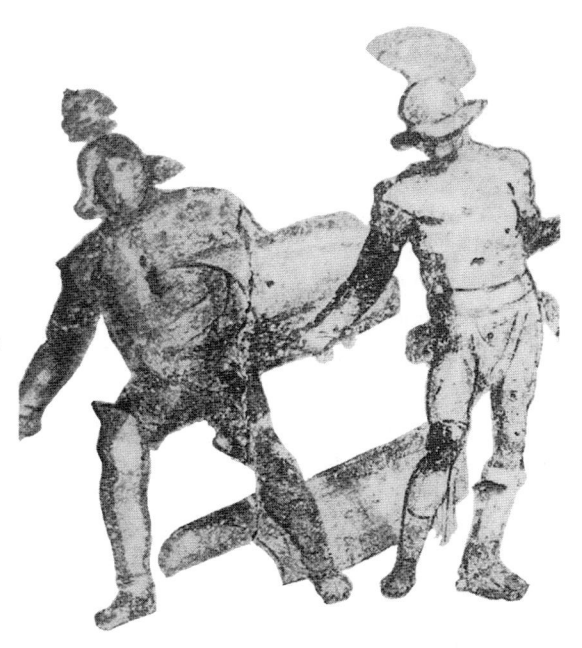

Moreover it is recommended that 'the blows should be accompanied, not thrown and even less riddled because they make you lose control of the sword and are ineffective; and having hit the target, the sword must be pushed, without withdrawing the arm, rather with the help of the whole person'.

This description seems to describe the action of a gladiator represented in a painting found on the external facade of the Caupona of Purpurius in Pompeii.[289] When the fighter lunges with the *gladius*, the torso rotates so that the shoulder and the right arm are in front of their left counterpart, so that the body, usually placed side on, assumes a frontal position.

The right foot moves forward in respect to the left in the attack, so that it can accompany the rotation of the torso and the whole weight of the body could be used to aid the penetrating action of the *gladius*. This statement is confirmed by Vegetius, who describes how:

> But when it comes to what they call 'to javelins', and the fighting is hand-to-hand with swords, soldiers should have the right foot forward, so as to draw the flank away from the enemy lest they be wounded, and to have the right hand closer so it can land a blow. Obviously, therefore, recruits should be equipped and protected with every ancient type of arms. For a man who does not fear wounds because he has his head and chest protected must acquire sharper courage for battle.[290]

Livy, speaking about the use of the *gladius*, relegates its use to a mechanical and repetitive activity, devoid of heroic acts and particular initiatives, comparing it twice to the action of a 'shovel'. During the Battle of Trasimene,

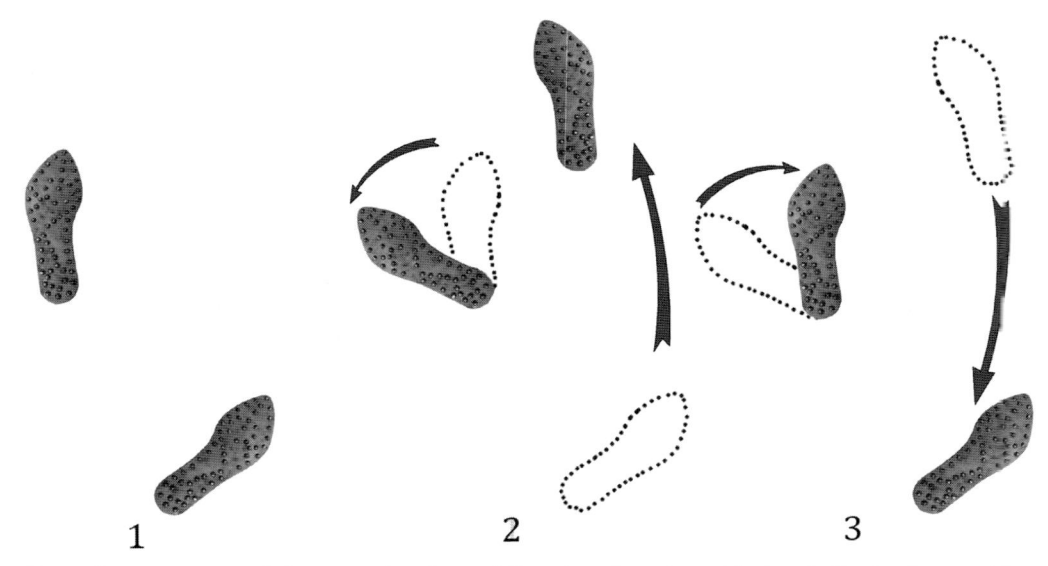

Fig. 9: Representation of the steps taken by a soldier when thrusting with the *gladius*. In the transition from the guard position (1) to the attack position (2), the right foot is brought in front of the left one, which simultaneously rotates slightly on its axis towards the outside. After the lunge, the right foot was retracted backwards (3) in order to assume the guard position again. (*Author's drawing*)

amidst the general consternation the consul himself ... brought such order as time and place permitted out of the confusion in the ranks, where the men were all turning different ways to face the various shouts; and wherever he could go and make himself heard, he tried to encourage them and bade them stand and fight. Their position, he said, was one from which vows and supplications to the gods could not extricate them, but only their own brave exertions: it was the sword [*ferrum*] that opened a way through embattled enemies, and the less the men feared, the less, in general, was their danger.[291]

The second reference is by the tribune Publius Sempronius Tuditanus who, after the defeat of Cannae, spoke in this way to the defeated soldiers and refugees in the camp: '... let us break out through these men that are clamouring in disorder and confusion at our gates. With a sword [*ferrum*] and a stout heart a man may pass through enemies, be they never so thick ... . Uttering these words he grasped his sword [*gladius*], and, forming a column, strode away through the midst of the enemy.'[292]

But if the *gladius* was the offensive weapon by definition, the shield was not only a defensive element, as it often intervened as an active part, completing the action of the *gladius*. This can be concluded from the fight between Gauls and Romans reported by Livy: 'it was a matter not so much of hands and swords [*gladiis*] as of making their way by pushing against one another with shields and bodies ...'[293]

This function is evident in various representations, mostly gladiatorial, in which the fighter raises the shield, bringing it into a horizontal position, to create a block for the opponent and prevent him from coming into direct contact. This action hindered the

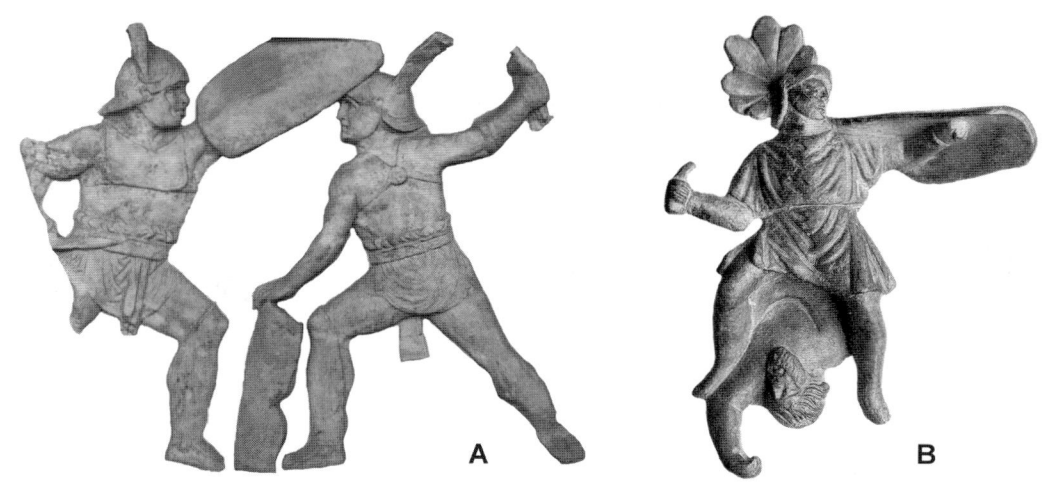

Fig. 10:
A) Fight between two *provocatores*. It highlights the technique of preventing the opponent from approaching by lifting the shield. This move allowed a slower approach, creating a difficult situation for those involved in it, in the attempt to induce the opponent to expose themselves and obtain the opportunity for the winning thrust. The scene represents the clash as if the two gladiators acted at different times: the fighter on the left, who will be the winner, is depicted during the attack, while the right gladiator, defeated, has already placed his shield on the ground as a sign of surrender. Marble relief from the first century BC, from the Tiber drainage. Museo Nazionale Romano delle Terme, Rome. (*Author's photo*)
B) This equestrian baldric appliqué is a demonstration of how this gladiatorial technique was also adopted by soldiers. It represents a Roman soldier fighting against Celtic or Germanic barbarians, one of whom lies dead at his feet. He holds the *scutum* horizontally, as if to keep the enemy at a distance. Ultimately, the shield was not only a defensive element but also an offensive weapon. Diocesan Museum of Leon, Spain. (*Author's photo*)

enemy from launching his attack, and at the same time gave the legionary time to bring his right arm back to prepare his own *gladius* for a thrust, to be launched at the right moment. When that moment had arrived, defined by a critical exposure of the rival, the legionary lowered his shield, which allowed him to shorten the distance and carry out his offensive move with a sword.

The 'Roman fencing' was framed in a very specific organised context and had to take place within regulated spaces, not too large, in order not to enable the penetration of enemy forces, but not too small either, in order to not limit the movements of the infantry. Polybius tells us that the armed Roman soldiers occupied a space of 3ft (89cm). The Greek author continues confirming that in 'their mode of fighting each man must move separately, as he has to cover his person with his long shield, turning to meet each expected blow, and as he uses his sword both for cutting and thrusting it is obvious that a looser order is required, and each man must be at a distance of at least three feet from the man next him in the same rank and those in front of and behind him, if they are to be of proper use'.[294]

The arrangement of the infantrymen within a legion is clear in the *stele* of Glanum from the Late Consular or Imperial Period, in which they appear arranged adjacent to one another, in successive rows, with the right hand on the *gladius*, ready to draw it from the scabbard, while the left hand holds the *scutum* used for protection (Fig. 11).

What has been said so far is, as anticipated, a didactic description of how a fight should develop. In practice, keeping the ranks of one battle array had to be very difficult. This passage from *De Bello Gallico* is very explanatory, illustrating how easy it was to lose the spaces needed for fencing movements, creating dangerous limitations to the combat itself. The situation was dramatic

Fig. 11: The legionary infantry was arranged in a precise, well-organised manner, to present a compact front to the enemy. Stele from Glanum, Gallo-Roman Museum of Fourviere – Lyon. (*Author's photo*)

> ... Caesar ... perceived that his men were hard pressed, and that in consequence of the standards of the twelfth legion being collected together in one place, the crowded soldiers were a hindrance to themselves in the fight; that all the centurions of the fourth cohort were slain, and the standard-bearer killed, the standard itself lost, almost all the centurions of the other cohorts either wounded or slain, and among them the chief centurion of the legion P. Sextius Baculus, a very valiant man, who was so exhausted by many and severe wounds, that he was already unable to support himself; he likewise perceived that the rest were slackening their efforts, and that some, deserted by those in the rear, were retiring from the battle and avoiding the weapons; that the enemy [on the other hand] though advancing from the lower ground, were not relaxing in front, and were [at the same time] pressing hard on both flanks ...

Thus, those leading the deployments, the centurions and the standard bearer, had been lost, while the soldiers, who were now gathered without space and possibility of action around the standards, suffered the attacks or sought to escape. Having understood the danger,

> Caesar advanced to the front of the line, and addressing the centurions by name, and encouraging the rest of the soldiers, he ordered them to carry forward the standards, and extend the companies [*manipulos laxare iussit*], that they might the more easily use their swords [*facilius gladiis utipossent*]. On his arrival, as hope was brought to the soldiers and their courage restored, while everyone for his own part,

Fig. 12: Bas-relief of the Augustan period, depicting *venatores* fighting against wild beasts. In a compulsive situation such as that of a battle, the aggression of barbarian enemies attacking without an organised military technique could be similar to that of the wild beasts shown in this representation. It should be noted that the shield is the main weapon used to block the attack of the 'enemy' which was then eliminated by a sword stroke. Furthermore, the position of the legs and torso was that of the soldiers deduced from the previous representations, useful to give the infantryman maximum stability to withstand the considerable impact of the attack. Villa Torlonia, Rome. (*Author's photo*)

in the sight of his general, desired to exert his utmost energy, the impetuosity of the enemy was a little checked.[295]

After restoring adequate spaces, the soldiers were able to return to the fight.

As we can easily guess, in the context of a fight it was not easy to maintain a perfect order of deployment, since the strength of the enemy attack, especially that of certain enemies, such as the Germans, was comparable to the assault of ferocious beasts. To understand what pressure the Roman soldiers had to endure during certain assaults, we can observe a gladiatorial scene from the Augustan age in which two *venatores* are attacked by two beasts (Fig. 12). The shield was used to block the enemy attack and support the weight of the beast (i.e. the barbarian), good reason for the *miles* to be planted with his feet firmly on the ground. The moment of stalemate, manifested by the enemy fury contained by the shield, was the right one to deliver the blow with the *gladius* on the exposed left side of the enemy.

Although the training of the soldiers was designed to avoid any individualism and maintain coordination with all the other *pedites*, each soldier had his own character, disposition and way of fighting. This observation comes from Caesar who, in addition to being a general who personally participated in the war, was a keen observer. While moving among the ranks, he stimulated the fight, checked that the infantry fought with ardour, and above all he observed the use of swords carefully, because from this he was able to understand the character of the soldier in front of him better: 'He looked upon the brands,/These reddened only at the point, and those/Streaming with blood and gory to the hilt/He marks the hand which trembling grasped the sword/Or held it idle, and the cheek that grew/Pale at the blow, and that which at his words/Glowed with the joy of battle.'[296] Knowing the psychology of a man in an act in which instinct takes over reason, such as when an individual is forced to kill and is risking his life in turn, certainly allowed him to understand how much he could trust each of his men. In fact, during a battle, the life of each one was based on the correct behaviour of the adjacent soldiers, the fellow soldiers, but above all 'to keep their ranks and not to desert their standards nor to give up without grave cause the position …'[297]

The first century BC ended leaving us a mature and very complex military formation, in continuous evolution and adaptation, an expression of a war machine so sophisticated that it has no comparison in the contemporary ancient world, nor even in the armies of later centuries. We will have to wait at least for the Napoleonic era, and in many respects even later, to find something similar in terms of military efficiency and organisation, an achievement that still arouses amazement in all those preparing to get to know these formidable people.

III(B).3 THE LATE CONSULAR *GLADIUS*

Around the middle of the first century BC, although the type of High Consular *gladius* is still present and has not abruptly disappeared, it begins to appear more typically and exclusively Roman, without similarities and admixtures from other cultures.

On closer inspection, this is not surprising nor is it in contradiction with the complex Italic landscape we know. In fact, at the end of the Consular Age, the whole of Italy was now fully Romanised and cultural homogenisation had long since reached its peak.[298]

Before starting the analysis of the evolutionary changes that the *gladius* underwent in the Late Consular Age, an overview of the archaeological evidence will be useful. All modern literature is inclined to consider the following specimens, all from the late Consular Age, as the most archaic known to date (in chronological order):

1) From Smihel, Slovenia (total length = 69.5cm, blade length = 62.2cm, max. width = 4.4cm), dating 185–165 BC;
2) From Smihel, Slovenia (total length = 75.5cm, blade length = 66.0cm), dating 185–165 BC;
3) From Alfaro, Spain (blade length = 55.0cm), generically dated to the Mid–Late Consular Age;
4) From Giubiasco, Switzerland, from grave 471, found complete with scabbard (total length = 79.5cm, blade length = 70.5cm, max width = 4.7cm, scabbard length = 73.7cm), dating to the second–first century BC;

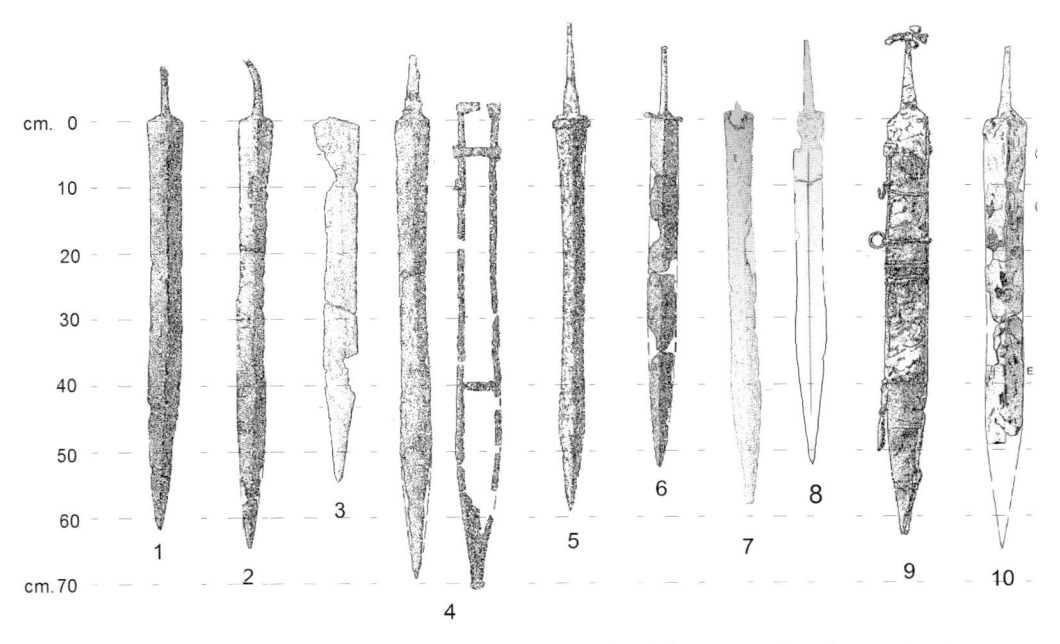

Fig. 1: Some of the examples of Late Consular *gladii* considered the most archaic by modern literature. For numbering refer to the text. (*Author's drawing*)

5) From Nidau, Switzerland (total length = 74.0cm), dating to the second–first century BC;
6) From Mouriès, France (total length = 64.0cm, max. width = 5.0cm), dated between 100 and 75 BC, from the grave of a Romanized Gaulish warrior;
7) From Sisak, preserved in the Zagreb Archaeological Museum (blade length = 60.0cm, max. width = 4.4cm), dated to the end of the second–first century BC;
8) From Sisak, preserved in the Zagreb Archaeological Museum (blade length = 53.0cm, total length = 64cm, max. width = 5.0cm), dated to the end of the first century BC;
9) From the island of Delos, Greece, still in the scabbard (total length = 76.0cm, max. width = 6.5cm), dated 75–69 BC;
10) From Osuna, composed of two fragments and missing the tip, of presumed length equal to about 64–65cm;

with the clarification that in this list, which in any case is not inclusive of all the specimens dating between the beginning and the end of the Consular Age, given the continuous discoveries in progress, specimens whose origin is not known are not included either.

III (B).3,1 The characteristics of the Late Consular gladius and the differences with the High Consular Age typology

▶ **Length and profile of the blade**
There are no substantial differences in the profile of the blade compared to the previous period, but lanceolate profiles exist alongside those with parallel cutting edges.

The tang is always barrel-shaped, as we have seen before. As previously mentioned, once the transition from the Monarchical to the Consular *gladius* was completed, any other type of tang disappeared, never to appear again.

Instead, attention should be focused on the length of the blades. A brief period appears to be attested in archaeological finds, starting from the late first century BC and only lasting a few decades, in which surprisingly short weapons, sometimes only 54–55cm in length, appear. It should be noted however, that although this small size is a typical feature of this century, it should not be considered as common to all the specimens,

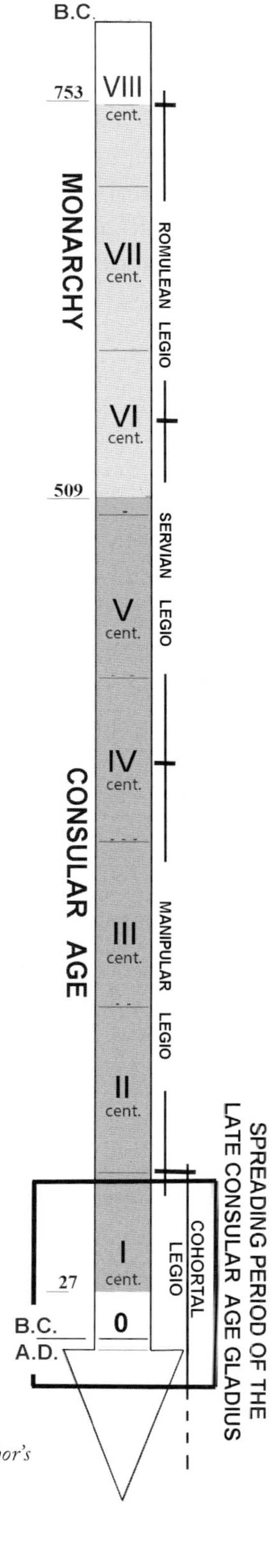

Graph 1: Chart showing the period of use of the Late Consular *gladius*. (*Author's drawing*)

since at the same time some weapons of a length more similar to the previous period exist. Very short blades can certainly be dated towards the end of the Consular Age, but longer ones can be found throughout the entire Consular Age.

Before proceeding further, it is necessary to consider the reasons behind this somewhat surprising innovation, which is obviously not accidental but more a consequence of precise tactical needs. We have seen that at the beginning of the first century BC, in the Roman social and military panorama, the first episode of the traumatic phenomenon of civil war intervened. Some factors are directly connected to this evolutionary aspect and which we can highlight as follows:

- throughout the first century BC, the clashes were particularly numerous and bloody, involving a very large number of legions and considerable military resources;
- the Roman legionary found himself facing his own comrades, with the same fighting techniques and the same offensive and defensive weapons;
- the legionary's professionalism was complete and deepened, making him highly trained in the use of his weapons and his physical performance;
- Vegetius describes in detail the type of training and, in particular, the agile movement of the recruit equipped with a shield and *gladius* and his attempts to learn how to strike the enemy on the calves, legs and face, without being hit in return;
- Vegetius again testifies that the training also focused on the fundamental ability to keep the ranks compact, even during the confusion of battle.

We must imagine the legionary of this period, engaged in a civil confrontation, as part of a compact line, placed tightly behind his shield which, together with the others, almost forms a wall. Moving his legs swiftly he shifts his stance to a more upright position, trying to hit the opponent's upper part from above; then moving into a more crouched position, useful for reaching the lower parts of the enemy, whilst thrusting between the narrow spaces left by the tight shields, and at the same time defending himself from identical blows.

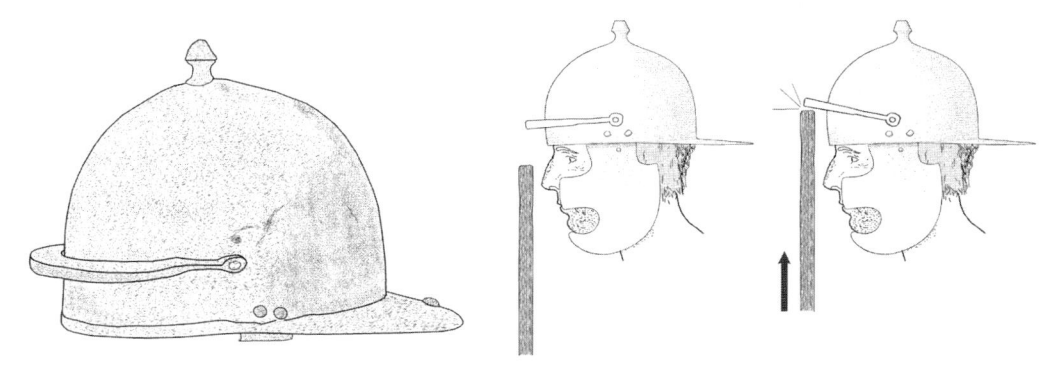

Fig. 2: Left: Roman helmet from the Rhine (Rheinisches Landesmuseum, Bonn, Germany) showing the typical articulated front bar. Right, operation of the front bar, with the possibility of sliding upwards in case of impact on the shield. (*Author's drawing*)

222   The Roman Gladius and the Ancient Fighting Techniques

Fig. 3:
Above: Difference in protection from thrusting blows above when comparing a Montefortino type A helmet (from thrust, left) and an Imperial one (from tip, right). Below: Crouched position of the legionary, for which it is necessary that the helmet would have a rather high neck guard, more or less at eye level. It is evident that both the helmet on the top left (from Niedermormter, late second–early third century AD) and the one on the right (from the Rhine, Mainz, second half of the first century AD) would be incompatible with this posture. (*Author's drawing, with the exception of the legionary, taken from Connolly*, The Roman Fighting Technique Deduced from Armour and Weaponry)

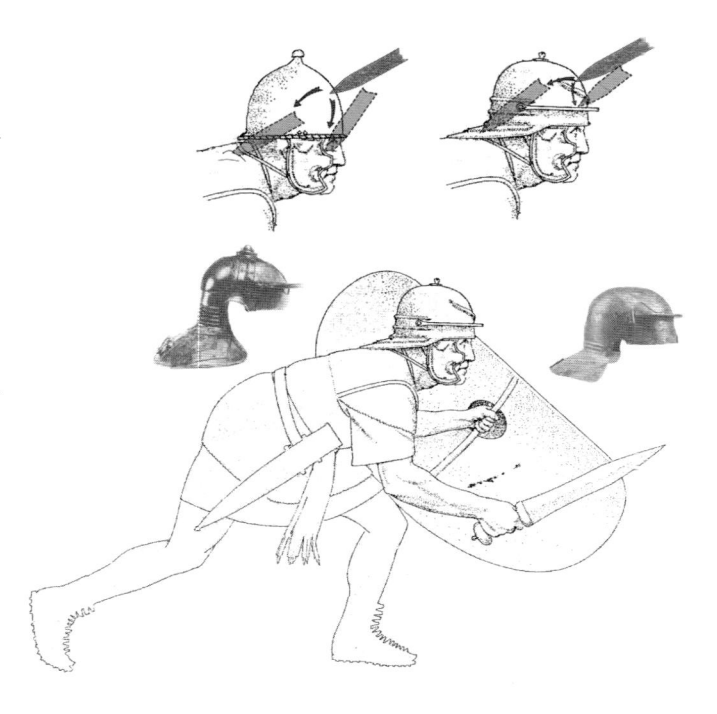

Even the helmets seem to represent the same scenario. The Montefortino helmet of type A and B[299] of the thrusting type, was no longer suitable for this type of combat and therefore gave way to its evolved types (types C–D–E–F according to the classification of H.R. Robinson). Perhaps the most archaic specimen found among the latter is that of Eich[300] (Mainz – Germany), which introduces particular characteristics. The bar on the forehead appears for the first time, an unusual Roman element with no equivalent in other cultures and which we know to be suitable for stopping the run of the points of sloping blades from above (cf. Chapter II.3.4 'The Monarchical *Gladius*').[301] Furthermore, since it is hinged and not fixed, it has the fundamental characteristic of being able to move upwards. This, together with the description by Vegetius, makes it clear that the soldier's face would have been particularly close to the upper edge of the shield, with his eyes just above it. There was a good chance this element might strike his helmet and the possibility of the helmet sliding upwards had to be prevented, in order to avoid the backward flexion of the neck, which would have had negative consequences.

The neck guard begins to widen for the same reason the front bar appears, but remains quite high, at the height of the cervical vertebra. As P. Connolly rightly observes, this is compatible with the crouched position we have previously described, which would not be possible with deeper neck rolls (as in the Imperial models, especially from the second century AD), which only allow an erect or almost erect position (Fig. 3).[302]

It is easy to understand that in this scenario, a long blade would have been a hindrance, and what was really needed was a short weapon, little more than a long dagger, only suitable for thrusting, so that the legionary could take the best advantage of all the small gaps between the shields. Blows from the side were not possible, and would have seriously risked injuring nearby comrades.

We can therefore say that the evolution of the *gladius* of this period was a direct consequence of the civil wars.[303]

▶ The blade's shoulders with straight profile

With the approach of the end of the Consular Age we also witness the progressive disappearance of the shoulders with a descending profile, which were constantly present in the High Consular Age, which are now replaced by straight ones, with a horizontal profile (Fig. 4-B).[304] This feature seems to have been greatly appreciated by the Romans, to the extent that in a short time it was almost always present in all of their edged weapons, *gladii* or *spathae*, until the end of the empire.

At the moment, it is not possible to find a clear historical reason to justify this change, although a one can be suggested by more or less personal deductions. The underlying logic seems to be basically that of a continuing process of structural simplification of the weapon that we have already seen in the transition from the Monarchical sword to the Consular one. In fact, fixing the guard (flat side towards the blade) on straight shoulders is very easy; one only needs to make sure that the two pieces are level to ensure excellent stability.

It should be noted that on some specimens, a sort of intermediate situation can be observed, namely substantially straight shoulders but with a slight downward curvature, which at present seem to constitute a moment of transition from one system to another (Fig. 4-A).

▶ The tripartite hilt and the 'washers' variant

Normally nothing changes in the conception of the hilt, which remains tripartite as in the High Consular Age. However, it is accompanied by a particular variant, which we will call 'washers'.

We have to wait until the end of the Late Consular Age to see this adopted by some Roman armouries, but its origins are to be found a little bit earlier. The archaeological

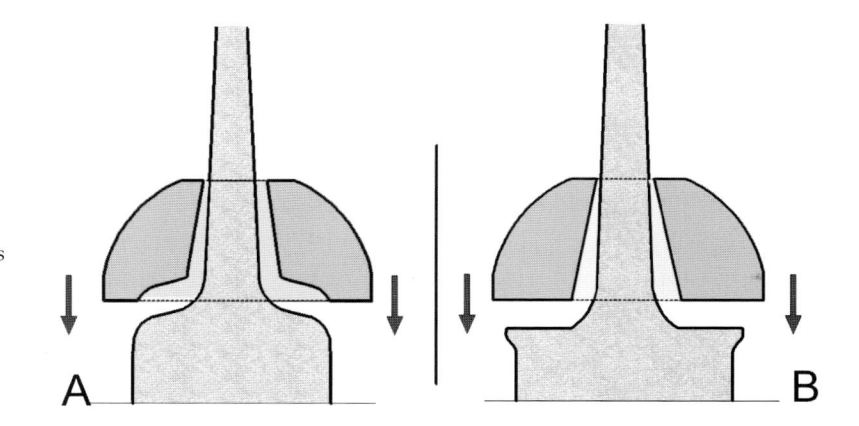

Fig. 4: A: Shoulders with slightly descending profile; B: Shoulders with straight profile. (*Author's drawing*)

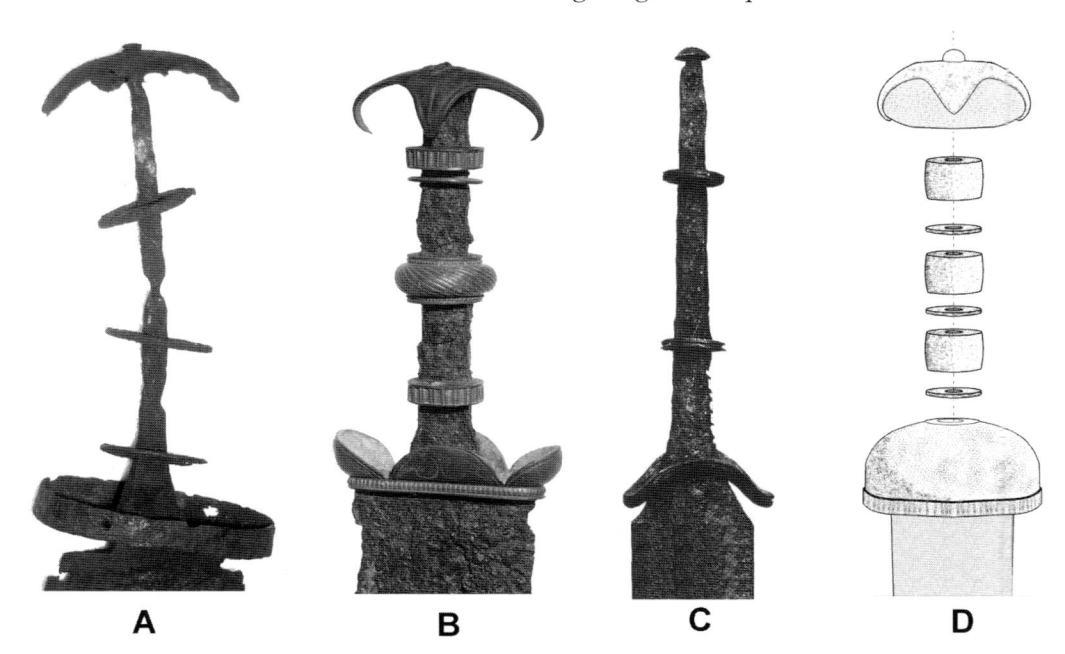

Fig. 5: A) Roman sword (private collection), B) Celtic sword from Hod Hill (British Museum, 929-1, 452), C) Celtic sword from Cashel (Ireland), D) Virtual reconstruction of a sword handle as a composite hilt with washers. Between A and B you can see the similarity both for the upper closing element and in the washers on the tang and finally for the lower plate enclosing the guard, now lost as it was evidently made of organic material. On the other hand, example C, of Celtic origin, shows the same washers as the Roman *gladius*, albeit only having two. Note the significant wear due to the rubbing of the central washer in the centre of the tang of specimen A (the latter is shown in the image out of the original position for photographic reasons), which caused it to collapse and tilt to the left. (*Author's drawing*)

Fig. 6: Details of Latenian swords of various periods showing a hilt with washers: specimens 1 to 5 still show the presence of washers on the tang, however in specimens 6 to 8 we notice residues of the organic material placed between the washers.
1: Killaloe; 2: Lisnachroger; 3: Edenderry; 4: Cashel; 5: Sligo; 6: British Museum catalogue no. 184 (no. P 1975, 5-31, Rudstone); 7: British Museum catalogue no. 210 (P 1991, 10-1, 13 Rudstone). This specimen still shows one of the horn elements, 28mm long, which however seems to have been made in such a way as to join the others missing without separation by washers. 8: British Museum catalogue n.127 (Coleford, not part of the BM collection). (*Author's drawing*)

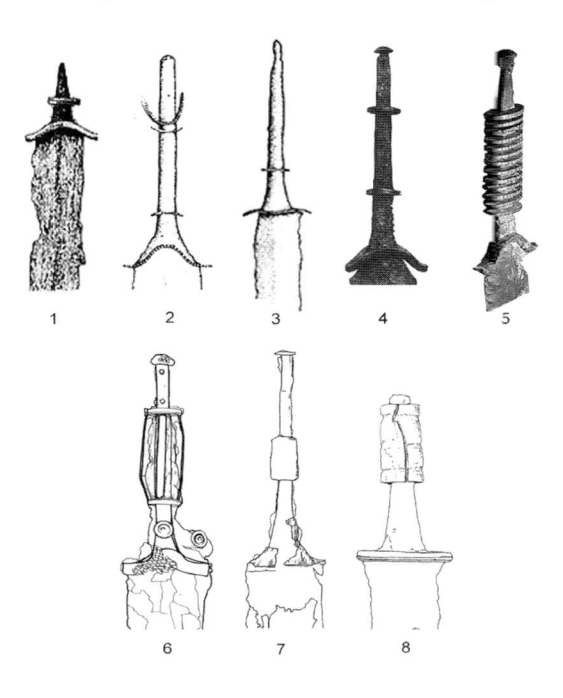

evidence shows that this type of handle had a good diffusion in Celtic armies, starting from the end of the second century BC, with many specimens from Gaul, Britain and into Ireland having been found, the influence of which is also found in the composition of the guard and the upper pommel.[305] In practice this means forming the handle not in a single piece, as in the Roman stereotype, but in three or four parts through the use of two or three washers separating elements made of organic material (Fig. 5).

In the current archaeological panorama, there are numerous specimens placed in a middle point between Celtic and Roman culture, leaving a certain margin of doubt about their real attribution, even if various scholars have interpreted them as belonging to auxiliary Gauls, and therefore as a form of Roman weapon heavily influenced by traditional Celtic elements.[306] Ultimately, however, this technology had some diffusion into the Roman military world.

III (B).3,2 The many types of gladii in the first century BC

▶ **The modern classification**
In the study of the various types of *gladius* of this period, we believe it is right to start from the modern classification, which almost unanimously divides the *gladii* of this period into two (or three) main types (Fig. 7), the so-called:

- 'Hispaniensis': wrongly considered to be of Hispanic derivation,[307] usually considered as the most archaic Roman sword and represented with the features and characteristics of what we have previously called the 'Early Consular' *gladius* – variant 'B' and therefore with a fairly long blade, lanceolate, often quite narrow and with a long tip;
- 'Mainz':[308] in use at least until the middle of the first century AD, presented as a *gladius* with a short and wide blade, often lanceolate too, with a long tip. C. Miks believes that it was possible to identify various subtypes (Mühlbach, Sisak, Classic, Wederath, Haltern-Camulodunum) which continued its use until the end of the second century AD.[309]

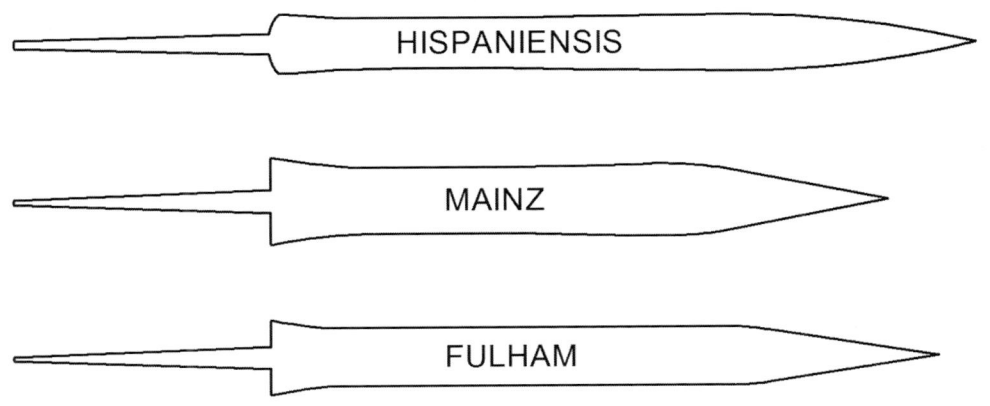

Fig. 7: Schematization usually accepted by modern literature of the three main types of *gladii* of the Late Consular Age–early Empire. (*Author's drawing*)

To these we can then add the 'Fulham', which takes its name from a specimen preserved in the British Museum and found in the Thames near the locality of the same name. Sometimes considered by some scholars a subtype of 'Mainz',[310] it does not differ much from it except for having parallel cutting edges.

▶ The real situation

Since the intention of our study is to strictly adhere to historical data, we have avoided starting from these reconstituted positions, also because the general modern classifications risk existing only to satisfy the needs of us modern people, rather than depicting historical reality, with the danger of misrepresentation. This was well expressed by Professor Alessandro Barbero:

> Historians are often convinced of things that then turn out to be totally invented. It happens that a series of authors begin to copy each other, often adding a small personal contribution, until it becomes true in itself and indisputable. Often we start from the belief that those who wrote that thing before us knew it well, especially if there are many who have supported it, and therefore it is true. Within some time it becomes commonplace even if it was simply born from a first invention.[311]

An examination free from external influences reveals a much less schematized and in some ways perhaps quite enigmatic picture, which leads us to state that the desire to identify a classification of *gladii* in which all (or almost all) of the specimens of this period can be included is practically impossible and certainly wrong, and it would have no grounds in historical reality or scientific utility. There are specimens traceable to the Mainz or Hispaniensis type as represented above, but they are the minority. What actually exists is a large variety in which all the characteristics that we have seen so far coexist. We therefore find specimens with a long blade with more or less parallel cutting edges; as well as very short and thin ones; specimens with a short but wide blade, both with parallel and lanceolate edges; and to make things even more variegated, blades with neither parallel nor lanceolate edges but slightly triangular ones, and so on. Ultimately, it is a 'potpourri' of characteristics, in which the centuries-old legacy blends with the new needs of the first century BC.

To make the concept clearer, we want to present a series of more or less contemporary specimens, which appear absolutely different from each other (Fig. 8). From the combined table we can easily deduce the coexistence of practically every variety of blade, but with two fixed points that represent constant characteristics: the long tip[312] and the barrel tang. We also note, as mentioned earlier, that oblique shoulders coexist with straight ones, the latter belonging to specimens that are normally less archaic.

The Consular Age 227

Fig. 8: Comparison between ten specimens all datable to the Late Consular Age – early Empire, with a table showing the characteristics of the various specimens (author's drawing).
1 = Historisches Museum der Pfalz – Speyer;
2 = Private collection, Italy;
3 = British Museum, London;
4 = Schweizerisches Landesmuseum, Zurich;
5 = Private Collection;
6 = Arheoloskj Muzej, Zagabria;
7 = Römisch-Germanisches Zentralmuseum, Mainz;
8 = British Museum, London;
9 = Present location unknown (see C. Miks A 516);
10= Národní Muzem, Praha.

Note:
a) the profile of the lanceolate edges is not very noticeable in the design due to the small size;
b) the profile of the edges is parallel, the sensation that it is lanceolate is given by the enlargement near the guard;
c) the profile of the edges is triangular, although not very pronounced. The small size of the drawing may mistakenly suggest it is parallel.

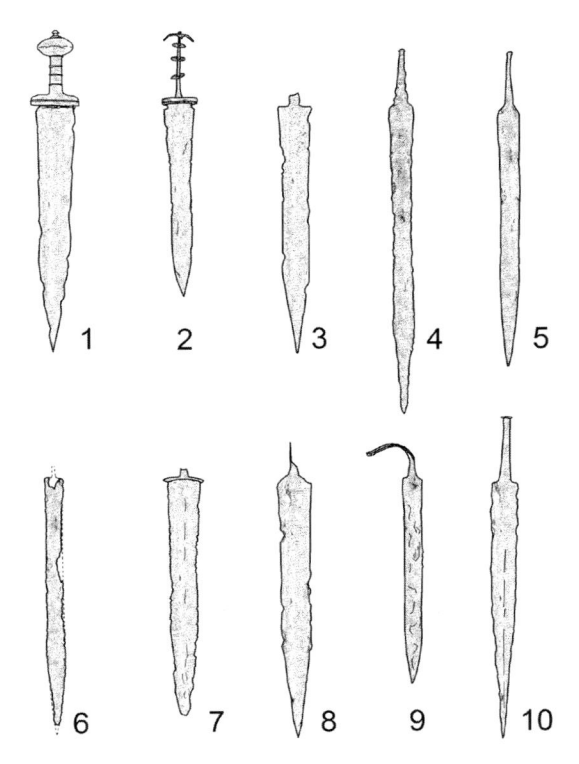

Specimen n.	Long		Blade Cutting Edges			Blade				Tip		Note
	Yes	No	Parallel	Lanceolate	Triang.	Long	Short	Narrow	Wide	Long	Short	
1	•				•	•			•	•		
2	•			•			•		•	•		
3	•		•			•			•	•		
4	•			•		•		•		•		a
5	•	•				•		•		•		b
6	•			•			•	•		•		a
7	•				•		•			•		c
8	•				•		•			•		
9	•		•				•	•		•		
10	•				•	•				•		

▶ **A possible explanation for the great variety of types**
The existence of this particular mixture of such different types requires a reflection on the reasons behind it. On closer inspection, this did not happen during the Monarchical Period but during it the weapons, both Italic and purely Roman, could be slightly different from each other, some longer, others a little shorter, but essentially all fairly homogeneous. Nor do things change much in the High Consular Age, whether

we are faced with type 'A' or 'B',[313] which are not dissimilar and above all suggest a similar use. However, in the first century BC, we are almost suddenly faced with the opposite situation, with an extreme variety of shapes and sizes. In consideration of the organisational care and the search for improvement in the Roman mentality this cannot simply be a coincidence, but certainly a consequence of precise needs

> ... But when they are to fight, they leave nothing without forecast, nor to be done off-hand, but counsel is ever first taken before any work is begun, and what hath been there resolved upon is put in execution presently.[314]

> Caesar proceeded to train his forces, not as a commander trains a veteran army with a magnificent record of victorious achievements, but as a gladiatorial instructor trains his recruits. How many feet they were to retreat from the enemy; the manner in which they must wheel round upon their adversary; the restricted space in which they must offer him resistance – now doubling forward, now retiring and making feint attacks; and almost the spot from which, and the manner in which they must discharge their missiles.[315]

These new needs can probably be deduced from the brief summary given in Table 2 on the types of enemies that Romans were facing in this century, often having completely different fighting methods. From the Gauls, with a variegated but poorly organised army of infantry and cavalry, to the elusive Parthians, to the Germans, to quite unusual enemies such as those of the slave revolt of Spartacus, to the Hellenistic army of Mithridates VI and above all to the Romans themselves in the Civil Wars.

Year (BC)	Enemy	Type of Army
89	Italics, Social War	Roman
89–85	Mithridates VI, First Mithridatic War	Various Greek and Near Eastern cultures (Greeks, Armenians, Sarmatians, Scythians, Thracians etc.)
87	Athenians, Siege of Athens	Greek
83–82	Romans, Civil War	Roman
82	Samnites, Civil War	Roman
80	Romans, Sertorian Wars	Roman
75–66	Mithridates VI, Third Mithridatic War	Various Greek and Near Eastern cultures (Greeks, Armenians, Sarmatians, Scythians, Thracians etc.)
73–71	Servile Wars	Unorganised with various armies
69	Tigranes II, Armenians	Near Eastern, of Parthian type
62	Romans, Cataline troops	Roman
58–51	Gauls, Conquest of Gaul	Infantry and cavalry, poorly organised

Year (BC)	Enemy	Type of Army
58	Germans, Ariovistus	Infantry, poorly organised
53	Parthians, Battle of Carrhae	Archers and heavy cavalry
49–45	Romans, Civil War	Roman
47	Egyptians, Battle of Nylus	Greek armament, Middle-Eastern mercenaries
44–31	Romans, Civil War	Roman
38	Parthians, Pacorus I	Archers and heavy cavalry
25	Cantabres	Celtic culture. Guerrillas and light weapons
11	Germans	Infantry, little organised

Table 2: Main enemies faced by the Romans during the first century BC, showing their multi-ethnicity and related fighting techniques.

Certainly the search for perfection in armament will have led those in charge to decide the characteristics of the weapon with which to equip the legionaries in relation to the enemy to be faced. The preparations, the equipment in general and the *gladius* in particular for a clash in the context of a civil war, where presumably a close confrontation '*ad gladius*' against armoured legionaries was expected, must certainly have been different from those against the servile army or the Parthians or Gauls.[316] Hence the range of enemies of the first century BC gave birth to an equally varied range of *gladii*.

This thesis would also explain why more archaic weapons seem to coexist with later ones. Types of *gladius* that for centuries had proven to be suitable against certain enemies would certainly have continued to be so if this enemy had remained substantially the same, but equally certainly they would be accompanied by others more suitable against opponents with different, previously unencountered, characteristics. For example, this is the case of the Gauls fought by Caesar, who despite centuries of evolution, were not very dissimilar from those of the Battle of the Allia at the beginning of the fourth century, and against whom the traditional helmets and long *gladii* could still be suitable, while against the legionaries of the civil wars the most modern pointed helmets and short *gladii* were required.

For the sake of completeness of our study, we consider it useful to report the occasionally recurring hypothesis that the different types of *gladius* are instead related to the different orders of the *velites*, *hastati*, *principes* and *triarii*, but this seems to have little historical basis since in the later first century BC the cohort had already been a reality for some time, while such *ordines* had disappeared in the first century BC.

III (B).3,3 An aid for dating: the analysis of characteristics

At the end of our excursus on the types of Monarchical and Consular *gladii*, we want to provide an aid to attempt the dating of a possible specimen without context. The dating of an archaeological find should always be based on scientifically verifiable data or at least, in the case of objects belonging to burials or part of complex deposits, looking for clues in accompanying material that can be datable, such as coins. However, in the case of a *gladius*, this is not always possible and often we are faced with finds with no context. In this case, we can still try to date it through a critical analysis of its characteristics, while always keeping in mind the limits of this system, which can potentially lead us towards errors and misunderstandings. For this purpose, we provide some schematic indications that are intended to help the scholar to achieve a result. The combination of the various characteristics and the relationship between them can suggest an approximate dating, which sensitivity and personal experience can and must refine (in the table and specifications that follow the numbers in square brackets refer to Graph 2).

Part of the Weapon	Characteristic	Suggested Dates (century BC)	Notes
Hilt	Crossed [1]	End seventh–early fourth	Monarchical *gladius*
	Tripartite [2]	From early fourth onwards	Consular *gladius*, of all periods (High and Late)
	With washers [4]	Second half of first	Also widespread in Celtic specimens
Tang	Flat and wide [7]	End seventh–early fourth	Monarchical *gladius*
	Barrel [8] [9] [10]	From early fourth onwards	Consular *gladius*, of all periods (High and Late)
Shoulders	Descending [8]	From early fourth onwards	Becoming increasingly rare from the beginning of the first century
	Straight [10]	From first century onwards	Never present before the first century
	Straight, slightly descending [9]	First half of first century	Probably limited to the end of second century and beginning of first
Blade: cutting profiles	Lanceolate [2]	End seventh–end of Consular Age	Present in all periods
	Parallel [2]	From early fourth onwards	From the arrival of the Celts onwards
	Slightly triangular [3]	From the second half of first onwards	Typical of the late Consular Age–Claudian dynasty period
Blade: width	From narrow to medium (3–5cm) [1] [2]	From early seventh onwards	Present in all periods
	Wide (over 5cm) [3]	From the end of Consular Age onwards	Typical of the late Consular Age–Claudian dynasty period

Part of the Weapon	Characteristic	Suggested Dates (century BC)	Notes
Blade: length	Long (over 53cm) [1] [2] [3]	From late seventh and onwards	Temporally ubiquitous
	Medium (between 44 and 53cm) [1] [2] [3]	From late seventh and onwards	Temporally ubiquitous
	Short (until 43–44cm) [3]	From the middle of the first onwards	Probably linked with the Civil Wars
Point: Length	Long and tapering [1] [2] [3]	From end of seventh century onwards	The characteristic element of the *gladius* until the High Imperial period
	Short and triangular	Not visible (only in the Imperial period)	Not visible in the period under consideration
Point: cutting profiles	Curvilinear [5]	Until the middle of the first century BC	The difference between the two profiles is often not very appreciable without careful examination
	Straight [6]	From the middle of first century BC onwards	

Table 3: Period of diffusion of the main characteristics of Roman *gladii* in the period covered by this book. Numbers in square brackets refer to Graph 2.

- Hilt:

In this case the understanding is simple, if we have a cross hilt [1], we are certainly dealing with a Monarchical *gladius* (without forgetting the vast diffusion of this weapon in central Italic culture) and therefore the date will certainly be between the end of the seventh – beginning of the sixth century BC and the beginning of the fourth century BC. Please refer to the appropriate chapter for a possible understanding of the culture which it belongs to (central Italic, Magna Graecia, Macedonian).

If, on the other hand, the handle is tripartite [2], or at least what remains of it suggests it, the weapon can range from the beginning of the fourth century BC onwards, potentially until the end of the Empire.

In the case of the hilt with washers [4], it can dateable between the second half of the first century BC to the High Imperial period.

- Tang:

Since it is closely related to the hilt, the same reasoning applies: if it is wide, flat and shaped according to the design seen for the Monarchical sword [1]–[7], the weapon is earlier than the beginning of the fourth century BC, if instead the shank is a barrel, [8] [9] [10], we have a date immediately after that.

- Shoulders:

The descending profile [8] is a clue that places us in a rather large period of time, from the beginning of the fourth century BC, to potentially up to the end of the first century BC (and even beyond).

However, we can say that after the Marian period this feature becomes increasingly rare. More definitive is the straight profile [10], which can never be found in the second half of the first century BC, and which therefore circumscribes the dating.

As for the intermediate type (substantially straight but slightly descending) [9], we do not have sufficient data to be able to give a reliable date. However, from the various other characteristics of the specimens that possess it, we can deduce that it was a sort of transition from one type to another, that can be placed between the second half of the second century and the Caesarian period, with all the need for caution that such a supposition imposes.

- Blade, cutting profile:

The lanceolate profile [1] [2] does not provide us with a particular date. In fact it can be found from the beginning of the Monarchical sword to the end of the Consular Age, disappearing only in the Imperial period. The straight one [2] [3] is a little more useful because in the Monarchical Period it seems to be absent, with the first appearances from the advent of the Italo-Celtic sword (early fourth century BC), to then persist over the centuries. Finally, the slightly triangular profile is a clear indication of a rather late blade, dating from the end of the Consular Age onwards.

- Blade width:

A particularly wide blade (5–7cm) is typical of the late period [3], from the end of the Consular Age onwards, while narrower blades are generally present in all periods [1] [2] [3].

- Blade length:

It is very useful when it is short [3], roughly within 43–45cm, indicating that we are in the Late Consular Age, about the middle of the first century BC onwards, and potentially even a few decades earlier. Longer blades [1] [2] are less straightforward, since we can find them in throughout the history even if they tend to be more archaic than the short ones. A blade longer than average can hardly ever be placed in the final period.[317]

- Point:

Always long and tapering (gladiolus leaf), at least in relation to its geometry and overall length, it constitutes a real watershed with the following Imperial period, in which we will see it decidedly shorter, but throughout the period of our study its length does not seem to provide us with useful indications for dating.

However, we can have useful information from the shape of the edges. With the approach of the final period these seem to tend towards a straight profile [6] (Fig. 9-B), while previously they tend more to an arch [5] (Fig. 9-A). Despite the truth of this characteristic, however, it is often not very accentuated, so the weapon has to be examined carefully to be correctly identified.

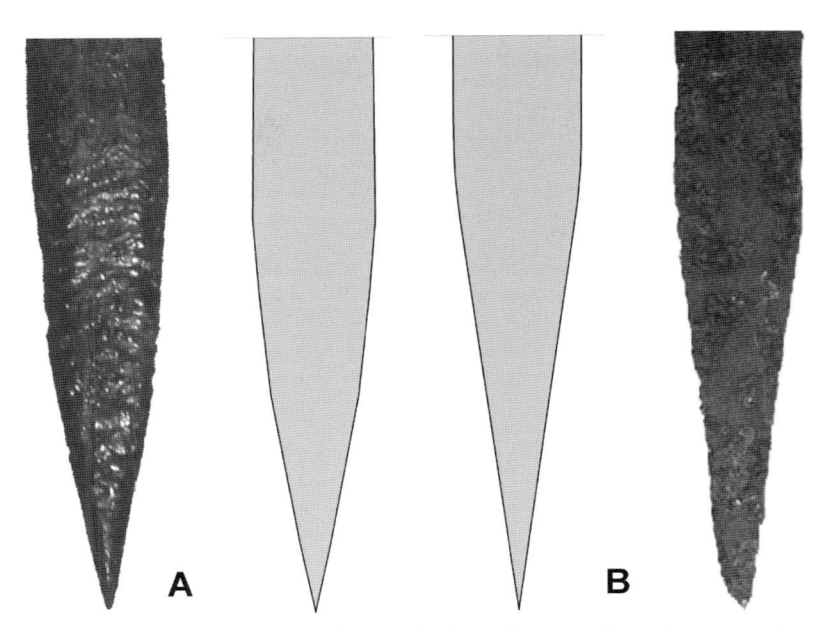

Fig. 9: Two types of points, both long and tapered, shown both on the authentic specimen and on a drawing, of which the first (A) shows the edges tending to an arch while in the second (B) they are substantially straight. (*Author's drawing*)

III (B).3,4 Suspension and wearing of the weapon in the Late Consular Age
The natural and inevitable evolution of the weapon suspension and wearing systems analysed so far, starting with the Bronze Age and passing through the centuries of the Monarchy and the High Consular Age, leads us finally to meet the most typical ones of the Roman world. These ultimately originated from the synergy of the main advantages of the archaic ring technologies and that with the *balteus*, which we have seen present among all the Italic peoples (including the Celts), at least from the sixth century BC. Once again we are faced with an intense cultural exchange and reciprocal influences of the various peoples who lived together in central Italy, blurring the borders of origin and classification.

We will first see how the *gladius* was worn in the Roman world and then move on to the more specifically technological part.

The ways of wearing the *gladius*
• Oblique and vertical position of the scabbard:
We have seen how the vertical position of the weapon, along the soldier's thigh, could create problems (hindrance during running, bouncing on the thigh, tendency to damage the scabbard, etc.), and how since the seventh century BC, all the central Italic populations and above all the Celts had tried to find a remedy to it by looking for the best way to keep it oblique. But if this is certainly true during action, it is equally true that the Roman legionary was normally in quieter situations, for which the vertical

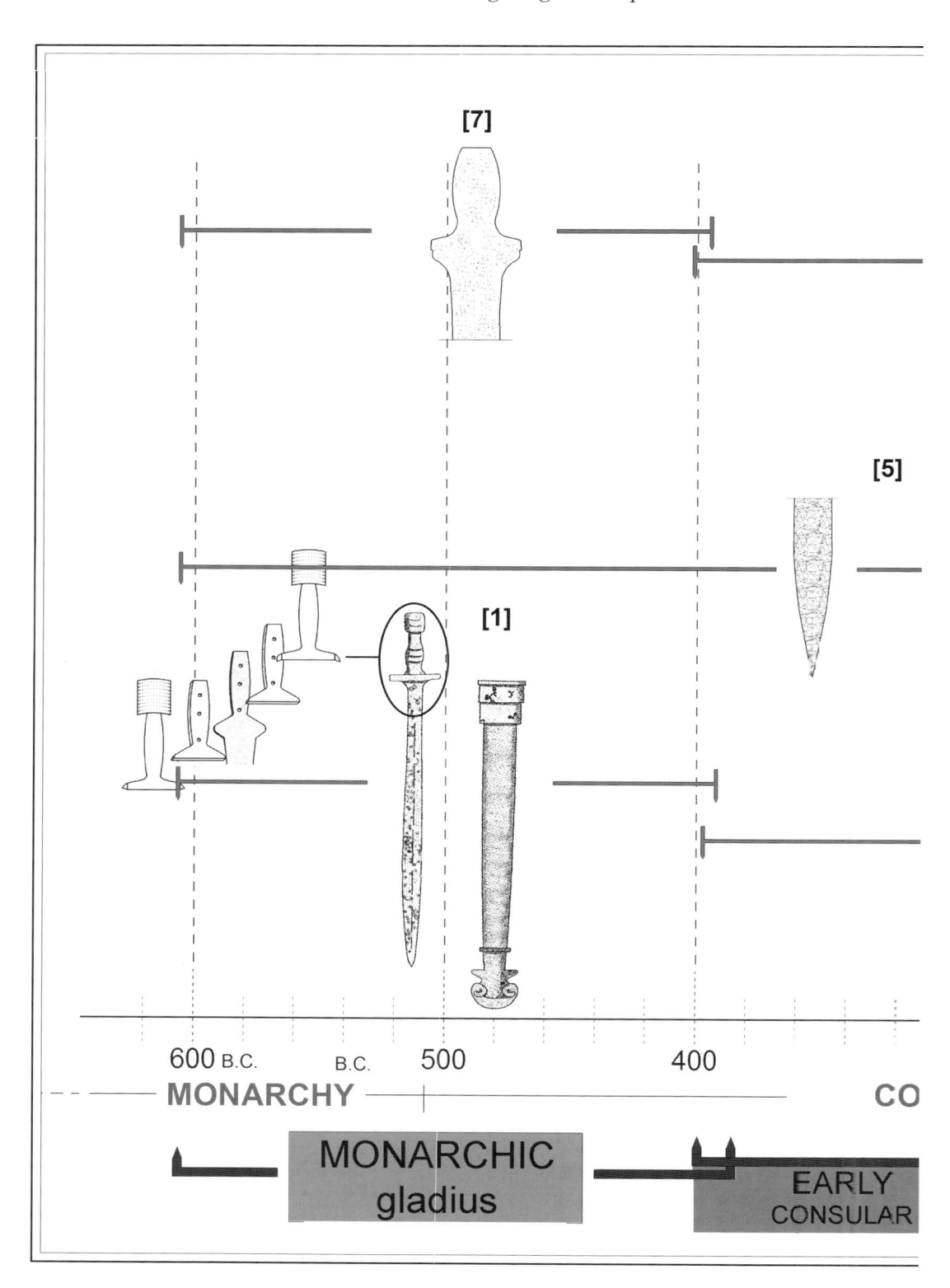

234 The Roman Gladius and the Ancient Fighting Techniques

600 B.C.   B.C. 500   400

MONARCHY   CO

MONARCHIC gladius

EARLY CONSULAR

The Consular Age 235

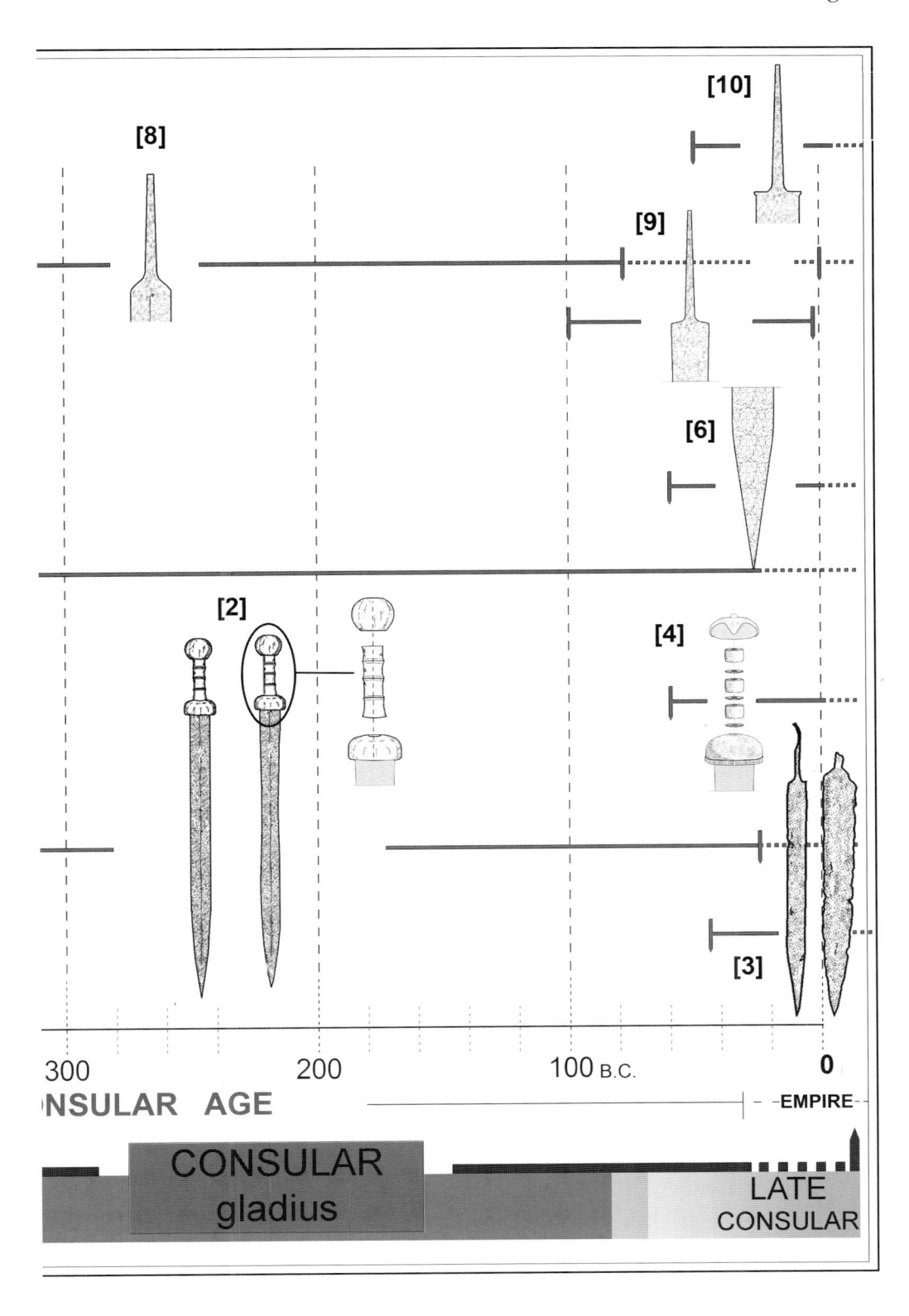

[10]
[8]
[9]
[6]
[2] [4]
[3]

300   200   100 B.C.   0
NSULAR AGE — EMPIRE
CONSULAR gladius   LATE CONSULAR

Previous Page: Graph 2: Dating periods of the various characteristics of the *gladius*:
- [1] *Gladius* with cross hilt, with composite handle and typical scabbard.
- [2] High Consular *gladius*, both in the variant with lanceolate and parallel edges, with tripartite handle.
- [3] *Gladius* of the Late Consular Age–High Empire with short blades (both wide and narrow, with lanceolate, parallel or triangular edges).
- [4] Handle with washers.
- [5] Long tip with pointed profile.
- [6] Long tip with straight profile.
- [7] Flat tang for cross hilt.
- [8] Descending shoulders and barrel shank.
- [9] 'Intermediate' shoulders, slightly descending, and barrel shank.
- [10] Straight shoulders and barrel shank.

(Author's drawing)

position is undeniably more comfortable as the scabbard does not protrude beyond the body. In a nutshell, we can say that:

- the vertical position is more suitable in moments of rest;
- the oblique position is instead more suitable for energetic movement, such as in battle.

There is precise evidence of this in the iconography, particularly relevant being the funerary *stelae* depicting standing soldiers,[318] said to be in military *habitus*,[319] for the most part from the Rhine region and dated placed between the first and third centuries AD (Fig. 10-1). They are an excellent representation of the appearance of the legionary, whether he is a simple soldier or an officer, especially those of the first century AD, since, as Franzoni affirms, they explicitly refer to the typical features of the military world, the uniform and weapons in first place,[320] while in the following periods 'the depiction of soldiers reflects less and less the war characteristics in favour of those in civilian clothes'.[321] In these the soldier, always represented in scenes that we could define as quiet and peaceful,[322] practically always wears the *gladius* (and the *pugio*) vertically.[323] To these we could add many other representations of moments of quiet, and they too invariably show the scabbards in a vertical position,[324] some of which can be seen in Fig. 10.

As for the *milites in procintu stantes*,[325] we also have many representations of these and in such situations we can see how the *gladius* was carried obliquely instead. The splendid relief of the Battle of Actium, from the 'Medinaceli' Frieze, illustrates this well.[326] Although the artist's aim was not the representation of the individual soldier as in the Rhine *stelae*, but of the battle scene as a whole, with consequent lack of the most minute details of the equipment, figures of marines in the heat of battle are clearly evident, showing the scabbard tilted forward (Fig. 11-1). Many other examples could be added to this,[327] some of them in Fig. 11.

If the indications we draw from it are on average fairly unambiguous and concordant, it is nevertheless necessary to specify how it is inevitable that in the variegated ancient world there are some exceptions and some representations that do not comply with this rule. For example, in the *Tropaeum Traiani*, which so faithfully adheres to the

Fig. 10: Depictions of legionaries at rest. Note the vertical position of the scabbard. 1: *Stele* of Annaius Daverzus; 2: Arch of Carpentoratum; 3 and 4: *Tropaeum Traiani* in Adamclisi (Romania), metopae XXII-IX. (*Author's photo*)

representation of the vertical or oblique position of the weapon depending on the situation, we have instead a metopa (XXXI-6) which seems to disagree with it, representing the legionary fully engaged with a Dacian warrior, the *gladius* unsheathed on the right, very similar to those in Fig. 12,4 and 12,5, but with his scabbard upright.[328]

- Side on which worn:

It is almost universally accepted that the *gladius* was carried on the right side by ordinary soldiers and on the left by the officers, from centurions upwards. This is certainly true as a general rule and the historical and archaeological evidence is a clear attestation of this. Polybius's testimony leaves no room for misunderstanding, when he states that 'Besides the shield they also carry a sword, hanging on the right thigh and called an Iberian sword'.[329]

To date, however, it is not entirely clear when this custom came into use among the Romans. What we know for sure is that it was a widespread practice among the Celts since very ancient times. Strabo attests that 'The Gallic armour is commensurate with the large size of their bodies: a long sabre, which hangs along the right side, and a long oblong shield, and spears in proportion … '.[330] He is referring to the Belgians, therefore a Transalpine Celtic tribe and not a purely Italic one, but his work, despite having been written at the time of Augustus, remains as valid testimony. On the other hand, his contemporary Diodorus Siculus states 'Some of them have iron cuirasses, chain-wrought, but others are satisfied with the armour which Nature has given them and go into battle naked. In place of the short sword they carry long broad-swords which are hung on chains of iron or bronze and are worn along the right flank.'[331] Moreover, many representations of armed Celts anticipate and confirm these literary descriptions, some of which can be seen in Fig. 12.[332]

But fairly archaic references to this custom are also found in a more purely Italic context. Among these, the Faliscan crater n. 9830001 AGR (Fig. 2-1 of Chapter III (A).3 'The Upper and Middle Consular *Gladius*', fourth century BC) and the two bronze statues preserved in the museum of Villa Giulia (Rome) depicting two Roman legionaries (Fig. 14-1 of Chapter III (A).3 'The Upper and Middle Consular *Gladius*', third century BC), to which can be added, among many other examples, an Etruscan cinerary urn in alabaster from Volterra (Guarnacci museum, inv. 427, middle of the third – second century BC), which re-proposes a scene of struggle between characters with a typical Italic ethnic connotation. In all these works we note that the infantryman carries the sword on his right side.

But if it is unquestionably true that this has been the rule for legionaries (but not for officers), it is worth asking whether it has always been as strict as is commonly held by modern literature.

> When, after this, they are gone out of their camp, they all march without noise, and in a decent manner, and everyone keeps his own rank, as if they were going to war. The footmen are armed with breast-plates, and head-pieces, and have swords

Fig. 11: Representations of legionaries in battle or in triumphal processions. Note the scabbard in a markedly oblique position. 1: Medinaceli frieze; 2: Arch of Augustus in Susa; 3: Glanum mausoleum (Saint Rémy de Provence); 4–5: *Tropaeum Traiani* in Adamclisi (Romania), metopae XXXI-3. (*Author's photo, except 2 and 3 Raffaele D'Amato*)

240 The Roman Gladius and the Ancient Fighting Techniques

on each side, but the sword which is upon their left side is much longer than the other, for that on the right side is not longer than a span.³³³

Josephus does not seem to give us unanimous information, even though he is describing the Roman army in a period somewhat outside that of our current reference. This apparent inconsistency finds numerous confirmations in the iconography, some of which can be seen in Fig. 13.³³⁴

Even if our current knowledge is still too modest, in the light of what is stated above it is possible to hypothesise that the position on the right, although predominant, was not an absolute and mandatory rule, but that it could still be accompanied by that on the left, both in the Imperial period rather than, probably, in the Consular one. This circumstance, however, is not that surprising given that the representations of various kinds, dating back to even very archaic periods, often show the sword of

Fig. 12: Evidence of Celtic warriors with sword hanging from the right side. 1: Terracotta figure of a Gaulish warrior (British Museum); 2: Alabaster cinerary urn, from Chiusi (Archaeological Museum of Florence, inv. 81692); 3: Stàmnos 1569 of the Akademisches Kunstmuseum (Bonn). (*From 'L'armamento dei Celti nel periodo della battaglia del Metauro', by D. Vitali*)

Fig. 13: Examples of the *gladius* carried on the left side instead of on the right. 1: Column of Marcus Aurelius. Note that the legionary in the centre of the scene carries his *gladius* hanging on his left side, while his fellow soldier has it on his right. 2: Detail of the Portonaccio sarcophagus. Notes that the legionary in the centre carries the scabbard on his left side, hanging from a baldric. (*Author's photos*)

a Monarchical type hanging from a *balteus* on the left (see Chapter II.3 'The Monarchical *Gladius*') thus justifying a custom perhaps in disuse but certainly not unknown. Furthermore, it should be remembered that even in the ancient world left-handers existed!

The suspension system technology

The components of the Roman hanging system consist of two parts: the first is an integral part of the scabbard and is basically made up of rings and bands (Fig. 14-1), the second is the complex structure of straps, belts and *baltei*, intended to be tied to the soldier's body and connected to the former (Fig. 14-2).

- **Component n. 1**: scabbard rings and bands

It is fundamentally very simple but at the same time extremely efficient (Fig. 15).

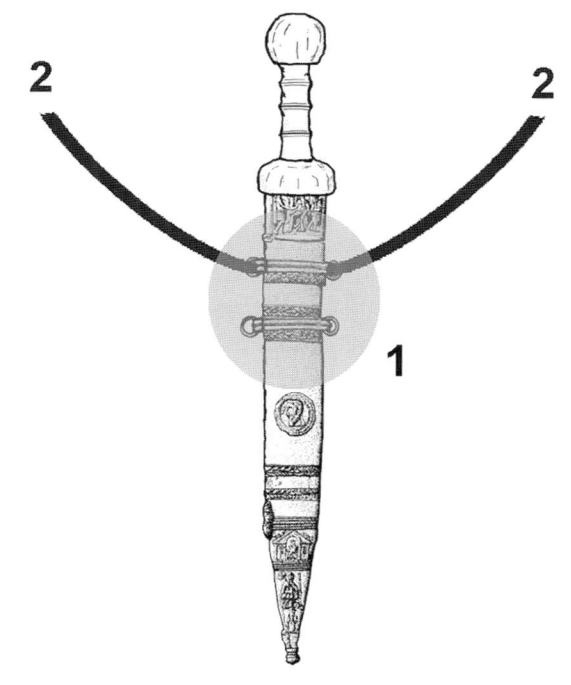

Fig. 14: Representation of the two main suspension components:
Component '1' – set of rings and sheath's bands;
Component '2' – set of belts and/or straps necessary for connection to the soldier's body. (*Author's drawing*)

Description:
Basically this consists of two pairs of small rings (Fig. 15-3) bound to the scabbard by means of metallic suspension bands (Fig. 15-5). The distance of the centre from the latter in the various analysed finds, shown in Table 4, are between 40mm and 100mm, with a greater concentration between 50mm and 75mm with an approximate average of 62mm.[335] This is not a mere random distance, but the best balance between the position and length of the belts necessary to angle the scabbard.

In fact, the arrangement of the four rings forms an imaginary quadrilateral which gives the possibility of generating – or not – a pair of forces capable of angling the scabbard: if the belts are both connected to a pair of rings on the same line, the traction does not generate rotation (Fig. 16-1), leaving the scabbard upright. Instead, by placing them on staggered rings, we obtain an inclination of the scabbard, resulting from the twisting of the imaginary quadrilateral (Fig. 16-2).

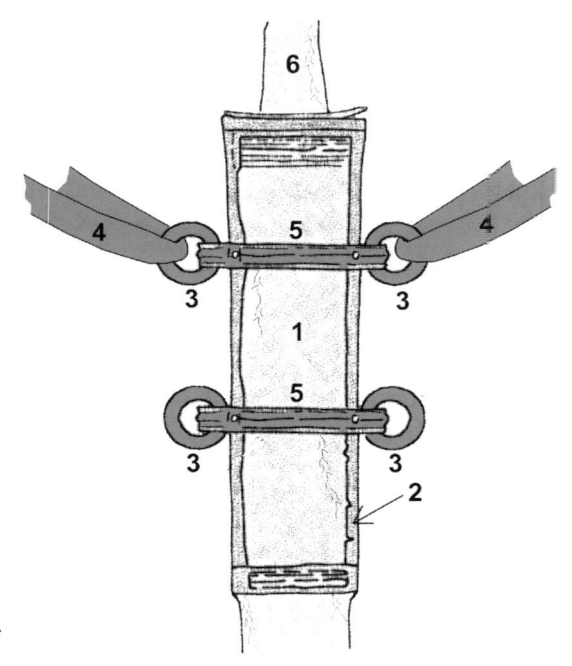

Fig. 15: Example of a pair of bands with four rings, which were used to connect the scabbard to the *balteus* or *cingulum* (based on the example from Berry-Bouy). 1: Scabbard; 2: Scabbard frame; 3: Suspension rings; 4: Suspension bands; 5: Straps; 6: Tang of the blade. (*Author's drawing*)

To make this happen easily, the distance between the upper and lower pairs of rings must not be too short, otherwise when too much tension was applied to them it would have, as a consequence, generated both excessive stress on the structure of the scabbard and a constriction on the soldier's body. However, it shouldn't be too long either, otherwise the lower strap would drop too much on the thigh, creating a hindrance, as well as an unsightly effect.

Specimen	Inv. No.	Date	Total length (mm)	Rings centre distance (mm)
Delos museum	inv. E. 1909	69 BC	760	80
Ornovasso (Verbano)	/	70–30 BC	840	100
Musée du Berry-Bourges	inv. 893.29.1	First century BC	730	74
Mittelrheinisches Landes Museum	11.4.1901	First century BC – First century AD	657	74
RMGZ – Mainz	0.15.391	First century AD	660	53
Mittelrheinisches Landes Museum	0.3162	First century AD	640 ca.	58 ca.

Specimen	Inv. No.	Date	Total length (mm)	Rings centre distance (mm)
So called 'Tiberius'- British Museum	GR 1866.8-6.1	First century AD	700	82
Het Valkhof Museum Nijmegen	GN.E.XIV.8°	First century AD	680	40
Narodni Museum Ljubljana	R17110	First century AD	665 ca.	40 ca.
Mittelrheinisches Landes Museum	R2580-81	First century AD	437	40
Mittelrheinisches Landes Museum	o.3166	First century AD	588	64
Mittelrheinisches Landes Museum	/	First century AD	542	56
Mittelrheinisches Landes Museum	1917/99	First century AD	670	76
Porto Novo – Corsica	/	First century AD	465 ca.	42 ca.
Pompei- museo archeologico Napoli	5757	First century AD	692	68
Pompei- Sovrint. Acheolog. Napoli	4541	First century AD	542	70
Rijkmuseum Van Oudhen- Leiden	1896/9.5	First century AD	642	50
Regionalmuseum Xanten	80/16861	First century AD	645	48

Table 4: Distances between the two pairs of rings (upper, and lower) in some of the examples of scabbards that maintain their original position unaltered.

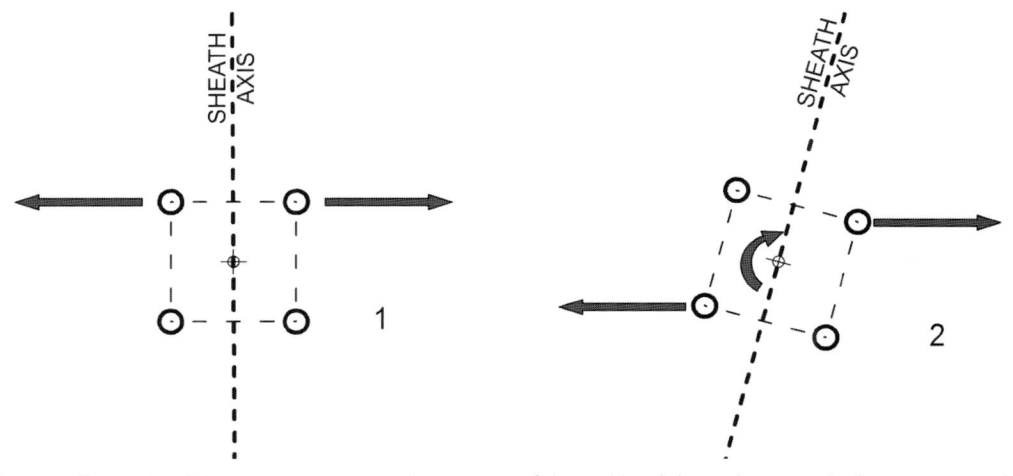

Fig. 16: Example of the consequences on the rotation of the scabbard depending on which rings are used to connect the belts. In configuration 1 the upper pair of rings are used, in this case the traction lies on the same level and therefore no rotation is generated. In configuration 2, on the other hand, the upper and lower ring are used, thus generating a misalignment of the forces and consequent rotation of the scabbard. (*Author's drawing*)

History and origins:
It is not easy to establish when the use of the four-ring system took over in the Roman military culture. We have already seen that the use of the 'ring' element is almost as old as the central Italic culture, almost dating back to the early Iron Age, even if of a somewhat different type, consisting of one or two large rings connected to short chains.

The first appearance of a complex version, more akin to the Roman system, can be found in Celtiberian territory, mounted on dagger scabbards with atrophied antennae, with a certain presence also in Andalusia, Portugal and Extremadura.[336] Many specimens are found still with their scabbard, some dating back to the end of the fifth and beginning of the fourth century BC, and on many of them the rings and bands are present. However, we note that they are practically never four in number but always a maximum of three, which suggests a similar type of suspension, but not entirely the same. The same technology can also be found on the *falcatae* scabbards starting from the mid-fifth century BC.

A particular variant appears in the Iberian territories in the late fourth–early third century BC, which seems to combine the more typical Celtic suspension system,

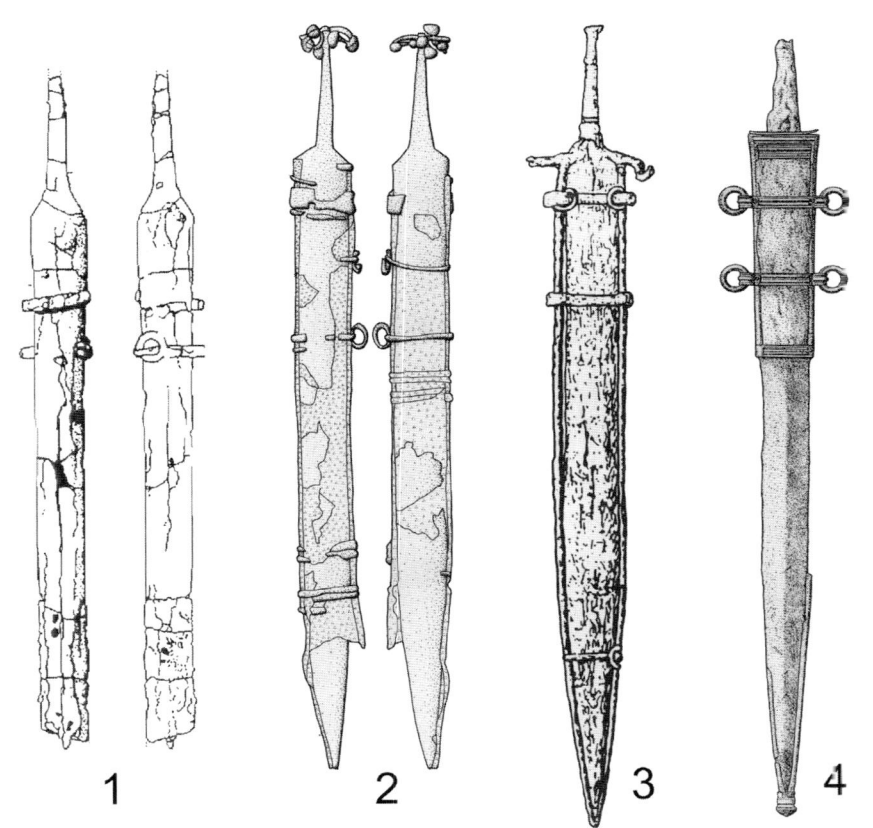

Fig. 17: *Gladii* from 1) La Azucarera; 2) Delos; 3) Ornavasso; 4) Fontilet-Berry Bouy (from 'Gladius hispaniensis: an archaeological view from Iberia' by S. Quesada Sanz).

involving the use of a bridge on the scabbard, with the one with rings[337] (Fig. 17-4). It deserves to be mentioned as it is considered by F. Quesada Sanz to be a proof of a first step in the evolution of the Celtic sword through Hispanic territory that 'leads to the creation of a model almost identical to the Roman republican sword in shape, size and suspension system'.[338] This statement, however, is scarcely acceptable as these specimens have only two rings, both on the left side of the scabbard. We have seen that the Celts wore the sword on the right side, but the aforementioned position of the rings seems to be suitable only for the left side, and in addition the two rings on the same side do not allow the weapon to be carried vertically. This is not the right place to investigate this, but once again we note that this apparently similar system probably in fact differs significantly from the Roman one. Added to this is the extreme rarity of similar specimens, with the consequence that it is scientifically very risky to use them as evidence of a widespread structural evolution, even more in Italy, where there are no clear traces of them.

To find the first Roman weapons showing the four-ring system we have to wait until the first century BC. Perhaps the most archaic is the specimen from La Azucarera, datable between 150 and 70 BC, Fig. 18-1.[339] However, there is doubt about the number of rings originally present on the scabbard, since the poor state of conservation makes it impossible to determine for certain whether the two bands had two or four rings.

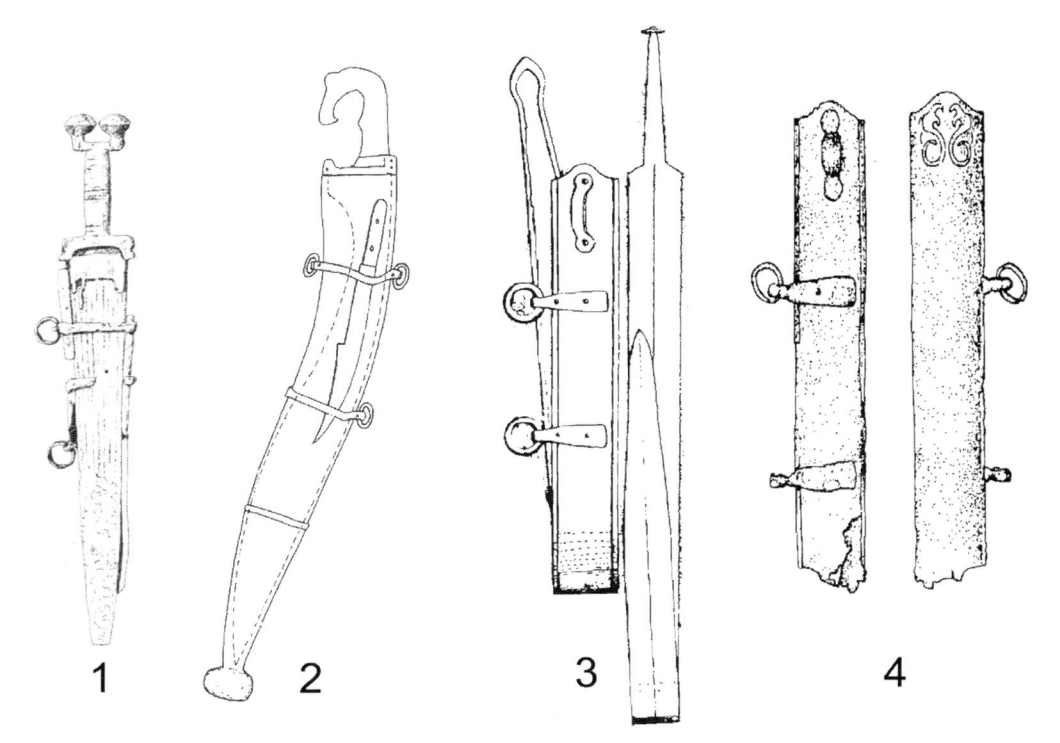

Fig. 18: 1) Dagger with atrophied antennae, from Aguilar de Anguita Illora; 2) Iberian *falcate*; 3) sword and scabbard from Arcobriga; 4) Quintanas De Gomaz scabbard (from 'Gladius hispaniensis: an archaeological view from Iberia' by S. Quesada Sanz)

The same situation applies more or less to the well-known *gladius* from the island of Delos (Fig. 18-2), probably the first specimen to be classified as '*hispaniensis*', dated to 69 BC. Much has been written about it,[340] but what we are interested in highlighting is that it too, perhaps like the specimen from La Azucarera and those from Quintanas de Gormaz and Arcóbriga, only shows two rings on the left side. As significant as it may be, we can consider it as nothing more than an 'undeveloped' stage of the Roman ring suspension.

Finally we come to the specimen from Ornavasso (Verabano, necropolis of S. Bernardo, tomb 31), singular for its considerable length, over 80cm, and for its unusual style of guard, dating back to between 70 and 30 BC. In this case we note the two bands, particularly distant from each other (see Table 3) and only the two upper rings, the lower ones having been lost. The first specimen with the complete apparatus is the one known as 'Fontillet, Berry-Bouy', preserved in the museum of Berry-Bourges, dated by C. Miks to the La Tène D2 period (around 70–30 BC) and to slightly later by P. Connolly (around 20 BC).[341]

From this moment, the archaeological presence of the four-ring suspension is quantitatively remarkable, with morphological characteristics that remain substantially unchanged until its gradual decline, around the middle of the second century AD.

Variants and exceptions
Alongside this consolidated archaeological panorama, iconography seems to give us sporadic attestations of exceptions to this four-ringed stereotype. In the lapidary of the basilica of S. Agnese Fuori le Mura in Rome, there is a relief from the end of the first century BC, with what is probably the panoply of a Romano-Celtic horseman, defined as such by the representation of a Celtic helmet with horns, next to two *gladii*, a large circular shield with *umbo* and two *vexilla* (Fig. 19-1). The scabbard of the two *gladii*, or at least the one on the left since the other is partially hidden by the shield, shows only an upper suspension band, with two rings.

In the frieze of the arch of Arausius (modern-day Orange, France), probably erected in 20–25 AD to commemorate the victories of Germanicus, there are reliefs with trophies of weapons in which we find several groups of *gladii* with their *cingula*. Also in this case, we can only find the upper suspension band and moreover with only one ring (Fig. 19-2).

As things stand, it is very difficult to establish whether this is only artistic licence and/or approximation, even if the lack of evidence in the archaeology and the rarity in the iconographic panorama itself seem to favour this hypothesis. In support of this, it must be said that wearing a *gladius* attached to a belt by means of a single ring would make the weapon extremely unstable, which is the exact opposite of the ideal situation. However, on the same monuments mentioned before, other *gladii* are represented with double suspension, which complicates the problem further.

However, there is a specimen – albeit unique – that could confirm this use of a single suspension band, the *gladius* with its scabbard from Levka (Bulgaria), preserved in the

National Museum of History in Sofia (Bulgaria),[342] which is fitted only with the upper band (Fig. 19-3).[343] But its uniqueness in an extensive archaeological panorama does not let us consider it as a significant variant, but only as an exception.

Modern literature has often wondered whether or not these four links were all used, even if not simultaneously, often seeking the answer in practical reconstruction tests of various more or less subjective suspension hypotheses.[344] In reality, historical evidence confirms a rather variable situation, with solutions that involve the simultaneous use

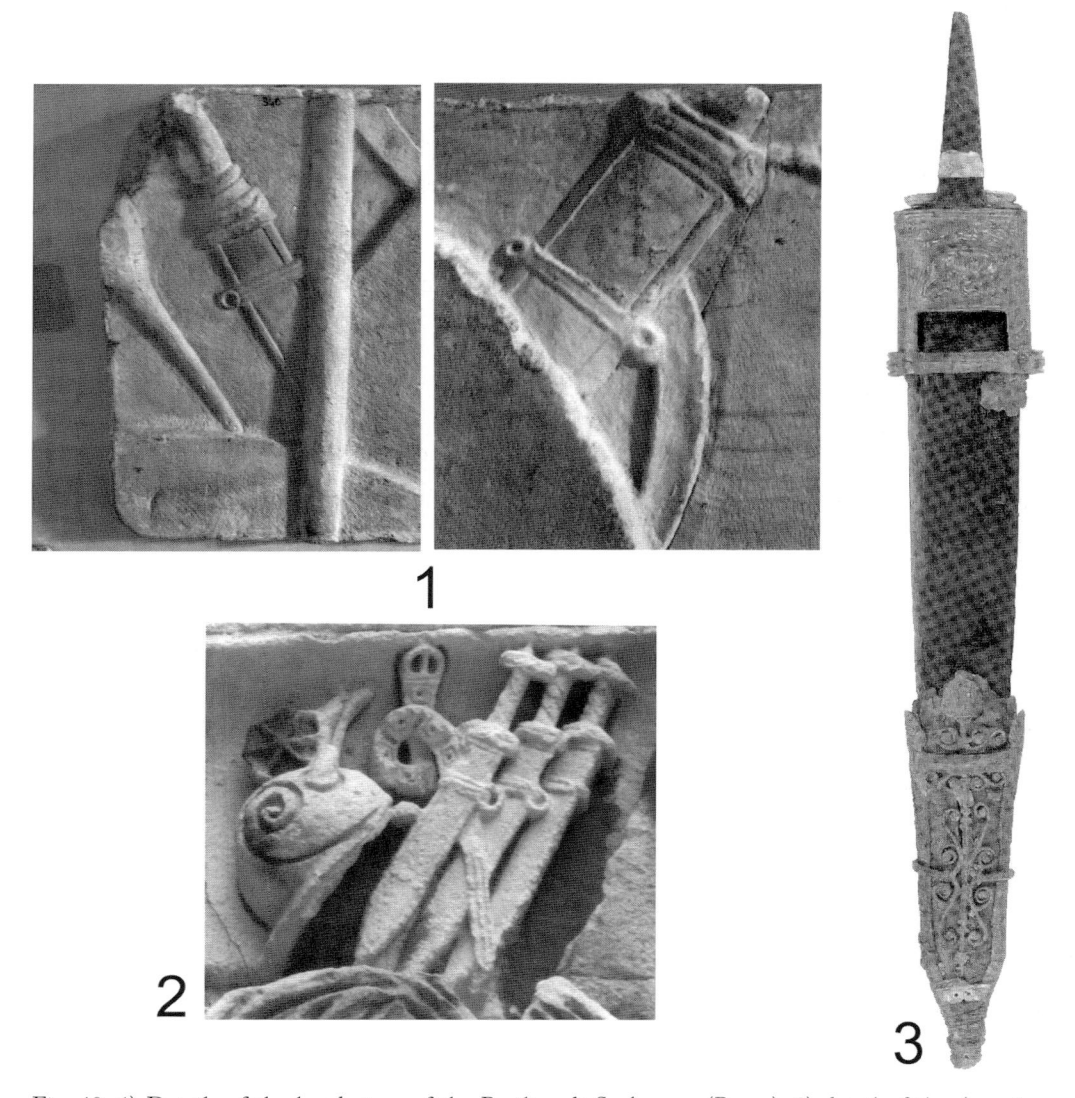

Fig. 19: 1) Details of the lapidarium of the Basilica di S. Agnese (Rome); 2) detail of the Arausius (Orange) Arch; 3) *Gladius* from Levka (Bulgaria)
(Photos nos 1 and 2 Raffaele D'Amato, no. 3 from 'Catalogue of National Museum of History' (Sofia, Bulgaria))

of all the rings, others only of three and finally only of two. However, all of them, as partially suggested by P. Connolly[345] too, provide for a different use depending on whether the scabbard is placed on the right side or on the left.

Component n. 2: belts and *baltei* for connection to the soldier's body

The complex n. 1 of rings and bands just described is in very close synergy with n. 2, which is made up of either a baldric[346] or a belt[347] (sometimes both together), of which we will now examine the various types and characteristics.

The suspension from the cingulum

| no. of rings used at the same time: | 2 |
| no. of belts necessary: | 1 |

As already stated, the *gladius* could also be suspended from a belt, called the *cingulum*. This was the typical legionary belt that encircled the waist and was often richly decorated with metal plates. From a practical point of view, its function was both to hold the *gladius* and the *pugio*, and to help to distribute part of the weight of the *lorica hamis conserta* on the hips, although its symbolic meaning was no less important. In fact, 'being one with the sword that was hanging from it'[348] meant it was means that supported the military symbol par excellence, the *gladius*, and consequently it took on the same status.[349]

We know that this technology derived from previous centuries, to the extent that we find evidence of it even in the Late Consular Age in the *stele* of the centurion Minucius Lorarius, who is portrayed with a single buckled belt, rather simple and apparently devoid of decoration. The Rhine funerary *stelae* seem to suggest that during the first century AD, two belts were used: one for the *gladius* and one for the *pugio*, even if this use gradually disappeared, returning to only one.

In any case, for our purposes, it is above all important to understand how the *cingulum* was connected to the rings and suspension bands of scabbard components previously seen and how this worked.

As some scholars[350] rightly point out, in reality the latter remains quite obscure. The Rhine *stelae*, although so rich in detail, do not really clarify the situation, but luckily we are helped by a splendid image from the temple of Baalshamin in Palmyra (Syria),[351] depicting a divine triad with Baalshamin Lord of the skies, himself in the centre, on his right the sun god Malakbel and finally on his left the moon god Aglibol (first half of the first century AD, Fig. 20-A). Looking at the detail of the *stele*, it can be seen that the weapon is carried slightly obliquely and that the straps pass through only two staggered rings, one upper and one lower. This shows us the practical application of the principle described above in Fig. 16, on the rotation of the scabbard depending on which rings are used to connect the belts. When the soldier is at rest, it is sufficient to connect the *cingulum* to only to the two upper rings of the scabbard (A and B in

Fig. 20: A: Baalshamin temple (Palmyra, Syria); B: detail of the *stele* of Tiberius Iulius Abdes Pantera in which *gladius* and *pugio* are clearly seen, each one hanging from a belt (*cingulum*). (*Author's photo*)

Fig. 21) so that it assumes a vertical position (Fig. 21 – 1), as we see in the Rhine *stelae* (Fig. 10-1). But if, on the other hand, the rear strap is connected to the lower ring (C in Fig. 21), the scabbard immediately leans forward (Fig. 21-2), which in turn is useful in combat.

This system, therefore, is connected to only two rings of the scabbard alternating out of three, namely A and B at rest, C and B in battle. The fact that there is a fourth can be explained by the possibility of carrying the weapon both on the left and on the right.

However, when examining the Rhine *stelae* some scholars support the alternative hypothesis that only 'the upper pair was the one attached to the belt during the first century AD'.[352] This opinion, however, does not seem to take into consideration that these works usually show men at rest, a situation that indeed requires the involvement only of the two upper links. In other cases, other interpretations are given without any historical or technical confirmation (Fig. 22).

This technology is quite similar in its final practical result to the Celtic one previously described, with the advantage of placing the metal structure of the scabbard under less stress, especially when worn at an angle. Good stability on the body was guaranteed even during violent movements, as well as avoiding the possibility that the scabbard would accidentally slip between the soldier's legs and the effect of dragging, when the blade was drawn from the scabbard, provided, however, that the straps used were short enough, as indeed the *stele* of Abdes Pantera suggests. The problems reported by J.P. Hazell in his study, when he states that if the scabbard was connected to the *cingulum* only through the upper pair of rings, without any help from the balcric, the sword was positioned a little lower, with little martial aspect, and also tended to hit the knees,[353] derive once again from the limited analysis of the Rhine *stelae*, without considering the

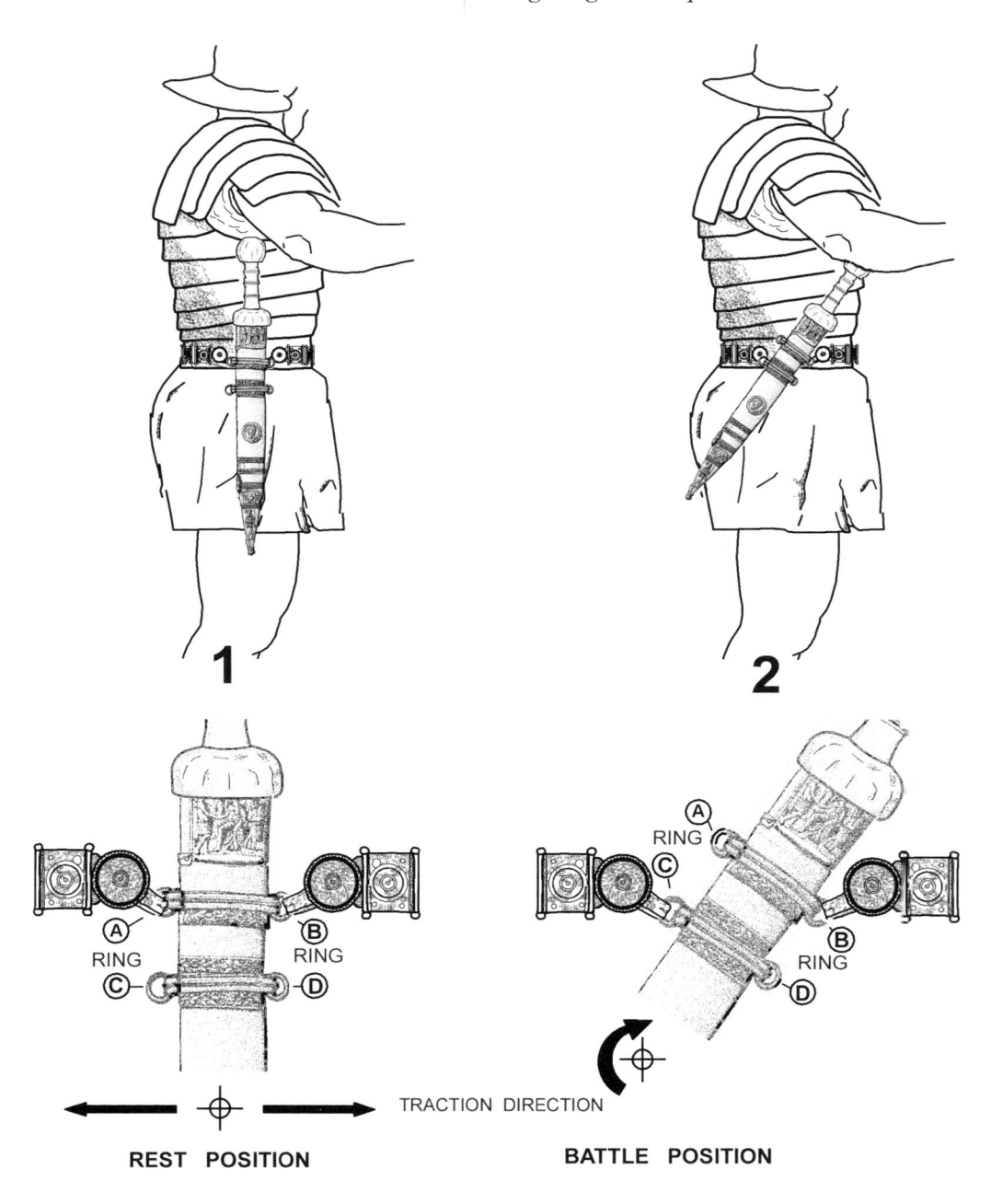

Fig. 21: Suspension at the *cingulum*. 1- Rest position; 2- Battle position.
Key: A and B: pair of upper rings; C and D pair of lower rings. (*Author's drawing*)

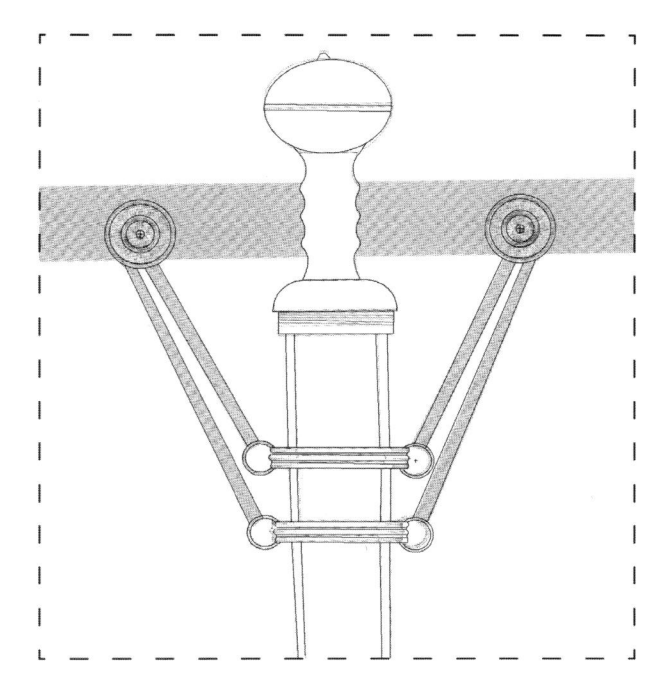

Fig. 22: This representation of the connection system of the scabbard to the *cingulum* is without historical and technical references. In this case, various problems arise: the two pairs of straps, upper and lower, unnecessarily perform the same function; it is not possible to place the weapon obliquely for battle; the scabbard is completely unstable, etc.) (Drawing from Istenič, *Roman Military Equipment from the River Ljubljanica*)

possible second oblique position of the scabbard. With this precaution, the problem, again reported by Hazell, of the difficulty of extracting a weapon with a blade longer than 54cm[354] from an upright scabbard is also overcome, because it is much easier from the oblique position.

Suspensions from a Roman balteus
It should first be noted that this system may apparently seem inconsistent from a temporal point of view to our studies, which are limited at the end of the Consular Age. In fact, it is widely believed that only from the end of the first century BC (the Early Principiate) did it seem to become common to wear only one belt (instead of two as in the previous period), with the sword now suspended from a baldric.[355] In reality this must be backdated, potentially considerably, not only because the *gladii* on the arch of Carpentoratum (which we have seen to be dated to the Caesarian period) clearly seem to use a *balteus* and not a *cingulum*, but above all because we know that the baldric had always existed in the Greco-Roman culture: it was created practically together with the sword itself. It is difficult to believe how the association between baldric and sword, after having been a constant for centuries, could disappear in a certain period and then reappear in the first century AD. It is more likely that the evidences of the Consular Age are only rarer, even if we have already seen some in Chapter II.3,3 'The Monarchical *Gladius*', which show the use of the baldric at the beginning and end of the third century BC.

Apparently the functionality of the *balteus* was modest and it is often thought that the sword carried in this way was too mobile. The re-enactors have discovered that, if

252 The Roman Gladius and the Ancient Fighting Techniques

it is worn on the left without ligatures, it has an alarming tendency to move, with the risk of ending up between the legs.[356] In reality, this belief arises from forming a model from archaeological evidence, which for obvious reasons are not real representations. These include the Portonaccio sarcophagus, where a clash between Romans and barbarians is depicted (last quarter of the second century AD). On the main side we can find a legionary engaged in piercing a barbarian with his *gladius*, with the scabbard simply hanging from a *balteus* on the left side, without the aid of belts or anything else (Fig. 14). The way it is depicted, it could not really remain in this position, but it would inevitably slide round the front of the soldier. It is very likely that the artist exercised a legitimate simplification, which, on the other hand, we often find, quite similarly, both on Trajan's Column and on that of Marcus Aurelius. However, the Portonaccio soldier is a *miles* or *centurio* of a mixed infantry and cavalry cohort, fighting on the ground after his horse has been killed, the sword being designed for a cavalry soldier, with a longer baldric inevitably carried on the left. Still, being now a monument deprived of colour and metallic details, the analysis of what remains does not allow a complete evaluation of the iconography.

Instead, there are two bas-reliefs that clearly show us how the *balteus* worked in reality with maximum efficiency, introducing us to two types of this suspension system that we will call the 'Modena' type and the 'Chieti' type.

'MODENA' TYPE *BALTEUS*	
No. of rings used at the same time:	3
No. of belts needed:	2

Fig. 23: A stone bas-relief in the Archaeological Museum of Modena. (*Author's photo, courtesy of the Museum*)

The Consular Age 253

In the lapidary of the Archaeological Museum of Modena, it is possible to admire the representation of a *gladius*, datable to the late Consular Age–Early Principiate by analogy of its scabbard with that from Vrhnika, found in the Ljubljanica river, commonly believed to be of the Augustan period.[357]

The binding technique of this *balteus* is very evident and is composed of two belts, one longer, ending with a fringe (the latter detail common in many representations), and a shorter one, on which the buckle is mounted (Fig. 24), which connect to some of the rings that we previously called 'component n. 1 – rings and suspension bands'.

The representation in Fig. 24 shows its quite simple working method. The two belts are both fastened to the pair of upper rings (A and B in Fig. 24). The longer strap passes over the shoulder on the opposing side to the one on which the scabbard is positioned to, continuing down and connecting to the second ring of the scabbard beneath the first one and positioned on the same side (D in Fig. 24); at this point the belt is turned around the waist and tied to the buckle of the shorter belt. We note that

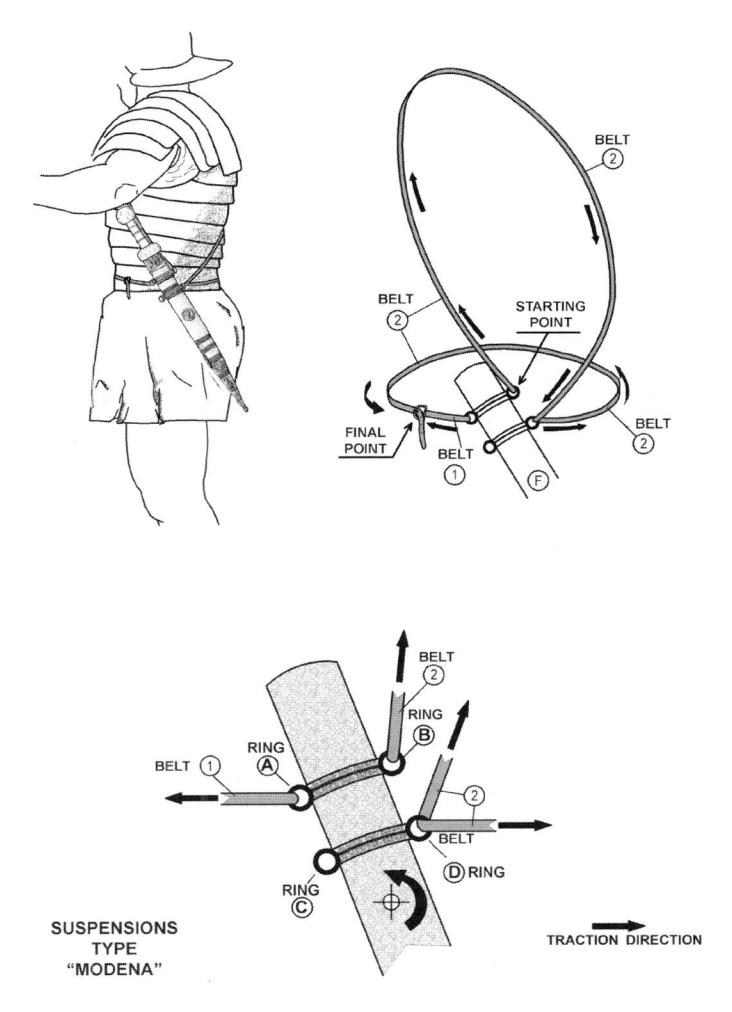

Fig. 24: 'Modena' type suspension type in battle position. (*Author's drawing*)

only three rings are used at the same time, and, in the case of the bas-relief, it is worn on the left side. To bring it to the right, it is enough to reverse the position of the two straps, so that the ring now at rest will be used (C in Fig. 24).

It is important to note that this wearing system apply its traction on staggered rings (A and D in Fig. 24), so that you can easily vary the scabbard's inclination. Indeed, in the case of a slightly stretched belt, it will assume an almost vertical or a slightly inclined position, but it will be sufficient to increase the traction, simply by moving the buckle a few holes, to incline it more: thus passing from the rest position to battle position with a simple movement of the hand.

'CHIETI' TYPE *BALTEUS*	
No. of rings used at the same time:	4
No. of belts needed:	1

The Chieti museum houses a bas-relief representing an oval shield with *umbo*, decorated with three circles interlaced with each other, with a *spathe* and a *balteus* on it.[358] On the background we can see a head of a *carnyx* (Celtic musical instrument) and draperies (Fig. 25). The style is typical of the second century AD, between Hadrian and Antoninus Pius.[359] If so, it shows the suspension of a cavalry *spatha*.

It introduces us to the second type of suspension with *balteus*, which involves the use of a single strap, in this case arranged in a way to carry the weapon on the right side. It starts by passing inside the D ring (remember that the rings referred to are those of the 'component n. 1 – suspension rings and bands' above), then goes behind the scabbard to slide inside the other ring C (C and D constitute the pair of lower rings, see Fig. 26). It then makes the typical turn behind the back and on the opposite shoulder (left in this case), and then goes back down on the chest to slide into ring A. Once again it passes

Fig. 25: A stone bas-relief from the Archaeological Museum of Chieti. (*Author's photo, courtesy of the Museum*)

The Consular Age 255

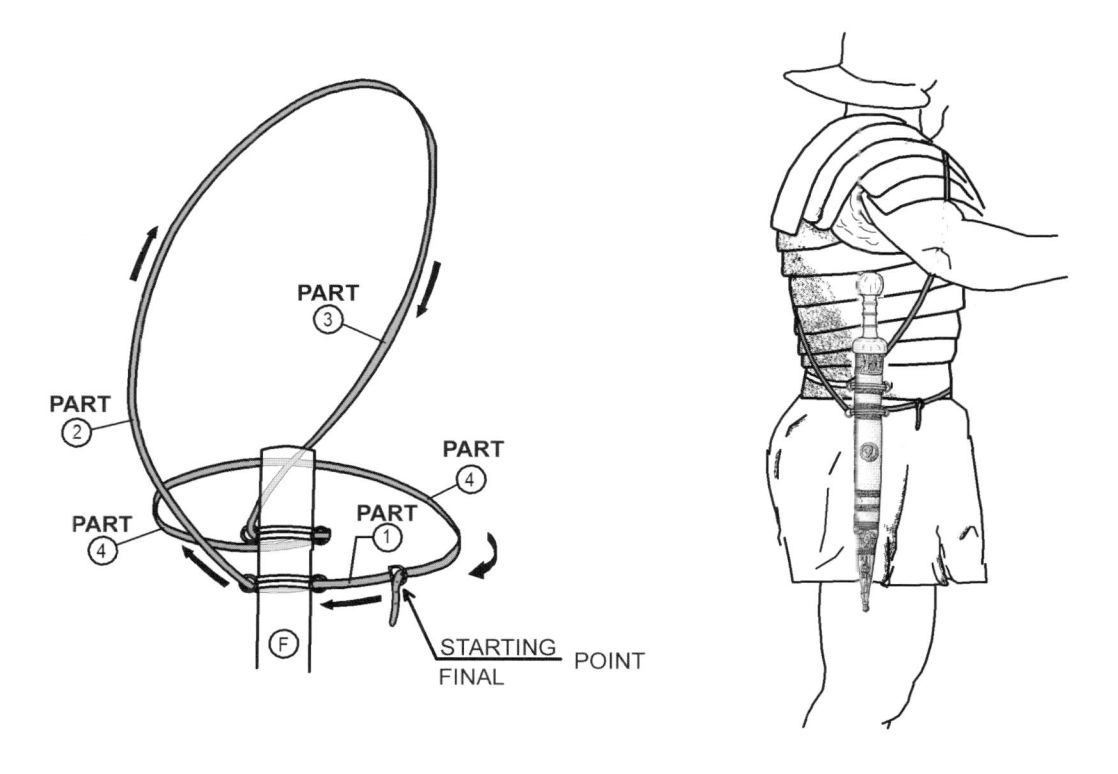

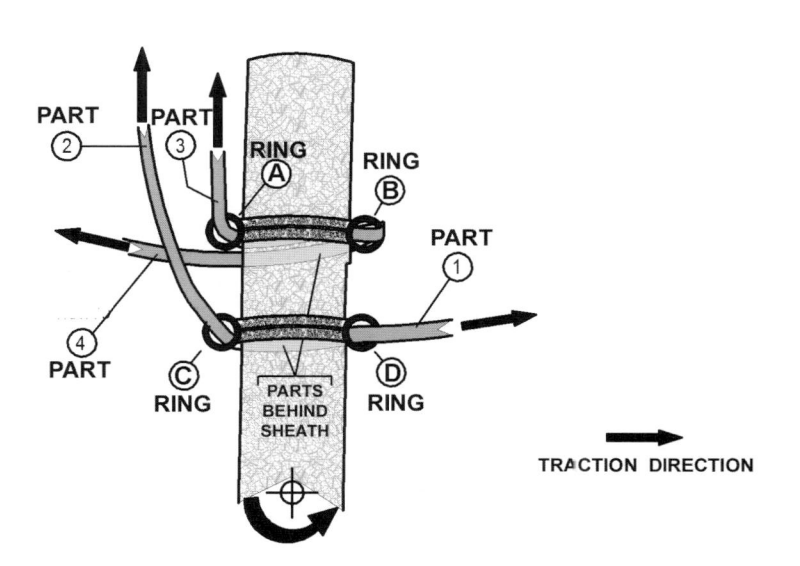

Fig. 26: 'Chieti' type suspension in rest position. (*Author's drawing*)

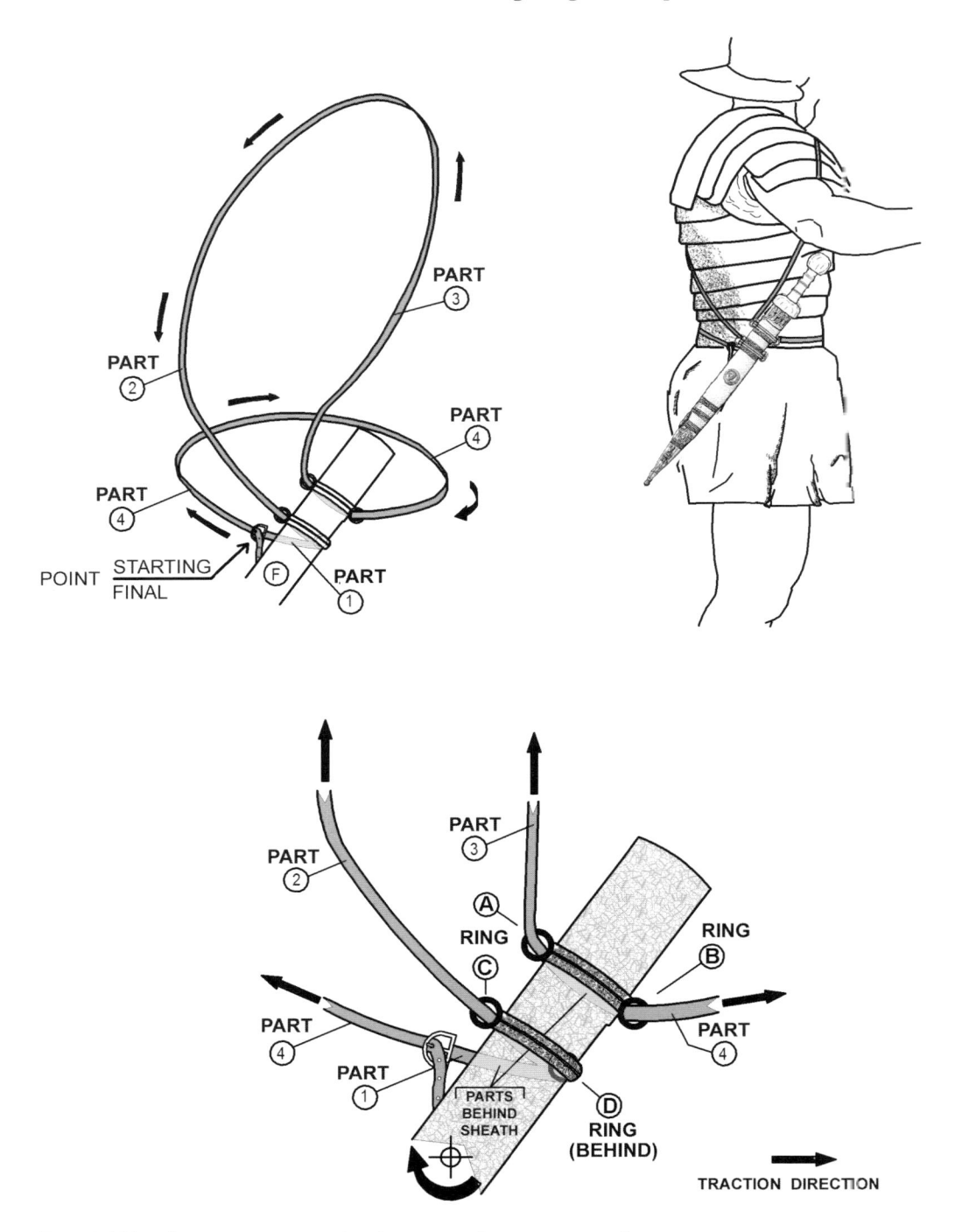

256 The Roman Gladius and the Ancient Fighting Techniques

Fig. 27: 'Chieti' type suspension in battle position. (*Author's drawing*)

behind the scabbard and slides into the last remaining ring B (A and B form the pair of upper rings, see Fig. 26).

At this point we find ourselves with the two ends on the same side of the scabbard (front), the first, shorter and with the buckle, placed at the bottom and the second, longer, at the top. There are now two possibilities for tying, depending on whether the rest or battle position is required.

- Resting position (vertical scabbard, Fig. 26): the upper longer end makes a complete turn behind the loins, passing under the scabbard, until it finally intercepts the buckle on the soldier's abdomen.
- Battle position (oblique scabbard, Fig. 27): this time it is the lower, shorter end going towards the rear of the soldier, always passing under the scabbard, even if, being very short, it will stop immediately behind it, at the height of the side (right in this case). The long end, on the other hand, will turn all around the body counter clockwise, first passing over the abdomen, then connecting to the buckle on the side.

Although it may seem that the straps passing under the scabbard are working in a strange and almost opposite way, in reality this is also the result of archaic traditions. In fact, on closer inspection, even in the previously seen Celtic systems (Fig. 13 of Chapter III (A) 3,4 'The High and Middle Consular *Gladius*') the same thing happened on both rings.

As in the 'Modena' type suspension, the greater the traction, the greater the inclination of the scabbard will be, and to bring the weapon to the left, it is enough to reverse the wearing in a mirror image.

Apparently this is a somewhat complex methodology, less immediate in the transition from the resting to the battle position, but in reality this derives only from the difficulty of explanation. Its practical application, once well understood, is in fact simple and fast.

It is important to note that both suspensions allow obtaining the resting and attacking positions in a fast and easy way, and also keep the scabbard very stable.

Anomalies and uncertain suspension systems
It would obviously be a mistake to think that we have exhausted all the possible suspension systems used in the complex Roman military world, particularly because the iconography and some archaeological finds seem to suggest the existence of variants. However, the information is not clear enough and at times in certain representations they seem to point towards unrealistic solutions, perhaps because they are influenced by a sort of artistic licence by those who created them.

However, we believe it is correct to try to mention them, framing them as 'anomalies and uncertainties'.

- 'Rear element' system:

The most interesting system is certainly what we could define as 'rear element', suggested first by the Rhine *stelae*, where the *gladius* is represented being attached to

Fig. 28: *Gladii* connected to the *cingulum* only: 1) From the relief of Pula (Croatia); 2) From the lapidary of S. Agnese Fuori le Mura (Rome); 3) From the Publius Aelius Mestrio *stele* (Magyar Nemzeti Mùzeum, Budapest, inv. R-D-138). (*Photo by Raffaele D'Amato*)

the belt without the aid of the so-called 'frogs'[360] and the rings of the scabbard, which often seem entirley unused.

We find similar situations in the depiction of a *gladius* on the relief of Pula (Croatia, Fig. 28-1) and in one of the marble fragments of the lapidary of S. Agnese Fuori le Mura (Rome, Fig. 28-2). More extreme cases are those of the *stele* of Publius Aelius Mestrio (Fig. 28-3) and that of the representation of the Gallic auxiliary of Vacheres, where we cannot see even the rings represented, although it should be observed that the former does not have high-quality details.

According to F. Grew, M.A. Phil and N. Griffiths,[361] also reporting the thesis of Lindenschmit[362] and Nylen,[363] it can be assumed that 'the belt passed directly through a metal fitting on the back of the scabbard, or through a system of straps stretched between the rings, but invisible from the front', a hypothesis also shared by M. Bishop.[364]

If we accept this hypothesis of a belt passing through a bridge element on the back, we have two possibilities:

- the artist has faithfully recorded reality and therefore these scabbards are sometimes equipped with two distinct systems (rings and rear bridge), so that the belt can be connected either to one or the other;
- or, more simply, the sculptor did not feel it necessary to deepen the detail of the connection between the scabbard and the belt, probably because it did not fall within the scope of his work.

The evidence from archaeological finds supporting the existence of this underlying element is indeed very weak, and indeed sometimes they seem to disavow it. The *gladius* of the soldier of Herculaneum, for example, although we know it was certainly connected to the *cingulum* because of a piece of it was still attached to the scabbard, shows no trace on the scabbard of any bridge or similar element (Fig. 29).

Given the substantial completeness of the find, it is very difficult to think that all trace, if any, has been lost. In this regard it should be mentioned that not even the other

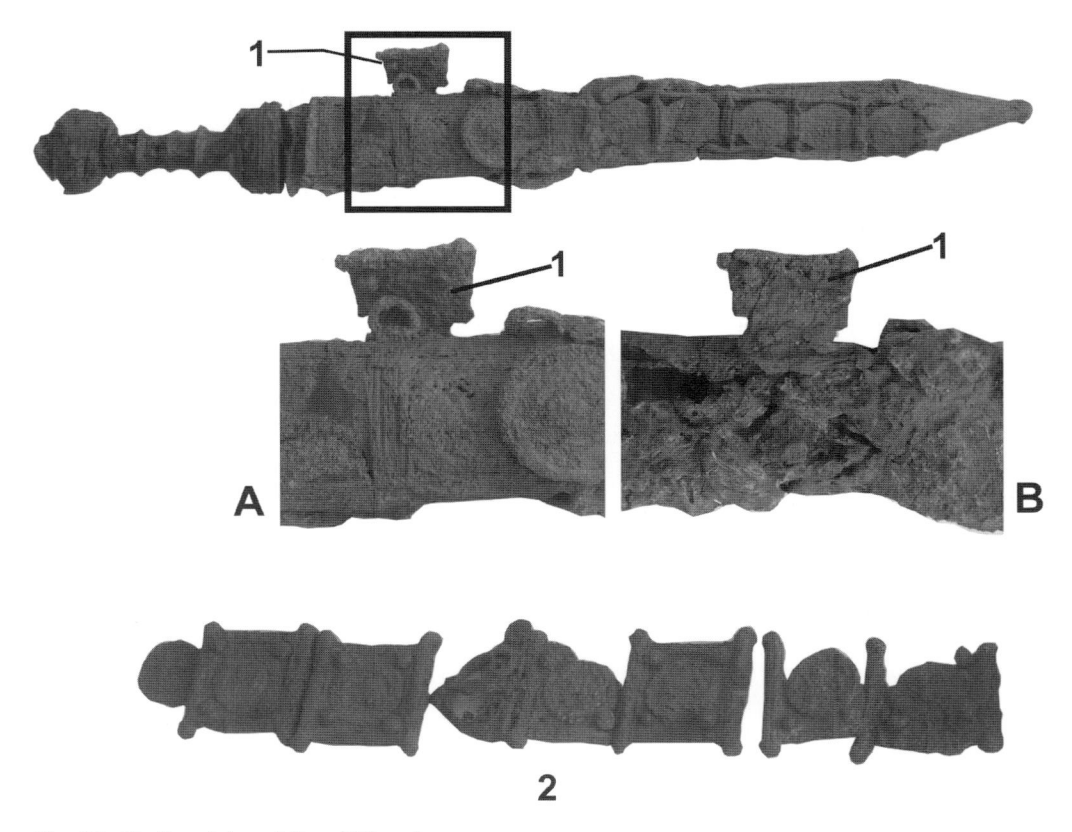

Fig. 29: *Gladius* of the soldier of Herculaneum.
A) Front view of the detail of the attachment point to the *cingulum*, a plate of which (1) has remained attached to the scabbard.
B) Same detail but seen from the back. (2) Other elements of the *cingulum*. (*Drawing by the author from Raffaele D'Amato photo*)

four specimens from Pompeii show certain clues, even if we do not know on what basis, of the bridge that is reported as present by some authors.[365] Only on one specimen[366] is there is band parallel to the two suspension bands connecting the pairs of rings (and therefore also parallel to the belt), placed just below the upper one and slightly raised almost to form a bow (Fig. 30- 3). But the very fact that it is parallel to the belt shows little utility for its connection to it, so that its function is absolutely uncertain.[367]

Even the specimen from the Ljubljanica River has an unusual fitting at the back, almost rectangular and bipartite, arranged transversely in respect of the scabbard (Fig. 30-1). It could be considered an unusual suspension without the help of the canonical rings on the scabbard, which are missing, even if it is assumed that they existed and have been lost over time.[368] For the sake of completeness, we cite a scabbard preserved in the Vatican Museums in Rome,[369] found at the end of the eighteenth century in the Pontine Marshes, which is equipped with an element that seems to have been made

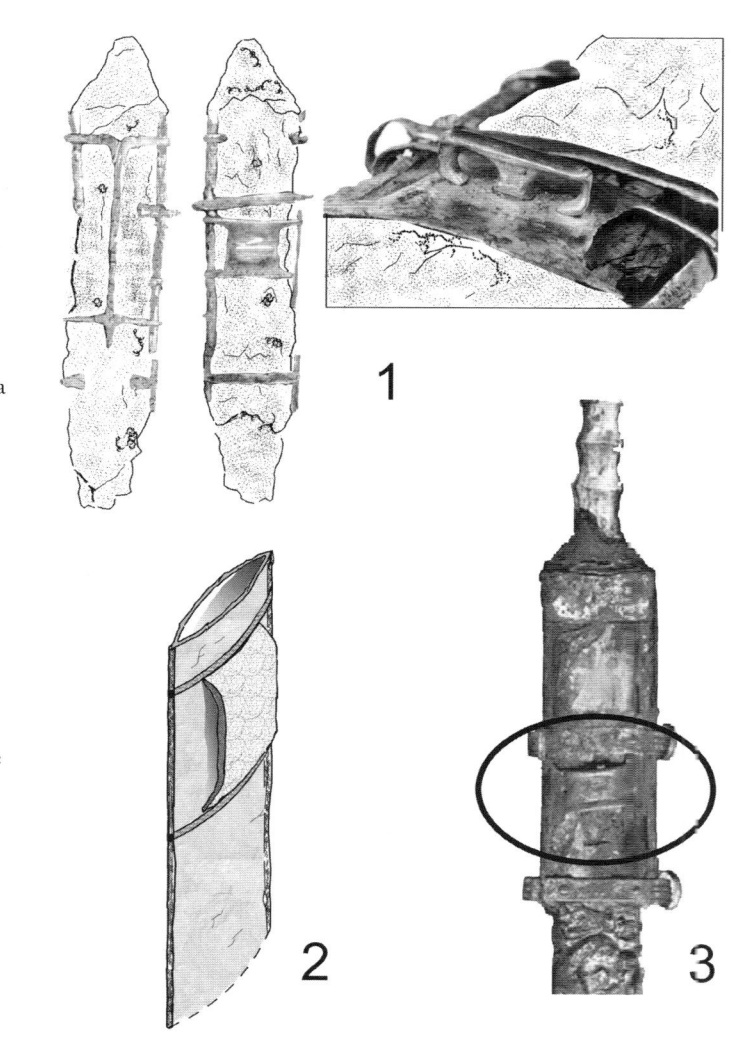

Fig. 30:
1) Specimen from Ljubljanica (Slovenia), an unusual bipartite element on the back. Augustan period (photo by Istenič, 'A Roman late republican gladius from the river Ljubljanica');
2) Fragmented example of a scabbard of possible Roman culture. Indefinite dating. On the back of the scabbard there is an element that seems to have been made especially for passing a belt (Vatican Museums, inv. 65776, author's drawing);
3) Back of the scabbard of one of the *gladii* from Pompeii, on which we see a horizontal band whose function is unclear.

precisely for the passage of a belt. In this case Roman manufacture is possible but not certain,[370] as well as its dating, and therefore it is not particularly helpful in this case.

As there is no other significant proof, the historical evidence is not enough to justify the real existence of this bridge on the scabbards, which was very common in later centuries on those of the *spathae*.

However, the existence of a contrast between the scarcity of archaeological finds and the undoubted frequency in iconographic representations is undeniable.

Ultimately, at the present state of knowledge we do not know precisely how the scabbard could connect to the *cingulum* or to the *balteus* in the case of non-use (or absence) of the suspension rings–bands complex of the scabbard.

- 'Artistic' systems with 'archaic *balteus*':

Iconography often gives us images of weapons suspended from a baldric in such a way that they can hardly work in reality, and seem to be more the result of the artist's legitimate desire to treat the scene as a whole, inspired by classical mythology and its stereotypes, than to report the technical details carefully.

Among the various examples we can mention is the splendid sarcophagus preserved in the Vatican Museums with the depiction of an Amazonomachy (Fig. 31-1). The hero, naked and engaged in battle, holds the drawn sword in his right hand, the scabbard hanging on his left side. We see it connected to a simple and subtle baldric in the most classic of the representations we have seen in Chapter II.3,3 'The Monarchical *Gladius*' and through a single ring. It is evident that the position as reproduced by the artist, almost at 45° angle, is physically impossible, since the scabbard tied in this way would obviously tend to be in a more accentuated vertical position.

We have already encountered the same single-ring solution in the frieze of the Arausius arch (Fig. 19 – 2).

On Trajan's Column, as well as on that of Marcus Aurelius, there is an abundance of *milites* in the most disparate poses that also carry their sword simply hanging from a *balteus*, without the aid of a belt or anything else. From some of these representations, we can clearly understand their limit and the lack of relevance to reality, such as those in Fig. 31. In this case, the weapon would have immediately slipped towards the soldier's knee, potentially also placing itself between his legs, hindering his movements. This consideration obviously applies in general in the representations and not only to this one, which we have taken only as an example.

Ultimately it is not possible to take all representations of 'artistic' suspensions with a simple baldric, of 'Homeric' flavour, into consideration, therefore it will be good to limit ourselves to the few examples reported, which however are well representative of this reality.

In conclusion, we can only consider that, despite their artistic splendour, they are not useful for our purposes nor do they return the description of suspension systems that could be used in the reality of a battle.

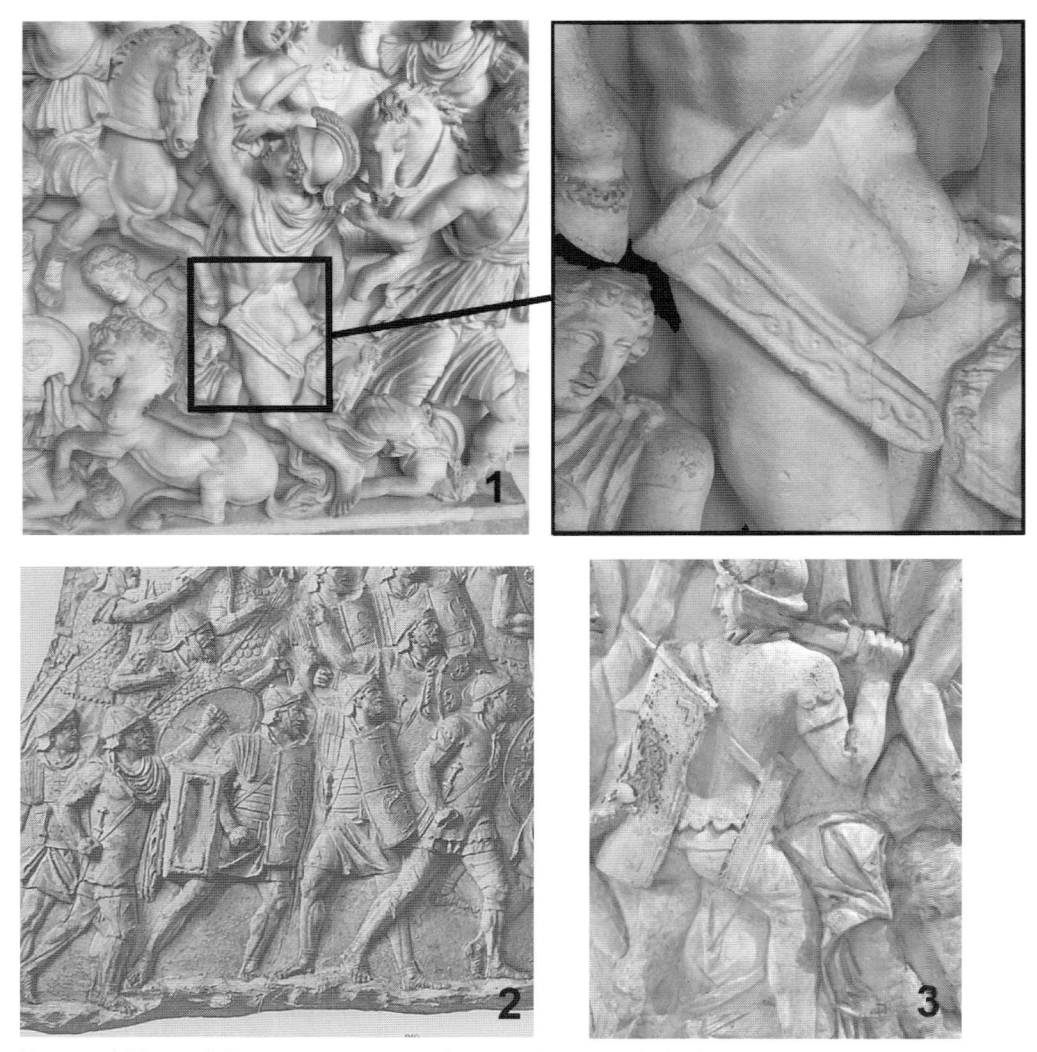

262   The Roman Gladius and the Ancient Fighting Techniques

Fig. 31: 1) Vatican Museums, amazonomachy sarcophagus, mid-third century AD, inv. 933;
2) –3) Trajan's Column. (*Author's photos*)

- System with *balteus* and *cingulum* used together:

It is worth mentioning what is considered to be one of the most intuitive and simple suspension systems, involving the simultaneous use of *cingulum* and baldric.
  Since the weapon simply hung on the latter without any other aid, it was virtually impossible to carry in a functional way; two variants of this system are mainly suggested and adopted:

- The first one is suggested by P.J. Hazell, with '*the upper rings attached to the cingulum, the sword weight was supported by linking the baldric to the lower rings*'.[371] (however, it should be noted that in the system drawing proposed by the author (Fig. 32) there

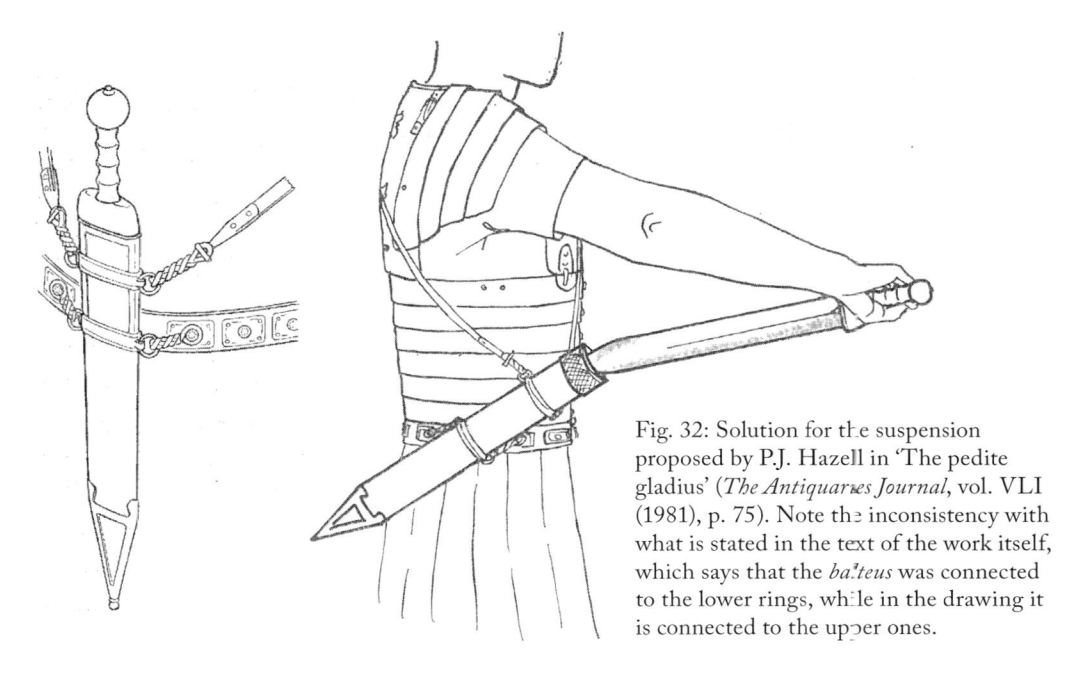

Fig. 32: Solution for the suspension proposed by P.J. Hazell in 'The pedite gladius' (*The Antiquaries Journal*, vol. VLI (1981), p. 75). Note the inconsistency with what is stated in the text of the work itself, which says that the *balteus* was connected to the lower rings, while in the drawing it is connected to the upper ones.

is an inconsistency, the baldric appearing attached to the upper rings and not to the lower ones).

In reality it should be observed that this solution has no historical basis but seems to be only a suggestion, in addition to the fact that both the bindings, as proposed, perform almost the same function, and moreover without allowing the sword to be tilted.

- The second variant is the one often adopted in the world of re-enactors, which sees the *cingulum* passing over the *balteus*, so as to exercise a sort of blocking (Fig. 33-3). In this case we are faced with the same limitations, i.e. there is no historical evidence and the oblique position is not possible.

If we analyse the classical sources,[372] we see that neither of these two variants is in use. If it is true that in them we find the coexistence between baldric and *cingulum*, nevertheless no connection between them is evident. The *cingulum* never connects with the baldric but seems to have the sole function of supporting the complex of the *baltea* and the *catellae*[373] and, probably, to represent the aforementioned military status symbol. But above all, unlike the custom of modern re-enactors, it passes under the baldric, and not above it (Fig. 33-1 and 2).

We have no other historical sources to understand with certainty how the suspension with *balteus* and *cingulum* combination worked, but the iconographic sources prove its existence. However, it is possible that the coexistence of these two elements, although certain, did not mean their collaboration in the suspension of the weapon.

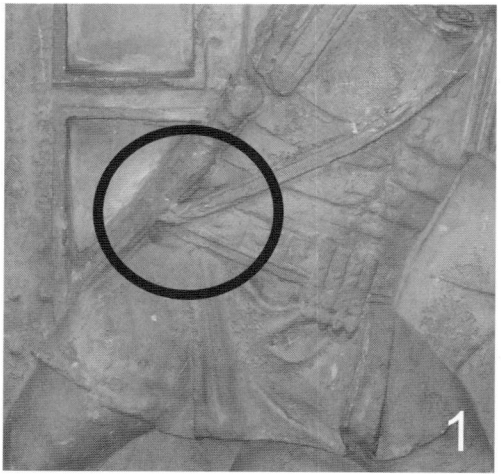

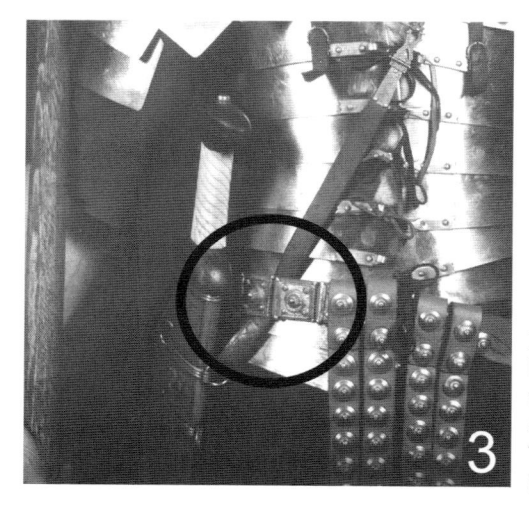

Fig. 33: 1 and 2) Details of Trajan's Column, in both of which we see that the *cingulum* passes under the *balteus*; 3) Position of the *cingulum* normally used by re-enactors, opposite to that on Trajan's Column, that is, passing over the *balteus*. (*Author's photo and drawing*)

This excursus has led us to understand how the suspension and carrying systems of the Roman *gladius* worked, first and foremost and once again, the result of centuries of combat experience, the roots of which seem to date back to the seventh century BC, among the Apennine and Piceni peoples in particular. The slow evolution and improvement of the most archaic systems had led to the achievement of the three fundamental objectives mentioned several times, common to all the suspension methods described: the possibility of passing easily from the vertical to the oblique position, the stability of the weapon on the soldier's body and finally its easy execution, testifying to the pragmatism of the Roman mentality.

III (C) THE CONSULAR AGE: CONCLUSIONS

The consular *legio* was not only a change linked to political events, but above all an adaptation to the new threats that the Romans had to face. With continuous territorial expansion, they had to face new people, whose facies, different from those of the *Latium Vetus*, used an innovative combat style. These differences and the disorientation of the first clashes were the stimulus for a tumultuous evolution of the Roman way of fighting, since the previous Servian *legio* was no longer capable of competing with such enemy forces. In the fourth century BC, following the clashes with the tumultuous Celts first and the warlike Samnite guerrillas later, the Romans understood the limits of this compact formation, although it had been decisive in opposing the Etruscan armies. The answer was the institution of the manipular Livian *legio*, which in some ways constituted a sort of return to a structure similar to the Monarchical *Legio Romulea*, with the distinction of the infantry in *antepilani* (*hastati* and *principes*) and *pilani* (*triarii*, *rorari* and *accensi*). But nevertheless in it there coexisted a significant depth of battle array, in analogy to the Servian one, and good adaptability of the deployment to enemy pressures. From the continuous dam of previous times, an elastic functioning was reached like 'the springs of a mattress'. Alongside all this we also see another fundamental novelty, namely the transition to an army no longer seasonal but made up of professionals, to whom salaries were paid.

However, we are still in the presence of a fairly compact formation, albeit more agile than the previous one, where age rather than wealth was the determining factor in the selection criteria, since it was linked to the concept of military valour, understood as experience and combat skills.

But towards the middle of the second century BC the moment came when this formation also showed its limits, represented by the fact that it was basically only suitable for a head-on collision, which was badly suited to further new war scenarios, whose protagonists were mainly Pyrrhus first and Hannibal later. Thus it was that the manipular *legio* of Polybius (or the pre-cohortal) was introduced, characterised by the fact that the maniples now become even more agile units capable of fighting independently, unlike those of the Romulean and the Livian one, who could only do it in concert with the others. Their independence was possible thanks to the fact that the number of infantry of each maniple was doubled compared to the previous ones. The strength of this new deployment was ultimately precisely this great adaptability, since its efficiency remained unchanged whether the complete legion was used or only a part of it, that is, the individual maniples.

Starting from the beginning of the first century BC, one of the fundamental and most traumatic moments in Roman history is approaching, namely the beginning of the Civil Wars. Together with the Marian reforms, of a short time before, and the terrible clashes with the Cimbri and the Teutons, they were able to profoundly change army and society. One of the consequences was the need to develop formations that, compared to the Polybian maniples, were equipped with ever greater fighting strength as well as autonomy, characterised by even more numerous and profound units, thus reaching the cohortal legion. Inside, the distinction between the various orders was only administrative and the soldiers had become high-level professionals in order to face increasingly skilled and formidable enemies, represented by the Roman soldiers themselves in the Civil Wars. This profound upheaval could not fail to have repercussions on armament in general and on the *gladius* in particular. Hence, after a few decades from the occurrence of the first of these events, the first helmets to protect against thrusts and new types of *gladius* began to appear. Next to the always-used 'Consular' type *gladii* we now see a large and almost confused variety appear, often characterised by the remarkable shortness of the blade, from which the typical Roman sword that will characterise the Imperial Period will derive.

In this chapter we have seen how the great skill of the Roman people was the ability to understand their limits and to find always the correct answers to overcome them, improving their formations and adapting their weapons, many times adopting them from their enemies. But all these changes always took place so that the fulcrum of all this was the *gladius*, a weapon to which the sense of strength and military virtue was traditionally connected.

Chapter IV

'De Falsis Originibus': On the Erroneous Derivation of the *Gladius* from Non-Italic People

The history of the origins of the Roman *gladius* (including the Italian sword with cross hilt) is rather controversial, in the sense that we frequently come across statements that the weapon derives from non-Italic people. The claims that still present the greatest credibility are not supported by direct evidence and are often questionable. For this reason we have dedicated this chapter to understanding and collating the various evidence, trying to overturn the numerous historical misunderstandings.

In this regard, we want to once again dwell on the intuitive but often ignored concept of how an object is formed by reflecting the culture and history of the people from which it was born. A high-quality artefact with 'winning' characteristics will always diffuse into other cultures. The transition will not only involve changes in its structural and functional prerogatives in groups of people with similar archaeological facies, as is the case with communities belonging to the same cultural lineage; on the contrary, when an object is adopted by communities with different traditions and facies, this inevitably involves essential changes in order to adapt the object to the social characteristics of the new community. This is a basic universal concept, in which the same object used by two different cultures can never be the same, but will always have differences deriving from assimilation into the culture, a fact that, in certain modern axioms, is often forgotten.

IV.1 ABOUT THE HELLENIC ORIGINS – THE SWORD WITH CROSS HILT IN HELLENIC LANDS

It is almost a unanimous opinion among modern historians that the sword with cross hilt is typically of Hellenic origin and culture, commonly called the *xiphos* (ξίφος), used by both the Greek hoplite and the Macedonian phalangite. In some cases we see this concept taken to extremes with the assertion that it passed on directly to the Roman army in the third century BC, ignoring all of the central Italic history of the previous four centuries.[1]

In reality, beyond appearances, there is no proof of this. Often, when reference is made to archaeological evidence, images of finds from the Picenum area are almost always proposed in the treatises (in particular from No. 69 of Campovalano), confusing the latter for Hellenic, while little or nothing was shared with that culture there. Furthermore, the numerous specimens found in Macedonian (but not Greek) funerary contexts are not correctly interpreted, nor is the data obtainable from vascular images. In this chapter, we will be analysing the various areas in which evidence can be found, such as classical literature, ceramography and the archaeological finds in Magna Graecia, Macedonia and Greece.

IV.1,1 Socio-political overview

Greek combat evolved greatly over time and with different aspects between the various Hellenic populations; to this day there are gaps and strong disagreements on what the real aspects of combat were.

In the Late Bronze Age (twelfth–ninth century BC) aristocratic leaders were carrying a sword and its use was well described by Homer in the *Iliad*. The sword, because of its high cost and the need to learn its use through training, which the subsistence economy did not permit, made it impossible to possess for anyone other for the *basileis* (the head of the community which in the central Italic world was represented by the *pater familias*) and the small circle of aristocrats, at the moment that marks the collapse of the palace civilisation and the transition to the so-called Hellenic Middle Ages. We are in a historical period in which combat took place between the 'heroes', the aristocrats, admirably described by Homer, among whom the sword coexisted both in the role of a weapon and as a symbol of power. An archaic Cretan citation allows us to understand the concept of aristocratic power and how weapons and wealth were its source:

> I have great wealth: a spear, a sword, and the fine leather shield which protects one's skin. For with this I plough, with this I harvest, with this I trample the sweet wine from the vines, with this I am called master of the serfs. Those who dare not hold a spear, a sword, or the fine leather shield which protects one's skin, all cower at my knee and prostrate themselves, calling me 'Master' and 'Great King'.[2]

Greece underwent a political change over the centuries, aristocratic power giving way to monarchical power which persisted until 510 BC, the year when the last Athenian tyrant fell, making way for democracy. During this socio-political evolution, the changed role of the armed individual, which was framed within a hoplitic type of group combat in which the spear and the shield were most important, was accompanied by a parallel reduction in the importance of the sword.[3] This change began and developed from the birth of the city-states, from the late eighth century BC, since war was no longer seen as a dispute between individual heroes but as a legal communal decision. This concept reached its zenith with the birth of democracy, since this idea of social equality was reflected in the military sphere, whereby all citizens without distinction of class fought for their *polis* with same weapons out of respect for the law rather than being forced to by a monarch. Herodotus says of the Greeks that: 'They are free, yet not wholly free: law is their master, whom they fear much more than your men fear you. They do whatever it bids; and its bidding is always the same, that they must never flee from the battle before any multitude of men, but must abide at their post and there conquer or die.'[4]

On the Erroneous Derivation of the *Gladius* from Non-Italic People 269

An army composed of a 'middle class', very different from the point of view of the class of origin,[5] did not allow specialised combat such as that developed by the Roman army. Although Aristotle asserted that 'it is proper that the government should be drawn only from those who possess heavy armour',[6] this seems more of an ideological statement than a practical one, since Socrates, although not belonging to the relevant census, served as a hoplite on various occasions, alongside Alcibiades, who instead was a *hippeus* (equestrian). Therefore, among the hoplites, there were not only citizens of considerable wealth, who had the economic capacity to pay for bronze armour, but also those from lower classes, who probably protected themselves with leather or linen armour rather than bronze, or perhaps borrowed it.

This premise on the rather varied composition of the Hellenic army, from a class point of view, must be associated with the consideration that, except for the Spartans, Greek soldiers were not professionals, since none of them was trained for war. Aristotle, at the end of the fourth century BC, explained Spartan military supremacy:

> the Spartans, although so long as they persisted by themselves in their laborious exercises they surpassed all other peoples, now fall behind others both in gymnastic and in military contests; for they used not to excel because they exercised their young men in this fashion but only because they trained and their adversaries did not … for they have rivals in their education now, but they used to have none before.[7]

Further evidence that the Greek army was made up of citizens and not of professional soldiers comes from Plutarch, in the context of a disquisition between the Spartan king Agesilaus and the allies of the Greek city-states (fifth century BC):

> When he heard once that the allies had come to be disaffected because of the continual campaigning (for they in great numbers followed the Spartans who were but few), wishing to bring their numbers to the proof, he gave orders that the allies all sit down together indiscriminately and the Spartans separately by themselves; and then, through the herald, he commanded the potters to stand up first; and when these had done so, he commanded the smiths to stand up next, and then the carpenters in turn, and the builders, and each of the other trades. As a result, pretty nearly all of the allies stood up, but of the Spartans not a single one; for there was a prohibition against their practising or learning any menial calling. And so Agesilaus, with a laugh, said, 'You see, men, how many more soldiers we send out than you do.'[8]

We can conclude that an army composed of varied classes, without homogeneity of armament and above all not being composed of professional warriors, could scarcely have based its combat on the sword. Fighting with sword involves training and learning specific techniques, which was not favoured in classical Greece. On the contrary, the presence of instructors in the army was opposed, because the specialised masters of arms (the *hoplomachoi*), were regarded thusly: 'a man who was a coward … his only gain would be in rashness, which would make his true nature the more conspicuous; while if he were brave, people would be on the look-out for even the slightest mistake on his part, and he would incur much grievous slander.'[9] In summary, instinctive combat was exalted, probably because in hoplitic training any individualistic ability would have had negative effects on training. There is a passage from Xenophon in which there is exaltation of the innate combat between various animals, man included:

> 'And now,' he continued, 'we have been initiated into a method of fighting, which, I observe, all men naturally understand, just as in the case of other creatures each understands some method of fighting which it has not learned from any other source than from instinct: for instance, the bull knows how to fight with his horns, the horse with his hoofs, the dog with his teeth, the boar with his tusks. And all know how to protect themselves, too, against that from which they most need protection, and that, too, though they have never gone to school to any teacher.'[10]

The sword used in an instinctive way essentially implies stabbing thrusts, like those that could be given with the *machaira*, rather than more complicated fencing, for which the *xiphos* was designed, and the use of which would have required a degree of training that the Greeks lacked. Hans van Wees says that the normal training of the hoplites was fundamentally different from that of a modern soldier and as such it is difficult to recognise even if well documented: they did mostly informal, private training, mostly aimed at general physical fitness rather than specialised combat skills.[11] We can find this reflected in an anecdote reported by Xenophon, in which King Agesilaus, to improve the training of his troops, awarded a prize to the best javelin thrower, the best archer and the best cavalryman; it is very interesting to note that among the hoplites the prize would have gone to the one who 'should be in the best physical condition'.[12]

Unlike in the Roman world, where training was imposed as a matter of discipline, in Greek military training competitiveness was encouraged, because it was much more important to obtain optimal physical condition through training, than exercise specifically for learning how to use a weapon.

It is very interesting to note how among all the Olympic disciplines, such as the javelin throw, pankration (a mixture of wrestling and boxing), boxing, wrestling, running and oplitodromy (a race for armed athletes), there is none linked to the use of the sword. Each sporting activity having a connection with military activity of men at arms, this absence should make us reflect and lead us to conclude that the use of the sword was little regarded, as it did not enhance the athletic skills of the participants in the competition. Probably the sword was only the weapon of last resort, to be wielded when it was not possible to carry out group combat, and in this context it was probably regarded negatively, because it favoured individual combat. As Aeschylus recalls (sixth century BC), the most important weapon that defined the Greek army, and that was used during the collision between the phalanxes, was the spear or *dory*, to the extent that the victory on the field of Plataea 'was due to the Doric spear'.[13] The sword was only used later, when the cohesion between the hoplites had broken down and the soldiers turned to hand-to-hand combat. The Greeks did not believe in the military strength of the sword, as when a certain Athenian decried the Spartan swords (μάχαιραι) for being so short, and said that jugglers on the stage easily swallowed them. King Agis, accordingly, replied: 'And yet we certainly reach our enemies with these daggers [ἐγχειρίδια].'[14] Although the speech of the Spartans also seems short, yet it certainly hits the point, and grasps the attention of the listener

The Spartan king probably exalted the role of swords because his army had widespread training in their use that was not found among the Athenians. Basically, the sword had less importance in the classical Greek military culture, unlike the Italic one. In any case, the sword, of whatever type it was, despite being a weapon of secondary importance, nevertheless had a certain diffusion and for this reason there were specialised factories, such as that of Demosthenes' father who owned more than thirty slaves as workers.[15] They were freely available for sale and in Sparta this was in the market square, in the ironware section, next to the spits and scythes.[16]

IV.1,2 The historical sources

Classical literature

The term '*xiphos*' can be found in the *Iliad*,[17] therefore dating it to the eighth century BC. Even if it had an extremely vague meaning in the ancient times, it was used to indicate the sword in general. It probably derived from the Mycenaean '*qsiphos*', with which the sword had been indicated since the Bronze Age. Since in our times this term is normally used in specific reference to the sword with a cross hilt, for ease of understanding in this chapter we will use one or the other term as synonyms.

The investigation of ancient literature on the presence and role of the sword in hoplite combat is not free from difficulties; first of all because the concept of a hoplitic phalanx, normally widespread among us today, is probably more of an abstract idea than a historical reality. As with the development of the Servian *legio* (Chapter II.2,2), hoplitism was a way of fighting that evolved over time and which reflected the socio-political mentality of the Greeks, where the spear (*dory*) was the main weapon, while the sword was relegated to a secondary role.

There are various quotations in which the use of a sword is reported, which always happens when formations break into a tangle of men who can fight only with them.[18] In the description of the Battle of Thermopylae (480 BC), Herodotus tells us that in the defence of the narrow pass against the soldiers of Xerxes 'By this time most of them had had their spears broken and were killing the Persians with swords [ξιφεσι]'.[19] The Greek historian continues the description by saying that 'in that place they defended themselves with swords [μαχαίρῃσι], if they still had them, and with hands and teeth. The barbarians buried them with missiles, some attacking from the front and throwing down the defensive wall, others surrounding them on all sides.'[20]

Another example is that of the Battle of Crimisus River, fought in Sicily in 341 BC. The clash occurred between the phalanx of the Sicilian Greeks, led by the Corinthian general Timoleon, and the Carthaginian phalanx, and when the two armies came to hand-to-hand combat, the use of swords required skill, no less than physical endurance:

> But these withstood his first onset sturdily, and owing to the iron breastplates and bronze helmets with which their persons were protected, and the great shields which they held in front of them, repelled the spear thrusts. But when the struggle came to swords [ξίφη] and the work required skill no less than strength, suddenly, from the hills, fearful peals of thunder crashed down, and vivid flashes of lightning darted forth with them.[21]

These are just two examples of classic quotations that report the use of the *xiphos*, but none of those analysed helps to understand what type of swords the Greek warriors used and therefore if we can find specific references to the sword with a cross hilt.

Pottery painting[22]
The study of Greek vase decoration is an important means of understanding how sociological aspects were interpreted by the ceramic artists of the time, who as Boardman states, 'allow a knowledge of the popular visual experience'.[23] The possibility of having a visual representation of everyday events in religious-mythological, military, artistic and civil areas, which the painter knew well and could easily identify with, is a means to understand the presence, diffusion and certain characteristics of the cross-hilted sword within that world.

First of all it is useful to point out that past and present are difficult to distinguish, because for the Greeks myth was a habitual means to explain contemporary situations or problems, which causes a certain difficulty in defining a scene as mythological or as a real fact, the first being a representative form of contemporary reality. We also encounter this problem in the depiction of armament, which is always contextual of the time the pottery was made, even if the scene depicts an ancient episode.[24] Thus from studying a vase and framing the pictorial style,[25] we find the weapons of the period in which it was painted, not of the story it tells. However, one should bear in mind that unfortunately the representation of swords is not always defined enough to allow a precise classification of the weapon.

The end of ceramic production came in the fifth century BC, due to various factors such as Athens' loss of economic and commercial strength after the Peloponnesian War (404 BC), the devastation of the population due to the plague and, definitively, the Macedonian takeover of all Greece by Philip II in the fourth century BC. It should be noted that, while the Greek potters copied Etruscan forms for the vases destined for the market of Etruria itself, the painters made no concessions in their representations nor did they take into account the destination market.[26] This observation by Boardman is very important because it shows us how, in the context of the armaments that we find depicted on Greek vases, it exclusively relates to the panoply of the Greek soldier, even when found in Etruria. The possible presence (or absence) of the *xiphos* on a Greek vase will therefore be a precise indicator of whether our sword was part of the panoply of Greek soldiers, and its frequency in the representations will indicate its degree of popularity.

The Corpus Vasorum Antiquorum
The basis for our analysis was the *Corpus Vasorum Antiquorum* (CVA), an international research project on Greek and Italic ceramics of the classical age, the textual descriptions and related images of which are collected in a database.[27] Working on the most complete list in the world has allowed the realisation of a reliable study: however, it was necessary to limit it only to the specimens published for Italy and Greece, given the total quantity of finds available within the *Corpus* (over 100,000). This exclusion of important collections may be considered as a limitation to the study, but it is necessary to make two considerations: the first being that the collections outside Greek and Italian territory group together finds that are very often without context; the second is that all of the ancient production – and therefore also the finds excluded from the study – originally came from one of these two territories, thus allowing our choice to obtain the same statistical value.

Ultimately, this study concerns the data of approximately 4,200 relevant vessels and fragments, sufficient to provide statistically reliable results and not invalidated by the possible contribution of those preserved in foreign collections.

Italic collection[28]
The vases kept in Italian museums are partly imported (therefore Greek in all respects), partly locally produced, but maintaining an Attic style, and finally a part is represented by pieces produced in Italy in local style.

The entire Italic CVA collection was analysed, consisting of about 3,700 specimens, of which only 483 (13.0 per cent) show weapons, which we have divided into the following subgroups shown in Table 1:

Kind of Weapon Brandished by the Warrior	Number	%
Cross-hilt sword	14	2.8
Only sword but not cross hilt	43	8.9
Only sword with a doubtful cross hilt	31	6.4
Spear and any sword (in the scabbard)	117	24.3
Only spear	278	57.6

Table 1: Distribution of weapons in Italic vascular representations.

The Italic pottery suggests the spear was the main weapon, supplied to 395 soldiers out of a total number of 483 armed men (81.7 per cent), of which 57.6 per cent are holding the *hasta* as the only weapon, compared to those in possession also of a sword, which are 205 (42.44 per cent), of which only a paltry 2.8 per cent are certainly equipped with a cross-hilted sword (Graph 1).

274 The Roman Gladius and the Ancient Fighting Techniques

Graph 1: Percentage of representations of the various weapons out of the total of Italic vases showing images of armed men.

- ONLY SPEAR 57,6%
- ONLY CROSSED HILT SWORD 2,8%
- UNCERTAIN SWORD 6,4%
- SWORD BUT NOT CROSSED HILT 8,9%
- SPEAR + SWORD INSIDE THE SCABBARD 24,3%

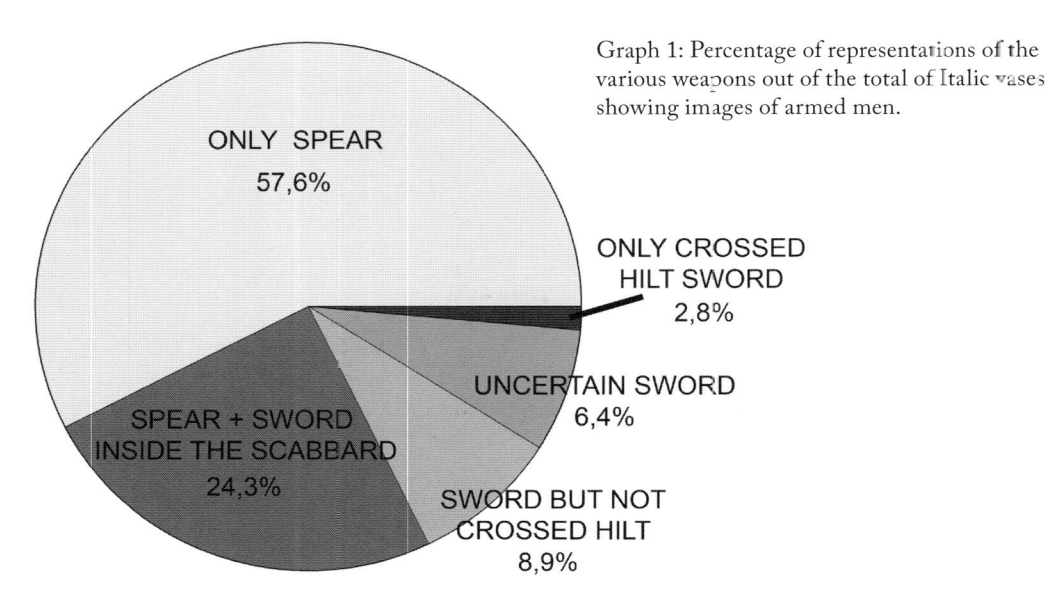

A further relevant notation is that many of these 483 representations, while showing the presence of weapons, refer to sacrifices or symbolic displays, not to episodes strictly connected to combat.

- Data on chronological distribution

A very important fact is the distribution over the centuries of images showing weapons, which we see shown in Table 2, as well as in Graph 2.

	Seventh century BC	Sixth century BC	Fifth century BC	Fourth century BC
Cross Hilt	0	1*	6 (20%)	6 (20%)
Different from Cross Hilt	2	57	25	3
Doubtful	0	20	30	5
Sword in the Scabbard	0	53	53	3
Only Spear	23	143	91	19

*End sixth century (c.520 BC)

Table 2: distribution over the centuries of the various weapons in Italic vascular representations.
Key:
- cross hilt = cross-hilted swords;
- no crossed hilt: presence of sword, in any role and position, but certainly not crossed hilt.
- doubtful = swords for which the attribution of crossed hilt is doubtful.
- sword inside the scabbard: in the scene there is a sword (of any type), not used but in the scabbard.
- spear only: the scene shows the spear as the only weapon.

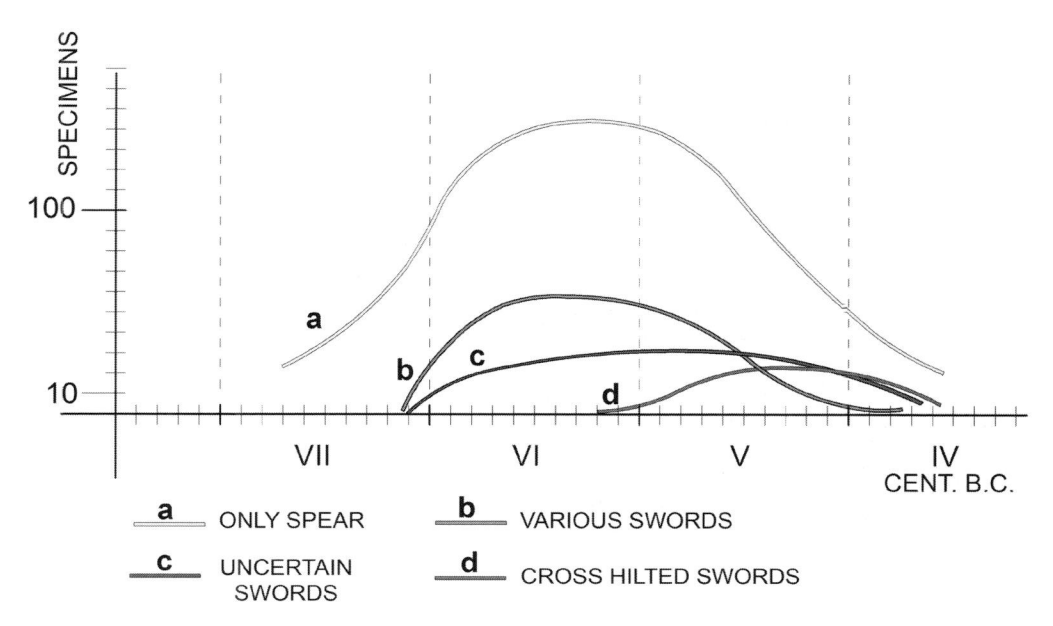

Graph 2: The numerical distribution of the various weapons over the centuries.

What immediately can be concluded is:

1. The spear has been present since the seventh century BC and persists in representations until the fourth century BC, with a peak between the end of the sixth and the beginning of the fifth century BC. Its representations greatly predominate over those of swords.
2. The sword is present only from the sixth century BC onwards, while in the seventh century it is almost absent.
3. The *xiphos* (or cross-hilted sword) is entirely absent until the end of the sixth century BC.

- Detailed data on the *xiphos*

Analysing the data in detail with reference only to the representations of *xiphoi*, we have obtained significant results regarding their geographical distribution and their use.

Etruria	Daunia	Rest of Magna Graecia	Other places	Greece (production)
12	9	4	1	5

Table 3: Distribution of the cross-hilted sword in various areas of Italy and Greece

If we remove the Etruscan and Daunian production, the presence of the *xiphos* in Attic production is very limited.

276   The Roman Gladius and the Ancient Fighting Techniques

This data shows a greater concentration in Etruria, but a certain interpretative variability must be taken into account since it is possible that the phenomenon depends only on the greater production of vessels, and therefore on the greater number of vessels arriving from these territories, or it could be consequent to a local Attic production that followed the taste of the client.

- Usage data:

On the thirty-one representations of *xiphoi* (Table 3) we found:

Fifteen swords in scabbards carried on the left side, while the warrior holds a spear. Sixteen swords actually held, whether in the scabbard or unsheathed, of which, in turn, eight specimens held but not in a combat scene, only symbolic, and eight specimens effectively used, in combat or in a sacrifice context.

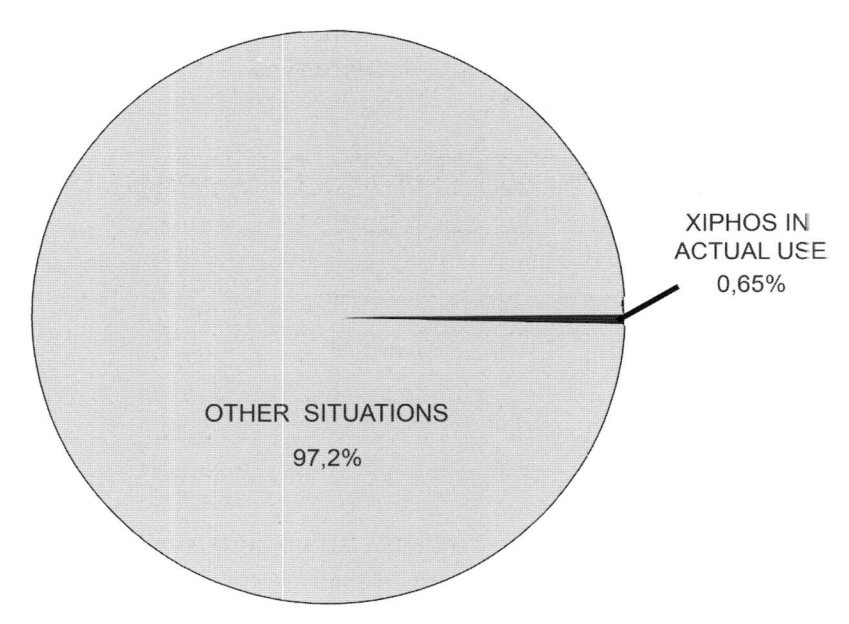

Graph 3: Percentage of representations of *xiphoi* in the total of representations of armed men.

It is therefore obvious that not only the presence of the cross-hilted sword was entirely marginal in the Italic vessel representations on Italic vessels (only 2.8 per cent of the total representations of armed men), but also that only a small part of these were represented in scenes of actual use (0.65 per cent of the total depictions of armed men, Graph 3). Moreover, of this small number, most of them are in scenes of sacrifice, and therefore the remaining, referable purely to combat, consists of a virtually undetectable percentage. Note the large difference in the presence of the spear, which consists of 395 representations (81.8 per cent of the total number of soldiers).

On the Erroneous Derivation of the *Gladius* from Non-Italic People 277

Greek collection[29]

Unfortunately the accessible database of Greek pottery is less rich than the Italian one, since many Hellenic museums, at the moment, have decided not to take part in the CVA project. However, about 500 significant vessels and fragments were examined, of which 58 (12.8 per cent) show weapons, more precisely:

Kind of Weapon Brandished by the Warrior	Number	%
Cross-hilt sword	0	0
Only sword but not cross hilt	0	0
Only sword with a doubtful cross hilt	2	3.4
Spear and any sword (in the scabbard)	5	8.6
Only spear	51	88.0

Table 4: Distribution of weapons in Greek vessel representations.

Also for Greece, the temporal distribution in the various centuries shows the spear widely represented in the manufactories from the seventh to the fifth century BC, while the sword is rarely present (Table 5).

	Seventh century BC	Sixth century BC	Fifth century BC	Fourth century BC
Cross Hilt	0	0	1	0
Different from Cross Hilt	0	0	0	2
Doubtful	0	0	0	0
Sword in the Scabbard	2	0	2	0
Only Spear	1	34	16	0

Table 5: Distribution over the centuries of the various weapons in Greek vessel representations.

The only representation of a *xiphos* is from the fifth century BC, but in this vase it is in the scabbard on the left side, while the warrior holds a spear; therefore the sword is in a subordinate and secondary position to the latter.

To briefly summarise what information was gathered from the above, we can say for sure that the preponderance of the subjects concern mythological aspects, because these 'legendary tales' were an integral part of the history of the Greeks, dating back to a remote past when men and gods shared their stories and heroes were actual living individuals who, with their real and magical powers, fought the ineluctable struggle of life against supernatural forces. The combats, on the other hand, are only a small minority of representations since they did not reflect everyday life, while the vases were often an inexpensive and widespread product that spoke to ordinary people. The results of the CVA study show the spear as the undisputed protagonist, with the sword relegated to a weapon of secondary importance and represented in multiple types.

278   The Roman Gladius and the Ancient Fighting Techniques

Among these, the *xiphos* (or cross-hilted sword) is not distinguished among the various types depicted, suggesting that this model was one of many variants available, and practically never used in combat scenes, having only a marginal role.

IV.1,3 The sword in the Greek world

The variety of swords in the ceramography
From the statistics of the vessel images we have suggested that within the Greek culture the *xiphos* was just one of the many types of sword, without any predominant role. A great variety of typologies emerge from the ceramography, some of which seem to go back to very distant times, without being able to identify any kind of standardisation of swords.

To emphasise this concept, we have reported an overview of some of the main types below, with traces to this area and at the same time with precise archaeological evidence, without the presumption of wanting to report them all.[30]

A) Bronze swords, probably of a type dating back to the tenth and ninth centuries BC
In this example we find one represented in a Chalcidian amphora from the sixth century BC, showing clearly the guard equipped with the classic bridge element, that can typically also be found in the *xiphoi* (or cross-hilted swords).

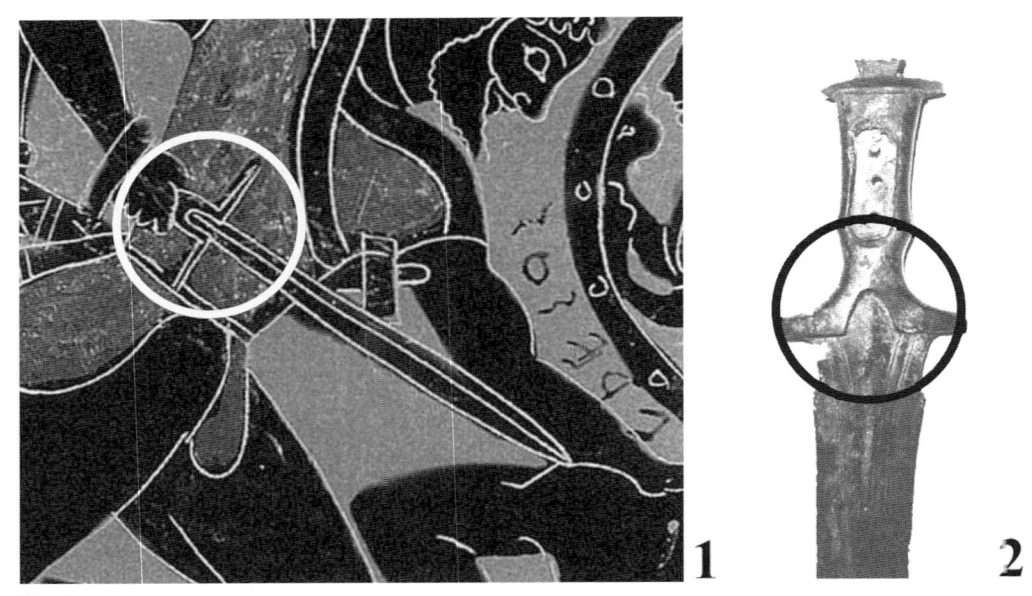

Fig. 1:
1) Chalcidian amphora with Diomedes killing Resus in Troy, sixth century BC. (Malibu Museum)
2) Bronze sword, tenth–ninth century BC.

B) Graeco-Etruscan daggers
Short swords with a characteristic T-shaped pommel with a small terminating sphere. Examples of this kind are also found in the Etruscan area, even if without particular diffusion.

On the Erroneous Derivation of the *Gladius* from Non-Italic People

Fig. 2:
1) CVA, Firenze, Archaeological Museum, III (1), Plate 98, 1-2, Inv. 70800, Record 26. The Theseus deeds, from Tarquinia, c.480.
2) Etruscan dagger, seventh–sixth century BC, 38cm long, iron and bronze.

C) Bronze swords of the second millennium BC

To understand the specimen shown here we will need to focus our attention on the scabbard. Although similar to that of the cross-hilted swords, it shows a very particular finishing element, made with metal wires variously arranged around the scabbard itself. It seems to derive from a very archaic Central European style, at least from the end of the second millennium. The handle, with the wide hilt, is certainly attributable to the cross-hilted sword.

Fig. 3:
1) Red figure cup, CVA Rhodes, early fifth century BC, London, Cleofrades painter.
2) Bronze sword scabbard, late second millennium BC.

280 The Roman Gladius and the Ancient Fighting Techniques

D) Archaic bronze daggers of Italic type

This type of dagger, probably in bronze, has clear archaic characteristics often found in southern Italy. Note the large 'umbrella' pommel and the bridge guard.

Fig. 4:
1) Relief on pottery from Mykonos of the seventh century BC (Mykonos Museum).
2) Tursi (MT) S Maria D'Anglona-Valle Sorigliano, grave 7, early eighth century BC.

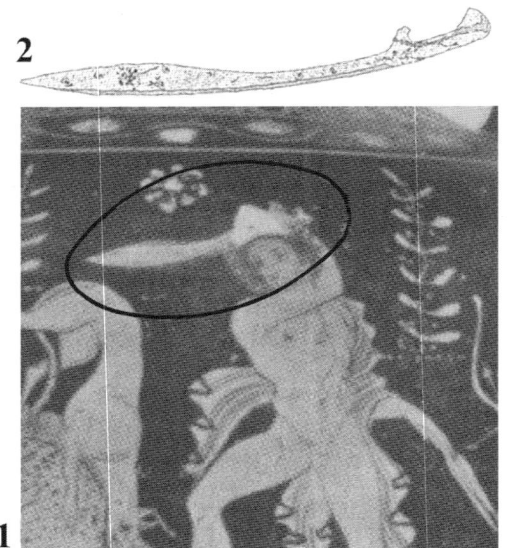

E) *Machaira*

The *machaira* (or *falcata*) is frequently present in archaeological findings both in Etruria and in Greece. The characteristic of this sword is its curved shape with the cutting edge on the inside. The terminal part of the blade is larger in order to assume a useful shape to accentuate the 'cut' effect. The action of this weapon was based on 'sabre' blows, favoured by a shift of the centre of gravity towards the point, with the purpose of accentuating the force of the blow.

Fig. 5:
1) CVA, Milan, Archaeological Museum, collection H. A., record 26.
2) Etruscan *falcata*, Villa Giulia Museum, Rome, c. sixth century BC.

On the Erroneous Derivation of the *Gladius* from Non-Italic People   281

F) Swords of oriental influence
We often find representations of short swords with a characteristic conical pommel, clearly of Middle Eastern influence, usually from the Luristan or Urartu culture. In reality, the vast majority are made of bronze, often cast in one piece, with a small blade.

Fig. 6:
1) CVA, Trieste, record 18, pot 402.
2) CVA, Milan, Apulian pottery, plate 1, pot 239.
3–4) Luristan and Urartu sword hilts, eleventh–seventh century BC.

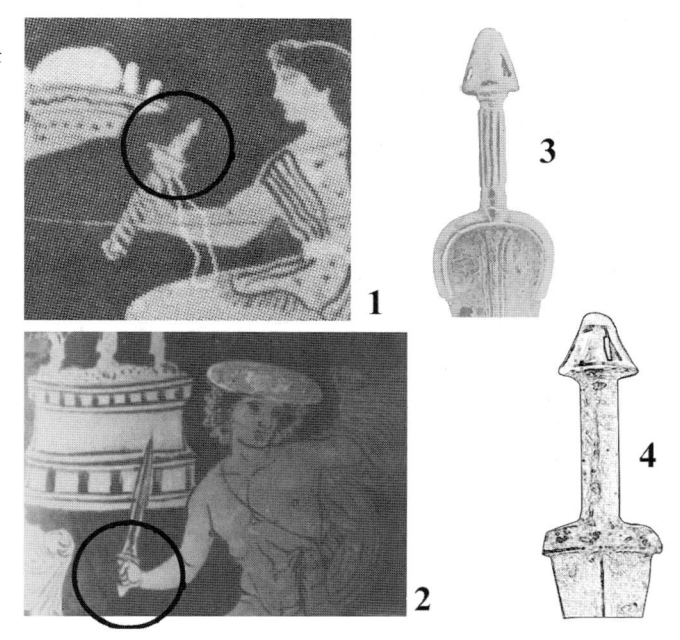

G) Swords of uncertain identity
It is not always easy to trace the actual type of sword that the artist wanted to represent. For example, Fig. 7 offers us a questionable weapon, since it would seem to have a typical cross-hilted sword handle but the pseudo-cylindrical pommel could indicate a weapon of more archaic and substantially different derivation. In the figure we see a specimen from the late Bronze Age with a fully compatible pommel.

The archaeological evidence
The study of the archaeological finds was based on the analysis of finds from Greece itself and from the two regions that were most affected by its influence, namely southern Italy (Magna Graecia) and Macedonia.

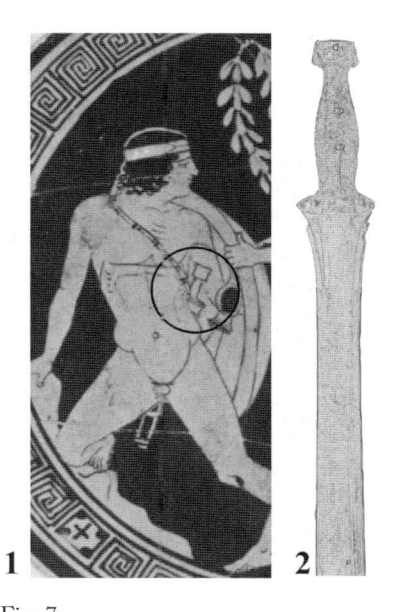

Fig. 7:
1) Attic red figure vase, CVA, Trieste, Archaeological Museum, record 25, 3909.
2) Bronze sword, Late Bronze Age.

Greece

While it is true that burying the dead with weapons was prohibited in Greece in very archaic times, thus depriving us of an important source of information, fortunately the votive shrines, the most famous of which were those of Delphi, Delos, Olympia and Samos, were established. As E. Polito observes

> the use of burying the dead with their weapons is widespread in Greece, although not generalised, until the end of the Geometric Age. The deposition with weapons disappears in the Archaic and Classical Age on the Greek continent, but it persists in peripheral areas, such as Macedonia, and appears again in Late Classical and Hellenistic tombs. The synchrony has been observed between the disappearance of weapons in depositions and the beginning of dedications of weapons in Panhellenic sanctuaries.[31]

In the latter, large quantities of objects of the most disparate nature had been offered for centuries, more or less from the eighth to the middle of the fifth century, in relation to the divinity to which they were addressed to and the reason for which they were offered in sacrifice: they could be public offerings, made by the entire community of a city, perhaps in gratitude for a battle won, as well as private donations from wealthy individuals or even individual soldiers.[32] After this period a radical change took place and votive gifts of arms unfortunately became extremely rare. The mention of the donor's name also disappeared from the dedications and at the same time there were inscriptions of ownership and dedications on metal bars of all weights (from 60g to 26kg). P. Siewert hypothesised that in this period a norm was promulgated which prohibited offering of weapons, which could instead have been melted down and dedicated in the form of bars.[33] One of the last finds datable with good certainty is a group of three *sauroteres*[34] taken as booty from the inhabitants of Thurii, dedicated between 444 and 433 BC.[35]

In any case, the period covered is sufficient since in the second half of the fifth century BC, the cross-hilted sword (or *xiphos*) had been present in Italy for at least a century and a half. If the hypothesis of its Hellenic origin was confirmed, archaeological data should testify to an abundance of finds in the same period in Greek territory. The votive deposits are places of exceptional

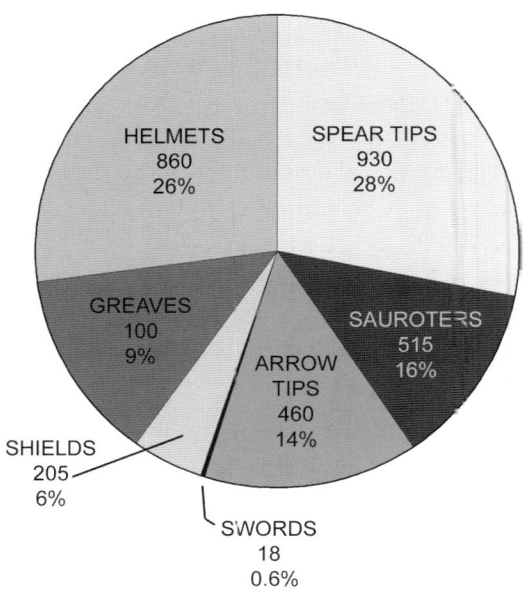

Graph 4: Weapons found in the sanctuary of Zeus in Olympia. Note the virtual absence of swords. (Data from Naso, *Italic finds in Greek sanctuaries*, p. 40.

archaeological value due to the large quantity of artefacts found and are therefore very valuable sources of information.

As an example we will only analyse the votive deposit of Zeus in Olympia, as weapons are the most common dedication in it with over 3,000 specimens found, an extraordinary number that has no comparison in all of Greece.[36]

Basically all the weapons present in the Greek panoply were found in it, but in significantly different quantities. Among the defensive types, helmets certainly prevail, most of which are of the Corinthian type, but there is no lack of Illyrian and Chalcidian types either; there is also an abundant number of greaves and in a decidedly more limited number, shields. Among the offensive types, the absolute majority are spears, approximately twice the number of arrows, but what is very unusual is the lack of swords,[37] of which there are only eighteen specimens out of over 3,000 weapons, equal to about 0.6 per cent (Graph 4).

However, it is important to consider the provenance of these weapons, whether they belonged to the deceased or his enemy, in the latter case probably offered as spoils of war. In this regard, the opinions of scholars do not always agree. E.G. Hatzi claims the armament of Olympia was ex-votos for the victories achieved by the various cities, offered by wealthy individuals, but also by the soldiers themselves, who donated part of their armour to the divinity as a sign of their gratitude.[38] This thesis seems corroborated by the famous helmet of Miltiades,[39] of the Corinthian type, which was offered by the famous general in the sanctuary of Zeus after his victory at the Battle of Marathon (490 BC), evidenced by the inscription engraved on the left cheek-guard.

However, A. Naso, although not discussing the origin of the helmet, believes that it could be an exception, since such private dedications of weapons or axes are rare in Olympia and ultimately helmets should be considered mostly as spoils of war.[40] This thesis seems to be confirmed by a Persian helmet, found near that of Miltiades, with an inscription stating that it was offered to Zeus by the Athenians and was from the loot taken from the Persians. Similarly a Corinthian helmet of Italic workmanship and a helmet of Etruscan type, both dedicated to Zeus by Hiero, tyrant of Syracuse, and his fellow citizens, are both spoils of war after the victory at Cuma in 474 BC.

The hypothesis that the dedications are part of war booty is reiterated by Naso when he observes that the pre-Roman Italic objects found in Greece are mainly Etruscan with some exceptions of weapons and personal objects from other parts of Italy, and these are to be considered as war booty from the conquered Italic populations by the Greek colonists in the clashes following their settlement on the coasts of southern Italy and Sicily.[41]

Both hypotheses seem to completely exclude each other, but they probably coexisted, so that these ex-votos were probably coming both from the spoils of war and, to a lesser extent, from the personal property of a private donor. In fact, 'the Greek tradition of dedicating weapons alternatively provides for personal weapons, limited to a single piece or a panoply, deposited in shrines, and that of looted weapons, chosen or piled up in stoai or other special environments'.[42] However, A.M. Snodgrass rightly points out that in this

284   The Roman Gladius and the Ancient Fighting Techniques

regard the historical period has its influence: 'In early times these were normally spoils, won from enemies, and perhaps previously erected to form a trophy on the battlefield; but by the Hellenistic period at least the habit of dedicating one's own armour, in gratitude for its protection, had arisen.'[43] It could therefore be observed that the two hypotheses lead to different conclusions; in the case of offerings of personal weapons by a Greek fighter, it is evident that they were of Hellenic culture, while in the case of weapons taken from the enemies, they should not be connected with the Argive armament.

On closer inspection this does not make much difference as both of these cultures usually wear only the typical Greek panoply, as demonstrated by their similar helmets (apart from rare exceptions). This is easily explained by the fact that in the hoplite period the rivalry between the Greek city-states was very strong and the cause of frequent clashes, in which armies of this culture therefore participated, for example the three Messenic Wars in the eighth, seventh and fifth centuries BC,[44] or the Peloponnesian Wars in the fifth century BC, at the Battle of Halki, in 429 BC, and various other warlike events of the same nature. 'In Greece, a concordant discord persisted, chronic from immemorial time: harmony existed in the sphere of sporting activity, in poetry, in philosophical and scientific thought, but otherwise it was a fratricidal war of all against all.'[45] Wars that can be defined as civil or at least intra-cultural, makes the above data perfectly referable to Greek culture alone.

Southern Italy (Magna Graecia)
Looking at the burials in southern Italy, the difference from those in central Italy regarding the presence of weapons (and swords in particular) stands out. In the south, despite the presence of sword-wielding people since the end of the ninth century BC,[46] the discovery of such weapons in the necropolis and in Ionic votive deposits is episodic and exceptional,[47] while on the contrary in central Italy the finds are abundant (see Chapter II.3 'The Monarchical Sword'). In these last territories there are almost no male tombs not containing the cross-hilted sword. As M. Ruggeri Giove states, 'the type of swords depicted on the statue of the warrior of Capestrano [the cross-hilted sword] finds innumerable confirmations in the archaeological reality [see Chapter II.3 'The Monarchical Sword']'.[48] Beyond this observation, another important fact emerges, namely that in the southern regions, especially Puglia and Basilicata, we rarely find swords with a military function and in some cases they are ceremonial and symbolic, normally placed within a panoply with the same characteristics.

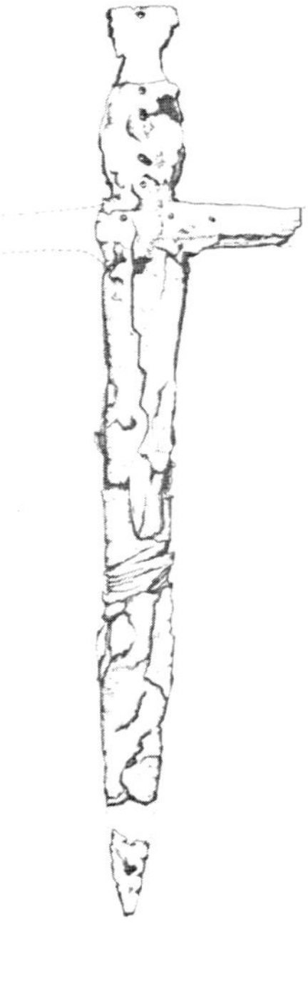

Fig. 8: Specimen from tomb 17/71 from Metaponto, loc. Crucinia, estimated length 42cm, end of sixth– beginning of fifth century BC. You can still see rivets passing through the metal, which allowed the fixing of the handle plaques, the same technique used in central Italy.

On the Erroneous Derivation of the *Gladius* from Non-Italic People   285

Some excellent examples are from Lucanian tombs, such as 421 of Banzi, datable to the beginning of the fourth century BC, and 107 of Braida di Vaglio, around the fourth century BC, both found together with greaves and other equipment, tomb 652 of Chiaromonte, with a rather short blade and accompanied by a Celtic-influenced *umbo*, and burial 566 of the necropolis of Metaponto, identifiable as a long-bladed sword.[49]

Also worth mentioning are the two specimens from tomb 608 of Metaponto Crucina (Fig. 9), which despite having less extreme morphological proportions than that previously mentioned, are equipped with a handle embellished with gold foils, in close analogy with Macedonian customs, as well as the sword of tomb 17/71 (Fig. 8), datable to the end of the sixth–early fifth century BC,[50] which although fragmentary still has sufficient elements of the handle remaining to make it clear that it was made in a similar way to those in central Italy, although with a much wider hilt, according to the style of these regions.

The cross-hilted sword in the context of Magna Graecia, and in particular in its north-eastern part, does not belong to a vast social class but to a small elite of aristocratic warriors, sometimes of the highest rank, to the point that in some cases, as in the necropolis of Braida di Serra di Vaglio (Basilicata), Bottini and Setani hypothesise that 'we are faced with the tombs of the Basilei, the Italic kings so far known only from the vague indications of the sources'.[51]

Ultimately, in the southernmost regions of the Italian peninsula, both in the Magna Graecia colonies and in those with a more indigenous cultural connotation (Enotri, Coni, Itali, Morgeti, Iapigi etc.), the archaeological situation seems to return a different

Fig. 9:
1) Pair of specimens from grave 608 of Metaponto Crucina.
2) Specimen from grave 421 of Banzi.
3) Specimen from grave 652 of Chiaromonte.
(not to scale)

social and military reality from the central-Italic one, absolutely compatible with that shown by the vase painting, namely:

- cross-hilted sword rarely present;
- the swords are mainly symbolic, alongside a secondary purely military use.

Macedonia

It is not easy to understand Macedonian life in the most archaic times, prior to Philip II, due to the almost total lack of written sources and the scarcity of archaeological evidence, although recent studies have now confirmed the presence of permanently settled and relatively large populations both in the coastal areas and inland.[52]

In the recently excavated important necropolises of Pydna, Pieria, Ierissos, Thermi, Sindos, Derveni and AyaParaskevi, all in the Thessaloniki Museum, in addition to Aigai and Archontiko near Pella, we frequently note the surprising wealth of tombs, with large numbers of objects of high quality,[53] proving the existence of a rather sophisticated society. They often contain valuable gold objects, such as diadems, bracelets, funeral masks, etc., or items covered with this precious material, such as helmets and swords. Gold appears closely linked both to the funeral sphere of high-ranking individuals, and to that of social representation, as well as a symbol of power and eternity.

We have archaeological data that allows us to understand what the weaponry of a Macedonian soldier was. The excavation of Seuthopolois (present-day central-southern Bulgaria, 1948–54), published by L. Ognenova-Marinova in 1984,[54] unearthed a bronze cheek-piece, six bronze arrowheads and eight iron spearheads, as well as twelve curved daggers, with precise parallels with the tombs of archaic Macedonia, such as the necropolis of Vergina[55] and that of Pella,[56] the latter in use from the end of the fifth–beginning of the fourth century BC, as well as those of Epirus.[57] In these burials of common infantry we note the total absence of the *xiphos* and only rarely do they contain a sword of a different type,[58]

On the other hand, our sword is almost always present in high and very high ranking burials. Some of the most characteristic specimens known to date come from:

- Pydna, datable to the second half–end of the fourth century BC, 67cm long;[59]
- Kaloyanovo (Sliven, Bulgaria);[60]
- Zagorsti (Novo Zagora, Bulgaria);[61]
- Zimnicea (Romania),[62] datable through a *kantharos* present in the same tomb to the third quarter of the fourth century BC, with an estimated length of 60cm (the specimen is incomplete);
- Veroia (Macedonia),[63] late fourth–early third century BC, although an earlier dating to the third of the fourth century is not excluded, due to an *unguentarium* with pseudo-Cypriote[64] decorations;
- Derveni (Northern Greece),[65] tomb B, late fourth–early third century BC;

On the Erroneous Derivation of the *Gladius* from Non-Italic People   287

- Kozani (Macedonia),[66] length 67cm, according to its first published description, and 63.3cm according to what is reported in the catalogue 'Treasure of Ancient Macedonia' (1978, 41, Fig. 11);
- Vitsa (Macedonia),[67] dated to the end of the fourth–early third century BC;
- Sciatbi Necropolis,[68] length of the surviving part 59cm and estimated total length about 65cm, datable to the late fourth century BC;
- Vergina (Macedonia),[69] *Megali Toumba*, four specimens in total, two of which are from the famous tomb and two from the adjacent pyre (length of one of the latter two: 60.5cm up to the centre of the hilt). Although this burial is commonly attributed to Philip II, all scholars are not in agreement: it could also be of Philip III or even of another sovereign.[70] In any case, given a certain imprecision, the later dating is from the third quarter of the fourth century BC;[71]
- Vergina (Macedonia),[72] *Stenomakri Toumba*, dated at the end of the fourth century BC;
- Apollonia Pontica (Bulgaria),[73] late fourth–early third century BC, 71.9cm in length, of which the blade is 57.8cm. This specimen is the only one to appear ritually folded, which is unusual in these localities.

Fig. 10:
1–4) Specimens from the tomb of Philip II (or III). 1 and 2 are from the tomb itself while 3 and 4 are from the funeral pyre.
   5) Specimen from tomb no. 194 of the necropolis of Pella (with enlargement of the handle).
   6) Specimen from tomb no. 9 of the necropolis of Pella (with enlargement of the handle).
(not to scale)

All the cross-hilted swords are from princely burials displaying gold decorations (where surviving) to emphasise that this weapon was limited to the noble class. To be precise, it can mainly be found in the burials of individuals belonging to rank of horsemen, with the sole exception of a specimen combined with a shield, placed next to a seated warrior and represented on sarcophagus no. 7 of the tomb of Ostrusha, which identifies him as an infantryman.[74]

Finally, it should be pointed out that the datable specimens are all limited to a rather short period, located around the second half of the fourth century BC or shortly after. Exceptions are the examples of Dedeli, Valandovo, Demir Kapjia, which are dated to the seventh–fifth century BC.

A surprising and in some ways unexpected analogy with what we saw in southern Italy stands out in Macedonia: here too the sword with a cross hilt (or *xiphos*) is present in moderate numbers and, in addition to its military function, also representative of the status symbol of the noble class. Another interesting parallel which makes the southern Italic *xiphoi* indistinguishable from the Macedonian ones is the frequent use of gold leaf decorations, associated with the funeral sphere.

The summary of this excursus on archaeological finds is as follows:

- In Greece there is essentially a reduced presence of finds of cross-hilted swords (swords of Marathon), regardless of whether they have real or a representative purpose.
- In southern Italy and Macedonia, on the other hand, we find a very similar situation with the presence of such weapons richly embellished with gold and having purposes also representative of the social status of the deceased. There are no archaeological indications that validly allow us to assume a military use nor the opposite (Table 6).

	Tactical Use	Representative Use
Greece	No	No
Magna Graecia	No	Yes
Macedonia	No	Yes

Central Italy	Yes	No

Table 6: Synthesis of the presence of archaeological finds in the three investigated areas, related to the type of use. The fourth row, relating to central Italy, has been added for comparison purposes.

These results are in agreement with those arising from the examination of the figural vases and curiously similar also in percentages.

IV.1,4 Migration of the sword with cross hilt

The sword with a cross hilt, after its appearance in central Italy, followed a unique migratory path to other places and among peoples such as in southern Italy and Greek and Macedonian territory, during which it underwent a transformation. Finally, it will return to its place of origin, but more as a symbol than for real use. This migration developed in three main phases.

First migration: from central Italy to southern Italy
The archaeological data from the graves of the seventh–sixth century BC has allowed us to understand that the cross-hilted sword originated within the Apennine cultural facies, where it developed over time. The discovery of numerous other artefacts dating back to later times, suggests that it also spread in culturally different territories.

From the seventh century BC, the Central Italic people began a process of migration towards southern Italy, since as Tagliamonte points out,

> the Etruscan and Greek cities of the coast or of the Campania hinterland and then, gradually, the more southern ones acted as polarisers for the indigenous world behind, in which the Italic component soon makes its appearance … The arrival of these people has already activated that process of 'italicization' as a cultural, but also ethnic-linguistic fact, since the seventh century BC which will culminate a few centuries later in the 'Samnitization' of the southern areas of the peninsula.[75]

This phenomenon continued in the sixth century,[76] but it was during the fifth century that it underwent a strong boost, especially by the Umbrian and Picenian populations. In this period, many cities in these territories, such as Otricoli, Amelia, Spoleto, Bevagna, Assisi, Gubbio, Todi, Terni etc, were endowed with mighty walls, an indication of insecurity and evidence of numerous conflicts. It is possible that the pressure from the Celts in the north and the development of Roman power in the west resulted in the impoverishment of the central Italian territory, which together with the limits of technological development at the time (which did not allow for economic growth proportional to demographic development), caused the migratory movements towards the south.

This instability explains the use of the '*Ver Sacrum*' (see Chapter II.1 'Monarchical Period – Historical Framework), a sacrificial-totemic-religious procedure with the aim of controlling the demographic weight of the population through young people in their twenties abandoning their original social nucleus in order to conquer a new territory in which to settle. To this religious procedure we must also add the non-ritualised dispersion of many civilians and armed men who respectively put their craft and military skills (as mercenaries) at the service of southern civilisations. In fact, while in the north and west a hostile front was created, respectively by the Celts and the Romans, in the south a great demand for civilian and military manpower was increased both for the expansionist policy of Dionysius I, and for the decrease in numbers of Greek colonists, as well as for the increased vitality and aggressiveness of the Apulian populations.

The migration of the Apennine people brought with it the traditions, customs, beliefs and everyday objects, along with the cross-hilted sword (or *xiphos*). The regions of Puglia (Japigia) and Basilicata (Lucania) were very important places for the transformation of the sword. While the indigenous peoples lived in the hinterland, among which the Apennine people migrated, the Greek colonies (Magna Graecia) were located along the coast, with which were established not only conflicting relationships, but also those of influence and trade, giving rise to great cultural mixture and economic development. Precisely in this 'border area', a crossroads of multiple cultures, where people and traditions met, clashed and merged, and confronted outsiders (Greeks and Illyrians), the metamorphosis of the sword took place, allowing it to assume the necessary qualities to take on 'international' characteristics. We have seen in the previous report on the archaeological findings how the burials of Puglia and Basilicata territories, with the presence of the cross-hilted sword, are numerically scarce and attributable only to high-ranking persons, around which other, poorer burials, belonging to warriors armed only with the spear, can be found. In the sixth century BC, the presence of prestigious Greek goods, mythical images of Hellenic culture and weapons belonging to the hoplite panoply can be noted. The adoption of the latter or parts of it, is considered by scholars as an expression of 'weapons to show off', an expression of rank, rather than being linked to an actual warlike function.[77] In fact, the great wealth and abundance of goods and weapons resulting from trade with the Greek populations brought a new way to stand out and flaunt power for those who held the top positions in society. This statement is also valid for females as well, in whose burials we find a large quantity of high-quality ornamental jewellery for this purpose.[78] The weapons now had to arouse fear, awe and admiration in those who saw them, and this aspect tends to prevail over the practical function, which was to kill and protect. A demonstration of this are the frequent finds of horse harnesses, a symbol of power despite the fighting taking place between foot soldiers, the ornamentation of the shields, the finely embossed greaves with theriomorphic motifs (snake heads) and the swords embellished with hilts and guards in ivory and gold.[79] This feature is very important; as we have already seen, it is precisely because of the migration of the *xiphos* towards the south, that a massive recourse to the custom of decorating weapons in burials with showy gold foils begins, a distinctive and peculiar trait of these areas, but completely absent in their territories of origin. Alfonsina Russo affirms that

> only the exponents of the Italic elites, characterised as horsemen, can show off splendid armour, embellished with metal inserts of different colours and with embossed decorations, the use of which seems to refer to particular occasions in which display of social status is required, as evidenced by the extraordinary repertoire of images present on the funeral paintings of Paestum. At the peak of exaltation of the social values attributed in life, the Lucan aristocrats are represented as horsemen who, exhibiting trophies and prisoners, are welcomed by their women on their return victorious from the war.[80]

Here therefore is a very important first step: in the sixth–fifth century BC our sword, now in southern Italy, begins to incorporate the influence of the Lucanian and Iapygian populations, as well as the influence of the Greek mentality, maintaining

Fig. 11: *Stele* from Paestum with horsemen returning from battle. Note how aristocrats are represented as knights. (*Courtesy National Museum of Paestum, author's photo*)

its morphological characteristics almost unchanged, but transforming itself from a weapon of war into a status symbol of the ruling class as well.

Second migration: from Southern Italy to the Macedonian world
The cross-hilted sword (we now find the length shorter in some specimens, in others the acquisition of the rounded point and very frequently a certain fragility of its handle) thus became a symbol of aristocratic power. The fact that it was enriched with precious decoration in gold and ivory made it suitable for being appreciated by the Hellenic culture.

These changes were facilitated by the extensive commercial contacts between Magna Graecia and the Greek peninsula, which mainly took place by sea, as Strabo also confirms: 'In the case of those who sail across from Greece or Asia, the more direct route is to Brentesium [Brindisi, a Salento city located in present-day Puglia]'.[81] There was probably also another route through the Illyrian region, which had always maintained strong links with the Italian coast across the Adriatic Sea, but for our studies which one was the main route is not important. The main thing is that the sword, thus modified, crossed the borders of the Italian peninsula, arriving and spreading in the Hellenic and Macedonian territory, moving from west to east, opposite to the usual one for ideological models and merchandise, but which we know to have happened.

To understand the reasons why our sword spread in the Kingdom of Macedonia, but had little penetration in Greece, we must keep in mind that in the fifth century BC Greece – the period of maximum diffusion of our sword in the Hellenic territory – 'democracy'[82] was born, while in Macedonia the monarchy persisted and the myth of the foundation of the nation was based on the sword.

In that historical-political-cultural context, the cross-hilted sword increased its status by being typical for the royalty in Lucania and Iapigia, and symbolised strength and the power of the Macedonian sovereigns but, at the same time, under this guise, it could not be accepted by democratic Greece. It is useful to note that there are many common traits between the Macedonian population and the central Italic one, identifiable in the period of foundation (the reign of the Μακεδονία is traced back to around the eighth century BC), in their pastoral origin,[83] and in the general characteristics of the territory and monarchy.

Regarding the origin of the Macedonian people, Herodotus tells that Perdiccas, the exiled king of Illyria, arrived in Macedonia and placed himself and his brothers (Gauanes and Aeropus) at the service of the king of Lebaea as a shepherd. Perdiccas, having performed portents, was considered dangerous by the sovereign who dismissed him 'pointing to the sunlight' to show how much he was willing to give him as compensation for his services, therefore a reward without content. The young man replied with a symbolic gesture: '"We accept what you give, O king," and with that he took the *machaira* which he had with him and drew a line with it on the floor of the house round the sunlight.'[84]

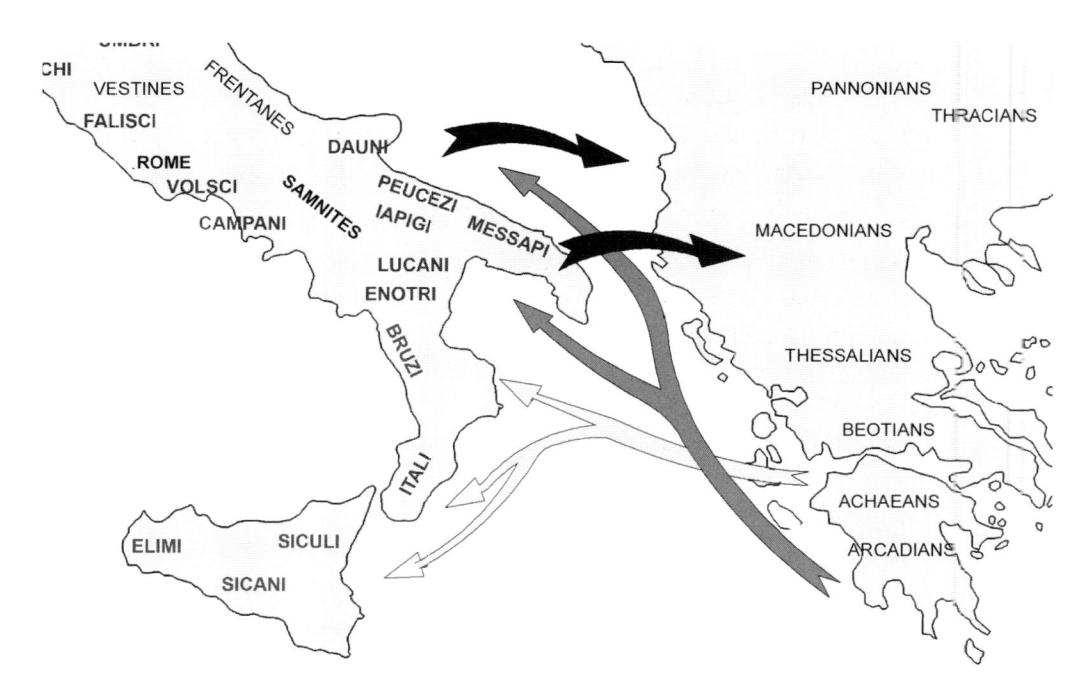

Fig.12: Main trade routes between the regions of Lucania and Iapigia and the Greek world.

The act Perdiccas performed with his sword was both of religious and political nature, since it symbolically marked taking of possession of royalty, represented by the light of the sun, from which the emblem of the royal power of Macedonia will derive and be the basis of the rites of foundation of Macedonian cities.[85] The sword was the means by which Perdiccas obtained the royal investiture. It was also the tool used by the Macedonians to make sacrifices, as well as the weapon of young people during the *ephebeia*, the rite of transition from the juvenile to the adult state.[86]

However, if the sword acquired a symbolic power in Macedonian society, it simultaneously lost its position in the military compared to the spear. This evolution took place above all thanks to Philip II (382–336 BC), father of Alexander the Great, who revolutionised the way of fighting of his own army and consequently its armament.

In describing the latter, the various ancient authors almost never make any mention of the sword, to the extent that some scholars believe that the Macedonian infantrymen were completely without it, even if this is impossible given the descriptions of the sources and the iconography of the sword in this age. Asclepiodotus (first century BC) writes that

> The best shield for use in the phalanx is the Macedonian, of bronze, eight palms in diameter, and not too concave; and their spear, moreover, is not shorter than ten cubits, so that the part which projects in front of the rank is to be no less than eight cubits — in no case, however, is it longer than twelve cubits, so as to project ten cubits ... [87]

and again,

> The infantry is divided into the corps of hoplites, the corps of targeteers, and the corps of so-called light infantry [*psiloi*]. Now the corps of hoplites, since it fights at close quarters, uses very heavy equipment — for the men are protected by shields of the largest size, cuirasses, and greaves — and long spears of the type which will here be called 'Macedonian'.[88]

Polienus (second century AD) explains that 'Philippus accustomed the Macedonians to constant exercise, before they went to war: so that he would frequently make them march three hundred stades, carrying with them their helmets, shields, greaves, and spears; and, besides those arms, their provisions likewise, and utensils for common use.'[89] Arrian (second century AD), in describing the Greek and Macedonian armament, says that 'the heavy infantry wear armour, round shields or oblong shields, swords [μαχαιραι] and spears, like the Greeks, or *sarissai*, like the Macedonians'[90] (note that the sword is not mentioned among the latter);

Finally Aelian (second–third century AD) offers the following description: 'Infantry can come in one of three forms: the hoplites [ὁπλίται], the peltasts [πελταστάι] and, thirdly, the psiloi [ψιλοί] or 'naked' troops [i.e. the light infantry and skirmishers]. The hoplites carry the most equipment of all of the different types of foot soldier, using, according to the Macedonian manner, round shields and long spears [δόρατα].'[91]

The only mention of swords we find is in the so-called 'Amphipolis decree',[92] 'those not bearing the weapons appropriate to them are to be fined according to the regulations: for the *kotthybos*, two obols, the same amount for the *konos*, three obols for the *sarissa*, the same for the *makhaira*, for the *knemides* two obols, for the *aspis* a *drachma* ...', but only the *machaira* is mentioned and not the *xiphos*.

The explanation of this lies in the fact that the Macedonian way of fighting was based on the *sarissa*, the long spear, with the purpose of stopping the enemy at a distance, causing it to break on an impenetrable wall of spears and at the same time prevent close contact between shields, delegating to the cavalry the task of attacking the enemy formation and destroying it.

Fig. 13: Macedonian noble burials. Note the predominant use of gold decorations. (*Courtesy of the Archaeological Museum of Pella, photo by the author*)

So the sword was used by the infantry rarely, since physical contact was avoided in combat, while it was perfect for the monarchs as a representation of their power, thus forming a socio-political-war framework completely compatible with archaeological data.

Third migration: the xiphos returns to its territories of origin
The cross-hilted sword, owned by the Macedonian aristocracy, became a symbol of its power and as such, precious specimens were part of the panoply of Philip II and his son Alexander the Great. The myth developed around the latter for his conquests on the borders of the known world at the time, in which he subdued and unified numerous peoples of different cultures, arousing admiration and desire for emulation on the part of all Roman generals. After his death (323 BC) the third migration of the cross-hilted sword began, which brought it back to Italic soil, but no longer as a real object but an idealised version. Having lost all connection with the physical reality of the object, it can be said that only its spirit returned, bearing a completely different symbolism from that which the Macedonian aristocrats gave themselves. From a symbol of military power on Italic soil (seventh–sixth century BC) it became an allegory of royal authority in Macedonian territory (fifth-sixth century BC) and then from the first century AD,

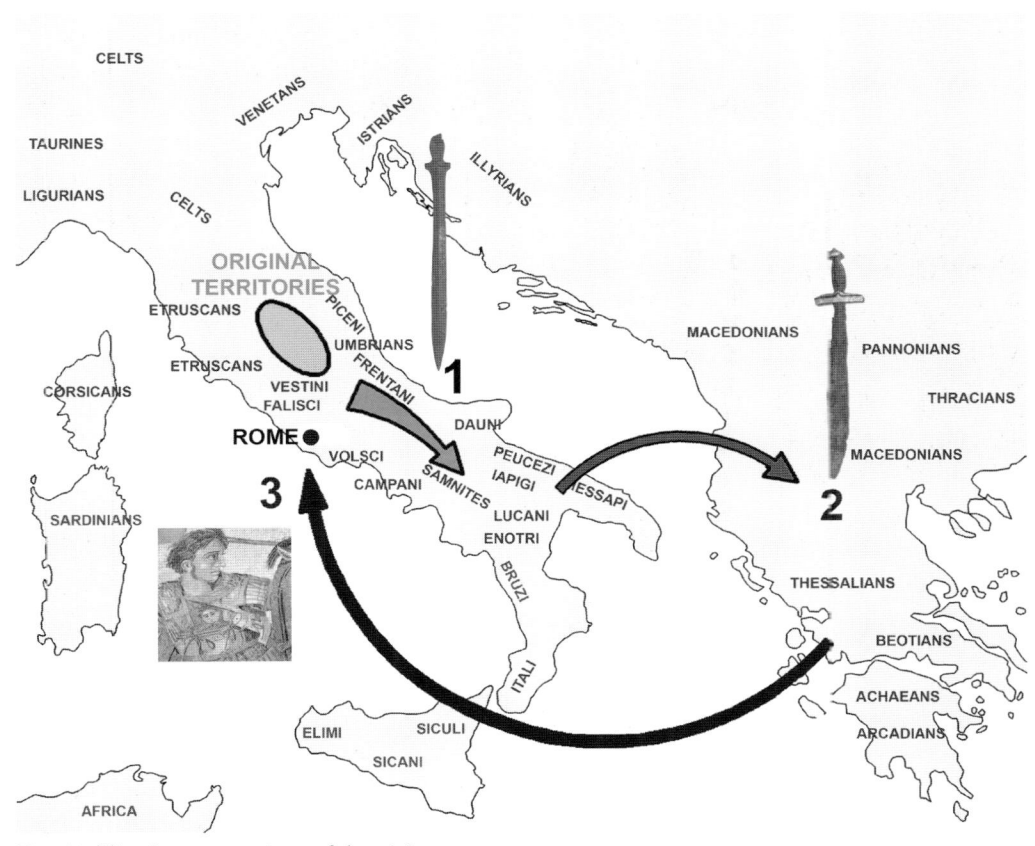

On the Erroneous Derivation of the *Gladius* from Non-Italic People 295

Fig. 14: The three migrations of the *xiphos*:

1) From the territories of origin, in central Italy, it migrates to the south of the peninsula;
2) Here it transforms, becoming also a status symbol, and then migrates to Macedonia;
3) In Hellenic lands this characteristic is accentuated, and then it returns to Rome in the form of an allegory of royal power.

in the Roman environment, the personification of imperial power, the unity of people and a symbol of harmony, as that belonged to Alexander the Great (as you can find described better in Chapter V 'The Symbolic Value of the *Gladius*'), adorning the statues of numerous Roman emperors for centuries.

IV.2 ABOUT THE HISPANIC ORIGINS – THE CORRECT INTERPRETATION OF '*GLADIUS HISPANIENSIS*'

A cornerstone of the modern literature is that the origin of the Roman *gladius* is Hispanic and that it was acquired by the Romans relatively late, at the end of the third century BC during the Second Punic War. This statement, which excludes the existence of the weapon in about four previous centuries of Italic history, is based exclusively on the fact that two classical authors occasionally define the *gladius* as '*hispaniensis*'.

As a consequence, great efforts are made to identify the alleged origins of the weapon in Spain and in support of this hypothesis often questionable proofs and statements are proposed. These situations are sometimes extreme, to the point of identifying the moment in which the Romans adopted the *gladius* (in this case defined precisely as *hispaniensis*) even to within a period of approximately six years, between the Battle of Cannae (216 BC) and the capture of Nova Cartago (210 BC), based only on a very short passage from a classical source, as if this had happened on the basis of a modern international contract and not as the result of a complex secular development.

All this partly reflects a common error, namely the excessive simplification of historical events, especially when they are not well understood. In fact, if this mental process is useful for forming a general view, it can become dangerous when an event, not sufficiently explored, is interpreted on the basis of isolated sentences from classical authors. The consequence is an erroneous interpretation, which if accepted and repeated uncritically by various authors, will be elevated over time to an axiom, a 'historical truth', and as an unfounded theory it is more difficult to challenge.

The path that we will follow in this chapter is to analyse the relations that the Roman *gladius* had with the Hispanic territory, relying only on rigorously scientific information, to obtain the explanation that is closest to the historical facts.

IV.2,1 Socio-political framework

Hispania was the term by which the Romans indicated the current Iberian peninsula, which Strabo defined as having a geographical shape like 'an ox-hide', where in the north the Pyrenees mountain range divided it from Celtic territory.[93] This territory was inhabited by numerous populations, each of them with a special archaeological facies, which together constituted a very varied ethnic group, a situation similar to that in Italy before the Roman supremacy. The populations that lived in the southern and eastern territories, the Turdetani and the Iberians (the latter composed of numerous tribes), were the most civilised ones, accustomed to greater commercial contacts with the Phoenicians, Carthaginians, Greeks and Romans, and were those who, having overcome Carthaginian rule, quickly accepted integration into the Roman world.

The Celts,[94] people of Indo-European descent with cultural characteristics similar to those present in Western Europe and Italy, were settled in the central and western areas of the peninsula. They were a warlike population with little tendency to urban development, whose social characteristics were in stark contrast to Roman ones, which is why they strenuously opposed Romanisation.

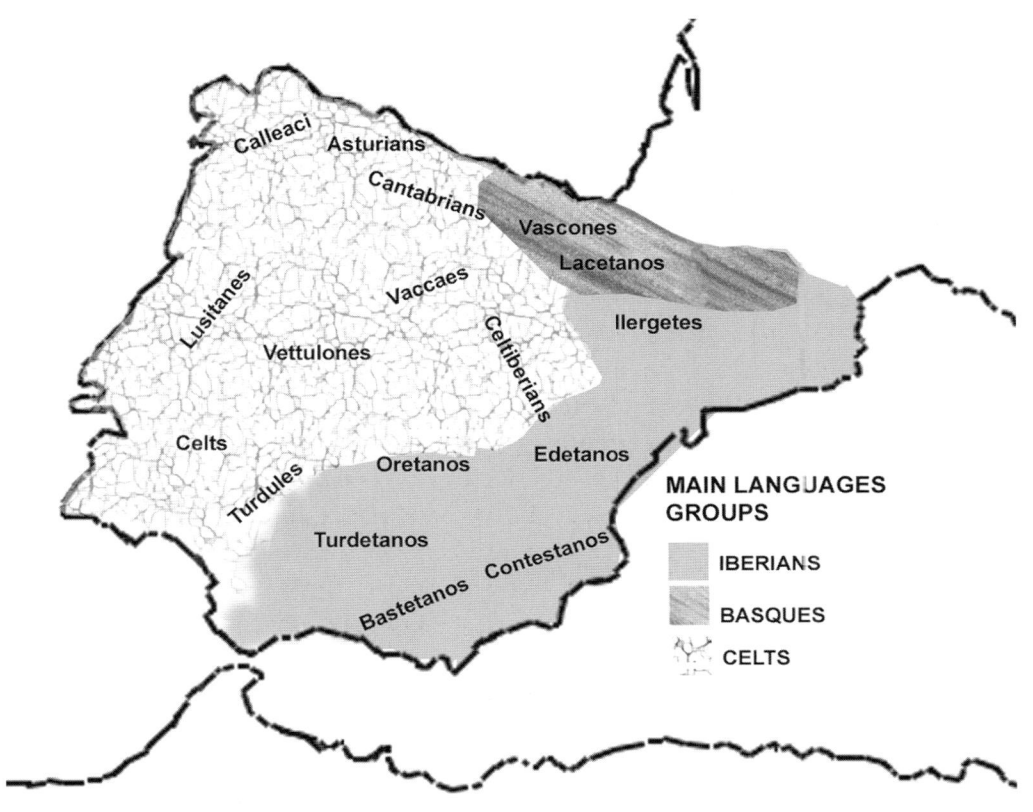

Fig. 15: Iberia before the Carthaginian conquest in 300 BC.

The Basques were the third *gens* that characterised Iberia, a population that lived in the valleys near the Pyrenees, whose poverty and isolation made them of marginal importance in the ancient history of this region.

As Martin Almagro-Gorbea states, the Roman conquest represented the last consequence, achieved not without resistance, of the process of 'Mediterraneanisation', or the general tendency towards forms of urban life, which began a thousand years earlier with the arrival of the Phoenicians and Carthaginians and culminated with the assimilation of the whole of Hispania into the Roman Empire, whose civilising effort contributed to unify peoples and to the reaching new horizons of historical development.[95]

It will be in this geographical and historical context that the definition *gladius hispaniensis* will be correctly interpreted.

IV.2,2 The historical sources

Hispaniensis non est Hispanicus
The study of the problem should start by understanding of what the Romans meant by the term '*hispaniensis*' and its subtle but fundamental difference with '*hispanicus*'.

These two terms are often considered synonymous, but in reality they indicate two cultures that are close but at the same time very distant, which leads astray valuable works such as, for example, that of F. Quesada Sanz, when he states that '… the term *hispaniensis* or *hispanicus* came in time to refer to any short, multi-purpose and robust double-edged sword with a straight blade …',[96] thus assimilating one term with another without making any distinction, or M. Bishop, who writes how 'The Romans believed that their short sword originated in Iberia, as the name *gladius hispaniensis* suggests',[97] misunderstanding its meaning.

Let us allow Flavius Sosipater Charisius, a Latin grammarian active in the mid-fourth century AD, to explain this fundamental difference: 'when we say "Hispanos" we mean the name of the people, instead with "Hispanienses" the name of those who live in the Hispanica province, so they are not *Hispanici*.'[98] He means that the natives, of purely Hispanic culture, are called '*Hispanos*', while those who live in the Iberian territory, but are of Roman origin and above all of Roman culture, are called '*Hispanienses*'. The same concept is expressed by Martial, who constantly claims his desire to belong to a Roman and urban tradition, who in the preface to '*Libris peregrinis*' (12,6) writes: 'Furthermore, what is most difficult for you, judge from my trifles with your [own] brilliance put aside, to prevent my sending to Rome, if you so determine, not a book from Spain, but a Spanish [book].'[99] In this case he highlights this subtle but fundamental distinction between *Hispaniensis*, Spanish by birth but Roman in form and spirit, of superior culture, and *Hispanus*, Spanish by race and origin and consequently rough and uncultivated.

We have further clarification from the study of the names taken from literary sources and in the inscriptions of those who followed Sertorius in the wars named after him fought in Spain. The army was mainly made up of real Italics, evidently exiles, and '*hispanienses*', that is, second and third generation Italics among the settlers previously transplanted to Spain.[100]

And again, the work *Bellum Hispaniense*, by an unknown author but certainly from the Caesarian period, deals with the civil war in Spain between Caesar and the sons of Pompey, therefore a conflict of Roman 'style and culture' (if we can say so) set in Iberia, and it is for this reason that it is called '*hispaniense*'.

This difference also appears indirectly in a passage from Seneca,[101] in which a statement by a veteran is described who, addressing Caesar who was struggling to recognise him, said '"I do not blame you, Caesar,"' answered the man, "for not recognising me; for when this took place, I was unwounded; but afterwards, at the battle of Munda, my eye was struck out, and the bones of my skull crushed. Nor would you recognise that helmet if you saw it, for it was split by a Spanish machaera."'[102] In this case, the author, in reference to a purely local weapon of indigenous culture and tradition, uses the term '*hispana*'.

Also Livy referred to the Hispanic native Alorcus during the siege of Saguntum in 219 BC, defining him as '*Alorcum hispanum*',[103] and a little further on, in reference to the native Spanish people, he uses the term '*Hispanis populis*'.[104]

In summary, we find the distinction of terms in *Latin Synonyms With Their Different Significations and Examples Taken From The Best Latin Authors*[105] where in section 1233, we find the following definition:

> Hispanus = Spanish, person born in Spain. Nec numero Hispanos, nec robore Gallos, nec callidiate Poenos, nec arribus Graecos superavimus (Cicero)
>
> Hispaniensis = an inhabitant of Spain although not native. Tacitus defines as Hispaniensis exercitus the Roman army stationed in Spain.

We can now understand why the ancient authors on some occasions used the term *gladius 'hispaniensis'*. It is clear that this term suggests that it is purely of Roman culture and tradition but is somehow related to Hispania.

We can identify this connection by making the words of Sandars our own: 'the expression *gladius hispanicus*, just like that of a "Toledo blade" in recent times, bore reference not to the type, which the Romans did not adopt, if my contention is correct, but to the quality of the weapon'.[106] Rapin also agrees with this interpretation.[107]

We have abundant and precise historical evidence of this, such as that of Philo of Byzantium who repeatedly praises the Hispanic blacksmiths for their skill in the construction of weapons and for their understanding of the related heat treatments. The Byzantine scientist states that the Spanish blacksmiths, to test the resistance of the swords, positioned them on the head and then bent them until they touched the shoulders, after which, if the swords straightened by themselves, they believed that the steel was good.[108] Furthermore, he reports that they also knew the different qualities of the steels made with minerals from various sources. The Hispanic ability in tempering also seems to be confirmed by Martial who, in reference to the construction of the *pugiones*, says 'This *pugio*, marked with serpentine veins, Salo, while it was hissing with heat, tempered with ice-cold water'.[109] Salo is the name of the Jalón river, in Celtiberian territory.

Diodorus Siculus and Ennius are also very clear about this. The Greek author, referring to the Iberian populations, tells us that:

> And a peculiar practice is followed by them in the fashioning of their defensive weapons; for they bury plates of iron in the ground and leave them there until in the course of time the rust has eaten out what is weak in the iron and what is left is only the most unyielding, and of this they then fashion excellent swords and such other objects as pertain to war. The weapon which has been fashioned in the manner described cuts through anything which gets in its way, for no shield or helmet or bone can withstand a blow from it, because of the exceptional quality of the iron.[110]

While the Latin author speaks to us of their ability to manufacture very sharp weapons: '*deducunt habiles gladios filo gracilento.*'[111]

On the other hand, the connection between these regions and their metallurgical tradition has ancient roots and it is true that from 800 BC onwards, the use of iron for the making of weapons and tools gradually spread to central Europe, where the oldest metallurgical centre was Noricum (Austria), around 400 BC. However, the centre of gravity had shifted towards the Celtic regions and Spain. It should also be considered that one of the main objectives of the bloody Hannibalic wars was the possession of the rich Iberian mining areas. Seven years after the conquest of Cartagena (209 BC), a defeat that forever expelled the Punics from Spain, thus preventing them from obtaining the crucial metals for weapons production, Scipio managed to defeat Hannibal's armies (202 BC),[112] this therefore being one of the factors that led the Romans to victory.

In relation to the conquest of Nova Carthago by Scipio, the way that the Romans treated the Spanish blacksmiths is very interesting. Polybius describes that

> [Scipio] after exhorting the citizens to be well disposed to the Romans and to be mindful of the kindness shown to them, he dismissed them all to their houses. Weeping and rejoicing at one and the same time, owing to their unexpected delivery, they made obeisance to Scipio and dispersed. He told the working men that for the time being they were public slaves of Rome, but if they showed goodwill and industry in their several crafts he promised them freedom upon the war against Carthage terminating successfully. He ordered them to enrol themselves in the quaestor's office, appointing a Roman superintendent over every thirty, the whole number being about two thousand.[113]

This forced labour is also confirmed by Livy who tells how

> of male free men about ten thousand were captured. from that number Scipio released those who were citizens of New Carthage and restored to them their city and also all the property which the war had spared to them. The artisans numbered about two thousand men. these he announced would be public slaves of the Roman people, with the not distant hope of freedom if they should actively exert themselves in providing the equipment for war.[114]

The purpose was to produce weapons:

> In order that there should be no lack of weapons for practice and for real warfare he [Scipio] paid particular attention to the artificers. As I before stated, he had appointed skilled supervisors [Hispanics] of the different sections of this branch, and he used himself to visit the workshops daily and personally distribute the materials required … the men in the town sharpening weapons, forging brass or carpentering, in a word, with everyone busily engaged upon the preparation of weapons, no one could have helped when he saw that town saying, in the words of Xenophon, that it was 'a workshop of war.'[115]

Finally, we consider a very important passage from the Byzantine Suda, as it seems to explain the reasons that led the Romans to rely on the Spanish blacksmiths in the construction of their weapons. This is a Byzantine document from the tenth century AD, considered perhaps a medieval rewriting of a now-lost book of Polybius, simply for its consistency with Books VI, 23.6 and III, 114.3. Originally written in Greek, some

Latin versions also exist,[116] even if their reliability is sometimes questioned by some authors both of the past[117] and present centuries;[118]

> The Celtiberians by far surpass other people in the fashion of their machairai, this has an effective point, and a powerful down-stroke with either edge. For this reason the Romans discarded their native swords after the wars with Hannibal, and adopted the Iberian weapon. They adopted the form, but the actual quality of the iron and the process of manufacture they were quite unable to reproduce.[119]

The crucial passage 'τήν μέν κατα σκευήν μετέλαβον' is sometimes translated 'the Romans have adopted the shape of those weapons …', but the basic meaning of the verb Κατασκευω is 'construction, technique, preparation, elaboration, structure',[120] so correct interpretation is that 'the Romans adopted the construction technique of those weapons' and not the shape.[121]

Therefore in these passages, we see the connection with Spain manifested in perfect agreement with the meaning of the term '*hispaniensis*', in fact:

- The Romans asked Hispanic blacksmiths to forge their weapons because they considered them to be skilled craftsmen, with great technical construction skills and high-quality iron;[122]
- however, they assigned them some controllers, Roman superintendents, so that they supervised their work as it was carried out according to their wishes;
- the high quantity of production, almost on a mass scale, may have led to give a distinctive definition to such weapons compared to those of Italian origin.

In other words, we are not in the presence of a mere purchase or even adoption of Iberian weapons, as erroneously believed, but of the commission abroad of what we could call a contract (in this case, forced) for the production of a weapon totally akin to the Roman tradition, albeit with local labour and metallurgy.

So ultimately this confirms the existence of the *gladius hispaniensis* and not the *gladius hispanicus*.

The classic sources and their interpretation
In light of the clarifications given to the interpretation of the term '*hispaniensis*' and the reasons that led the Romans to use it, we can analyse the individual passages of classical literature that refer to the definition of the Hispanic sword to understand its real meaning:

Livy, *Ab Urbe Condita*
- XXXVIII,21: referring to a clash with the Gauls by the consul Gnaeus Manlius Vulso, in the Galatian War (189 BC) 'This type of soldier [the *veles*] carries a three-foot shield and, in his right hand, javelins which he uses at long range; he is also equipped with a Spanish sabre.'[123]

- XXXI, 34: In reference to a clash between the Macedonians and Roman cavalry in 200 BC, 'since they were used to fighting with the Greeks and Illyrians, when they had seen bodies chopped to pieces by the Spanish sword, arms torn away, shoulders and all, or heads separated from bodies, with the necks completely severed, or vitals laid open, and the other fearful wounds, realised in a general panic with what weapons and what men they had to fight'.[124]

Both quotations refer to events chronologically very close to the conquest of Nova Carthago, following which the Romans had their weapons produced by Spanish smiths, therefore Livy's use of the term *hispaniensis* to define troops equipped with *gladii* of this origin. To be precise, it should be noted that the second quotation (XXXI, 34) refers to a longer cavalry weapon, which modern people would more properly call a sword (*spatha*), and not to the infantry *gladius*, the object of our study. These are the only two citations in which explicit reference is made to *gladius hispaniensis*.

Polybius, *The Histories*
VI-6: in his famous work, in the book in which he describes the Roman armament, he says that 'Besides the shield they also carry a sword, hanging on the right thigh and called a Spanish sword'.[125]

First of all, it is important to note once again the chronological concordance. Polybius refers to a period very close to the aforementioned events, since he himself lived almost at the same time.

However, being written in Greek, the account does not allow us to detect that subtle distinction between Hispanic natives and naturalised Romans, since the Greeks called all the inhabitants of Spain *Iberi*, and Spain itself *Iberia*. We can only imagine that it referred to a weapon *hispaniensis* by assonance and concordance of period and to what was asserted by Livy.

Livy, *Ab Urbe Condita*
VII-10: we have kept this passage by the same author separate from the others, since it is the only one in all classical literature that seems to refer specifically to a native Hispanic weapon. It describes the duel between Torquatus Manlius and a Gaul in 361 BC: '… The young man's friends then armed him; he assumed the shield of a foot-soldier, and to his side he buckled a Spanish sword, convenient for close fighting'. In the Latin we see the term used '*hispano gladio*' and not '*hispaniensi gladio*'.[126]

However, its apparent clarity is deceptive. It is not first-hand information from Livy, but copied by him from Quintus Claudius Quadrigarius,[127] who was not a true historian. His work, written in the first half of the first century BC, had more fictional than historiographic intentions, aimed mainly at glorifying the deeds of his *gens Claudia* and the rhetorical narration of military actions.[128] But Livy himself tells us[129] that Quadrigarius in turn was not the primary source, since he only made a translation of Acilius's *Annales*,[130] a work originally written in Greek in the first half of the second century BC. The original draft is lost, but this is not too serious a limitation because it will certainly have used the only adjective provided by this language (*Iberikè*), which does not provide, as already mentioned, the distinction between *hispaniensis* and *hispanicus*.

Ultimately, the anecdote was first written in Greek, then translated by Quadrigarius after about a century using the term '*hispano*' in his own initiative and not on the linguistic basis of the original version nor obviously on the direct experience that the author could have of weapons used by Torquatus, and then slavishly taken up by Livy a few decades later and finally (we report for the sake of completeness) also by Aulus Gellius in his work *Noctes Atticae*,[131] from the Antonine period.

As with the previous passage by Polybius, the value for our studies is therefore very limited but nevertheless there is an interesting fact. Although the narrated event is very archaic, far preceding the events of arms production in Spain, when it was written (the original version) was, however, once again very close to it.

IV.2,3 The archaeological panorama

The study of weapons of purely Hispanic culture and tradition is very important in order to confirm – or possibly question – the previous assertions, since some of them and their related technological components are often considered irrefutable witnesses to the Hispanic origins of the *gladius*. In this culture there are various types of swords, some of which have characteristics that differ considerably from the *gladius*, others less so, but as we can see, for all of them there are doubts that they could be considered the archetype of the Roman sword.

Swords in the Iberian Peninsula
- Atrophied Antennae Swords' (Fig. 16-A):
Some authors specifically refer to the 'Atrophied Antennae Sword' as the direct progenitor of the *gladius*, a weapon datable from the fifth to the third century BC (G. De La Chica, *El armamento de los Iberos*, p. 316; Connolly, *Greece and Rome at War*, pp. 130–1; Feugère, *Weapons of the Romans*, pp. 16–19). F. Quesada Sanz responds to this by considering only type VI to be acceptable but with great effort and many doubts: 'they are therefore very short swords … and much shorter that the c.62cm Roman Republican Gladii … the

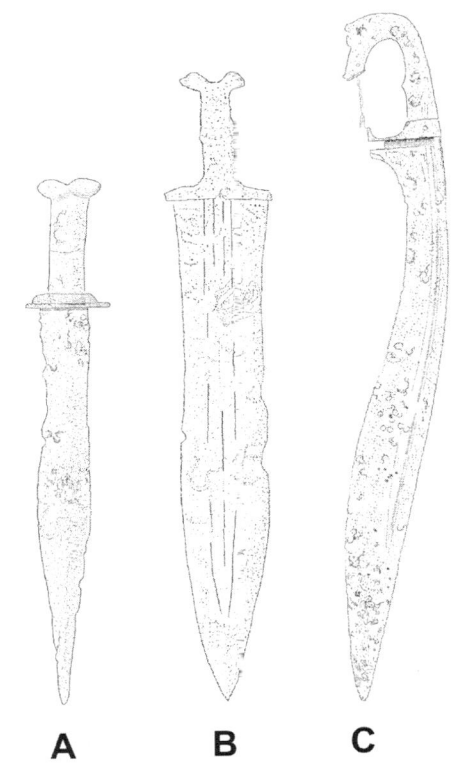

Fig. 16: A) Iberian 'Atrophied Antennae' dagger. B) Iberian 'Frontòn' sword. C) Iberian *falcata*.

examples of Republican Roman swords ... recently discovered have virtually nothing in common with these swords ...'[132] It should be added that the type of handle is completely different and in addition, being practically daggers, their use is also substantially different from that of the *gladius*.

- The 'Frontòn Sword' (Fig. 16-B):

Other authors indicate instead the so-called 'Frontòn' sword type (Aguilera and Gamboa, *Las necròpolisibèricas*, p. 13; Connolly, *Greece and Rome at War*, p. 150), which, however, is excluded by various authors including Quesada Sanz, for three reasons: first of all because from the end of the third century it had already been in disuse in Iberia for one century, being a very ancient type datable to the fifth – fourth century BC; second, for the shape and dimensions of the blade which are completely different (it is very wide in relation to the length); and finally for the structure of the handle, flat and rhomboid, which is completely different from the simple tang of the *gladius*.[133]

- The Falcata (Fig. 16-C):

In some cases we see authors, always Spanish, refer to the *falcata* (A. Arribas, *Los Iberos*, p. 58; A. Guadàn, *Las armasen la moneda ibérica*, p. 36; S. Broncano, *La necròpolis ibérica de El Tesorico*, p. 97 etc.). This is a particularly risky thesis, as Quesada Sanz rightly points out it has absolutely nothing to do with the *gladius*, being a curved sabre.[134] This weapon is incidentally related to similar Etruscan and Greek models, not forgetting that there is a considerable distance in time between the two. In fact, while in Etruria specimens dating back to the seventh century BC have been found and it was immediately adopted in Greece towards the sixth century BC, but we have to wait until the middle of the fifth century BC to see it appear in Iberian territory,[135] although shortened in length. The length ranges from 75–80cm on the Etruscan specimens and 52–55cm on the Iberian ones. However, they were all weapons devoted to slashing blows, in no way related to the Roman sword.

These three types of swords, with all the numerous subtypes that the modern literature identify, substantially cover the entire Iberian landscape, the remaining ones being of marginal presence. What emerges is that despite the efforts made by some authors, it is practically impossible to see any link with the Roman *gladius*.

- The Celto-Iberian Sword

In some cases we have interesting references to the Celtic of La Tène I and II sword types (A. Schulten, 'Las Guerras de 154-72 BC', p. 5; D. Fletcher, *Problemas de la Cultura Ibérica*, p. 59; A. Brühn de Hoffmayer, *Arms and Armor in Spain*, p. 46; P. Coussin, 'Les Armes Romaines', p. 227), called by some also as 'of Hispanic imitation'. Quesada Sanz argues that 'the prototype of the *gladius hispaniensis* is a Celtiberian sword whose remote origin is not in the characteristic Iberian types of the 5th–4th centuries BC, but in the Celtic La Tène I sword substantially modified in accordance with local tastes from the late fourth century BC in the Meseta and the Southeast'.[136]

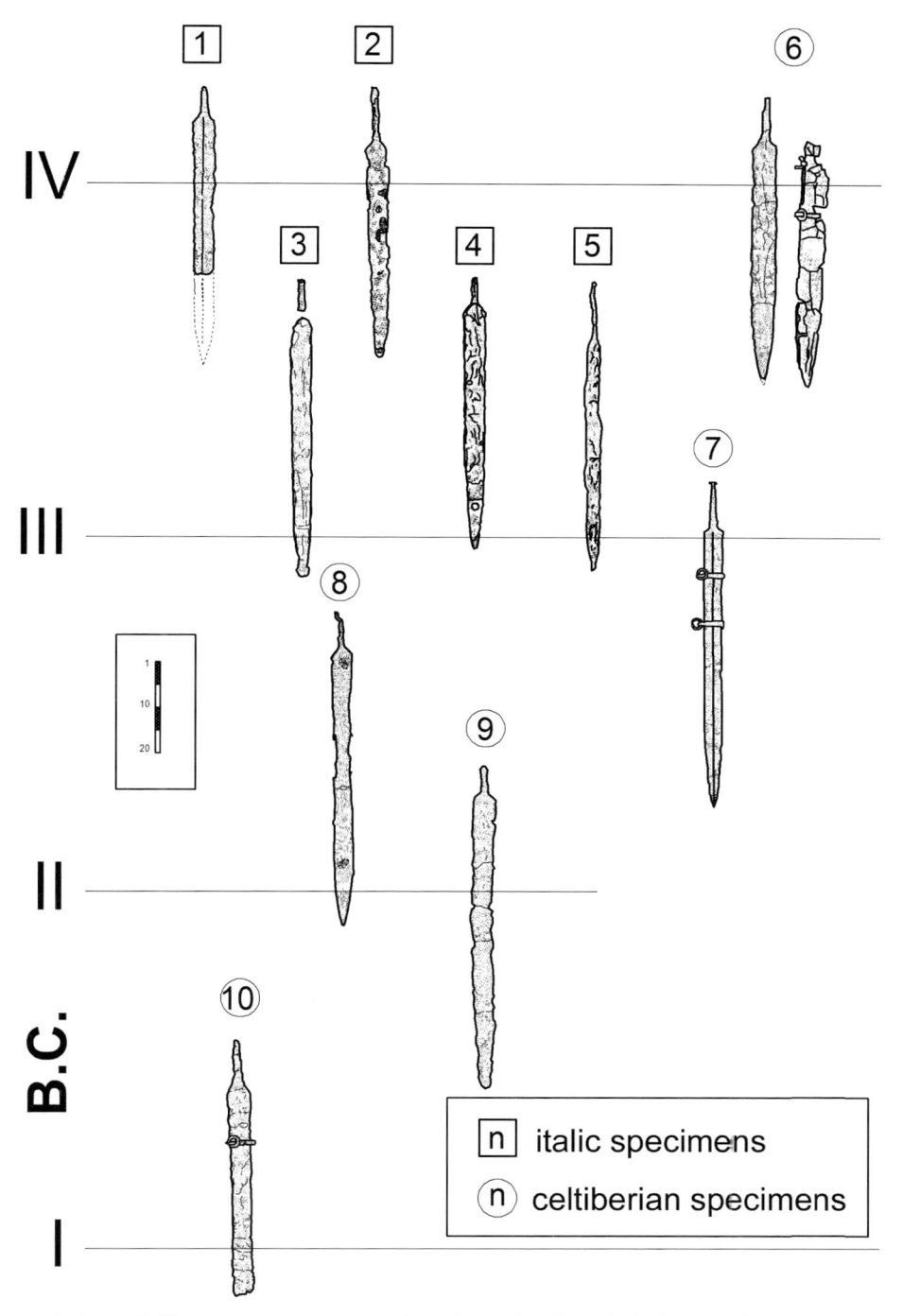

On the Erroneous Derivation of the *Gladius* from Non-Italic People 305

Fig. 17: Italic and Hispanic specimens in chronological order: 1) S. Vittore fourth century BC. 2) Bazzano fourth century BC. 3) Pietrabbondante fourth–third century BC. 4) Pietrabbondante fourth–third century BC. 5) Pietrabbondante fourth–third century BC. 6) Cigarralejo end fourth century BC. 7) La Osera early third century BC. 8) Gomaz third–second century BC. 9) Cabecico second century BC. 10) La Azucarera second–first century BC.

This thesis of the *gladius* deriving not directly from Hispanic weapons but from the Celtic sword mediated by Iberia is also taken up by P. Connolly: 'the basic premise of F. Quesada Sanz's paper on the origins of the Spanish sword that the *gladius hispaniensis* was never a short sword and probably evolved from a Spanish adaptation of the Celtic long sword must be right.'[137]

However, Quesada Sanz himself raises some doubts, one of an archaeological-cultural nature, related to the extreme rarity of this type of weapon in Hispanic territory: 'There is only one possible objection to our proposal: the apparent scarcity of La Tène swords in the Iberian Peninsula: it seems odd that the Romans adopted a type of sword very rare among the Celtiberians',[138] and another of a chronological nature, being a weapon 'old-fashioned in the mid-third century BC'.[139]

The five main specimens found in modern-day Spain that are commonly considered as evidence of this particular origin are the one from Cigarralejo (grave 54, end fourth century BC., total length 63cm), La Osera (grave 201, end fourth–early third century BC, total length 71.5cm), Gomaz (grave 'N', third–second century BC, total length 68.4cm), Cabecico (grave 142, second century BC, total length 70cm) and La Azucarera (second–first century BC, fragmented, remaining length 55.5cm) (Fig. 17).

The main characteristics of a Celto-Iberian sword are the spiked tang, the blade with substantially parallel edges and sharp point, with descending shoulders and of medium length, all factors that we now know well since it is nothing more than the Italo-Celtic sword or High Consular *gladius* (in particular, Type A), which has been extensively discussed in the appropriate chapter. These are the characteristics well known in central Italy, but which on the other hand have nothing to do with those of the swords of purely Hispanic culture, as seen above.

It is also necessary to think about the chronology. In a purely Italian context, one of the most archaic examples is that from tomb 5 of Presenzano (unpublished, Archaeological Museum of Teanum Sidicinum in Teano – CE),[140] datable to the first half of the fourth century BC. Instead, in a more purely Roman context, we have the example of the sword of S. Vittore, from the last quarter of the fourth century BC (see Chapter III (A).3 'The High and Middle Consular *Gladius*'). On the other hand, the most archaic Iberian specimens (from La Osera and Cigarralejo), are about some decades more recent, while all the others are about one century more recent (Fig. 17). In short, in Italy the birth of this sword seems much more archaic and when the Romans came into contact with the Iberians during Hannibal's wars, at the end of the third century BC, it had already been created in Rome by an Oscan craftsman at least a century earlier, and almost two if we want to refer more generally to the central Italic territory.

Moreover, while in the Hispanic territory they seem rare as previously seen, on the contrary they were widespread in central Italy. As Vitali also reminds us 'all the Celtic or Celtic territories in the Umbrian, Etruscan, Middle Adriatic, Ligurian, Venetic and Rhaetian world, have returned more or less high percentages (of swords) and more or less significant types'[141] (see Chapter III (A).3 'The High and Middle Consular *gladius*').

Therefore, considering the considerable difference of diffusion between the two territories, Italic and Iberian, the chronological differences, the affinity with the Italic tradition and the foreignness in the Iberian one; all of this suggests that the historical path of this weapon traces that described for the *falcatae*, i.e. the opposite of that normally considered: weapons transited from the central Italic territory to the Iberian one, perhaps via Celtic mercenaries or similar.

This explains Quesada Sanz's aforementioned legitimate perplexity – 'it seems strange that the Romans adopted a type of sword very rare among the Celtiberians' – as in fact, they did not adopt it but instead exported it. From this it is possible to formulate a hypothesis that is perhaps extreme but certainly plausible. The few specimens found in Celtiberia were not weapons of native warriors but belonged to Italic 'foreigners', perhaps mercenaries. The Iberians not only never influenced the Romans with this sword, but it was also never really present within their culture.

The metal frame scabbard
The construction technology of the Roman sword scabbard, which consists of a structure made with a guttering frame with a 'U' section, intended to accommodate the two closing valves of organic material (Fig. 18), is usually considered as definite proof of the Hispanic derivation of the *gladius*.

Quesada Sanz says that 'the recent discovery of new republican Roman *gladius* in Slovenia, Israel and Egypt, confirms the hypothesis that the Roman republican *gladius hispaniensis* was inspired by a late version of the sword La Tène I, modified in Celtiberia in the shape of the blade and the structure of the scabbard [the specimens cited show this type of frame scabbard]'[142] and 'at the end of the fourth and then the third century. BC a sword model substantially identical to the Roman *gladius* was generated in Hispania, as a modification of the Latin sword. These changes mainly concerned the length of the blade (which stopped at 60cm, instead of continuing to lengthen as it happened in France during La Tène II) and the scabbard materials, the metal ones being replaced by those in leather or wood with metallic frame'.[143]

Kavanagh also[144] agrees with these statements, bearing witness to some Hispanic weapons 'fully concordant with known examples of republican Roman swords' (Quintanas del Gomaz necropolis, tomb 54 of Cigarralejo, and tomb 210 of La Osera). Mike Bishop states that 'Therefore, what the Romans seem to have taken from the Celtiberian weapons was the form of the blade and the frame scabbard'[145] and, referring to the so-called 'Pompeii' sword, which no longer has the frame scabbard unlike the previous 'Mainz' type, he maintains that it was thereby breaking a tradition that stretched right back to the Celtiberian frame scabbards of the third century BC.[146] P. Connolly dedicates a paragraph of his work to the question, in which he claims, referring to the late Consular Roman scabbards, that 'these are all Hispanic-type metal frame from the third century BC'.[147] Without going further, it will be sufficient to say that modern literature has almost unanimously added to these, but almost always only by handling this thesis uncritically.

Fig. 18: Scabbard construction
1) Edge guttering with 'U' section.
2) Scabbard sheets.
3) Suspension bands for the ring fastenings.
4) Suspension rings.

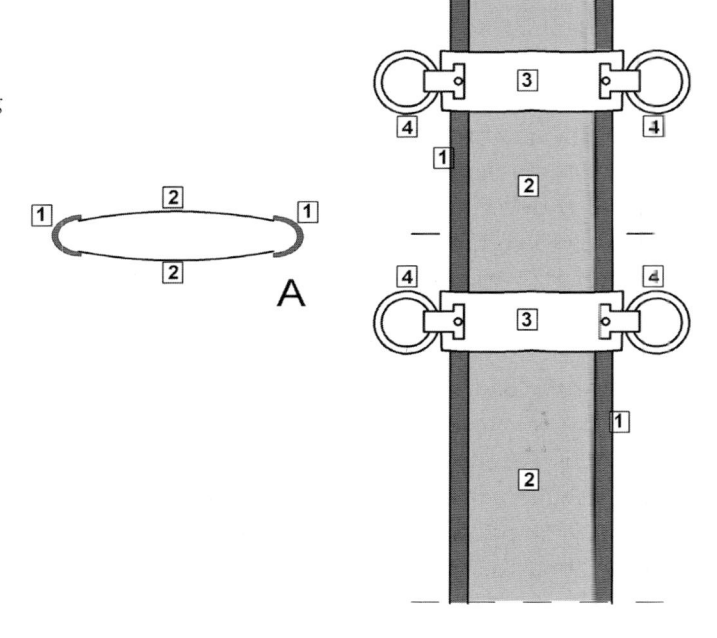

In general, the motivation behind this theory is that this way of assembling the scabbard had been present in Spain, and particularly in the Meseta,[148] since relatively recent times, about the second half of the third century BC. As Kavanagh tells us, only Quesada Sanz, in partial correction of the above, has the doubt that perhaps the framed scabbards could be of Italic influence, so that those of some Hispanic Latenian specimens could be the product of Roman influence and not vice versa.[149] This doubt is certainly well founded. In fact, if it is absolutely certain that this technology was widely used in these Hispanic regions, an in-depth study of the central Italic archaeological panorama returns an equally and abundant chronologically well antecedent picture in finds.

In this area, this technology appeared about four centuries earlier in the scabbards of stamen daggers,[150] widespread in the central Apennines, in Picenum and surrounding areas, up to the Faliscan-Capenate countryside and in the Sabina Tiberina, in close proximity to Rome. Like the cross-hilted swords, they are weapons very little known by modern scholars, especially non-Italians, even if they are particularly characteristic and widespread in these areas. We have important information from the aforementioned work by P.F. Stary[151] (see Chapter II.3 'The Monarchical *Gladius*') in 1981, and from few others that followed.[152]

At the present time, the knowledge we have indicates their appearance at the beginning of the seventh century BC through a specimen found in tomb 73 of the necropolis of Monte Cerreto in Narce, which is probably the most archaic known,[153] but immediately afterwards registered a massive presence in numerous other necropolises.[154] We record hundreds of finds in the burials of at least seventy-four necropolises in Lazio, Molise and Abruzzo (see Fig. 11 – Chapter II.3 'The Monarchical *Gladius*'), for example, in the one of Fossa (L'Aquila), where 500 tombs have been excavated, in that of Campovalano (Teramo) more than 600, in that of Alfedena (L'Aquila) almost 1,500 and so on, in which specimens of swords and daggers still in their scabbard are not at all rare, many of them made with this technique. This technology is certainly not limited to the period of diffusion of stamen daggers and cross-hilted swords but continues its existence for centuries in Italic and Roman culture, starting from the Consular Period up to the High Empire.

Among the many specimens, an excellent example is the sheath of the pseudo-Roman sword found in SoknopaiouNeusos (El-Fayyum, Egypt),[155] datable to the end of the first century BC–early first century AD, of which the terminal part of the scabbard has survived, showing a perfect analogy with those of the daggers with stamens especially from the Abruzzo area, type 3,[156] from about the sixth to seventh century BC (Fig. 19).

Finally, for the sake of completeness, it should be noted that an examination of Celtic weapons in contemporary continental Europe shows that this technology was never adopted in their scabbards, allowing their influence on the Italic populations to be excluded. Celtic scabbards were invariably made with two overlapping metal sheets on the edges, to cover the entire surface, without the support of any perimeter structure.

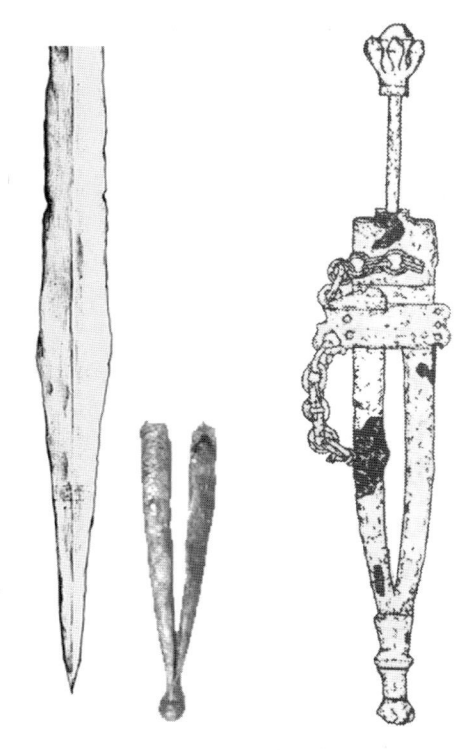

Fig. 19: left: Part of the pseudo-Roman sword found in Soknopaiou Neusos (El-Fayyum, Egypt) and its scabbard, datable to the end of the first century BC–early first century AD (drawing by Davoli and Miks 'A new Roman sword from Soknopaiou Nesos'). Right: Type 3 stamen dagger, still in the scabbard, from tomb 16 of the necropolis of Opi (AQ), in the Abruzzo region, dating back to the seventh century BC (drawing by Weidig, 'I pugnali a stami, considerazioni su aspetti tecnici, tipologici, cronologici e distribuzione in area abruzzese'). Note the marked similarity of the construction technology of the two scabbards.

The construction technique of the frame scabbards appears ultimately of purely central Italic origin, very well mastered and appreciated by all the numerous local populations, such as the Piceni, Vestini, Equi, Sanniti, Peligni, Frentani, Marsi, Marrucini etc. and preceding the Celtiberian one by at least three to four centuries (Fig. 20).

Indeed it can be said that when the Romans came into contact with the Hispanics during the Second Punic War, not only did they already know this technique for many centuries but the last part of the period of their use, identifiable with the end of the first century BC, was approaching.

Once again we can legitimately assume that, just as the *falcata* and the Italo-Celtic swords moved from Italy to Spain, the same happened to this scabbard technology.

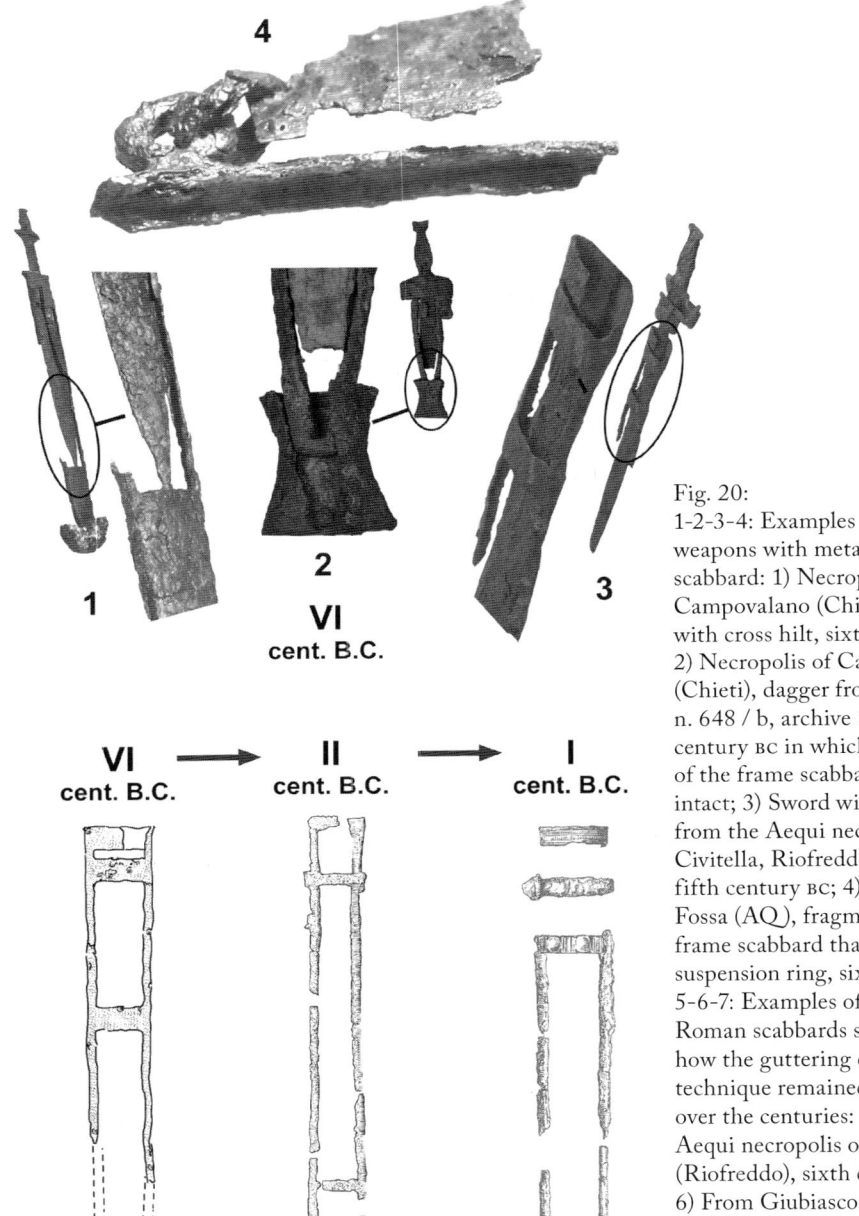

Fig. 20:
1-2-3-4: Examples of Italic weapons with metal frame scabbard: 1) Necropolis of Campovalano (Chieti), sword with cross hilt, sixth century BC; 2) Necropolis of Campovalano (Chieti), dagger from tomb n. 648 / b, archive 16848, sixth century BC in which the structure of the frame scabbard is preserved intact; 3) Sword with cross hilt from the Aequi necropolis of Casal Civitella, Riofreddo (Rome), sixth–fifth century BC; 4) Necropolis of Fossa (AQ), fragment of a metal frame scabbard that still retains the suspension ring, sixth century BC. 5-6-7: Examples of Italic and Roman scabbards showing how the guttering construction technique remained unchanged over the centuries: 5) From the Aequi necropolis of Casal Civitella (Riofreddo), sixth century BC; 6) From Giubiasco (Switzerland), second century BC; 7) From Idrija PriBaci (Slovenia), first century BC. (Photos and drawings by the author, with the exception of n. 6 (from M. Bishop, *Roman Military Equipment, from the Punic Wars to the fall of Rome*) and n. 7 (from C. Miks, *Studien zur Römischen Schwertbewaffnung in der Kaiserzeit*)

IV.3 CONCLUSIONS

The most important concept that emerges from this dissertation is that the *gladius* was an entirely Roman weapon and had no Greek or Iberian origin.

The spread from East of civilisation, of ideas and of a large part of trade, has led scholars to believe that the finds of the cross-hilted sword in Macedonia and Magna Graecia were proof of a similar path developed for the *gladius*. But the archaeological reality and historical sources allow us to ascertain how, in this case, the diffusion took place in the opposite direction, similarly to trade which by definition is always bi-directional. Very interesting is the concept that the sword used by the central Apennine populations, aimed purely for war, was integrated by the Hellenistic culture after a metamorphosis, for which it became an emblem of aristocratic power.[157] But if this sword, so decorated and embellished, managed to penetrate the customs of the populations of Magna Graecia and Macedonia,[158] contrary to what the ceramography and the finds of the Greek votive deposits apparently demonstrate, this diffusion did not occur completely in Greece, where in some areas the development of democracy effectively prevented the acceptance of a monarchical symbol.

Also significant is the idealisation of the Macedonian sword which, because it was in the possession of Alexander the Great, became a symbol of what the Hellenistic conqueror represented for the Romans, an emblem of strength and unity of the conquered people, adopted in the statuary by various emperors as a means of propaganda. On the other hand, the generals and emperors adopted it too in the form of *Parazonium*.

In regard of the Iberian origin, even in this case the sources and archaeological data reveal a straightforward truth, confirming the doubts of some modern authors, including H. Sandars, who argues how 'the Romans did not adopt any Iberian swords' and 'this statement is mythical and in no respect based upon fact'.[159] Unfortunately, the majority of modern authors have uncritically adopted the simpler thesis that the *gladius hispaniensis* refers to the origin and not the one, perhaps less intuitive, which refers to the technology and geographical area of manufacture. In fact, as Plutarch narrates in relation to the clashes between Sertorius and Metellus in the war of 79–76 BC fought in Spain, '… Sertorius was admired and loved by the Barbarians [i.e. the Hispanici], and especially because by introducing Roman arms and formations and signals he did away with their frenzied and furious displays of courage, and converted their forces into an army, instead of a huge band of robbers'.[160] With this passage the author testifies to us that it was the local Hispanic populations who abandoned their own weapons, obviously different, passing to the Roman combat system, including the adoption of 'armament', thereby improving their structure and military efficiency. But even Athenaeus of Naucrates, albeit indirectly, confirms this concept, narrating how

> the Romans … retained their ancestral customs, they took over from their subjects whatever remnant of noble discipline they could find, leaving to them that which was useless, in order that they might never become capable of attaining to the

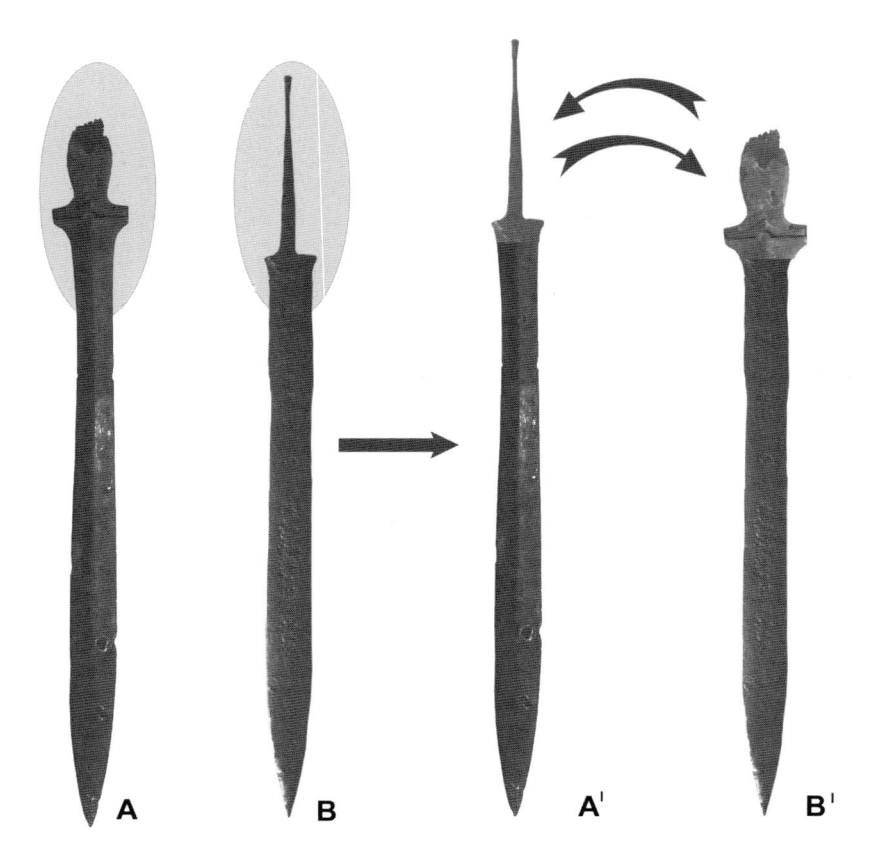

Fig. 21: Virtual exchange of the tang between a Monarchical *gladius* (A) and a Late Consular (B) (A' and B' the results after this exchange).

recovery of what was lost ... From the Etruscans, also, who attacked in close formation, they took over the close battle; from the Samnites they learned the use of the oblong shield, from the Spaniards, the use of the javelin, and so on, learning different things from different people, and bringing them to greater perfection.[161]

The author, in referring to the various weapons adopted from the various peoples, would certainly not have omitted to mention the most important one for the Romans, the *gladius*, the exclusion of which from this list is an implicit admission of its extraneousness from Iberian culture.

In conclusion it is also appropriate to take up and complete an important concept already partially exposed by Aguillò. The author's opinion is that too much importance has been given to the term '*hispaniensis*' and that more modern authors than classical ones have spoken of this type of *gladius*.[162] Considering that the quotations on the Hispanic *gladius* are a very few that basically could be connected to a single event, limited in time and location (the taking of Nova Carthago in Hispania), we believe this concept to be acceptable.

To conclude, we would like to propose a very particular example to help people to understand the importance of the concept of tradition applied to the technological and structural progress of the *gladius*, according to which over the centuries the weapon, in the context of its evolution, has remained firmly attached to the indigenous characteristics of the swords owned by the ancient ancestors, among which the Capestrano warrior remains as the classic reference.

To prove our claim, we virtually exchanged the grip of a sixth century BC Monarchical sword with that of one from the Caesarian period (Fig. 21). With this done, the two weapons, virtually modified, can be easily confused with each other, one could be backdated by five centuries as well as the other post-dated in the same way. We have used this small experiment to demonstrate that the atavistic cross-hilted sword, originally from the central Italic areas, continued to exist until the end of the Consular Age, even though it evolved in some of its technological characteristics, demonstrating the fragility of theses that propose more or less exotic origins.

Chapter V

The Symbolic Value of the *Gladius*

In the course of human history, the sword has been one of the main objects in numerous mythological tales, magical rituals and heroic cults, an object that has been held to symbolise values shared by whole communities. The importance of this artefact is inherent in its use, since it allowed the owner to cause the death of another human being, implying a power that in ancient cultures frequently had a direct connection with the divine. According to the cultural facies and the historical period examined, the relationship that man had with the sword was different, a phenomenon that can also be found in the relationship the Romans had with the *gladius*, special and quite distinct from the mentality of the people who preceded it and those who took over after the fall of the Empire.

V.1 THE *BELLUM SACRUM* AND THE SYMBOLISM OF THE SWORD IN THE PRE-ROMAN AGE

Fighting between humans has the unnatural purpose of killing the enemy, a different objective from that which occurs between animals of the same species, where combat is symbolic, used only as a rite of confrontation to establish the hierarchy of the strongest.[1] Man's awareness of working *contra naturam* has led archaic peoples to 'invent' ceremonies and rituals that could justify, and religiously permit, this action.

Since ancient times, war has found a justification in the divine will and, while the warrior becomes a sacrificial victim and at the same time a divine instrument, his weapon takes on a sacred character. The confirmation for this can be found in the meaning of the word 'sword' in its Latin form '*ensis*', which derives from the Indo-European '*nsi*', while in Sanskrit, a language also belonging to the Indo-European family, it is '*asì-*', with the meaning, in addition to the specifically military one, of 'sacrificial knife for animals' too.[2] The term *spatha* is also of Indo-Eofuropean derivation, coming from '*spa-*', while in Sanskrit it is '*sphà*', with the meaning of 'extending',[3] the sword being an extension of the killer's hand and enabling contact with the victim. From this linguistic analysis we can see how the sword, since the Bronze Age, has been considered as 'a specific means of killing human beings'[4] unlike other offensive weapons such as axes, arrows, bows, javelins or slings[5] that derive from working or hunting tools. The ancient combat between men was part of a sacrificial act, called the '*bellum sacrum*', in which the divinity decided the outcome of the event, while the priest[6] and/or the commanding officer[7] interceded to predict the outcome of the clash, propitiate victory and favour the defeat of the enemy. On these occasions, amulets and war cries were used to repel and frighten evil spirits in the context of a 'sacred horror'. Therefore the duel was the moment that defined who was the hero and who was the loser between the fighters, an outcome that reflected the will of the divine discords on Olympus. The Homeric duels, fought by Hector, Achilles, Agamemnon, Ajax and many others, are proof of how the pagan gods were at war with each other, leaving men at their mercy, thus justifying the killing of a fighting hero as the result of an extra-human will from which man could not escape. In a Heraclitean fragment, Πόλεμος, 'war', is even defined as the 'father of all things', while in Plato the concept of a conflict between souls and flesh appears for the first time. This was taken into the Jewish-Christian theology in which the idea of the war between God, understood as the highest good, and Satan, who represents the highest evil, exists. They were considered as leaders of squadrons of angels and demons who fight on the celestial and on the earthly plane.[8]

Therefore, in a context where the clash did not have effects limited to the human being but also involved the supernatural part, propitiatory rites, both religious and superstitious, were essential to obtain divine approval. For this reason the weapons, which were nothing more than the means with which the supernatural will was expressed, had their own religious and apotropaic value, and thus were subjected to blessings and purifying rites.

As an example, the British Museum holds a group of weapons (two spearheads, one of which is illustrated, and a Cuma-type sword) (Fig. 1) which belonged to a chieftain of the initial phase of the Iron Age in a southern area of the *Latium Vetus* (Cassino–Frosinone). The unusual character of these objects is in the anthropomorphic representation of the figural spear, where the eyes, the nose and the mouth and a headdress are highlighted, a fact that gives a superhuman meaning to the figure.[9]

This weapon being a decorative object can be excluded for the reason that the engravings could not have been seen from a distance. The weapons had an esoteric symbolic-evocative-religious meaning, which ensured its wearer divine protection and at the same time favoured the defeat of his opponent.[10] Similarly, the antenna sword (Fig. 2) also presents, albeit in a stylised way, an anthropomorphic representation. The hilt symbolically reproduces a man in which the small apical knob represents the head, the antennae

Fig. 1: Group of weapons from Cassino (Frosinone) in the collections of the British Museum.
A) Figural spearhead, cat. n. PRB WG 1138, h approx. 37cm.
B) Cuma-type sword, cat. n PRB WG1136, h approx. 36cm.
The weapons had been owned by a *pater familias* and the anthropomorphic spear assumed an esoteric meaning that gave protection and at the same time strength to the one carrying it.
(Drawing from *Prehistoric Metal Artefacts from Italy – 3500–720 BC – in the British Museum*)

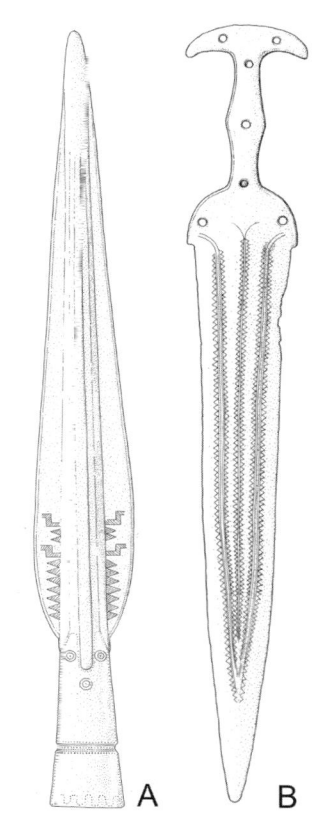

are the arms, the handle the body and the hilt with descending shoulders the legs, a representation that can be more easily understood by observing some types of Celtic swords that explicitly represent this sort of figure. In this context, the blade, extending from between the warrior's legs, can be considered as the phallus, and as proof of this consideration the sword was inserted into the sheath, called *vagina* in Latin, from which the name of the female genitalia derives. Probably this symbology is not accidental, but refers to the concept expressed above, in which the soldier in a battle could take on the connotation of the officiant of a sacrifice, when he killed an enemy, or of a sacrificial victim himself, when he was mortally hit. The blade/phallus that penetrated the body not so much caused the death of the enemy warrior, as it symbolically induced his transformation and glorification (that is, he was regenerated). According to M. Gimbutas, the Indo-Europeans '… worshiped the swiftness of arrow and spear and the sharpness of the blade. The touch of the axe blade was thought to awaken the powers of nature and transmit the fecundity of the Thunder God. The frightening black God of Death and the Underworld marked the warrior for death with the touch of his spear tip, glorifying him as a fallen hero.'[11]

So the *pater familias*[12] controlled and protected the tribe which had given him political, military and sometimes even religious power. Among the various objects that exalted his role as a leader

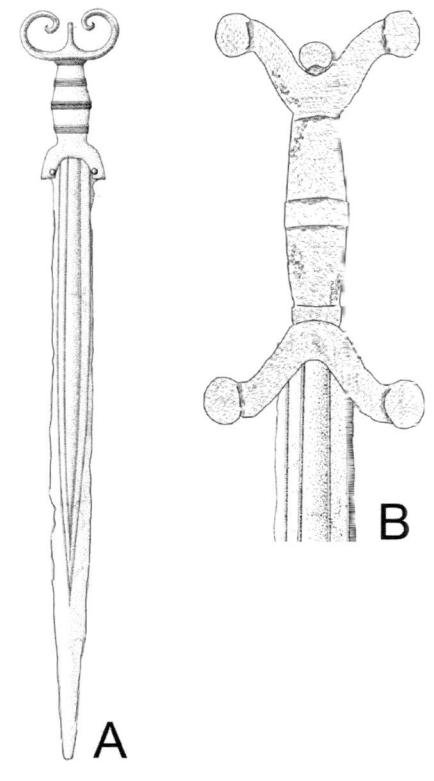

Fig. 2: Two swords from the Bronze Age, the first (A), called an antennae sword, is also typical of the Italic territory, while the second (B) is typically Celtic. Unusually, both are clearly representing an anthropomorphic interpretation of the hilt, where the blade takes on a phallic meaning in the context of the symbolic and religious action that the killing of the enemy assumed. (*Author's drawing*)

there was certainly the sword, an object which due to its high cost, with consequent limitation to its diffusion and favouring a real advantage to the physical strength of those who owned it, had a strong connotation of power and symbolic value.

Other elements that allow us to include the sword among the objects that marked social prestige are the confirmation of the refined decoration of the blades and their scabbards, the presence of ivory or bone handles and the richness of the panoplies in which they are found, where they are often accompanied by helmets and greaves.[13] Furthermore, being a weapon that due to its characteristics provides close contact with the enemy and consequently requires skill to use, it involved training that only people linked to the aristocracy could afford. In fact, all those who depended on a job aimed at a mere survival did not have either the economic capacity to purchase it or the time to obtain the necessary skills to use it.

V.2 ROMAN PRAGMATISM: *BELLUM IUSTUM* AND THE *GLADIUS*

A characteristic of the Roman people was their extremely pragmatic approach to religious, social and military matters, to the extent that Cicero stated that '... in the case of a state in its external relations, the rights of war must be strictly observed. For since there are two ways of settling a dispute: first, by discussion; second, by physical force; and since the former is characteristic of man, the latter of the brute, we must resort to force only in case we may not avail ourselves of discussion.'[14] On the basis of this affirmation we note that, although the belief in the religiosity of war persisted among the Romans, therefore involving the divine part, it was fundamentally a typically human matter, thus framing it judicially and defining it as a violation of religion and law. We should not fall into the common mistake of thinking that the Romans were a more belligerent people than their contemporaries, based only on some famous Latin phrases especially by unknown authors, such as '*si vis pacem, para bellum*' ('if you want peace, prepare for war') and '*divide et impera*' ('divide and conquer', with the meaning of putting the various people and commanders in opposition to each other). First of all, war for the Romans was a negative concept, and we can frequently detect this from the ancient authors such as Virgil, in the *Aeneid*, who deprecates the '*crimina belli*'[15] and the '*scelerata insania belli*'[16] and comments that '*nulla sanus bello*',[17] since the *bellum* can be '*horridum*',[18] '*asperum*',[19] '*crudele*',[20] '*cruentum*'[21] and '*triste*',[22] But war was also seen negatively within religion, to the extent that Virgil again places it in the sphere of the '*nefas*',[23] defining it as one of the greatest and most terrible evils that afflict mankind.[24] Unfortunately, the Mantuan poet observed that the conflict became a sad necessity in the face of the injustice which men refuse to repair, and in this case, only after having made the gods ascertain the *aporia* through rituals, which were repeated unchanged in these times, war was declared.

But the Roman people by definition did not seek the dominion and oppression of the subjugated people through war, as Cicero affirmed, anticipating Virgil's approach, a universal peace among peoples, which could be obtained through Roman supremacy and the divine will. War was only the last resort. The synthesis of the thought derives from Roman priestly documents, which were admirably enunciated by Francesco de Martino, who exalted 'the political-religious vocation of the [Roman] people, whose supreme goal was peace and friendship with the foreigners'.[25]

The *Bellum Iustum* is nothing more than an explanation of the organisational needs of the Roman people. In it one can find a precise classification of roles: what belonged to the divinity was very distinct from what was human, in addition to the obligation to follow correct legal practice in the disputes between states, aimed at not losing the protection of the gods. The concept of *Iustum*, therefore, seems more as the pursuit of a logical approach rather than a religious or juridical practice, which is also reflected in the way of conceiving of war and consequently in how the fight develops. The *gladius* therefore became *Regimen castrorum*[26] (commander of military camps), the weapon on which all Roman combat was based, becoming a symbol of its people.

V.3 THE SWORD, FROM WEAPON TO POLITICAL PROPAGANDA

The sword with which the 'Warrior of Capestrano', a central-Italic Bruttian-Picenian leader of the second half of the sixth century BC, was armed and which we know to be the *gladius* of the legionaries of the Monarchical Period, was a sword also used by other peoples.[27] What we are witnessing is not so much its diffusion beyond the borders of Italy, as seen in Chapter II.3, but the fact that this weapon did not always have the same meaning, taking on different connotations depending on the people who used it. So while the special characters of the object remained unchanged, the associated use and meaning varied.

From being a combat item of the Osco-Umbrian populations (practical use) it evolved to be an 'expression of the military condition of the aristocratic oligarchy'[28] (symbolic use, without excluding the practical one) for the *gentes* who lived in the Italic regions of Puglia and Basilicata and above all for the Macedonian military elite, acquiring an ideal meaning (political propaganda) for the Romans after Alexander the Great.

The acquisition of the symbolic role of 'Power' was accompanied by the weapon losing certain practical functions, such as the pointed tip in the models of artistic representation, and by the acquisition of decorative elements in ivory and gold that elevated its intrinsic value and which consequently made it a status symbol, as well as a symbol of power. It is within this concept that the cross-hilted sword will 'arm' King Philip II (found in his tomb), his son Alexander the Great and all his friends and noble knights on horseback (see the so-called 'Sarcophagus of Alexander'[29]).

The cross-hilted sword is portrayed in some mosaics in Pella (Macedonia), the capital of the Macedonian Empire of Philip II and Alexander, acknowledging its role as a symbol of royal power. In fact, by showing the weapon Alexander will be able to stop the lion's assault because the ferocious feline, an allegory of the force of nature, will recognise the sovereign as the one who controls the whole empire. The lion is represented turning his aggressive attentions towards the friend of the Macedonian king, who is about to kill him with a *machaira* (not with the sword) which is accompanied by a cross-hilted sword scabbard (the scabbard and his naked heroism making him a noble).

Another work full of allegorical and symbolic elements is the mosaic from the Villa del Fauno in Pompeii, in which Alexander is shown defeating Darius III of Persia. Exhibited in the most visible part

Fig. 3: Cross-hilted sword found in the tomb of Philip II of Macedon, father of Alexander the Great. Note how the handle is decorated with damascening and gold trimmings, thus enhancing the value of the weapon and therefore the prestige of the one who held it. (*Photo by Raffaele D'Amato*)

Fig. 4: The Sarcophagus of 'Alexander', actually the burial of the king of Sidon. In these two details, of the Battle of Issus, we can see two fighters, who we guess to be of noble lineage by their possession of horses and the panoply, both with cross-hilted swords. (*Photo by the author, courtesy of the Istanbul Archaeological Museum – Turkey*)

of the Pompeian *domus* in the context of a decorative and symbolic programme, it is a pictorial copy from the end of the fourth century BC of a second century BC original, probably attributed to Philoxenus of Eretria. In this work Alexander the Great is armed with the sword discussed previously, but we can also note the presence of a second Italic sword lying in the foreground as if it had been lost by a fighter: it appears unsheathed,

Fig. 5: Lion-hunting mosaic executed with the fluvial pebble technique (House of Dionysus, Pella, Macedonia – Greece, fourth century BC). Alexander, to the left of the lion, with the *petasos* typical of the Macedonian imperial family, threatens the beast with the cross-hilted sword in his left hand (symbol of his status) while holding a spear with his right hand; Hephaestion, a general and a friend of Alexander, placed to the right of the lion, is in the act of striking the lion with a *machaira*, but which strangely has a scabbard typical of the Italic sword. (An artistic error or a sign of inferiority of rank compared to Alexander? The *machaira* scabbard was made in the same way but with flexible material, as in the Macedonian tombs of Kallikles and Liso). (*Author's photo, courtesy of the Archaeological Museum of Pella*)

with the blade facing the Persian army (the enemy), with the probable meaning of indicating the direction in which the fighting is taking place, while the scabbard is symbolically turned towards the Macedonian army, with the meaning of protection.

While for Philip II the sword, like the golden diadem, was one of the various objects symbolising royal power and prestige, Alexander the Great saw the weapon as means to 'magically' obtain the strength it represented and that resided in it. In this regard, the episode in which Alexander took possession of the temple of Athena in Troy, by depositing the weapons of the Homeric heroes, testifies that the king was convinced that he was taking on their strength,[30] spreading the concept whereby the sword 'becomes more and more a symbol of an excellence in the broad sense and of a broader ideal of heroism'.[31]

A further interpretative evolution of our sword occurred in Roman times, when 'the archaic *gladius* became the symbol of a myth'. In fact, the image of Alexander the Great was idealised by many ancient authors such as Ptolemy who, to enhance his exploits alongside the Macedonian leader, described him as a conqueror without weakness,[32] or Klitarchos, who 'does not trace the history of a king, but the exploits of a hero',[33] depicting him as a character predestined for glory and the conquest of the known world.

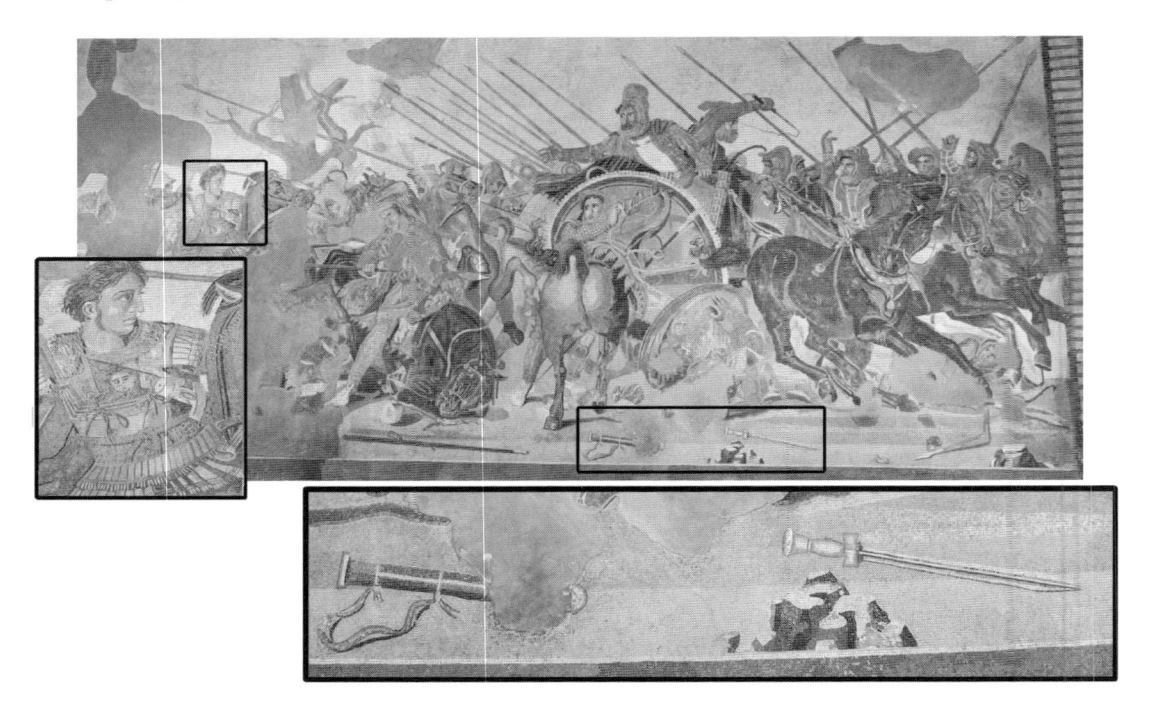

Fig. 6: Mosaic of the Battle of Issus discovered in the House of the Faun in Pompeii, preserved in the National Archaeological Museum of Naples. The mosaic, which alludes to either the Battle of Issus or Gaugamela, is believed to be a copy of the original pictorial by Philoxenus of Eretria, made in Alexandria in the second half of the second century BC and imported to southern Italy. Alexander the Great is armed with a cross-hilted sword; an identical sword can be seen in the foreground on the battlefield to symbolically indicate the enemy army (unsheathed sword) with the 'friendly' one (scabbard) to the left. (*Mosaic from the Domus del Faunus (Pompeii) preserved in the National Archaeological Museum of Naples. Author's photo*)

Later on the Greek and Roman authors[34] took up these sources sublimating the myth, identifying in Alexander the hero who developed monarchical power and who would unify the world through great military enterprises, a great empire made up of different people and cultures, something that, as we know, only Rome would be able to achieve later on. This concept became an obsession for the Roman generals and emperors who constantly pursued this idea in order to be able to emulate and surpass the myth of Alexander the Great, the creator of a universal empire.[35]

We can therefore note that the Central Italic sword, having been used by Alexander the Great, became the symbol *par excellence* of what the conqueror represented in the eyes of the Romans themselves: greatness, conquest and unification of subordinate peoples. It is within this vision that we hypothesise the explanation of the use of the archaic sword in imperial statuary portraiture, treated like a model of a decorative element and useful for sending a message of political propaganda. In fact, like the various elements that characterise a statue, as stated by Cadario, 'from the body of the statue the observer did not expect physical realism but more "objective information" on his public role, career and business'.[36] For this reason, a 'language of statues' was created in which the *status* (attitude), the *imago* (the face), the *esthes* (dress), the *hypodesis* (footwear) and even more the 'attributes'[37] of the statue such as the *patera* (bowl), the scroll, the *lituus* (a kind of trumpet), the sceptre, the globe, the map, the lightning bolt and the weapons (in our case the *gladius*), gave rise to a conventional message that could be read easily by the observer. However, while we know the meaning of some of these statuary messages well, our knowledge is incomplete for others. For example the depiction of a *lorica* evoked the idea of military success, while the 'armed nudity' that was initially linked to the Hellenistic message of sovereignty, progressively delineated the heroic, or divine, condition portrayed during the Augustan period. On the contrary, the meaning of a sword in the hands of imperial figures, which had archaic characteristics that do not correspond to the types of contemporary *gladii* in the sculptural work, has never been defined. Most likely the sword could be interpreted as a symbol of *Pax Augusta*, peace in the empire: being held 'upside down', with the tip pointing backwards and upwards, in a position that is anything but threatening, issuing the message of non-belligerence and employing the sword possessed by Alexander the Great, in relation to the universality of his conquests, possibly symbolising harmony over the whole empire. On the other hand, it was the sword which was defined as *parazonium* and held by Hellenistic officers, as well as by the Roman ones of the Consular Age. In this way we discover how this sword adorns numerous imperial statues that have come down to us.[38]

Characteristically, the statues of the Imperial Period are often portrayed with obvious and sometimes serious 'errors', especially with the *gladius* when compared to the archaeological finds of the seventh–sixth centuries BC. There are two explanations that we can hypothesise from this: the first is that the Roman archaic *gladius* was actually like the one represented in the Imperial statuary, different from the Piceni-Abruzzese finds, while the second is a result of an artistic difficulty in reproducing an object that no longer existed when the statue was made, but remained in the collective imagination solely as a symbolic element. In the latter case, it is hypothesised that

322   The Roman Gladius and the Ancient Fighting Techniques

Fig. 7:
A) Statue from Pompeii of Marcus Claudius Marcellus (42–23 BC), favourite nephew and designated successor of Augustus. He holds the sword with the handle upside down and the point upwards, resting on the forearm, in an attitude that is anything but offensive. As always, the point is typical while both the pommel with a spherical shape and the guard, with the shape of two volutes, appear different from the archaeological reality of the usual *gladius* in that period, which is logical, because they were swords reserved for senior officers, emperors and commanders. It appears very small, because it is not the *gladius* of the troops but that of a superior officer. (*Author's photo, courtesy of the Archaeological Museum of Naples*).
B) Bronze statue of Nero Claudius Drusus Germanicus (15 BC–19 AD), discovered and preserved in Amelia (Terni). A member of the Julio-Claudian dynasty, Germanicus was a valiant general, destined by the will of Augustus himself to ascend the imperial throne. He is represented in a triumphal costume, as a victorious general, covered by the muscled *lorica* (*Statos*) according to the model also used for Augustus in the statue from Prima Porta. The sword, of which the original piece has not been assembled to the statue for technical-conservation reasons and of which there is a copy on the statue, appears very faithful to the archaic finds. It should be noted that, being a military representation, the *gladius* is worn as a combat weapon, linked to its *balteus*, and not, as in the previous representations, upside down, sending a message of peace. (*Author's photo, courtesy of the Archaeological Museum of Amelia, Terni*)

any knowledge of the object and its Italic origin had been lost, while contemporaries remembered that it was owned by Alexander the Great, essentially as an ideal element. But this is not conceivable. Beyond the different forms of archaic *gladius* that may have existed, its continuity in the Roman world of the Consular Age (and throughout all the period) is attested by the Etruscan urns, which show – given the detailed representation of the weapons and armaments depicted – as this *gladius* was used simultaneously with the new types and became the sword of military commanders through a connection with the Hellenistic world. These more than any other embodied the tradition and conservativeness of the *antiqui mores*, and therefore exhibited, even on the battlefield, a sword linked to the ancient traditions of Rome. The strong symbolic charge that characterised this weapon can also found in the Dioscuri, who are frequently represented with it.[39]

Roman portraiture shows them in heroic nudity, as part of a message of '*Concordia*' between peoples, specifically between the Roman people and the Latin League, the sword resting on the forearm with the point facing upwards, in the meaning of the absence of belligerence. The Greek myth of the Dioscuri is intertwined in the Roman world with the Battle of Lake Regillus (496 BC), where the twins, placing themselves at the head of the Roman cavalry, led the Capitoline forces to victory against the Latin people. It is difficult to trace military aid from alleged Greek cavalry during the battle as some authors hypothesise,[40] while reading the *Foedus Cassianum*, the resulting peace treaty, suggests another idea. After this battle there were neither losers nor winners, contrary to what Roman historiography claims, but on the contrary, the bond of friendship and alliance with the Latin League was exalted so as to bring it metaphorically back to that of the divine twins. The Dioscuri, inseparable twins in deeds, affection and destiny, metaphorically represented the Roman and Latin people who, united by a single origin and a common history, were to be projected towards a common destiny.

With the Imperial period the path of idealisation of the cross-hilted sword had ended, first being transformed into a myth and later being the bearer of a message of political propaganda. The message of *Pax Augusta* and of *Concordia* between the people, issued by the imperial authorities and decreed by the Divinities, thus defined the new role of the sword.

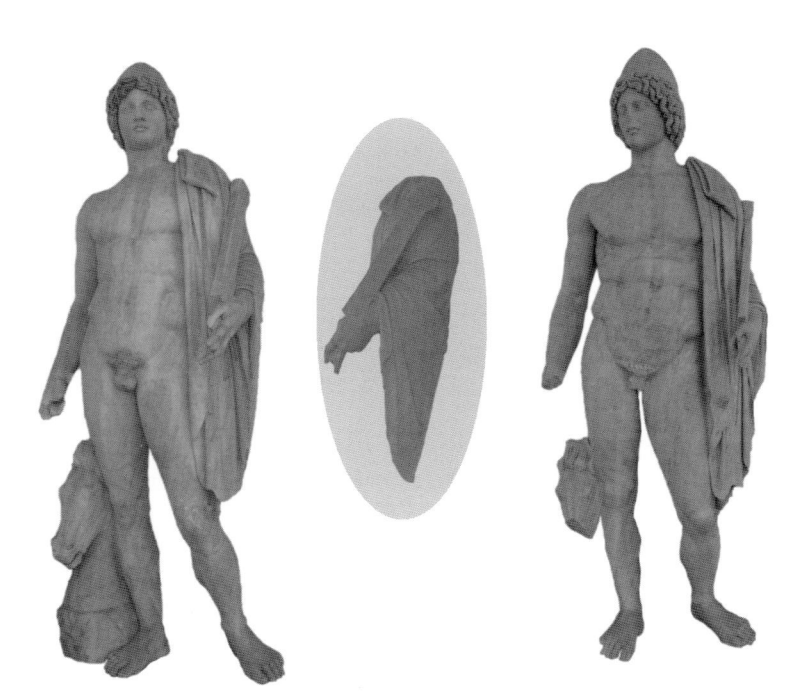

Fig. 8: Relief from the altar dedicated to the nymph Juturna, located near the remains of the temple of the Dioscuri and the House of the Vestals (Hestia) in the place where the Dioscuri were seen giving water to their horses after the battle at Lake Regillus. This is the location where the Twins announced the Roman victory. Rome, second century BC. (*Author's photo*)

V.4 THE *GLADIUS*, A DEMOCRATIC SWORD

The Roman people established a revolutionary relationship with the sword, not only compared to that conceived in the Bronze Age, but also to that of the people who followed them, such as the variegated populations belonging to the age of migration, the Merovingians or the infantrymen of the medieval period in the West.

The great revolution and discontinuity that we find between the Roman people and the others was that the relationship of the *miles* with the sword was of a 'democratic' type, in the sense that it armed almost all of the soldiers who made up the legion, without being a symbol of power and therefore of privilege. In fact, the equipment was always regulated by the state, distributed in such a way that all infantrymen needing a sword in their armament had one.

The concept of heroism, in the sense of exalting the abilities of the individual at the expense of the united army, was strenuously fought against, with rare episodes limited to the Monarchical and High Republican Periods. Torquatus Manlius who, disobeying orders, left the ranks to fight the Tuscan Geminus Macio in a duel, certainly showed his worth because he won the duel, but was punished in an exemplary way because his behaviour had jeopardised the army that based its strength on unity and organisation. The strength of the Roman army was inherent in a planned and well-harmonised combat by the various components in combination, not relegated to individual skills and inventiveness, where each individual infantryman was nothing more than a cog in a larger mechanism, useful to amplify its defensive capacity and its offensive action.

This approach favoured the development of a particular relationship between the soldier and his sword, and as might be expected, a completely different one compared to other peoples and in different eras. The relationship was in some respects detached and free from any spiritual-religious bond. In fact, the salvation and strength of a Roman soldier was based on the functioning of the legion, the efficiency of which depended on personal survival and victory in battle, and not on the prowess with which the infantryman managed to wield his sword. The mystical relationship was therefore not with the *gladius*, but towards what represented the

Fig. 9: A mystical relationship did not develop between the infantryman and his own sword, but with the *Signa* and the *Imagines* which ultimately personified the power of Rome. Legionary Eagle between two *Signa* belonging to the *Legio X*. Silver plate. (*Private collection, author's photo*)

legion and the emperor, such as the *Signa* and the *Imagines* of the imperial family, which, preserved in the chapel of the *castra* (the *aedes* or *sacellum*), were the objects of veneration by the soldiers (Fig. 9).

It is in this context that we can understand how the weapons, even if in the first centuries they were purchased by the *miles* themselves, were supplied by an approved producer, to the extent that the cost was withheld from their *stipendium*.[41]

We can certainly affirm that this 'democratic' distribution of weapons prevented the development of a magical-religious relationship between the soldier and his *gladius*, a relationship that we do find with the *pater familias* of the Bronze Age as well as after the fall of Rome with the knights of the Medieval West.

V.5 THE SYMBOLOGY OF THE *GLADIUS* FOR THE ROMANS

Every commonly-used object, especially if it is widespread, lends itself to allegories, features in allocutions and even becomes a 'sacred means' through which ceremonial rites are celebrated. Although the *gladius* had an important role in the life of the Roman people, since it had always maintained a connotation of practical use, it never acquired any symbolic power. At most it acquired an allegorical meaning of force, action, death and power. The myth to which the cross-hilted sword was subjected to was a different phenomenon to what we are affirming now, as it did not treat the sword so much as an object, but what Alexander the Great represented, an ideal for the Romans. To facilitate understanding of this idea, we have decided to divide this section into subsections.

Oratory
Cicero, as well as Erasmus of Rotterdam, used the saying '*plumbeus gladius*'[42] to define weak arguments in oratory. In fact, a *gladius* made of lead, when hitting an enemy, would have easily bent and been ineffective, unlike an effective sword with steel blade which would have penetrated straight through without bending, becoming lethal.

Military life: warships
The *rostrum*, the bronze ram mounted on the prow of warships, was metaphorically assimilated by the Romans to the action of the *gladius*, since its action, the breaking through of the side of the enemy ship, was based, like our weapon, on the thrust. This is not our personal opinion, but it is what the Romans themselves conceived, so much so that in numerous stone bas-reliefs, representing a beaked ship, we find the

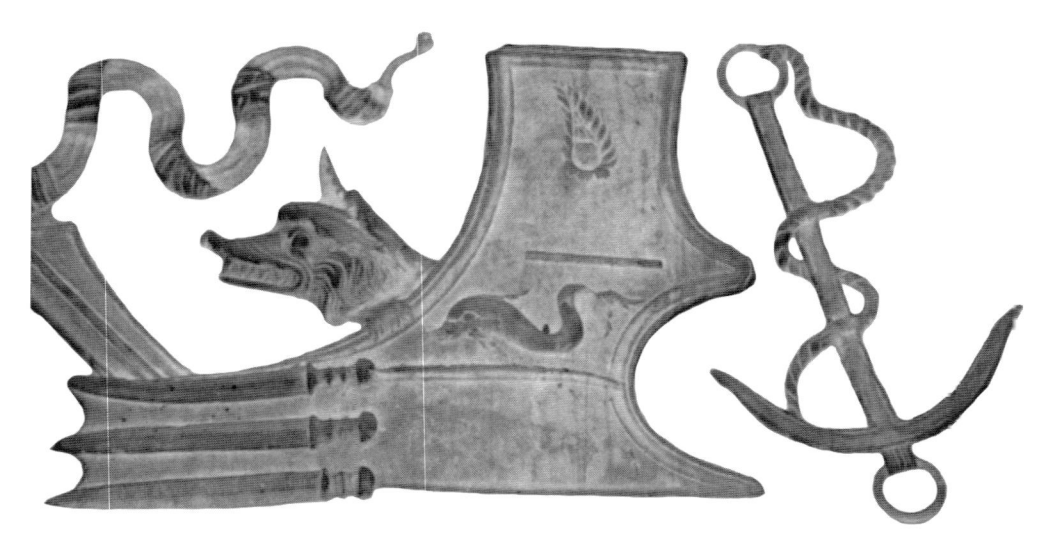

Fig. 10: *Rostrum* of a Roman warship: detail of a marble frieze from the Augustan period with naval emblems in bas-relief. This frieze is in the Capitoline Museums, set in the wall in the highest part of the walls of the 'Sala dei Filosofi'. (*Author's photo*)

sea ram decorated on its sides by some *gladii*, whose points are aligned with that of the *rostrum*.[43]

The metaphorical association between the action of a naval weapon and one adopted by the infantry was not a Roman invention. In fact, the *rostrum* was a means of war used by the Phoenicians long ago and was slavishly copied by the Capitoline people during the First Punic War both from a technical and symbolic point of view.

On a Phoenician *rostrum*, found near the island of Levanto, where the Battle of the Egadi was fought, there is an inscription dedicated to the god Baal[44] which reads: 'And could the spear produce a great damage, Baal furiously pushes this *rostrum* against its target, so that the shield could be weakened hit in the centre.'[45] The meaning that we can conclude, as explained by Garbini, the decipherer of the inscription, is that the Phoenician god could defeat the Roman ship, armed with a spear (metaphorically the *rostrum*), with which he would have had to pierce the enemy shield (the side of the Roman ship) and killing the men behind (the Roman soldiers).

From this inscription we can understand the difference in mentality between the Carthaginian people, who linked the action of the *rostrum* to the divine sphere, to the hand of Baal or to the trident of Poseidon,[46] and the more pragmatic one of the Romans who in their *rostra* avoided any link with the divine, relating them only to their fighting capacity, the thrust given by their main weapon, the *gladius*.

Military life: the army

In descriptions of military activities, we have numerous references to the *gladius* which testify how this weapon permeated the way of thinking and acting of the Roman soldiers. There is an episode occurring during the secession of the Plebs on the Aventine in 449 BC, in which the plebeian tribunate was reminded to maintain its original defensive character and not that of attack, having to use 'a shield rather than a sword',[47] linking the concept of 'action' to the *gladius*.

Julius Caesar affirmed that 'as it rebounded no less to the honour of a good general, to gain the victory by his conduct, than by the sword',[48] referring to the concept that the power of arms alone was not sufficient to gain victory.

Referring to the proclamation of Vitellius as emperor, in the Year of the Four Emperors, there is an anecdote in which the general used this weapon to invest himself with the authority of command, and the fact that it had belonged to Julius Caesar made this action mythical:

> Therefore hardly a month had passed, when the soldiers, regardless of the hour, for it was already evening, hastily took him from his bedroom, just as he was, in his common house-clothes, and hailed him as emperor. Then he was carried about the most populous villages, holding a drawn sword of the Deified Julius, which someone had taken from a shrine of Mars and handed him during the first congratulations.[49]

328   The Roman Gladius and the Ancient Fighting Techniques

It must be considered that with the exception of the earliest centuries, the *gladius* was the fulcrum of the military life of every infantryman, distinguishing him and accompanying him in the various phases of his career, from the oath of loyalty to his rising through the ranks, and in many cases, to his death.

Ammianus Marcellinus, in describing the solemn promise that Augustus Julian asked his soldiers to make before waging war on Constantius, narrates that the oath hinged on the threat made with his own *gladius*:

> And when all had been bidden to take the usual oath of allegiance, aiming their swords at their throats, they swore in set terms under pain of dire execrations, that they would endure all hazards for him, to the extent of pouring out their life-blood, if necessity required; their officers and all the emperor's closest advisers followed their example, and pledged loyalty with like ceremony.[50]

An oath under threat was also adopted by Scipio to prevent the young nobles from leaving Italy at a critical moment in the war against Hannibal: 'held his drawn sword over the heads of the conspirators and vowing that he would treat as a public enemy whoever should not swear at his dictation, compelled them all to bind themselves with an oath not to abandon Italy … '[51]

But this use of the sword to make a solemn promise was not intended only as a means of compulsion, but also as an exaltation of strength, as when Primipilus Marcus Flavoleius in inciting the soldiers 'he held up his sword and took the oath traditional among the Romans … '.[52]

Fig. 11: The military folding chair (*Sella Castrensis*), having to accommodate a solider with his *gladius*, had a lateral loop in the seat, such as to allow the weapon to be worn. This loop was not necessary in the *Sella Curulis*, which was for the high magistrates in *Toga Praetexta*, who therefore did not carry the *gladius*. (*Photo and drawing by the author*)

But if the beginning of a *miles*'s service took place under the protection of a *gladius*, 'a warrior's death' was considered glorious if it occurred 'due to a barbarian sword'[53] or through one's *gladius*, since in the case of a military defeat suicide was the only way to spare the *Familia* dishonour, as Brutus did, aware of the defeat at Philippi,[54] or Varus, after the defeat at Teutoburg.[55]

Thus, a sword could decree both the beginning of a military career and the honourable end of a soldier, since it essentially defined his military *auctoritas*. It represented the virile strength of a Roman soldier and this was perceived in the same way a man brags about his sexual member. It is in this perspective that the loss of a weapon or the punishment inflicted through the deprivation of the scabbard should be understood, because the humiliation felt by a Roman soldier on those occasions can be compared today to being naked in public and humiliated for our dishonourable state.

The strong bond of the soldier to his *gladius* is found when Frontinus tell that 'Marcus, son of Cato the Censor, in a certain battle fell off his horse, which had stumbled. Cato picked himself up, but noticing that his sword had slipped out of its scabbard and fearing disgrace, went back among the enemy, and though he received a number of wounds, finally recovered his sword and made his way back to his comrades.'[56] But even more unequivocally we find these considerations in Livy when he describes a punishment imposed on some soldiers by the consul Marcus Claudius Marcellus, who 'To the cohorts which had lost their standards he ordered barley to be issued, and as for the centurions of the maniples whose standards had been lost, he made them stand aside with drawn swords and no belts; and he ordered that on the morrow they should all, infantry and cavalry, present themselves under arms.'[57]

As a final example to emphasise the meaning of authority and power evoked by the *gladius*, we report our thesis on the different shape of the *Sella Curulis* compared to that of the *Castrensis*, the folding seats of the highest offices of the state, respectively civil and military. While the symbol of power of a major magistrate was given by the *fasces* and the *toga praetexta*, elements that did not hinder the use of the *Sella Curulis*, whose seat was rectangular in shape, which would not allow the accommodation of a military officer girded with his symbol of power represented by the *gladius*. The sword did not allow without difficulty the act of sitting, and this was the reason why in the *Sella Castrensis* the seat was modified with a gap in one side, useful for allowing the *gladius* to be housed whilst worn.

Exceptional events

That the *gladius* was associated with the concept of 'military power' is confirmed by Livy when, reporting a series of evil omens that struck Rome during the Second Punic War, described that 'in Gaul a wolf had snatched a sentry's sword from its scabbard and run off with it'.[58] To the Romans a *gladius* that was stolen from its scabbard by a wild animal symbolised Hannibal (the wolf) who had the ability to remove military strength from the Romans (the *gladius*). We recall the other exceptional events that occurred at the same time, such as lightning striking the Temple of Hope in the Forum of Rome or how stones had rained in the Picenum. All these facts, premonitions of disastrous events, required for their expiation, the purification of the city, the immolation of victims, offerings of gold and a bronze statue to the gods as well as a *lectisternium* (a sacred banquet), prayers and votive offerings.

The *gladius* as an instrument of punishment and execution

The *gladius* was also an instrument of capital punishment, as Vegetius explains, that 'But if extreme necessity urges the medicine of the sword [*ferri medicinam*], it is just to follow ancestral custom and punish the ringleaders of crimes, so that fear extends to all, but punishment to few.'[59] While during the Monarchical and Republican Period the ordinary tool for beheading was the axe, present in the *fasces*, during the Empire it was the *gladius*. In the latter period, only the emperor, or the governors of the provinces, could issue the death sentence, which was defined as *ius gladii*, literally 'the right of the sword', executed with the formula *gladio animadverti placet*,[60] meaning 'give him the coup de grace with the *gladius*'.

In the Etruscan Sanctuary of Fucoli, in Chianciano Terme (province of Siena – Tuscany), a ritual axe from the Hellenistic period was discovered, having a shape with a head set back from the profile of the handle, which is typical of those of the seventh century BC used for human and animal sacrifices.[61] What is peculiar about this religious or judicial instrument is the gold damascened decoration on the blade, which represents the Monarchical *gladius*. Even if the damascened representation is not complete (the sword's handle is partially missing), the weapon as a whole is quite recognisable, with the blade aligned with that of the axe. The latter in its archaic form and the sword in its contemporary value, co-present in the same object, could have had the meaning of a function that can be superimposed on the two weapons, namely that of both being sacrificial weapons. The possibility that this had been used for carrying out the death penalty is a probable hypothesis. In 297 BC, the consul Quintus Fabius Maximus Rullianus, 'in the case of two legions which had given way before the foe … chose men by lot and beheaded them in the sight of their comrades'.[62] The position of the depiction of *gladius* on the axe would also suggest that the sword blow was not

Fig. 12: Ritual axe found in the Etruscan Sanctuary of Fucoli, Chianciano (Siena, Tuscany) of the Hellenistic period but with the same archaic shape of axes of the seventh century BC. The blade of the axe shows a cross-hilted sword in gilded damascening, referring to a superimposed function of the blade, probably linked to the death penalty. (*Author's drawing*)

Fig. 13: Martyrdom of Achilleus (fourth century AD), a small column carved in marble, found in the Basilica of AghiosNereus and Achilleus, representing the martyr with his hands tied, while the executioner (*speculator*) raises his sword to behead him. Rome, Catacombs of Domitilla. (*Author's photo*)

a cutting one, as in the axe blow or in the Medieval executions in which the head was cut off, but pointed, probably through a blow that went to penetrate the clavicular dimple. This method would seem to be contradicted by the *Martyrium Lugdunensium*, describing the persecution of Christians in the cities of Lyon and Vienne around 177 AD, in which the execution was by cutting off the head.

Relating to the death sentence, there is an anecdote about Caligula, told by Suetonius, who tells that the emperor kept two notebooks 'with different titles, one called "The Sword" and the other "The Dagger", and both containing the names and marks of identification of those whom he had doomed to death'.[63] Probably the distinction was between those destined for a public, legal punishment, marked in the list of the sword, compared to those to be eliminated by assassins, in the list of the dagger.

Justinian's codes give us an indication of a certain number of crimes and offenders that were punished with the sword, such as adultery,[64] acts of immorality against nature,[65] assassins,[66] poisoners,[67] public officials who exercised extortion,[68] the *subscribendarius* and the *optio* accomplices of cheating people, those who were awarded the *Annona* without having the right to it,[69] secretaries who falsified certificates,[70] deserters,[71] those who consulted the deities,[72] those who offered sacrifices to false gods[73] and the Christians who refused to practise the cult and the rites of the official religion,[74] defamers,[75] informers,[76] those who sold a free man as a slave,[77] the *plagiarii* (those who stole a slave or enslaved a freedman or a free man)[78] etc

The *damnatio ad gladium*, on the other hand, was a death sentence that did not take place at the hands of an executioner, but through a combat as a gladiator. Those who were condemned to this fate were armed with a weapon and forced to fight to the death; whoever survived was forced to continue to clash with another, and so on until there was only one criminal left who was then executed. We can conclude that the death penalty issued with the *ius gladii* was a 'dignified death' to which only free men, the *honestiores*, were sentenced, since all the others, the *humiliores*, low-ranking citizens and slaves, were punished in a far more atrocious way, framed in the *summa supplicia*.[79] In fact, during the aforementioned martyrdom of Lyons, the governor 'had consecrated to beheading those of them who were in possession of Roman citizenship, while the others were cast out to wild beasts',[80] and also the Apostle Paul, as a Roman citizen, suffered beheading in Rome, at the *Aquæ Salviæ* along the Via Laurentina, unlike the other proto-martyrs who were not Roman citizens.[81]

V.6 THE SYMBOLISM OF THE SWORD AFTER THE FALL OF THE ROMAN EMPIRE

The fall of the Roman Empire coincided with the affirmation of the Christian religion and the disintegration of both civil and military organisation in the West, in a climate of extreme economic and social uncertainty. The *gladius*, which until that moment had assumed a meaning linked to its ability as an efficient, not sacred, weapon, gradually took on a different meaning, since over time it was idolized acquiring a symbolic charge, historically not commonly found in other weapons.

By analysing the causes of these changes better, we can see that in the Late Empire the Roman army became more and more composed of barbarian elements that fought for pay, rather than in a spirit of devotion to the state, creating the basis for the constitution of the mercenary militia typical of the medieval period. The phenomenon of mercenaries arose from the inability of urban centres to defend themselves and from the attitude of the barbarian populations to warrior practices. These companies were characterised by the heterogeneity of the elements that made them up and by their mobility, aimed at finding new economic resources for self-sustenance, for which they offered military protection or looted those centres that had refused to employ them.

In the West the salvation of the individual militiaman and of the group was no longer linked to an imperial organisation on which the pay, armament and security of the entire army depended, but to the commander who led the army, as well as to the possibilities of individuals to arm themselves. Gradually a sort of elite was created based on fighting ability, where the most skilled and charismatic ones also became richer and therefore with greater possibilities to equip themselves with better weapons, decorated in an artistic and valuable way. In this context, the ostentation of a weapon became a symbol of power and privilege, a very important phenomenon since the aggregation of the group was based on strength and valour.

Thus, we can see how the sword became a means of defining the rites of passage within society among the Germans, becoming the symbol of social freedom: in fact, it was given to the young man when he came of age, as well as becoming a gift of exchange between spouses.[82] Attila gained command of the Huns when he was given a sword found by a shepherd which he attributed to Mars and claimed as a heavenly favour.

The sword therefore, in addition to its meaning linked to its lethal capacity, gradually took on a mystical meaning, since it allowed the salvation of its owner. With this historical premise we can understand Ammianus Marcellinus when he reports that among the Alans, 'No temple or sacred place is to be seen in their country, not even a hut thatched with straw can be discerned anywhere, but after the manner of barbarians a naked sword is fixed in the ground and they reverently worship it as their god of war, the presiding deity of those lands over which they range'.[83] The sword stuck in the ground thus became an object of devotion, as we can also find among other peoples, such as the Scythians, unable to form an abstract idea of the divinity, so they worshipped the god of war symbolised by an iron scimitar,[84] as well as in Caucasian and Germanic folklore (during the oath ritual),[85] or also in the legend of King Arthur and that of San Galgano.[86]

The link between military and religious symbolism became stronger and stronger, also favoured by the shape of the medieval sword which, with its pronounced guard, was easily associated with a cross. Following this connection, in the Sacred Scriptures the sword became a symbol of the Lord's strength, justice and vengeance: St. Paul invites us to take 'the sword of the Spirit, which is the word of God'[87] while the Christ of the Apocalypse is represented radiant as the sun with a *gladius* coming out of his mouth. In this case the weapon takes on the role of a symbol of purifying fire and illuminating truth as a lightning bolt. This significant representation can be found in various churches, including the Bourges Portal and in many miniatures.[88]

In medieval traditions, the sword that belongs to Christian knights and heroes takes on the value of a noble weapon, favouring the development of a personal relationship such that the fighter will give his sword a mythical name, a fact completely foreign to the Roman mentality. Thus from historical traditions, as from the *Chansons de geste*,[89] we find that 'Excalibur'[90] was the sword of King Arthur, 'Altachiara', also called the 'Gioiosa', was in the possession of Charlemagne, as 'Gioiosa' was also the sword of Lancelot, while 'Durendal'[91] was that of Roland, the paladin of Charlemagne.

The *gladius*, as a 'democratic' weapon in an organised combat, had by now ceased to exist in the Western world, because heroic combat, in which the sword had acquired a symbolic value, had (once again) taken over, and an empathy between the knight and his blade developed that we could define a mystical, an inconceivable fact for the Roman soldier. In the East, where the Empire did not collapse, the existence of an organised Roman army lasted at least until the eleventh century. Swords (*spathia*) were supplied to infantrymen and horsemen mainly by the state, and only with the advent of mercenaries and of the feudal Pronoia also in Byzantium, the bond with the sword was intensified as a mystical element of worship and divine protection in battle.

In summary, the fall of the Roman Empire in the West also had consequences for the *gladius* and provoked its end, both from the ideological and military point of view, as a democratic weapon of an organised community for the purposes of war. Nevertheless, throughout the course of the Middle Ages, the word mainly used to define the sword was *gladius*, in memory of the historical importance that this weapon had for the peoples who had been within the orbit of the *Res Publica Romana*.

Conclusion

When the Emperor Hadrian asked what the *gladius* was, the philosopher Epictetus replied that it was the '*Regimen castrorum*', 'the leader of the military camps'.[1] For a sword to be considered as the point of reference for all soldiers, implies a great cultural revolution since it involves an aggregation of the armed forces focusing on the 'means' of combat, and consequently on its 'method' of use.

In the past, the way of conceiving of the sword was different and this was due to the strong mystical-religious value to which it rose, since the blade is the means for a man to take the life of another human being. The sacredness of the object is also underlined by the fact that for example in the Bible, the sword is mentioned more than 500 times,[2] becoming a symbol of the Lord's strength, justice and vengeance. We can therefore understand how this object, more than any other, has been affected by the cultural influences of the people who have used it, becoming a 'litmus test' of the habits and the way of thinking for the people who have based their military actions on it.

In many phases of human history, the possession of a sword was limited to the elites, since being a precious object that required training, it excluded most of the population who lived on lesser resources. This explains why the sword was usually wielded by a 'hero' whose actions were considered almost superhuman, who in various historical periods assumed the connotation of the *pater familias*, Alexander the Great, the German warriors or medieval knights, making the weapon a symbol of strength and power.

But for the Roman people the *gladius* was never connected to religion and since the most archaic times it armed all of the infantry of a legion, thus assuming a 'democratic' status, which culturally we can define as a modern vision of a way for conceiving of war, an innovation which, however, was lost with the fall of the Empire, at least in the West.

The practical essence of the *gladius* as a military weapon is well indicated by Seneca when he stated that 'You will speak of a sword as good [*gladius bonus*] not when its sword-belt is of gold, or its scabbard studded with gems, but when its edge is fine for cutting and its point will pierce any armour'.[3] To be efficient the *gladius* had to have the right qualities such as being light (*levis*)[4] and short, to allow the soldier to be agile during combat, and to have a point on which its deadly action was based on. All of this was associated with a simple suspension system, designed to be less awkward during everyday life and be of least hindrance during action. These characteristics, summarised in a few lines, were the result of an evolutionary process that began before the birth of Rome among the Apennine peoples of central Italy and lasted throughout the history of the Roman Empire. Since the seventh century BC, the cross-hilted sword was widespread in the Picene warrior burials and its presence spread throughout central Italy, differing from the swords present in the north of the peninsula, characterised by a longer blade, and from those in the south, which were shorter and similar to daggers. This sword, which draws its origins from the Safine culture, will be the Monarchical *gladius*, which in the course of its history will be influenced by both Celtic and other populations.

The affirmation of this object by the Roman people will be favoured by their way of thinking, which led them disdain instinctive fights, such as the Celtic way based on slashing strikes, and to prefer the efficiency of sharp and cutting blows instead (*punctimcaesim que condiscant*).[5]

But this way of fighting required training as the soldier had to learn to strike without exposing himself to harm (*ne qua parte ipse pateret ad plagam*)[6] in an organised formation in which the 'soldiers, closely packed and in fully-manned lines stood their ground fast and firm, like towers and renewed the battle with greater vigour; and being intent upon avoiding wounds, they protected themselves like murmillos, and with drawn swords pierced the enemy's sides, left bare by their frenzied rage'.[7] But what Ammianus described was nothing more than the culmination of a slow and progressive evolution that began with the birth of Rome, where the military organisation was nothing more than a reflection of the archaic social and political structure of the city.

The Romulean battle-array was created by distinguishing the armed men into three age groups and therefore according to their military ability, constituting three *acies*, aimed at containing the 'swarm' attacks of those people who did not yet have an organised social structure. The most widespread weapon among the infantrymen was the spear, but the actual combat centred around the *gladius*, which was supplied to all of the *principes* and which in this period still coexisted with the Italic cross-hilted sword and possibly with some ancestral bronze swords. At the height of the Monarchical Period, the clash with the Etruscan hoplite armies condemned these three Romulean *acies* to failure. The Romans were able to prevail over the fearsome Tyrrhenians only by evolving their own battle array, which was made much deeper, and by moving the soldiers who were equipped with complete panoply to the front line, thus making it possible to contain the Etruscan force. But the combat formation of the Capitoline army was not just a passive propulsion made up of shields and spears, since it was based on the *gladius* with which all the infantry of the various Servian classes were now equipped. With the passage of time, new enemies and different combat modes emerged in the Consular Age, which were a stimulus for further evolution. The guerrilla warfare of the Samnites, the fury of the Celts and the cunning of Hannibal based on 'disrespect' for Italic military traditions, led to the front of the legions becoming progressively leaner which, now based on the *ordo* and no longer on the *acies*, was now better able to adapt to the course of the battle. The development was completed towards the end

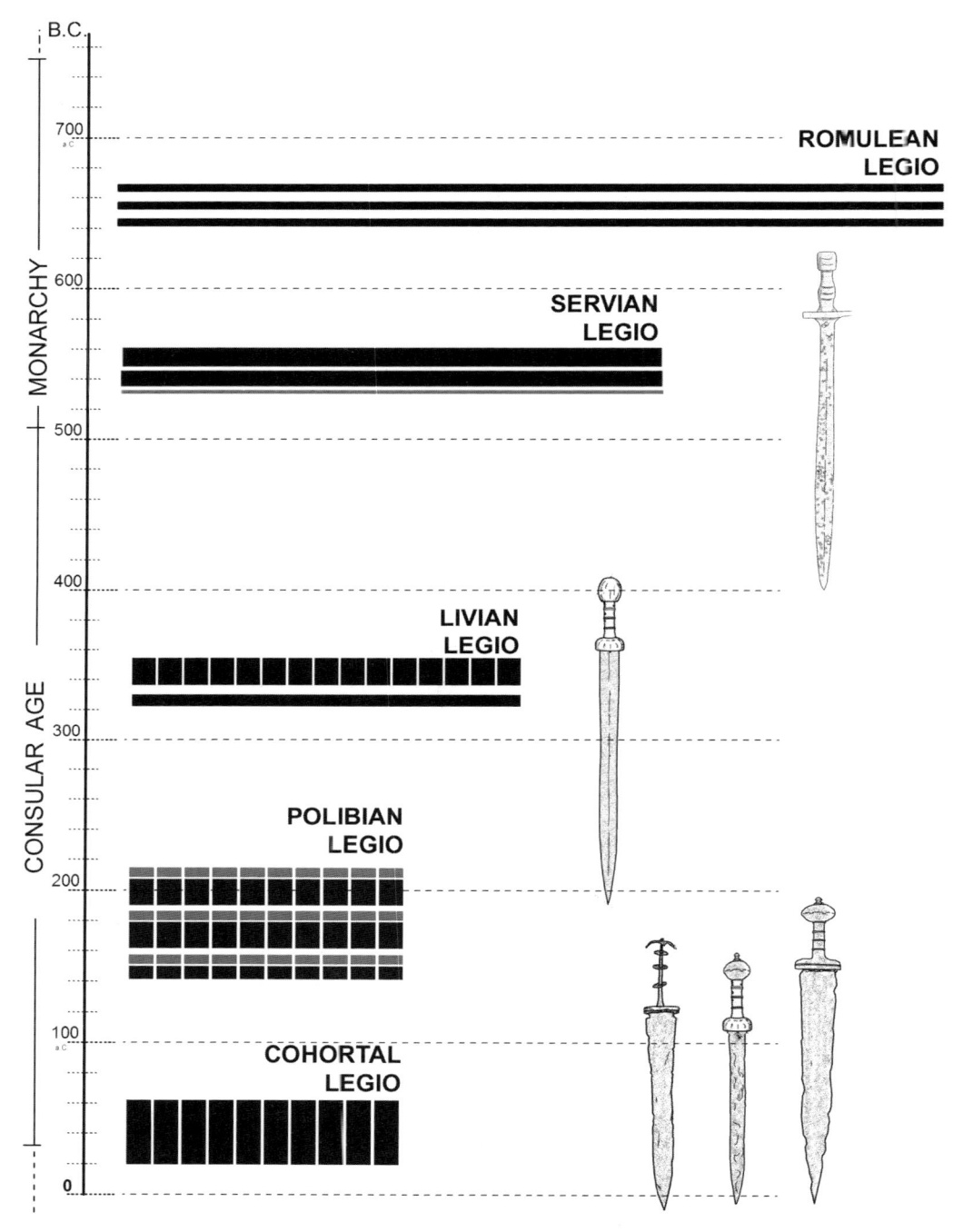

336 The Roman Gladius and the Ancient Fighting Techniques

Diagram 1: Overview of the evolution throughout the period examined in this book of the various types of legions and *gladii*. Note how, with the passage of time, the formations progressively lose their width but at the same time aim at a greater depth of the battle array.

of the Consular Age with the creation of the cohorts, autonomous fractions of the legion that could be used to manage the progress of the battle in various situations, including attack and defence, while the conflict was in full swing. The changes in the way of conceiving the military battle array were the cause of important modifications to the *gladius* itself, including the important influence of the Celtic people settled in the central-Italic territories. The blade remained substantially unchanged in shape and size, but an important innovation in the form of the barrel shank appears, accompanied by the practical and ergonomic tripartite handle. The elaborate and typical handle of the Monarchial sword was replaced by a handle that was easier to construct, making it more suited to mass production. In the final part of the Consular Age another radical change took place, due to the fact that the Romans also had to fight against each other in the context of the Civil Wars. Consequently, we see types of *gladius* more suitable for this tighter, very close-quarters combat style appear, with the difference of the blade being formed with a thrusting point, when compared to the previous models. In fact, the main feature is that the weapons were particularly short, easy to handle in very confined spaces. However, it should be noted that in the latter period the short

Fig. 1: Precision and organisation, which turned out to be the winning force of the army, was a prerogative of the Roman mentality, as can be seen in the construction of a landfill. *Mons Testaceus* is a 36m-high landfill from the Imperial era, located at the Emporium, the ancient river port of Rome. The artificial hill is made up of fragments of amphorae, essentially from oil-production, where the food residues that impregnated the terracotta made them not reusable, due to the decomposition processes that caused a bad smell. For this reason, most of the amphorae, after being emptied of their contents, were broken, piled up and 'disinfected' with lime to limit the release of unpleasant odours. Here is the example of the 'Monte dei Cocci' (current name of the ancient landfill) to better understand the organisational mind of the Roman people, applied to a landfill. (*Author's photo*)

types co-exist with specimens of the most varied shapes and sizes, in addition to those typical of previous centuries, a fact that can probably be explained by the need to adapt the functionality of the weapon to the many types of combat, connected to the many corresponding types of enemies of the first century BC.

We can therefore say with a certain confidence that, although the Roman combat became more and more articulated over time, it was always based on an orderly deployment and with fencing at the heart, characterised by 'organisation' and 'technique', which for the Capitoline people was a *modus cogitandi*. We find this approach on a civil level not only in the institution of the *Ius* (law) but also in the various technical, cadastral, metrological and topographical aspects, as well as, in the religious sphere, in the context of the *Cultus Deorum* (the cult of the gods) consisting of scrupulous cultic practices.[8] Everything in Roman daily life had to be planned and as a symbol of this vision we have reported the evidence of the *Mons Testaceum* (called the 'Testaccio' by modern Romans), an artificial hill in the centre of Rome, which is nothing more than a landfill. It is the most explicit example of the efficient Roman way of thinking, which in order to eliminate the no longer usable amphorae, they juxtaposed the fragments with 'maniacal precision' in order to optimise the space occupied.

The *gladius* proved to be a profoundly Italic weapon, where the use of the epithet *Hispaniensis* (referring to those who lived in the Iberian territory, but who were of Roman origin and culture) was only to define an attribute of quality. A historical reference that has been given more importance by modern authors than by the ancient ones which, when misinterpreted by attributing a Hispanic origin to the weapon, involves denying much of its essence and culture. What emerges at the end of our study is ultimately what we already said in the introduction, namely the history of a people that coincides with that of its sword. The *gladius* is probably one of the artefacts that more than anything else reflects the Roman mentality since its history follows the same path of conceiving the life and institutions of the people, including the art of waging war.

Notes

Introduction

1. The term *gladius* is used mostly in prose and not in poetic forms (a case is mentioned in Ennius, one in Ovid, one in the *De Bello Civili* of Lucan as can be seen in the entry 'Gladius' in *Thesaurus Linguae Latinae* vol. VI 2, p. 2011, lin. 48 –p. 2028, lin. 29, Imprimatur 5. XI.30, author Koch). On the contrary *ensis* as shown in *Thesaurus Linguae Latinae*, vol. V 2, p. 608, lin. 20 – p. 611, lin. 13, imprimatur 23. VI. 34, author Hörmann is '*voxferepoetarum* …' ('almost exclusive voice of the poets'). For *mucro* the situation is more complex because it has many meanings, used both in prose but above all in poetry. In prose, *mucro* is the technical word for the point of the *gladius*. In rhetoric it is used with the meaning of 'tip' but naturally lends itself to a figurative use, estranged and poetic: in fact there are many poets cited: Ennius (archaic), Lucretius, Virgil, Propertius, Ovid (classics), Dracontius (late antiquity) in *Thesaurus Linguae Latinae*, vol. VIII, p. 1555, lin. 55 – p. 1556, lin. 82, imprimatur 6. XII. 63, author van den Hout – B).
2. The Greek names related to the definition of the sword are: Ἀκινάκης, straight short sword, used by the Easterners (*Akinakes*); Ἀορ, word used by the poets, synonymous with ξίφος; Κοπίς, curved sabre, very often impossible to distinguish from the μάχαιρα; Μάχαιρα, curved sabre in Homer and the classical authors distinguished from the ξίφος, but both words became synonymous, especially in Polybius; Ξίφος, straight sword, usually double-edged; this is the classic sword of the Greeks; Ξιφομάχαιρα, long sword before *Esychius*; Ξυήλη, short Spartan sword; Σπαθη, the larger part of the sword, then used improperly to indicate a larger sword; Φάσγανον, dagger, then sword in Homer and Sophocles (from *Dictionnaire des Antiques Grecques et Romaines de Daremberg et Saglio*, Université Toulouse, Jean Jaurès, col. 1600–1601).
3. Wilhelm Corssen, philologist (1820–75). He studied the Italic languages (*De Volscorum lingua*, 1858); and is still important for many parts of his work (1868–70) on pronunciation, vocalising and accentuation of Latin, while the part on the Etruscan language (1873–5) has been superseded.
4. Pietro Ottorino Pianigiani (1845–1926) was a magistrate of the Kingdom of Italy and an important Italian linguist, particularly famous for his studies of etymology and philology. He was the author of the *Vocabolario Etimologicodella Lingua Italia*, one of the most celebrated and best-known etymological dictionaries of the Italian language, first published in 1907.
5. Varro, *De Lingua Latina*, V, 16.
6. Isidore of Seville, *Etimologie o origini*, XVIII, 6, 1.
7. Pliny the Elder, *Naturalis Historia*, XXI, 108.
8. Ibid., XXXII, Chapter 15.
9. Armando Battiato, 'Contributo all'identificazione degli organismi acquatici riportati nel libro IX del *Naturalis historia* di Plinio il Vecchio', pp. 10–60.

Chapter 1: The Archaic Period

1. Eleonora Fioroni, *Il mondo degli oggetti*, p. 11.
2. Gimbutas, *La civiltà della dea, il mondo dell'antica Europa*, vol. 2 Stampa alternativa/nuovi equilibri, p. 150. The word Kurgan literally means 'tumulus', used by the author to indicate the culture of the semi-nomadic shepherds who built grave mounds in the shape of a rounded hill.
3. Villar, *Gli indoeuropei e le origini dell'Europa*, p. 52.
4. These notions derive mainly from the archaeological studies of Marija Gimbutas, but have been essentially confirmed by many other scholars (James Patrick Mallory, *In Search of the Indo-Europeans*,

New York: Thames and Hudson, 1989) and by recent genetic studies applied to various populations. From the DNA studies of analysing human evolution, based on mitochondrial DNA, which is transmitted only by the mother, and on the Y chromosome, transmitted only by the father, it can be seen how the Kurgan peoples, carriers of the Y-DNA R1a haplogroup, had a contact which then evolved into a clash/migration with the people carrying the Y-DNA R1b (Natalie Myres, 'A major Y-chromosome haplogroup R1b Holocene effect in Central and Western Europe', *European Journal of Human Genetics*, doi: 10.1038 / ejhg.2010.146) (J. Chiaroni, P. Underhill, L.L. Cavalli-Sforza 'Y chromosome diversity, human expansion, drift and cultural evolution', *Proceedings of the National Academy of Sciences of the United States of America* 106 (48): 20174: 20179). This migration of the population with the haplogroup Y-DNA R1b was the basis of the widespread colonisation of the Italic territory, essentially in its U152 clade (David K. Faux, 'Y-Chromosome Marker S28 / U152 Haplogroup R-U152' available at https://www.davidkfaux.org/R1b1c10_Resources.pdf).

5. Phase 1: around 4300–4000 BC it was deduced that there was a great migration from the steppes of southern Russia (area of the lower course of the Volga river) which infiltrated the territory to the west of the Black Sea until it reached the Danubian and Balkan area.
Phase 2: The second wave came from the steppes of southern Russia towards Transcaucasia, Iran and part of Anatolia and caused a second infiltration in Central Europe (3500 BC).
Phase 3: The third wave of the Kurgan people originated after 3000 BC from southern Russia and consisted of such a massive invasion as to induce drastic changes in ethnic groups, favouring the bases of the birth of the Indo-European people, being characterised by the movement towards the Aegean and the Adriatic Sea.

6. As per the evidence presented in the article by Francesco Fedele 'La società dell'età del Rame nell' area alpina e prealpina', after the second half of the fourth millennium, numerous evidences of human presence existed, among which the find of the man of Tisenjoch ('Otzi') is particularly important.

7. Villar, *Gli indoeuropei e le origini dell'Europa*, p. 481.

8. To understand the importance of weapons in this society, see Gimbutas, *La civiltà della dea: il mondo dell'antica Europa'* vol. 2, p. 198, who defines it as 'bellicose, exogamic, patriarchal, patrilineal and patrilocal, with a strong clan and hierarchical organisation, which gives prominence to the warrior class'.

9. In the millennial history of man, only by the Roman people first and in modern times later will be realised a cultural unification of peoples and different ethnic groups who populated and live in this territory.

10. Transhumance was a pastoral practice in many Italian regions until the last century, which consisted of a 'pastoralism transmigrating with the seasons', along the sheep tracks, i.e. the shepherds' roads. The flocks were moved to the coastal regions in the winter and to the mountainous areas in the summer season to enjoy the best climate and pastures.

11. Tagliamonte, *I figli di Marte*, pp. 55–66.

12. From Villar, *Gli indoeuropei e le origini dell'Europa*, p. 480: 'The fascinating thing is the archaeologist thinking that it coincides with the plan of a Roman camp, offering this as proof that the inhabitants of the Terremare are the ancestors of the Romans, who would have begun their penetration towards the south starting from the fourteenth century BC.'

13. Cardarelli, 'Terremare: l'organizzazione sociale e politica delle comunità', pp. 653–60; Cremaschi, 'Foreste, terre coltivate e acqua. L'originalità del progetto terramaricolo', pp. 34–44.

14. The term 'Apennine civilisation' was used by U. Rellini for the first time to distinguish the populations of central and southern Italy from the Terremare civilisation. In fact, at an earlier stage, the school of L. Pigorini attributed to the Terramare civilisation the diffusion of the Indo-European culture from north to south in the Italian peninsula.

15. As Anna Maria Bietti Sestieri (*l'Italia nell'eta' del bronzo e del ferro*, p. 128) says 'The Apennines are not a barrier, but rather the main linking factor and element of relative cultural homogeneity'.

16. Herodotus, *The Histories*, I, 94 and IV, 49.

17. Pliny the Elder, *Naturalis Historia*, 3, 112.

18. A correct classification of the facies populating the Italian peninsula, together with their evolution and extinction, is a subject that is still impervious and a source of contradictions among the numerous scholars who have been involved with the study. For the understanding of the Bronze Age we relied on the 'ethno-linguistic' definitions of Paleo-Umbrian, Safine and Umbrian-Safine which, although not accepted by the specialists in the field, allow the average reader to have a good understanding of the historical framework. This exposition has been based upon Ancillotti and Cerri, *Le tavole di Gubbio e la civiltà degli Umbri*.
19. Pliny the Elder, *Naturalis Historia*, 3, 50.
20. Herodotus, *The Histories*, I, 94, 6–7.
21. Didier Marcotte, *Géographes grecs. Tome 1: Introduction générale. Ps.-Scymnos, Circuit de la terre*. Texte établi et traduit par D.M (Paris: Les Belles Lettres, 2000, Collection des universités de France, seerie grecque 203), p. 221.
22. Dionysius of Halicarnassus, *Roman Antiquities*, I, 27.
23. Cazzella et al., 'Riunione Scientifica; 40, Istituto italiano di preistoria e protostoria', p. 805
24. Sestieri, *L'Italia nell'età del bronzo e del ferro*, p. 153.
25. Strabo, *Geographica*, V, 2,1 and V, 3,4.
26. Our references to the *Latium Vetus*, unless otherwise mentioned, have been based upon Anna Maria Bietti Sestieri, 'L'Italia nell'età del bronzo e del ferro'. Ordinary Professor of European Proto-History at the University of Salento, awarded the 'Europa Prize' by the Prehistoric Society in 1996, she is presently the most quoted scholar of this historical-geographical reality, which she describes meticulously starting from the archaeological data known today in her treatise.
27. Sestieri, 'Archeologia della morte fra età del bronzo ed età del ferro in Italia'.
28. The importance of Ficana, as a rival of Rome for the ford of the Tiber, is witnessed by its destruction in the seventh century BC by Ancus Martius (Dionysius of Halicarnassus, *Roman Antiquities*, III, 38); when repopulated two years later by the Latin people, it was destroyed, the walls demolished, the buildings burnt and the population deported to the Aventine Hill.
29. Claudia Cecamore, 'Il santuario di Iuppiter Latiaris sul monte Cavo: spunti e materiali dai vecchi scavi'.
30. The Tiber river became a *limes*, a boundary between the Etruscan and Latin people, a Latin term (*rivals*) that outlines this situation of contrast, since the word indicates people who lived on the banks of the same river between whom conflicts easily arose. From the genetic-etymological vocabulary of the Italian language of Giovanni B. Bolza.
31. Torelli, *La forza della tradizione*, p. 161.
32. Varro, *De re rustica*, 2.10.3.
33. This consideration is based upon the analysis of the outfits from the male burials of the Latium III stage, the one closest to the one analysed here, since as cremation was widespread during this period, we cannot otherwise have accurate information.
34. A limitation of the ancient Roman documents is that they date back no later than the third century BC, since many of them were handed down orally and the records of public interest of the priestly college of the *pontifices*, kept in the *Regia*, were partially destroyed by a fire caused by the Celtic attack in 390 BC. The lost parts were recompiled by the *Pontifex Maximus* P. Mucius Scevola around 130 BC, and reused by Latin historians, although modern scholars criticise the objectivity of these recompilations, mainly aimed at enhancing some events or characters or backdating events to increase their authority. We consider it correct, beyond any modern criticism, to stick as closely as possible to the events narrated in antiquity which, however 'not perfectly congruous', we consider more reliable than many modern ruminations, since they have the merit of having been thought of and written by those who lived in a historical period close to that described.
35. Lendon, *Le ombre dei guerrieri*, p. 13.
36. Alessandro Cavalli, 'Tradizione' from Treccani, *Enciclopedia italiana*.
37. Ancillotti and Cerri, *Le tavole di Gubbio e la civiltà degli Umbri*, p. 345.
38. Ibid., pp. 72–3.
39. See the references to the chapter of the origins of the Picenian graves from the Necropolis of Molaroni-Servici of Novilara and the Quattro Fontanili at Veii.

40. According to Ulpian (*Digesta* 50.16.195.2) 'The '*familia*' is a number of person who, either by nature or by law, are subjected to the power of one person, the *pater familias*' ('*iure proprio familiam dicimus plures personas, quae sunt unius potestate aut natura iure subiectae*').
41. Bettini and Short, *Con i Romani, un'antropologia della cultura antica*, p. 124.
42. The *Iliad*, despite being a text of Greek language and traditions, narrates facts similar to those of the contemporary Italic world. The society that is described is that of the Bronze Age, homogeneously widespread both in the Greek and in the Italic territory, so much so that it can be taken as a starting point for anthropological and duel descriptions.
43. Homer, *Iliad*, XV, 488–492.
44. Ibid., XX, 104–105.
45. Hobbs, *L'arte della guerra nella Bibbia*, p. 59.
46. Hector, shepherd of the host (Homer, *Iliad* X, 406; XIV, 423).
47. Homer, *Iliad*, XI, 492–497.
48. Plutarch, *Parallel Lives*, 'Romulus', 16, 4–5: 'But Romulus, after considering how he might perform his vow in a manner most acceptable to Jupiter and accompany the performance with a spectacle most pleasing to the citizens, cut down a monstrous oak that grew in the camp, hewed it into the shape of a trophy, and fitted and fastened to it the armour of Acron, each piece in its due order. Then he himself, girding his raiment about him and wreathing his flowing locks with laurel, 6 set the trophy on his right shoulder, where it was held erect, and began a triumphal march, leading off in a paean of victory which his army sang as it followed under arms, and being received by the citizens with joyful amazement. This procession was the origin and model of all subsequent triumphs, and the trophy was styled a dedication to Jupiter Feretrius.'
49. *Spolia prima o opima* (Livy, *Ab Urbe Condita*, I, 10; Dionysius of Halicarnassus, *Roman Antiquities*, II, 34, 4) if the Roman general himself won the duel, *spolia secunda* if another officer, *spolia tertia* if a simple *miles* (Varro, quoted by Festus, *De verborum significatu*, p. 189) and *spolia provocatoria* if the duel was provoked by the enemy's general.
50. Homer, *Iliad*, XI, 265 and 541.
51. Ibid., XI, 390.
52. Augusto Botto Micca, *Omero medico*, Viterbo, 1930, quoted by Maurizio Martinelli, *La lancia, la spada, il cavallo,*, p. 249.
53. Armando Cherici, 'Corredi con armi, guerra e società a Orvieto, pp. 187–9. Academia.edu
54. A.M. Adam and A. Rouveret, 'Les cité étrusques et la guerre au V siecle avant notre ère', in *Crise et transformation des Societes Archaiques de l'Italie antique au V siècle avant J.C.*, Rome, 19–21 November 1987, pp. 327ff.
55. The *Carmen Saliare* is a fragment in archaic Latin, whose text was recited by the Salian Priests.
56. Festus, P. 205M, Lindsay: '*Pilumno e Poploe in carmine saliare Romani, velut pili suti assueti: vel quia praecipue pellant hostis.*
57. On the origin of *Quirinus* there were since ancient times different interpretation as narrated by Plutarch himself: 'To the surname of Quirinus bestowed on Romulus, some give the meaning of Mars, others that of Citizen, because the citizens were called Quirites; but others say that the ancients called the spear-head (or the whole spear) "quiris," and gave the epithet Quiritis to the Juno whose statue leans upon a spear, and the name Mars to a spear consecrated in the Regia, and a spear as well as a prize to those who performed great exploits in war; and that Romulus was therefore called Quirinus as a martial, or spear-wielding, god', Plutarch, *Parallel Lives*, 'Romulus' 29, 1–8. Following the most likely theories the name of the god was linked with that of the *curia* (*co-viria*) and *quirites* (*co-virites*) with the meaning of patron of the *curias* and of the men gathered in them.
58. Ibid.
59. Festus, 55, 3 from notes to the fragments of the orations of Marcus Porcius Cato, note 120.
60. Paul Kruger 21 *ad. Edictum Digesto* 8.3,7.
61. 'Romulus, once, in trial of his strength, cast thither from the Aventine hill a spear, the shaft of which was made of cornel-wood; the head of the spear sank deep into the ground, and no one had strength to pull it up, though many tried, but the earth, which was fertile, cherished the wooden

shaft, and sent up shoots from it, and produced a cornel-trunk of good size, Plutarch, *Parallel Lives*, 'Romulus', 20, 24–30.
62. Sextus Pompeius Festus (p. 55 L) specifies that: 'with the *hasta caelibaris* is covered the head of a bride. This needle was made of a javelin drawn from the body of an overthrown and killed gladiator. It meant that the wife had to be united to the husband as the javelin had been united to the gladiator; perhaps also she recalled that the matrons are under the protection of Juno Curita, so nicknamed for what she wore the javelin called *curis* in the language of the Sabines; perhaps with the wish that the wife would give birth to valiant men; perhaps, finally, it meant that, by marriage law, the wife is subject to the husband, because the javelin and the spear sum up all the armour and are the symbol of command. It is for this reason that they are gifted to valiant men, and that captives are sold under it', Fayer, *La familia romana*, pp. 490ff.
63. Many definitions linked to the hasta are an excerpt from Goffredo Bendinelli, *Enciclopedia Italiana* 1930, under the entry 'Asta'.
64. The *xiphos* (ξίφος) was the generic thrusting sword.
65. Short sword, dagger.
66. The *phasganon* was the double-edged sword with leaf-shaped blade, suitable for thrusting and cutting. In the late Bronze Age, this distinction disappeared and the Greek word *xiphos*, derived from *qsiphos*, indicated both the thin-bladed swords and those with a wider blade, suitable for more varied fencing.
67. Dumézil, *Gli dei Germani*, pp. 71–84
68. Homer, *Iliad*, Book XXII, 306–309.
69. Ibid., Book XXII, 311–325.
70. Ibid., Book VII, 273: 'And now had they been smiting with their swords in close fight.'
71. Angelo Martinoti, 'Il simbolismo dell'ascia', p. 318.
72. Horace, *Odes*, IV, 4, 17–22.
73. Virgil, *Aeneid*, VIII, 193–306; Ovid, *Metamorphoses*, IX, 185–5.
74. From the collection of Latin texts on works of land surveying of the fifth century AD, a fragment of the Book of Vegoia, dating back to the second century BC (but certainly referring to much more archaic definitions), is of considerable interest describing the concept of borders and property, their sacredness and the divine punishment for not respecting them: 'Know that the sea has been separated from the Sky. Now when Jupiter had claimed the land of Etruria, he established and ordained that the plains be surveyed and the fields bounded. Knowing human avarice and the passions that land excites, he willed that everything be marked with boundary stones. When someday someone, moved by the avarice of the ending eight saeculum, will scorn the property that was allotted to him and will cover that of the others, men by guilty manoeuvres will violate, touch, or displace these boundaries. But whoever will have touched them, extending his property and diminishing that of another, for this sacrilege will be condemned by the gods. If slaves shall do this, they shall be moved to a lower status by their owner. But if this is done with the knowledge of the master, the household will be immediately uprooted, and the whole of his family will perish. The people responsible will be afflicted by the worst diseases and wounds and their limbs will be weakened. Then even the land will be shaken by storms or whirlwinds and many landslips. The crops will be frequently laid low and cut down by rain and hail, they will perish in the heat of the summer, they will be killed off by blight. There will be civil strife amongst the people. Know that these things happen, when such crimes are committed. Therefore do not be either a deceitful or treacherous. Place restraint in your heart.'
75. Hobbs, *L'arte della guerra nella Bibbia*, p. 109.
76. Ibid., p. 66.
77. The considerable distance in time between the events narrated and recording them in writing would explain the presence of numerous chronological inconsistencies. In fact, as Fausto Codino says, the oral tradition is by its nature conservative: in all probability the poet will never have seen that helmet in life; the singer preserves as far as he can, but when he enriches or modifies his traditional texts he has no other model than the present reality; one can understand how in the *Iliad* the old and the new are mixed, and therefore it is difficult to obtain the picture of a specific

era from the twenty-four books; each generation has left its traces, and in the end one gets the impression that these armies went to equip themselves in a historical museum of weapons (from Morelli, 'Omero medico?').

78. Fausto Codino, *Prefazione all'Odissea* (Ediz. Einaudi), pp. 7–8.
79. Van Wees, *L'arte della guerra nell'antica Grecia*, pp. 252–3.
80. Maurizio Martinelli, *La lancia, la spada, il cavallo*, p. 242
81. Homer, *Iliad*, XII, 167–170.
82. Ibid., XI, 498–501.
83. Ibid., XIV, 368–377.
84. Bettalli, 'Ascesa e decadenza dell'oplita', p. 5.
85. Van Wees, *L'arte della guerra nell'antica Grecia*, p. 253.
86. Francesco di Sandro Altoni, probably a teacher of Cosimo I, Gran Duke of Tuscany, composed the manuscript in the first half of '500: *Monomachia, trattato dell'Arte di scherma*, pp. 216ff.
87. The rock pictures of Valcamonica present the greatest expressiveness in the Iron Age and where the duel takes place between infantrymen, with or without helmets, armed with a sword and a small shield. The most accepted hypothesis is that they are ritual fights in the context of funeral ceremonies, and in some cases the arms appear 'U- shaped, a intended to express mobility in combat. In addition to the sword and shield we can detect various other weapons (axes and daggers);
88. On some of these images you can see two armed men where the shield clearly highlights the '*brocchi*', the prominent bosses used to block the opponent's sword. In these depictions the armed men are alone, without the other fighter, but depicted with various swords, two lanceolate-shaped, one with a triangular blade and the third with a rounded point.
89. On the bronze vessel of Bisenzio an armed dance is depicted, which according to the most accredited hypotheses seems connected to the *Salii* ritual. The warriors danced but, at the same time, fought each other with the spear and a small shield around a chained animal placed in the centre of the lid. In the censer cart, from the necropolis of Olmo Nello of Bisenzio, we see an armed pair in the act of fighting a duel with sword and buckler, protected by helmets and a high belt. They are positioned on a mobile wheel probably connected to a mechanism that rotated it during the movement of the trolley itself. This suggests to us the dynamic with which the skirmish took place, as if the armed men rotated in a circle during the fight, similarly to what is described for Renaissance *brocchiero* fencing;
90. For a better understanding of these artworks see also: T. Cittadini, C. Gastaldi, A. Marretta, U. Sansoni, 'Valcamonica, immagini dale rocce', Ed. Skira; Martina Antonella Scubla, 'Lo scudo bilobato nei contesti archeologici dell'Italia antica, materiali e questioni connesse', Tesi di Laurea Anno Accademico 2012-13, Università degli Studi di Milano, Facoltà degli Studi di Filosofia e Lettere, Corso di Laurea triennale in Scienze Storiche, Relatore Prof.ssa Giovanna Bagnasco Gianni; Cherici, 'Armi e armati nella società Visentina con note sul carrello e sul cinerario dell'Olmo Bello'.
91. Hanson, *The Other Greeks*, p. 231.
92. Hamblin, *Warfare in the Ancient Near East to 1600 BC*, p. 247.
93. Campi, *Di alcune spade in bronzo trovate nel Veneto, nel Trentino e nel Tirolo*, pp. 20ff.
94. Undset, *Die altesten Schwertformen*, pp. 1ff.
95. Naue, 'Armi italiane nella collezione Naue in Monaco', pp. 94ff.
96. Colini, 'Suppellettile della tomba di Battifolle ed altri oggetti arcaici dell'Etruria', pp. 13ff.
97. Naue, *Die vorromischen Schwerter aus Kupfer, bronze und Eisen*.
98. Peroni, *Die Schwerter in Italien – Le spade nell'Italia continentale*.
99. We recall that the Bronze Age is conventionally divided into ancient (EBA) twenty-second–seventeenth century BC; middle (MBA) sixteenth–fifteenth century BC; recent (LBAII) fourteenth–eleventh century BC' and final (LBA IIB) tenth–seventh century BC. Followed by the Early Iron Age (IA1);
100. For example, in the duel described in the *Iliad* between Peneleos and Lycon, when the latter struck the crest of his opponent's helmet, the sword hilt broke and at that point he was killed by Peneleos with a thrust to the neck (Homer, *Iliad*, XVI, 330–341). On this technological problem, see Snodgrass, *Arms and Armour of the Greeks*, p. 18.

101. Also called 'Naue II' or 'Griffzungenschwert'.
102. Oakeshott, *The Archaeology of Weapons*, p. 31.
103. Ibid., p. 26.
104. Caesar, *De Bello Gallico*, II, 30.
105. Ibid., IV.
106. Burton, *The Book of the Sword*, pp. 127–8.
107. D'Ercole, *Eroi e Regine, Piceni Popolo d'Europa*, p. 116.
108. Martinelli, *La lancia, la spada, il cavallo*, p. 109.
109. Pellegrini, 'Alcune considerazioni sulla produzione metallurgica nella valle del Flora dall'Eneolitico alla prima età del ferro', pp. 8–9.
110. Peroni, *Die Schwerter in Italien – Le spade nell'Italia continentale*, pp. 23–5.
111. Ibid., p. 77.
112. Ibid., p. 87.
113. Lunigiana is a small Italian region located between the north of Tuscany and the south of Liguria, inhabited in pre-Roman times by the Senguani, often better known as the Liguri Apuani, who irrevocably sided with Hannibal during the Second Punic War;
114. Saliola and Casprini, *Pugio – Gladius Brevis Est*, p. 68.
115. Demontis, *Il Popolo di Bronzo*, p. 20.
116. Pliny the Elder, *Naturalis Historia*, III, 68–70.
117. Oakeshott, *The Archaeology of Weapons*, pp. 41–2.
118. Howard, *Bronze Age Military Equipment*, p. 235.
119. Homer, *Iliad*, XV, 313–134, 709.
120. Ibid., XIII, 712–718.
121. Ibid., XIV, 479.
122. Drews, *The End of the Bronze Age*, p. 142.
123. Howard, *Bronze Age Military Equipment*, pp. 313–24.

Chapter II: The Monarchic Period (753–509 BC)

1. Plutarch says that: '... After the rout of the enemy, Romulus suffered the survivors to escape, and moved upon their city itself. But they could not hold out after so great a reverse, and suing for peace, made a treaty of friendship ... abandoning their salt-works along the river ...': Plutarch, *Parallel Lives*, 'Romulus', 25, 24–31.
2. The Sabines were one of the three tribes from which Rome was formed; the episode of the abducting of the Sabine Women and the consequent Battle of Lacus Curtius are testaments to the contrasts occurring between these two groups. Three of the eight monarchs were of Sabine origin: Titus Tatius who ruled the city together with Romulus, followed by Numa Pompilius and Ancus Marcius.
3. According to Plutarch, 'The people, too, were arranged in three bodies, the first called Ramnenses, from Romulus; the second Tatienses, from Tatius; and the third Lucerenses, from the grove into which many betook themselves for refuge, when a general asylum was offered, and then became citizens. Now the Roman word for grove is "lucus." That these bodies were three in number, their very name testifies, for to this day they call them tribes, and their chief officers, tribunes.' Plutarch, *Parallel Lives*, 'Romulus', 20, 2.
4. Dionysius of Halicarnassus, *Roman Antiquities*, II, 7.
5. Varro, *De Lingua Latina*, V, 56.
6. Livy, *Ab Urbe Condita*, ed. Scandola (1994), I, 13, 8.
7. Ibid., I, 1, 5.
8. Dionysius of Halicarnassus, *Roman Antiquities*, I, 31.
9. Maurizio Martinelli, *La lancia, la spada, il cavallo*, p. 243.
10. Dionysius of Halicarnassus, *Roman Antiquities*, I, 57, 4.
11. Cherici, 'Etruria - Roma: per una storia del rapporto tra impegno militare e sapienza politica nelle comunità antiche', p. 164.
12. Dionysius of Halicarnassus, *Roman Antiquities*, III, 2, 3.

13. Ibid., V, 37, 2.
14. Ibid., III, 2, 3.
15. Ibid., III, 41, 5.
16. Ibid., V, 37, 2.
17. Ibid., VIII, 12, 2.
18. Ibid., III, 34, 4.
19. Ibid., II, 15, 1.
20. Ibid., II, 3, 4–5.
21. Ibid., VI, 62, 3.
22. Diodorus Siculus, *Bibliotheca Historica*, VIII, 6, 3.
23. Harris, *Rome in Etruria and Umbria*.
24. Plutarch, *Parallel Lives*, 'Romulus', 3, 1–6: 'But the story which has the widest credence and the greatest number of vouchers was first published among the Greeks, in its principal details, by Diocles of Peparethus, and Fabius Pictor follows him in most points. Here again there are variations in the story, but its general outline is as follows …'. Dionysius of Halicarnassus, *Roman Antiquities*, I, 74, 1–2: ' … As to the last settlement or founding of the city, or whatever we ought to call it, Timaeus of Sicily, following what principle I do not know, places it at the same time as the founding of Carthage, that is, in the thirty-eighth year before the first Olympiad [813 BC]; Lucius Cincius, a member of the senate, places it about the fourth year of the twelfth Olympiad [728 BC], and Quintus Fabius (Pictor) in the first year of the eighth Olympiad [747 BC]. Porcius Cato does not give the time according to Greek reckoning, but being as careful as any writer in gathering the date of ancient history, he places its founding four hundred and thirty-two years after the Trojan war [751 BC].'
25. Dionysius of Halicarnassus, *Roman Antiquities*, II, 15.
26. Livy, *Ab Urbe Condita*, ed. Scandola (1994), I, 8, 1–4.
27. Hobbs, *L'arte della guerra nella Bibbia*, p. 55.
28. In Rome we find various divinities that served to protect different people but laid the foundations for the identity of a new lineage. This statement derives from the study of the cults present on the Quirinalis hill, which in various numbers were located on its top: on the *Collis Mucialis* the cult of Semo Sancus Dius Fidius, a Sabine deity similar to Jupiter, was practised; on the *Collis Saluteris* there was a shrine dedicated to Salus (health); on the *Collis Latiaris Iuppiter Latiaris* (Jupiter of Latium), of very ancient origins, was venerated who had previously been venerated on the *Mons Albanus*; and on the *Collis Quirinalis*, at the point indicated by Romulus, the *sacellum* for the cult of Quirinus was built, an aboriginal divinity perhaps equivalent to Mars, who at the time of the birth of Rome became the protector god of the *curiae*, the divinity that sanctioned the union of the Romans and Sabines, and in which Romulus was deified after his death. S.M. Bruzzesi, 'The reconstruction of the topographical structure of the 6th Augustus of Rome from the republican period to the late ancient age', PhD thesis in Ancient History 2013, Doctoral Coordinator Prof.ssa Maria Malatesta, Supervisor Prof. Francesca Cenerini p. 38 and following Alma Mater Studiorum - University of Bologna.
29. Strabo, *Geographica*, V, 3,4. With regard to the ceremony of the *Feriae Latinae* on the *Mons Albanus*, please see the description of a bronze vase from Bisenzio dating back to the eighth century BC, which according to some scholars represents the investiture ceremony of the head of the Latin League (see Chapter I.2 'The Archaic Fighting Techniques').
30. The wide-brimmed headgear, a sign of royalty or noble lineage, can be seen in many representations such as the clay decorated antefix of the Etruscan palace in Murlo (Siena), the hat worn by King Arkesilas on a Laconic cup, and many depictions of ancient Italy, from Daunia to Capestrano to the Bolognese situles (Sassatelli, 'L'arte delle situle', p. 103). In wartime the headgear was certainly replaced by a helmet, a prestigious object frequently found in the burials together with the sword, the armour (*kardiophylax*) and the shield placed to cover the *dolium* (Torelli, *La forza della tradizione*, p. 208).
31. The *Salii*, priests assigned to the cult of Mars, Quirinus and members of the imperial family, represent one of the many examples of how certain influences, coming from non-Roman people,

had entered the customs and become characteristic of the Capitoline community, to the extent of remaining unchanged over the centuries. These priests with their rites were present in Latium well before the birth of Rome and persisted in their way of dressing, dances and songs for so long that in later times their words in archaic Latin were no longer understood by the Romans themselves. Horace, *Epistulae*, II, 1, 86.

32. Torelli, *La forza della tradizione*, pp. 68–70.
33. Like the *Salii* priests, the Vestals, consecrated to the goddess Vesta, wore a dress that was based on an archaic one, identical to the wedding dress in which the deceased of the first half of the eighth century BC were buried. The custom of burying young women in their wedding dress is one that remained unchanged in Italy until the last century. In the eighth-century BC female pit tombs, it is possible to find the typical arrangement of the *fibulae* around the head and chest, as well as the use of six braids, which we typically find in the dress of the Vestal Priestess.
34. The *apex* was a high cap contracted into the shape of a cone, fitted with a point made of olive wood and fastened with chinstraps, the *apiculae* (Dionysius of Halicarnassus, *Roman Antiquities*, II, 70).
35. The *ancile* was the shield given by Mars Gradivus to King Numa Pompilius as a pledge of Rome's eternal invincibility. According to the legend, the sacred shield, together with eleven other copies made by the blacksmith Mamurius Veturius, was entrusted to the custody of the *Salii*, a priestly college of young patricians instituted by King Numa himself. Ovid, *Fasti*, III defines the *ancilia* in the following way: 'And called it *ancile*, because it was cut away (*recisum*)'.
36. The axe, a typical weapon of the Neolithic and early Bronze Age, in this context loses its military role in favour of a ritual function. Axes are found in particularly sumptuous burials, and not only male, with probable priestly functions, so much so as to suggest that they had become a sign of priestly rank or the symbol of political power in memory of ancient warrior values (testified by the *stele* of Avele Feluske).
37. A confirmation of this concept was found in the burial of a young male 16–20 years of age, who exceptionally held simultaneously military, religious and civil powers. The burial discovered in Quadrato di Torre Spaccata, a peripheral area of Rome, presented a complete miniature outfit, consisting of the symbols of military power, made up of a full panoply comprising a sword, a spear, three shields (two of which were bilobed and one circular) and a pair of greaves, while the religious one was represented by a sacrificial knife with a serpentine blade in addition to the already mentioned *ancilia*; finally, the civil authority, linked to the control and administration of the metal resources of the community, was evidenced by the presence of a small group of casting slag and bronze fragments (A. De Santis, 'Le sepolture di età protostorica a Roma', *Bull Com* CII, 2001, pp. 269–80; EAD).
38. Strabo, *Geographica*, 5.3.1.
39. Dionysius of Halicarnassus, *Roman Antiquities*, II, 49, describes the Sabines as Umbrians pushed towards central-South Italy.
40. Strabo, *Geographica*, V, 250,
41. Ibid., V, 3, 1. Pliny the Elder, *Naturalis Historia*, III, 13, 110.
42. Dionysius of Halicarnassus, *Roman Antiquities*, II, 49, 3.
43. Strabo, *Geographica*, V, 4, 12.
44. Varro, *De Lingua Latina*, VII, 29. Strabo, *Geographica*, V, 4, 12.
45. Even today the writer Ignazio Silone, who was born in Abruzzo, defined these mountains as 'the most domineering characters of Abruzzo life'.
46. G. Tagliamonte confirms this observation by stating that this warrior and, as we shall see, raiding connotation (ethnic, of group and individual) of the Italic population is inextricably welded, in that vision of geographic determinism typical of much of ancient historiography, to the mountainous and wild nature of the country inhabited by them (in *I figli di Marte*, p. 46)
47. Pliny the Elder, *Naturalis Historia*, III, 12, 106.
48. Livy, *Ab Urbe Condita*, ed. Scandola (1994), II, 22, 3.
49. Ibid., VII, 29, 5.
50. Ibid., IX, 13, 7.
51. Strabo, *Geographica*, V, 4, 2.

52. Dionysius of Halicarnassus, *Roman Antiquities*, II, 49, 5.
53. Franca Parise Badoni and Maria Ruggeri Giove, *Alfedena. La necropoli di Campo consolino: Scavi 1974-1979*, Ministero per i beni culturali e ambientali, Soprintendenza Archeologica dell'Abruzzo, 1980.
54. Anna Maria Sestieri, 'Dai circoli ai tumuli: rilettura delle necropoli abruzzesi', *Quaderni di Archeologia d'Abruzzo* 1/2009, p. 45.
55. Livy, *Ab Urbe Condita*, ed. Scandola (1994), I, 10, 3–5.
56. The Antemnates were a people of probable Sabine origin settled near Rome.
57. Livy, *Ab Urbe Condita*, ed. Scandola (1994), I, 11, 2.
58. Ibid., I, 15, 2.
59. The tales of the Old Testament are set in a time period from 1800 BC to 400 BC, although the related documents come from later times. More precisely the period of the Judges (pre-monarchic) goes from circa 1200 BC until 1040 BC, when Saul, first king of Israel, received the throne; the monarchy lasted until the destruction of the Temple of Jerusalem by the Babylonians in 586 BC.
60. Hobbs, *L'arte della guerra nella Bibbia*, pp. 138–9.
61. Livy, *Ab Urbe Condita*, ed. Scandola (1994), I, 5, 7.
62. Dionysius of Halicarnassus, *Roman Antiquities*, I, 79, 12.
63. Ibid., I, 80, 2.
64. Ibid.
65. Anon., *Origo Gentis Romanae*, XXII, 3.
66. Plutarch, *Parallel Lives*, 'Romulus', 8, 7.
67. Varro, *De Lingua Latina*, V, 16.
68. Ovid, *Fastii*, 115–118.
69. Iohannes Lydus, *De magistratibus populi Romani tres*, ed. R. Wuensch, Lipsia, 1903, I, 9.
70. Varro also confirms this military structure giving the definition of '*milites*': "'*milites*" (soldiers) at first the legion was made of three *milia* ['thousand'] and the individual tribes of Titienses, Ramnes and Luceres sent their *milia* of *milites*': Varro, *De Lingua Latina*, V, 16, 89.
71. Plutarch, *Parallel Lives*, 'Romulus', 13, 1–6.
72. Battaglia and Ventura, *De rebus militum*, Vol. I, pp. 59–60.
73. Livy, *Ab Urbe Condita*, ed. Scandola (1994), I, 16, 1.
74. Ibid., I, 28, 7. Mettius was the Alban king who betrayed Rome in the battle against the Fidenates and Veientes.
75. Jean le Lydien, *Des magistratures de l'état romain*, texte établi, traduit et commenté par Michel Dubuisson et Jacques Schamp, Vol. III, LesBelles Lettres, Paris, 2006.
76. Ovid, *Fasti*, III, 113–114.
77. Livy, *Ab Urbe Condita*, ed. Scandola (1994), II, 50, 1.
78. Ovid, *Fasti*, III, 127-132.
79. Varro, *De Lingua Latina*, V, 16, 89
80. Ennius, *Annals*, 284.
81. Livy, *Ab Urbe Condita*, ed. Scandola (1994), VIII, 8.
82. Polybius, *The Histories*, VI, 23, 16.
83. Varro, *De Lingua Latina*, V, 16. Note: the derivation of *pilum* from *perilum* is a form invented by Varro to explain the connection between *pilum* and *perire*.
84. Martinelli, *La lancia, la spada, il cavallo*, p. 93, quoted in Robert Drews, *The End of the Bronze Age, Changes in Warfare and the Catastrophe c.a. 1200 B.C.*.
85. Vegetius, *L'arte della guerra romana*, I, 20, 14.
86. Polybius, *The Histories*, VI, 21, 7.
87. Varro, *De Lingua Latina*, V, 16.
88. Livy, *Ab Urbe Condita*, ed. Scandola (1994), VIII, 8.
89. Plutarch, *Parallel Lives*, 'Romulus', 14, 28–31.
90. The Emperor was called *Princeps*, the first member of the Senate was called *Princeps Senatus*, the *princeps prior* (*primus pilus*) was the commander of the first *manipulus* of the first *cohors*, the *centurio princeps prior* and *posterior* commanded respectively the third and fourth *centuria* of each *cohors*, the

princeps praetorii was the administrative chief of the *legio*, the *princeps castrorum* was the commander of the Praetorian camp, the *princeps castrorum peregrinorum* was the commander of the *Frumentarii* camp and the *princeps officii* was the head of the administrative offices.

91. Scardigli, *La lancia, il gladio, il cavallo*, p. 69.
92. Varro, *De Lingua Latina*, V, 16.
93. Ibid. The Varro quotation comes from a fragment of the *Frivolaria*, Leo, II, p 535.
94. Pliny the Elder, *Naturalis Historia*, VIII, 74; IX, 63.
95. Suetonius, *Twelve Caesars*, 'Augustus', 40, 5.
96. Plutarch, *Parallel Lives*, 'Numa', 19, 21–22.
97. Ancillotti and Cerri, *Le tavole di Gubbio e La Civiltà degli Umbri*, p. 274.
98. Ibid., p. 238: 'Many structures of Umbrian-Sabine origin are visible in Roman social life … homothetic are the "*tota*" iguvina and the Roman "*civitas*", the "*trifu-*" iguvina and the Roman "*tribus*", the "*arsmo-*" iguvini and the Roman "*comitia curiata*", the "*ocri-fisio-*" iguvinus and the Roman "*arxtarpeia*", the "*poplo totar iouinar*" and the "*populus romanus*", the '*catera-*' iguvine and the Roman "*centuriae*", the "*ner-*" iguvini and the Roman "*principes*" (veterans), the "*natin-*" iguvinae and the Roman "*gentes*", the "*ueiro-*" iguvinus and the Roman "*vir*" as civic subject.'
99. *Tabula* VI, rear face, row 59.
100. In the *Tabulae*, to indicate the leader of the family, master of the property and of the members of the nuclear family, the word '*ueiro*' is employed, corresponding to the Roman '*vir*'. In the case of '*ner-*' the army veteran is meant.
101. The past participle of '*sihitir*' is '*kinkto-*', directly connected to the Latin '*cincto*'.
102. Pisani, *Le lingue dell'Italia antica oltre il latino*, pp. 178–9.
103. Werner, *Nascita della nobiltà. Lo sviluppo delle élite politiche in Europa*, pp.150, 170–2.
104. PF 159 PL *Censio hastaria dicebatur cum militi multae nomine ob delictum militare indicebatur quod hastas daret* –Ammenda hastaria was the imposition on a soldier to deliver up the *hasta* as a fine for a military transgression.
105. Martinelli, *La lancia, la spada, il cavallo*, p. 231.
106. Cherici, 'Armati e tombe con armi nella società dell'Etruria padana: analisi di alcuni monumenti', pp. 213–16.
107. Van Wees, *L'arte della guerra nell'antica Grecia*, pp. 274–5.
108. Plate 1.b.20.
109. Ancillotti and Cerri, *Le tavole di Gubbio e la civiltà degli umbri*, p. 52.
110. Reisoli, *Ardant du Picq*, pp. 89–98.
111. Ardant du Picq quotes the example of Hannibal at Cannae and Caesar at Pharsalus, who were victorious despite having numerically inferior armies.
112. Vegetius, *L'arte della guerra Romana*, I, 26.
113. Livy, *Ab Urbe Condida*, ed. Scandola (1994), II, 48.
114. Ibid.
115. Ibid., II, 50.
116. Reisoli, *Ardant du Picq*, p. 91.
117. Martinelli, *La lancia, la spada, il cavallo*, pp. 100 and 228.
118. Plutarch, *Parallel Lives*, 'Romulus', 21, 3–5.
119. Reisoli, *Ardant du Picq*, p. 93.
120. Ibid.
121. Who, 'when they were face to face and had surveyed each other, they challenged mutually to single combat before battle, while their armies remained quiet under arms': Plutarch, *Parallel Lives*, 'Romulus', 16, 16–18.
122. Dionysius of Halicarnassus, *Roman Antiquities*, IV, 15, 1-2.
123. 'I had … twenty-five splendid decorations […], nine of whom I voluntarily encountered and overcame when they challenged someone of our men to fight in single combat': ibid., X, 37, 3.
124. 'For when the Barbarians were besieging Clusium, Fabius Ambustus … committed the youthful folly of taking up arms for the Clusians and challenging the bravest of the Barbarians to single combat': Plutarch, *Parallel Lives*, 'Numa', 12, 35–41.

125. 'The Roman, following him up while he was still holding his shield aloft, drove his sword home from underneath and slew the Gaul': Dionysius of Halicarnassus, *Roman Antiquities*, XV, 1, 3
126. Livy, *Ab Urbe Condita*, ed. Scandola (1994), VII, 9, 8.
127. Ibid., VII, 10, 2.
128. Ibid., VII, 10, 7.
129. Ibid.
130. Ibid., VII, 10, 9–10.
131. Ibid., VIII, 7, 8.
132. Ibid., VIII, 7, 15–16.
133. Ibid., VIII, 7, 17.
134. Ibid., I, 37, 3.
135. Machiavelli, *Discorsi sopra la deca di Tito Livio*, pp. 1288–9.
136. Dionysius of Halicarnassus, *Roman Antiquities*, II, 13, 1–3.
137. 'Postumius, ordering his followers to dismount, formed a compact body of six hundred men, and observing where the Roman battle-line suffered most, being forced downhill, he engaged the enemy at those points and promptly crowded their ranks together ...', Dionysius of Halicarnassus, *Roman Antiquities*, VI, 34, 2. Against the Volscians, in the fifth century BC, the Roman horsemen were ordered 'to dismount, drew them up and kept them with him to observe any part of the line that might be hard pressed and to go to its relief; and they proved to be the cause of the very brilliant victory which the Romans then gained ...', ibid., VIII, 67, 2–5.
138. Ibid., VI, 11, 3.
139. Dionysius of Halicarnassus writes *ippikôis xíphesi makrotérois oũsi*, where the word *xíphos* is a generic word for swords, so the translation as saber, single-edged sword, is a free interpretation of the translator.
140. Dionysius of Halicarnassus, *Roman Antiquities*, VIII, 67, 2–5.
141. Livy, *Ab Urbe Condita*, ed. Scandola (1994), I, 42, 5.
142. The Centuriate assemblies were a popular assembly where all Roman citizens, plebeians and patricians, could exercise their political rights. The assemblies were divided into *centuriae*, divided into the five census classes; the class with the most *centuriae* was the 5th, while the 1st was the least numerous.
143. Livy, *Ab Urbe Condita*, ed. Scandola (1994), I, 43, 9. The same concept in Dionysius: 'I will order all the citizens to give in a valuation of their property and everyone to pay his share of the taxes according to that valuation ... for I regard it as both just and advantageous to the public that those who possess much should pay much in taxes and those who have little should pay little ... ', Dionysius of Halicarnassus, *Roman Antiquities*, IV, 16, 4.
144. According to Livy's description, the sword is present in the panoply of the soldiers of the first three classes, while for Dionysius of Halicarnassus also for the 4th. Despite this divergent information, the spread of the *gladius* within the Servian army is highly significant.
145. Livy, *Ab Urbe Condita*, ed. Scandola (1994), II, 30, 10-15.
146. Battaglia and Ventura, *De rebus militum*, Vol. I, pp. 99–104. To this hypothesis we have reported a correction relating to the 4th class, merged with the *leves* as in Battaglia and Ventura, while in this case we have decided to include them in the body of the *scutati*.
147. The *situlae* have a very large area of diffusion, even if they are unanimously referable to the culture of the Venetians. The decoration with the embossed technique includes depictions of military parades, ceremonial processions, banquets and activities such as hunting and rural work, which can be traced back to an aristocratic tradition of ostentation of power. It seems that Villanovan-Etruscan art greatly influenced the art of *situlae*, as suggested by Giovanni Colonna by connecting the first and oldest embossed work attributable to the art of *situlae*, the work of an artisan, to the jingle of the tomb of the Ori in Bologna made in Bologna but of cultural roots of the northern Etruria of the seventh century. (G. Sassatelli, 'The art of *situlae*', pp. 99 ff.).
148. Cherici, 'Armati e tombe con armi nella società dell'Etruria padana: analisi di alcuni monumenti', p. 197.
149. Livy, *Ab Urbe Condita*, ed. Scandola (1994), VIII, 8, 8, 3.

150. *Ineditum Vaticanum*, Jacoby cap. 3 (rr. 14-17). The passage refers to a certain Kaeson, a Roman ambassador who, during the First Punic War, explained in his passage the theory of the ability of the Romans to appropriate the inventions of other peoples, especially in the military sphere.
151. Atheneus of Naukratis, *Dipnosophistarum*, VI, 106, 16–18.
152. Tyrtaeus 10-12 by G. Paduano (ed.), Zanichelli, Bologna.
153. D'Acunto, *Il mondo del vaso Chigi*, pp. 83–4.
154. Marco Bettalli, *Mercenari, il mestiere delle armi nel mondo greco antico*, Carrocci – Saggi, pp. 422–3: 'The hoplite taken individually or in small groups, but not organised in the phalanx, is in fact an entity without sense; if we want to give credit to Herodotus (III 120.3), Polycrates took possession of Samos after rebelling with 15 hoplites, too few to think of forming a phalanx; not to mention the epibathai, the hoplites mounted on ships, who used to fight in groups of about 10 men. This should also make us reflect on the nature of the hoplite battle, a subject of extreme problematic, facing which I think it is necessary to re-evaluate the moment of individual combat to the detriment of the rugby-type push, the othismòs, a hypothesis that leads to unsurpassed incertitude, at least in the opinion of the writer.'
155. Machiavelli, *Discorsi sopra la prima deca di Tito Livio*, p. 1277.
156. In John Miles Paddock's study of helmets found on Italian soil and dated from the sixth century BC to the first century AD, the author excluded the Corinthian helmet from his analysis *a priori*, because it is considered to be an exceptional finding not typical of the Italic culture. Among the hoplite helmets are listed the discovery of sixteen Italo-Chalcidian specimens, of which six were in the Etruscan territory and the rest in southern Italy, while the Pseudo-Corinthians are all related to the Apulian and partly Campanian territory (southern Italy). Paddock, *The Bronze Italian Helmets: The Development of the Cassis from the Last Quarter of the Sixth Century* BC *to the Third Quarter of the First Century* AD, pp. 37, 78ff, and 265ff.
157. Maurizio Martinelli, *La lancia, la spada, il cavallo*, p. 47.
158. Fausto Zevi, 'La tomba del guerriero di Lanuvio', pp. 417–20.
159. Polito, *Fulgentibus armis*, p. 25.
160. This heroic conception is widely present represented in the Etruscan tombs of Tarquinia and Chiusi, on Vulcii pottery and in the description of Dionysius of the votive games of 496 (or 499) BC. Zevi, 'La tomba del guerriero di Lanuvio', p. 420.
161. Red-Attic figure pottery, decorated by the Berlin painter, an artist active in Athens, coming from the Necropolis of Cava della Pozzolana, Cerveteri, dated to 500–490 BC. For the scholars, the crater was realised on commission and the subjects adopted, articulated according to a coherent narrative scheme, had to take on a particular meaning, interpretable in light of the historical moment in which they are located: around the fourth–third century BC Falerii is committed to defending his freedom against Rome. In this picture (the depiction of the Trojan War) can be symbolised the contrast between the Falisci, descendants of the Argive Halesus, and the Roman barbarians. 'Sulle orme di Eracle', catalogue of the exhibition.
162. People north of Rome, inhabitants of Ager Faliscus.
163. Livy, *Ab Urbe Condita*, ed. Scandola (1994), VIII, 8, 3.
164. Jacoby, *Ineditum Vaticanum*, FGrHist 839, F 1, 3, 14-17. On the temporal framing of the text, von Armin in fact thought that in particular Chapters 3 and 5 could be drawn from a tradition going back to Fabius Pictor, while the work would have been written in the first–second century AD. Jacoby speculates a composition in the first century BC. Mazzarino proposes a date of around 100 BC. M.A. Cavallaro, a pupil of Mazzari, proposed to identify the author as Cecilius of Caleatte, which would move the date towards the end of the first century BC or the beginning of the first century AD (M.A. Cavallaro, 'Dionisio, Cecilio di Kale Akte e l'Ineditum Vaticanum', in Helikon 13–14 (1973–4), pp. 118–40). Gabba (*Dionigi e la storia di Roma arcaica*, Milan: 1996) finally proposed a post-Augustean date, in particular basing on the contents of the first chapter, that argues with Dionysius of Halicarnassus and the idea that the political life is mainly based on the oratory ability.
165. Mazzarino, *Pensiero Storico Classico*, II, 2, pp. 148–9. The Italian historian underlines how the Philhellene named Dicearcos, author of the *Ineditum Vaticanum*, exalts the Romans' ability to adapt and assimilate the tactics of other peoples.

166. Livy, *Ab Urbe Condita*, ed. Scandola (1994), VIII, 8, 3.
167. Jacoby, *Ineditum Vaticanum* cap. 3 (rr. 14-17): 'very capable of assimilating the methods of others, they learned the phalangitic order from the Etruscans [and] the combat on horseback from the Samnites'.
168. Atheneus of Naukratis, *Dipnosophistarum*, VI, 106, 16–18, G. Kaibel, Leipzig 189: 'And from the Tyrrhenians they derived the practice of the entire army advancing to battle in close phalanx.'
169. Pani and Todisco, *Storia romana dalle origine alla tarda antichità*, p. 47.
170. Varro, *De Lingua Latina*, I, 77.
171. Isidore of Seville, *Etimologie o origini*, XVIII, 14.
172. Pliny the Elder, *Naturalis Historia*, VII, 56, 201; Isidore of Seville, *Etimologie o origini*, XVIII, 54.
173. Varro, *De Lingua Latina*, VII, 35; Festus, *De verborum Significati*, p. 403.
174. Armando Cherici, 'Etruria - Roma: per una storia del rapporto tra impegno militare e capienza politica nelle comunità antiche', p. 167.
175. This fundamental movement will be discussed at length later on.
176. Garlan, *Guerra e società nel mondo antico*, p. 140.
177. Dionysius of Halicarnassus, *Roman Antiquities*, IV, 41, 1.
178. Ibid., IV, 43, 1.
179. Ibid., IV, 43, 2.
180. Ibid.
181. Livy, *Ab Urbe Condita*, ed. Scandola (1994), I, 52, 3.
182. Ibid., VIII, 6, 15.
183. Ibid., I, 52, 6.
184. Battaglia and Ventura, *De rebus militum*, Vol. 1, pp. 141–59.
185. Dionysius of Halicarnassus, *Roman Antiquities*, IV, 51, 4
186. In Cherici, 'I Piceni e l'Italia medio adriatica', p. 526.
187. Connolly, *Greece and Rome at War*, p. 104.
188. The Saties were one of the most important aristocratic families of Vulci in the fourth century BC.
189. The original is now in Rome, at Villa Albani.
190. The images depict the duels between the sons of Oedipus (Etheocles and Polinikes) and between Marce Camitlnas and Cneve Tarchuines Rumach, whose name is undoubtedly evocative of that of the Tarquinii kings of Rome. This is followed by a series of monomachies having as protagonists Larth Ulthes who kills Laris Papathnas Velznach, Rasce who slaughters Pesna Aremsnas Sveamach and Avle Vipnas who stabs Venthikau Plsachs, in which we can see an episode of archaic history that saw Rome and some allied cities opposed to the Vulcii. The Vulcii emerged victorious from this confrontation, establishing a phase of dominance over Rome itself. And again, one of the scenes represents the monomachy of Marce Camitlnas, who we see overwhelming Cnaeve Tarchuinies Remach, or Gnaeus Tarquinius from Rome, normally considered by Etruscologists to be a member of the Roman Tarquinii family.
191. Lugdunum speech I, 8-27 (0 Corpus Iscriptionum Latinarum, XIII, 1668, Dessau, *Iscriptiones Latinae Selecta*, p. 212).
192. The suffix '-na', in fact, in Etruscan means the belonging of one term to another, in the specific case the word 'Macstr-na' therefore means 'servant of his master'.
193. Andrea in *Eroi etruschi e miti greci*, p. 57.
194. Sgubini in *Eroi etruschi e miti greci*, pp. 15ff.
195. Eutizi, 'Protagonisti dello scavo e personaggi nel sepolcro', p. 36.
196. Cherici, 'I Piceni e l'Italia medio adriatica'.
197. Giove, *Warriors and Kings of Ancient Abruzzo*, p. 34.
198. Among them for instance Christian Miks in *Studien zur romischen, Schwerbewaffnung in der Kaiserzeit*, p. 31, and Peter Connolly in *Greece and Rome at War*, p. 63, both referring to the same specimen;
199. The 'ratio' is the length / width ratio, the higher it is the more slender the blade is, and obviously on the contrary, the lower it is the more squat the blade appears.
200. Late Bronze Age (twelfth–tenth century BC).

201. Saliola and Casprini, *Pugio – Gladius Brevis Est*, Chapter V.
202. Eteocles and Polynices were twin brothers, sons of Oedipus, who become enemies to the point of slaughtering each other due to their father's curse. Their struggle metaphorically represents the one between the Etruscan factions for the control of Rome.
203. Livy, *Ab Urbe Condita*, ed. Scandola (1994), I, 25.
204. Ibid., I, 26.
205. Ibid., VII, 10.
206. Vegetius, *Epitoma Rei Militari*, I-XI, 7; ' … Against the post as if against an adversary the recruit trained himself using the foil and hurdle like a sword and shield, so that now he aimed at as it were the head and face, now threatened the flanks, then tried to cut the hamstrings and legs, backed off, came on, sprang, and aimed at the post with every method of attack and art of combat, as though it were an actual opponent … .'
207. In the case of the first two blades from the left in Fig. 3 there would be an increase of only 1.2–1.5cm^3 of iron, corresponding to about 10–12g.
208. Most of the armament known from the archaeological documentation of these areas is combat equipment, but occasionally appear specimens which, due to their morphological characteristics or rich decoration, allow us to legitimately assume that they are weapons not for real use but intended exclusively for display, or parade weapons acquired as luxury goods or ceremonial gifts and exhibited as insignia of rank (Tagliamonte, 'Lo sviluppo di una società aristocratica: il ruolo delle armi', pp. 113–14). This specimen and its scabbard are precisely part of these, as tomb 69 is one of the most sumptuous of the entire necropolis of Campovalano, certainly attributable to a *princeps*. That such a specimen is even less representative of the real cross-hilted sword, is the fact that it underwent heavy restoration in the 1970s, of which unfortunately it is no longer possible to access the report, but which seem to have substantially altered the original proportion so as to potentially make it quite distinct from its original geometry. Comparing it to the average of the numerous other blades that have remained unchanged that we have seen to be around 55–58cm, it differs greatly from it, resulting in much larger, longer, wider and heavier blade.
209. In reality, centuries later, during the Late Empire we will see the reappearance in the *spathae* of very showy and round scabbard chapes, reminiscent of those of our cross-hilted sword.
210. Grave 648/b, Chieti Museum, inv. 16848.
211. This technology will be explored extensively from the historical point of view in Chapter IV.
212. Saliola and Casprini, *Pugio – Gladius Brevis Est*, cap. V.
213. Among them for instance, Istenič, *Roman Military Equipment from the River Ljubljanica*, p. 40. This publication contains significant inaccuracies and errors, apparently connected to the restricted knowledge of Italian history of the first millennium BC.
214. See for instance ibid., p. 32.
215. P.F. Stary, *Zur Eisenzeitlichen Bewaffnung und Kampfesweise in Mittelitalien* (ca. 9. bis 6.Jh. v. Chr.), Marburg, 1981.
216. Landolfi, 'I Piceni' in *Italia omnium terrarum alumna: la civiltà dei Veneti, Reti, Liguri, Celti, Piceni, Umbri, Latini, Campani, e Iapigi*, 1988; Papi, 'La necropoli di Alfedena e la via d'acqua del Sangro', 1988; Sgubini Moretti, 'Pitino. Necropoli di Monte Penna: tomba 31', *La civiltà picena nelle Marche*, Ripatransone: Maroni Editore, 1992.
217. Stary, *Zur Eisenzeitlichen Bewaffnung und Kampfesweise in Mittelitalien*.
218. Apenninea, east of Rome.
219. Grave 8 and 10 (end seventh century BC), graves 3 and 13 (early fourth century BC) 21 and 23 (late seventh–early sixth century BC).
220. Weidig 'I pugnali a stami, considerazioni su aspetti tecnici, tipologici, cronologici e distribuzione in area abruzzese', p. 121.
221. Ibid., p. 125.
222. To date they have been found in seventy-four necropolis, which have returned hundreds of specimens.
223. Maria Ruggeri Giove, 'Alfdena, la necropoli di Campo Consolino'.
224. Ibid.

225. Sabino Moscati, *Gli Italici – l'arte*, Jaca Book, 1983, p. 210.
226. Giove, *Warriors and Kings of Ancient Abruzzo*, p. 34.
227. Vincenzo D'Ercole and Elica Cella, 'Il Guerriero di Capestrano', in Ruggeri Giove, *Guerrieri e re dell'antico Abruzzo*, p. 34.
228. Note that some authors believe they are spears rather than javelins, but the evident presence of the hook for the *amentum* makes the second interpretation more feasible.
229. Unfortunately, details of the precise location of their discovery has been lost.
230. Nn. inv. 251-2752-2753/S.
231. Livy, *Ab Urbe Condita*, ed. Scandola (1994), VIII, 4 (… *si consanguineos nos Romanorum esse* …).
232. Ibid., VIII, 6.
233. Ibid., VIII, 8.
234. Ibid.
235. Ancient Roman and central Italic coinage, temporally following the *aes rude* and preceding the *aes grave*
236. R. D'Amato, *I centurioni Romani*, Goriziana, 2012, p. 11.
237. The 'Statere' originally indicated the set of two unit weights which, placed on either side of scales, determined their balance. Over time it became the unit of measurement for gold and consequently for coinage.
238. Virgil, *Aeneid* XII, 398–411.
239. An ancient pre-Roman Italic people, settled near modern-day Ardea, a few kilometres south of Rome.
240. The choice of depicting the cross-hilted sword in a first-century fresco can be traced back to a historical memory of the archaic weapon or, as described in the chapter on the symbolic value of the sword, to an exaltation of the Trojan hero armed with the same type of weapon borne by Alexander the Great; the fact is that in the late Consular era the swords of senior military commanders still preserved such a shape.
241. Saliola and Casprini, *Pugio – Gladius Brevis Est*, pp. 67–8.
242. I. Fossati, *Gli eserciti etruschi*.
243. The work obviously is not from the Monarchical period but much later, its testimonial value on this type of suspension remains however intact, as the artist wanted to represent a much more archaic reality here.
244. Strabo, *Geographia*, V,2,7.
245. Gianluca Tagliamonte 'Lo sviluppo di una società aristocratica: il ruolo delle armi', p. 115.
246. Joachim Weidig in 'I pugnali a stami, considerazioni ed aspetti tecnici, tipologici, cronologici e distribuzione in area abruzzese' says that 'the presence of two chains in all the examined specimens can be observed. We have no evidence of a suspension made with a single chain, as proposed in the reconstruction of the Grossi sheath, 1990.'
247. Ibid., p. 110.
248. In reality, the term axe is improper, the latter having the blade perpendicular to the handle. The right term is 'adze', but since in the common lexicon it is practically never used and could be misleading, we will continue to use the term 'axe'.
249. To prunderstand this concept, just think of a collision or braking with the car at high speed, the shorter the stopping distance/time, the more violent the impact or braking is.
250. Settled in the regions of Asia Minor and Mesopotamia.
251. Plutarch, *Parallel Lives*, 'Camillus', 40, 4.
252. The human arm moving in a horizontal trajectory is not able to reach a speed even comparable to that obtainable with a vertical blow
253. Martinelli, *La lancia, la spade, il cavallo*, p. 67.
254. Giuliano De Marinis, 'Pettorali metallici a scopo difensivo nel villanoviano recente', *Atti e memorie dell'Accademia La Colombaria*, XLI, 1976.
255. At least a hundred specimens come from the Abruzzo area, with the characteristic of admirable geometric decoration, similar to the Villanovan shields. For further information see Raffaela Papi, Dischi corazza abruzzesi a decorazione geometrica nei musei italiani (Rome: 1990)

256. De Marinis and La Rocca, *Il sepolcreto dell'Esquilino*, p. 153.
257. Moscati, *Gli Italici, l'arte*, p. 211;
258. Polybius, *The Histories*, VI, 23, 14-15.
259. Martinelli, *La Lancia, la spade, il cavallo*, p.76.
260. The importance of the Tiber for the Romans is described by Cicero (*De Re Publica*, II, 10): 'Could anything display divine ability more than Romulus' embrace of the benefits of the coast while avoiding its vices by placing his city on the bank of a large river that flows strongly into the sea throughout the year? In that way, the city could import essentials by sea and export its surplus produce; it could also use the river to receive the necessities of civilised life not only from the sea but carried downriver from inland. Romulus therefore seems to me to have divined that this city would someday be the home and center of the greatest empire; for a city located in any other part of Italy would not so easily have exercised so much power.'
261. The Pons Sublicius was initially a bridge made of tied wooden planks (as can be seen from the Volscian word '*sublica*'), which could be easily removed for a easier control of the territory.
262. Valerius Maximus, *Facta e dicta memorabilia*, I, *ex*. I.
263. Giorgio Ruffolo, *Quando l'Italia era una superpotenza*, p. 10.
264. Livy, *Ab Urbe Condita*, ed. Scandola (1994), I, 8.
265. Epigraph containing part of Claudius's speech, from Lugdunum (Lyon) Col. I, linn. 9-12. The emperor emphasised to the senators that in the royal age the throne was transmitted not only between individuals belonging to various families, but also to other peoples (Romulus was succeeded by the Sabine Numa, and the throne of Ancus Marcius had welcomed the Etruscan Tarquinius Priscus; he also highlighted how Tarquinius Priscus, whose father was Greek and the mother a decayed noble woman, in Rome '*regnum adeptus est*', despite not having, elsewhere, the possibility of holding offices, while Servius Tullius, who in Etruscan was called Mastarna, was the son of a slave, and in Rome he became king, with great benefit for the community
266. Dionysius of Halicarnassus, *Roman Antiquities*, II, 15: 'Secondly, finding that many of the cities in Italy were very badly governed, both by tyrannies and by oligarchies, he undertook to welcome and attract to himself the fugitives from these cities, who were very numerous, paying no regard either to their calamities or to their fortunes, provided only they were free men.'
267. Tacitus, *Histories*, IV 74, 4.
268. Dionysius of Halicarnassus told that already in the time of Romulus there was a tendency to assimilate freed slaves. *Roman Antiquities*, 19, 4.
269. Ibid., II 16; XIV 6: Tacitus, *Annals*, XI 24, 4.
270. Polybius, *The Histories*, VI, 25, 11.
271. Sylloge inscriptionum Graecarum, 543.

Chapter III: The Consular Age

1. Livy, *Ab Urbe Condita*, ed. Scandola (1994), I, 8, 7.
2. Dionysius of Halicarnassus, *Roman Antiquities*, II, 8,1.
3. The Italian word *paga* (pay) comes from the Latin *pacare*, with the meaning of reassuring the person who must have something, and the proof of this is found in the term *quietanza* (receipt). *Stipendium* (salary) is a word composed of the Latin word, *stips* (*obolo*, small coin) and the verb *pendere* (to pay) for which to salary (*stips-pendium*) properly means 'to pay with small coins'. In addition to the salary, the soldiers also had the right to the periodic distribution of salt, hence the term salary (*salario*), which in Italian is more linked to a salary for manual work than the salary for an intellectual job (*stipendio*);
4. Livy, *Ab Urbe Condita*, ed. Scandola (1994), IV, 59, 11.
5. Ibid., IV, 60, 1.
6. In 326 BC the *Poetelia Papiria* law abolished enslavement for debt.
7. It was decided that no Roman could possess more than 500 *iugeri* of *ager publicus* (public land, owned by the state) which mostly derived from military conquests, and this greater availability meant that even the lower classes had the possibility of receiving land to cultivate.
8. In 312 BC the censor Appius Claudius Caecus for the first time included in the register of senators some plebeians, thus proceeding with the abolition of the distinction between ordinary senators

(*patres*) and adjunct senators (*conscripti*), allowing the latter the right to vote, which they previously had not enjoyed.
9. Livy, *Ab Urbe Condita*, ed. Mazzocato (1997), II, 23.
10. Ibid., V, 5.
11. Ibid., IV, 59.
12. Ibid., V, 10.
13. The *tributum* was a tax charged on all citizens in order to provide for the needs of war.
14. Polybius, *The Histories*, VI, 39, 12-15.
15. Ibid., XIII, 3, 3-8.
16. Livy, *Ab Urbe Condita*, ed. Mazzocato (1997), V, 37, 7-8.
17. Ibid., V, 38, 2.
18. Ibid., V, 38,
19. Ibid., X, 16, 6-8.
20. Ibid., VII, 12, 11.
21. Dionysius of Halicarnassus, *Roman Antiquities*, XIV, 10, 1.
22. T. Mommsen, *Storia di Roma antica* libro II, 'Dall'abolizione dei re di Roma sino all'unione d'Italia', Biblioteca Sansoni, cap. IV (La caduta della potenza Etrusca – i Celti), p. 415.
23. Plutarch, *Parallel Lives*, 'Camillus', 40, 4.
24. Dionysius of Halicarnassus, *Roman Antiquities*, XIV, 10, 2.
25. Livy, *Ab Urbe Condita*, ed. Mazzocato (1997), IX, 13.
26. Brizzi, *Il guerriero, l'oplita, il legionario, gli eserciti nel mondo classico*, p. 48.
27. Livy, *Ab Urbe Condita*, ed. Mazzocato (1997), IX, 31, 9.
28. Brizzi, *Il guerriero, l'oplita, il legionario, gli eserciti nel mondo classico*, p. 79.
29. Livy, *Ab Urbe Condita*, ed. Mazzocato (1997), VIII, 8, 3.
30. *Ineditum Vaticanum*, p. 118.
31. Sallust, *De coniuratione Catilinae*, 51.
32. Ateneo di Naucrati, *I Deipnosofisti* o *I dotti a banchetto*, Prima traduzione italiana commentata su progetto di Lucio Canfora, Salerno Editrice, Roma, VI, 106.
33. Plutarch, *Parallel Lives*, 'Romulus', 21, 1.
34. Guattani, *Monumenti Sabini*, Vol. 3, pp. 131–2
35. Polybius, *The Histories*, VI, 23, 2-5.
36. '[The Macedonians] were armed with round shields and long spears, the Romans had the large shield called the scutum, a better protection for the body, and the javelin, a much more effective weapon than the spear whether for hurling or thrusting.' Livy, *Ab Urbe Condita*, ed. Scandola (1994), IX, 19, 7
37. Martinelli, *La lancia, la spada, il cavallo*, Vol. 7, p. 48.
38. Ibid., Vol. 7, p. 53.
39. Livy, *Ab Urbe Condita*, ed. Scandola (1994), I, 30.
40. Ibid., VI, 12
41. Ibid., VII, 16-17.
42. A A Vari, La Tomba di François, Francesco Roncalli: La decorazione pittorica, Ed Quasar, Pag. 86.
43. Dionysius of Halicarnassus, *Roman Antiquities*, VI, 10, 2
44. Ibid., VI, 10-12.
45. Livy, *Ab Urbe Condita*, ed. Scandola (1994), VIII, 8. The entire quotation, analysed point by point, is taken from this chapter of the Latin author.
46. Maurizio Martinelli, *La lancia, la spada, il cavallo*, p. 48.
47. The Romans and the Latins, who after Tarquinius Superbus had acquired the same technical approach to combat and that now opposed each other, had 'a force of equal size used to be supplied by the Latins, now, however, they were hostile to Rome. The two armies were drawn up in the same formation, and they knew that if the maniples kept their order they would have to fight, not only *vexilla* with *vexilla*, *hastati* with *hastati*, *principes* with *principes*, but even centurion with centurion... (Livy, *Ab Urbe Condita*, ed. Scandola (1994), VIII, 8, 15). But the Romans prevailed 'with respect to courage [*animos*]' (Ibid., 8, 13).

Notes 357

48. Caesar, *De bello civili*, I, 72, 3: ' ... as it was as much the duty of a commander to win by policy and by the sword...'
49. Polybius, *The Histories*, VI, 21, 7.
50. Livy, *Ab Urbe Condita*, ed. Scandola (1994), VIII, 8, 5-6.
51. Marquardt, 'Das Militarwesen'.
52. Polybius, *The Histories*, VI, 23.
53. Sextus Julius Frontinus, *Stratagemata*, II, 4.
54. Ibid., II, 5, 4.
55. Livy, *Ab Urbe Condita*, ed. Scandola (1994), VIII, 8, 5-6.
56. In this case Livy seems to add up only the number of infantry and centurions, leaving out the standard bearers, (60+2)+(60+2)+(60+2)=186. For more information on this problem, see the related paragraph 'The numbers of the Livian Legion).
57. Livy, *Ab Urbe Condita*, ed. Scandola (1994), VIII, 8, 7-8.
58. Varro, *De lingua Latina*, VI, 3.
59. Livy, *Ab Urbe Condita*, ed. Scandola (1994), VIII, 10.
60. Vegetius, *L'arte della guerra romana*, I, 20, 14-15.
61. Livy, *Ab Urbe Condita*, ed. Scandola (1994), VIII, 11, 7.
62. Vegetius, *L'arte della guerra romana*, I, 20, 16-17.
63. Plautus, 'Trinummus', act II, scene IV, 456: '*Ferentarius amicus est sine dubio, qui fert aliquid amico commode*'.
64. Varro, *De lingua Latina*, V, 16. (Frivolaria fragment, Leo, II) '*Agite nunc, subsidite omnes quasi solent triarii*'.
65. Plautus, 'Fabularum fragmenta', Leo II.
66. Varro, *De lingua Latina*, VII, 58.
67. Livy, *Ab Urbe Condita*, ed. Scandola (1994), VIII, 9, 13-14.
68. Nonius Marcellus, *De compendiosa doctrina*, from two verses of Lucilius found in books VII and X. The translation is uncertain because, being fragments, the context is missing: '*pone paludatus stabat rorariu velox. Quinque hastae aureolo cinctu rorariu veles*': 'behind stood the agile *rorarius* covered by a military cloak ... the *rorarius veles* armed with 5 light spears worn in the gilded belt. '
69. Varro, *De lingua Latina*, VI, 89, and VII, 58: 'The accensi, Cato writes, were attendants ; the word may be from *censio* "opinion", that is, from *arbitrium* "decision", for the *accensus* is present to do the arbitrium of him whose attendant he is.'
70. Nonius Marcellus, *De compendiosa doctrina*, 520, 11 ff.
71. Livy, *Ab Urbe Condita*, ed. Scandola (1994), VIII, 10, 2-7.
72. Varro, *De lingua Latina*, VII, 56.
73. Livy, *Ab Urbe Condita*, ed. Scandola (1994), VIII, 8, 3-8.
74. Niebuhr, *Romische Geschichte*, vol. 3, pp. 110–21 and 543–52.
75. Ibid.
76. Marquardt, 'Das Militarwesen'.
77. H. Delbruck, *Geschichte der Kriegskunst im Rahmender politischen Geschichte*, vol. 1 (Das Altertum, 3rd ed., Berlin 1920), pp. 259–91.
78. P. Faccaro, 'La storia dell'antichissimo esercito romano e l'età dell'ordinamento centuriato', in *Atti del secondo Congresso Nazionale di Studi Romani*, vol. 3, Rome, 1931, pp. 91–7.
79. De Sanctis, *Storia dei Romani*, vol. 1, pp. 247–9, 354–7 and 403–06; vol. 2, pp. 56–61, 192–212 and 314–15.
80. The word '*recursus*', which means folding, is the term used by Livy in *Ab Urbe Condita*, VIII, 38, 10-11 to express the retreat of an exhausted maniple from the fight, moving behind a soldier who is ready to replace him.
81. Livy, *Ab Urbe Condita*, ed. Scandola (1994), VIII, 8, 9-10.
82. Livy, *Ab Urbe Condita*, ed. Mazzocato (1997), VIII, 8.
83. Ibid., VIII, 38, 10-11.
84. Ibid., IX, 32, 8-9.
85. Livy, *Ab Urbe Condita*, ed. Scandola (1994), IX, 39.

86. Ibid., VIII, 8, 3-14. Apart from this technical description, there is another example, again by Livy, in the description of the Battle of Vesuvius in 340 BC against the Latins, in which the consul Publius Decius Mure sacrificed himself to the gods of Mani (*devotio*) for the victory of the Roman people. The battle was going in favour of the Latins, and after the death of his colleague, Titus Marlius, aware that the enemies were superior in strength 'cried out to the Roman triarii: "rise up now and with fresh strength confront the weary enemy, remembering your country and your parents, your wives and your children, remembering the consul who lies dead that you may conquer." When the triarii had got to their feet, fresh and sound in their glittering armour, a new and unforeseen array, they received the antepilani into the gaps between their files, and, raising a shout, threw the enemy's front ranks into disorder, and thrusting their spears into their faces, disposed of the fine flower of their manhood and went through the other maniples almost scatheless, as though their opponents had been unarmed, penetrating their masses with such slaughter as scarce to leave a fourth part of their enemies alive …' (Ibid., VIII, 10, 2-7). In this incident, the *triarii* do not perform a purely defensive function, which we could define as a 'porcupine', but a real attack through which they managed to disrupt the enemy formations.
87. Maurus Servius Honoratus, *In Vergilii carmina comentarii*, XII, 121.
88. In the case that *pilata* mean shields, since the same word is used in Greek, it must be translated that the rear manoeuvre of the infantry armed with *hastae* occurred from the ranks of shielded infantrymen.
89. Machiavelli, *Discorsi sopra la prima deca di Tito Livio*, vol. 2, pp. 1321–2. 'The greatest mistake that those men make who arrange an army for an engagement is to give it only one front, and commit it to only one onrush and one attempt (fortune). This results from having lost the method the ancients employed of receiving one rank into the other; for without this method, one cannot help the rank in front, or defend them, or change them by rotation in battle, which was practised best by the Romans.'
90. Battaglia and Ventura, *De rebus militum*, Vol. II, pp. 53–2.
91. Vegetius, *L'arte della guerra romana*, II, 13, 4-7.
92. The problem of the divergence between the numbers of the unit described by Vegetius compared to those reported by Livy is due to the fact that Vegetius mixed different and chronologically distant sources, giving rise to a picture with contrasting and discordant aspects, see Elisabetta Todisco, 'Rassegna di studi militari 1989-1994' in *Epigrafia e Territorio, Politica e Società – Temi di antichità romane IV*, ed. Mario Pani. pp. 377–8.
93. Battaglia and Ventura, *De rebus militum*, Vol. II, p. 57.
94. Livy, *Ab Urbe Condita*, ed. Scandola (1994), VIII, 8.
95. Polybius, *The Histories*, VI.
96. Dionysius of Halicarnassus, *Roman Antiquities*, VIII, 86, 4.
97. Ibid., VI, 10, 2.
98. The *pezeteri* were the Macedonian infantry armed with the *sarissa*, a long spear measuring about 5-7m.
99. Brizzi, *Il guerriero, l'oplita, il legionario, gli eserciti nel mondo classico*, p. 47.
100. Polybius, *The Histories*, XVIII, 30, 9-10.
101. Ibid., XVIII, 31, 5-6.
102. Ibid., XVIII, 32, 3-5.
103. Livy, *Ab Urbe Condita*, ed. Mazzocato (1997), XXI, 49, 13–50, 1.
104. Ibid., XXI, 47, 1.
105. Ibid., XXI, 5.
106. Polybius, *The Histories*, XVIII, 28, 6-8.
107. Dionysius of Halicarnassus, *Roman Antiquities*, V, 42, 2.
108. Livy, *Ab Urbe Condita*, ed. Mazzocato (1997), XXVI, 4.
109. Ibid., XXXVIII, 20-21.
110. Polybius, *The Histories*, VI, 22.
111. Livy, *Ab Urbe Condita*, ed. Mazzocato (1997), XXXI, 35.
112. Ibid

Notes 359

113. Polybius, *The Histories*, II, 30
114. Livy, *Ab Urbe Condita*, ed. Mazzocato (1997), XXXVIII, 12-14.
115. Ibid., XXVIII, 33, 5.
116. Ibid., XXX, 33.
117. Ovid, 'Libellus in ibis', 45.
118. Vegetius, *L'arte della guerra romana*, III, 13.
119. Cicero, *Epistolae ad Familiares* IX, epistola XX.
120. Polybius, *The Histories*, VI, 21, 9-10.
121. Ibid., VI, 24, 3-6.
122. Ibid., VI, 23.
123. Ibid., II, 33, 2-6.
124. An example of cavalry duties can be found in this passage from Livy: (12) '… the Roman cavalry charging into the middle of the enemy threw his infantry into confusion, and at the same time barred the passage for the Spanish horse (17-18) … the Romans never relaxed the pursuit until they had stripped the enemy of his camp… .' Livy, *Ab Urbe Condita*, ed. Mazzocato (1997), XXIX, 2.
125. Polybius, *The Histories*, VI, 25.
126. Ibid., III, 117, 5-6.
127. Ibid., III, 115, 3.
128. Ibid., III, 107, 9-12.
129. Scipio, in Africa, reinforced the V and VI Legions who had fought at Cannae with suitable soldiers and brought their number up to 6,200. Livy, *Ab Urbe Condita*, ed. Mazzocato (1997), XXIX, 24, 13.
130. Polybius, *The Histories*, VI, 21, 10; see also II, 24, 3; III, 107, 9-11; VI, 20, 8.
131. Napoléon Bonaparte, *Précis des guerres de Jules César*, p. 80.
132. Andrea Zambelli, *Delle differenze politiche fra i popoli antichi ed i moderni*, part I: *La guerra* Vol. 2, Bravetta, 1839, pp. 471–93.
133. Polybius, *The Histories*, XVIII, 32, 10-12.
134. Ibid., XV, 9, 6-10.
135. Livy, *Ab Urbe Condita*, ed. Mazzocato (1997), XXVIII, 2, 6-7.
136. Polybius, *The Histories*, XV, 15, 7.
137. Livy, *Ab Urbe Condita*, ed. Scandola (1994), IX, 19, 7.
138. Ibid., X, 14, 14-18.
139. Polybius, *The Histories*, III, 115, 11-12.
140. Livy, *Ab Urbe Condita*, ed. Mazzocato (1997), XXX, 34, 10-11.
141. Polybius, *The Histories*, XV, 14, 1-5.
142. Ibid., XV, 12, 8-9.
143. Ibid., XV, 9, 9-10.
144. Livy, *Ab Urbe Condita*, ed. Mazzocato (1997), XXXVII, 42.
145. Ibid., XXVIII, 2, 6-7.
146. Ibid., XXVIII, 2, 8.
147. Polybius, *The Histories*, XV, 13, 2-3.
148. Livy, *Ab Urbe Condita*, ed. Mazzocato (1997), XXX, 34.
149. Ibid., XXII, 4, 7 -5, and 7-8.
150. Vegetius, *L'arte della guerra Romana*, I, 26.
151. Livy, '*Ab Urbe Condita*', ed. Mazzocato (1997), XXIV, 48.
152. Cicero, *Tusculanae*, opera 1, XLV 109.
153. Livy, *Ab Urbe Condita*, ed. Mazzocato (1997), XXXVII, 43.
154. The *contubernium* was the smallest unit of the Roman army, consisting of eight soldiers.
155. The exact interpretation of Roman hoplitism has been widely discussed in Chapter II.2 'The Fighting in the Monarchic Period'.
156. The spread of the early Consular *gladius* is not well known by modern authors, as attested by Janka Istenič in 'Roman Military Equipment from the river Ljubljanica', p. 32 saying that 'we know very little of the development of Roman swords and scabbards before the Augustan period'.

157. It should always be borne in mind that it is impossible to confine similar evolutionary processes to excessively precise and restricted periods, which therefore must be taken with due care
158. Di Fazio and Cherici, 'L'armamento dal guerriero celtico al legionario romano', p. 46.
159. Grassi, *I celti in Italia*, p. 9.
160. For many scholars the term '*gladius*' itself is of Celtic derivation and replaces the very ancient '*ensis*', which will remain confined to epic poetry alone, as well as '*sagum*', which will serve to indicate the short military coat of raw wool.
161. '*Nuovissimi forestieri*' (very new foreigners).
162. Livy, *Ab Urbe Condita*, ed. Mazzocato (1997), V, 33: 'I would not deny that the Gauls were conducted to Clusium by Arruns or some one else living there, but it is quite clear that those who attacked that city [i.e. the Senones] were not the first who crossed the Alps. As a matter of fact, Gauls crossed into Italy two centuries before they attacked Clusium and took Rome. Nor were the Clusines the first Etruscans with whom the Gaulish armies came into conflict; long before that they had fought many battles with the Etruscans who dwelt between the Apennines and the Alps.'
163. In fact, Livy asserts that at the moment when the Senones poured into Clusium before arriving in Rome, 'The people of Clusium were appalled by this strange war, when they saw the numbers, the extraordinary appearance of the men, and the kind of weapons they used, and heard that the legions of Etruria had been often routed by them on both sides of the Po ... sent ambassadors to ask the senate for assistance ... .' (*Ab Urbe Condita*, V, 35). Still, during the tragic clash on the Allia river (390 BC) the Romans ' almost before they had seen their untried foe ...' (*Ab Urbe Condita*, ed. Mazzocato (1997), V, 38).
164. Ibid., V, 33.
165. Pliny the Elder, *Naturalis Historia*, XII, 5.
166. Such as a tomb in Orvieto of the sixth century BC belonging to a character whose name, Catacus, betrays its clear Celtic origins (Grassi, *I celti in Italia*, p. 15). Equally important is tomb no. 15 of the necropolis of Gravellona Toce (loc. Piemonte) which, next to examples of typical local ceramics, presents a Latenian sword and a schnabelkanne (type of jug for domestic use) in bronze with a siren attacking, whose dating is placed by Peroni in the full fifth century BC (R. Peroni, *Studies on the chronology of the civilisation of Este and Golasecca*, Sansoni, 1975, pp. 344, 350 and 351).
167. The Biturges, Arverni, Senones, Aedui (sub-group of Insubres), Ambarri, Carnutes and Aurleci.
168. However Livy in *Ab Urbe Condita*, V, 34, 9 mentions a pre-existence of the Insubri with respect to the expedition of Bellovesus, therefore this tribe, so important in the subalpine Celtic history in the following centuries, would have been settled in the Cisalpine even before the sixth century BC.
169. Ibid., V, 35, 1.
170. Mainly Salluvii, Boi and Lingones, who however could have been added in slightly later times.
171. Cherici, 'Forme di contatto mondo celtico e non celtico', p. 382.
172. Austin and Vidal-Naquet, *Economie et Sociétés en Grèce ancienne*.
173. Strabo, *Geographica*, IV, 6, 3.
174. Polybius indeed (*The Histories*, II, 22, I) tells us that they 'are called Gaesatae because they serve for hire, this being the proper meaning of the word'. Fabius Pictor is even more explicit ('Annales' - Oros. IV,13,5) '*Gaesatorum quod nomen non gentis, sed mercenariorum Gallorum est*'.
175. This author (in *Histories*, VII, 165, I) reconstructing the scenario of the Battle of Hymera in 480 BC, tells us that ' Terillus son of Crinippus, the tyrant of Himera ... who had been expelled from Himera by Theron ... brought [in Sicily] against Gelon three hundred thousand Phoenicians, Libyans, Iberians, Ligyes, Elisyci, Sardinians, and Cyrnians [a Celtic population located between the Pyrenees and the Aude], led by Amilcas son of Annon, the king of the Carchedonians'.
176. Cherici, 'Forme di contatto mondo celtico e non celtico', p. 386.
177. Ibid., p. 372.
178. V. Kruta, 'I Celti', pp. 263–311.
179. Bergonzi, *La Romagna tra il VI e il IV sec. a.C.- nel quadro della protostoria dell'Italia centrale*, p. 83. To this we can add other particularly representative indications of the adoption of Italic social customs, such as the use of the funeral banquet, which is widespread among the peninsular tribes, in direct contact with the cultures that had developed the model. We are therefore witnessing the

deposition of banquet services in grave goods, a practice previously completely foreign to Celtic culture, whose greater or lesser complexity was related to the social status of the deceased. Another apparently insignificant object but with great testimonial value is the strigil, the athlete's tool, typical first of Greek culture and then the Roman, which we find widespread from the fourth century BC in the burials of the Cenomani, the Boi, the Senones and the Insubrians, which stands as a symbol of participation in the rites and customs of Mediterranean cultures. The deposition of this object in the grave goods of the deceased represents it as a full part of the refined peninsular civilisation. This does not happen in the transalpine groups, isolated from the main trade routes (for example those of the necropolis of Marzabotto and Carzaghetto), in the tombs of which all those elements of Etruscan-Italic derivation typical of those of the Boi and Senones are completely absent and of the areas as far north as the Po.

180. The Battle of Talamon was fought in 225 BC between the Romans and a Celtic coalition (the Boi, Insubransi, Taurini and Gaesati);
181. The Battle of Clatidium was fought in 222 BC between the Romans and the Insubrians.
182. Cherici, 'Forme di contatto mondo celtico e non celtico', p. 380.
183. The Falisci were an ancient people of central Italy, bordering on the Etruscans For an exhaustive source of data on Volterra and Faliscan painting, please refer to: Beazley, *Etruscan Vase Painting*; M. Cristofani, 'Itinerari iconografici nella iconografia volterrana', pp. 175-192; Corpus Vasorum Antiquorum, F 33, pp. 19–20.
184. Number 9830001, s. Corpus Vasorum Antiquorum, F 33, tav. 1.
185. Servadei, 'L'immagine del Celta nella pittura vascolare etrusca', p. 294.
186. Ibid., p. 294; For the study of such kind of shield see P.F. Stary, *Ursprung und Ausbreitung der eisenzeitlichen Ovalschilde mit spindelormigen Schildbuckel*, 1981.
187. The image of this specimen shows a warrior from behind, naked, equipped with an oval shield with a central spine and with a trace of a probable narrow spear on the right. The nudity, as well as the facial features and the blond and bristly hair, seem to denote him as a Celt, however the sword is hanging not from a chain at the waist, but from a baldric worn over the right shoulder, which points towards an Italic origin. Still ambiguity, therefore, which rightly raises perplexity among scholars, with M. Harari, editor of the piece in 'Immagine inedita di guerriero celta su un frammento vascolare da Spina', pp. 167–70; who supports the Celtic ethnic connotation and U. Hockmann (in *Gallierdarstellung in der Etruskischen Grabkunst des 2 Jhs. v. Chr.*', 1990, p. 204, note 16), who instead rejects this interpretation.
188. This work, attributable according to Beazley in *Etruscan Vase Painting*, pp. 49–50, 98–9, pl. 6 Fig. 5 to the Vatican Painter G111, depicts two converging armed horsemen. The character on the right shows the classic Celtic characteristics, such as once again the nakedness (at least in the parts of the body not covered by the long oval shield), the long sword and the decorations of the shield, but the harness that adorns the neck of his horse, made up of chains with disc studs, is instead common in the Etruscan context (as reported by Cristina Servadei, 'L'immagine del Celta nella pittura vascolare etrusca', p. 295). The same goes for his partner (or opponent), who also wears an Italic-type helmet.
189. Trying to define clear connotations in objects without knowing the importance of the interaction between Central-Italic people frequently leads many authors to wrong interpretations.
190. Grassi, *I Celti in Italia*, pp. 65ff.
191. Tagliamonte, *Spade di tipo lateniano in contesti sabellici*, p. 241.
192. Tagliamonte, 'Dediche di armi nei santuari del mondo sannitico', pp. 115–16.
193. P.F. Stary, 'Keltische Waffenauf der Appennin-Halbinsel', *Germania* 57 (1979), p. 110; Poppi L.Kruta 'Spade lateniane dell'Italia centrale in collezioni francesi', pp. 472–4; Dore, 'L'armamento lateniano in Italia: riflessioni e proposte per un corpus', pp. 39–40.
194. Very widespread among the Celts but scarce in the Sabellian culture.
195. Tagliamonte and Raccar, 'Materiali di tipo e di ascendenza lateniana nel medio e basso adriatico', p. 213. The only tomb attributable to a purely Celtic male subject is no. 1411 of Bazzano. In the necropolis of Camerano (province of Ancona, Marche, in the Picenum territory) 103 Picene burials have been unearthed, datable to between the end of the sixth and the middle of the third century

BC among which were excavated eight males with iron swords having Italo-Celtic characteristics. With the exception of these weapons, these burials are similar to the other contemporary ones, with which they have in common all the other characterising elements, such as the NE-SW orientation, the pit with four-sided recess, the *stele*, the upside-down position of the spear (i.e. with the tip downwards), the placing of a small knife inside a clay pot, etc.

196. Zuffa, 'I Galli sull'Adriatico', p. 141.
197. Nicosia, Sacco, Tondo, 'La Spada di San Vittore'.
198. A pre-Roman centre, it had great importance as a port close to Mount Conero, where products from the trans-Adriatic area and from the Aegean regions flowed.
199. Tagliamonte and Raccar, 'Materiali di tipo e di ascendenza lateniana nel medio e basso adriatico', p. 213.
200. In the vast collection of the British Museum, which by its nature and scale we can assume as an excellent representative of the stereotype of La Tène swords, weapons from the fourth century BC until the Roman conquest are present, with over 200 specimens of different shapes, weights and lengths, with various metallographic and construction compositions, classified into seven main categories. All are invariably made with a tanged hilt connected to the blade by descending shoulders, all forged in a single piece.
201. Such as, for example, a specimen from Castione dei Marchesi (Fidenza, Parma), dating back to the end of the Bronze Age – early Iron Age, as well as a dagger from tomb no. 87 of the necropolis of Caracupa (Latina, Latium), in iron, dated to the eighth century BC. and placed together with another sword (Peroni, 'Die Schwerter in Italien', specimen no.395), all made with thorn tangs and descending blade shoulders (Luigi Pigorini, 'Le spade e gli scudi delle terremare dell'età del bronzo e delle necropoli laziali della prima età del ferro', *Bullettino di paleontologia italiana* anno IX, n. 6-7, luglio 1883, tav. III Fig. 17).
202. However, a good rule of thumb when talking about the weapons of the ancient world is not to make the mistake of considering this as an absolute rule, since isolated specimens can be encountered that will derogate from it in all or in part.
203. It should be noted that a similar specimen, in ivory, was found in the so-called 'warrior's tomb' in the Celtic necropolis of Sion (Switzerland), but it is an isolated specimen.
204. Preserved in the Museum 'Giovanni Antonio Sanna' on Sassari.
205. A. Allegrucci, *I Senoni e la spada Lateniana – uno sguardo sull'affermarsi della spada lunga celtica in territorio italico fra il IV ed il III sec. a.C.*
206. Dionysius of Halicarnassus, *Roman Antiquities*, V, 47, 1. The episode refers to 503 BC during the consulate of Postumius and Agrippa, the year of a victorious battle against the Sabines. We should be careful not to confuse the state supply of weapons with the direct production of the same through, in fact, state armouries, which was not known before the third century AD, while the recourse to private armouries is far older. That is, soldiers did not physically purchase weapons based on personal taste from an armourer, as was the case in Greece or among the Celts, but were provided by the state with the most suitable equipment, the cost of which was deducted from their salary (Battaglia and Ventura, *De rebus militum*, Vol. I, p. 33.
207. Sim and Kaminski, *Roman Imperial Armour*, p. 41.
208. Battaglia and Ventura, *De rebus militum*, Vol. I, p. 30.
209. Circa 450–100 BC.
210. Istenič, 'A Roman late republican gladius from the river Ljubljanica (Slovenia)', p. 171.
211. In particular, example 1 from Smihel, as well as no. 6, the famous gladius from Delos, no. 9, although less visible as it is still inserted in the scabbard, and finally n'.10.
212. Although in this first period the Celtic swords were shorter than those of the cavalry of La Tène III (second–first century BC), which reached lengths of 90cm and more, we are always in the presence of rather long weapons.
213. F. Mathieu, 'sperimentazioni di archeologia ricostruttiva'.
214. In physics the torque formula is $Mt = S$, where S = applied force, r = radius or distance of the force from the torsion point. To give an example to have an intuitive understanding, think of the action

of tightening a bolt with a wrench: it is clear that the longer the wrench is, the less effort is made to perform the action and vice versa.
215. System of two equal and opposite forces acting on parallel lines of action. The distance between these two lines is called 'arm' (equivalent to 'r' in the formula referred to in the previous note). A couple acting on a body determines its rotation.
216. Simplifying, in this case we define 'arm' the distance between the point where the force is applied and the fulcrum of the lever.
217. In reality, in this work the presence of belts is clear and constant but there are no weapons hanging from them. However, this seems to be due to the fact that these could have been miniatures in bronze or iron applied to the marble relief, but of these only the related holes survive.
218. A.M. Adam and V. Jolivet, *Emprunts et échanges de certains types d'armament entre l'Italie et le monde non-mèditerranéè aux V et IV siècle avant J.C.*, Paris, 1986, pp. 129–44.
219. Two copies of the document were found, one in the Forum of Augustus in Rome and the second in Arretium (modern-day Arezzo).
220. Degrassi, 'XIII, Fasti et Elogia, III, Elogia', *Inscriptiones Italiae*, pp. 22–4, n° 17 and pp. 64–6, n°83; cfr 'Corpus Inscriptionum Latinarum, I², p. 195, nn. XVII-XVIII; Corpus Inscriptionum Latinarum, XI, 1831; Dessau, *Inscriptiones Latinae Selectae*, n. 59.
221. Plutarch, *Parallel Lives*, 'Marius', VI, 6.
222. Sallust, *The Jugurthine War*, 85, 29-35.
223. Ibid., 84, 1.
224. Plutarch, *Parallel Lives*, 'Marius', IX, 1.
225. Sallust, *The Jugurthine War*, 86, 1-2.
226. We must emphasise that 1,500 asses already corresponded to a small property, not enough to support a medium-sized family, making us understand how the reform instituted by Gaius Marius was the natural evolution of a process that had begun long before.
227. Sallust, *The Jugurthine War*, 86, 1-2.
228. Virgil, *Eclogues*, I, 5-75.
229. Cicero, *Tuscolanae*, II, 37.
230. Plutarch, *Parallel Lives*, 'Marius', XIII, 13,1. Sextus Julius Frontinus, *The Stratagems*, IV, 7.
231. Valerius Maximus, '*Mirabilia*, II, 3, 2.
232. Sextus Julius Frontinus, *The Stratagems*, 4.2.2.
233. Sallust, *The Jugurthine War*, XLIX, 6.
234. Plutarch, *Parallel Lives*, 'Marius', XI, 2-3.
235. Ibid., XI, 13.
236. Ibid., XVI, 3-4.
237. Ibid., XX, 8-10.
238. Appian, *The Civil Wars*, I, 34-35 (150-159).
239. Plutarch, *Parallel Lives*, 'Caesar', XXXV, 6.
240. Ibid., XXIX, 7.
241. Ibid., XVII, 4.
242. Lucanus, *Pharsalia*, VII, 503.
243. Ibid., I, 1-7.
244. Horace, *Epodes*, VII.
245. Ibid., XVI.
246. Armitage, *Guerre civili, una storia attraverso le idee*, p. 12, referring to Osgood, *Caesar's Legacy*, p. 3, in which is quoted P.A. Brunt, *Italian Manpower, 225 BC-AD 14* (Oxford University Press, Oxford 1971), pp. 509–12. Eutropius, *Roman History*, V, 9, 2.
247. Ibid., V, 9, 2.
248. Frontinus (*Stratagems*, II, 5, 31) certifies the presence of Roman-style armed cohorts in the army of Sertorius during the siege of Lauro (see chapter 18). As for the *tesserae* (identification marks used especially by soldiers) compare Polybius, VI 34, 8-11; Justinus, III 5, 10.
249. Plutarch, *Parallel Lives*, 'Sertorius', XIV, 1-2.
250. Ibid., XII, 6-7.
251. Lucanus, *Pharsalia*, VII, 257-263, 318-322.

252. The numbers reported by Eutropius in *Roman History* are less: Pompey could count on 40,000 infantry, and 1,100 allied cavalry from all over the East; Caesar lined up 30,000 infantry and 1,000 horsemen.
253. Varro, *De Lingua Latina*, V, 16, 88.
254. Polybius, *The Histories*, XI, 23, 1.
255. Varro, *De Lingua Latina*, V, 88.
256. Pseudo-Caesar, 'La lunga guerra civile, Alessandria-Africa-Spagna', BUR 2009, ed. Luigi Loreto, La guerra d'Africa, 17, 1-2.
257. Aulus Gellius, *Noctes Atticae*, XVI, 4, 6.
258. Plutarch, *Parallel Lives*, 'Sertorius', XIII, 1.
259. Ibid., XII, 6-7.
260. The Eburoni were a tribe of Gallia Belgica.
261. Caesar, *De Bello Gallico*, VI, 34, 1-2 and 5-6.
262. Caesar, *De Bello Civili*, I, 43, 4.
263. Plutarch, *Parallel Lives*, 'Lucullus', 20, 1-4.
264. Caesar, *De Bello Gallico*, V, 15, 4.
265. Caesar, *De Bello Civili*, III, 93, 8.
266. Ibid., I. 45, 7-8.
267. Plutarch, *Parallel Lives*, 'Lucullus', 27, 7.
268. Caesar, *De Bello Civili*, I, 43, 3.
269. Caesar, *De Bello Gallico*, VI, 40, 2-3.
270. Pseudo-Caesar, 'La lunga guerra civile, Alessandria-Africa-Spagna', Ed BUR 2009, ed. Luigi Loreto, La guerra d'Africa, 15, 3.
271. Ibid., 17, 1.
272. Caesar, *De Bello Civili*, II, 41, 5-6.
273. Frontinus, *Stratagems*, IV, 27.
274. Although Polybius (v. XI, 23, 1 cited above) refers the coexisting *velites* to a cohort, we can believe that the body was disposed of with the establishment of the cohorts, not only because Caesar's commentaries never mention them, but also for a statement by Livy who describes them as of a body that no longer existed in his time (Livy, *Ab Urbe Condita*, ed. Mazzocato (1997), XXX, 32: '*Ea tunc levis armatura erat ...*' describing the *velites* in the Battle of Zama).
275. Vegetius, *L'arte della guerra romana*, II, 6, 1-2.
276. Ibid., II, 6, 9.
277. Appian, *The Civil Wars*, I, 82.
278. Pseudo-Igynus, 'De munitionibus Castrorum' 1, Appendix II of Giuseppe Cascarino (ed.), *Castra, campi e fortezze dell'esercito romano* (Il Cerchio, 2010), p. 229.
279. Plutarch, *Parallel Lives*, 'Sertorius', XVI, 5-8.
280. Dionysius of Halicarnassus, *Roman Antiquities*, XIV, 11, 3.
281. Polybius, *The Histories*, X, 20, 1-7.
282. Vegetius, *L'arte della guerra romana*, 1. XI.
283. Caesar, *Bellum Africanum*, 71, 1.
284. Vegetius, *L'arte della guerra romana*, 2. XXIII. 4.
285. Antonio Manciolino, *Opera Nova*, ed. Marco Rubboli and Alessandro Battistini (Il Cerchio, 2008), pp. 103–16, 'tu, spadaccino, devi tenereil piede manco innanzi ... tu raccoglierai il piede destro appresso il manco. Indi scorrerai innanzi con il piede manco sanza tirare anchora alcuno colpo. Perché trovandoti il tuo nemico così stretto, di due cose l'una fargli serà forza, overo tirare, overo fuggire a l'indietro. ma poniamo che gli tirasse una stoccata con il manco innanzi, a cotale stoccata più contrari potrai fare'.
286. Francesco di Sandro Altoni, Plate Chapter V of Book II: the half-sword 'fosse quando la spada non feriva di lontano (perché) gli mancava l'essenza della spada se bene ne haveva la forma'.
287. The statements of Francesco di Sandro Altoni are freely translated from the vernacular prose of the Renaissance period, taken from *Monomachia, trattato dell'arte di scherma*, ed. Alessandro Battistini, Massimo Rubboli and Jacopo Venni, p. 224.

288. Vegetius, *L'arte della guerra romana*, 1. XII.
289. Pompeii House IX 12, 7 a Pompei.
290. Vegetius, *L'arte della guerra romana*, 1. XX. 23-25.
291. Livy, *Ab Urbe Condita*, ed. Mazzocato (1997), XXII, 5.
292. Ibid., XXII, 50.
293. Ibid., XXXIV, 46.
294. Polybius, *The Histories*, XVIII, 30, 6-8.
295. Caesar, *De Bello Gallico*, II, 25, 1-3.
296. Lucanus, *Pharsalia*, VII, 557-577.
297. Caesar, *De Bello Civili*, I. 44, 3.
298. We should remember that the *Lex Plautia Papiria*, which granted Roman citizenship to all the inhabitants of the peninsula, was promulgated in 89 BC.
299. For the classification of Montefortino helmets, always refer to H. Russell Robinson.
300. Connolly, *The Roman Fighting Technique Deduced from Armour and Weaponry*, pp. 360–1.
301. In reality something similar appears in some slightly more archaic purely Celtic specimens, as for example in those from Mihovo (Slovenia) and Port bei Nidau (Switzerland), which also show a protrusion of the front edge of the helmet, but it is too small to perform the same function and moreover it is not hinged but fixed.
302. Connolly, *The Roman Fighting Technique Deduced from Armour and Weaponry*, p. 362.
303. Finally, for completeness, we report the thesis of D. Battaglia and L. Ventura about the reduction of the length of the blades. For these authors it is a consequence of the introduction of gladiatorial techniques within the Roman army, which is well documented by classical sources: 'The introduction of the gladiator therefore had a whole series of consequences on Roman armament. First of all, the shield: one particularly voluminous to compensate the inexperience of the *hastati*, was reduced in height. While the shield was maintaining, in its rectangularity (or sub-rectangularity) shape, an important capacity to obstruct the opponent's blows, now the armed arm could climb over this protection with less amplitude than before, increasing on the one hand a more easy handling and the frequency of attacks, allowing on the other hand the use of shorter swords, therefore lighter and more manageable. The *gladius hispaniensis* gradually disappeared between 60 and 20 BC, replaced by models inspired by it but shorter by 10–15cm, such as the Pompei and Mainz. Since, by virtue of the shorter weapon and greater self-confidence, even the distance of the melee was reduced, it was easier to undergo in turn targeted thrusts to the neck and shoulders; similarly to gladiatorial ones, therefore, more and more cantilevered elements on the helmets began to develop, first with an increase in the neck guard, later with the appearance of a front bar. Even the cheek-guards gradually increased in size, in order to more efficiently protect the faces of the soldiers.' (Dario Battaglia and Luca Ventura, *De Rebus Militum*, Vol. II, p. 202). However, we believe that with this approach the cause-effect relationship has been reversed, that is, the introduction of gladiator training (among other things limited in time and geographical spread) was one of the various responses to certain socio-military needs and events and not the cause.
304. There are obviously some exceptions, which in any case become increasingly rare with time.
305. With particular reference to the type of swords called 'group IV' or 'of Brigantes' by Stuart Piggott in 'Swords and scabbards of the British early Iron Age', *Proceedings of the Prehistoric Society*, 16, pp. 1–28.
306. Including Lionel Pernet, *Armements et auxiliaires gaulois*, pp. 104–05. An excellent example is a well-known specimen from Hod Hill (south Britain) which shows the substantially complete neck, devoid of the organic parts only. The three washers on the tang, in bronze, of generous size and exquisite workmanship, are well preserved, considered by Bill Maning as a Roman gladius with a modified handle, even if the width of the blade is still compatible with a purely Celtic weapon. Regarding the weapons of this peculiar location, the theory of Fraser Hunter ('Iron Age swords and Roman soldiers in conquest period Britain', in *JRES* n. 17, p. 16) is that they may have belonged to local warriors enlisted in the Roman army or adopted directly by the auxiliaries, however limited to the period of Claudius and Nero.

307. See Chapter IV '*De falsis originibus*, On the erroneous derivation of the Gladius from non-Italic peoples'.
308. For a more exhaustive dissertation on this type of sword see Bishop, *The Gladius – The Roman Short Sword*, pp. 12–17.
309. Miks, *Studien zur römischen, Schwerbewaffnung in der Kaiserzeit*.
310. Ibid.
311. Alessandro Barbero, in the conference 'La paura dell'anno mille', in Festival della Mente di Sarzana, 2013.
312. For the appearance of shorter blades we have to wait about the middle of the first century AD.
313. We should remember that the type 'A' is the variant with parallel edges while the 'B' has lanceolate ones.
314. Josephus, *De Bello Iudaico*, III, 99-101.
315. Pseudo Caesar, *Bellum Africanum*, 71, 1-2: '*Caesar contra eius modi hostium genera copias suas non ut imperator exercitum veteranum victoremque maximis rebus gestis, sed ut lanista tirones gladiatores condoce facere: quot pedes se reciperent ab hoste et quemadmodum obversi adversariis et in quantulo spatio resisterent, modo procurrerent modo recederent comminarenturque impetum, ac prope quo loco et quemadmodum pila mitterent praecipere*'.
316. For a similar adaptation of a weapon to the needs of combat, with reference to the Roman *pugio*, see Saliola and Casprini, *Pugio – Gladius Brevis Est*, Chapter IV.
317. Cavalry *spathae* are obviously an exception, but they are not the subject of our study.
318. Called in the usual scientific language 'stehende soldaten'.
319. In Italian '*in abito militare*', that is, depicting the fully-equipped soldier.
320. Claudio Franzoni, *Habitus atque Habitudo Militis*, L'Erma di Bretschneider, 1987, p. 129.
321. Saliola and Casprini, *Pugio – Gladius Brevis Est*, p. 75
322. In some cases in the company of other characters, perhaps of his own family, as in the *stele* of Firmus and C. Faltonius Secundus, represented in the company of two slaves.
323. An exception is the *stele* of the centurion Minucius Lorarius, which shows the sword slightly angled forward, perhaps only because the artist wanted to represent the effect of the hand resting on the hilt. Indeed what should be emphasised here is the horizontal position of the *pugio*, unique among all the depictions.
324. Among these, of particular interest is the arch of Carpentoratum, erected to commemorate the victories of Caesar in Gaul (at least according to the thesis of D'Amato and Sumner, in *Arms and Armour of the Roman Imperial Soldier*, p. 20; but not everyone agrees on the reasons for its construction. Gilbert Picard proposed that the arch was built to symbolically commemorate the Augustan victories in the East and in the northern regions), showing two *gladii* in their scabbards in a resting position, vertical, with four rings and the balteus (Fig. 11-2). On the well-known *Tropaeum Traiani*, in Adamclisi (Romania), then, in some metopes (XXXIX, XLIV and others) we see a row of legionaries marching, therefore not in battle, who carry the *gladius*, on the right, almost vertically (Fig. 11-3 and 11-4). To these we can add from the same monument, the relief of two legionaries or more probably standing praetorians, with a beautiful *scutum* resting at their feet, the *paenula* and the *gladius* on the left, obviously vertical. We close the quotations of scenes on the resting position by recalling the beautiful depiction of legionaries marching on Trajan's Column, each with lorica segmentata, the helmet hanging on the right shoulder and the *impedimentum* on the *furca*, as well as that of the column of Marcus Aurelius, very similar and equally beautiful. Both show the legionaries with the *gladius* on the right side, in a vertical position.
325. *In procinctu stare* = be ready to fight (from Enciclopedia Treccani).
326. Lunensis Marble, Cordoba. Earl of Cardona collection, cat. IX,5.4.
327. We would like to mention among these that of the mausoleum of Glanum (Saint Rémy de Provence), dating back to the Augustan period (30–25 BC), where in the battle scene of the north frieze you can see the *milites* carrying the scabbard forward, and hanging from a *balteus* on the left side (Fig. 11-3). To this can be added the image on the arch of Augustus (Susa, Turin, Fig. 11-2), datable to 19–8 BC and erected by the king of the Ligurian tribes of the Cozii, Cotius, to celebrate the alliance with Augustus. It is particularly notable also because it is the oldest depiction of *lorica*

Notes 367

segmentata (on this subject, see D'Amato and Sumner, Arms and Armour of the Roman Imperial Soldier, p. 41), which is seen worn by a long line of *milites in procintu stantes*, who all wear the sword in an oblique way, always on the left.

328. It is possible to hypothesise that this derives from a need of the artist, as it – if oblique – would have been partially hidden behind the shield, unlike that of the same metopa XXXI-3 which, on the other hand, does not remain hidden.
329. Polybius, *The Histories*, VI,23,6.
330. Strabo, *Geographica*, IV,4,3.
331. Diodorus Siculus, *Bibliotheca Historica*, V,30,3.
332. We recall a terracotta figurine of a Gallic warrior, of Egyptian production, preserved in the British Museum, which shows him naked, simply covered with a cloak, carrying a large oval shield with a central spine and the sword on the right side hanging from a belt at his waist; some naked male figures with long hair, identifiable as Celtic *bàrbaroi* (on it see D. Vitali, 'L'armamento dei Celti nel periodo della battaglia del Metauro', p. 118, as well as Adam-Jolivet, 'A propos d'une scène de combat sur un vase falisque du musée du Louvre', 1986, pp. 166–77), represented on some Etruscan urns from Volterra and Chiusi, which can date from the middle of the third to the second century BC; the warrior of the stàmnos 1569 of the Akademisches Kunstmuseum in Bonn (about which see Beazley, *Etruscan Vase Painting*, pl. 24, Fig. 1), whose suspension on the right side by means of a belt close to the waist is very evident, and finally the Celtic warriors represented in some steles of the Etruscan necropolis of Bologna (burial grounds in Giardini Margherita, Arnoaldi and Certosa), dating back to the end of the fifth–beginning of the fourth century BC.
333. Josephus, *De Bello Judaico*, III,5,5.
334. On the *Tropaeum Traiani* some legionaries are represented with the *gladius* on the left and the same is visible on the Arch of Augustus in Susa (Fig. 12-2), as well as in a representation of the column of Marcus Aurelius (Fig. 14-1, even though it should be noted that this is unique among all the armed forces of this column and that of Trajan, who instead represent it practically always on the right). We find it still on the left in some scenes of the Glanum mausoleum and the Portonaccio sarcophagus (Fig. 14-2). Another apparent ambivalent situation is found on the Rhine *stelae* of the *aquiliferi*, among which, next to those of Genialis, Luccius Faustus and Luccius Germanus carrying the weapon on the right, we find those of Pintaius and Lucius Sertorius Firmus, who instead wear it on the left.
335. Data refers to eighteen specimens showing the original and unaltered position of the rings and bands.
336. Quesada Sanz, *Armas del la antiqua Iberia* (2010), p. 80.
337. We find it on a typically Celtic specimen from Quintanas de Gormaz, modified precisely according to this Hispanic way (Quesada Sanz 'Gladius hispaniensis: an archaeological view from Iberia', p. 258), as well as on that from the necropolis of Arcóbriga, burial 'D' (Fig. 18-3) and on that from tomb 54 of El Cigarralejo.
338. Ibid., p. 263.
339. A. Iriarte and others in,'El depósito de armas de la Azucarera (Alfaro, La Rioja)' in *Cuadernos de Arquelogia de la Universitad del Navarra*, n. 4, 1986, p. 182 believe to date it to the Sertorian wars, while F. Quesada Sanz potentially dates it back to the middle of the second century BC (in ' Gladius hispaniensis: an archaelogical view from Iberia', p. 261); Its belonging to the Roman culture derives from the fact that it was found with a Montefortino-type helmet, a shield boss and a helmet crest holder, very rare elements in contexts of the Meseta (Quesada Sanz, 'Gladius hispaniensis: an archaeological view from Iberia', p. 261).
340. For more information on this specimen, as well as on the others mentioned below, see C. Miks, *Studien zur römischen Schwertbewaffnung in der Kaiserzeit*. In detail, for the Delos specimen, see p. 563 (A123).
341. Connolly, 'Pilum, Gladius and Pugio in the Late Republic', p. 49.
342. N. inv. 37324.
343. Although it cannot be entirely excluded that the lower one has simply been lost.

368   The Roman Gladius and the Ancient Fighting Techniques

344. Among the various works see P.J. Hazell, 'The pedite gladius', *The Antiquaries Journal*, Vol. VLI (1981), p. 73; Eric Nylem, 'Early gladius sword found in Scandinavia', *Acta Archaelogica*, XXXIV, 1963, pp. 212–28; Bishop and Coulston, Roman Military equipment, p. 74; Quesada Sanz, 'Gladius hispaniensis: an archaeological view from Iberia', p. 259.
345. Connolly, 'Pilum, Gladius and Pugio in the Late Republic', p. 53.
346. Latin *balteus*.
347. Latin c*ingulum*.
348. Stefanie Hoss, 'Sharp dressed men: the Roman military belt as fashion item', *Journal of Roman Military Equipment Studies*, Vol. 18 (2017), p. 85.
349. The *cingulum* connoted the wearer's belonging to the army, to the point that its negative form, *discintus*, had such a negative meaning that the term remained in use in the Italian language to indicate a person with sloppy clothes and in disorder. Frontinus shows us that in those times, even amongst civilians, 'an appearance in public with a belt badly worn was a bad sign for the person, from this come the words *cintus*, *praecintus* and *succintus*, with the meaning of diligent, active, skilful while on the contrary *discintus* was synonymous with inept, limp, indolent, that is, a person with a bad meaning' (R.P. Vaglia, in the translation 'The Stratagems' di S. G. Frontino, 2013, p. 150, n. 120). In a purely military context, to deprive someone of the belt was a precise infamous punishment, which could be imposed on a single legionary as well as on an entire unit. 'L. Piso, because Gaius Titius, commander of a cohort, had given way before some runaway slaves, ordered him to stand daily in the headquarters of the camp, barefooted, with the belt of his toga cut and his tunic ungirt … . (Frontinus, *The Stratagems*, IV, 133) 'Sulla ordered a cohort and its centurions, though whose defences the enemy had broken, to stand continuously at headquarters, wearing helmets and without uniforms' (Frontinus, *The Stratagems*, IV, 133) and again '[L. Curius, in the Dardanian War around Dyrrachium] … *then he compelled the mutinous legion to advance without arms*'(Frontinus, *The Stratagems* IV, 75).
350. Among them Bishop, *The Gladius – the Roman Short Sword*, p. 47.
351. The Baalshamin Temple in Palmyra was built in 131 AD as part of a synthesis of the Eastern and Roman architectural style. An inscription made by the Senate of Palmyra in Greek and Palmyrene commemorates the benefactor Male Agrippa who built this temple and the visit of the Emperor Hadrian. In this perspective of syncretism, the representation of oriental divinities with attributes, such as those of the *gladius*, typically Roman, which was in any case also used by the Palmyrene troops, is justified.
352. Bishop, *The Gladius – the Roman Short Sword*, p. 48.
353. Among the various works, P. J. Hazell, 'The pedite gladius', *The Antiquaries Journal*, Vol. VLI (1981), p. 75.
354. 21in in the original text.
355. Bishop, *The Gladius – the Roman Short Sword*, p. 47.
356. Ibid., pp. 46–7.
357. Istenič, 'A Roman late republican gladius from the river Ljubljanica (Slovenia)', p. 171.
358. Not on public display. Courtesy of the museum management.
359. The authors would like to thanks Dr. Vincenzo Lemmo for such interpretation and dating.
360. A sort of disc-shaped belt elements, to which the sheath straps are connected. There is no Italian technical term to indicate these elements, which appear as a sort of disc attached to the belt. They are normally indicated with the English term 'frogs'.
361. Francis Grew and Nick Griffiths, T*he Pre-Flavian Military Belt: the Evidence from Britain*, Cambridge University Press, 2011, p. 52.
362. L Lindenschmit, *Tracht und Bewaffnung des römischen Heeres während der Kaiserzeit* (1882), p. 10.
363. Nylen, 'Early gladius sword found in Scandinavia', p. 225.
364. Bishop, *The Gladius – the Roman Short Sword*, p. 47.
365. G. Ulbert, 'Gladii aus Pompeij: vorarbeiten zu einen corpus römische Gladii', *Germania* 47 (1969), pp. 115–18, source later quoted by Grew and Griffiths in *The Pre-Flavian Military Belt: the Evidence from Britain*, p. 52 and in general, from Bishop too in, *The Gladius – the Roman Short Sword*, p. 47.

366. Museo archeologico di Napoli, inv. 5757, C. Miks pl. 29, A592, even if this text does not show the rear of the weapon but only the front.
367. Various interpretations have been given, such as reinforcement for the scabbard, hooking for a *balteus*, or a place to store a knife or whetstone (in the style seen on the 'Warrior of Capestrano'), but no hypothesis is convincing.
368. Istenič, 'A Roman late republican gladius from the river Ljubljanica (Slovenia)', p. 177.
369. Inv. 65776;
370. Indeed, there is a *spatha* dated to the late third century AD, preserved in the Universitetets Historiska Museet - Lund showing a similar element. See C. Miks, *Studien zur römischer Schwertbewaffnung in der Kaiserzeit*, A659.
371. P.J. Hazell, 'The pedite gladius', *The Antiquaries Journal*, Vol. VLI (1981), p. 76.
372. Especially on Trajan's Column and the Antonine column.
373. See D'Amato and Sumner, *Arms and Armour of the Roman Imperial Soldier*, p.100, quoting the relvant passages by Pliny the Elder that describe these particular aprons of Roman military belts.

Chapter IV: 'De Falsis Originibus': On the Erroneous Derivation of the Gladius from Non-Italic Peoples

1. Istenič, 'A Roman late republican gladius from the river Ljubljanica (Slovenia)', p. 32.
2. Van Wees, *L'arte della guerra nell'antica Grecia*, pp. 73–4.
3. Hanson, *L'arte occidentale della guerra. Descrizione di una battaglia nella Grecia classica*, Chapter X.
4. Herodotus, *The Histories*, VII, 104,4-5.
5. On this aspect see Bettalli, 'Ascesa e decadenza dell'oplita', ορμος, ricerche di Storia Antica n.s. 1-2008/2009. Academia.edu.
6. Aristotle, *Politics*, 1297b1-1.
7. Ibid., 1338b25-39.
8. Plutarch, *Moralia*, 214 B 72.
9. Plato, *Laches*, 182e-184c.
10. Xenophon, *Cyropaedia*, 2.3.9-10.
11. Van Wees, *L'arte della guerra nell'antica Grecia*, p. 153.
12. Xenophon, *Hellenica*, 3.4.16.
13. Aeschylus, in *The Persians*, 817.
14. Plutarch, *Parallel Lives*, 'Licurgus', XIX, 4.
15. Demosthenes, 27.9.
16. Xenophon, *Hellenica*, 3.3.7.
17. For example Homer, *Iliad*, vv. 194, 210, 220.
18. Herodotus, *The Histories*, VII, 224, 1.
19. Ibid.
20. Ibid., VII, 225, 3.
21. Plutarch, *Parallel Lives*,'Timoleon', XXVIII, 1.
22. Most of the general information on Greek ceramography was drawn from the studies of John Boardman, one of the most distinguished scholars of ancient Greek art and particularly of pottery and vase painting.
23. John Boardman, *Storia dei vasi greci*, Istituto Poligrafico e Zecca dello Stato Libreria della Stato, 2005, p.173;
24. Ibid., p. 179.
25. The pictorial styles, in a nutshell, are divided into: 'Geometric Style' (tenth–eighth century BC), characterised by linear motifs such as labyrinths, swastikas, 'key' patterns, etc, patterns that probably derived from the ones easily woven on the frame. Human figures appear only in the eighth century BC, when it is not unusual to find Homeric duels with the sword as the main weapon. 'Orientalising style' (eighth–seventh century BC) was the result of the first contacts with the East, such as the Mesopotamian empires and Syria, of Phoenician trade and the influence of specialised artisans, always of oriental origin, who migrated to the Greek peninsula. Because of this influence, Greek artists abandoned the rigid geometric schematics and the human figures reached a high

maturity of representation. It was at this stage that the production, from being purely local, began to have a market outside its own city of origin, and Corinth was one of the most representative centres. The 'Black Figure' style (seventh–sixth century BC), introduced from Corinth, was soon adopted by Athens which imitated its production. The figures were made of black paint on a clay background and could be highlighted through the use of engravings or the addition of white and red pigments. In the sixth century, the export of Athenian vases to the Greek colonies, nearby Etruria and other parts of Greece began a trade that soon became impressive in volume. The 'Red Figure' ceramics (sixth–fourth century BC) progressively replaced the black one, exclusively for aesthetic reasons. In fact, the artist had the opportunity to create decorations richer in detail thanks to the chromatic variation, which favoured its diffusion especially in the thriving Western market. Also worth mentioning are the 'Apulian Ceramics' (fifth–third century BC), a typical production of the Lucanian territory (south-eastern Italy). The first potters and decorators were probably Greeks, but after a first phase a local style was developed where the figures, of great refinement, are in the context of a decoration that plays a role of great importance, thus making them easily distinguishable from the Athenian ceramics that are devoid of such floral patterns. The 'Ceramics with relief decoration' and 'Undecorated ceramics' (from the eighth to the sixth century BC) were a production where the decorations were impressed directly on the vase, or applied on top of moulded separately.

26. Boardman, *Storia dei vasi greci*, p. 5.
27. Currently free access online at www.cvaonline.org, where more than 100,000 specimens are catalogued.
28. The analysed data came from the following museums: Adria (M. Civico), Agrigento (M. Arch. Regionale), Bologna (M. Civico), Chiusi M. Arch. Nazionale), Como (Civico M. Arch. Giovio), Gela (M Arch. Nazionale), Genova (M. Civico d'archeologia ligure di Genova), Grosseto (M. Archeologico), Capua (M. Campano), Bologna (M. Civico), Ferrara (M. Nazionale), Fiesole (Collezione Costantini), Firenze (M. Archeologico), Gioia del Colle (M. Arch. Nazionale), Lecce (M. Provinciale), Milano (M. Civico Archeologico e Collezione H.A.), Napoli (M. Nazionale), Orvieto (M. Faina), Palermo (M. Nazionale e Collezione Mormino), Parma (M. Nazionale d'Antichità), Rodi (M. archeologico dello spedale dei cavalieri di Rodi), Roma (M. Naz. Villa Giulia, M. Preistorico L. Pigorini, (M. Capitolini), Siracusa (M. Arch. Nazionle), Taranto (M. Nazionale), Tarquinia (M. Nazionale), Trieste (Civico Museo di storia e arte), Torino (M. d'Antichità), Umbria (M. Comunali), Verona (M. del Teatro Romano), Vibo Valenzia (M. Statale Vito Capialbi).
29. The data analysed come from the Museums of Athens (National Museum) and Thessaloniki (Archaeological Museum).
30. The description of the vases refers to the cataloguing of the CVA.
31. Polito, *Fulgentibus Armis*, pp. 23–5.
32. Hatzi , *The Archaeological Museum of Olympia* p. 88, with reference to the Olympia Sanctuary.
33. P. Siewert, 'Votivbarren und das Ende der Waffen- und Geräteweihung in Olympia' AM 111 (1996), pp. 141–8.
34. The *sauroteres* were the spike at the other end of a spear from the spear head.
35. Naso, 'Reperti Italici nei santuari Greci', p. 41.
36. For the particular importance of the sanctuary of Olympia in relation to the military sphere, see U. Sinn, 'Olympia. Die Stellung der Wettkämpfeim Kult des Zeus Olympios', *Nikephoros* 4 (1991), pp. 31–54.
37. Baitinger, *Die Angriffs waffen aus Olympia*.
38. Hatzi, *The Archaeological Museum of Olympia*, p. 86;
39. H. Baitinger argues in 'Waffen und Bewaffnung aus der Perserbeute in Olympia', in AA 1999, pp. 125–39, the validity of the attribution to the famous Greek general, hero of Marathon, and not to a namesake;
40. Naso, 'Etruschi e Italici nei santuari greci', p. 334.
41. Naso, 'Reperti Italici nei santuari Greci', p. 39.
42. Polito , *Fulgentibus armis*, pp. 94–5.
43. Snodgrass, *Arms and Armour of the Greeks*, p. 59

Notes 371

44. A beautiful example of a bronze *sauroter*, offered as an ex voto at Olympia, bears an inscription that testifies to it as part of the booty stolen by the Messenians from the Spartans during these wars.
45. Silvestri, *La Vittoria disperata, la seconda guerra punica e la nascita dell'Impero di Roma*, pp. 120–1.
46. See for example the graves no. 230 e 454 of Incoronata – San Teodoro, no. 7 of Anglona – Valle Sorigliano, some of Chiaromonte – contrada San Pasquale, no. 31 of Anglona.
47. De Siena, 'La realtà militare nelle colonie greche', p. 33.
48. Giove, *Warriors and Kings of Ancient Abruzzo*, p. 34.
49. De Siena, 'La realtà militare nelle colonie greche', p. 31.
50. Bottini, *Armi. Gli strumenti della guerra in Lucania*, pp. 123–4.
51. Bottini and Setari, *Basileis, antichi re in Basilicata*, p. 61.
52. Grammenos, *The Kingdom of Macedonia*.
53. Grammenos, *The Gold of Macedon*.
54. Nankov, 'An ivory scabbard chape from Seuthopolis rediscovered: evidences for a xiphos from early Hellenistic Thrace?', p. 44.
55. Ibid., p. 45. The 300 tombs explored in the Vergina necropolis present some interpretative chronological limits, since the necropolis was used for a very extended period ranging from 1000 to 500 BC, in addition to the fact that some mounds were reused in the Hellenistic period.
56. Lilibaki and Akamatis, *Pella, Capital of the Macedonians*, p. 42.
57. L. Ognenova-Marinova, *"Илирийският" надпис от Северна Албания*, p. 166.
58. Man. Andronikos, 'An early iron age cemetery at Vergina, near Berorea', University of Thessalonike, p. 95. The author classifies them as 'northern type' of central Europe, one of which is visible in Table VI, Fig. 12; It is worth remembering what has already been said in note 1, that in this chapter we are using the term '*xiphos*' as a synonym for 'cross-hilted sword' as it is commonly understood in this way, although the true meaning of the term is much more vague.
59. Descamps-Lequime and Charatzopoulou, *Auroyaume d'Alexandre le Grand. La Macedoine antique*.
60. Nankov, 'An ivory scabbard chape from Seuthopolis rediscovered: evidences for a xiphos from early Hellenistic thrace?', p. 44.
61. Ibid.
62. A. Alexandrescu; 'La nécropole Gète de Zimnicea', *Dacia* XXIV (1980), pp. 19–126.
63. I. Touratsoglou; 'Το ξίφος της Βέροιας' in *Ancient Macedonia*, 611 (1986).
64. Trakatelli, 'The Category of the so-called Pseudo-Cypriote Amphoras and Their Distribution in Cyprus, Greece and the Black Sea', pp. 85–6.
65. P. Themelis and I. Touratsoglou, ΟΙ ΤΑΦΟΙ ΤΟΥ ΔΕΡΒΕΝΙΟΥ. ΑΘΗΝΑ. 1997, 84, Fig. 94.
66. *Treasures of Ancient Macedonia*, Archaeological museum of Thessalonike, 1979, 43, Fig. 9.
67. Vokotopoulou, Βιτσα 'Τα Νεκροταφεία Μιας Μολοσσικής Κώμης', Fig. 87 a, pl. 299a.
68. Breccia, *La necropoli di Sciathi*, p. 172, Fig. 78.
69. Andronikos, *Vergina. The Royal Tombs and the Ancient City. Athen*, pp. 144–5, Fig. 99.
70. Borza and Palagia, 'The Chronology of the Macedonian Royal Tombs at Vergina', pp. 81–125.
71. Damyanov, 'An early Hellenistic xiphos from Apollonia Pontica', p. 31.
72. Andronikos, *Vergina: The Royal Tombs and the Ancient City. Athens*, pp. 142–4. See also, A. Kottaridi, *Aigai, the Royal Metropolis of the Macedonians*, Athens, 2013 p. 271;
73. Damyanov, 'An early Hellenistic Xiphos from Apollonia Pontica', pp. 23–36.
74. Valeva, *The Painted Coffers of the Ostrusha Tomb*, p.103, Fig. 1a, 1b, pl. 11-1.
75. Tagliamonte, *I figli di Marte*, p. 68.
76. As attested by Strabo in *Geographica*, VI,I,2: 'the Samnitae had grown considerably in power, and had ejected the Chones and the Oenotri, and had settled a colony of Leucani in this portion of Italy' (a Samnite ethnic group);
77. Bottini, *Armi, gli strumenti della guerra in Lucania*, pp. 49–51.
78. Bottini and Setari, *Basileis, antichi re in Basilicata*, p. 15.
79. Nava, 'Il ritratto aristocratico: il guerriero indigeno nel mondo arcaico', p. 40
80. Russo, 'L'arte della guerra tra IV e III secolo a.C.', p. 58.
81. Strabo, *Geographica*, VI, 7.

82. The novelty of the Athenian constitutional system, started as early as the sixth century by Solon and before the Persian wars from Clistenes, it lies in the fact that power is no longer held by noble families by lineage or eminent by wealth.
83. Herodotus, *The Histories*, VII, 137-138.
84. Ibid., VIII, 137, 5.
85. Quintus Curtius Rufus, *History of Alexander* 4.8.6.
86. Plutarch, *Parallel Lives*, 'Licurgus', 28.
87. Asclepiodotus, Tactics (Technètaktikè), 5.1, 2, Ed. Soc. Dante Alighieri, Antonio Sestili (ed.):
88. Ibid., 1, 2.
89. Polienus 'Stratagems' 4.2.10;
90. Lucius Flavius Arrianus, 'L'arte tattica – trattato di tecnica militare', ed. Antonio Sestili, Aracne Editrice, III, 2-4.
91. Aelianus, 'Tactics', Ed. Soc. Dante Alighieri, ed.Antonio Sestili, II, 7-9.
92. A surviving fragment of an inscription on marble that reported some rules of behaviour in the Macedonian army, datable to about 200 BC.
93. Strabo, *Geographica*, 'Iberia' III, 1,3.
94. The Celts, together with the Iberians, constituted the main population of Hispania, as Martial reported (10, 65: *Hiberis et Celtis genitus*).
95. Almagro-Gorbea 'Uno scenario bellico', p. 52.
96. Quesada Sanz, 'Gladius hispaniensis – an archaelogical view from Iberia', p. 268.
97. Bishop, *The Gladius – the Roman Short Sword*, p. 8.
98. *Ars Grammatica*, 135,12 sgg: 'Nam- cum- dicimus-'Hispanos',- nomen- nationis- ostendimus-; cum- autem- 'hispanienses', cognomen –eorum-, qui- provinciam- Hispanum- incolunt-, etsi- non -sint – Hispani'.
99. '*Quod tibi difficillimum est, de nugis nostris iudices nitores eposito, ne Romam, siit adecreveris, non Hispaniens emlibrum mittamus, sed Hispanum*'.
100. Pasquale Martino, 'Nella tranquilla città di Cheronea', 1992, in 'Sertorius' (Plutarch).
101. Seneca, *De Beneficiis*, 5,24.
102 '*Necgaleam illam si videres, agnosceres, machaeraenimhispana divisa est.*'
103. Livy, *Ab Urbe Condita*, XXI, 12, '*temptata deinde per duos est exigua pacis spe, Alconem Saentinum et Alorcum Hispanum*'.
104. Ibid., XXI, 19.
105. By M. Jean Baptiste and Gardin Dumesnil, 1809.
106. Sandars, *The Weapons of the Iberians*, pp. 58–62.
107. Rapin, 'L'armement celtique en Europe: chronologie de son evolution technologique du V au I s. av. J.-C'.
108. Philo of Byzantium, *Mochlica* 72: 11 f.
109. Martial, *Epigrams*, XIV – 33 '*Pugio, quemcurva signat brevis orbita vena. Stridentem gelidis hunc Salo tinxit aquis*'.
110. Diodorus Siculus, *Bibliotheca Historica* V, 33-34.
111. Ennius, *Annals*, VII, fragment 143, where '*gracilento*' should be translated as 'thin, sharp'.
112. Giardino, *I metalli nel mondo antico, introduzione all'archeo metallurgia*, p. 6.
113. Polybius, *The Histories*, X, 17, 7-10.
114. Livy, *Ab Urbe Condita*, XXVI, 47.
115. Polybius, *The Histories*, X, 20, 4-7 (Scipio). 'And arms he had in abundance, both those captured at (New) Carthage and those which after the capture of that city he had caused to be made by impounding a large number of artisans' (Livy, '*Ab Urbe Condita*', XXVII, 17); 'The city itself rang with preparations for war, since artisans of all kinds were shut up in public workshops. the general inspected everything with the same care; now he was on the fleet and the docks, now he was with the legions as they ran; now he was giving his time to viewing the work that was done from day to day in shops and arsenal and on the docks, with the utmost rivalry, by the great multitude of artisans' (Livy, *Ab Urbe Condita*, XXVI, 51);

116. *Celtiberi gladiorum fabrica excellunt: quippe eorum gladii et mucrone sunt valido, et ad caesi mutra quem anuferiendum apti quam obrem Romani iam inde ab Hannibalicis temporibus, abiectis ensibus patriis, Hispanici gladii usum ascrivere: ac fabricam quidem imitati sunt, bonitatem autem ferri et reliquam curam asse qui haud quaquam potuerunt.*
117. For instance, this passage from *Biografia Universale Antica e Moderna, ossia Storia per alfabeto della vita publica e privata di tutte le persone che si distinsero per opere, azioni, talenti, virtù e delitti...*, XV, near G.B. Missiaglia, Venezia, 1829, p. 341: 'L'opera di Suida è una compilazione fatta quasi senza scelta o senza discernimento. Ignoranti copisti accrebbero ancora più gli errori del primo autore, inserendo nel testo delle note le quali altro non fanno che rendere più oscuri i passi cui dovrebbero dilucidare. Ad onta di tutti i difetti che a diritto in esso si notano, tale *Lessico* non lascia d'essere d'un'alta importanza, atteso il numero grande di frammenti che vi si trovano di scrittori non giunti sino a noi, nonché per le particolarità che contiene intorno ai poeti' [Suida's work is a compilation made almost without choice or without discernment. Ignorant copyists increased the errors of the first author even more, inserting notes in the text which do nothing but obscure the passages they should explain. In spite of all the defects that are rightly noted in it, this Lexicon does not cease to be of high importance, given the large number of fragments that are found there from writers who have not come down to us, as well as for the particularities that it contains around the poets].
118. Among them Sandars, *The Weapons of the Iberians*, pp. 58–62, who doubts its reliability because it is too late and arguably from Polybius.
119. *Suda Bizantina – 'fragmenta ex incertis libris'*, Fragment 179.
120. Montanari, *Vocabolario della Lingua Grecca*.
121. Translation and profeesional advice of Dr. Lorenzo Del Monte, New York Unversity (USA).
122. Iberian iron and the skill of the Spanish artisans would remain fundamental but would be only one of the many resources of the *Res Publica*. Let's not forget that Pliny, in listing the iron and steel centres with the best materials, mentions localities in the Iberian Peninsula (Bilibilis and Turiaso) alongside others in Central Europe (Noricum), Italy (Como and Sulmona), until he gets to the distants Parthians and to the steel of the Seres (not better identified but understood to be the Far East, Pliny, *Naturalis Historia*, 34,142) and, speaking of the latter two, he states that 'none of the other kinds of iron are made of the pure hard metal, a softer alloy being welded with them all' (Ibid., 34,145). The Romans even imported steel from the area of what is now Hyderabad (India), although they believed it came from China.
123. *Hic miles tripedalem parmam habet et in dextera hastas, quibus eminus utitur; gladio Hispaniensi est cintus; quod spe decollato pugnandum est, translatis in laevam hastis stringit gladium.*
124. *Nam qui hastis saggittisque et rara lanceis facta volnera vidissent, cum Graecis Illyriis que pugnare adsueti, postquam gladio hispaniensi detruncata corpora diuisa a corpore capita patientiaque viscera et foeditate maliam volnerum viderunt, ad versus quae tela- quos que viros pugnandum foret pavidi volgo cernebant.*
125. μάχαιρα ... .Ιβηρικην.
126. *Armant inde iuvenem aequales; pedestre scutum capit, Hispano cingitur gladio ad proprio rem habili pugna.*
127. Roman annalist who lived in the Late Consular period, around the first half of the first century BC.
128. Peter, *Historicorum Romanorum Reliquiae*, vol. 1, frr. 10,42,56.
129. In *Ab Urbe Condita*, XXV, 39,12: 'Claudius, qui annales Acilianos ex graeco in latinum sermonem uerit ... [Claudius Quadrigarius, who translated the annals of Acilius from Greek into Latin]' and XXXV,14,5 '*Claudius, secutus Graecos Acilianos libros* [Claudius, following the work of Acilius, written in Greek ...]'.
130. Roman historian also devoted to politics, who lived in the first half of the second century BC, a great connoisseur of the Greek language.
131. IX,13.
132. Quesada Sanz, 'Gladius hispaniensis – an archaeological view from Iberia', pp. 255ff.
133. Ibid.
134. Ibid.
135. Connolly, *Greece and Rome at War*, p. 63; Quesada Sanz, *Armas del la antiqua Iberia*, p. 68.

374 The Roman Gladius and the Ancient Fighting Techniques

136. Quesada Sanz, 'Gladius hispaniensis – an archaeological view from Iberia', p. 268.
137. Connolly, 'Pilum, Gladius and Pugio in the late Republic', p. 56.
138. Quesada Sanz, 'Gladius hispaniensis – an archaeological view from Iberia', p. 266.
139. Ibid., p. 258.
140. Tagliamonte and Raccar, 'Materiali di tipo e di ascendenza lateniana nel medio e basso adriatico italiano', p. 213.
141. Vitali, 'L'armamento dei Celti nel periodo della battaglia del Metauro', p. 122.
142. Quesada Sanz, 'Hispania y el ejército romano repubblicano. Interacción y adopción de tipos metálicos', p. 392.
143. Ibid., p. 398.
144. Kavanagh ' Armas de la Hispania prerromana', p. 154.
145. Bishop, *The Gladius – the Roman Short Sword*, p. 10.
146. Ibid., p. 22.
147. Connolly, 'Pilum, Gladius and Pugio in the late Republic', p. 53.
148. Quesada Sanz, *Armas de la antique Iberia*, p. 99.
149. Kavanagh, 'Armas del la Hispania prerromana', p. 155.
150. Stary, *Zur Eisenzeitlichen Bewaffnung und Kampfesweise in Mittelitalien (ca. 9. bis 6.Jh. v Chr.)*.
151. Ibid.
152. Landolfi, 'I Piceni'; Papi R., 'La necropoli di Alfedena e la via d'acqua del Sangro'; Sgubini Moretti, 'Pitino. Necropoli di Monte Penna: tomba 31'.
153. J. Weidig, 'I pugnali a stami, considerazioni su aspetti tecnici, tipologici, cronologici e distribuzione in area abruzzese, p. 121.
154. It is perhaps possible that this technique was mastered in central Italy even before the appearance of stamen daggers, perhaps since the early Iron Age in the Aquila area, as the short swords of the Fossa necropolis of the early Iron Age may suggest.
155. See Davoli and Miks 'A new roman sword from Soknopaiou Nesos'.
156. Of the 'windowed' or 'cage' type. See Weidig, 'I pugnali a stami, considerazioni su aspetti tecnici, tipologici, cronologici e distribuzione in area abruzzese', pp. 115 and 120;
157. 'The sword, especially when decorated with ivory, silver or gold ornaments, was an object of prestige, denoting the extraordinary social status and religious status of its owner', Ioannes Graekos, 'War and hunting: the world of the Macedonian king and his companions', taken from the catalog *Heracles to Alexander the Great - treasures from the royal capital of Macedon, an hellenic kingdom in the age of democracy*, Ashmolean Museum of Oxford and the Hellenic Ministry of Culture and Tourism, p. 83.
158. We should remember that in the period under study Greece and Macedonia were two different cultural entities.
159. Horace Sandars, 'The weapon of Iberians', *Archeologia*, 1913, pp. 58–62.
160. Plutarch, *Parallel Lives*, 'Sertorius', XIV, 1-2.
161. Atheneus of Naucrates end of second century AD, *I Deipnosofisti o I dotti a banchetto*, VI, 106. First Italian translation commented on project of Lucio Canfora, Salerno Editrice, Rome.
162. Juan Cabré Aguilló, 1943, p. 21.

Chapter V: The Symbolic Value of the *Gladius*
1. A typical example of symbolic combat is the confrontation of two male deer, with the antlers, for the domination of the herd and the possession of the females, at the end of which the defeated male runs away and disappears into the bush.
2. Villar, *Gli indoeuropei e le origini dell'Europa*, p. 131.
3. Dizionario etimologico, Rusconi Libri.
4. James, *Rome and the Sword*, p. 19.
5. Ibid.
6. The *Salii* were one of the most remarkable priestly colleges in ancient Rome and had the task every year of opening and closing the time that could be dedicated to war. For the ancient Romans, the war period ranged from March (the rituals of the *Salii Palatini* in this month marked the passage

of citizens from *civis* to *miles* under the protection of Mars) to October, in which the Roman citizen returned, as *civis*, to dealing with productive activities under the protection of the god Quirinus: the rites led by the *Salii Quirinales* marked this moment by purifying men, weapons and animals who had participated in military activities.
7. The commanding officer, representing the whole unit, performed sacrifices and performed haruspicine acts in his role as '*Pullarius*'.
8. Di Petta and Sarlo, *Guerra*, Universo del Corpo, 1999.
9. It should be noted that this interpretation is not unanimously shared, since there are other examples of spears with the same type of decoration which, however, do not seem to have any connection with anthropomorphic forms.
10. Sestieri, 'Fattori di collegamento interregionale nella prima Età del Ferro: indizi di un'ideologia condivisa, legata alle armi, dal Lazio meridionale alla Puglia'.
11. Gimbutas, *La civiltà della dea, il mondo dell'antica Europa, vol. 2*, pp. 201–02.
12. On the figure of the *pater familias* in detail see Chapter I.2,1.
13. Peroni, *Le spade nell'Italia continentale – Die Schwerter in Italien*, p. 87.
14. Cicero, *De officiis*, I, 34.
15. Virgil, *Aeneid*, 7, 339.
16. Ibid., 7, 461.
17. Ibid., 11, 362.
18. Ibid., 6, 86.
19. Ibid., 1, 14.
20. Ibid., 8, 146.
21. Ibid., 11, 474.
22. Ibid., 7, 325; 7, 545; 8, 29.
23. Ibid., 2, 217; 10, 900.
24. Ibid., 6, 273.
25. De Martino, *L'idea della pace a Roma dall'età arcaica all'impero*.
26. *Altercatio Hadriani Augusti et Epicteti philosophi* LLA 635.5, par.: 8, p. 104.
27. For more details see Chapter II.3 and Chapter IV.1.
28. Nava, 'Il ritratto aristocratico: il guerriero indigeno nel mondo arcaico', p. 41.
29. The Pentelic marble sarcophagus shows the Battle of Issus and hunting scenes. it is believed to be the burial of Abdalonimus, appointed king of Sidon by Alexander, through his friend and companion Hephaestion.
30. Polito, *Fulgentibus armis*, p. 22.
31. Ibid., p. 37.
32. Goukowsky, *Essai sur les origines du mythe d'Alexandre*, p. 144, from Claude Mossé, *Alessandro Magno, la realtà e il mito*, p. 177.
33. Ibid., p 139, from Mossé, *Alessandro Magno, la realtà e il mito*, p. 177.
34. The Greek authors such as Diodorus, Plutarch and Arrian, as well as the Roman ones such as Quintus Curtius Rufus and Justinus/ Trogus, as Claude Mossé writes, saw in the figure of the Macedonian the founder of this new world. Mossé, *Alessandro Magno, la realtà e il mito*, p. 183.
35. We remember how, in the Consular Age, Scipio Africanus was identified as a new Alexander, while Pompey, to whom the epithet 'The Great' was added after his victories in Asia, celebrated a triumph with a splendour reminiscent of the Macedonian (Appianus, *Mithridates*, 117); Julius Caesar, confronting the figure of Alexander, regretted how the Macedonian, at his age, already reigned over so many people and he did not (Plutarch, *Parallel Lives*, Caesar', 11, 5); Mark Antony called one of Cleopatra's children Alexander, and it was probably not a casual choice; in the Imperial era the myth persisted, so much so that Octavian/Augustus wanted to visit the mausoleum of Alexander the Great honouring him and placing a gold crown on the head of the body (Suetonius, *Twelve Caesars*, 'Augustus', 18) as well as being gratified by wearing a seal on which was the effigy of the Macedonian; Caligula, on the other hand, loved to wear the Macedonian's armour stolen from his mausoleum (Suetonius, *Twelve Caesars*, 'Caligula', 52) and finally Trajan, after the Dacian campaign, claimed that he had gone farther than Alexander.

36. Matteo Cadario, 'Il linguaggio dei corpi nel ritratto romano' from the catalogue *Ritratti, le tante facce del potere*, ed Eugenio LaRocca, Claudio Parisi Presicce with Annalisa Lo Monaco. Mostra dei musei capitolini 2010.
37. Even Cicero (*Ad Atticus*, 115, 17) and Dione di Prusa (*In Defense of Rhodes*, 31, 156), explaining what could help identify a portrait, did not emphasise only the physiognomy of the face, but also clothes and accessories' from Cadario, ibid.
38. There are numerous statues from the Imperial era with the sword of Alexander the Great including a marble sculpture of Julius Caesar, a work of the second–third century AD preserved in the Archaeological Museum of Naples; it is visible in a statue from Pompeii of Marcus Claudius Marcellus, favourite grandson and designated successor of Augustus (Archaeological Museum of Naples); it completes the military representation of the bronze statue of Amelia (Terni) which portrays the victorious general Nero Claudius Drusus Germanicus; the archaic *gladius* dresses, in the context of heroic nudity, the statue of the Emperor Titus from Herculaneum (Archaeological Museum of Naples), but also the statues of the emperor Lucius Verus and Marcus Aurelius, as well as that of the emperor Commodus, in a work of the second–third century AD, idealised in the personification of Achilles while killing Troilus (Archaeological Museum of Naples);.
39. The myth tells that when Pollux, son of Tindarus and therefore of human origin, died in battle, Castor, son of Zeus therefore immortal, gave half his life to his dead brother, so they remained united forever, one day in the world of the living and the following in that of the dead.
40. Scardigli, *La lancia, il gladio, il cavallo*, p. 85.
41. Adrian Goldsworthy, *Storia completa dell'esercito romano*, Logos, 2007, p. 95.
42. *Ad Atticus* 1.16. Erasmus of Rotterdam, from *Adagia*, 1,1,51.
43. The representation of naval *rostra* whose tip is depicted with *gladii*, is frequent in Roman sculpture. We highlight this metaphorical association on a funerary stone found along the Via Emilia of the first century BC, preserved today in the Museum of Modena, where three *gladii* per side decorate the *rostrum* of the warship; on a marble bas-relief kept in the Palatine Museum in Rome, also from the first century BC, in which is sculpted a Roman ship crammed with armed men; in two distinct friezes kept in the Sala dei Filosofi of the Capitoline Museums in Rome, from the Augustan era, where in one is represented a sword hilt from which three blades branch off, while in the other three distinct blades are carved; as well as on a marble sculpture part of a monument from ancient Ostia, also of the Augustan age, where two *parazonia* and a central *gladius* are reproduced on the side of the rostrum.
44. Baal, which means 'Lord' and who entered the Phoenician pantheon through the Middle Eastern peoples, was often considered as the god of lightning, personifying the benign god who brought rains irrigating the fields.
45. The inscription was translated by Prof. Giovanni Garbini, who deduced that it is a copy of a fragment of a literary text and not a simple votive invocation. In fact, the phonetic assonances and the use of highly sought-after words are typical elements of all ancient poetry, especially Phoenician and Hebrew.
46. The Israeli *rostrum* of Phoenician or Ptolemaic origins (fourth–third century BC) found in Atlit, south of Haifa, presents on the side the image of a weapon, in this case the trident of Poseidon
47. Livy, *Ab Urbe Condita*, ed. Mazzocato (1997), III, 53. 9.
48. Caesar, *The Civil War*, 1, 72, 2.
49. Suetonius, *Twelve Caesars*, 'Vitellius', 8.1.
50. Ammianus Marcellinus, *Historiae*, 21.5.10.
51. Livy, *Ab Urbe Condita*, ed. Mazzocato (1997), summary of book XXII.
52. Dionysius of Halicarnassus, *Roman Antiquities*, IX, 10, 4.
53. *Scriptores Historiae Augustae* (Aelius Lampridius) - XVIII: Alexander Severus 62, 1.
54. Plutarch, *Parallel Lives*, 'Brutus', 52, 3-8. 'Some, however, say that it was not Brutus himself, but Strato, who at his very urgent request, and with averted eyes, held the sword in front of him, upon which he fell with such force that it passed quite through his breast and brought him instant death.'
55. Velleius Paterculus, *Roman History* II, 119, 3.

56. G. Frontinus, *Stratagems*, ed. Roberto Ponzio Vaglia, new ed. Edoardo Mori, Casa Editrice Sonzogno Milano, 168.
57. Livy, *Ab Urbe Condita*, ed. Mazzocato (1997), XXVII, 13.9.
58. Ibid., XXI,62.
59. Vegetius, *L'arte della guerra romana*, 3, IV, 9.
60. Acta martyrum Scilitanorum 14; Acta Cypriani 3,6; Acta Maximiliani 3,1.
61. Torelli, *Exterminatio*, pp. 805–19. At Academia.edu
62. Frontinus, *The Stratagems*, IV, 1, 35.
63. Suetonius, *Twelve Caesars*, 'Caligula', 49.3.
64. Ammianus Marcellinus XXVIII, 1.16. The senator Cetegus convicted of adultery had his head cut off.
65. *Codex Theodosius*, IX, 7, 3; *Institutiones*, IV, 18, 4.
66. *Institutiones*, IV, 18, 5; *Codex Theodosius*, IX, 14, 3 referring to the *Lex Cornelia de Sicariis*.
67. *Institutiones*, IV, 18, 5 referring to the *Lex Cornelia de Sicariis*.
68. *Codex Theodosius*, I, 7, 1.
69. Ibid., VII, 4, 1.
70. Ibid., XIV, 17, 6.
71. Ibid., VII, 18, 4.
72. Ibid., IX, 16, 4,
73. Ibid., XVI, 10, 4.
74. Acta martyrium, Acta procun solaria sancti Cypriani episcopi et martyris, IV.
75. *Codex Theodosius*, IX, 24, 10.
76. Ibid. X, 10, 10.
77. Ibid., IX, 6, 3.
78. Ibid., IV, 18, 10.
79. The *summa supplicia* (the ultimate forms of execution to which non-Roman citizens could be subjected) were the *vivicrematio* (the fire), the *damnatio ad bestias* or *ad ludum* (being fed to wild beasts or destined to combat as gladiators), the *damnatio ad metalla*, also defined as *proxima morti poena* (sentenced to work in the mines until death), the *damnatio ad furcam* (hanging) and the *damnatio in crucem* (crucifixion), which was abolished by Constantine, considering it inhuman, due to his Christian piety.Elio Tavilla, 'La pena di morte nella cultura penale di diritto romano: fondamenti ed eredità', p. 57.
80. *Martyrium Lugdunensium* V, 1, 47.
81. Acts of the Apostles, 22, 25-29: 'But when they had strapped him down Paul said to the centurion on duty, "Is it legal for you to flog a man who is a Roman citizen and has not been brought to trial?" When he heard this the centurion went and told the tribune; "Do you realise what you are doing?" he said. "This man is a Roman citizen." So the tribune came and asked him, "Tell me, are you a Roman citizen?" Paul answered "Yes". To this the tribune replied, "It cost me a large sum to acquire this citizenship." "But I was born to it," said Paul. Then those who were about to examine him hurriedly withdrew, and the tribune himself was alarmed when he realised that he had put a Roman citizen in chains'.
82. Tacitus, *Germania*, 10, 18.
83. Ammianus Marcellinus, *Res gestae*, XXXI, 2, 23.
84. Herodotus, in *The Histories* IV, 62, 1-2, tells that the Scythians sacrificed horses and herds to an old iron sabre, the symbol of Ares.
85. Corso, 'Danze popolari', *Enciclopedia italiana*, XII, p. 368; H. Meschke, Schwerttanz und Schwertspiel im germanischen Kulturkreis, Leipzig 1931
86. The two legends both date back to the twelfth century AD. The most famous myth is that of King Arthur's sword in the stone (and the twelve knights of the Round Table), connected to the Breton cycle and to the ascertained Celtic and Druidic components of these legends. According to some authors, the origin of Arthur is due to a pagan Gallic god called Artor while for others he was a Celtic warrior of the sixth century AD named Artorius, a Romano-British military leader, who defended his land from the invasion of the Angles and the Saxons. In Italy there is the legend of

Galgano Guidotti, who as a brave knight consecrated his life to the Lord, renouncing material goods and retiring to a hermit life. He retired to the Montesiepi hill (Siena) where he stuck his sword in a rock emerging from the ground, as a renunciation of war and as a representation of the Cross in front of which to pray.
87. Ephesiansi, 6, 17.
88. Chevalier and Gheerbrant, *Dizionario dei simboli, miti, sogni, costumi, gesti, forme, figure, colori, numeri*.
89. Epic of literary genre that developed in France from the eleventh century.
90. In the works of the Breton cycle, Excalibur was given to King Arthur by a supernatural entity the Lady of the Lake, so that the sovereign could build a new kingdom characterised by high knightly values, while the scabbard had the supernatural power to protect the one who wielded it from being wounded in battle.
91. In the *Chanson de Roland* it is said, then, that Durandal had some sacred relics in the pommel, a tooth of S. Peter, the blood of St Basil, the hair of St. Dionysius and a piece of clothing of the Virgin Mary, which gave it divine power. Rolland, on the verge of death, tried to destroy it so as not to let it fall into enemy hands, but thanks to the incredible powers of the steel, the paladin was unsuccessful and was forced to throw it into a river.

Conclusion

1. *Altercatio Hadriani Augusti et Epicteti philosophi* LLA 635.5, par. 8, p. 104.
2. James, *Rome and the Sword*, p. 20.
3. Seneca, *Epistulae morales*, IX, 76.
4. Tacitus, *The Histories*, 1, 79, 4.
5. Vegetius, *Epitoma rei militaris*, 2, 23, 4.
6. Ibid., 1, 11, 6.
7. Ammianus Marcellinus, *Res Gesta*, 16, 12, 49.
8. Worship practices, if celebrated incorrectly, had to be repeated to avoid upsetting the proper balance between men and gods.

Bibliography

Ancient Sources

Aelianus, *Manuale di tattica*, edited by Antonio Sestili, Soc. Dante Alighieri, 2011.
—— Matthew, C., *The Tactics of Aelian or On the Military Arrangements of the Greeks. A New Translation of the Manual that Influenced Warfare for Fifteen Centuries*, Barnsley, 2012.

Aeschilus, *I persiani* edited by Monica Centanni, Feltrinelli, 2014.
—— Aeschylus, *Persians. Seven against Thebes. Suppliants. Prometheus bound*, The Loeb Classical Library, Cambridge, MA: Harvard University Press, 2009.

Ammianus Marcellinus, *Storie*, edited by Giovanni Viansino, Mondadori, 2008.
—— Ammianus Marcellinus (Amm. Marc.), *The Histories - Res Gestae (Hist.)* Latin text and English translation by J.C. Rolfe, The Loeb Classical Library, 3 vols, London, 1939–1950.

Anonymous, *Acta S. maximiliani martyris*, edited by Enrico di Lorenzo, Loffredo, 1980.

Anonymous, *Altercatio Hadriani Augusti et Epicteti philosophi*, edited by William Daly Lloyd and Walther Suchier, The University of Illinois Press, 1939.

Anonymous, *Inedito Vaticano*, edited by H. von Arnim, Hermes, 1982.
—— *Ineditum Vaticanum*, by H. von Arnim (ed.), Hermes, 27. Bd., H. 1 (1892), pp. 118–30.

Anonymous, *Le cose della guerra*, edited by Andrea Giardina, Arnoldo Mondadori, 1989.
—— Anonymous, *On the war - De Rebus Bellicis in anonimo, Le cose della guerra*, edited by Andrea Giardina, Milan, 1989.

Anonymous, *Origo gentis romanae – Un'altra storia di Roma*, edited by Mario Lentano, Nuova Universale, 2015.
—— *Origo Gentis Romanae – the origin of the Roman race*, edited by Kyle Haniszewski, Lindsay Karas, Kevin Koch, Emily Parobek, Colin Pratt and Brian Serwicki, Canisius College, Buffalo, New York, 2004.

Anonymous, *Scrittori della storia augusta*, edited by Paolo Soverini, Turin: UTET, 1983.
—— *Scriptores Historiae Augustae* (*SHA*), Latin and English text in *Historia Augusta*, in three volumes, The Loeb Classical Library, Harvard University Press 1921–1932, translated by D. Magie.

Anonymous, *Suidae Lexicon*, edited by Ada Adler, B.G. Teubneri, 1938.

Appian, *Le guerre civili*, edited by Atto Rupnik, Idee Nuove, 2004.
—— Appian (App.), *Roman History – Ρωμαϊκά* (Civil Wars – Εμφύλιος πόλεμος); *Mithridatic Wars – Mithridateios* (*Mithr.*); *Gallic Wars – Keltikê* (*Kelt.*), Greek text in Appian. *The Foreign Wars*, L. Mendelssohn, Leipzig, 1879; English translation in White, H., Appian, *The Foreign Wars*, New York, 1899.

Aristotle, *Politica*, edited by Federico Ferri, Bompiani, 2016.
—— Barker, Sir Ernest, *The Politics of Aristotle*, Oxford: Oxford University Press, 1995.

Arrianus Lucius Flavius, *L'arte tattica – trattato di tecnica militare*, edited by Antonio Sestili, Aracne Editrice, 2012.
—— De Voto, J.G., *Flavius Arrianus, Teknh Taktika and Ektasis kata Alanon* (The Expedition against the Alans), Chicago, 1993.

Aesclepiodotus, *Manuale di tattica (Technètaktikè)*, edited by Antonio Sestili, Soc. Dante Alighieri., 2011.
—— *Aeneas Tacticus: Aesclepiodotus*, edited by William Heinemann, The Loeb Classical Library, 1962.

Atheneus of Naucratis, *Dipnosophistarum*, edited by George Kaibel, Leipzig, 1890
——, *I Deipnosofisti o I dotti a banchetto*, edited by Luciano Canfora, Rome, Salerno Editrice, 2001.

—— Athenaeus, *The Deipnosophistae*, edited by C.B. Gulick, The Loeb Classical Library, 7 vols, Harvard University Press, 1927–1941.

Bastiaensen Antonius Adrianus Robertus, *Atti e passioni dei martiri*, edited by Silvia Ronchey et al., Mondadori, 1987.

—— *Acta Martyrum*, ed. Ruinart P. Theodorici, opera ac studio collecta selecta atque illustrata, Ratisbon, 1859.

—— *Acta Martyrum*, in *Acta SS.; Analecta Bollandiana; Bibliographica hagiographica graeca, Bibliographica Latina*, Brussels, 1895–1898.

—— *Acta Martyrum selecta, Ausgewählte Martyreracten und andere Urkunden aus der Verfolgungszeit der christlichen Kirche*, in Latin and Greek, edited by O. von Gebhardt, Berlin, 1902.

—— 'Les Actes des Martyrs, Supplément aux Acta Sincera de D. Ruinart', *Mémoires de l'Académie des Inscriptions et Belles Lettres* XXX, Paris, 1882.

Caesar, *Bellum Africanum = De bello caesarianum*, edited by Antero Reginelli/ prod. Narcissus.me. – 2015.

——, *De bello civile*, edited by Fernando Solinas, Arnoldo Mondadori, 1987.

——, *De bello Gallico*, edited by Carlo Carena, Arnoldo Mondadori, 1987.

—— Caesar (Caes.), The Wars (*Commentaries on the Gallic War – De Bello Gallico* (BG); *Commentaries on the Civil War – De Bello Civile* (BC); *On the African War – De Bello Africano* (BA); *On the Hispanic War – De Bello Hispaniensi* (BH); *On the Alexandrine War – De Bello Alexandrino* (BAL). Latin text in *Commentarii de Bello Gallico*, edited by Otto Seel, Leipzig, 1961, *Commentarii belli civilis*, edited by A. Klotz, Leipzig, 1927. English text in *De Bello Gallico & Other Commentaries*, translated by W. A. MacDevitt, introduction by Thomas De Quincey, London & Toronto, 1940.

Cicero Marcus Tullius, *Epistole ad Attico*, edited by C. Di Spigno, UTET, 2005.

——, *Epistularum ad familiares*, edited by Dante Nardo, Patron, 1966.

——, *Tusculanae*, edited by L. Zuccoli Clerici, BUR, 1996.

—— Cicero, *The Letters to his Friends III, books XIII-XVI*, The Loeb Classical Library, Cambridge, MA: Harvard University Press 1979, translated by W.G. Williams.

—— Cicero, *The Letters to his Friends I, books I-VI*, The Loeb Classical Library, Cambridge, MA: Harvard University Press 1990, translated by W.G. Williams.

—— Cicero, *The Letters to his Friends II, books,* The Loeb Classical Library, Cambridge, MA: Harvard University Press 1979, translated by W.G. Williams.

—— Cicero, *Letters to Atticus I-II-III*, The Loeb Classical Library, Cambridge, MA: Harvard University Press 1967, 1980–1984, translated by W.G. Williams and E.O.Winstedt.

—— Cicero, *Tusculan Disputations*, The Loeb Classical Library 141, Cambridge, MA Harvard University Press, 1927, translated by J.E. King.

Demosthenes, *Orazioni*, edited by Ilaria Sarini, BUR, 1992.

—— Demosthenes, *Orations*, Vol. I: Orations 1-17 and 20: Olynthiacs 1-3. Philippic 1. On the Peace. Philippic 2. On Halonnesus. On the Chersonese. Philippics 3 and 4. Answer to Philip's Letter. Philip's Letter. On Organization. On the Navy-boards. For the Liberty of the Rhodians. For the People of Megalopolis. On the Treaty with Alexander. Against Leptines. The Loeb Classical Library 238, Cambridge, MA: Harvard University Press, 1930, translated by J. H. Vince.

Diodorus Siculus, *Biblioteca storica*, edited by Giuseppe Cordiano and Marta Zorat, BUR, 2014.

—— Diodorus Siculus, *Bibliotheca historica*, Ed. primam curavit Imm. Bekker, alteram L. Dindorf. Rec. F. Vogel. Vol. I–V. Lipsiae: Teubner, 1883–1906.

Dio Cassius, Storia Romana, edited by Giuseppe Norcio, BUR, 2005.

—— Cassius Dio, *Roman History – Romaika (Rom.)*, Greek and English text in The Loeb Classical Library, 9 vols, Cambridge, MA: Harvard University Press, 1914–1927, translated by Ernest Cary.

Dionysius of Halicarnassus, *Le antichità Romane*, edited by Francesco Donadi, Gabriele Pedullà and Elisabetta Guzzi, Einaudi, 2010.

—— Dionysius of Halicarnassus, *Roman Antiquities – Rhomaike Archaiologia (Rom.)*, The Loeb Classical Library, Cambridge, MA: Harvard University Press, 1913–1937.

Ennius Quintus, *Annali*, edited by E. Flores, Liguori, 2000.

—— *The Annals of Quintus Ennius*, edited Otto Skutsch, Oxford University Press, 1985.

Eutropius, *Storia di Roma*, edited by Fabrizio Bordone, Sant'Arcangelo di Romagna : Rusconi, 2014.
—— Justin, Cornelius Nepos, and Eutropius, *Eutropius, Abridgment of Roman History. Literally translated ... by the Rev. John Selby Watson*, London: George Bell and Sons, 1886, pp. 401–505.
Opere di M. M. Porcio Catone con traduzione e note. Frammenti delle opere perdute di M. Porcio Catone accresciuti, tradotti ed illustrati con note dal prof. Ab. Giovanni Berengo Venezia, Antonelli, 1846 In 8°, br. edit., pp. XXVI-374 colonne-CCLXXXIV (contenenti i " Frammenti delle opere perdute di M. Porcio Catone accresciuti, tradotti ed illustrati con note dal prof. Ab. Giovanni Berengo"). Coll. "Biblioteca degli scrittori latini"
Fragmentary Republican Latin, Volume III: Oratory, Part 1. Edited and translated by Gesine Manuwald. The Loeb Classical Library 540. Cambridge, MA: Harvard University Press, 2019.
Filon of Byzantium, *Greek and Roman Artillery. Technical Treatises*, edited by E.W. Marsden, Oxford, at the Clarendon Press, 1971.
Frontinus Sextus Julius, Stratagemmi, edited by Ponzio Vaglia, Sonzogno, 1919.
—— Frontinus (Front.), *Stratagems, Strategemata* (*Strat.*) Latin and English text in The Loeb Classical Library, Frontinus, Strategems-Aqueducts of Rome, Cambridge, MA: Harvard University Press, 1950 (1997), Translation by C.E. Bennett.
Herodotus, *Le storie*, edited by Aristide Colonna and Fiorenza Bevilacqua, UTET, 1996.
—— Herodotus, *The Histories*, Moscow, Idaho: S. Hayes St, 2013, translated by George Rawlinson.
Homer, *Iliade*, edited by Rosa Calzecchi Onesti, ET Classici Einaudi, 2014.
—— Homer, *Iliad*, edited by S. Lombardo and S. Murnaghan, Indianapolis, 1997.
Horatius Flaccus Quintus, *Epodi*, edited by E. Mandruzzato, BUR, 1985.
—— Horace, *Odes and epodes*, Harvard University Press, 2004, translated by N. Rudd.
Isidorus of Sevilla, *Etimologie o origini*, edited by Angelo Valastro, UTET, 2014.
—— Isidore of Seville, *The Etimologies of Isidore of Seville*, edited by S.A. Barney, W. Lewis and J.A. Beach, Cambridge, 2006
Josephus, *Guerra giudaica* edited by Giovanni Vitucci. – Cles (TN) : Mondadori, 2009.
—— Josephus, *The Jewish War – Bellum Judaicum* (*BJ*); *Against Apio – Contra Apionem* (*Contra Ap.*).
English texts in *The Works of Josephus*, translated by William Whiston, Peabody, 1987.
Lucanus, *La guerra civile*, edited by Renato Badali, UTET, 2015.
—— Lucan, *Civil War – Pharsalia* (*Phars.*), Latin and English text in The Loeb Classical Library, Lucan, The Civil War, Cambridge, MA: Harvard University Press,1928, translated by J.D. Duff.
Marzialis Marcus Valerius, *Epigrammi*, edited by E. Merli and M. Scandola, BUR, 1996.
—— Martial (Mart.), *Epigrams – Epigrammata* (*Ep.*); *Apophoreta* (*Apoph.*) ; *The Book of the Spectacles – Liber Spectaculorum* (*Lib. Spect.*)
Latin and English texts in
Martial, *Epigrams*, Vol. I, Books 1-5, The Loeb Classical Library, Cambridge, MA: Harvard University Press, 1993, translated by D.R. Shackleton Bailey.
Martial, *Epigrams*, Vol. II, Books 6-10, The Loeb Classical Library, Cambridge, MA: Harvard University Press,1993, translated by D.R. Shackleton Bailey
Martial, *Epigrams*, Vol. III, Books 11-14, The Loeb Classical Library, Cambridge, MA: Harvard University Press, 1993, translated by D.R Shacketon Bailey.
Maurus Honoratus Servius, *Servii grammatici Qui feruntur in Vergilii carmina commentarii / recensuerunt Georgius Thilo et Hermannus Hagen*, New York: BG Teubner, 1881.
—— Maurus Servius Honoratus, *Commentary to Aeneid – Commentarii in Vergilii Aeneidos libros* (*Comm.*) edited by Thilo Georgius, Leipzig: Teubner, 1881.
Nonius Marcellus, *De compendiosa doctrina*, edited by John Henry Onions, Nabu Press, 2010.
Ovidius P. Naso, *Fastorum libri VI. Tristium lib V. Ex Ponto libri VI. et libellum in Ibin. Ad usum scholarum* edited by Thoma Vallaurio, 1870.
—— Ovid (Ov.), *The Festivals – Fasti*; *Metamorphoses* (*Met.*); *Sorrows – Tristia*
Latin and English texts in
Ovid, *Metamorphoses*, Books I-VIII, The Loeb Classical Library, Cambridge, MA: Harvard University Press, 1916 (1999), translated by F.J.Miller.
Ovid, *Metamorphoses*, Books IX-XV, The Loeb Classical Library, Cambridge, MA: Harvard University Press, translated by F.J. Miller

Ovid, *Tristia, Ex Ponto*, The Loeb Classical Library, Cambridge, MA: Harvard University Press, 1968, translated by A.I. Wheeler.
Ovid, *Fasti*, The Loeb Classical Library, Cambridge, MA: Harvard University Press, 1989, translated by J.G. Frazer.
Patercolus Caius Velleius, *Storia Romana*, edited by Renzo Nuti, BUR, 1997.
—— Velleius Paterculus, *Compendium of Roman History. Res Gestae Divi Augusti*, The Loeb Classical Library 152, Cambridge, MA: Harvard University Press, 1924, translated by Frederick W. Shipley.
Plato, *Lachete*, edited by Giovanni Reale, Bompiani, 2015.
—— Plato, *Laches. Protagoras. Meno. Euthydemus*, The Loeb Classical Library 165, Cambridge, MA: Harvard University Press, 1924, translated by W.R.M. Lamb.
Plautus T. Maccius, *Pseudolus-Trinummus*, edited by Giovanna Faranda, Mondadori, 2000.
—— Plautus, *The Little Carthaginian. Pseudolus. The Rope*, The Loeb Classical Library 260, Cambridge, MA: Harvard University Press, 2012, edited and translated by Wolfgang de Melo.
Pliny the Elder, *Storie naturali*, edited by Francesco Maspero, BUR Rizzoli, 2003.
Pliny the Elder, *Natural History – Historia Naturalis* (*HN*)
Latin and English text in, Pliny (the Elder) *Natural History*; in 10 volumes, The Loeb Classical Library Cambridge, MA: Harvard University Press, 1938-1962, translated by H. Rackham.
Plutarch, *Moralia*, edited by Emanuele Lelli and Giuliano Pisani, Bompiani, 2017.
—— Plutarch, *Moralia, Volume I: The Education of Children. How the Young Man Should Study Poetry. On Listening to Lectures. How to Tell a Flatterer from a Friend. How a Man May Become Aware of His Progress in Virtue*, The Loeb Classical Library 197, Cambridge, MA: Harvard University Press, 1927, translated by Frank Cole Babbitt.
——, *Vite parallele*, edited by Domenico Magnino, UTET, 1992.
——, *Vite parallele*, edited by Carmine Ampolo and Mario Manfredini, Mondadori, 2008.
Plutarch, *Parallel Lives – Paralieloi Bioi* (*Caesar* (*Caes*); *Cicero* (*Cic.*); *Crassus* (*Crass.*); *Caius Marius* (*Mar.*); *Fabius Maximus* (*Fab. Max.*); *Lucullus* (*Luc*); *Pompey* (*Pomp.*); *Sertorius* (*Sert.*); *Sulla* (*Sull.*)
Greek and English text in Plutarch, *Parallel Lives* in 11 volumes, The Loeb Classical Library, Cambridge, MA: Harvard University Press, 1914-1926, translated by B. Perrin
Polybius, *Storie* edited by Roberto Nicolai, Rome: Grandi tascabili economici Newton, 1998.
—— Polybius, *Histories – Pragmateia (Prag.)*.
Greek and English text in, Polybius, *Histories* III, Books 5-8, The Loeb Classical Library, Cambridge, MA: Harvard University Press 1923, translated by W.R. Paton.
Polienus, *Gli Stratagemmi*, edited by Elisabetta Bianco, Dell'Orso, 1997.
—— Polyaenus, *Stratagems of War*, edited and translated by Peter Krentz and Everett L. Wheeler, 2 vols, Chicago, 1994.
Pseudo-Scimnus, *Circuit de la terre*, edited by Didier Marcotte, Paris, 2000.
Rufus Quintus Curtius, *Alexander the Great*, edited by Tania Gergel, Penguin Publishing Group, 2009.
Sallustius Caius Crispus, *La guerrra giugurtina*, edited by Giovanni Garbugino, Garzanti, 2007.
——, *De coniuratione Catilinae'*, edited by L. Storoni Mazzolani, BUR, 1976.
—— Sallust, *Catiline's War – Bellum Catilinae* (*Cat.*); *Jugurthine War – Bellum Jugurthinum* (*Jug.*), *The Histories – Fragmenta Historiarum* (*Hist.*)
Latin and English text in Sallust, *War with Catiline, War with Jugurtha. Selections from histories. Doubtful works*, The Loeb Classical Library, Cambridge, MA: Harvard University Press, 1921, translated by J.C. Rolfe.
Seneca Lucius Annaeus, *De Beneficiis*, edited by M. Menghi, Laterza, 2008.
—— Seneca, III, *Moral Essays, De Beneficiis*, The Loeb Classical Library, Cambridge, MA: Harvard University Press 1935, translated by J.W. Basore.
Strabo, *Geografia, Iberia e Gallia*, edited by Francesco Trotta, BUR Rizzoli, 1996 – Vol. III and IV.
——, *Geografia, l'Italia*, edited by Anna Maria Biraschi. – [s.l.] : BUR Rizzoli, 2000 – Vol. V-VI.
—— Strabo, *Geography – Geographica (Geogr.)*.
Latin and English text in
Strabo *Geography*, II, Books 3-5, The Loeb Classical Library, Cambridge, MA: Harvard University Press, 1923, translated by H.L. Jones.

Strabo, *Geography*, II, Book 17 and general index, The Loeb Classical Library, Cambridge, MA: Harvard University Press, 1932, translated by H.L. Jones.
Suetonius, *Vite dei dodici Cesari*, edited by Gianfranco Gaggero, Rusconi, 1994.
—— Suetonius (Suet.), *The Twelve Caesars – De Vita Caesarum Augustus* (*Aug.*); *Caesar* (*Caes.*); *Galba*; *Nero*.
Latin and English text in Suetonius, *The Lives of the Caesars*, in two volumes, The Loeb Classical Library, Cambridge, MA: Harvard University Press, 1914, translated by J.C. Rolfe.
Tacitus, *Germania*, edited by Bianca Ceva, BUR, 2006.
—— Tacitus I, *Agricola. Germania. Dialogue on Oratory* The Loeb Classical Library, Cambridge, MA: Harvard University Press, 1914, translated by M. Hutton and W. Peterson.
Theodosius Flavius, Codice teodosiano [Online] // ancientrome.ru.
—— *Codex Theodosianus* (*Cod.Theod.*), Latin text in *Theodosiani libri XVI cum constitutionibus Sirmondianis*, edited by Th. Mommsen, P.M. Meyer and P. Krueger, 1-2. Berolini (Berlin), 1954 and 1962;
Titus Livius, *Ab Urbe condita*, edited by Mario Scandola, Biblioteca Universale Rizzoli, 1994.
——, *Ab Urbe condida*, edited by Gian Domenico Mazzocato, Newton, 1997.
—— Livy, *History of Rome from the Founding of the City – Ab Urbe Condita*, The Loeb Classical Library, Cambridge, MA: Harvard University Press, 1924-1949.
Valerius Maximus, Facta et memorabilia, edited by L. Canali, Medusa Edizioni, 2006.
—— Valerius Maximus, *Nine Books of Memorable Deeds and Sayings – Memorabilia, Factorum et Dictorum Memorabilium Libri Novem* (*Mem.*)
Latin and English text in Valerius Maximus, *Memorable Doings and Sayings*, in two volumes, The Loeb Classical Library, Cambridge, MA: Harvard University Press 2000, translated by D.R. Shackleton Bailey.
Varro Marcus Terentius, *De Lingua Latina*, edited by A. Traglia, UTET, 1979.
—— *M. Terentii Varronis de lingua latina librorum quae supersunt*, Leipzig, 1833.
—— Varro, *On the Latin Language* in two volumes, The Loeb Classical Library, Harvard University Press 1938, translated by R.G.Kant
Varro Marcus Terentius, *De re Rustica*, edited by A. Traglia, UTET, 1979.
—— Cato-Varro, *On Agriculture*, The Loeb Classical Library, Cambridge, MA: Harvard University Press, 1934, translated by W.D. Hooper and H.B. Ash.
Vegetius, *L'arte della guerra romana*, edited by Marco Formisano, BUR, 2003.
—— Vegetius, *Epitome of Military Science*, edited by N.P. Milner, Liverpool, 1993.
Latin text in Vegetius, *Epitoma Rei Militaris*, edited by M.D. Reeve, Oxford, 2004.
Virgilius Maro Publius, Bucoliche edited by M. Geymonat, Garzanti, 1981.
—— Virgil (Virg.), Latin and English text in Virgil, I, *Eclogues. Georgics. Aeneid*, The Loeb Classical Library, Cambridge, MA: Harvard University Press, 1916, translated by H. Rushton Fairclough.
—— *Eneide* [Libro] edited by Fo Alessandro. – Torino : Einaudi, 2012.
——, *Opera omnia*, edited by A. Forbiger, Parts I–III, Lipsiae:Teubner, 1873–1875.
Xenophon, *Ciropedia*, edited by Franco Ferrari, BUR, 2001.
—— Xenophon, *Cyropaedia*, Harvard University Press, 1914, translated by Walter Miller.
——, *Elleniche*, edited by Giovanna Rocchi Daverio. – [s.l.] : BUR, 2002.
—— Xenophon, *Hellenica*, Harvard University Press, 1918, translated by Carleton, L.Brownson

Modern Works
Dizionario etimologico, Rusconi, 2012.
Corpus Vasorum Antiquorum [Online] // https://www.cvaonline.org/cva/ / prod. Union Academique Internationale [et al.], 2000.
Adam, A.M., and Rouveret, A. 'Les cité étrusques et la guerre au V siecle avant notre ère', *Crise et trasformation des Societes Archaiques de l'Italie antique au V siecle avant J.C. Actes de la table ronde de Rome*, Rome: Collection de l'école française de Rome, 1987.
Aillagon, Jean-Jaques (ed.), *Roma e i barbari*, Venice: Skira. Catalogo della mostra a Palazzo Grassi, 2008.

Alexandrescu, Alexandrina D., 'La nécropole Gète de Zimnicea', *Dacia* XXIV, 1980.
Allegrucci, A., *I Senoni e la spada lateniana, uno sguardo generale sull'affermarsi della spada lunga celtica in territorio italico fra il IV e III sec. a.C.*. [Online] // http://zweilawyer.com/2011/02/10/la-spada-lateniana-2/ / prod. Campagnano Gabriele.
Almagro-Gorbea, Martin, 'Uno scenario bellico', in Arce, Javier, Ensoli, Serena, and La Rocca, Eugenio, *Hispania Romana, da terra di conquista a provincia dell'Impero*, Milan: Electa, 1997.
Altoni, Francesco di Sandro, *Monomachia, trattato dell'Arte di scherma*, edited by Battistini, Alessandro, Rubboli, Marco, and Venni Jacopo, Il Cerchio, 2014.
Ancillotti, Augusto, and Cerri, Romolo, *Le tavole di Gubbio e la civiltà degli Umbri*, Perugia: Edizioni Jama, 1996.
Andreae, Bernard, 'La tomba Francois ricostruita', in Sgubini, Anna Maria Moretti, *Eroi Etruschi e Miti Greci – gli affreschi della tomba di Francois tornano a Vulci*, Cooperativa Archeologica, 2004.
Andronikos, Manolis, 'An early iron age cemetery at Vergina, near Berorea'.. – [s.l.] : University of Thessalonike.
——, *Vergina. The royal tomb and the ancient city*, Athens, 1984.
Armitage, David, *Guerre civili, una storia attraverso le idee*, Donzelli Editore, 2017.
Arribas, Antonio, *Los Iberos*, AYMA, 1965.
Austin, Michel, and Vidal-Naquete, Pierre, *Economie et Sociétés en Grèce ancienne*, Armand Colin, 1972.
Badoni, Franca Parise, and Ruggeri Giove, Maria, 'Alfedena. La necropoli di Campo consolino: Scavi 1974-1979'. [Rapporto] : Report di scavi. . – [s.l.] : Ministero per i beni culturali e ambientali, Soprintendenza Archeologica dell'Abruzzo, 1980.
Baitinger, Holgher, *Die Angriffswaffenaus Olympia*, Berlin–New York: 2001.
Barbero, Alessandro, Conferenza 'La paura dell'anno mille'. // in Festival delle Mente. – Sarzana : [s.n.], 2013.
Battaglia, Dario, and Ventura, Luca, *De rebus militum – la tattica della legione romana dagli alberi al tramonto: la monarchia*, Ars Dimicandi, 2012.
——, *De rebus militum, la tattica della Legione romana dagli albori al tramonto: la Repubblica*, Ars Dimicandi, 2014.
Battiato, Armando, 'Contributo all'identificazione degli organismi acquatici riportati nel libro IX del Naturalis historia di Plinio il Vecchio', *Bollettino Accademia Gioenia Sci. Nat.*, Catania: Università degli Studi di Catania, 2012. – 374 : Vol. 45.
Beagon, Mary, 'Scienza greco-romana: Plinio, la tradizione enciclopedica e i mirabilia'. // Treccani, l'Enciclopedia Italiana..
Beazley, J.D., *Etruscan Vase Painting*, Oxford: Clarendon Press, 1947.
Bendinelli, Goffredo, 'Asta', *Enciclopedia Italiana*, 1930.
Bergonzi, Giovanna, *La Romagna tra VI e il IV sec. a.C.- nel quadro della protostoria dell'Italia centrale*, Bologna: University Press, 2015.
Bettalli, Marco, 'Ascesa e decadenza dell'oplita'. [Rivista] // ορμος, Ricerche di Storia Antica.. – [s.l.] : Università degli Studi di Palermo, 2008–9.
Bettini, Maurizio, *Il racconto dei miti classici*, Il Mulino, 2015.
——, and Short, William, *Con i Romani, un'antropologia della cultura antica*, Il Mulino, 2014
Bietti Sestieri, Anna Maria, *L'Italia nell'età' del bronzo e del ferro – dalle palafitte a Romolo (2200-700 a C.)*, Carocci, 2010.
——, 'Archeologia della morte fra età del bronzo ed età del ferro in Italia. Implicazioni delle scelte relative alla sepoltura in momenti di crisi o di trasformazione politico-organiszativa', in Nizzo, Valentino (ed.), *Atti dell'Incontro Internazionale di studi in onore di Claude Levi-Strauss*, Museo Nazionale Preistorico Etnografico 'Luigi Pigorini', 2010.
——, 'Fattori di collegamento interregionale nella prima Età del Ferro: indizi di un'ideologia condivisa, legata alle armi, dal Lazio meridionale alla Puglia', *Rivista di Scienze Preistoriche*, 2006.
Bishop, Mike C., *The Gladius – The Roman Short Sword*, Oxford: Osprey Publishing, 2016.
Boardman, John, *Storia dei vasi greci*, Istituto Poligrafico e Zecca dello Stato Libreria della Stato, 2005.
Boettcher, Alexander, *Acta Proconsularia Sancti Cypriani*, GRIN Verlag, 2008.

Bolza, Giovanni Battista, *Vocabolario genetico-etimologico della lingua italiana*, Vienna: Stamperia di Corte e di Stato, 1852.
Bonaparte, Napoléon, *Précis des guerres de Jules César : Ecrit à Saint-Hélène par Marchand sous la dictée de l'Empereur*, Les Perséides, 2009.
Borza, Eugene, and Palagia, Olga, 'The Chronology of the Macedonian Royal Tombs at Vergina', Jahrbuch des Deutschen Archaologischen Instituts, 2008.
Bottini, Angelo, *Armi. Gli strumenti della guerra in Lucania*, Edipuglia, 1991.
——, and Setari, Elisabetta, *Basileis, antichi re in Basilicata*, Naples: Electa, 1995.
Breccia, Evaristo, *La necropoli di Sciatbi*, Le Caire, Impr. de l'Institut français d'archéologie orientale, 1912.
Brizzi, Giovanni, *Il guerriero, l'oplita, il legionario, gli eserciti nel mondo classico*, Il Mulino, 2013.
Broncano, Santiago Rodríguez, *La necròpolis ibérica de El Tesorico*, Noticiario arqueológico hispánico, 1985.
Brühn de Hoffmayer, Ada, *Arms and Armor in Spain*, Instituto de Estudios sobre Armas Antiguas, Consejo Superior de Investigaciones Científicas, Patronato Menéndez y Pelayo, 1972.
Brunt, P.A., 'Italian Manpower, 225 h.C.-a.D. 14', *L'Antiquité Classique*, 1972.
Buranelli, Francesco (ed.), *La tomba Francois di Vulci*. Mostra organiszata in occasione del centocinquantesimo anniversario della fondazione del Museo Gregoriano Etrusco, Vatican City: Quasar, 1987.
Burton, Richard F., *The Book of the Sword*, 1884.
Campi, Luigi, *Di alcune spade in bronzo trovate nel Veneto, nel Trentino e nel Tirolo*, Parma, 1888.
Cardarelli, Andrea, 'Terremare: l'organizzazione sociale e politica delle comunità', in Brea, M. Bernabò, Cardarelli, A., and Cremaschi, M., *Le Terramare. La più antica civiltà padana*, Electa, 1997.
Cartwright, C.R. and Lang, Janet, *British Iron Age Swords and Scabbards*, British Museum Pubns Ltd, 2005.
Cavalli, Alessandro, 'Tradizione', *Enciclopedia italiana* 'Treccani'.
Cazzella, A. (et al.), 'Riunione Scientifica; 40, Istituto italiano di preistoria e protostoria', *Atti della XL riunione scientifica : strategie di insediamento fra Lazio e Campania in eta preistorica e protostorica*, Florence: Istituto italiano di preistoria e protostoria, 2007.
Cecamore, Claudia, 'Il santuario di Iuppiter Latiaris sul monte Cavo: spunti e materiali dai vecchi scavi', *Bull. della Comm. Arch. Comunale di Roma* Vol. XCV, Rome: Erma di Bretschneider, 1993.
Cherici, Armando, 'Armati e tombe con armi nella società dell'Etruria padana: analisi di alcuni monumenti', in Della Fina, M. (ed.), *Atti del XV Convegno Internazionale di Studi sulla Storia e l'Archeologia dell'Etruria* 2007.
Cherici, Armando, 'Corredi con armi, guerra e società a Orvieto'. [Rivista] // Academia.edu.
——, 'Armi e armati nella società Visentina con note sul carrello e sul cinerario dell'Olmo Bello', *Annali della Fondazione per il Museo 'Claudio Faina'*, Vol. XII, Quasar, 2005.
——, 'Etruria – Roma: per una storia del rapporto tra impegno militare e capienza politica nelle comunità antiche', *Gli etruschi a Roma, fasi monarchia e alto repubblica. Atti del XVI Convegno Internazionale di Studi sulla Storia e l'Archeologia dell'Etruria* Vol XVI. Annali delle fondazione per il museo 'Claudio Faina', 2009.
——, 'Forme di contatto mondo celtico e non celtico; riflessi culturali e socio-economici del mestiere delle armi', *Atti del XXIV convegno di studi etruschi ed italici*, Marsiglia: 2002.
——, 'I Piceni e l'Italia medio adriatica', *Atti del XXII convegno di studi etruschi ed italici*, 9–13 April 2000.
Chevalier, Jean, and Gheerbrant, Alain, *Dizionario dei simboli, miti, sogni, costumi, gesti, forme , figure, colori, numeri* BUR, 1999.
Cittadini, T. (et al.) 'Valcamonica, immagini dalle rocce'. // 2013. - [s.l.] : Skira.
Colini, Angelo G., 'Suppellettile della tomba di Battifolle ed altri oggetti arcaici dell'Etruria', *Bollettino di Paletnologia Italiano*, 1906.
Colonna Aristide e Bevilacqua Fiorenza [Libro].
Colonna, G., 'La Romagna fra Etruschi, Umbri e Pelasgi', *La Romagna tra il VI e IV sec. a.C. nel quadro della protostoria dell'Italia centrale*, Bologna, 1982.

Connolly, Peter, 'Pilum, Gladius and Pugio in the late Republic', *Journal of Roman Military Equipment Studies*, M. C. Bishop at the Armatura Press, 1997.
———, *The Roman Fighting Technique Deduced from Armour and Weaponry*, Exeter: University of Exeter Press, 1991.
———, *Greece and Rome at War*, Barnsley: Frontline Books, 2012.
Corso R. 'Danze popolari'. [Sezione di libro] // Enciclopedia Italiana / aut. libro Cappelletti Vincenzo e Nisticò Gabriella.
Coussin, Paul, 'Les Armes Romaines. Essai sur les Origines et l'Evolution des Armes individuelles du Légionnaire romani', *Reveu belge de Philologie et d'Histoire*, 1926.
Cremaschi, Mauro, 'Foreste, terre coltivate e acqua. L'originalità del progetto terramaricolo' in Bernabò Brea, Maria and Cremaschi, Mauro, *Acqua e civiltà nelle Terremare, la vasca votiva di Noceto*, Trento: SKIRA, Università degli studi di Milano, 2004.
Cristofani, Mauro, *La grande Roma dei Tarquini*, L'Erma di Bretschneider, 1990.
———, 'Itinerari iconografici nella iconografia volterrana', *Atti del XIX Convegno di Studi Etruschi e Italici*, Volterra, 1995.
D'Acunto, Matteo, *Il mondo del vaso Chigi. Pittura, guerra e società a Corinto alla metà del VII secolo a.C.*, Boston: De Gruyter, 2013.
D'Amato, Raffaele, *I centurioni Romani*, Goriziana, 2012.
———, and Sumner, G., *Arms and Armour of the Imperial Roman Soldier. From Marius to Commodus, 112 BC – AD 192*, London: Frontline Books, 2009.
Damyanov, Margarit, 'An early Hellenistic xiphos from Apollonia Pontica', *Archaeologia Bulgarica* Vol. XIX, 3, 2015.
Davoli, Paola, and Miks, Christian, 'A new roman sword from Soknopaiou Nesos', *ISAW Papers*, New York University, 2015.
De Marinis, Giuliano, 'Pettorali metallici a scopo difensivo nel villanoviano recente', *Atti e memorie dell'Accademia La Colombaria*, 1976.
———, and La Rocca, E. , *Il sepolcreto dell'Esquilino*, Rome, 1976.
De Martino, F., 'L'idea della pace a Roma dall'età arcaica all'impero', *VIII Seminario Internazionale di Studi Storici 'Da Roma alla Terza Roma*, Rome, 1988.
De Sanctis, Gaetano, *Storia dei Romani*, Fratelli Bocca, 1907.
De Siena, Antonio, 'La realtà militare nelle colonie greche' in *Genti in arme. Aristocrazie guerriere della Basilicata antica*, Rome: De Luca Edizioni d'Arte, 2001.
Degrassi, Atilius, 'Fasti et Elogia', *Inscriptiones Italiae*, Libreria dello Stato, 1937.
Della Fina, G.M., De Lucia Brolli, M., and Mercuri, M.A., *Sulle orme di Eracle*, Rome: Quasar, 2014.
Demontis, Angela, *Il Popolo di Bronzo*, Condaghes, 2006.
D'Ercole, Vincenzo, *Eroi e Regine, Piceni Popolo d'Europa*, De Luca, 2001.
———, and Cella, Elica, 'Il Guerriero di Capestrano', in Ruggeri Giove, Maria, *Guerrieri e Re dell'Abruzzo antico*, Carsa, 2007.
Descamps-Lequime, Sophie, and Charatzopoulou, Katerina, *Au royaume d'Alexandre le Grand. La Macédoine antique*, Paris: Exposition présentée au musée du Louvre, Somogy Editions d'Art, 2011.
Dessau, Hermann, *Inscriptiones Latinae Selectae*, Nobel Press, 2012.
Di Fazio, Massimiliano, and Cherici, Armando 'L'armamento dal guerriero celtico al legionario romano', *International Congress Of Classical Archaeology: Meetings between Cultures in the Ancient Mediterranean*, Rome: MIBAC Ministero per i Beni e le Attività Culturali, 2008. – Vol. Volume speciale.
Di Petta, Gilberto, and Sarlo, Ottavio, 'Guerra' // Enciclopedia Treccani. – 1999.
Dore, Anna, 'L'armamento lateniano in Italia: riflessioni e proposte per un corpus', *Ocnus. Quaderni della Scuola di Specialiszazione in Beni Archeologici*, 1995.
Drews, Robert, *The End of the Bronze Age, Changes in Warfare and the Catastrophe ca. 1200 B.C.*, Princeton, New Jersey: Princeton University Press, 1993.
Dumézil, Georges, *Gli dei dei Germani*, Adelphi, 1974.
Elio, Tavilla, 'La pena di morte nella cultura penale di diritto romano: fondamenti ed eredità', *Beccaria. Revue d'histoire du droit de punir* Vol. 1, Geneve: Michel Porret, 2015.
Ennio, Quinto, *Annali*, edited by E. Flores, Liguori, 2000.
Erasmus of Rotterdam, *Adagi*, edited by E. Lelli, Bompiani, 2013.

Eutizi, Emanuele, 'Protagonisti dello scavo e personaggi nel sepolcro', in Moretti Sgubini, Anna Maria, *Eroi etruschi e miti greci. Gli affreschi della Tomba François tornano a Vulci*, Vulci, 2004.
Fayer, Carla, *La familia romana. Aspetti giuridici e antiquari. Sponsalia matrimonio dote: parte II*, Rome: L'Erma di Bretschneider, 2005.
Feugère, Michael, 'L'equipment militaire d'époque républicaine en Gaule', *Military Equipment in Context – Journal of Roman Equipment Studies* Vol. 5, Leiden: Van Driel-Murray, 1994
——, *Weapons of the Romans*, Tempus, 1997.
Fioroni, Eleonora, *Il mondo degli oggetti*, Lupetti, 2001.
Fletcher, Vallas Domingo, *Problemas de la Cultura Ibérica*, Istituto de arqueologia Rodrigo Caro, 1960.
Fossati, Ivano, *Gli eserciti etruschi*. Editrice Militare Italiana, 1987.
Fraccaro, P. 'La storia dell'antichissimo esercito romano e l'età dell'ordinamento centuriato', *Secondo Congresso Nazionale di Studi Romani*, Roma, 1931.
Gardin Dumesnil, Jean Baptiste, *Latin Synonyms with Their Different Significations and Examples Taken from the Best Latin Authors*, London: Richard Taylor and Co., 1809.
Garlan, Yvon, *Guerra e società nel mondo antico*, Bologna: Il Mulino, 1985.
Giardino, Claudio, *I metalli nel mondo antico, introduzione all'archeo metallurgia*, Laterza, 2010.
Gimbutas, Marija, *La civiltà della dea, il mondo dell'antica Europa* Vol. 2, edited by Mariagrazia Pelaia, Stampa alternativa/Nuovi Equilibri, 2013.
Goukowsky, Paul, *Essai sur les origines du mythe d'Alexandre*, Nancy: Université de Nancy, 1981.
Grammenos, D.V., *Gold of Macedon*, John S. Latsis Public Benefit Foundation, 2007.
——, *The Kingdom of Macedonia*, John S. Latsis Public Benefit Foundation, n.d.
Grassi, Maria Teresa, *I celti in Italia*, Longanesi, 1991.
Grew, Francis and Griffiths, Nick, *The Pre-Flavian Military Belt: the Evidence from Britain*, Cambridge University Press, 2011.
Guadàn, Antonio Manuel, *Las armas en la moneda ibérica*, Cuaderno De Numismatica, 1979.
Guattani, Giuseppe Antonio, *Monumenti Sabini*, Tipografia C. Pulcinelli, 1828.
Hamblin, William J., *Warfare in the Ancient Near East to 1600 BC (Warfare and History)*, Routledge, 2006.
Hanson, Victor Davis, *The Other Greeks: The Family Farm and the Agrarian Roots of Western Civilisation*, University of California, 1995.
——, *L'arte occidentale della guerra. Descrizione di una battaglia nella Grecia classica*, Garzanti Editore, 2009.
Harari, M., 'Immagine inedita di guerriero celta su un frammento vascolare da Spina, in Celti ed Etruschi nell'Italia centro-settentrionale dal V secolo a.C. alla romanizzazione', *Atti del Colloquio internazionale, Bologna 12–14 April 1985*, Bologna, 1987.
Harris, William Vernon, *Rome in Etruria and Umbria*, Oxford: Oxford University Press, 1971.
Hatzi Georgia E., *The Archaeological Museum of Olympia*, Athens: John S. Latsis Public Benefit Foundation & Eurobank EFG, 2008.
Hobbs, T.R., *L'arte della guerra nella Bibbia*, Alessandria, 1997.
Howard, Dan, *Bronze Age Military Equipment*, Barnsley: Pen & Sword Military, 2011.
Hunter, Fraser, 'Iron Age Swords and Roman Soldiers in Conquest Period Britain', *Journal of Roman Equipment Studies* No. 17, 2016.
Istenič, J., *Roman Military Equipment from the River Ljubljanica – Typology, Chronology and Technology*, Narodni Muzej Slovenije, 2019, vol. Catalogi et monographiae 43.
——, 'A Roman late-republican *gladius* from the river Ljubljanica (Slovenia)', *Arheološki vestnik* Vol. 51, 2000.
James, Simon, *Rome and the Sword, How Warriors And Weapons Shaped Roman History*, Thames & Hudson, 2011.
Kavanagh, Eduardo, 'Armas de la Hispania preromana'. [Articolo]. – Mainz: RGZM Römisch-Germanisches ZentralmuseumLeibniz-Forschungsinstitut für Archäologie, 2016.
Kruta, Poppi L., 'Spade lateniane dell'Italia centrale in collezioni francesi', *Celti ed Etruschi nell'Italia centro-settentrionale dal V sec. a.C. alla romanizzazione, Atti del Colloquio internazionale*, Bologna, 1985.
Kruta, Venceslas, 'I Celti' in *Italia omnium terrarum alumna. La civiltà dei Veneti, Reti, Liguri, Celti, Piceni, Umbri, Latini, Campani e Iapigi*, Milan: Libri Scheiwiller – Credito Italiano, 1988.

Landolfi, M., 'I Piceni' in *Italia omnium terrarum alumna: la civiltà dei Veneti, Reti, Liguri, Celti, Piceni, Umbri, Latini, Campani, e Iapigi*, Milan: Libri Scheiwiller – Credito Italiano, 1988.

Le Lydien, Jean, 'Des magistratures de l'état romain', in Dubuisson. Michel, and Schamp, Jacques, *L'antiquité Classique* Vol. III, Paris, 2006.

Lendon, Jon, *Le ombre dei guerrieri, strategie e battaglie nell'antichità antica*, edited by C. Caneva, UTET, 2006.

Lilibaki-Akamatis, I.M., and Siganidou. M., *Pella, capital of the Macedonians*, John S. Latsis Public Benefit Foundation, 1997.

Machiavelli, Niccolò, *Discorsi sopra la prima deca di Tito Livio, Dell'arte della guerra e altre opere*, edited by Rinaldo Rinaldi, UTET, 2006.

Manciolino, Antonio, *Opera Nova*, edited by Marco Rubboli and Alessandro Battistini Il Cerchio, 2008.

Marquardt, J. 'Das Militarwesen', in Mommsen, Theodor, and Marquardt, J., *Handbuch der romischen Alterthumer*, Berlin, 1884.

Martinelli, Maurizio, *La lancia, la spada, il cavallo, il fenomeno della guerra nell'Etruria e nell'Italia centrale tra l'età del bronzo ed età del ferro*, Florence: Centro stampa Regione Toscana, 2004.

Martinoti, Angelo, 'Il simbolismo dell'ascia', academia.edu.

Mazzarino, Santo, *Pensiero Storico Classico*, Bari: Laterza, 2011.

Meschke, H., *Schwerttanz und Schwertspiel im germanischen Kulturkreis*, Leipzig, 1931.

Miks, Christian, *Studien zur romischen, Schwerbewaffnung in der Kaiserzeit*, VML Vlg Marie Ledorf, 2007.

Mommsen, Theodor, *Storia di Roma antica* 4, edited by D. Baccini, G .Burgisser and G. Cacciapaglia, Florence: Sansoni, 1972.

Montanari, Franco, *Vocabolario della lingua greca*, Loescher Editore, 2013.

Morelli, E., 'Omero medico?', *Riv Chir Mano* Vol. 42, 3, 2005.

Moscati, Sabatino, *Gli Italici – l'arte* Jaca Book, 1983.

Mossé, Claude, *Alessandro Magno, la realtà e il mito*, Laterza, 2008.

Nankov, Emil, 'An ivory scabbard chape from Seuthopolis rediscovered: evidences for a xiphos from early Hellenistic Thrace?', *Archaelogia Bulgarica*, Vol. XI, 2007.

Naso, Alessandro, 'Reperti italici nei santuari greci', *Krise und Wandel. Süditalien im 4. und 3 Jh. v.Chr.», Internationaler Kongress anlässlich des 65. Geburtstages von Dieter Mertens*, Rome, 2006.

———, 'Etruschi e Italici nei santuari greci', *Atti del convegno internazionale di studio*, Udine, 2003.

Naue, Julius, 'Armi italiane nella collezione Naue in Monaco', *Bollettino di Paletnologia Italicno* 1896.

———, *Die vorromischen Schwerteraus Kupfer, bronze und Eisen*, 1909.

Nava, Maria Luisa, 'Il ritratto aristocratico: il guerriero indigeno nel mondo arcaico' in *Genti in arme – Aristocrazie guerriere della Basilicata antica*, Ed De Luca., 2001.

Nicosia, Emanuele, Sacco, Dante, and Tondo, Manuela, 'La Spada di San Vittore-Das Schwert von San Vittore' in *Waffen fur die gotter, krieger prophaen heiligtumer*, Tiroler Landesmuseum, 2012.

Niebuhr, Barthold George, *Romische Geschichte*, Berlin, 1832.

Ninou, Kate, *Treasures of Ancient Macedonia*, Archaeological museum of Thessalonike, 1979.

Nizzo, Valentino, 'Aspetti dell'ideologia guerriera a Roma e nel Latium Vetus durante l'età di Romolo', *Atti del XXIX Corso di Archeologia e Storia Antica del Museo Civico Albano. L'esercito e la cultura militare di Roma antica* edited by Simona Carosi. Albano, 2010.

Nylen, E., 'Early gladius sword found in Scandinavia', *Acta Archaeologica* Vol. XXXIV, 1963.

Oakeshott, Ewart, *The Archaeology of Weapons*, The Boydell Press, 1960.

Ognenova-Marinova, Lyuba, "Илирийският" надпис от Северна Албания, Bulgarian Academy of Sciences, 1958.

Osgood, Josiah, *Caesar's Legacy: Civil War and the Emergence of the Roman Empire*, Cambridge University Press, 2006.

Paddock, John Miles, *The Bronze Italian Helmets: The Development of the Cassis from The Last Quarter Of The Sixth Century BC to the Third Quarter of the First Century AD*, University of London, Institute of Archaeology, 1993.

Pani, Mario, and, Todisco, Isabella, *Storia romana dalle origine alla tarda antichità*, Casocci editore, 2008.

Pellegrini, Enrico, 'Alcune considerazioni sulla produzione metallurgica nella valle del Flora dall'Eneolitico alla prima età del ferro', *Preistoria e Protostoria in Etruria* Vol. II, Milano 1995.
Pernet, Lionel, *Armements et auxiliaires gaulois (IIe et Ier siècle avant notre ère)*, Monique Mergoil, 2010.
Peroni, Renato, 'Culti, comunità tribali e gentilizie, caste guerriere e figure di eroi e principi nel secondo millennio in Italia ed Europa centrale ed Egeo' in Marzatico, F., and Gleirscher P., *Guerrieri, principi ed eroi*, Museo Castello Buonconsiglio (2004).
Peroni, Vera Bianco, *Die Schwerter in Italien – Le spade nell'Italia continentale*, Monaco, 1970.
Peter, Hermann, *Historicorum Romanorum Reliquiae*, Lipsiae Stutgardiae Teubner, 1914.
Piggott, Stuart, 'Swords and scabbards of the British early Iron Age', https://doi.org/10.1017/S0079497X00018880. – Cambridge University Press, 2014.
Pisani, Vittore, *Le lingue dell'Italia antica oltre il latino*, Turin: Rosenberg & Sellier, 1964.
Polito, Eugenio, *Fulgentibus armis – introduzione allo studio dei fregi d'armi antichi*, Rome: L'Erma di Bretschneider, 1998.
Quasten, Johannes, *Patrologia*, Marietti, 1980.
Quesada Sanz, Fernando, 'Hispania y el ejército romano republicano.Interacción y adopción de tipos metálicos Hispania and the Republican Roman Army. Interaction and adoption of weapon types', *Sautuola* Vol. XII, 2007.
——, 'Gladius hispaniensis – an archaelogical view from Iberia', *Journal of Roman Military Equipment Studies* 8, 1997.
Rapin, André, 'L'armement celtique en Europe: chronologie de son evolution technologique du V au I s. av. J.-C', *Gladius* Vol. XIX, 1999.
Reisoli, Gustavo, *Ardant du Picq*, Turin: Officina grafica Pasquale Scarrone, 1929.
Rocco, Marco, *L'esercito romano tardoantico: persistenze e cesure dai Severi a Teodosio*, Libreriauniversitaria. it, 2014.
Ruffolo, Giorgio, *Quando l'Italia era una superpotenza – Il ferro di Roma e l'oro dei mercanti*, Einaudi, 2008.
Ruggeri Giove, Maria, *Warriors and Kings of Ancient Abruzzo*, Pescara: Carsa, 2007.
——, *Alfadena La Necropoli Di Campo Consolino. Scavi 1974-1979*, Sovrintendenza archeologica dell'Abruzzo, 1980.
Russo, Alfonsina, 'L'arte della guerra tra IV e III secolo a.C.' in Genti in arme – Aristocrazie guerriere della Basilicata antica, De Luca, 2001.
Saliola, Marco, and Casprini, Fabrizio, *Pugio – Gladius Brevis Est*, Rome: Arbor Sapientiae, 2012.
Sandars, Horace, 'The weapons of the Iberians', Archeologia, 1913.
Sassatelli, G., 'L'arte delle situle', in: Venetkens. Viaggio nella terra dei Veneti antichi'. [Libro]. – Venezia : [s.n.], 2013. – Vol. Catalogo della Mostra, Padova 2013.
Scardigli, Marco, *La lancia, il gladio, il cavallo – uomini, armi e idee nelle battaglie dell'Italia antica*, Mondadori, 2010.
Schulten, A., *Numantia. Die ergebnisse der Ausgrabungen 1905-1912*, Munich: 1914–1931.
——, 'Las Guerras de 154-72 BC', Fontes Hispaniae Antiquae IV, Libreria anticuaria luces de Bohemia, 1937.
Scubla, Martina Antonella 'Lo scudo bilobato nei contesti archeologici dell'Italia antica, materiali e questioni connesse'. [Relatore Prof.ssa Giovanna Bagnasco Gianni] // Tesi di Laurea Anno Accademico 2012-13.. – Facoltà degli Studi di Filosofia e Lettere, Università degli Studi di Milano : [s.n.].
Servadei, Cristina, 'L'immagine del Celta nella pittura vascolare etrusca' in Vitali, Daniele, *L'immagine tra mondo celtico e mondo etrusco-italico: aspetti della cultura figurativa nell'antichità*, Bologna: Alma Mater Studiorum, 2003.
Sgubini Moretti, A.M., 'Pitino. Necropoli di Monte Penna: tomba 31', *La civiltà picena nelle Marche*, Ripatransone: Maroni Editore, 1992.
——, Eroi etruschi e miti greci. Gli affreschi della Tomba François tornano a Vulci'.. – Vulci : [s.n.], 2004.
Siewert, P. 'Votivbarren und das Ende der Waffen- und Geräteweihung in Olympia'. [Sezione di libro]. – [s.l.] : MDAI, 1996.
Silvestri, Mario, *La Vittoria disperata, la seconda guerra punica e la nascita dell'Impero di Roma*, BUR, 2015.
Sim, David, and Kaminski, Jaime, *Roman Imperial Armour, the production of early imperial military armour*, Oxbow Books, 2012.

Simeoni, Manuela 'Ares, Marte e gli altri – Capire le relazioni tra divinità del mondo antico per capire il carattere originario di ciascuna'.Giorno Pagano Europeo della Memoria, – 30 June 2013.
Snodgrass, Antony M., *Arms and Armour of the Greeks*, The Johns Hopkins University Press, 1999.
Stary, Peter F., *Zur Eisenzeitlichen Bewaffnung und Kampfesweise in Mittelitalien (ca. 9. bis 6 Jh. v. Chr.)*, Mainz am Rhein: P. von Zabern, 1981.
Tagliamonte, Gianluca, 'Armamento e guerra nell'Italia medio-adriatica preromana', *Quaderni di archeologia d'Abruzzo*, 2010.
———, 'Dediche di armi nei santuari del mondo sannitico', *Formas e imàgenes del poder en los siglos III y II a.C.: modelos helenísticos y respuestas indígenas, Actas del Seminario*, Madrid, [s.n.], 2004.
———, *I figli di Marte – mobilità, mercenari e mercenariato – Italici in Magna Grecia e Sicilia*, Giorgio Bretschneider, 1994.
———, 'Lo sviluppo di una società aristocratica: il ruolo delle armi' in *Eroi e Regine – Piceni popoli d'Europa*,De Luca, 2001.
———, *Spade di tipo lateniano in contesti sabellici*, Congedo Editore, 2008.
———, and Raccar, Marina 'Materiali di tipo e di ascendenza lateniana nel medio e basso adriatico' *Piceni ed Europa* edited by Mitja Guštin, Peter Ettel and Maurizio Buora, 2007.
Torelli, Mario, *La forza della tradizione, etruria e Roma, continuità e discontinuità agli albori della storia*, Longanesi, 2011.
———, 'Exterminatio', *Scienze dell'Antichità*, 2007–08.
Trakatelli, L., 'The category of the so called Pseudo-Cypriot amphoras and their distribution in Cyprus, Greece and the Black Sea', *International conference, Networks in the Hellenistic world: according to the pottery in the Eastern Mediterranean and beyond*, Cologne and Bonn: Nina Fenn, Christiane Romer-Strehl, 2011.
Undset, J., *Die altesten Schwertformen* ZFE, 1890.
Valeva, Julia, *The Painted Coffers of the Ostrusha Tomb*, Sofia: Bulgarski houdozhnik., 2005.
Van Wees, Hans, *L'arte della guerra nell'antica Grecia*, Goriziana, 2012.
Villar, Francisco, *Gli indoeuropei e le origini dell'Europa*, Il Mulino, 2008.
Vitali, Daniele, 'L'armamento dei Celti nel periodo della battaglia del Metauro', in Luni, Mario, *La battaglia el Metauro, tradizione e studi*, Quattroventi, 2003.
Vokotopoulou, J. 'Βίτσα. Τα Νεκροταφεία Μιας Μολοσσικής Κώμης'. [Libro]. – Atene : [s.n.], 1986.
Vv. Aa. 'Eroi e Regine – Piceni popoli d'Europa'. [Libro]. – [s.l.] : De Luca, 2001.
Vv. Aa. I Piceni e l'Italia medio adriatica' 2000 [Atti di convegno] // Atti del XXII convegno di studi etruschi ed italici. – Ascoli Picena-Teramo-Ancona : Ist. Editoriali e Poligrafici, 9-13 aprile 2000.
Weidig, J., 'I pugnali a stami, considerazioni su aspetti tecnici, tipologici, cronologici e distribuzione in area abruzzese', *Ricerche di archeologia medio-Adriatica: 'le necropoli, contesti e materiali* a cura di Gianluca Tagliamonte Cavallino Lecce : Congedo Editore, 2008.
Werner, Karl F., *Nascita della nobiltà. Lo sviluppo delle élite politiche in Europa*, edited by Pico S. e Santamato S.. – Turin: Einaudi, 2000.
Zevi, Fausto, 'La tomba del guerriero di Lanuvio', *Spettacles sportifs et sceniques dans le monde etrusque-italique*, Publications de l'Ecole francaise de Rome Vol. 172, 1993.
Zuffa, Mario, 'I Galli sull'Adriatico', in *I Galli e l'Italia*', Catalogo della Mostra, Rome: 1978